Guatemala and Belize

© Robert Frerck/Odyssey

Mexico with its prickly pear and its serpent; Mexico
blossoming and thorny, dry and lashed by hurricane
winds, violent in outline and color, violent in eruption
and creation... Mexico is a land of crimson
and phosphorescent turquoise shawls. Mexico is a land of
earthen bowls and pitchers, and fruit lying open to a
swarm of insects. Mexico is an infinite countryside of
steel-blue century plants with yellow thorns... Mexico, the
last of the magic countries, because of its age and its
history, its music and its geography..."

Pablo Neruda
Confieso que he vivido: Memorias. 1974. Translated as
Memoirs by Hardie St. Martin. 1977.

Travel Publications

Michelin North America
One Parkway South, Greenville SC 29615, U.S.A.
Tel. 1-800-423-0485
www.michelin-travel.com
TheGreenGuide-us@us.michelin.com

Manufacture française des pneumatiques Michelin

Société en commandite par actions au capital de 2 000 000 000 de francs
Place des Carmes-Déchaux – 63000 Clermont-Ferrand (France)
R.C.S. Clermont-Fd B 855 200 507

© Michelin et Cie, Propriétaires-éditeurs, 2000

Dépôt légal Novembre 2000 – ISBN 2-06-000082-3 – ISSN 0763-1383

Typesetting : NORD COMPO, Villeneuve d'Ascq
Printing and binding : I.M.E. Baume-les-Dames
Cover design: Agence Carré Noir à Paris 17ᵉ

THE GREEN GUIDE:
The Spirit of Discovery

The exhilaration of new horizons, the fun of seeing the world , the excitement of discovery: this is what we seek to share with you. To help you make the most of your travel experience, we offer first-hand knowledge and turn a discerning eye on places to visit.

This wealth of information gives you the expertise to plan your own enriching adventure. With THE GREEN GUIDE showing you the way, you can explore new destinations with confidence or rediscover old ones.

Leisure time spent with THE GREEN GUIDE is also a time for refreshing your spirit and enjoying yourself.

So turn the page and open a window on the world. Join THE GREEN GUIDE in the spirit of discovery.

Contents

Dear Reader

Introduction

Geography – Economy – Time Line – Indigenous
Presence – Art and Architecture – Literature – Cinema – Music and Dance – Traditions – Handicrafts and Food

Region 1: Mexico City

Region 2: Central Mexico

Region 3: Central West

© Robert Frerck/Odyssey

Santa Prisca Parish Church, Taxco

© Robert Frerck/Odyssey

Sunday Market, Chichicastenango, Guatemala

Tonantzintla Church, Facade Detail, Puebla

© Robert Frerck/Odyssey

King Pacal of Palenque, Museum of Anthropology

© Robert Frerck/Odyssey

5

Maps and plans

LIST OF MAPS AND PLANS

The World (1635)

Using this guide

● This guide is divided into three sections: Mexico, with nine regions, Guatemala and Belize. Within these, each **Entry Heading** is followed by a population figure, map reference, and tourist information phone number ▯.

● Following the names of sights mentioned in this guide, there is useful information in *italics*: sight location addresses, recommended visiting times, opening hours, admission charges (The P$ signifies Mexican pesos; Q$, the Guatemalan quetzal; BZ$, the Belizean dollar; and USD$, the US dollar.), telephone numbers and web addresses, when available. Symbols used in sight descriptions include the metro ⓜ, on-site parking *(estacionamiento)* ▣, on-site eating facilities ✗ and camping facilities △.

● Mexico City offers **digressions**, entertaining breaks from sightseeing, which are marked by a purple band and indicated on maps by a purple dot ❶ with the number identifying it on the map. Letters in parenthesis, such as (BX), indicate the coordinates for principal sights on the maps.

● Sections with a blue background offer practical information, such as available transportation, contact information for visitors bureaus and recreation opportunities, for a city or region.

● Cross-references to destinations described elsewhere in the text appear in SMALL CAPITALS; consult the **Index** at the back of the guide for the appropriate page number.

● We welcome corrections and suggestions that may assist us in preparing the next edition. Please send your comments to Michelin Travel Publications, Editorial Department, P. O. Box 19001, Greenville, SC 29602-9001 or to our web site: www.michelin-travel.com.

Legend

★★★ **Worth the trip**
★★ **Worth a detour**
★ **Interesting**

Sight Symbols

━━●━━━━━━ Recommended itineraries with departure point

⛪ ✡	Church, chapel – Synagogue		▣	Building described
○	Town described		▭	Other building
AZ B	Map co-ordinates locating sights		▪	Small building, statue
▪ ▲	Other points of interest		◎ ♣	Fountain – Ruins
⚒ ⌒	Mine – Cave		🛈	Visitor information
🌾 ⚓	Windmill – Lighthouse		⚓ ⚓	Ship – Shipwreck
☆	Fort – Mission		☀ ⩗	Panorama – View

Other Symbols

🛣 Interstate highway (USA)		🛣 US highway		180 Other route
🍁 Trans-Canada highway		401 Canadian highway		Mexican federal highway

═══	Highway, bridge	═══	Major city thoroughfare
═══	Toll highway, interchange	═══	City street with median
═══	Divided highway	═══	One-way street
───	Major, minor route	■■■	Pedestrian Street
15 (21)	Distance in miles (kilometers)		
2149/655	Pass, elevation *(feet/meters)*	⧓	Tunnel
△6288(1917)	Mtn. peak, elevation *(feet/meters)*	══╪══	Steps – Gate
✈ ✈	Airport – Airfield		Drawbridge – Water tower
⛴	Ferry: Cars and passengers	🅿 ✉	Parking – Main post office
⛵	Ferry: Passengers only		University – Hospital
←←◗	Waterfall – Lock – Dam	🚆 🚌	Train station – Bus station
—··—··—	International boundary	●	Subway station
------	State boundary, provincial boundary	❶	Digressions – Observatory
🍇	Winery	▭ ⊞	Cemetery – Swamp

Recreation

■-○-○-○-■ Gondola, chairlift		〔- -〕 ►	Stadium – Golf course
🚂 Tourist or steam railway		▭ ▭	Park, garden – Wooded area
⛴ ⚓ Harbor, lake cruise – Marina		🌀	Wildlife reserve
Surfing – Windsurfing		🐾 ⩗	Wildlife/Safari park, zoo
🤿 Diving – Kayaking		------	Walking path, trail
🎿 Ski area – Cross-country skiing		🚶	Hiking trail
	🎠 Sight of special interest for children		

Abbreviations and special symbols

PG	Government Palace	PM	City Hall	POL	Police station
		PN	National Park		
🏛	Archaeological site	Ⓜ	Metro-Mexico City	✉	Covered market
🚻	Restrooms	✗	Restaurant	🅿 Parking	🏇 Horse racetrack

All maps are oriented north, unless otherwise indicated by a directional arrow.

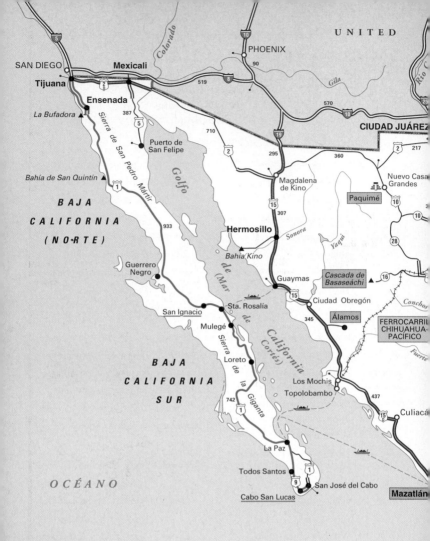

UNITED

Colorado

5
10 PHOENIX

SAN DIEGO
Mexicali
90
Gila
Rio C

Tijuana
519
8
25

Ensenada
2
570

La Bufadora ▲
387
710
CIUDAD JUÁREZ

5
Sierra de San Pedro Mártir
19
2 217

Puerto de
San Felipe
295
360
Nuevo Casa
Grandes

Bahía de San Quintín ▲
Golfo
Magdalena
de Kino
Paquimé
10

1
BAJA
15
307
10

CALIFORNIA
(NORTE)
933
Hermosillo
28

Sonora

Bahía Kino

Guerrero
Negro
de
(Mar
Cascada de
Basaseachí ▲
16

Guaymas

San Ignacio
Sta. Rosalía
15
Ciudad Obregón
Conchos

Mulegé
de
345
Álamos
FERROCARRIL
CHIHUAHUA-
PACÍFICO

BAJA
California
Loreto
Fuerte

CALIFORNIA
Sierra de la
Gigante
(Cortés)

SUR
Los Mochis

1
742
Topolobambo
437
15
Culiacá

La Paz

OCÉANO
Todos Santos
1

9
San José del Cabo
Mazatlán

Cabo San Lucas

PACÍFICO

Principal Sights

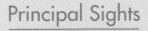
WORTH THE TRIP ★★★

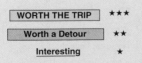
Worth a Detour ★★

Interesting ★

Place names in black type indicate the cities and sights
described in the guide (see Index).

De   in Deutsh
En   in English
Es   en Español
Fr   en Français
It   in Italiano
Ne   in het Nederlands
Po   em Português

0   200 km
0   100 mi

Suggested Regional Tours

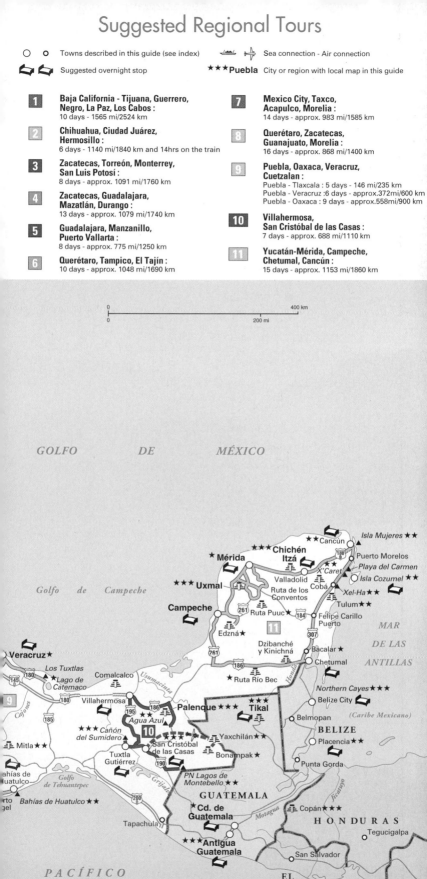

○ ● Towns described in this guide (see index)   ⛴ ✈ Sea connection - Air connection

◄ ◄ Suggested overnight stop   ★★★ **Puebla** City or region with local map in this guide

1 **Baja California - Tijuana, Guerrero, Negro, La Paz, Los Cabos :**
10 days - 1565 mi/2524 km

2 **Chihuahua, Ciudad Juárez, Hermosillo :**
6 days - 1140 mi/1840 km and 14hrs on the train

3 **Zacatecas, Torreón, Monterrey, San Luis Potosí :**
8 days - approx. 1091 mi/1760 km

4 **Zacatecas, Guadalajara, Mazatlán, Durango :**
13 days - approx. 1079 mi/1740 km

5 **Guadalajara, Manzanillo, Puerto Vallarta :**
8 days - approx. 775 mi/1250 km

6 **Querétaro, Tampico, El Tajín :**
10 days - approx. 1048 mi/1690 km

7 **Mexico City, Taxco, Acapulco, Morelia :**
14 days - approx. 983 mi/1585 km

8 **Querétaro, Zacatecas, Guanajuato, Morelia :**
16 days - approx. 868 mi/1400 km

9 **Puebla, Oaxaca, Veracruz, Cuetzalan :**
Puebla - Tlaxcala : 5 days - 146 mi/235 km
Puebla - Veracruz :6 days - approx.372mi/600 km
Puebla - Oaxaca : 9 days - approx.558mi/900 km

10 **Villahermosa, San Cristóbal de las Casas :**
7 days - approx. 688 mi/1110 km

11 **Yucatán-Mérida, Campeche, Chetumal, Cancún :**
15 days - approx. 1153 mi/1860 km

Panoramic View of Orizaba Peak

Introduction
to Mexico

Mexico: Country of the Unexpected

From the Pacific Ocean to the Caribbean Sea, deserts to tropical jungles, and high plateaus to snow-covered volcanoes, Mexico invites us to discover a different world, full of magic and tradition: **Mexican time and space**. The endless, picturesque out-of-the-way places of this country stimulate our senses and imagination. Mexico's multiple and contrasting voices reflect the cheerfulness and vitality of its people, who proudly preserve the roots of their ancestral cultures.

Country of Contrasts – In addition to the political borders with the United States to the north (marked by the Rio Grande), and Guatemala (marked partly by the Usumacinta River) and Belize to the south, natural and social boundaries abound. Mexico's landscapes—snow-covered volcanoes, vast deserts, high mountain ranges, immense valleys, white sandy beaches overlooking waters with diverse shades of blue, forests and jungles, rivers and waterfalls—fuse with its indigenous past, the mixing of heritages that occurred with the arrival of the Spaniards, and the interventions of the United States and France. Mexico offers a stunning diversity of physical and cultural traits, which makes this place a land of contrasts, where reality and fantasy converge.

The Mexicans – Getting to know the Mexican people is a memorable experience. Their warmth, hospitality and ingenuity are matched only by their cheerful informality and drive. Mexicans have their own concept of time, and *"ahorita"* or *"al ratito"* (in a little while) are frequently heard as indefinite measures of minutes, days or never. One could say that Mexico is the country of the unexpected. No wonder André Breton characterized it as "surreal."

Brigitta L. House

Sunday Market, Mexico City

Mexico Today

Area	1,958,201sq km/1,214,085sq mi 10,000km/6,200sq mi coastline , 5,073sq km/3,145sq mi of islands
Population	91,158,290 (55% of the population consists of mestizos, 20% of indigenous peoples, 15% of Caucasians and 10% of other races)
Time Zone	GMT: -8, -7, -6 and –5; a summer schedule is observed *(p 399)*
Languages	Spanish (official); indigenous languages and dialects are also preserved
Capital	Mexico City (Federal District)
States	31 plus the Federal District *(map p 50)*
Government	Democratic, representative and federal republic, consisting of three powers: Executive (president), Legislative (senators and deputies) and Judicial (Supreme Court of Justice and tribunals)
Religion	Catholic (predominant); freedom of worship
Climate	Ranges from a desert climate in the north to a tropical climate in the south *(p 391)*
Economy	Primary sources of income: services (including tourism), industry, mining, petroleum, farming, ranching and fishing *(p 22)*

Geographical Features

Shape and Relief – *Map pp 20-21*. Mexico's terrain resembles an inverted triangle with an elongated shape stretching from northwest to southeast at the **Isthmus of Tehuantepec**, formerly known as the Nudo Mixteco (Mixtec Knot) for its complex mountain ranges and geological origins.

From the northern and southern ends of this great continental body jut out two uniquely shaped peninsulas, Baja California and Yucatán. These landmasses are connected to the mainland by narrow isthmuses of barely 150km/93mi in width. **Baja California**, bathed by the Pacific Ocean and the Gulf of California (Sea of Cortés), consists of a narrow strip of land with steep cliffs, mountainous bays and desert zones of over 1,000km/620mi in length and an average width no greater than 100km/62mi. The **Yucatán**, on the southeastern end, is shaped like a rhomboid and constituted by an enormous limestone plain that covers over 100,000sq km/62,000sq mi, surrounded by the waters of the Gulf of Mexico and the Caribbean Sea, with extensive coastal plains, innumerable lagoons, inlets and reef formations.

Mountain Ranges, Plains and Plateaus – From the air, the Mexican terrain resembles a crumpled piece of paper. Hundreds of creases run along mountain ranges, deep canyons and steep cliffs, where it is still possible to find pristine regions. This panorama can be appreciated in 60% of the Mexican territory, which consists of towering mountain chains that run parallel to the coastlines of the Gulf of Mexico and the Pacific Ocean. In order of importance and area, they include the **Sierra Madre Occidental**, the **Sierra Madre del Sur**, the **Sierra Madre Oriental** and the **Sierra Volcánica Transversal** on the 19th parallel. The latter is also known as **Eje Neovolcánico** (Neovolcanic Axis) because it comprises the country's highest peaks, which form a natural barrier from east to west. They include **Pico de Orizaba** (Orizaba Peak) (5,747m/18,850ft), Mexico's tallest, also known as Citlaltépetl, "Montaña del Amanecer" (Sunrise Mountain); **Popocatépetl** (5,452m/17,883ft) or "Cerro que Humea" (Smoky Mountain), which since 1994 has lived up to its name by increasing its volcanic activity and covering the sky with enormous smoke clouds; **Iztaccíhuatl** (5,386m/17,666ft) or "Mujer Dormida" (Sleeping Woman); and the **Nevado de Toluca** (4,690m/15,383ft), also called Xinantécatl, "Montaña del Ocaso" (Sunset Mountain) or "Lugar de los Nueve Cerros Nevados" (Place of the Nine Snow-Covered Peaks). The summits of these elevations are covered with snow year-round. Despite their location in subtropical latitudes, dense jungles thrive at the foot of the volcanoes. A similar paradox occurs with desert landscapes found in tropical regions, such as the depression of the Balsas River at the point where it flows into the Pacific Ocean.

The great mountain chains previously cited also contain two huge plateaus: in the north-central part, the **Altiplanicie Mexicana** (2,000–2,500m/6,560–8,200ft) and, to its south, bound by mountain spurs, the **Meseta de Anáhuac** (2,240m/7,347ft). The less important and less extensive low plains comprise the Gulf and Pacific coasts, into which flow the streams of the Sierra Madre Oriental and the Sierra Madre Occidental.

Natural Regions and Flora – Mexico's northern desert zones include rocky deserts in **Baja California** and sandy deserts in Sonora and Sinaloa, mostly populated by cacti. By contrast, dense forests, consisting of both pine and oak trees, abound in the mountains, sierras and plains that extend throughout Mexico. Sharp contrasts of tall and medium forests, covered with fog almost year-round, characterize the sides of the mountain ranges, which generally present roughly cut slopes down to sea level (such as those of the Sierra Madre Oriental, called **Huastecas**, found in San Luis Potosí, Tamaulipas, Hidalgo and Veracruz). Vast, arid groves and pastures abounding in prickly pears and agave plants, as well as wide spaces dedicated to extensive cattle ranching, are found in the **Altiplanicie Mexicana** (Mexican High Plateau), primarily in Chihuahua, Coahuila, Durango and Zacatecas. Isolated mountain elements, such as rocky crevices shaped by erosion, occasionally interrupt these open spaces.

The **Meseta de Anáhuac** (Anáhuac Plateau) comprises extensive plains with a few mountain spurs of lesser importance, as well as the marshy valleys of Chapala, Yuriria and Cuitzeo, which thrive in the diverse agricultural activities in the Bajío. These activities benefit from the Lerma-Santiago River, which nurtures the land until it reaches the Pacific Ocean in San,Blas, Nayarit, and the Moctezuma Pánuco River, originating in the northern part of the Valley of Mexico and flowing into the Gulf of Mexico. Savannas, low thorny jungles, and medium and low jungles, with ceiba trees, palm trees, mangrove trees and bulrushes, line the **Pacific** and **Gulf coasts**. They are bathed by the Grijalva, Usumacinta, Papaloapan and Coatzacoalcos rivers, which flow into the Gulf, and by the Balsas River (important for generating hydroelectric power) between the states of Guerrero and Michoacán.

A canopy of jungles to the north and to the south, mostly unexplored, covers the limy soil of the **Yucatán**. The coastlines of this platform hold lagoons of calcareous and coral origins, interconnected with the sea, both underground and at the surface. Due to infiltration phenomena, this peninsula does not experience superficial draining, which explains the formation of the **cenotes**.

SAN DIEGO

PHOENIX

UNITED STATES

3078 △

PENINSULA

Colorado

Gila

Ciudad
Juárez

Río Grande

I. Cedros

Golfo

Hermosillo

SIERRA

Chihuahua

3102 △

de

DE

(Mar de Cortés)

California

Sierra
Tarahumara

MADRE

Altiplanicie

BAJA

CALIFORNIA

23°27' Tropic of Cancer

2164 △

Cabo San Lucas

Durango

OCCIDENTAL

Mexicana

2956 △

San Luis Potosí

R. Gde. de Santiago

19°

Cabo Corrientes

GUADALAJARA

Lerma

Nevado
de Colima

V. Tancítaro

Sierra

SIERRA

OCÉANO

PACÍFICO

Nevado de Colima
4240m/13911ft

Volcán de Fuego

Volcán Tancítaro
3860m/12664ft

5000m
16404ft

2000m
6562ft

Río Tepalcatepec

Río Cutzamala

Sea Level
Pacific Ocean

Balsas
Depression

Cross section following Parallel 19° North

OF AMERICA

DALLAS

Jackson

Mississippi

Alabama

Rio Colorado

Brazos

Brazo

HOUSTON

NEW ORLEANS

SIERRA

MADRE

ORIENTAL

MONTERREY

Matamoros

4054 △

GOLFO DE MÉXICO

Tropic of Cancer   23°27'

Pánuco

Tampico

Meseta del Anáhuac

Mérida

Cancún

I. Cozumel

Golfo de Campeche

Península

de Yucatán

MAR

19°

MÉXICO
de Toluca   Iztaccíhuatl
                 V. de
                 Malinche

Popocatépetl   Puebla   Pico
                              de Orizaba

Volcánica

Veracruz

Chetumal

DE LAS

2703 △

3414 △

Transversal

1879 △

Oaxaca

Istmo de

Tehuantepec

Grijalva

Usumacinta

2784 △

Belmopan

BELIZE

ANTILLAS

(Caribe
Mexicano)

capulco

MADRE   DEL   SUR

Golfo
de Tehuantepec

Sierra Madre de Chiapas

GUATEMALA

Ciudad de
Guatemala

HONDURAS

EL
SALVADOR

Iztaccíhuatl
5386m/
17159ft

Popocatépetl
5452m/17930ft

Pico de Orizaba
5747m/18406ft

Sierra de Monte Alto

evado de Toluca
4690m/15387ft

Ajusco
3930m/
12894ft

Volcán de Malinche
4461m/14636ft

Valley
of Toluca

Valley
of Mexico

Valley
of Puebla

Sea Level
Gulf of Mexico

500 km

250 mi

Scarlet Macaw

Fauna – Broadly defined, America's two extensive fauna regions, the **Nearctic** and the **Neotropical**, find their boundaries in Mexican territory, at the height of the Sierra Volcánica and Mexico's southern depressions. This region is known as the **Mexican zone of transition**. It allows a mixture of both elements, thus forming a complex zoographical partnership. While **bears**, **wolves** and **coyotes** are most characteristic of the Nearctic mammals, **monkeys**, **deer**, **jaguars** and **armadillos** abound in the Neotropical fauna. Animals found in both American regions include the **puma**, **ocelot** and **lynx**, as well as a wide variety of **reptiles**, such as the caimans of the coastal lagoons, and birds with beautiful plumage, such as flamingos, **macaws** and parrots.

National Parks – Mexico's great wealth of flora and fauna has motivated the creation of a significant number of national parks. However, not all of them offer camping facilities. The objective of these sites is to delimit the wildlife reserves to prevent the extinction of certain species; manage archaeological remains, caves and zones of geological interest; regulate hunting; and control forest exploitation of wood species, such as the forests of precious woods found in the tropical regions. The most noteworthy parks include Basaseáchi in Chihuahua; Lagos de Montebello in Chiapas; Eduardo Ruiz in Michoacán; Lagunas de Chacahua, in Oaxaca; and Garrafón in Isla Mujeres.

Economy

Tourism – Mexico's most important activities with respect to its national production are its **services** (businesses, restaurants and hotels), with 65.5% of the Gross Domestic Product (GDP). A leading industry in Mexico's economic growth, tourism occupies third place (after petroleum and manufactured goods) in foreign income.

The yearly flow of incoming foreign visitors reaches 22 million, mainly from the United States. Mexico possesses an adequate infrastructure of hotels and services, particularly at those sites most frequented by tourists. Vestiges of pre-Hispanic art, colonial cities, beaches, indigenous cultures and their colorful handicrafts are some of the highlights that attract tourists.

Industry – Industrial activity holds second place in generating the country's national product, with 28.8% of the GDP. The most important industries include textiles, food, iron and steel, transportation equipment, chemical products and machinery. These industries are concentrated in the major cities, such as Mexico City, Monterrey, Guadalajara, Puebla and Veracruz.

Another important aspect of Mexico's economy is the **maquiladora industry** (manufacturing), found in major cities along the border with the United States. These operations are dedicated to assembling or transforming raw materials, electrical equipment, clothing and transportation equipment, which are imported temporarily and then returned to their country of origin (mainly the United States) once the final product is obtained.

Mining – Mexico's traditional mining wealth is determined by its geological structure. The most important mining centers are located in the country's northern mountain regions. Although this activity's importance has decreased, Mexico still occupies first place worldwide in **silver** production and figures among the world's top five producers of zinc, mercury, fluorite and sulfur.

Petroleum and **natural gas**, the most significant resources in the nation's mining industry, are managed by **Petróleos Mexicanos (PEMEX)**, the country's largest enterprise. Today the primary regions of exploitation are located in southern Mexico (in Tabasco, Chiapas and the marine platform of Campeche) along with the coastal region of the Gulf of Mexico (Tamaulipas and Veracruz), which produces 2,858 million barrels of crude oil daily. Mexico ranks among the world's five top exporters of "black gold."

Agriculture – In spite of Mexico's urban and industrial growth, agriculture still plays an important role in the livelihood of many Mexicans. It employs 60% of the nation's economically active population, and it is extremely diverse, encompassing products from both tropical regions and temperate and cold areas. The country's six main products include **corn**, **beans**, **wheat**, **sugar cane**, **coffee** and **sorghum**. The first two are the staples

Harvesting Corn, Oaxaca

of the Mexican diet, and almost half of the arable land is dedicated to their cultivation. Wheat and sugar cane are also staples of general consumption. Coffee, on the other hand, constitutes the main agricultural export. Sorghum stands out for its positive impact in the development of poultry and hog farming.

Ranching – The ecological conditions in most regions of Mexico favor cattle ranching activities, which are practiced throughout the country. Of particular commercial importance, bovine breeding is popular primarily in northern Mexico (Chihuahua, Durango, Sonora and Zacatecas) and a significant amount of live cattle is exported to the US. In the rest of the country, the sale of livestock generally is targeted to meet the needs of the domestic market.

Fishing – The nation's most productive region, in terms of fishing resources, is the northwestern coast (Ensenada, Guaymas, Mazatlán and La Paz). Sardines, tuna, shrimp, oysters and lobsters, among other species abound. **Shrimping** represents more than one third of the value of all the fish caught in Mexico, and it is the primary fishing export. Important ports include Tampico, Veracruz, Progreso and Cozumel.

We welcome corrections and suggestions that may assist us in preparing the next edition. Please send us your comments:
  Michelin Travel Publications
  Editorial Department
  P. O. Box 19001
  Greenville, SC 29602-9001
  TheGreenGuide-us@us.michelin.com

Time Line

Origins

50,000 BC	First migration of Asiatic peoples to America via the Bering Strait.
12,000 BC	Tepexpan man. The most ancient remains found in Mexico.
9,000 BC	Corn harvesting begins.
7,000 BC	Probable beginnings of sedentary communities and agriculture.

Pre-Hispanic Era

1800–200 BC — **Pre-Classic Era**

Establishment of communities in the central part of the continent, known as Mesoamerica. These communities lived off fishing, gathering, hunting and farming, mainly of corn, beans, chili peppers and pumpkins. Development of the **Olmec culture** south of the Gulf of Mexico. The Olmecs were very influential and soon dominated other towns and villages. Origins of settlements in the Maya lowlands and building of foundations in Monte Albán.

200 BC–AD 900 — **Classic Era**

Maximum development of pre-Hispanic civilizations and consolidation of Mesoamerican cultures' characteristics in the arts, ceramics, writing, the calendar, medicine, mathematics and astronomy. Formation of ruling theocratic castes. **Polytheistic religion** is converted into the integrating nucleus of all aspects of indigenous life. Splendor of Teotihuacán, Monte Albán (Zapotec), Mitla (Zapotec), Uxmal, Palenque, El Tajín, Cobá, Bonampak, Yaxchilán; decline of the great cities of Cacaxtla and Xochicalco.

900–1521 — **Post-Classic Era**

Demographic growth and the impoverishment of farmers, combined with the invasion of nomadic groups originating from the north, unleashes a crisis that is halted two centuries later with the implementation of **military governments**; the latter favors the worship of merciless gods who demand human sacrifices. Emergence of metallurgy. Mesoamerica reaches its maximum expansion. Great development of the Toltecs in Tula. Height of Mitla (Mixtec) and Monte Albán (Mixtec).

1325 — **Founding of Mexico-Tenochtitlán**: Mexica (or Aztec) rule is initiated within and beyond the Mesoamerican territory.

The Conquest

1511 — The crewmembers of a Spanish vessel are shipwrecked near Jamaica and captured by the Yucatán Maya, among them **Jerónimo de Aguilar** who later encounters **Hernán Cortés** and serves as his interpreter.

1517 — Exploratory expedition is led by **Francisco Hernández de Córdoba** along the Yucatán coastline.

Epic of Mexico, Mural by Diego Rivera, National Palace

1518	**Juan de Grijalva** navigates from the island of Cozumel to Cabo Roxo in the Tamiahua Lagoon, along the Mexican coast, thus acquiring his first impression of Mesoamerica's grandeur.
1519	Mesoamerica's population: 25 million inhabitants. **Alfonso Álvarez Pineda** travels along the coast of the Gulf of Mexico, from Florida to the Pánuco River.
Feb 1519	The governor of Cuba, **Diego de Velázquez**, sends Hernán Cortés to the Yucatán coast. While in Tabasco, Cortés meets **La Malinche**, who together with Jerónimo de Aguilar, serves as the key to the Conquest of Mexico, for Aguilar speaks Spanish and Maya, and La Malinche speaks Maya and Náhuatl.
April 1519	Cortés founds the first Spanish settlement named the **Villa Rica de la Vera Cruz** (Rich Village of Vera Cruz), sinks the ships and initiates an inland exploration, defeating **Xicohténcatl** and the Tlaxcaltec people, whom he converts into his powerful allies against the Aztec Empire.
Nov 1519	The Spaniards arrive at Tenochtitlán. **Moctezuma II** receives them peacefully, lodges them in the Axayácatl Palace and showers them with honors and gifts. A few days later, Cortés takes Moctezuma II prisoner.
1520	Upon finding out that Pánfilo de Narváez has arrived with orders to replace him, Cortés goes on his search to combat him, leaving Pedro de Alvarado in charge of Tenochtitlán. The latter allows the celebration of a religious feast, which ends in a battle known as the **Matanza del Templo Mayor** (Killing at the Great Temple). The Spaniards are surrounded; while trying to escape, they are discovered and attacked, resulting in a bloody massacre; this event is known as **La Noche Triste** (Sad Night).
May 1521	With the help of 450,000 Tlaxcaltecs, the Spaniards, after defeating other Aztec fortifications, initiate the siege of Tenochtitlán, which lasts 75 days.
August 1521	**Fall of Tenochtitlán**.

■ La Malinche

The famous character of La Malinche—Cortés' translator, advisor and mistress—facilitated the meeting between the Spaniards and the Aztecs. She, along with 20 other maidens, was a welcoming gift offered by Tabscob, a Maya ruler who lived in the area known today as the state of Tabasco. In 1522 she gave birth to Martín Cortés, son of the conquistador and one of the first mestizos on the American continent.

© Bob Schalkwijk /Col. INBA

Colonial Era

1522–1536	The Spaniards conduct a series of expeditions to strengthen and expand their dominion.
1524	Spiritual conquest is initiated with the arrival of 12 **Franciscan friars**, who are followed by **Dominicans** (1526) and **Augustinians** (1533). They undertake a gargantuan task, as they deal directly with the indigenous peoples, learn their language, gain their trust and facilitate the fusion of cultures.
1528	King Charles V establishes in New Spain the first *audiencia* (high court), which assumes judicial and governmental powers.
1531	A second *audiencia* is formed, where the seat of Royal Authority is initiated, a task that is continued by the first two viceroys: Mendoza and Velasco.
1539	First print shop is introduced.
1553	Inauguration of the **Real y Pontificia Universidad de México** (Royal and Pontifical University of Mexico) which held the same privileges as the University of Salamanca and housed five schools.
1566	Conspiracy of **Martín Cortés**. Upon realizing that the Spanish Crown has centralized all the decision-making and power, and that they have been stripped of their privileges, the conquistadors decide to rebel.
1571	Founding of the **Tribunal del Santo Oficio** (Holy Office Court).
1651	**Sor Juana Inés de la Cruz**, renowned Mexican poetess, is born in San Miguel Nepantla.
1692	**Insurrection in Mexico City**. The people set afire the viceroys' palace and city hall.
1767	Expulsion of the Jesuits by orders of King Charles III.
1809	**Conspiracy of Valladolid** by Captain García Obeso, Lieutenant Mariano Michelena and Private Vicente de Santa María; they attempt to form an assembly that will govern the country in the name of Ferdinand VII.
1810	**Conspiracy of Querétaro**. The plotters from this city rely on the support of Spanish magistrate Miguel Domínguez and his wife **Josefa Ortiz de Domínguez**; they meet regularly to address topics linked to their desire for independence. The meetings' participants include Aldama and Allende; the latter informs Father Miguel Hidalgo of the outcome.

Independence

Sept 1810	**War of Independence** (1810–21).
	In the atrium of the Parish Church of Dolores, located in the state of Guanajuato, Father **Miguel Hidalgo y Costilla** rises up in arms against the Spanish government to fight for Mexico's independence. In Atotonilco he grabs the banner of the Virgin of Guadalupe and is followed by an army of civilians heading toward Mexico City; Ignacio Allende, Juan Aldama, Mariano Jiménez and Mariano Abasolo accompany him.
1811	The insurgents are defeated at the battle of the Bridge of Calderón; their leaders are forced to head north in search of backup, but in Acatita de Baján, Ignacio Elizondo betrays them. Hidalgo, Allende, Aldama and Abasolo are tried, and all, except Abasolo, are sentenced to the death penalty. By then, a great number of rebels have spread throughout the country. They include Amo Torres in New Galicia, Father José María Mercado in Nayarit, José María González Hermosillo in Sonora, Rafael Iriarte in Zacatecas and Father **José María Morelos** in the south. The latter is the most brilliant of all. Successor of Hidalgo in the armed battle, he seizes almost the entire territory of the present state of Guerrero; the Galván brothers, the Bravo brothers and **Vicente Guerrero** join him.
1814	Constitution of Apatzingán is proclaimed, but never goes into effect.
1817	Continuation of the armed struggle led by Francisco Xavier Mina, Mier y Terán, Vicente Guerrero and Torres.
1821	**Agustín de Iturbide** proclaims the **Plan de Iguala** or the Plan of the Three Guarantees: one religion, union of all social groups, and Mexico's independence with a constitutional monarchy.
Aug 1821	Viceroy Juan de O'Donojú signs the Treaty of Córdoba, which ratifies the Plan de Iguala.
Sept 1821	Independence is consummated with the triumphant entry into Mexico City by the **Trigarante Army** led by Agustín Iturbide, and the first independent government is formed.

1822–23	**First Empire**: Iturbide is crowned emperor under the name of Agustín I, whose empire extends from Oregon and the Colorado River to Panama.
	At the beginning of 1823, **Antonio López de Santa Anna** creates the **Plan de Casa Mata**, a project to establish the Republic. Former insurgents and Bourbonists of the Conservative Party join in this effort, which results in the demise of the empire on March 19, 1823. Iturbide is exiled to Liorna, Italy. The Kingdom of Guatemala opts for its separation and independence.
1824	The **Constitution of Mexico**, which established the Federal Republic, becomes law.
1836	Texas, New Mexico and California declare their independence.
1846–48	During the presidency of General Antonio López de Santa Anna, a war breaks out against the US and ends with the signing of the **Treaty of Guadalupe**, through which Mexico recognizes the independence of Texas, New Mexico and California. Combined, these states made up more than half of the Mexican territory.
1855	Ignacio Comonfort, president pro tem. The era of anarchy and chaos ends.
1856	The promulgation of the **Leyes de Reforma** (Reform Laws) is initiated to achieve the separation of church and state.
1857	The Constitution is proclaimed; as a result Ignacio Comonfort is elected president and liberal **Benito Juárez** is elected vice-president. The Plan of Tacubaya, led by General Felix Zuloaga, incites the conservatives to rebel. Comonfort, seeking the nation's peace, abolishes the Constitution and divides his own party.
1858–61	**Reform War**. With an improvised army and many deficiencies, the liberal party, headed by **Benito Juárez**, dives into a struggle for legality and against the conservatives. Juárez flees and later installs his government at the port of Veracruz, combating for three years the conservative forces that had declared General Miguel Miramón president of Mexico.

Don Benito Juárez
(c.1860)

Teixidor: Cruces Y Campa/INAH

1859	In Veracruz, Juárez issues the **Reform Laws**-signifying nationalization of all ecclesiastical property except church buildings; recognition of marriage as an event requiring a civil contract; establishment of the Registrar's Office; secularization of all cemeteries; and freedom of worship.
1861	The economic crisis leads President Juárez to suspend payment of the national debt; this propels the creditor nations (France, England and Spain) to sign the **Tratados de La Soledad** (Treaties of Solitude), by which France does not abide, thus initiating the invasion of Mexico.
1862	At the **Cinco de Mayo Battle** in Puebla, the French are defeated by the Mexican Army, and it is not until almost a year later that Napoleon's forces are able to break the city's resistance. Juárez abandons the capital and establishes his government in Paso del Norte (the present-day Ciudad Juárez), where he remains for the duration of the Second Empire.

Maximilian of Hapsburg
(c.1860)

Teixidor: Cruces Y Campa/INAH

1864	**Second Empire: Maximilian of Hapsburg** is declared Emperor of Mexico. He signs the Treaty of Miramar with Napoleon III, in which he agrees to pay the cost of the intervention, an exorbitant amount, and which dictates the policy his government should follow.
1867	Maximilian finds himself unprotected by France and wishes to abandon the throne, but the conservatives convince him to remain in power. He is attacked by the Republicans and decides to center his power in Querétaro. He is finally captured and executed alongside Miramón and Mejía on the hill of Las Campanas. The Republic is restored with Juárez as president.
1873	Under the administration of Lerdo de Tejada, the **Rebelión de los Cristeros** (a revolt led by militant Catholics) takes place in Guanajuato and Jalisco, in protest to the provisions of the 1859 Reform Laws.

The Porfiriato 1877–1911

General **Porfirio Díaz** remained in power for 33 years, achieving an economic boom and greater exploitation of Mexico's mining and petroleum industries. He accomplished important public works and attracted foreign capital. During the *Porfiriato*, Mexico's middle and upper classes, attracted to French art and culture, went to the extent of mimicking the French architectural style with mansards and inclined roofs, in a country that had never seen snow. The paternalism of General Díaz' dictatorship did nothing to halt abuses and censorship of the press, the seizing of farmlands, and the submission of peasant farmers to work for haciendas under unjust conditions.

1893	To obtain England's recognition of his government, Díaz cedes part of the Mexican territory, which is annexed to Belize.
1908	Díaz-Creelman interview; Díaz declares that his legitimate successor should emerge from the organization of Mexicans in true political parties, from a free and open electoral fight. Díaz's words provoke the creation of opposition parties.
1910	**Francisco I. Madero** formulates the **Plan of San Luis**, a revolutionary treaty that calls for free suffrage, no reelection, and an armed uprising for November 20.

General Porfirio Díaz
(c.1910)

Fondo Coloniales/INAH

The Revolution

1910–20	President Díaz is defeated and abandons the country on a ship to Europe. Armed Revolutionary Movement.
1911	In the south, several groups take up arms; the Figueroa brothers in the state of Guerrero seize the capital city of Chilpancingo, and **Emiliano Zapata** announces the **Plan of Ayala**, demanding a solution to the agrarian problem with his motto *"Tierra y Libertad"* (Land and Liberty). However, the revolution reaches its greatest victory in the north, with the capture of Ciudad Juárez. Madero assumes the presidency.
1913	**Decena Trágica** (Tragic Ten Days): the ten days during which Mexico City is under siege. **Victoriano Huerta** betrays Madero and signs the Pact of the Citadel, or Pact of the Embassy. Madero and Pino Suárez are forced to resign; Pedro Lascurain is declared interim president; Madero and Pino Suárez are apprehended and, two days later, assassinated. When Huerta assumes the presidency, the armed struggle resumes. **Venustiano Carranza** assumes the title of First Chief of the Constitutionalist Army and launches a campaign against Huerta. Carranza is accompanied by revolutionary caudillos, including **Álvaro Obregón**, who leads the campaign in the west, **Pablo González** in the east, and **Francisco Villa** (more commonly known as Pancho Villa) in central Mexico, who at the helm of the Northern Division fights the most brilliant battles against the federal army.
1917	A new **Constitution** is decreed. It guarantees an eight-hour workday, freedom to teach, and other provisions. Venustiano Carranza is elected constitutional president.
1919	Emiliano Zapata is ambushed and slain.
1920	Congress declares Adolfo de la Huerta provisional president of the Triumphant Revolution. A national reconstruction task begins.
1923	Francisco Villa is assassinated.

Fondo Casasola/Fototeca del INAH

Pancho Villa in Presidential Chair alongside Emiliano Zapata,
Mexico City (December 6, 1914)

1926	Provoked by tensions between church and state, the **Rebelión Cristera** is initiated during the administration of General Plutarco Elías Calles.
1929	Formation of the first, official political party called the Partido Nacional Revolucionario (National Revolutionary Party), today known as the **Partido Revolucionario Institucional (PRI)** (Institutional Revolutionary Party).
1938	General **Lázaro Cárdenas'** administration brings a halt to the armed struggle that broke out in 1910. Cárdenas achieves peace with the *Cristeros* (militant Catholics), decrees the expropriation of oil companies, and creates the Exporting Company of National Petroleum. A year after it is nationalized, the railroad company is handed over to the Railroad Workers Union. Education and culture receive greater support.
1946	The PRI paves the way for a civil government, with **Miguel Alemán Valdés** as president (1946–1952).
1968	Student movement, repression and killing of students in Tlatelolco. Olympic Games are held in Mexico.
1970–76	Luis Echevarría Álvarez, president of Mexico. **World Cup** held in Mexico for the first time (1970).
1976–82	José López Portillo, president of Mexico. Nationalization of the Bank (1982).
1982–88	Miguel de la Madrid Hurtado, president of Mexico.
Sept 1985	Two earthquakes devastate Mexico City and other towns.
1986	Significant reduction in oil prices. Mexico enters the General Agreement on Tariffs and Trade (GATT). World Cup held in Mexico for the second time.
1988–94	Carlos Salinas de Gortari, president of Mexico.
1994	Armed rising in Chiapas led by the Ejército Zapatista de Liberación Nacional (EZLN) (National Liberation Zapatista Army), under the leadership of Subcomandante Marcos; the **North American Free Trade Association (NAFTA)**, signed by Canada, the United States and Mexico, goes into effect; strong devaluation of the Mexican peso, the worst of the 20C.
1994–2000	Ernesto Zedillo Ponce de León, president of Mexico. Era of economic recovery and democratic transition.
1997	**Cuauhtémoc Cárdenas**, member of the Democratic Revolutionary Party (Partido de la Revolución Democrática–PRD), wins first elections for Mayor ("Head of Government") of Mexico City.
June 1999	Two earthquakes shake up the states of Oaxaca, Tlaxcala, Guerrero and Puebla, particularly affecting the city of Puebla.
July 2000	**Vicente Fox Quesada**, member of the center-right National Action Party, or PAN (Partido de Acción Nacional), defeats the presidential candidate of the 71-year ruling PRI.

Addresses, telephone numbers, opening hours and prices published in this guide are accurate at press time. We apologize for any inconvenience resulting from outdated information. Please send us your comments:
  Michelin Travel Publications
  Editorial Department
  P. O. Box 19001
  Greenville, SC 29602-9001
  TheGreenGuide-us@us.michelin.com

Indigenous Presence

What is Mesoamerica?

In 1943 anthropologist Paul Kirchoff coined the term **Mesoamerica**, "Middle America," to name the geographical region of the ancient cultures that developed in North and Central America. The zone stretched from the state of Sinaloa to Honduras, whose inhabitants shared similar customs. Due to its vastness, Mesoamerica is divided into the following cultural regions *(map p 33)*.

Mexico and Other Civilizations

Mexico	BC	Other Civilizations
First settlers of America.	50,000	
	30,000	Paleolithic period. Cave paintings in southwestern France and northern Spain.
	3000–1750	Flourishing of Babylon. Cheops Pyramid, Chephren Pyramid and the Great Sphinx.
Flourishing of the Olmecs.	1820–200	
Archaic cultures: Copilco, Cuicuilco.	1520–200	
Beginnings of Monte Albán.	8C	Olympic Games in Olympia.
First settlement of the Maya lowlands.	500	
	447–432	Construction of the Parthenon.
Beginnings of Teotihuacán.	200–150	

Mexico	AD	Other Civilizations
	circa 72–80	Construction of the Coliseum in Rome.
Splendor of the Maya culture.	100–800	
Apogee of Teotihuacán.	200–500	
	330	Founding of Constantinople.
Great development in Monte Albán.	400–800	
	532–537	Construction of Hagia Sophia in Istanbul.
Splendor of Xochicalco.	800	Crowning of Charlemagne as emperor in Rome.
Height of the Toltec culture: Tula.	1000	
	1000–1150	Peak of the Romanesque period.
Foundation of Mexico-Tenochtitlán.	1325	
	1163–1235	Construction of Notre Dame Cathedral in Paris.
	1492	Columbus "discovers" America.
	1508–1512	Michelangelo paints the Sistine Chapel.
Hernández de Córdoba explores the Yucatán coast.	1517	Luther's Protestant Reformation.
Cortés reaches Veracruz.	1519	Mannerism flourishes.
Fall of Tenochtitlán (Aztec Empire).	1521	
	1527	Pizarro discovers the Inca Empire.
	1540	The Society of Jesus is founded. The Portuguese arrive in Japan.
Discovery of Zacatecas; beginnings of mining success.	1545–1563	Council of Trent; Counter Reformation.
	1598	Escorial Monastery is built.
	1656	Diego de Velázquez paints *Las Meninas*.
	1661–1710	Versailles Palace is built.
The conquistadors begin to resent Spain, which eventually leads to the War of Independence.	1740	
Jesuits are expelled from New Spain.	1767	Jesuits are expelled from Spain and its empire.

West — Different peoples have inhabited the region between the south of Sinaloa and the state of Guerrero. During the pre-Classic period, the **Purépechas**—settlers in the area of Michoacán, whom the Spaniards called **Tarascans**—stood out in western Mesoamerica. In comparison with their contemporaries, these indigenous peoples possessed an advanced technological capacity. They used copper for decoration and arms manufacture, which made them one of the most difficult groups to subdue during the pre-Hispanic era. The architecture of the Purépechas was well developed, as is seen in their capital city of Tzintzuntzan. Their excellent ceramics adopted abstract plant motifs and had a fine, brilliantly colored finish.

In the present-day states of Colima and Nayarit, artistic forms were modeled after domestic animals. Such was the case of the **tepezcuintle**, dogs fattened to feed certain sectors of the population.

	1776	US gains independence from England.
	1789	French Revolution.
Capture of Iturrigaray.	**1808**	Napoleonic invasion of Spain.
War of Independence.	**1810–21**	Bourbon monarchy in Spain.
		Napoleon abdicates at Fontainebleau.
Independence is consummated with Iturbide's Plan of Iguala.	**1821**	Greek War of Independence against the Turks.
Agustín de Iturbide's Empire.	**1822–23**	Reestablishment of absolutism in Spain.
Guadalupe Victoria, Mexico's first president.	**1824–29**	
Loss of Texas, New Mexico and California during Santa Anna's presidency.	**1836**	Second Industrial Revolution. Proclamation of the French Republic. Marx and Engels publish *The Communist Manifesto*.
Reform Laws	**1859**	Darwin· *The Origin of the Species*.
French intervention, Cinco de Mayo Battle in Puebla.	**1862**	
Empire of Maximilian of Hapsburg.	**1864**	
	1865	End of the American Civil War. Lincoln is assassinated.
The Republic is reinstated, with Juárez as president.	**1867**	Marx: *Das Kapital*.
	1874	First exhibition of Impressionist painters.
The Porfiriato (Dictatorship of Porfirio Díaz).	**1877–1910**	End of the Carlist War in Spain. Setting up of the Triple Alliance and the Triple Entente.
First workmen's strikes.	**1906**	
	1907	Pablo Picasso paints *Les Demoiselles d'Avignon*.
Mexican Revolution.	**1910–1920**	First World War. Russian Revolution. Futurism and Dadaism.
Manifesto of the Painters and Sculptors' Union, point of departure for mural paintings.	**1922**	
	1924	Surrealist Manifesto in Paris.
Establishment of the Partido Nacional Revolucionario (National Revolutionary Party), today the Partido Revolucionario Institucional (PRI) (Institutional Revolutionary Party).	**1929**	The Great Depression.
Presidency of Lázaro Cárdenas. Expropriation of foreign oil companies.	**1934–1940**	Spanish Civil War; Beginning of World War II.
	1959	Cuban Revolution.
Student movement, Olympic Games.	**1968**	Violent student movements worldwide.
	1969	First landing on the moon.
	1973	End of the Vietnam War. Picasso dies.
Earthquake devastates Mexico City.	**1985**	
	1989	Fall of the Berlin Wall.
	1991	Dissolution of the USSR. Persian Gulf War.
500th anniversary of the "discovery" of America.	**1992**	
First elections for Head of Government (Mayoralty) of Mexico City.	**1997**	China repossesses Hong Kong.

Central Plateau – The abundant natural resources and strategic advantages derived from occupying a central location have made the plateau the seat of the most powerful groups in Mexican history.

During the pre-Classic period, in places such as **Tlatilco**, its inhabitants modeled statuettes related to agriculture; and in other places, such as Cuicuilco, the first great stone foundations were built.

During the Classic period, one of the most formidable religious metropolises of the ancient world flourished at Teotihuacán, the cultural capital of Mesoamerica. From the monumental temples built atop artificial mountains that blend with the peaks on the distant horizon, the ruling priests wielded religious power that extended as far as Guatemala. The sober and austere spirit of the era was reflected in architecture by the **talud-tablero** configuration on the pyramids' facades, which consisted of a series of inclined walls *(taludes)* surmounted by horizontal panels *(tableros)*.

Political instability, war and famine may have caused the fall of the City of Gods in the 8C AD. This catastrophe did not bring about the demise of Cholula or Cacaxtla, but it caused the subsequent rebirth of Xochicalco, where one of Mesoamerica's most famous *taludes* was carved.

During the early post-Classic period, Tula began to exercise its hegemony by exalting military values that were expressed architecturally in **warrior-shaped columns**, defensive walls and tombstones depicting heart-devouring animals. However, nomadic invasions halted this development, forcing its Toltec inhabitants to migrate south and settle in faraway Chichén Itzá, a site where the Maya masterfully interpreted the religion of the plateau.

After burning Tula, the Chichimecs from the north moved on to **Tenayuca** and later to Texcoco, where they created a powerful kingdom.

In 1325 the **Mexicas** (or **Aztecs**) founded the greatest religious, administrative and cultural center of pre-Columbian America, México-Tenochtitlán. Its imposing stone sculpture reveals a strong temperament: carved vases to contain sacrificial blood, reliefs with fire serpents or scenes of self-sacrifices, and gods wearing the skin of their victims or covering their faces with tragic masks.

Gulf of Mexico – The Gulf basin, with a richly varied flora and fauna, witnessed three highly developed civilizations during the pre-Hispanic era. Considered the mother culture of Mesoamerica for having laid the basis for its cultural development, the **Olmec** civilization was established (1800 BC) in the region with the heaviest rainfall in the country. For this reason, only a few, poorly preserved archaeological remains have survived to the present date.

The Olmecs produced monumental sculptures with astonishing **colossal heads**, including the jaguar as their principal deity. They maintained a strong social hierarchy and were the first to carve a stone calendar. The leading ceremonial centers of the Olmec culture consisted of San Lorenzo, La Venta and Tres Zapotes.

In the Center of Veracruz, during the Classic period, the **Totonacs** settled in the city of El Tajín and furthered trading with the inhabitants of the plateau. They also carved yokes, palms and funeral axes, which contrast with the contagious merriment of their **caritas sonrientes** (little smiling faces) modeled in clay.

The apogee of the **Huastec** (or **Huaxtec**) culture occurred during the post-Classic period, north of the Gulf, where they fought repeatedly against the Mexica. Their relative independence allowed them to concentrate their religious beliefs on fertility, producing sculptures of figures with prominent sexual organs and gods associated with agricultural wealth.

Oaxaca – In the mountainous state of Oaxaca, numerous communities existed without common cultural links, a fact that can still be observed in their ethnic variety. During the pre-Hispanic era, the **Zapotecs** predominated in the southeast and later the **Mixtecs** in the northwest. Both located their principal ceremonial centers in the heart of Monte Albán, Mitla and Yagul. Monte Albán warrants special interest because of its ingenious construction plan atop a hill and also because it served both as a city and cemetery. In the entire region, art encompassed great architectural innovations. Massive structures harmonized with the use of the terrain and the **tablero escapulario**, which originated in Teotihuacán and contained a vast panel on which moldings in the form of simple frets were applied as decoration, allowing the play of light to create a chiaroscuro effect. The development of high-quality **goldsmithing** in this region stands out for its extremely fine filigree. Other decorative arts using feathers, clay sculpture and stone carving testify to the creativity of local craftsmen.

Maya – One of the most extraordinary civilizations of the ancient world, the Maya inhabited the present-day Mexican states of Yucatán, Quintana Roo, Campeche, Tabasco and Chiapas, and the countries of Belize, Guatemala, Honduras and El Salvador. Their admirable adaptation to an inhospitable climate and dense vegetation testifies to their complex and brilliant artistic and cultural development.

Constant observation of the stars' movements in the heavens, coupled with the enigmatic environment in which the Maya lived, may have contributed to their interpretative perceptiveness, as their magical expressions continue to astound and perplex researchers.

Cultural Regions of Mesoamerica

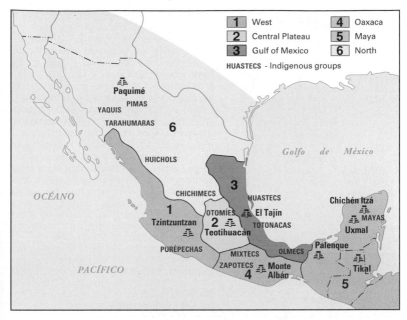

1 West		**4** Oaxaca	
2 Central Plateau		**5** Maya	
3 Gulf of Mexico		**6** North	

HUASTECS - Indigenous groups

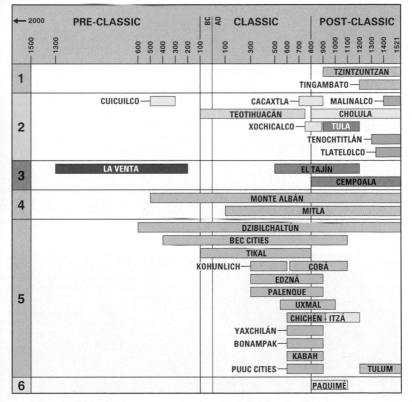

Predominant Cultures

Purépecha		Totonac	
Mexica		Zapotec-mixtec	
Teotihuacan		Olmec	
Toltec		Maya	
		Others	

33

Stela from Yaxchilán, Chiapas

Amidst these verdant settings, the monumental ceremonial centers such as Uxmal, Palenque and Yaxchilán remain as silent testimonies of the ancient Maya's ornamental riches, evidenced in their mural paintings, beautiful stucco masks, and decorated building facades with sober frets and elaborate cresting. The **Mayan arch** (or false arch), a triangular-shaped arch consisting of corbeled stone slabs meeting at the summit in a point or a slight curve *(photo p 330)*, demonstrates their ingenuity. This skillful architectural solution allowed for the dome-shaped ceilings that covered the temples. Special mention should be made of the exceptional **calendar glyphs** and sculptures, as well as their richly stylized and decorated ceramics. In some cases, the ceremonial centers were complemented with numerous **processional roadways**, which, in the Yucatán peninsula, connected different cities, creating an extensive network of **sacbés** (limestone roads) that facilitated the trade of merchandise.

Other Maya centers of greater splendor, characterized by their very lofty and imposing architecture, as well as their finely carved **stelae**, include Tikal and Quiriguá (both in Guatemala), Copán (in Honduras), and Caracol and Lamanai (both in Belize).

Northern Cultures

In northern Mexico, inhabited by semi-nomadic groups, such as the **Chichimecs** who lived by gathering and hunting, aridity was a major factor that impeded cultural development comparable to that of Mesoamerica. The so-called Desert Cultures led such a precarious existence that only in sites like Paquimé did they achieve extraordinary cultural expressions, as seen in their **ornamented ceramics** decorated with very simple aquatic and plant motifs, and in a few remnants of their basketwork.

From the end of the Classic period, the Chichimec invasions of Mesoamerica fostered their cultural and ethnic mixing, radically changing the future of the Central Plateau settlers, who subsequently were forced to defend their vulnerable northern frontier. The mythical island of **Aztlán** is located in this region. It was from here that the Chichimec tribes departed in search of the promised México-Tenochtitlán, which would later become the powerful Aztec Empire.

Present-day Indigenous Groups

Many of the 56 present-day groups, which comprise almost 10 million people, existed during the pre-Hispanic era. Their location within the national territory, as well as the climatic and topographical characteristics of the regions they inhabit, determine their lifestyles, including habitats, clothing, craftsmanship and economic activities, which consist mainly of agriculture and poultry farming.

Zapotec Woman and Child, Tlacolula, Oaxaca

Principal Indigenous Groups

Group	Location	Language	Handicrafts	Dances & Traditions
Amuzgos	Border between Guerrero and Oaxaca	Amuzgo	Textiles	Dances of the 12 Couples, the Conquest, Moors & Christians
Cucapá, Kiliwa, Cohimí, Pai Pai, Kimiai	Baja California Norte	Yumana family	Weavings with leather, beads, istle, wood and palm fiber	
Cuicatecs	In the northwest of Oaxaca state	Cuicatec	Textiles and pottery	Male dancers dressed as women (Huehuetones)
Chichimecs	San Luis de la Paz, Guanajuato	Chichimec	Woolen blankets and istle bags	La Checa game
Chinantecs	In the north of Oaxaca state, at the foothills of the Sierra Madre Oriental	Chinantec	Textiles	
Chontals	In the southwest of Oaxaca state	Chontal or Tlequistlatec	Textiles and pottery	Dance of the Little Horse
Huastecs	San Luis Potosí (SLP) & in the northern part of Veracruz	Huastec	Articles made of palm and agave fibers	Dances of the Huehues, Malinche, Blacks, Rebozos, Wands, etc.
Huichols	Jalisco, Nayarit and Durango	Huichol	Textiles, gourds and work in worsted wool	
Lacandons	Jungle of Chiapas	Lacandón	Bows and arrows	Renewal of the braziers
Maya	Campeche, Yucatán and Quintana Roo	Maya	Embroidery and sisal work	Jaranas, Dance of the Pig's Head
Mazahuas	Mexico City, Mexico State, Morelos, Michoacán	Mazahua	Carpets, throw rugs, bedspreads and tablecloths	
Mazatecs	Basin of the Papaloapan River	Mazatec	Textiles	
Mixes	In the northwest of Oaxaca state	Mixe or Ayook	Textiles and pottery	Dances: Los Negritos, the Conquest and the Tiger
Mixtecs	In the northwest of Oaxaca, Puebla and Guerrero	Mixtec	Articles made of palm leaves	Dances of the Puddles, the Blondes and the Chicholos
Nahuas	Mexico City, Hidalgo, Puebla, Morelos, Tlaxcala, SLP, Veracruz and Guerrero	Náhuatl	Bark paintings (amates), textiles and tin figures	Tlacoleros, the Snake, Ribbon Dance and agricultural rites
Otomís	Puebla, Hidalgo, Mexico State, Guanajuato, SLP	Otomí	Textiles, embroidery and basketry	
Pimas	In the southwestern part of Chihuahua and eastern part of Sonora	Pima	Basketry	
Tarahumaras	Mountainous knot of the Sierra Madre Occidental	Tarahumara	Work in palm, wood, ceramic and wool textiles	Dance of the Pascola, the Matachines and the Deer Dance
Tarascans (Purépechas)	Michoacán plateau	Tarascan or Purépecha	Work in wood, metal, pottery, hats and wool articles	Dances: Los Negritos, The Little Old Men
Tepehuans	Nayarit and Durango	Tepehuan	Simple pottery	Dance of the Matachines
Triques	In Oaxaca's southwestern part	Trique	Textiles	
Tzeltals	Center of Chiapas	Tzeltal	Weavings, wood-carvings and ceramics	
Tzotzils	San Juan Chamula, Chiapas	Tzotzil	Textiles, embroidery, pottery	
Yaquis	In Sonora's southeastern part	Yaquí	Ceramics and basketry	Dances: the Deer, the Pascola and the Coyote
Zapotecs	Valley of Oaxaca	Zapotec	Textiles and pottery	Feather dances

Their political and social organization is complex, given that many of these groups adhere to modern legal structures while maintaining a parallel traditional government based on customs passed down from father to son. Other groups remain autonomous or unassimilated. Although some of the indigenous communities are integrated linguistically, others remain monolingual. Their religious rituals best exemplify **cultural syncretism**. Despite the predominance of the Catholic religion, rites and elements that originated in the pre-Hispanic past are always present in their festivals and ceremonies. This religious feeling also permeates their music and dances.

Art and Architecture

Pre-Hispanic – In the pre-Hispanic settlements, **ceremonial centers** played a prominent role in relation to the size of the towns and cities, as they aimed for height and a panoramic view. In these centers surrounded by broad esplanades for public rituals and open-air market facilities, the sumptuous quarters of the rulers and priests, secular buildings and imposing tiered or pyramidal foundations were constructed. Only the nobility and the ruling elite could access the temples built atop the pyramids. The location of the vast majority of these ceremonial centers was determined by the orientation of the temples and roads in relation to the sunrise or sunset, in accordance with **astronomical phenomena** and agricultural cycles.

Owing to the custom of using ancient mounds as a foundation for new structures, the ruins visible today constitute the last construction phase of a superimposed structure. Construction materials generally included adobe, mortar used as an agglomerate, and precisely cut stone blocks, which are all the more impressive in light of the pre-Hispanic peoples' technological limitations, such as the lack of beasts of burden, the wheel and metal tools.

Most of the principal facades were painted, as were the statues and floors, because color held special meaning in the ancient inhabitants' unique vision of the world. With an amazing feel for composition and movement, they used drawings to express the poetic language of their relationship with nature on stelae, walls and **codices**.

Toward the end of the Classic period, **ball games** began to emerge, usually in double-T-shaped courts. The players in this religious ceremony attempted to pass a rubber or wooden ball, symbolizing the sun, through stone rings, which generally were built into the walls of the ball court. In some cultures the ritual ended in the sacrifice of one of the contenders.

Through these expressions of Mesoamerican art, archaeologists have inferred a sophisticated polytheistic religion, which acted as an integrating force. The whole world of forms that the craftsmen masterfully rendered in the **ritual ceramics** embodies a deep spiritual dimension, from the graceful female figurines associated with fertility, to the elaborate polychrome vessels destined to accompany the dead into the other world. Ancient Mexicans led a complex **spiritual life** in which their relationship with the forces of nature was essential for survival. To venerate their gods, they fashioned offerings

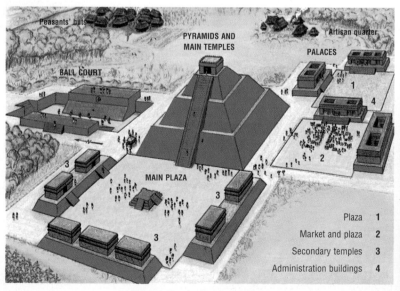

Peasants' huts

PYRAMIDS AND
MAIN TEMPLES

Artisan quarter

PALACES

BALL COURT

1

4

3

MAIN PLAZA

3

2

3

Plaza	1
Market and plaza	2
Secondary temples	3
Administration buildings	4

Components of a Ceremonial Center

of wood, bone and rock crystal. In later eras they also worked with gold, silver and copper, on which the artisan's skill dominated the materials, as can also be seen in the stone reliefs, so finely created that at a first glance they appear to be made of plasterwork.

Many **sculptures** abound with fretwork, scrolls and details that portray realistically and accurately the most important deities, rulers and historical events. Stucco modeling was also developed into a fine art, especially in the regions where stone was scarce, in which case a mixture of lime, sand and water served to adorn friezes, pillars and stairways. On the periphery of the great ceremonial centers, **artisans** lived and worked in particular districts according to their specialty. **Peasants**, on the other hand, lived in modest adobe and straw huts located near their farmlands. Of these constructions only a few vestiges remain.

Sixteenth Century – The art that emerged after the Conquest reflects the imposition of European customs on the indigenous peoples. In its evangelizing zeal, the Catholic Church served as chief patron of the arts, resulting in a minimization of secular arts, with the exception of architecture.

Under the friars' direction, **monasteries** were built, including structures unknown in Europe. For example, the

1 Open-air chapel
2 Posas or corner chapels
3 Atrial cross

Atrium — Chruch — Cloister — Refectory — Kitchen

Components of a Monastery

atrium served to accommodate hundreds of worshipers who listened to mass celebrated in the **open-air chapel**.

Another innovation consisted of the **capillas posas** (also known as **corner chapels** for their placement in each corner of the atrium) where worshippers paused or rested while carrying an effigy of the *Santísimo* (The Most Holy) during the processions, conducted out in the open within the confines of the atrium. The corner chapels contain small rooms with two entrances so that one may enter through one door, hold the ceremony and exit through the other door, which directly faces the next chapel. Built as basilicas or with a single nave, the **churches** embodied a mixture of styles: Romanesque, Gothic and Renaissance, with variations in the Plateresque style, or following architect Herrera's style. According to 16C chroniclers, the churches were covered with ornate wood ceilings, many of them carved in the Mudejar style, and with coffered ceilings. However, due to the ease with which fires consumed these ceilings, they were gradually replaced by smooth or ribbed cannon vaults that have survived to the present day. Although from the exterior the monasteries resembled fortresses, they lacked the installations of a true fortification, rendering them defenseless. The **cloisters** also vary in style and many of them preserve mural paintings on such subjects as the New Testament or the saints.

As for sculpture, gigantic wooden **altarpieces** were carved and then gilded and adorned with ornate Mannerist images combined with oil paintings on wood. Master painters, such as **Simón Pereyns**, Andrés de la Concha, Juan de Arrué, the brothers **Baltasar Echave** and others, created works of a medieval flavor with Flemish or Italian influences.

Seventeenth and Eighteenth Centuries – At the end of the 16C, architecture in Mexico underwent a transformation when the secular clergy replaced the traditional priests, and new parish churches were founded. The massive conventual structures were replaced by more modest constructions, adopting the **Latin cross** as the standard design, wherein a transept bisects the single nave and separates it from the presbytery. A cupola, supported by pendentives, rises above the intersection. This allows for the sacristy and registry room to be built on either side of the front wall, and the priests' quarters on one side of the nave.

© Bob Schalkwijk

Corner Chapel, Calpan, Puebla

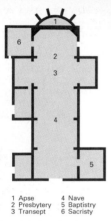

1 Apse   4 Nave
2 Presbytery   5 Baptistry
3 Transept   6 Sacristy

Latin Cross Floor Plan

Also new were the **convents**, in which there is no main portal, but rather two side entrances to accommodate the high altar and the choirs, both high and low, at opposite ends of the interior. Generally very spacious, the cloisters were veritable women's cities, given that some convents housed over 300 nuns, in addition to the servants who attended them.

Baroque architecture in New Spain was more decorative than structural, as few buildings presented a layout different from the traditional Latin cross. The period began with a variation of the Baroque style, known as restrained or transitional, because of its rather subdued ornamentation and limitation in terms of formal innovation. Its development began around 1640, with the spread of the **Solomonic** phase (so called due to its helicoidal or spiral columns) and, especially, with the more spectacular Baroque architectural forms, such as the **pilastra estípite**—a pilaster with an inverted truncated pyramid shape—which evolved within the **Churrigueresque** style. Created in Spain by Don José Benito de Churriguera, this type of pilaster was introduced in Mexico by architect Jerónimo de Balbás in the 18C. All the churches of this period covered their facades in this style, and all the altarpieces included the estípite pilaster. The most common ornamentation inside the churches was the **altarpiece**—made of carved and gilded wood. Some of them recounted true lessons of sacred history or emphasized the importance of the characters and founders of the religious orders.

An important decorative supplement, **plasterwork** was used to express, through exquisite pieces, new forms of Christian art. In New Spain two different forces influenced these forms. On the one hand, the vision of the emerging cities reflected the slow and painful process of cultural and human interchange, while struggling to preserve the artistic solutions fashionable in Europe. For example, the Capilla del Rosario (Rosary Chapel), a magical mirror in the city of Puebla, reflects an excessive ornamental wealth in which strokes of a popular nature can be discerned. On the other hand, clinging to popular interpretations, a tendency surfaced toward unheard-of forms and styles. This aspect is represented by Tonantzintla, where the imagination and construction techniques of the indigenous peoples confront a foreign art style and, with extraordinary wisdom and absolute ingenuity, manage to blend pre-Hispanic subjects and Christian forms, achieving a Baroque masterpiece.

From the 16C onward, **neo-Hispanic sculpture** acquired a strictly religious nature. Executed in stone—both in figures and in high reliefs and bas-reliefs—this form of art adorned the churches' facades. Sculpture in wood also reached great expressive strength.

Secular architecture, prominent particularly in the beautiful city palaces, consisted primarily of a single design: a central courtyard surrounded by four bays. By the 18C, an additional second floor fulfilled the owners' increasing residential needs, leaving the ground floor for the servants' rooms and rental space. Made of *tezontle* (a reddish volcanic stone with a porous texture) and quarry stone, their facades oftentimes boasted elaborate carvings. These buildings offered a touch of elegance to the cities of that era.

Nineteenth Century – From the middle of the 18C, **Neoclassical** art gained popularity, and several artists even attempted to found an academy, but lack of support from the Spanish and colonial authorities halted their plans. Nonetheless, Neoclassical forms began to appear in many works, as witnessed in the paintings of **Miguel Cabrera** or the architectural structures of **Ortiz de Castro**. However, the purity of the Greco-Roman styles—the symmetry, sobriety and harmony—never materialized with such definition because the pervasive Baroque influence persisted in the Neoclassical style.

In 1783 the Real Academia de las Bellas Artes de México (Royal Academy of Fine Arts of Mexico) was founded, under the auspices of King Charles III of Spain. In honor of its royal founder, the academy became known as the **Academia de San Carlos**. Among the European professors selected to instruct the students

© Bob Schalkwijk

Sagrario Metropolitano, Mexico City

figure sculptor and architect **Manuel Tolsá**, painter **Rafael Ximeno y Planes** and medallion engraver **Jerónimo Antonio Gil**. Tolsá played a leading role in architecture, both secular and religious. Credited with many important works in Mexico City, including the completion of the **Catedral Metropolitana** (Metropolitan Cathedral), the **Palacio de Minería** (Mining Palace) and the sculpture of King Charles IV, known as **El Caballito** (The Little Horse). He also designed the plans for the **Hospicio Cabañas** (Cabañas Hospice) in Guadalajara.

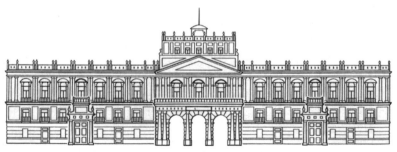

Palacio de Minería, Mexico City

Francisco Eduardo Tresguerras (1759–1833) stands out among the most famous architects of the period. Also a painter, sculptor, musician and poet, he exercised great influence in central Mexico.
Although the fervor for the Neoclassical style did not last long due to the War of Independence, among other factors, it destroyed many Baroque creations, which were considered to be in poor taste.
From 1810 on, New Spain's constant state of war resulted in a sharp decrease of artistic production.
In 1884 Porfirio Díaz reestablished peace, allowing the arts to flourish once again. Meanwhile, in 1847, the Academia de San Carlos was reorganized and a new group of European instructors arrived in Mexico. Prominent among them were painters **Pelegrín Clavé** and **Eugenio Landesio**. Also notable, **Juan Cordero** studied in Rome but left his most important work in Mexico, today exhibited in the National Art Museum, the Museo Nacional de Arte (MUNAL).
Landesio's best student, **José María Velasco**, was an outstanding Mexican landscapist considered the most brilliant painter of the 19C, with exceptional talents as a draftsman and colorist. His works, also on display at the MUNAL, reflect a nationalist line of thought. A second group emerged years later, including artists such as Felipe Sojo, Luis Coto and Martín Soriano.
Spanish master sculptor Manuel Vilar directed the School of Sculpture, but without Clavé's success. Another prominent sculptor, **Miguel Noreña** created the Monument to Cuauhtémoc, presently on the Paseo de la Reforma (Mexico City).
In architecture, the period was not particularly notable. Although the renowned Italian architect, Javier Cavallari, lectured at the Academy, he did not succeed in producing a significant number of outstanding students. **Lorenzo de la Hidalga** was the most prominent creator of many architectural works, including the cupola of the church of Santa Teresa La Antigua, on the eastern side of Plaza de la Constitución, and the pedestal of the sculpture called *El Caballito* (Mexico City).

Twentieth Century – Toward the end of the 19C and the beginning of the 20C, during the *Porfiriato* (Porfirio Díaz's dictatorship), Mexico began to cultivate an atmosphere of openness, with aims of becoming a "civilized country" and gaining avant-garde status. Among the people who had traveled to Paris or to the German cities, with Romanticism and Symbolism then in vogue, the most notable included **Jesús Contreras**, **Germán Gedovius** and **Julio Ruelas**. The latter, a painter, draftsman and engraver, stands out for being a loyal exponent of Symbolism and the decorative forms of Art Nouveau in paintings. Contemporaries in the field of engraving included **Manuel Manilla** and **Guadalupe Posada**, who through their expressive strength that denoted a certain irony in their representations, became the harshest critics of the culture of the *Porfiriato*. Outside of the Academy of St. Charles, **Joaquín Clausell** managed to create, through his love of nature and use of bright colors, a Mexican Impressionism that was fairly removed from French Impressionism.
Later emerged such prominent artists as **Diego Rivera** and his wife **Frida Kahlo**, **José Clemente Orozco**, **David Alfaro Siqueiros** and **Gerardo Murillo** (Dr. Atl). With them ended the search for Mexican painting fostered by European influences and began an introspective look at national sources of inspiration. Of humble origins and scarce resources, painter **Saturnino Herrán** possessed a powerful expressionist capacity, which he transmitted to his student **Francisco Goitia**.
In 1921, during the regime of Álvaro Obregón, José Vasconcelos was appointed Secretary of Education and marked the determinant factors for founding the "Escuela Mexicana de Pintura" (Mexican School of Painting). Vasconcelos offered the walls of

public buildings as a venue to display a Revolutionary art, called **Mexican mural painting**, which would exalt the people. It succeeded as no other artistic expression had ever before succeeded in America. In addition to Mexico's three greatest muralists-Rivera with his analytical drawings, Orozco with his marked expressionism and Siqueiros, an important theorist of the mural painting movement-many more distinguished muralists surfaced, among them Alva de la Canal, Fernando Leal, Fermín Revueltas, **Juan O'Gorman**, Pablo O'Higgins and Alfredo Zalce. Another contemporary, **Rufino Tamayo**-master of color-worked independently. Although he was criticized for not producing nationalist paintings, his work best conveyed the profound intimate feelings of the Mexican people. Subsequently **José Luis Cuevas**, **Pedro** and **Rafael Coronel**, **Manuel Felguérez**, Vicente Rojo, Alberto Gironella and Francisco Toledo conducted their own individual searches in the arts. In recent years, the new avant-garde currents worldwide have also had an impact on national production, as can be seen in alternative media to painting and sculpture, such as installation, object art and all its derivations.

At the beginning of the 20C, **architecture** was executed mainly by foreigners, with a few exceptions, such as architect **Antonio Rivas Mercado** who designed the Monument to Independence, popularly called El Ángel. Later new styles would emerge, such as **Neocolonial**, **Art Nouveau** and a tendency toward emulating **French** designs, all used in the new districts or suburbs surrounding the center of Mexico City. Since the administration of General Lázaro Cárdenas, architecture embarked on an innovative path, with Functionalism, which **Luis Barragán** rendered in a very personal and unique style. The best example of aesthetic integration during this era is the Ciudad Universitaria (University City), where architects, painters and sculptors united to construct the nation's most extraordinary house of studies.

Later, with the use of concrete and glass, architects such as **Ricardo Legorreta**, **Teodoro González de León**, **Abraham Zabludowsky** and **Pedro Ramírez Vázquez** created novel forms and spaces.

In the field of sculpture, Mexico has produced great artists, such as Ignacio Asúnsolo and, more recently, **Francisco Zúñiga**, Baltazar Martínez, Julián Martínez Sotos and Sebastián.

Art and Architectural Terms

Altarpiece: A work of art that decorates the space above and behind an altar.

Apse: the generally rounded end of a church behind the altar.

Atlantes: supports in the form of carved male figures.

Atrium: a forecourt or open central courtyard.

Azulejos: glazed, patterned, ceramic tiles.

Bastion: a projecting part of a fortification built at an angle or against the line of a wall.

Caryatid: a support in the form of a draped female figure.

Chancel: the part of the church containing the main altar.

Churrigueresque: a lavish and exuberantly decorated architectural style used by Don José Benito de Churriguera and those who imitated him in 18C Spanish architecture.

Cloisters: covered passages connecting the church to the chapter house, refectory and other parts of the monastery. Typically, they consist of a wall on one side and an open arcade or colonnade on the other.

Coffers: recessed panels formed in ceilings, vaults and domes.

Coro: the part of a chancel containing the stalls and used by canons and other members of the clergy.

Curtain wall: a stretch of wall between two towers or bastions.

Estípite: a pilaster in the shape of a truncated inverted pyramid.

Gable: the decorative, triangular upper portion of a wall that supports a pitched roof.

Gargoyle: a spout in the form of a grotesque human or animal figure projecting from a roof gutter to throw rainwater clear of a building.

Gilded: overlaid with a thin covering of gold.

Groined vaulting: a vault showing the lines of intersection of two vaults or arches (usually pointed).

Lintel: a horizontal piece that spans an opening, usually a window or door.

Merlon: the solid part of an embattled parapet between two crenels.

Mudejar: an architectural style, which flourished in Spain from the 13C to the 16C, characterized by the conservation of Christian art elements and the use of Moorish ornamentation.

Nave: usually the main part of the interior of a church.

Ogee arch: an arch in the form of a convex and concave curve.

Pendentive: one of the four triangular members that supports a dome over a square space.

Pier: vertical shaft supporting an arch.

Pilaster: a rectangular structure that resembles a pillar or column, but only projects a fraction of its width from the wall.

Plateresque: a style that originated in Spain in the 16C and is derived from *plata*, or silver. It is used to describe finely carved decoration as in the work of silversmiths.

Polychrome: decorated in several colors usually to achieve striking effects.

Presbytery: the part of a church that is reserved for the officiating clergy and is separated from the nave by a partition or screen .

Retablo: an altarpiece; marble, stone or wood decoration for an altar.

Sacristy: place in a church where the sacred vessels and vestments are kept.

Solomonic: helicoidal columns.

Stucco: a type of molding mix, consisting mainly of plaster, used for coating surfaces.

Talud-tablero: an architectural formula, characteristic of Mesoamerican architecture, consisting of facades where horizontal plains are staggered over slanted pyramid walls.

Transept: the part of a church at right angles to the nave that gives the church the shape of a cross. It consists of the transept crossing and arms.

Literature

Pre-Hispanic Period – The literature of Mesoamerica reflects the worldview, the socio-political evolution, the history, and the philosophical and ethical thinking of pre-Hispanic peoples. It is expressed pictographically, ideographically and, in some cases, orally. During the colonial era, friars and historians, indigenous peoples and mestizos, undertook the task of analyzing and interpreting such varied works—an endeavor that continues to the present day.

Matrícula de Tributos, Page from the *Códice Lámina*, Mexica Culture

© J.L. Rojas Martínez/Museo Nacional de Antropología

Two fundamental works underlie the Maya culture. They are the **Popol Vuh**, an epic tale infused with a profound, mythical and supernatural essence about the origins of the Maya, and the **Books of Chilam Balam**, a series of chronicles written by priests to document historical events, in accordance with the astronomical calendar. In drama, the book of *Rabinal Achi* is particularly notable.

In Náhuatl literature, many works have been preserved, including the *Veinte himnos de Tepeapulco (Twenty Hymns of Tepeapulco)*, the *Poema de Quetzalcóatl (Poem of Quetzalcóatl)*, the **codices** and *Cantares mexicanos (Mexican Songs)*, which recount myths, legends, proverbs and riddles, the concept of life and the world, moral rules and social formalities.

Colonial Era – After the Conquest, the chronicle became the first genre to be cultivated. The best examples are the *Cartas de relación (Letters Reporting the Discovery and Conquest of New Spain)* by **Hernán Cortés**, and *La historia verdadera de la conquista de la Nueva España (True History of the Conquest of New Spain)* by **Bernal Díaz del Castillo**. **Fray Bernardino de Sahagún** documented Mexican ethnography and archaeology in his *Historia general de las cosas de la Nueva España (General History of New Spain)*. Missionaries **Motolinía** and **Fray Bartolomé de las Casas**, among others, recorded native customs in their attempts at understanding the indigenous culture in order to more effectively teach the new religion.

Theater was used primarily as a means of propagating the Catholic faith. In the context of this new colonial society, **Juan Ruiz de Alarcón** stands out for having developed an original style, full of wit, reflection and ethical concerns, as seen in his play *La verdad sospechosa (The Truth Suspected)*. The flourishing of literary life in New Spain benefited from the arrival of the printing press in 1535 and the founding of the University in 1553. In the 17C, although Europe's Renaissance ideas from the 16C and 17C influenced many literary works, the end result, a truly Mexican literature, abounded in history, legends, symbolism and allegories. **Sor Juana Inés de la Cruz**, a nun with great intellectual gifts and sensitivity, wrote poetry, *Redondillas y sonetos (Quatrains and Sonnets)*, prose, *Carta a Sor Filotea de la Cruz (Reply to Sister Filotea)*, and plays, *Los enredos de una casa (The Obligations of a Home)*, all with equal mastery. Of no lesser importance are the works of **Carlos de Sigüenza y Góngora**, a historian, poet, scientist and prominent figure of his era.

In the 18C Jesuits **Landívar, Clavijero** and **Alegre** led a reactionary movement against the literary decadence that continued to predominate. They cultivated fine Latin poetry and translated the classics. Clavijero and Alegre also excelled in documenting history.

Nineteenth Century – During the first decade, due to political and social events between liberals and conservatives, pamphlets became the main instrument for propaganda, both for the insurgents (with a plain yet spontaneous style) and for the royalists (with a refined and cultured style).

José Joaquín Fernández de Lizardi, editor of the newspaper *El Pensador Mexicano (The Mexican Thinker)* wrote the first profoundly Mexican novel: *El periquillo sarniento*, in which a feeling of social moralization prevails.

In 1836 **José María Lacunza** and **Rodríguez Galván** founded the Academia de San Juan de Letrán (Academy of St. John Lateran), giving a new impulse to literature through the study of grammar, versification, serious criticism and new theses.

Political confrontations continued and, from this opposition, a literary division arose. On the one hand, Romanticism, with innovative or revolutionary tendencies, was initiated by **Fernando Calderón**, followed by **Guillermo Prieto** and culminated in the tragic figure of **Manuel Acuña**. On the other hand, the poetry of **José Joaquín Pesado** and the novels of **Ignacio Ramírez**—both humanists of refined culture and exquisite style—represented Classicism. Political peace achieved during the *Porfiriato* resonated in the newspaper *El Renacimiento (The Renaissance)* where writers of the most diverse ideological schools, such as **Manuel Payno**, **Roa Bárcenas** and **Justo Sierra**, collaborated. Newspapers, journals and pamphlets became the ideal means for supporting political campaigns, attacking the opposition, censoring customs, criticizing prominent individuals and awakening feelings of patriotism.

The novel as an artistic form was infused with nationalistic themes in the works of **Ignacio Manuel Altamirano** *(Clemencia and El Zarco)*, **Emilio Rabasa** *(La Bola)*, **José López Portillo Rojas** *(La parcela)*, **Rafael Delgado** *(La calandria)* and **Federico Gamboa** *(Santa)*.

Sor Juana Inés de la Cruz, Museo Nacional de Historia, Mexico City

© Bob Schalkwijk

Modernism developed in Mexico with the works of **Manuel Gutiérrez Nájera**, **Salvador Díaz Mirón** and **Amado Nervo**, who contributed to the journal *Azul*. This literary movement reached its peak with the *Revista Moderna*, which published articles by leading writers, such as **Olaguíbel**, characterized by an exalted individualism, an obsession with death, skepticism and an intense yearning for everything new.

Twentieth Century – The Mexican Revolution (1910) served as a major source of inspiration for narrative writings in the years following the armed struggle. Important works include **Mariano Azuela's** *Los de abajo (The Underdogs)* and **Martín Luis Guzmán's** *El águila y la serpiente (The Eagle and the Serpent)*.

At the beginning of the century, the founding of the Ateneo de la Juventud (Athenaeum of Youth) prompted a movement of literary renewal, a reaction to the educational and philosophical principles based on positivism. It features the works of three great writers: humanist and philosopher **José Vasconcelos**, prose writer of great strength and depth, author of *Ulises Criollo (A Creole Ulysses)*; critic and commentator **Alfonso Reyes**, author of *El deslinde (The Demarcation)*; and eloquent essayist **Antonio Caso**, renowned for his work titled *La persona humana (The Human Being)*. The diverse tendencies of more recent decades surfaced in journals such as *Contemporáneos*, which aimed to introduce Mexican literature to Europe's avant-garde currents and promote the stylistic renovation initiated by poet **Ramón López Velarde**, author of *Suave Patria*. To this group belong **Jorge Cuesta**, **Rodolfo Usigli** and the great poet **Carlos Pellicer**, whose style exudes sensuality.

Octavio Paz – (1914–98) 1990 Nobel Laureate in Literature, author of *El laberinto de la soledad (The Labyrinth of Solitude)* and a cultured man with a profound understanding of the problems of his time—led poets and novelists in rejecting their contemporaries' aestheticism. The *Revista Taller* served as a forum for publishing their works and opinions.

In the mid 20C, the revolutionary novel reappeared with *Al filo del agua (The Edge of the Storm)* by **Agustín Yáñez**, precursor and inspiration of the present generation of writers: **Rosario Castellanos** *(Balún Canán, Oficio de tinieblas)* with an intimate and pure feminine style; **Carlos Fuentes** *(La región más transparente – Where the Air Is Clear; La muerte de Artemio Cruz – The Death of Artemio Cruz)*, initiator of the modern urban novel and expert in Mexican culture; **Jorge Ibargüengoitia**, author of *Los relámpagos de agosto (Lightning in August)*, with his ironic style; and **Juan Rulfo** *(Pedro Páramo)*, father of Magical Realism.

Mexico's prominent playwrights include **Vicente Leñero**, **Emilio Carballido** and **Luisa Josefina Hernández**. Among the country's most notable short story writers figure **Edmundo Valadés**, **Juan José Arreola** and **Francisco Rojas González**. **Alí Chumacero**, **Efraín Huerta**, **Jaime Sabines** (1926–99) and **José Emilio Pacheco**, also a writer of prose, contribute to the nation's poetic heritage.

Toward the end of the 20C began to emerge intellectual development, social and political analyses, and Mexico's most important historians and political scientists, including **Carlos Monsiváis**, **Enrique Krauze**, **Fernando Benitez**, **Elena Poniatowska**, **Héctor Aguilar Camín** and **Ángeles Mastretta**.

Further Reading

General

Eternal Mexico by Robert Frerck. Chronicle Books, 1996.

Passport Mexico: Your Pocket Guide to Mexican Business, Customs and Etiquette by Randy Malat. World Trade Press, 1996.

Art, History and Civilization

Ancient West Mexico: Art and Archaeology of the Unknown Past by Richard Townsend. Thames & Hudson, 1998.

The Aztecs: People of the Sun by Alfonso Caso. Univ. of Oklahoma Press, 1970.

Contemporary Mexican Painting in a Time of Change by Shifra M. Goldman. Univ. of New Mexico Press, 1995.

Distant Neighbors: A Portrait of the Mexicans by Alan Riding. Vintage Books, Random House, 1986.

Mexican Contemporary by Herbert J.M. Ypma. World Design Series, 1997.

Mexican Modern Art by Luis Martín Lozano et al. National Gallery of Canada, 1999.

Mexican Muralists: Orozco, Rivera, Siqueiros by Desmond Rochfort. Chronicle Books, 1998.

Mexico: A Higher Vision by Michael Calderwood et al. ALTI Publishing, 1992.

Mexico: Biography of Power. A History of Modern Mexico 1810–1996 by Enrique Krauze. Harper Collins, 1997.

The Wind that Swept Mexico: The History of the Mexican Revolution 1910–1942 by Anita Brenner and George R. Leighton. Univ. of Texas Press, 1985.

Famous Mexicans: Bibliographies

Dreaming with his Eyes Open: A Life of Diego Rivera by Patrick Marnham. Knopf, 1998.

Frida: A Biography of Frida Kahlo by Hayden Herrera. Harper & Row, 1983.

Octavio Paz: Homage to the Poet by Kosrof Chantikian. Kosmos, 1997.

Cuisine

Food from My Heart: Cuisines of Mexico Remembered and Reimagined by Zarela Martinez. IDG Books Worldwide, 1995.

The Art of Mexican Cooking: Traditional Mexican Cooking for Aficionados by Diana Kennedy. Bantam Books, 1989.

The Cuisines of Mexico by Diana Kennedy. Harper Collins, 1989.

Recipe of Memory: Five Generations of Mexican Cuisine by Victor M. Valle. New Press, 1995.

Ecotourism and Adventure Travel

A Bird-Finding Guide to Mexico by Steve N.G. Howell. Cornell Univ. Press, 1999.

The Dive Sites of Cozumel and the Yucatan by Lawson Wood. Passport Books, 1997.

Mexico's Volcanoes: A Climbing Guide by R.J. Secor. Mountaineers Books, 1993.

Tropical Mexico: The Ecotravellers' Wildlife Guide by Les Beletsky. Academic Press, 1999.

Novels by Mexican Authors

The Crystal Frontier: A Novel in Nine Stories by Carlos Fuentes. Harvest Books, 1998.

The Death of Artemio Cruz by Carlos Fuentes. Farrar, Straus & Giroux, 1991.

The Labyrinth of Solitude by Octavio Paz. Evergreen, 1985.

Like Water for Chocolate by Laura Esquivel. Doubleday, 1992.

Massacre in Mexico by Elena Poniatowska. Univ. of Missouri Press, 1996.

Mexican Postcards by Carlos Monsiváis. New Left Books: 1997.

Pedro Páramo by Juan Rulfo. Grove Press, 1994.

Tear this Heart Out by Ángeles Mastretta. Riverhead Books, 1997.

The Underdogs: A Novel of the Mexican Revolution by Mariano Azuela. Signet Classic, 1996.

Cinema

Although the seventh art has had a fluctuating history in Mexico, it has managed to leave an indelible mark on the imagination of the Mexican people.

Toward the second decade of the 20C, Mexican silent movies flourished. This set the stage for talking pictures, whose initial purpose was to portray a nationalistic perspective (as occurred in the visual arts) through recurrent themes of Mexico's history. The quality and success achieved placed Mexican cinema on the world map. While initially modest and low-budget, with a folkloric perspective of the country, Mexican films began to evolve upon finding genres that appealed to the public. These included the *ranchera* comedy (for example, Fernando de Fuentes' *Allá en el rancho grande*), whose cast typically consisted of a beautiful "Maria" and a mariachi singer who fell in love on a ranch or hacienda setting; historical themes (especially revolutionary ones, with movies such as *Vámonos con Pancho Villa, El Compadre Mendoza* and *La sombra del caudillo*); urban domestic strife *(Una familia de tantas)*; cabaret musicals *(Aventurera, Salón México)*; and social themes *(Janitzio, Los Caifanes)*.

The decade from 1935 to 1945 marked the period of the **Golden Age of Mexican Cinema**. Both the support of US firms that invested significant amounts of money and the movie stars of the period were decisive factors in the Mexican cinema's artistic expansion, which earned it international fame and placed it at the top of the Hispanic box office charts.

Golden Age actors with a strong following included **Dolores del Río, María Félix, Lupe Vélez, Jorge Negrete, Pedro Armendáriz, Arturo de Córdova, the brothers Soler** and the unforgettable **Pedro Infante**. Joining them were carnival or popular theater comedians, such as **Mario Moreno "Cantinflas"** *(Ahí está el detalle)* and **Germán Valdés "Tin Tan"** *(El rey del barrio)*. The 1940s saw the emergence of four of Mexico's most important cinematographers: **Emilio "el indio" Fernández** *(Enamorada)*, **Julio Bracho** *(Distinto amanecer)*, **Roberto Gavaldón** *(Macario)* and **Alejandro Galindo** (1906–99, *Campeón sin corona, Espaldas mojadas)*. Together with photographer **Gabriel Figueroa**, director Fernández succeeded in combining artistic expression and a high aesthetic quality *(María Candelaria)*. His films received important international awards and helped popularize Mexican cinema in Europe.

During the Spanish Civil War, many Spanish republicans fled to Mexico and other Latin American countries. Most notably, movie director **Luis Buñuel** contributed to Mexican film through his unique interpretation of the nation's reality *(Los olvidados, Ángel exterminador)*.

The movie industry suffered a series of crises in the 1960s, experienced a sharp decline starting in 1977, and, with a few exceptions from independent filmmakers, practically came to a halt by 1982. This downswing was partly due to the quasi monopoly of the Mexican government, but also to distribution problems. Not until the late 1980s did Mexican cinema begin showing signs of rebirth, with such innovative producers and directors as Arturo Ripstein, Felipe Cazals, Jorge Fons, Jaime Humberto Hermosillo, Alfonso Arau, Alexandro Jodorowski, Alfonso Cuarón, Gabriel Retes, María Novaro, Carlos Carrera, Roberto Sneider and Guillermo del Toro.

Since 1971, during the months of November and December, Mexico City has hosted the **International Film Festival**, where the nation's most popular movies are recognized.

■ Reel Matters

Did you know that the Mexican movie *Like Water for Chocolate*, based on Laura Esquivel's novel of the same name and directed by her then-husband Alfonso Arau, was the most successful foreign-language film shown in the United States in 1993? Set in early-20C Mexico, with an underlying thread of magical realism, this sensuous film recounts the tale of Tita, the youngest daughter in an all-female family. Following tradition, her tyrannical mother forces her to forsake true love and care for her until her death. As a result, Tita unconsciously channels her suppressed emotions and passions into her extraordinary, mouth-watering culinary creations. This concoction of flavors, smells and sensuality will captivate male and female viewers alike.

Other Mexican movies that have enjoyed international acclaim include *El Mariachi* (1992), directed by Robert Rodríguez; *Danzón* (1992), directed by María Novaro; Sundance Film Festival award-winner *Santitos* (*Little Saints*, 1997) based on María Amparo Escandón's novel *Esperanza's Box of Saints* and directed and produced by Alejandro Springall; and *Sexo, Pudor y Lágrimas* (*Sex, Shame and Tears*, 1999), the highest grossing Mexican film of all times, directed by Antonio Serrano.

Music and Dance

Music runs through the veins of the Mexicans and reflects their customs, beliefs and environment. In the pre-Hispanic era, documented by 16C chroniclers, music played magical, secular and ceremonial roles, the latter being the most purified and elevated expression. Percussion and wind instruments, such as **rattles** and **huéhuetls** (drums made from tree trunks), **flutes** made from sugar cane, clay **whistles** and sea conchs, predominated. Chants and dances served to exalt the ritual of their beliefs, faith, hopes and fears. Although many of the instruments of that era are still used in some festivals, the mixture of native instruments with those introduced in Mexico by the Spaniards, immigrants and slaves from other countries provided a unique flavor to Mexican music.

From the Conquest onward, pre-Hispanic music fused with religious music brought by the friars, who used it as a means of evangelization and forbade any type of musical expression whose purpose was not the exaltation of the Catholic Church.

After the War of Independence, European artists began to arrive in Mexico, bringing with them new musical genres such as Italian opera. However, not until the arrival of **Manuel M. Ponce** did musical production with marked European influences, sprinkled with nationalistic characteristics, truly begin to gain strength. Ponce studied traditional Mexican music and began to incorporate these elements in his compositions, achieving works of great quality with a touch of modernism. As with the other arts of the period, an introspective look at Mexico's own resources also characterized the musical field. This movement made way for such notable musicians as the theoretical **Julián Carrillo**; the nationalistic **Carlos Chávez**; **Silvestre Revueltas**, considered by many as Mexico's greatest musician for his melodic richness and his great temperament; **José Pablo Moncayo**, known for the *Huapango*; and **Blas Galindo** and **Carlos Jiménez Mabarak**.

Popular music, banned during the colonial era due to its secularism and indigenous and African origins, made a comeback and managed to evolve after the War of Independence. The ballads, marches, *corridos*, *boleros*, *sones*, *huapangos* and *jarabes* became the voice of the people, the heart of the nation. These cheerful, lively and romantic rhythms were expressed by composers such as **Agustín Lara**, a poet-musician who filled the entire era around the 1930s with his music. Jalisco's mariachi music, with representatives such as **José Alfredo Jiménez**; the merry *sones* from Huasteca and Veracruz; the nostalgic marimba music from the Isthmus and the romantic *trova* of Yucatán all stand out as examples of the nation's creativity in this field.

Mexican music and dances constitute veritable feasts for the eyes and ears, on account of the colorful costumes worn by the participants and the rhythms and dances performed. The regional costumes evolved from indigenous attire and others from blends and additions made by the Spaniards and *mestizos*. For example, the **China Poblana** (Chinese woman from Puebla), reproduces the colors of the flag with sequins and, according to popular legend, was made by a woman of Asian descent who moved to the city of Puebla in the 18C. According to the locals, Emperor Maximilian of Hapsburg designed men's **charro costumes**—the best known and most readily identified with Mexicans—in the 19C, based on the ancient *chinaco* (warrior) costume. Today only *charrería* (rodeo) events, regional dances of the state of Jalisco, such as the **jarabe tapatío** (Mexican hat dance), and mariachi performances warrant the use of *charro* costumes. The **Ballet Folclórico de México** (Folkloric Ballet of Mexico) embodies all these expressions and throughout the year presents them at Mexico City's Palacio de Bellas Artes (Palace of Fine Arts), with a wide range of national dances and musical interpretations.

© Robert Frerck/Odyssey

Ballet Folclórico de México

In recent years **rock** music has swept the nation with performances by such popular bands as **El Tri**, **Café Tacuba**, **Maldita Vecindad**, **Los Caifanes** (now called **Jaguares**) and **Santa Sabina**, which have incorporated in their music social themes and messages that appeal to young people. Boleros and traditional music have also regained the spotlight through the efforts of present-day composers, such as **Juan Gabriel** and **Armando Manzanero**, as well as younger interpreters, such as the popular **Luis Miguel** and **Alejandro Fernández**.

Traditions

Festivals and Fairs – On every day of the year a festival is held somewhere in Mexico. While most of these festivals and fairs have religious origins, celebrations fill all aspects of life, including art, work and business. They all bear the purest sentiments of the people. (For a list of Mexico's most important traditions, see the **Calendar of Events**, under Practical Information.)

San Marcos, one of Mexico's major **fairs**, is celebrated in Aguascalientes *(p 159)*, with a wide variety of events. These include *palenques*, with diverse shows, mariachi music and **cockfights**, during which razor blades are tied to the roosters' legs so they can fight to the death in a small encircled area.

Some fairs hold **temporadas taurinas** (bullfighting seasons) with famous bullfighters. This tradition, which originated in Spain, was introduced in America during the colonial era. Since then, livestock fairs have gained nationwide recognition, with those of Mexico City, from November to February, and Aguascalientes, Querétaro and Tlaxcala considered the most important.

On the evening of September 15 (national month) Mexico celebrates **Independence Day**, the most popular national **festival**. The president of Mexico cries out *(da el Grito)* from the central balcony of the National Palace, in remembrance of the initiation of the armed struggle of 1810, and sounds the historic bell of Dolores while waving the national flag. The townspeople gather at the city's central plaza *(zócalo)*, to celebrate with fireworks and music. The following morning, a military parade marches through the city's main streets. Each state with a plaza and governor, or municipal president, celebrates this day in a similar manner.

Religious Events – Among Mexico's religious events, the **Day of the Virgin of Guadalupe**, celebrated on December 12 in the Villa de Guadalupe (Mexico City) transcends and strengthens the identity and nationalism of the Mexican people. Thousands of worshipers travel here from all corners of the nation, and from abroad, to visit the Virgin in her Basilica, located at the foot of the Tepeyac Hill. On this day Mexico witnesses infinite demonstrations of respect and veneration for the Virgin of Guadalupe, expressed through pilgrimages, promises, rosaries, dances and songs—such as **Las Mañanitas**, a popular birthday song.

Carnivals constitute another festivity celebrated in an atmosphere of cheerfulness and merriment. Held before Lent, carnivals invite everyone to give free rein to their pleasure before entering the period of fasting and austerity. The most famous carnivals are those of the ports of Veracruz and Mazatlán, where preparations take place many months in advance to decorate carriages, streets, shops, etc., which are then shown off in parades and dances, 24 hours a day. Needless to say, nobody sleeps during carnival!

Holy Week festivals are celebrated throughout Mexico, the best known being held in the Iztapalapa District (Mexico City), San Luis Potosí, Taxco and the villages of the Tarahumaras. On Maundy Thursday, worshippers conduct the visit of the seven houses. On Good Friday, the crucifixion is remembered. On Easter Saturday, the penultimate day of the festivals, the townspeople organize **quemas de Judas** (cardboard dolls filled with firecrackers and then lit to remember when Judas betrayed Christ), substituting the dolls with figures of politicians or characters from daily life. On Easter Sunday, the resurrection of Christ is celebrated.

Another unique religious event is that of **Corpus Christi**, better known as the day of the mules, whose tradition dates back to colonial times. On this day it was customary to pay tithes to the Spanish Crown. Those who could not pay with money would do so in kind, descending the hills with their donkeys loaded with merchandise in order to pay this tax. Today Mexicans celebrate this day by going to the Catholic churches with their children in native dress with *huacales* (crates) of fruit, turning this event into a popular evening festival.

At Christmas, Mexicans traditionally sing **Pastorelas**, shepherds' songs that also originated during the colonial era as a means to evangelize Mexico's original inhabitants. The **Posadas** (Mexican Christmas festivities) are held from December 16–24, in remembrance of the hardships that St. Joseph and the Virgin Mary encountered while trying to find a place where the Baby Jesus could be born. These parties include the indispensable **piñatas**, clay pots decorated with colorful paper and filled with candy and seasonal fruits. The Spanish friars of the 16C introduced this custom in Mexico, wherein the piñata embodies evil, and blindfolded men crack it open with a wooden stick that symbolizes religion, thus receiving its contents as a prize.

Another popular event is the Day of the Dead, a mixture of ancient pre-Hispanic and Christian rituals that reflects Mexicans' profound feelings towards death.

Tianguis and Markets – In the Náhuatl language the word *tianguis* means "market." During the pre-Hispanic period, Tenochtitlán and Tlatelolco stood out as the principal markets. The Spaniards described in their chronicles the way they functioned, their cleanliness and orderliness. Those of colonial times followed Old World patterns and established themselves in the main plazas, beside the public buildings, as occurred with the market in Mexico City, located on the main square. Most villages dedicate one day of the week to the market. Important for their colorful aspect and atmosphere are those of **San Cristóbal de las Casas** and **San Juan Chamula**, both in Chiapas; the market of **Tehuantepec** in Oaxaca; and that of the city of **Guanajuato**.

Handicrafts and Food

Handicrafts – Handicrafts constitute one of the deepest and most authentic expressions of the Mexican people. Their origins date back to pre-Hispanic times, and during the colonial era they evolved under the impact of new techniques and occupations, adopting the distinct features that characterize them today. The enormous variety of Mexican handicrafts corresponds to the country's many different regions, thus composing a multicolored spectrum of styles, symbols and traditions.

Food – Mexico possesses a great gastronomic tradition, the origins of which may be traced back to ancient Mexico, with the so-called Corn Cultures, characterized by a diet based on **corn**, **beans** and **chili** (hot peppers)—the famous Mesoamerican trilogy. Other popular foods include the meat of wild and domestic animals, fish, insects such as the *escamoles* (larvae of a species of ant), maguey worms and grasshoppers, as well as a wide variety of fruits and vegetables.

During the Conquest, New Spain's cuisine was enriched with the introduction of fruits, cereals, spices, coffee, beef and lamb, among others. The nuns took particular advantage of the fusion of the two cultures to create some of the delicious dishes still enjoyed to this day. These include the **desserts** that originated mainly in the convent kitchens of the colonial era; handcrafted **sweets**; **breads** with whimsical shapes and amusing names; and **beverages**, such as tequila, *mezcal*, *pulque*, beer, cool drinks made from a wide variety of tropical fruits and *atole*-a drink made of corn flour and sometimes mixed with chocolate *(champurrado)*. The blending of ingredients and dishes offers an almost magical range of flavors, smells and colors, which make Mexican cuisine one of the most diverse in the world.

From Mexico to the World – Mexico has offered the world a wide variety of products. These include **avocados**, **sesame seeds**, **peanuts**, **cocoa** (used to prepare the different types of *mole* sauces and chocolate), **pumpkins**, **sweet potatoes**, **chayote**, **gum**, **chili** (the national spice, available in the following varieties: *ancho*, *chipotle*, sweet, *guajillo*, *jalapeño*, *mulato pasilla*, *piquín*, *poblano* and *serrano*), **beans**, **guava**, **jícama** (a medicinal and edible plant), **maguey**, **mamey**, **mangoes**, **nopales** (prickly pear), **papaya**, **tomatoes**, **jitomates** (a kind of tomato), **tuna** (fruit of a type of cactus), **vanilla**, **zapote** (sapodilla fruit), **maize** (white, red and blue) and its endless derivatives, such as **elote** (ear of tender corn sold in all Mexican plazas); **tortillas** (essential for making appetizers); **guajolote** (turkey) and **tobacco**.

Mexican **antojitos**, appetizers resembling Spanish *tapas*, are readily available throughout the nation's eateries, from a street vendor's stand to the most luxurious restaurants. These hors d'oeuvres are made primarily from corn flour, the main ingredient in tortillas, tostadas, enchiladas, gorditas and tacos. Each state has its own specialties.

Zapotec Woman, Oaxaca

HANDICRAFTS AND MAIN DISHES

Region 1: Mexico City

Mexico City and Surroundings

Handicrafts – Leatherwork: articles for Mexican cowboys *(charros)*. **Basketwork:** wicker baskets and furniture. **Metalwork:** laminated copper, wrought iron, tin (picture frames, lamps), steel (knives, machetes, daggers). **Toys:** polychrome cardboard, cardboard Judas, papier-mâché figures of fantastic animals *(alebrijes)*, rag dolls, puppets, piñatas. **Masks:** paper, with headdresses of tin flowers and ribbons.

Dishes – Mexican *puchero* (beef and vegetable soup); *ensalada de nopales* (prickly pear salad); *chicharrón* (deep-fried pork rinds); *revoltijo* (rosemary cooked in *mole* sauce—a complex blend of chili, chocolate and ground nuts—with shrimp, *nopales*, or prickly pears, and potatoes); tamales; appetizers; *alegrías* (amaranth seed cakes); *pepitorias* (squash seeds in caramel); *muéganos* (round flour fritters with syrup); *merengues*; *buñuelos* (paper-thin, fried flour tortillas bathed in syrup).

Region 2: Central Mexico

Hidalgo

Handicrafts – Textiles: *huipiles* (women's tunics), *tilmas* (ponchos), *rebozos* (plain stoles). **Toys:** wooden (furniture, articulated dolls). **Masks:** polychrome wood.

Dishes – *tinga* (a spicy stew with tomatoes and red sausage); *mixiotes de pollo* (spiced chicken wrapped in maguey leaves); *zacahuiles* (tamales wrapped in large banana leaves); *chinicuiles* (fried worms from the maguey cactus); *escamoles* (ant eggs, eaten in a broth with chili, cactus or eggs, also eaten toasted); *barbacoa* (marinated lamb wrapped in maguey leaves and baked in a pit); *pastes* (popovers made with a sweet filling or ground beef, potatoes and chili); sweets made with nuts.

State of Mexico

Handicrafts – Ceramics: glazed and polychrome clay (Metepec). **Textiles:** embroidery and pulled-thread work with indigenous influence, *huipiles*, *tilmas* (ponchos), belts, sashes and decorative cords, sarapes and woolen blankets, plain and fine *rebozos* (Tenango), knotted throw rugs (Temoaya). **Basketwork:** willow (fruit baskets). **Metalwork:** silver jewelry (necklaces, bracelets, rings). **Glasswork:** blown glass (Texcoco). **Toys:** clay (whistles, crèches), *alebrijes*, rag dolls.

Dishes – *chorizos toluqueños* (stuffed tripe from Toluca); *moronga* (blood sausage cooked with onions and chili); *barbacoa*; cheese; candied fruits.

Morelos

Handicrafts – Textiles: Plain *rebozos*. **Metalwork:** tin (picture frames, lamps). **Toys:** rag dolls. **Masks:** wood combined with other materials (hair, hide, wire); with headdresses of tin flowers and ribbons.

Dishes – *clemole* (broth with tomato and chili); *longaniza en salsa verde* (cured pork sausage with green chili sauce); *cecina* (jerked beef); ice cream.

Puebla

Handicrafts – Ceramics: glazed, Majolica, tiles, ceremonial black pottery for the Day of the Dead. **Wood:** furniture with shell and metal inlays. **Textiles:** embroidered shirts, ponchos, plain *rebozos*. **Leatherwork:** articles for *charros*. **Basketwork:** straw hats, wicker baskets and furniture. **Metalwork:** silver offerings, tin (picture frames, lamps). **Bark Paintings** *(amates)*: white, polychrome. **Toys:** clay (whistles, crèches), wooden (furniture, articulated dolls). **Masks:** wood combined with other materials (hair, hide, wire) with headdresses of tin flowers and ribbons.

Ornamented Talavera Ceramic Vase from Puebla (18C)

Dishes – *mole poblano* (a chicken casserole dish cooked in a sauce with various types of chili, chocolate, almonds, peanuts, tomatoes and other spices); *chiles en nogada* (peppers stuffed with meat in white walnut sauce); *tinga* (stewed beef with onions, tomatoes and potatoes); tamales; camotes (boiled sweet potatoes).

Querétaro

Handicrafts – Metalwork: silver offerings and wrought iron.

Dishes – *albóndigas en chipotle* (meatballs in chili sauce); *barbacoa*; *chilaquiles* (casserole dish made of chopped fried tortillas with sauce and cheese); *gorditas*.

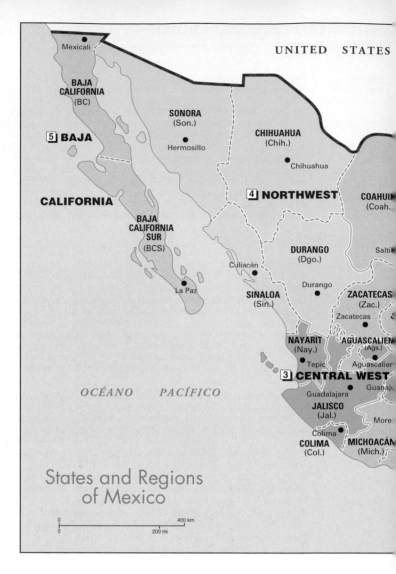

States and Regions of Mexico

0 — 400 km	0 — 200 mi

Tlaxcala   Handicrafts – **Wood:** polychrome canes. **Textiles:** sarapes and woolen blankets. **Masks:** polychrome wood.

Dishes – *pollo a la Tocatlán* (chicken with tomatoes wrapped in maguey leaves); *barbacoa*; maguey worms; *escamoles*; *tlacoyos* (corn tortilla stuffed with beans); mole verde (sauce prepared with chili and green tomatoes); *huauzontles* (vegetable stuffed with cheese and topped with sauce).

Region 3: Central West

Aguascalientes Handicrafts – **Textiles:** embroidery and pulled-thread work (blouses, sheets, tablecloths). **Toys:** wood (furniture, articulated dolls).

Dishes – *barbacoa de lomo* (barbecued pork wrapped in maguey leaves, then buried, covered with coals and left to cook for a full day); meats and poultry in wine; guava paste.

Colima   Handicrafts – **Leatherwork:** articles for *charros* and for everyday use (wallets, handbags).

Dishes – fish and seafood (shrimp tacos); *pozole blanco* (broth with hominy, pork and chili).

Guanajuato   Handicrafts – **Ceramics:** Majolica and tiles. **Textiles:** plain *rebozos*. **Leatherwork:** articles for *charros* and for everyday use (wallets, handbags). **Basketwork:** wicker baskets and furniture. **Metalwork:** silver offerings, laminated copper, tin (picture frames, lamps). **Toys:** polychrome cardboard, wood (furniture, articulated dolls). **Masks:** cardboard.

OF AMERICA

QUERÉTARO
(Qro.)
Querétaro

HIDALGO
(Hgo.)

2 **CENTRAL MEXICO**

Pachuca

MÉXICO
(Mex.)

1
MEXICO
CITY
(D.F.)

TLAXCALA
(Tlax.)
Tlaxcala

Toluca

Cuernavaca

Puebla

MORELOS
(Mor.)

PUEBLA
(Pue.)

6
ORTHEAST
Monterrey

UEVO
EÓN
NL)
Ciudad
Victoria

TAMAULIPAS
(Tamps.)

'S POTOSÍ
PL)
San Luis Posotí

Golfo   de   México

Mérida

9 **YUCATÁN**

YUCATÁN
(Yuc.)

ANAJUATU
to.)

Jalapa

QUINTANA
ROO
(Q. Roo)

Campeche

VERACRUZ
(Ver.)

7
TABASCO
(Tab.)
GULF
OF
MEXICO

CAMPECHE
(Camp.)

Chetumal

Villahermosa

hilpancingo

Belmopan

BELIZE

GUERRERO
(Gro.)

Oaxaca

8 **PACIFIC COAST**

CHIAPAS
(Chis.)

OAXACA
(Oax.)

Tuxtla
Gutiérrez

GUATEMALA

Cd. de Guatemala

HONDURAS

Dishes – **Appetizers**: tacos, *quesadillas*, *chalupas* (tortillas with beans, tomato sauce, chicken and onions); *birria* (mutton broth with oregano and *jitomates*); meats with beer; *cajeta* (caramel made from goat's milk).

Jalisco
Handicrafts – **Ceramics**: glazed and burnished clay. **Wood**: *equipales* (willow chairs with rush or leather seats), furniture with shell and metal inlays. **Textiles**: embroidery and pulled-thread work (blouses, sheets, tablecloths), plain *rebozos*. **Leatherwork**: articles for everyday use (wallets, handbags). **Basketwork**: wicker baskets and furniture. **Metalwork**: silver offerings, laminated copper. **Glasswork**: blown glass, red-colored blown and cut lead crystal. **Toys**: clay (whistles, crèches). **Masks**: polychrome wood.

Dishes – *caldo tlalpeño* (chicken broth with avocado and chili); *birria*; *tostadas* (fried corn tortillas covered with beans, poultry or beef, lettuce, onions, cheese, sour cream and tomato sauce); tamales; *pozole* (hominy soup); *dulce de leche* (milk sugar candy); *borrachos* (wine-flavored candies); *arrayanes* (fruit-flavored drops); *atole* (sweet corn beverage).

Nayarit
Handicrafts – **Masks**: polychrome wood; multicolored and lacquered (Huichols).

Dishes – *pescado zarandeado* (charcoal-grilled fresh fish with chili); *pozole blanco* (white hominy soup); fish and seafood.

51

Region 4: Northwest

Chihuahua   **Handicrafts – Ceramics:** burnished clay. **Wood:** stringed musical instruments, guitars (Tarahumaras). **Textiles:** sarapes and woolen blankets (Tarahumaras). **Leatherwork:** articles for everyday use (wallets, handbags). **Basketwork:** wicker baskets and furniture.

Dishes – seasoned meats; turnovers stuffed with ground beef; *rajas* (slices of various vegetables) with cheese; Mennonite cheese.

Durango   **Handicrafts – Leatherwork:** articles for everyday use (wallets, handbags). **Glasswork:** blown glass.

Dishes – *menudo* (tripe soup with oregano, cloves and chili); pork loin with maguey syrup; *dulce de membrillo* (quince candy) and *jamoncillos* (milk sugar bars).

Sinaloa   **Handicrafts – Textiles:** *rebozos.*

Dishes – chilorio (shredded pork with chili and spices); *pescado zarandeado* (fish); seafood barbecue; red tamales.

Sonora   **Handicrafts – Textiles:** sarapes and woolen blankets. **Leatherwork:** articles for everyday use (wallets, handbags). **Masks:** topped with dried deer heads.

Dishes – *caldillo de cecina* (jerked beef broth); fine strips of meat; *machaca* (beef jerky); *conejo campirano* (rabbit); *champurrado* (chocolate-flavored *atole*); *coyotas* (sweet tortillas).

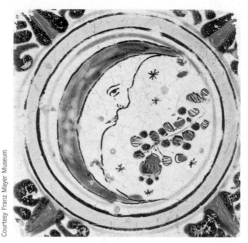

Courtesy Franz Mayer Museum

Ceramic Tile (c.17C), Puebla

Region 5: Baja California Peninsula

Baja California and Baja California Sur   **Handicrafts – Miscellaneous:** articles of shells, conchs and corals; leather work; woodcarvings; palm weavings; clay and salt works; ceramics (Yumana) and basketwork (Kimai).

Dishes – fish and seafood (clams, shrimp, lobster); *capirotada* (bread pudding with raisins).

Region 6: Northeast

Coahuila   **Handicrafts – Textiles:** sarapes and woolen blankets.

Dishes – *machaca con huevo* (beef jerky with scrambled eggs); *menudo norteño* (spicy tripe soup); *tasajo* (beef jerky, very similar to *cecina*); *jamoncillos* (milk sugar bars).

Nuevo León   **Handicrafts – Leatherwork:** articles for everyday use (wallets, handbags). **Glasswork:** blown glass.

Dishes – *cabrito a las brasas* (roasted kid); barbecued meat; *glorias* (custard tarts).

San Luis Potosí   **Handicrafts – Ceramics:** glazed. **Textiles:** embroidery and pulled-thread work (blouses, sheets, tablecloths), plain and fine *rebozos*. **Glasswork:** nuggets *(de pepita)*.

Dishes – *patlache* (a tamal wrapped in banana leaves); *enchiladas potosinas* (cheese tortillas with red chili sauce); *barbacoa; dulce de tuna* (cactus fruit candy).

Tamaulipas	**Handicrafts – Textiles:** leather (clothing articles made of deer or goat suede). **Miscellaneous:** figures with seashells; basketwork.

Dishes – fish and seafood (crab stuffed with crabmeat stewed with tomatoes); roast meat Tampiqueña-style (seasoned with sour orange juice and served with enchiladas and black beans).

Zacatecas	**Handicrafts – Wood:** furniture with shell and metal inlays. **Textiles:** embroidery and pulled-thread work (blouses, sheets, tablecloths). **Metalwork:** wrought iron, steel (knives, machetes, daggers).

Dishes – *birria; barbacoa; enchiladas zacatecanas; pipián* (a type of *mole* made with pumpkin seeds and chili); *gorditas; puchero vaquero* (beef and vegetable stew); *cabrito* (kid); *alfajor* (almond, coconut or nut paste).

Region 7: Gulf of Mexico

Tabasco — **Handicrafts – Miscellaneous:** articles of palm and wicker; engraved gourds; leatherwork and furriery.

Dishes – *pejelagarto asado* (roast fish resembling a reptile); *chilpachole* (spicy shrimp soup with corn and tomatoes); *tamales de chipilín* (tamales with spicy herbs); *plátanos machos fritos* (fried green plantains); chocolate.

Veracruz — **Handicrafts – Basketwork:** palm hats. **Bark paintings** *(amates)*: polychrome.

Dishes – fish and seafood, *huachinango a la veracruzana* (red snapper with tomato sauce, olives, chili and fine herbs); *chilpachole* (crabs in chili sauce); *ceviche* (raw fish marinated in limejuice, onions, tomatoes, chili and cilantro); *carne de mono de Catemaco* (smoked and grilled pork meat); coffee.

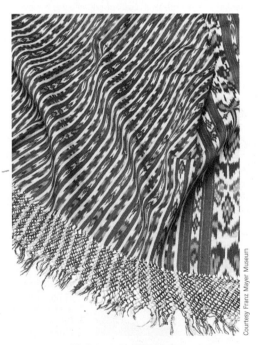

Courtesy Franz Mayer Museum

Silk Rebozo (c.19C), Mexico

Region 8: Pacific Coast

Chiapas — **Handicrafts – Ceramics:** with pre-Hispanic features, no glazing. **Wood:** percussion musical instruments (marimbas). **Textiles:** embroidery and pulled-thread work with indigenous influence, *huipiles* (women's tunics). **Metalwork:** gold jewelry (necklaces, bracelets, rings); tin (picture frames, lamps). **Masks:** with headdresses of tin flowers and ribbons. **Wax work.**

Dishes – tamales; *olla podrida* (spicy hotpot with beef, pork, chicken and vegetables); *cochinito al horno* (roast pork spiced with garlic and chili); *putzaze* (tripe and liver with tomatoes).

Guerrero	**Handicrafts – Ceramics:** with pre-Hispanic features, no glazing. **Textiles:** ponchos. **Basketwork:** willow (fruit baskets); palm hats. **Metalwork:** silver jewelry—necklaces, bracelets, rings (Taxco). **Lacquer work:** inlaid (Olinalá). **Bark Paintings** *(amates)*: polychrome. **Masks:** lacquered orangewood.

Dishes – fish and seafood (large oysters, clams, red snapper), *ceviche*; *pozole verde* (green hominy soup); tamarind; *cocada* (coconut pudding).

Michoacán	**Handicrafts – Ceramics:** glazed, burnished clay, ceremonial black pottery for the Day of the Dead. **Wood:** white wooden furniture decorated with knife-carvings, *equipales* (willow chairs with rush or leather seats), miscellaneous articles (miniature windmills, combs, letter openers), stringed musical instruments, guitars (Paracho). **Textiles:** embroidery and pulled-thread work with indigenous influence, *huipiles* (women's tunics), embroidered shirts, belts, sashes and cords. **Basketwork:** willow (fruit baskets), rice and wheat straw (Pátzcuaro, Tzintzuntzan), istle and henequen (throw rugs, carpets, etc.), wicker baskets and furniture. **Metalwork:** gold jewelry (necklaces, bracelets, rings), hammered copper (formerly Santa Clara del Cobre, today Villa Escalante). **Lacquer Work:** with gold leaf decorations (Pátzcuaro); striped (Uruapan). **Toys:** clay (whistles, crèches), rag dolls. **Masks:** lacquered orangewood.

Dishes – white fish, trout, *charales* (deep-fried freshwater fish); stuffed chili peppers (with cheese or beef); *carnitas* (deep-fried pork); *corundas* (small triangular tamales filled with cheese); *uchepos* (tender corn tamales served with cheese); *ates* (fruit jellies); *morelianas* (baked tortillas with milk sugar candy); *chongos zamoranos* (a famous Mexican confection).

Oaxaca	**Handicrafts – Ceramics:** glazed, burnished clay. **Wood:** miscellaneous articles (miniature windmills, combs, letter openers) **Textiles:** embroidery and pulled-thread work with indigenous influence, *huipiles*, embroidered shirts, ponchos, belts, sashes and cords, sarapes and woolen blankets, plain *rebozos*. **Leatherwork:** articles for everyday use (wallets, handbags). **Basketwork:** willow (fruit baskets), palm hats. **Metalwork:** silver offerings, gold and silver jewelry (necklaces, bracelets, rings), religious jewelry, tin (picture frames, lamps), steel (knives, machetes, daggers). **Bark paintings:** polychrome. **Toys:** clay (whistles, crèches), multicolored reeds, *alebrijes* (papier-mâché figures). **Masks:** polychrome wood, with headdresses of tin flowers and ribbons. **Wax work.**

Dishes – mole negro (meat in a spicy chili sauce); mole amarillo (pork with a spicy vegetable sauce); manchamantel (meat cooked with fruit); chapulines (dried grasshoppers with chili); tasajo; tamales; cecina; Oaxacan cheese; egg bread; chocolate; buñuelos (fritters); coffee.

Region 9: Yucatán Peninsula

Campeche	**Handicrafts – Basketwork:** *jipijapa* palm hats.

Dishes – fish and seafood (jumbo shrimp, *pámpano empapelado*, *esmedregal*, or salted fish).

Quintana Roo	**Handicrafts – Textiles:** embroidery and pulled-thread work with indigenous influence, hammocks.

Dishes – fish and seafood (sea snails, lobsters, dogfish turnovers).

Yucatán	**Handicrafts – Ceramics:** with pre-Hispanic features, no glazing. **Textiles:** embroidery and pulled-thread work with indigenous influence, hammocks. **Basketwork:** willow (fruit baskets); istle and henequen (rugs, runners), jipijapa hats, Panama hats. **Metalwork:** gold jewelry (necklaces, bracelets, rings).

Dishes – *sopa de lima* (chicken broth with fried tortilla); chicken and *cochinita pibil* (suckling pig); *panuchos* (fried corn tortillas stuffed with beans, chicken or suckling pig and covered with red onions marinated in vinegar and chili sauce); *papadzules* (tacos stuffed with hard-boiled eggs in squash seed sauce); *huevos motuleños* (fried eggs over a tostada with beans, peas, cheese, ham, sauce and green plantains); *queso relleno* (stuffed cheese).

Pollo Pibil, Typical Dish from Mérida

World Heritage List

In 1972, the United Nations Educational, Scientific and Cultural Organization (UNESCO) adopted a Convention for the preservation of cultural and natural sites. To date, more than 150 States Parties have signed this international agreement, which has listed over 500 sites "of outstanding universal value" on the World Heritage List. Each year, a committee of representatives from 21 countries, assisted by technical organizations (ICOMOS – International Council on Monuments and Sites; IUCN – International Union for Conservation of Nature and Natural Resources; ICCROM – International Centre for the Study of the Preservation and Restoration of Cultural Property, the Rome Centre), evaluates the proposals for new sites to be included on the list, which grows longer as new nominations are accepted and more countries sign the Convention. To be considered, a site must be nominated by the country in which it is located.

The protected cultural heritage may be monuments (buildings, sculptures, archaeological structures, etc.) with unique historical, artistic or scientific features, groups of buildings (such as religious communities, ancient cities); or sites (human settlements, examples of exceptional landscapes, cultural landscapes) which are the combined works of man and nature of exceptional beauty. Natural sites may be a testimony to the stages of the earth's geological history or to the development of human cultures and creative genius, or represent significant ongoing ecological processes, contain superlative natural phenomena or provide a habitat for threatened species.

Signatories of the Convention pledge to cooperate to preserve and protect these sites around the world as a common heritage to be shared by all humanity.

Some of the most well-known places which the World Heritage Committee has inscribed include: Australia's Great Barrier Reef (1981), the Canadian Rocky Mountain Parks (1984), The Great Wall of China (1987), the Statue of Liberty (1984), the Kremlin (1990), Mont-Saint-Michel and its Bay (France – 1979), Durham Castle and Cathedral (1986).

In Mexico, UNESCO World Heritage sites are:

Mexico City and State of Mexico

Mexico City – historic center (1987)
Xochimilco – historic center (1987)
Teotihuacán – archaeological site (1987)

Central Mexico

Querétaro – historic center (1996)
16C monasteries on the hillsides of the Popocatépetl Volcano (1994)
Puebla – historic center (1987)

Central West

City of Guanajuato and its mines (1988)

Northwest

Paquimé, Chihuahua – archaeological site (1999)

Baja California Sur

Cave painting of the Sierra de San Francisco (1993)
Whale sanctuary in El Vizcaíno Biosphere Reserve (1993)

Northeast

Zacatecas – historic center (1993)

Gulf of Mexico

Tlacotalpan, Veracruz (1999)
El Tajín, Veracruz - archaeological site (1992)

Pacific Coast

Morelia – historic center (1991)
Monte Albán, Oaxaca – archaeological site (1987)
Oaxaca – historic center (1987)
Palenque, Chiapas – archaeological site (1987)

Yucatán

Uxmal, Yucatán – archaeological site (1996)
Chichén Itzá, Yucatán – archaeological site (1988)
Sian-Ka'an Biosphere Reserve, Quintana Roo (1987)

Plazuela del Baratillo, Guanajuato

Sights

Region 1

MEXICO CITY

A City of Vivid Contrasts

Handicrafts and Food, p 48. Called the **Distrito Federal** (or simply *el D.F.*) by Mexicans, this capital city carefully preserves architectural traces of its pre-Hispanic and colonial past just as proudly as it shows off its well-engineered and beautifully designed modern buildings.

Here, on the streets and in the memory of the inhabitants, the most important and transcendent events of the past are ever present. Churches, palaces and historic monuments, as well as traditional festivities, patriotically proclaim how Mexico gained its independence from Spain in 1810, while solemnly commemorating the bloody social revolution of 1910 that marked the beginning of the modern era. Today, Mexico City serves as the country's political and cultural center.

From the beginning its inhabitants have faced and overcome adversity with faith, stoicism and courage. Nevertheless, at present the dire situation of one of the world's biggest cities (with a population of approximately 20 million in the D.F. and surrounding area) cannot be ignored. This metropolis that novelist Alfonso Reyes once called "the region with the clearest air" is now the most polluted and the most overpopulated. Despite its urban problems, Mexico City endures as one of the most important and exciting cities in the western hemisphere, offering an incredible array of entertainment: elegant theaters, modern movie cinemas, traditional *cantinas* and bars, and a very active nightlife. Thanks to the variety of its stores and markets, shoppers can embark on a fantastical journey of colors and tastes: from the peddlers just outside the Metropolitan Cathedral to handicraft markets in the city center; from the spacious avenues of Polanco and the fashionable *Zona Rosa* districts with their elegant boutiques to luxury malls such as Santa Fe (the biggest in Latin America) and Perisur.

Ciudad de México

Plaza de la Constitución

OVERVIEW OF MEXICO CITY

Geographical Notes

El Distrito Federal, the smallest geographic entity in Mexico, is bordered to the north, east and west by Mexico state, and to the south by the state of Morelos. Situated in a large elevated valley, the **Meseta de Anáhuac** (2,240m/7,305ft), the city is protected to the east by the legendary twin volcanoes Popocatépetl, "Smoky Mountain," and Iztaccíhuatl, "Sleeping Woman." The Ajusco mountain range marks its southern limit. On clear days, all these peaks can be spotted from different vantagepoints throughout Mexico City. Officially, the capital is divided into political districts, though one could also say that Mexico City has formed one enormous metropolis by gradually overtaking other cities as it overran its original boundaries.

Historical Notes

Foundation of México-Tenochtitlán – *Central Plateau, p 33*. The origins of Mexico City date back to AD 1325 when the Mexicas discovered the central islet of Lago de **Texcoco** (Lake Texcoco), where they were to settle, according to the prophesies of the god of war, Huitzilopóchtli. Legend suggests that the tribe came from **Aztlán**, a place never traced geographically and from which derived the name **Aztecs**. After a saga of almost two hundred years of wandering, involving attempts to settle in different parts of the valley, notably Tula and Chapultepec, and innumerable wars against already settled tribes, the Mexicas finally saw on the islet the divine sign they had awaited: an eagle devouring a snake while standing on a *nopal* (prickly pear cactus). This vision would become Mexico's national emblem.

The Mexicas took possession of the small island, which had not been claimed due to its inhospitable and muddy terrain. Gradually, through wars and alliances, they extended their territory until it became México-Tenochtitlán, the grandiose and enormous lake city that greeted the Spanish conquistadors.

The Floating City – México-Tenochtitlán-"the cactus field where Mexitli (another name for Huitzilopóchtli), son of the Sun and Moon dwells"-was composed of a series of small islands, which the Mexicas linked through a complex network of canals that facilitated transport by canoes and provided clean water. The Mexicas also built clay roads, aqueducts, bridges, and **chinampas** (floating gardens). The latter was fundamental for the Mexicas' territorial expansion and urban demarcation. Chinampas consisted of floating landmasses, a type of artificial islet made from the lake's vegetation and solidified with mud and roots. Each one measured approximately 75m/82yd in length and 10m/11yd to 20m/22yd in width. At first used only for farming, they later served as the foundation for many different structures. Today, this unique phenomenon can be admired in Xochimilco.

59

© Bob Schalkwijk

Mexico-Tenochtitlán Mural by Luis Covarrubias

The principal city or islet was divided into four districts or **calpullis**. Each district possessed a municipal building called a *Tecpan* and different types of constructions, such as temples, palaces, public buildings and residential quarters. A walled main plaza, or **Gran Teocalli**, stood in the island center. Four principal thoroughfares connected the main islet to the others at each cardinal point. Present-day Tlatelolco, located to the north of the central islet, was settled in AD 1331 as a commercial district, or *tianguis*, by a different indigenous group that managed to remain independent from the Mexicas until 1473.

The Aztec Empire – In less than two centuries, the once insignificant tribe of the Aztecs became Mesoamerica's greatest power. Through their superior skills of war and consolidation of power by a tributary, or taxation system, the Aztecs extended their rule from the areas surrounding present-day Mexico City into Central America. México-Tenochtitlán's religious concepts and values governed its urban, social and political structure, and all civil activities were based on the will and wishes of the Aztec deities.

When the Spaniards arrived, they marveled at the architectural beauty of the city, which by then was comprised of nearly 20,000 buildings. The conquistadors were also amazed by its urban distribution-which reminded them of Venice-by its social, political, and economic system, and by its large population, which far surpassed that of any European city of the time. Such an advanced and grand civilization would pose a great challenge for the conquering Europeans.

The Sixteenth and Seventeenth Centuries – After the Spanish Conquest of México-Tenochtitlán on August 13, 1521, Hernán Cortés insisted on building the new city on the same islet. He kept the same swampland surrounded by canals, but demolished the few remaining structures. Cast out to the city's fringes, the natives were relegated to an almost slave-like existence. The conquistadors used military force and the imposition of Christianity as their two most powerful weapons for domination. Evangelization, a key factor throughout colonial times, began in 1524 with the arrival of the first Franciscan friars.

The buildings of the second half of the 16C and the early 17C were, therefore, of a military and religious nature. However, few traces of these remain due to a series of long and devastating floods that struck the city during the second decade of the 17C.

Neo-Hispanic Mexico – In 1637, after the latest flood waters had receded, reconstruction began on the city. New Renaissance and Baroque architectural styles were adopted, followed later by the Churrigueresque and Plateresque, all of European influence. From this time until the mid 18C many monasteries were built with open-air chapels where the indigenous people were indoctrinated and educated. Hospitals and hospices for each of the races, aqueducts, public services and grand Spanish residences also appeared.

The neo-Hispanic city began to take on an original character. Not only were the materials different from those used in Europe (most of them were taken from the former pre-Hispanic structures), but the natives' manual labor was also unique. Not understanding the concepts of a culture and religion so different from their own, they created their own interpretation of European architectural styles. This phenomenon, called **arte tequitqui** (Tequitqui art), occurred all over Mexico and can be admired in most buildings of the time, not only in Mexico City, but also in the provincial colonial cities.

Neoclassical Apogee – Later, in the mid 18C, economic prosperity ushered in the Neoclassical style, which changed the city's appearance. Originating in France, this new architectural style, influenced by the Renaissance and the Enlightenment, was embraced by Mexico's **Real Academia de San Carlos de Bellas Artes** (St. Charles' Royal Academy of Fine Arts), founded in 1785. Large palaces arose as residences for the nobility and the bourgeoisie, many new streets were paved, and numerous monuments were erected. However, to make way for these new structures, architecturally significant Baroque buildings were demolished or remodeled.

Independence and its Impact – In 1810, after three centuries of supposed order and tranquillity, a social movement emerged that would change Mexico's destiny: the struggle for Mexican Independence. Thus, during the first decades of the 19C, urban development came to a halt. Later, in 1859, the Reform Laws (Leyes de Reforma) were passed, transferring all clerical properties into state hands. This transition spawned a new period of popular urban development. The demolition of many of the monasteries, whose lands were divided and sold, made way for new streets, greatly changing the city's layout and appearance. Unfortunately, the destruction resulted in the loss of many colonial buildings.

The Porfiriato – The last third of the 19C took place under the dictatorship of Porfirio Díaz. During this era, known as the "Porfiriato," the fruits of the country's economic boom were channeled into creating a more international image, with the goal of making the capital comparable to any great European city. This modernization brought with it positive changes such as public lighting, trams, water treatment plants, paving and sewage lines. Architects, masons and blacksmiths, as well as the best materials, were brought from Europe to create new buildings of noble character.

Twentieth Century – In 1910 the Mexican Revolution broke out, and the following ten years brought misery to the people and destruction to many cities.
At the beginning of 1920, a nationalist spirit emerged that spawned the muralist painting movement. **José Vasconcelos**, head of the Department of Public Education, was the first to encourage painters to decorate the inside walls of buildings, thus enriching Mexico's cultural heritage.
In the early 1930s, the population explosion spurred architects to design larger, more functional buildings. This style prevailed for some 20 years.

Contemporary México – Due to overcrowding and an utter lack of adequate planning, the city has deteriorated under a series of rapid changes. Although some of these, such as the metro system, have worked, others have been catastrophic, as was the case with poorly built public housing.
The idiosyncrasy of the Mexican people is no less complex than the city itself. As a result of three centuries of colonization, the *mestizo* race (a blend of Hispanic and indigenous blood) bears the weight of a certain amount of passive resignation contrasted with an active will to survive. The combination of these conflicting tendencies has created a very peculiar phenomenon whereby Mexicans live stoically with unbearable conditions for years until their patriotism, solidarity and fighting spirit takes over, spurring them into action. Very often this reaction is prompted by the emergence of leaders *(caudillos)* or by the sudden onset of disastrous life-threatening situations. Thus, after a powerful earthquake shook Mexico City in 1985, the citizenry pulled together, as never before, to assist those who lost everything. The quake's destruction prompted the creation of a new city, making the inhabitants more conscientious, better organized and supportive, creating groups and movements that would positively transform the capital and the country.
Presently, Mexico City faces the historic challenge of solving its problems through a democratic process. In July 1997, for the first time, democratic elections were held to elect the city's governmental chief, who previously had been appointed by the president. **Cuauhtémoc Cárdenas** (son of the famous former president Lázaro Cárdenas) candidate for the Partido de la Revolución Democrática (PRD), won the election by defeating the candidate for the traditional ruling party, the Partido Revolucionario Institucional (PRI). Equally important, for the first time, private citizens instead of government employees managed the electoral process.
Thus, Mexico City stands as a modern metropolis with a rich legacy of contrasting cultures, historical eras and pre-Hispanic roots. Today it invites visitors to explore the vestiges of its many hidden treasures.

PRACTICAL INFORMATION

Getting There

By Plane – **Mexico City's International Airport:** 6km/3.7mi northeast of the city center; **information:** ☎ 55-71-36-00 & 57-84-48-11. National arrivals: ext. 2303; international arrivals: ext. 2341; for orientation and information on airlines, and to report grievances or complaints: ext. 2260 *(year-round daily)*. Transportation to the city center: by taxi *(requires prepayment; tickets sold at "taxi" booth in main concourse; P$79)*. Buses to Cuernavaca, Puebla, Toluca, San Miguel de Allende, Celaya, Querétaro, León and Irapuato leave from stop located at Concourse D; tickets are sold at boarding. Car rental agencies in terminal.

By Bus – There are four main bus terminals for travel to almost every town in Mexico: **Central del Norte** (North Central), Eje Lázaro Cárdenas, 4907, ☎ 55-87-15-52; **Central del Sur** (South Central) Av. Taxqueña, 1320, ☎ 56-89-97-45; **Terminal del Oriente** (Tapo) (East Terminal) Ignacio Zaragoza, 200, ☎ 57-62-52-10, and **Central del Occidente** (West Central) Av. Río de Tacubaya ☎ 52-71-45-19. **Ticket Bus** sells bus tickets for travel to the southeastern end of Mexico City and accepts payment by credit cards or direct payment at the ticket booth; for schedules and rate information ☎ 51-33-24-24 *(daily 9am–11pm)*. Grey Line Tours, Londres, 166, Col. Juárez, offers daily bus trips to Taxco and Acapulco ☎ 52-08-11-63 *(daily 7am–10pm)*.

By Train – Connects the city with the rest of the country. **Estación de Ferrocarriles Nacionales de México** (Mexico's National Train Station), Av. Jesús García, 140, Col. Buenavista; for information and reservations ☎ 55-47-10-84.

Getting Around

Public transportation – The **METRO** *(pp 72-73)* connects the entire city by means of a network of 9 lines and 2 railways (Routes A and B for travel to the state of Mexico) with 154 stations *(Mon–Fri 5am–3am, Sat 6am–1am, Sun & holidays 7am–3am; P$1.50)*. Orientation and information on routes and location of tourist sights ☎ 56-27-49-51 *(Mon–Fri 9am–8pm)* and at METRO information desks at the following stations *(Mon–Fri 8am–2:30pm, 3–8pm; except holidays)*: Balderas, Chapultepec, Zócalo, Centro Médico, Tacuba, Chabacano, La Raza, Pino Suárez, Hidalgo and Insurgentes. Metro stations are well lit, and the subway system runs smoothly and efficiently. Visitors should avoid traveling during rush hour; the metro is least crowded from 10am–4pm, on weekends & holidays.

Buses *(daily 6am–midnight; P$2–$4)* connect all points around the city. Buses for handicapped people and senior citizens *(daily every 30min; free)*. Express buses run on major thoroughfares (Reforma, Insurgentes and Presidente Masaryk). Buses are usually crowded, especially during rush-hour traffic; exact fare is required. Be aware that route and bus numbers change frequently. **Bus stops** are found near metro exits. For schedules and information on routes ☎ 55-25-93-80 (Infotur). **Trolleybus** connects various points, generally with stops near metro exits *(daily 5am–11pm; P$1.50)*. **Buses for handicapped people** leave Universidad metro station for Central del Norte with intermediate stops *(daily 6am–11pm, every 30min)*. For information or to report grievances and complaints ☎ 55-39-28-00.

Fast-train leaves Taxqueña station for Xochimilco (formerly Embarcadero) with 18 intermediate stations that connect with the southern bus terminal, the Aztec stadium, the pier, museums, the handicrafts market and the flower market *(year-round Mon–Fri 5am–11pm; Sat–Sun and holidays 6am–11pm; P$1.50)*. For route information ☎ 55-73-19-54 or contact the Tourist Information Desk at Taxqueña station *(open year-round daily 6am–10pm)*.

Car – *(City Map pp 66-67)* Avenida Insurgentes traverses Mexico City from north to south, in both directions; Paseo de la Reforma from east to west, in both directions; and Periférico encircles the city as a two-way beltway with high-speed lanes. The city is also crisscrossed by a series of one-way axes, called *ejes viales* that link north with south and east *(oriente)* with west *(poniente)*. The **speed limit** varies according to street, axis and beltway or according to school or hospital zones; observe the speed limits indicated at each place. When renting a car in Mexico City, indicate the days you want to use the vehicle, because cars can not be driven on certain days. Street parking is not advisable; any vehicle parked illegally is likely to be disabled by the police; a fine has to be paid before the vehicle is released.

Public parking – Some areas, such as the Zona Rosa, have **parking meters** *(P$1/15min)*. Parking garages are located at: Plaza de Bellas Artes, Lázaro Cárdenas (Eje Central) and Av. Juárez *(7am–3am)*; Plaza Garibaldi, Lázaro Cárdenas, corner of República de Perú *(daily 24hrs)*; Plaza Morelos, corner of Balderas and Dondé, beside the Mercado La Ciudadela *(daily 24hrs; P$12–$14/hr)*.

Intersection of Bucareli and Paseo de la Reforma

Taxis – Green and yellow taxis–predominantly Volkswagen Beetles–cruise the major tourist areas. The US Embassy recommends that instead of hailing taxis from the street, visitors use taxi stands or **radio taxis:** Servi-taxi ☏ 55-16-60-20; Radiomex (ecological and executive) ☏ 55-74-45-96. Taxis are required to be equipped with a meter. Fares are reasonable; tipping is usually not expected. **Tourist taxis** stationed at hotels can be hired by the hour or day at prearranged rates; inquire at hotel's front desk.

General Information

Tourist Information – **Tourist Information Center (SECTUR)**, Masaryk, 172, ☏ 52-50-01-23, 52-50-00-27 or 52-50-85-55 or *www.mexico-travel.com (Mon–Fri 9am–9pm, Sat 10am–3pm)* offers information and brochures on entertainment, places of interest and festivals. **Infotur SECTUR** operates a multilingual tourist information hotline ☏ 52-50-01-51 *(daily 24hrs)*. Offices of the Attorney General (Agency 61) at Florencia, 20, Zona Rosa ☏ 51-30-81-49 and 51-30-81-54 *(daily 24hrs)* will help in cases of theft, loss or replacement of documents. For further assistance, contact your embassy.

Accommodations – The Official Accommodations Guide, *Guía Oficial de Hospedaje en México*, can be obtained from **SECTUR** and is on sale at Sanborns stores. **Reservation service: SECTUR**, Pte. Masaryk, 172, Col. Polanco ☏ 52-55-31-12 and 01-800-903-92 00 *(year-round Mon–Fri 9am–6pm, Sat 10am–1pm)*. Mexico City accommodates millions of visitors year-round; thus, it is recommended that hotel reservations be made well in advance. Most visitors, business travelers and tourists stay near Chapultepec Park, Paseo de la Reforma and Zona Rosa. Here most hotels offer such amenities as air conditioning, cable TV, radio, minibars, in-room safe deposit boxes and room service. Visitors can also expect hotels to have purified water.

Hotels: *(Reforma and Polanco districts; P$1,200 & up)* Camino Real ☏ 52-03-21-21, Presidente Intercontinental ☏ 53-27-77-00, Fiesta Americana ☏ 57-05-49-11, Four Seasons México ☏ 52-30-18-18, María Isabel Sheraton ☏ 52-07-39-33, J.W. Mariott ☏ 52-82-88-88, Nikko ☏ 52-03-48-00. **Zona Rosa hotels:** *(P$800–$2,100)* Calinda Quality Geneve ☏ 52-11-00-71, Krystal ☏ 52-28-99-28, Imperial ☏ 57-05-49-11, Westin Galería Plaza ☏ 52-11-00-14. **Zona Sur hotels:** *(P$1,600–$2,200)* Paraíso Radisson ☏ 56-06-42-11, Royal Pedregal ☏ 57-26-90-36, Continental Plaza ☏ 56-81-12-90. **Historic hotels:** *(P$900–$2,000)* Hotel de Cortés *(p 85)* ☏ 55-18-21-81, Hotel Majestic ☏ 55-21-86-00, Gran Hotel de la Ciudad de México *(p 71)* ☏ 55-10-40-47. *Rates are daily for double occupancy and subject to change. A 10% sales tax and 5% room tax are added to all bills.*

Press – Newspapers (Spanish language): *Reforma, El Universal, El Heraldo, La Jornada, Excélsior* and *El Financiero*. English language publications: *The News* and *Mexico City Times*. Foreign newspapers: *New York Times, Wall Street Journal, The Washington Post, USA Today* and *Le Monde*. The *Tiempo Libre* entertainment and cultural guide is available at most hotels.

Currency Exchange *(p 392)* ☏

American Express, Paseo de la Reforma, 234
(Mon–Fri 9am–6pm, Sat 9am–1pm)   52-07-72-82

Casa de Cambio Tíber, Paseo de la Reforma, 318
(Mon–Fri 8:30am–3pm, Sat 8:30am–2pm)   52-07-94-85

Casa de Cambio Tamibe, Niza, 11, Zona Rosa
(Mon–Fri 8:30am–4:30pm, Sat 10am–2pm)   55-14-37-31

Money Center, Londres, 227
(Mon–Fri 8:30am–6pm, Sat 8:30am–2pm)   52-08-34-23

Major banks will also exchange some foreign currency (fee). Visitors can obtain Mexican pesos with international credit cards at **ATM machines** located at Mexico City's International Airport: national arrivals (Concourse A) and international arrivals, (Concourses E & F), in most hotels, and outside banks (24hr entrance is provided by sliding credit card into device located on or near the door).

Sightseeing – Numerous companies offer organized **tours** of the city and nearby sights. Most excursions are narrated (English) and last either 1/2 day or a full day. Gray Line Tours *(daily; departures from their offices at Londres, 166; for schedules & prices ☏ 52-08-11-63)*. American Express *(daily; departures from Hotel Fiesta Americana, Reforma, 80; for schedules & prices; ☏ 57-05-15-15)*. Mexico Travel Advisors *(daily; departures from Génova, 30; for schedules & prices; ☏ 55-25-75-20)*. INAH organizes cultural excursions throughout Mexico; for further information, contact the Museo Nacional de Antropología ☏ 55-53-23-65 or *www.cnca.gob.mex/inah/servicio/paseos.html*. **Tren turístico** offers a train ride through the city *(daily 10am–5pm; departures from Av. Juárez, 66, corner of Revillagigedo; during weekdays, the train departs with a minimum of 8 people, during weekends every 30min or every hr, depending on demand; P$28; for more information and reservations ☏ 55-12-10-12 to 14)*. Knowledgeable guides can be hired with the assistance of SECTUR *(p 43)*, for information ☏ 52-50-01-23 (English-speaking operator). **Tourist taxis** *(taxis turísticos)* are stationed at most hotels and can be hired by the hour, by the day, or for excursions outside the city at pre-arranged fares. Drivers serve as guides (some are certified by SECTUR) and most speak English. Tourist taxi-cabs are licensed by SECTUR and have blue license plates.

Shopping – *(Markets p 95)* For **handicrafts** at reasonable prices, including jewelry, pottery and leather goods from all over Mexico, shoppers can visit various markets: Mercado de La Ciudadela *(p 83)*, Bazar Sábado *(p 105)*, Buenavista, Aldama, 187; Fundación Nacional de Artesanías (FONART); Tiendas Oaxaca, Calzada de Tlalpan, 2191; Mercado Insurgentes *(p 96)*. In the Zona Rosa a number of stores and **international boutiques** offer jewelry, handicrafts, clothes, souvenirs, and leather goods. Well-established **department stores** are located at Liverpool and Palacio de Hierro at 20 de Noviembre and Venustiano Carranza. At Londres, 136 a bustling **market** *(open daily)* offers an abundance of quality handicrafts and souvenirs at reasonable prices. Tane, Amberes, 70, is known for its exceptional silver jewelry. Dealers and artisans sell **antiques and collectibles** *(weekends only)* in the Plaza del Ángel, Londres, 161.

Shopping Centers *(open daily 11am–8pm)*: **South:** Galerías Insurgentes, corner of Insurgentes Sur and Parroquia; Plaza Coyoacán, corner of Av. Universidad and Río Churubusco; Plaza Loreto, corner of Río Magdalena and Av. Revolución; Centro Comercial Perisur, corner of Periférico Sur and Av. Insurgentes Sur. **North:** Plaza Satélite, corner of Periférico Norte and Circuito Centro Comercial, Ciudad Satélite. **West:** Plaza Centro Comercial Santa Fe (the newest shopping center), Av. Vasco de Quiroga, Col. Santa Fe; Pabellón Polanco, corner of Jaime Balmes and Homero, Col. Polanco; Plaza Molière, corner of Molière and Horacio.

Entertainment – Consult the arts and entertainment section of local newspapers *(p 43)* for schedules of cultural events, addresses of theaters and concert halls. To purchase **tickets**, contact the box office or Ticketmaster ☏ 53-25-90-00. Your hotel may also help in obtaining tickets. Palacio de Bellas Artes is home to the National Symphony Orchestra and Ballet Folclórico Company, and offers concerts and opera performances *(season Jan–March & Aug–Oct)*; for performance schedules ☏ 55-12-36-33. Nezahualcóyotl Hall ☏ 56-22-71-25, part of the University Cultural Center, hosts various artists and groups. The Mexico City Philharmonic performs at Ollín Yoliztli Hall ☏ 56-06-43-63. International symphonies, ballet and pop artists all perform at the National Auditorium in Chapultepec Park ☏ 52-80-92-50. Teatro Metropolitano ☏ 55-10-39-64, concerts and shows. **Ticket sales:** in person at the box office or from Ticketmaster ☎ 53-25-90-00 and at Ticketmaster outlets at El Palacio de Hierro, Mixup and Discolandia stores.

Theaters: Local dancers, singers and comedians perform at numerous venues throughout the city. Most plays are performed in Spanish: Teatro Blanquita, Avenida Lázaro Cárdenas (Eje Central), 16; Centro Teatral Manolo Fábregas, Velázquez de León, 31 and Serapio Rendón, 15; Teatro de los Insurgentes, Insurgentes Sur, 1587; Teatro San Rafael, Melchor Ocampo, 40; Teatro Silvia Pinal, Coahuila, 79.

Mariachis: Plaza Garibaldi; Restaurante Arroyo, Insurgentes Sur, 4003 *(open daily 8am–7pm)*; Restaurante Las Delicias, Insurgentes Sur, 1027 *(open Tue–Sun 1pm–3am)*; Bar El Jorongo, Paseo de la Reforma, 325 *(open daily 6pm–midnight)*.

Charreadas: Lienzo Charro del Pedregal, Camino a Santa Teresa, 306, ☎ 56-66-69-95, offers horse shows, including elegantly dressed *charros* (Mexican cowboys) and traditional folk singers.

Nightlife – The **cantinas**, a national institution, are the meeting places par excellence where strangers, warmed by drink, break the ice and forge great friendships. Live music and appetizers *(botanas)* are essential elements of the cantinas. People usually go there for lunch during the week, but those with afternoon free time may go to play a few games of dominoes or get involved in prolonged conversations.

If you choose to go out at night, the Historic Center offers good options. One of the best known places, **Plaza Garibaldi**, is excellent for dining, drinking and listening to Mariachi music. Facing the square the **Teatro Blanquita**, an old variety theater, now hosts popular shows. **La Ópera** bar is one of the most traditional.

Cantinas – **El Nivel** – *Moneda, 2, corner of Seminario, Centro Histórico. Mon–Sat 10am–midnight.* The oldest cantina in Mexico City, founded in 1872, with license no. 1. **La Guadalupana** – *Higuera, 14, between Caballo Calco and Ibáñez, Colonia del Carmen, Coyoacán. Mon–Fri noon-midnight, Sat noon–11pm, noon–6pm.*

Bars – **La Ópera** – *5 de Mayo, 10, corner of Filomeno Mata, Centro Histórico. Mon–Sat 1pm–midnight, Sun 1–6pm.* **Bar Mata** – *Filomeno Mata, 11, 3rd floor, corner of 5 de Mayo, Centro Histórico. Daily 8pm–2am.* **Bar Milán** – *Milán, 18, corner of General Prim, Col. Juárez, Centro Histórico. Tue–Sun 9pm–3am.* **El Hijo del Cuervo** – *Jardín Centenario, 17, between Tres Cruces and Carrillo Puerto, Col. del Carmen. Daily 1pm–noon.*

Exhibition sports – **Bullfights:** *(Nov–Mar, Sun 4pm)* Plaza México, Augusto Rodín, 241, Ciudad de los Deportes ☎ 55-63-39-61. **Soccer:** *(Feb–May & Sept–Nov)*, Estadio Azteca, Calzada de Tlalpan, 3465 ☎ 56-17-80-80 and at the Estadio Azul, Indiana, 255, Col. Nápoles. **Auto-racing:** *(year-round)* Autódromo Hermanos Rodríguez, Puerta, 5, Ciudad Deportiva, Col. Magdalena Mixhuca ☎ 56-49-24-99. **Tickets** for all attractions at box office or through Ticketmaster ☎ 53-25-90-00

Recreation – Adventure Kingdom *(Reino Aventura)* ☎ 57-28-72-00, Carr. Picacho-Ajusto, 1500 *(year-round Tue–Thu 10am–6pm, Fri–Sun 10am–7pm)* and La Feria. **Mountaineering:** excursions led by local guides, including transportation, equipment and provisions to Iztaccíhuatl Volcano, can be arranged through Gray Line Tours *(p 62)*, or Confederación Deportiva Mexicana ☎ 55-19-20-40 *(2pm–9pm)* and through Outward Bound, Garrison NY ☎ 914-424-4000. **Parks** ideal for cycling, hiking, swimming, boating and picnics include Chapultepec Park, Parque Nacional El Ajusco, Carretera Ajusco (20km south), Parque Nacional del Desierto de los Leones and Xochimilco *(p 110)*.

Useful Phone Numbers ☎

Emergency (police, fire department, ambulance)	**080**
Public Safety	060
Fire	57-68-37-00
Red Cross	53-95-11-11
AMA (Mexican Automobile Association)	55-88-70-55
Medical Emergency	55-39-72-00
Rescue Squad and medical urgency	57-22-88-05
Public Ministry Agency (specializing in tourist aid)	51-30-81-49

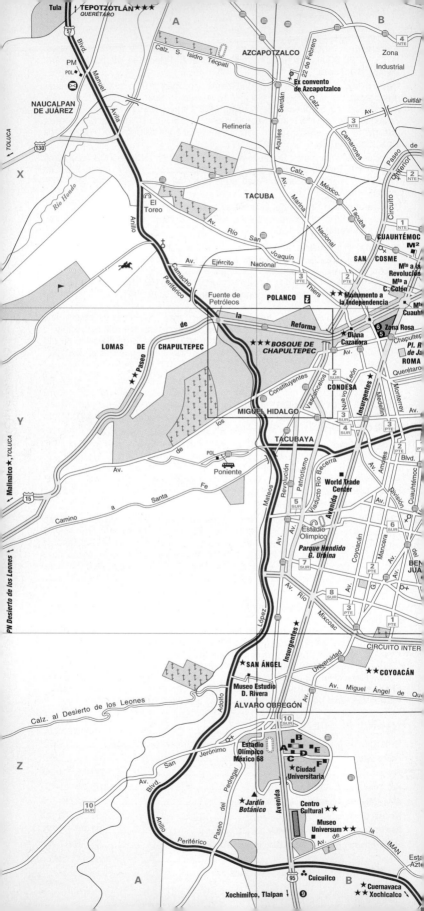

CENTRO HISTÓRICO★★★

Mexico City's Historic Center, declared a World Heritage Site in 1987, still preserves wonderful examples of the pre-Hispanic and colonial periods that coexist harmoniously with extraordinary 20C buildings. In pre-Hispanic times, the Gran Tenochtitlán stood here, later giving way to the Spanish Conquistadors' luxury palaces, enormous religious complexes and stunningly beautiful churches.

★★★① PLAZA DE LA CONSTITUCIÓN, AND SURROUNDINGS,
🚇 line 2 – Zócalo

★★★**Plaza de la Constitución (El Zócalo)** – *Photo p 59*. In pre-Hispanic times this plaza played a prominent role in the life of Aztec society, as part of the Templo Mayor (Great Temple). During the colonial era it witnessed the enactment of magnificent secular and religious festivals and the construction of architectural masterworks. Since then its appearance has changed according to the whims of rulers and architects. Now a concrete plaza with a large flagpole, the Zócalo hosts the daily raising and lowering of the flag by the National Guard.

From 1706 to 1843 the plaza housed a statue of King Charles IV of Spain and a building called **El Parián**. General Santa Anna, however, had these taken down and in their place planned a monument to Independence of which only the *zócalo* (base) was ever built. (By analogy, the word *zócalo* is frequently used to designate the main plaza of any city or town in Mexico.) In the 19C, the plaza was a popular place with shade trees, a bandstand and a trolley station. East of the Cathedral, a splendid construction, the **Nacional Monte de Piedad**, an institution of public welfare, occupies the site of Moctezuma's ancient home, which Hernán Cortés had reserved for his personal use after the Conquest. Completing the surroundings, on its southern edge, the "twin" buildings of the **Antiguo Edificio** and **Nuevo Edificio del Departamento del Distrito Federal (DDF)** (Old and New Government Offices of the Federal District) join the cathedral and Government Palace in delimiting the giant plaza. Throughout-and despite-all these changes the Zócalo has remained the heart of the city, full of life and zest, and the scene of popular celebrations especially during important national holidays such as **Independence Day** (Sept 16), the parade on **Revolution Day** (Nov 20), and New Year's festivities. It has also, in recent years, become the focal point for social and political rallies and protests, thus serving as a silent witness to Mexican history.

★★★**Catedral Metropolitana** – *Northern edge of the Plaza de la Constitución. Open Oct–Mar Mon–Sat 7am–6pm; Apr–Sept Mon–Sat 7am–7pm, Sun & holidays 7am–8pm. Closed May 1 & 5, Sept 1 & 16, Nov 20.* The first cathedral of New Spain, begun by order of Hernán Cortés in 1524 and consecrated in 1532, was a rather primitive structure. Thus, it was demolished in 1626 and replaced by the Catedral Metropolitana. The first stone of the present imposing building, designed by Claudio de Arciniega, was laid in 1573. The cathedral was completed in 1813 when Manuel Tolsá added the cupola and the upper balustrades.

Facade – One of the city's finest Baroque facades boasts three doors with Doric columns. The relief above the main door represents *La Asunción* (The Assumption of the Virgin Mary); the relief on the southwestern door depicts *La Entrega de las Llaves* (Jesus Giving Peter the Keys to the Kingdom); and the one on the third door corresponds to the nave of the church. Master sculptor, Manuel Tolsá, created the clock and the sculptures *Fe, Esperanza y Caridad* (Faith, Hope and Charity) that crown the facade. Damián Ortiz designed the 18C towers.

Interior – The cathedral's imposing and solid exterior complements its luxurious interior. However, at present only certain chapels and altars can be appreciated while the building is being leveled.

Five naves make up its layout: the two side aisles have seven chapels each, while the adjoining aisles are used for processions. The great height, the choir, and the altars that adorn the central nave render it outstanding.

Although the **chapels★** can only be viewed from the aisle, the first on the left, called the Capilla Santos Ángeles y Arcángeles (Chapel of the Saint Angels and Archangels), is remarkable due to its golden altarpiece.

Toward the north wall stands the altar dedicated to *El Señor de los Perdones* (Lord of Mercy), beside the magnificent **Altar de los Reyes★★★**, an elaborate gilded wooden altarpiece in the Baroque-Churrigueresque style. This stunning work of art, begun by Jerónimo de Balbás in 1718, took 19 years to complete. Two examples of neo-Hispanic art: Juan Rodríguez Juárez's *La adoración de los Reyes* (The Adoration of the Magi) and *La Ascensión de la Virgen* (The Ascension of the Virgin Mary), surrounded by reliefs of several kings, queens and saints, grace the center.

The main altar stands at the center of the principal nave, which is connected to the **choir★★**, the grille of which was crafted in Macao. Inside, arranged in a semi-circle, the wooden **choir stalls** reach east and west on either side of the 18C organ. The present choir, a replica of the original destroyed by a 1967 fire, has been restored through the work of master craftsman Miguel Ángel Soto Rodríguez and his team, which took place from 1978 to 1984.

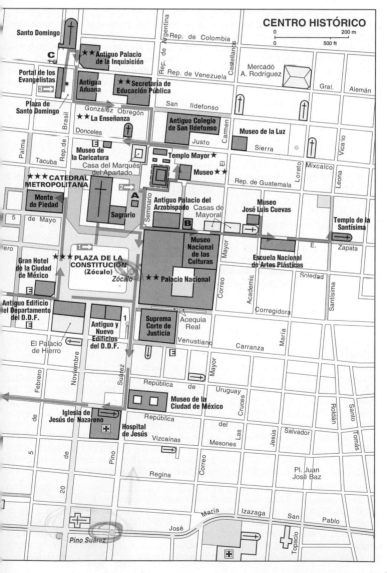

Leveling Work – From the beginning of its construction in 1573 to the completion of its vaults in 1667, the cathedral has undergone settling at different levels, from the high altar to the west tower. The initial inclination of 0.8m/2.6ft grew to 1.58m/5.2ft from the 17C to the 19C. By the 20C, the inclination measured 2.4m/7.9ft.

To halt further cracking and settling, architects implemented a leveling system, whereby material is extracted from the higher spots to make them level with the lower ones. Pilasters have also been laid underground to strengthen the foundations.

Preventive scaffolding has been placed inside to avoid structural problems during the leveling work. Although workers plan to remove the scaffolding by the year 2000, leveling will continue on an ongoing basis as a maintenance procedure.

Despite these repairs, the cathedral still looks out imposingly onto the Plaza de la Constitución

Sagrario Metropolitano (Metropolitan Sacrarium) – *Photo p 38. Just off the cathedral's eastern side.* From 1749 to 1768 Mexican architect Lorenzo Rodríguez built this sacrarium with red quarry stone and limestone reliefs. This bold contrast allows it to be distinguished easily from the main body of the cathedral. Its twin portals illustrate the beauty of the Baroque **facade★★**, representing the Twelve Apostles *(south)* and the Twelve Prophets *(east)*. The building has been closed to the public since 1993.

★★**Palacio Nacional** – *East side of the Plaza de la Constitución. Open year-round daily 9am–5pm. Closed national holidays.* ☎ *52-28-15-42.* From the earliest times, this site of the National Palace has served as a center of political power. In the pre-Hispanic era the homes of Moctezuma II stood here. After the Conquest, the grounds were reserved for Hernán Cortés, and later, in 1562, it became the viceroys' palace. In 1692 the southern wing was destroyed during a popular revolt. Soon after, Viceroy Gaspar de la Cerda had it reconstructed. During Revillagigedo's administration, the edifice was remodeled, and in 1852 the northernmost gate was built during Mariano Arista's administration, thus its name, the "Puerta Mariana." In 1926 it was again remodeled, with the addition of a third floor and a new facade, this time according to architect Petriccioli's plans.

The palace contains various courtyards: the south gate leads to the president's offices *(not open to the public)*; while the central gate opens onto the main courtyard where a replica of the original colonial fountain stands.

Main Staircase – On the walls of the main staircase, Diego Rivera (1886–1957) painted his outstanding **La epopeya de México★★★** *(photo pp 24-25)*. Created from 1929-35, the mural immortalizes the stages of Mexico's struggle within the framework of Rivera's own ideology.

A powerful portrayal of the battles of the Conquest of Mexico between Spaniards and natives, the **west mural** also depicts scenes of the Evangelization and the Inquisition. Five arches featuring various moments in Mexican history compose the upper part of the mural. From left to right one can see the **French Intervention** and the execution of Maximilian of Hapsburg in 1867; the **Porfirista era**; the **War of Independence** and the **Mexican Revolution**; the period of **La Reforma** (1857–62) and, finally, the **United States Invasion** (1847–48).

The **north mural** portrays the legend of Quetzalcóatl and recounts pre-Hispanic indigenous life.

On the **south mural**, Diego Rivera branded his impression of class struggle: the peasant farmers' struggle, workers' strikes, the fascists, labor, socialism, science, dictators, and rich politicians. Notice the figures of painter **Frida Kahlo** and her sister, accompanied by children.

North Corridor – Both sides of this corridor, which leads to the Secretaría de Hacienda y Crédito Público (Treasury Department) protocol areas, feature a pair of **grisailles** (use of the chiaroscuro technique) depicting what Mexico has given the world. To their right, a series of nine murals are devoted to pre-Hispanic cultures: the Gran Tenochtitlán, Totonac culture, and Cortés' landing at Veracruz, which portrays a disfigured person who may represent Hernán Cortés.

The **Museo del Recinto Parlamentario** *(open year-round Mon–Fri 9am–8pm; closed national holidays)* displays several documents from the period of the Reform Laws and personal papers of Benito Juárez. Visitors can also appreciate the beautiful semicircular chamber, where the Constitution of 1857 was drafted.

Suprema Corte de Justicia – *Pino Suárez, 2. Open year-round Mon–Thu 10am–5:30pm, Fri 10am–4:30pm. Closed national holidays. By permission only.* ☎ *55-22-36-40 ext. 222.* The Supreme Court, which borders the Plaza de la Constitución to the southeast, was built from 1935–1945 on the plot of land where once stood a market. Its architect, Antonio Muñoz García, gave it a restrained Neoclassic look. Inside, over the main staircase, José Clemente Orozco's mural paintings-the most notable being **La justicia**—adorn the walls. In the northern wing, over the library entrance, stands out **La guerra** (War), a mural painting by George Biddle. Outside, across the street, visitors can appreciate a monument to the **Fundación de México-Tenochtitlán (1)** (1970).

Museo de la Ciudad de México – *Pino Suárez, 30. Open year-round Tue–Sun 10am–6pm. Closed national holidays.* ☎ *55-22-36-40.* Formerly known as the Palacio de los Condes de Calimaya (Palace of the Calimaya Counts), the present-day museum, a beautiful two-story house, displays photos, murals, scale models and artifacts illustrating the city's history and culture, as well as pre-Hispanic collections. It was remodeled by architect Francisco Guerrero y Torres in 1780. The building's facade boasts a **large door**, imported from the Philippines, which bears the coats of arms of the original families who resided here. A huge **snake head**, probably from the Templo Mayor, was built into the corner foundation.

Interior – Formerly "the lords' courtyard," the main courtyard today contains a fountain adorned with a double-tailed Nordic mermaid. At the foot of the stairs, a lion and lioness ward off evil spirits. On the third floor sit the chapel, sacristy, and music room, and on the roof one finds the **studio**★ of Joaquín Clausell (1866–1935), possibly the only Mexican Impressionist painter in the early 20C.

Iglesia de Jesús de Nazareno – *República del Salvador, 119, beside the Hospital de Jesús. Open year-round daily 8am–2pm & 4–6pm. Closed May 1, Sept 16 & Nov 20.* Originally called the Iglesia de Nuestra Señora de la Pura y Limpia Concepción (Church of Our Lady of the Immaculate Conception), the building owes its current name to a quaint legend about the sculpture of Jesus carrying his cross, which was sent by lottery to this church where it remained for years. Inside, a small urn to the left of the high altar contains the **remains of Hernán Cortés**. On the ceiling above the choir, José Clemente Orozco's **mural**★, *Apocalypse* (1942–44) depicts the horrors of World War II.

Hospital de Jesús – *Passageway of the Calle 20 de Noviembre, 82. Open year-round Mon–Fri 9am–3pm, Sat 9am–noon. Closed national holidays.* ☎ *55-42-65-01.* Founded by Hernán Cortés in 1524, this first hospital in the Western Hemisphere continues to carry out its mission to this day. Its two interior courtyards are surrounded by arcades and separated by a staircase at the foot of which stands a **bust** of the conquistador. The upper level contains a **mural** by Antonio González Orozco depicting Cortés' first encounter with Moctezuma, supposedly on the very site where the hospital was founded. The Salón de Patronato, or boardroom, in the main offices on the ground floor, was once the church's sacristy. Note, above the portraits of Hernán Cortés, one of Mexico's most beautiful (16C) **coffered ceilings**★ made from gilded precious woods.

Ex Templo de San Felipe Neri – *República del Salvador, 49. Closed from Dec 16 to Jan 2 and national holidays.* A small plaza that breathes peace and tranquillity houses these two churches dedicated to Saint Philip Neri, **San Felipe Neri El Viejo** and **San Felipe Neri El Nuevo**. While the latter still preserves its magnificent Churrigueresque **facade**★, only the Baroque portal—which boasts a **relief** of its patron saint—and a plain bell tower remain on the older church, completed in 1668. San Felipe Neri El Nuevo houses the Miguel Lerdo de Tejada Library. Colorful **frescoes** by the Russian-born Vlady Kibalchich, entitled *Las revoluciones (The Revolutions)*, cover its 2sq km/1.2sq mi of surrounding walls.

★**Antigua Casa de los Condes de San Mateo Valparaíso (Offices of Banamex)** – *Isabel la Católica, 44, corner of V. Carranza. Open year-round Mon–Fri 9am–5pm. Closed national holidays.* ☎ *52-25-60-88.* Completed in 1772, this stately residence-one of the most famous mansions of the colonial era-was built by architect Francisco Antonio de Guerrero y Torres.
The enormous house bears an elegant front decorated with wrought-iron balconies, the characteristic family coat of arms, and a small corner tower with a statue of Our Lady of Guadalupe.
The large wooden gate, or **portón**, opens onto an enormous patio with a distinctive **double spiral staircase**★, that could be used by both nobility and servants.

Gran Hotel de la Ciudad de México (formerly El Centro Mercantil) – *Av. 16 de Septiembre, 82.* To the extreme right of the Plaza de la Constitución stands this representative example of the French architectural style popular during the Porfiriato, built by engineers Daniel Garza and Gonzalo Garita from 1895 to 1899. Whereas its exterior boasts several striking pink quarry stone columns, its luxurious **interior**★ contains Art Nouveau elements, such as the iron balustrades, the side elevators and a staircase. The plant motifs and bright colors of the **stained-glass window** adorning the ceiling create a stunning effect. A similar **window** can be seen at the nearby Palacio de Hierro department store *(Calle 5 de Febrero)*, one of the first stores of this type to be built in Mexico City (1868).

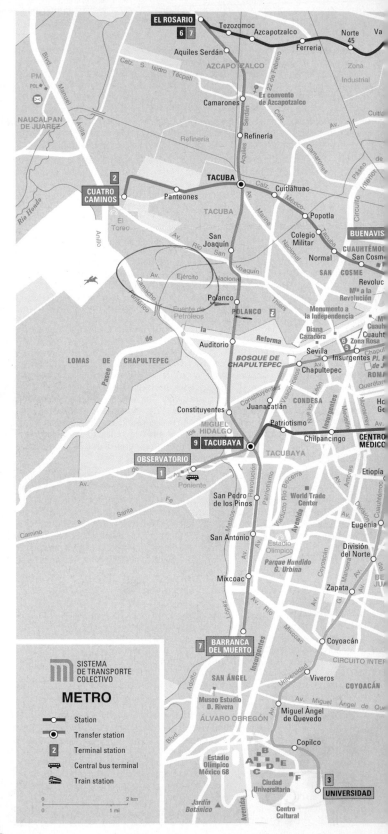

METRO

SISTEMA
DE TRANSPORTE
COLECTIVO

○—○ Station

◉ Transfer station

2 Terminal station

🚌 Central bus terminal

🚆 Train station

0 ——— 2 km
0 ——— 1 mi

★ ② TEMPLO MAYOR AND SURROUNDINGS
Ⓜ *line 2 – Zócalo*

★**Templo Mayor** – *Calle Seminario and República de Guatemala, beside the cathe-dral. Open year-round Tue–Sun 9am–5pm. Closed Jan 1, May 1 and Sept 16. P$20.* ☏ *55-42-06-06.* The Great Temple, facing west, preserves the remains of its two main altars: the red one dedicated to **Huitzilopóchtli**, god of war, and the blue one to **Tláloc**, god of rain. The temple underwent constant expansion due to floods and because each new pre-Hispanic ruler built on top of the previous temple, resulting in seven temples, one on top of the other.

This unique structure belonged to a sacred space, or main plaza, which covered 500sq m/545sq yd and housed 78 buildings. The model, **Maqueta de la Zona Lacustre del Altiplano (A)**, outside the archaeological site in the small plaza, east of the cathe-dral, familiarizes visitors with the layout of México-Tenochtitlán and the location of the Templo Mayor.

Archaeological Site – A replica of the **Coyolxauhqui**, whose discovery in 1978 prompted archaeologists to dig on this site, marks the starting point of the tour. Beginning with stage IVb of the Templo Mayor, the visit continues on to stage IV, which cor-responds to the rule of Moctezuma Ilhuicamina I, and Stage III in which we find reproductions of warriors leaning against the temple's staircases. It is believed that these may represent the Centzonhuitznahuas, enemies of Huitzilopóchtli.

Stone masonry reflects the progress from one period to the next, most notably in the staircases, stone carving and architecture.

The primitive temple with its two shrines, the southern dedicated to Huitzilopóchtli and the northern to Tláloc, belong to stage II. In front of the shrine to the god of war stands an altar of sacrifice, whereas a blue **Chac-mool** sculpture sits before the god of rain.

Just after the shrines lies the Patio Norte (stage VI), which consists of three more shrines: to the right **Tzompantli**, displaying rows of stone skulls on three of its sides; to the left, a foundation with two staircases facing east and west; and towards the back the **Templo Rojo** (Red Temple), better viewed from the other side. In stage V stands the **Recinto de los Guerreros Águila** (Building of the Eagle-Warriors); its poly-chrome sidewalks, decorated with carved figures, are still well preserved.

★★**Museo del Templo Mayor** – This specially designed modern museum traces the history of México-Tenochtitlán-from the departure of the Mexicas from the mythical Aztlán, to the Spanish Conquest.

Beginning on the first floor, the **model** of the main plaza gives visitors an idea of the Templo Mayor's place within the ceremonial center. Do not miss the **Nobel Peace Prize** medal left in Mexican safekeeping by Guatemalan leader Rigoberta Menchú until more peaceful conditions prevail in her own country.

Eight attractive halls in the museum illustrate the history of the Mexicas, the stages of construction of the Templo Mayor, and the artifacts uncovered during excava-tions.

The most outstanding pieces include the **tzompantli**, a stucco-finished wall of stone skulls, located at the entrance; the **Coyolxauhqui**, in the second hall; the **dios Murciélago** (Bat god) and jade **masks from Teotihuacán**, in the third hall; the original sculptures of the **guerreros águila** (eagle warriors) belonging to stage III, at the entrance to the fourth hall; and, the sculptures of Mictlantecuhtli (god of death) found in 1994 in the Casa de las Águilas (Eagles' home).

★★★**Coyolxauhqui** – *To be viewed from the fourth level.* While excavating the southern part of the Templo Mayor at the foot of the temple of Huitzilopóchtli, archaeolo-gists uncovered one of Mexico's most beautiful and impressive artifacts on February 21, 1978. According to legend, **Coyolxauhqui**, the Moon Goddess, was the daughter of **Coatlicue**, goddess of the earth and of death. One day, as she swept the temple on Coatepec hill, Coatlicue picked up exquisite feathers and put them in her bosom, and thus became pregnant. Coyolxauhqui incited her brothers, the stars, the **400 surianos**, or the **Centzohuitznahuas**, to go up the hill and kill their pregnant mother, Coatlicue, for having defamed them. They decided to kill her before her son was born. Coatlicue feared for her life, but the son in her womb calmed her by speaking to her from within. Just as they were about to kill Coatlicue, **Huitzilopóchtli** sprang from her womb, in full battle-dress and, brandishing a fiery serpent, wounded Coyolxauhqui-that is, the moon-and cut off her head. She fell down the hill, breaking into pieces. Immediately the warrior chased away his brothers, the stars. Those who survived were dispersed into the heavens.

Weighing eight tons and measuring 3.1m/10ft by 3.3m/10.7ft, the monolith alluding to this legend portrays the Moon-goddess at the moment she falls from the hilltop after being beheaded by her brother Huitzilopóchtli. A testimony to the artistry of the Mexica craftsmen, the relief's proportions are faultless. In the center, the motionless torso shows the scars of dismemberment. Arms and legs swirl

Coyolxauhqui, Museo del Templo Mayor

around at a surprising pace; the graceful droop of the head is prolonged in its feathered headdress; drops of blood appear. The belt is adorned with a skull, and her cheeks are decked in rattles, a feature that gives this goddess her name.

Antiguo Palacio del Arzobispado – *Calle Moneda, 4. Open year-round Tue–Sun 10am–6pm. Closed national holidays. P$8.* ☎ *52-28-12-43.* This imposing palace with a Baroque facade once belonged to Fray **Juan de Zumárraga** who established the Archbishopric of Mexico here in 1530. Zumárraga's reception of native Juan Diego, during which the latter announced the apparition of Our Lady of Guadalupe, took place at the palace. Following the 1629 floods, the building was buried and had to be rebuilt on top of the original first floor; nevertheless, the high walls and merlons were preserved. In 1867 it was turned into government offices. Since 1994 it has housed the **Museo de la Secretaría de Hacienda y Crédito Público** *(same times and charges as the Antiguo Palacio).* Artists such as Manuel Felguérez, Pedro Coronel, Francisco Zúñiga, Rufino Tamayo, Chávez Morado, Raúl Anguiano and Diego Rivera contributed works to the permanent collection as payment of their taxes.

Casa de la Primera Imprenta (B) – *Lic. Primo Verdad, 10. Open year-round daily 10am–5pm. Closed national holidays and during UNAM's summer and winter breaks.* ☎ *55-22-16-75.* This site housed a factory where cathedral bells were made in 1530. The first printing press on the American continent was founded in 1539 through the initiative of the Sevillian printer Juan Cronmberg, who sent his typographer Juan Paoli to Mexico.

Museo Nacional de las Culturas – *Moneda, 13. Open year-round Tue–Sun 9:30am–5:30pm. Closed national holidays.* ✗ ☎ *55-42-01-87.* During the 19C, Emperor Maximilian established the Public Museum of Natural History, Archaeology and History in the old Casa de la Moneda (Mint), completed in 1734. The collections were divided in 1909, leaving only pre-Hispanic and colonial history, until in 1964 they too were moved to the Museo Nacional de Antropología in Chapultepec Park. Presently, the National Museum of Cultures exhibits a general panorama of the world's most important cultures. Worthy of special attention is the **Africa** salon on the second floor. Rufino Tamayo's 1938 **mural** of the Mexican Revolution adorns the entrance.

Museo José Luis Cuevas – *Academia, 13. Open year-round Tue–Sun 10am–6pm. Closed national holidays. P$8.* ✗ ☎ *55-42-61-98.* The Ex Convento de Santa Inés, founded under the patronage of the marquises De la Cadena, was the city's first convent. It has a checkered history: built in 1598; opened as a convent in 1600; rebuilt by Manuel Tolsá in 1798; used as public housing from 1867 to 1915; and, finally, declared a historical monument in 1932. The Sala Erótica (Erotic Art Hall) includes works by the Mexican painter, engraver and sculptor José Luis Cu~ as well as interesting temporary exhibits. Cuevas' statue of a giant wor~ *giganta* (1991), enriches the courtyard.

Escuela Nacional de Artes Plásticas (formerly Academia de San Carlos) – *Academia, 22, corner of Moneda. Open year-round Mon–Fri 8am–7pm. Closed national holidays.* ☎ *55-22-00-42.* Originally a hospital, this building was remodeled in the mid 18C by the Italian Xavier Cavallari to house the San Carlos Academy by order of King Charles III of Spain. Relief medallions with the busts of Raphael, Michelangelo and Charles III embellish the facade. Note the plaster reproductions of classical Greek and Renaissance sculpture under the interior courtyard arcades. At present, the National School of Fine Arts offers graduate courses here.

Templo de la Santísima – *Calle de la Santísima, corner of E. Zapata. Open year-round daily 7am–1:30pm & 4:30–7pm.* Historians believe that architect Lorenzo Rodríguez, who also built the Sagrario Metropolitano, designed this church, constructed between 1755 and 1783. Its **facade★** is one of the most splendid examples of the Baroque *estípite* style, appropriately highlighted by an image of the *Santísima Trinidad* (Most Holy Trinity) showing God the Father's head crowned with a papal tiara. This attractive church suffers the same fate as the cathedral: settling due to its weight and the unstable nature of the ground.

★★③ **SANTO DOMINGO AND SURROUNDINGS**
Ⓜ *line 2 – Zócalo*

Plaza de Santo Domingo – Conceived from its inception as an open space, this plaza is considered one of the most ancient in all of Mexico. During the colonial period, important buildings—such as the religious complex of Santo Domingo, the Customs House and the Palace of the Holy Inquisition—directly influenced city life. Today, the plaza preserves a popular feel and, fortunately, continues to be protected by its beautiful historic structures. A central fountain, built in 1900, holds a statue of Doña Josefa Ortiz de Domínguez, *la Corregidora* (spouse of the royal representative) of the city of Querétaro.

The arcade on the western part of the plaza was built in the 17C and, since then, has housed diverse commercial establishments. In the 18C it took on the name of **Portal de los Evangelistas** (The Evangelists' Arcade) in honor of the public scribes who set up desks there to write for the illiterate. This tradition continues to this day and enhances the plaza's popular flavor. Besides the scribes, the arcade is crammed with small businesses—both shops and peddlers—that offer stationery and printing. Every day, dozens of people traverse the plaza. Some of them relax on the benches; others "confess" their most intimate secrets to the "evangelists" so they can commit to paper their statements, be they amorous proposals, tax returns or any other type of document.

Templo de Santo Domingo – *República de Brasil and B. Domínguez. Open year-round daily 8am–8pm.* This was the first monastery founded by the Dominican order in New Spain. At the outset, the friars settled on the site where today stands the Antiguo Palacio de la Inquisición (Former Palace of the Inquisition). However, they were subsequently obliged to abandon these premises when the monastery, constructed in 1590, deteriorated due to earthquakes and floods. Thus, a new religious complex was built on the north side of the plaza. It lasted from 1736 until its demolition in 1861, when by decree of the Reform Laws many religious structures were destroyed. Today only the church and the Capilla del Señor de la Expiración (Chapel of the Lord of Expiration) remain standing.

Main facade – A relief of St. Dominic, protected by saints Peter and Paul, graces the center of this Baroque facade. The **side portal** depicts St. Dominic and St. Francis, trying to prevent the collapse of the church of Lateran.

Interior – Manuel Tolsá created the outstanding Neoclassical high altar. The transept contains altarpieces dedicated to the Virgen de Covadonga (left) and to the Virgen del Camino (right). An excellent painting of Santo Domingo en Soriano by Fray Alfonso López de Herrera embellishes the altarpiece located on the right side. Some of the chapels boast works of famous painters. The Divine Providence Chapel features a painting by Miguel Cabrera; the Chapel of the Rosary-main chapel-displays one of Villalpando's works; the Chapel of the Sacred Heart exhibits a painting by López Herrera; and the Chapel of the Virgin of Guadalupe exhibits a creation by Juan Correa.

The **Capilla del Señor de la Expiración (C)** sits on the southwestern corner that housed the church's atrium in the exact same place where once stood one of the original 16C corner chapels. The present-day facade dates from the 19C.

★★**Antiguo Palacio de la Inquisición** – *República de Brasil, 33. Open daily 10am–6pm. Closed Maundy Thursday, Good Friday and during UNAM's summer and winter breaks.* ☎ *55-29-75-42.* The Court of the Holy Office of the Inquisition was established in New Spain in 1571 in reaction to a conspiracy led by Hernán Cortés' son, Martín, whose intention was to gain independence from Spain. Thus, the court functioned more as an arm for political control and repression than as a persecutor of heretics. Because the pope had entrusted the court to the Dominican Order, the Inquisition was established in this plaza. Initially, several lots were rented to build the necessary facilities, including torture chambers, prisons and dungeons. For many years, the present-day Calle de República de Venezuela was called **Cárcel de la Perpetua** (Perpetual prison), because it contained cells whose inmates had received life sentences. Public punishments were carried out in the Plaza Mayor, today known as the Zócalo; the stake was located in front of the Church of San Diego, beside the Alameda.

In 1732 the rented lots were sold off, and architect Pedro de Arrieta was commissioned to construct a new **building** for the Inquisition. He introduced such innovations as the octagonal entrance and the use of interlaced and false arches. The new seat of the court reopened in 1736.

Since 1854 the building has belonged to the National School of Medicine, and in 1879, a third story was added. In addition to the school's various departments, the structure today houses the **Museo de la Medicina Mexicana**, which illustrates the development of medicine in Mexico-from pre-Hispanic times to the 20C. The interior **courtyards** and the prison ruins are also open to the public.

Antigua Aduana – *República de Brasil, 31. Open year-round Mon–Fri 10am–6pm, Sat–Sun 10am–3pm.* ☎ *55-12-17-07.* During most of the colonial era, the Customs House stood on the property of the Marquis of Villamayor. In 1888 the customs system was abolished and various public offices occupied the building. Since 1951 it has belonged to the Secretaría de Educación Pública (SEP). Inside, a **mural** by David Alfaro Siqueiros, *Patricios y patricidas* (Patricians and Patricides, 1946) graces the walls and ceiling of two spacious courtyards, linked to each other by a staircase.

★★**Secretaría de Educación Pública (SEP)** (Department of Public Education) – *República de Argentina, 28. There is an information booth at the main entrance. Same times and charges as the Antigua Aduana.* The present-day main offices of Mexico's Department of Public Education stand on the site of what functioned for almost three centuries as the Convento de la Encarnación, founded in 1594 and inhabited by the Conceptionist nuns. With the enactment of the Reform Laws, the building's rooms were turned into classrooms. In 1921 the SEP was created during the presidency of Álvaro Obregón. The Minister of Education, José Vasconcelos, ordered the building's reconstruction. In 1993 the building was renovated to house the SEP headquarters, which covers one whole square block. In the first courtyard, a small **site museum** exhibits artifacts found during the renovations.

★★**Murals** – Vasconcelos hired Diego Rivera from 1923 to 1928 to decorate nearly 200 panels covering more than 1.5sq km/0.9sq mi This gargantuan task was Rivera's first major endeavor upon returning from an extended stay in Europe. Hence, the clearly visible influence of Cézanne, Picasso, Giotto and the Futurist school.

Patio del Trabajo – *First building upon turning onto the República de Argentina.* The ground floor depicts scenes from Mexican rural life, most notably the *Liberación del peón* (The Liberation of the Peasant) and *La maestra rural* (The Country Teacher), which highlight the progress made by the 1910 revolutionary movement. On the upper floor, due to the lack of wall space, Diego Rivera chose not to use color and instead produced grisailles (chiaroscuro technique), whose main theme focuses on intellectual, scientific and artistic activities. On the third floor, additional paintings by Rivera exalt various Mexican heroes. Whereas the corners of the Patio del Trabajo hold works from European and Asian cultures, those of the Patio de Juárez represent the arts.

Staircase – *South wall.* Along the walls of all three floors, Rivera illustrated the rich variety of Mexican scenery, from the coasts to the high plateau.

Elevators – *North wall.* Rivera took advantage of the dim light in the elevator shaft to create a vision of the Yucatán cenote and the Baths of Tehuantepec, thus displaying his technical prowess in finding such an artful solution to the challenge of decorating such a dark space.

Patio de las Fiestas – *Patio de Juárez.* The ground floor exhibits depictions of traditional Mexican fiestas. On the northern wall hang representations of Tehuantepec, Oaxaca, as well as frescoes by Jean Charlot and Amado de la Cueva. On the second floor, the apprentices of the master muralist painted the coats of arms of the Mexican states. Rivera decorated the third wall with lyrics from a revolutionary ballad *(corrido).* On the south wall, *El arsenal* portrays Rivera's inner circle: Frida Kahlo, David Alfaro Siqueiros, Tina Modotti and Julio Antonio Mella.

★★**Templo de la Enseñanza** (Nuestra Señora del Pilar) – *Donceles, 102. Open year-round Tue–Sun 7am–7pm.* This small church formed part of the first convent and school of the Compañía de María in New Spain. Constructed during the second half of the

Templo de la Enseñanza, Interior

© Bob Schalkwijk

18C, the building is considered one of the city's Baroque jewels, for which reason it achieved the status of National Monument in 1931. Whereas the church's portal draws attention due to its narrow proportions, the interior preserves in perfect state its original ornamentation and nine **altarpieces**. This structure differs from other convents in two regards: the nave does not run parallel to the street, and the **choir grilles** flank the high altar. Andrés López (18C) created the tapestries that adorn the grilles. This former convent now houses the General Notary Archives and the Colegio Nacional.

Museo de la Caricatura – *Donceles, 99. Open year-round daily 10am–6pm. Closed national holidays.* ☎ *57-02-92-56.* This 16C building, declared a Historic Monument in 1931, was opened to the public in 1987 as a museum of temporary exhibits. The year 1999 gave way to the inauguration of a permanent hall, whose collection offers a detailed overview of the history of caricature in Mexico, through some of the most representative works of this genre. The exposition covers the Independent Period (1826–76), satire during the Porfirismo, caricature of the Revolution, *caudillismo* (rule by a caudillo) and the *maximato*, as well as humoristic critique, organized by six-year periods during the 20C. The second floor houses the permanent collections of the Salón de la Plástica Mexicana.

Antiguo Colegio de San Ildefonso – *Justo Sierra, 16. Open year-round Tue–Sun 10am–6pm. Closed national holidays. P$20.* ✗ ☎ *57-02-63-78.* Formerly the Escuela Nacional Preparatoria, the building presently serves as a museum and cultural center. Founded by the Jesuits in 1588 and rebuilt at the beginning of the 18C, its facade features two Baroque portals with striking reliefs: San Ildefonso (St. Hildephonsus) receiving the chasuble *(west)* and St. Joseph as protector of the Jesuits *(east)*.

The **interior** comprises three courtyards—the Lower School, the Middle School, and the Upper School—adorned with beautiful **mural paintings★★★**. David Alfaro Siqueiros' murals stand out on the staircase of the first courtyard, while on the murals that decorate the walls of the three floors that comprise the third courtyard, José Clemente Orozco gives free rein to his sense of the ridiculous and tragic. *La alegoría de la Virgen* (The Allegory of the Virgin, 1922) by Fermín Revueltas and *El desembarco de la Cruz* (The Descent from the Cross, 1923) by Ramón de Alva de la Canal grace the main entrance. Whereas the left-hand wall of the staircase on the third floor exhibits Jean Charlot's mural *La masacre en el Templo Mayor* or *La conquista de Tenochtitlán*, the right-hand wall displays Fernando Leal's mural *Fiesta del Señor de Chalma* (1923). In the **Anfiteatro Simón Bolívar**, Diego Rivera graced the stage with his first mural, *La Creación* (1922). The **Salón Generalito** *(third floor of the main courtyard, left side)* boasts magnificent **choir stalls** which once belonged to the Church of St. Augustine, as well as a gallery of neo-Hispanic portraits.

Museo de la Luz – *Corner of El Carmen and San Ildefonso. Open Mon–Fri 9am–3:30pm; Sat–Sun 10am–4pm. Closed from Dec 17 to Jan 7 and national holidays. P$10.* ☎ *57-02-31-83.* This museum is located in the former church of St. Peter and St. Paul, founded by the Jesuits in the 16C. In 1922, José Vasconcelos commissioned Roberto Montenegro to decorate the building's pilasters, arches and vaults. A mural by the same painter graces the rear part of the museum. The chapel's cupola was painted by Xavier Guerrero and the stained-glass windows were designed by both artists and executed by Eduardo Villaseñor. From 1944 to 1977, this edifice was home to the National Periodicals and Newspaper Library. After nearly 20 years of abandonment, the building was renovated to house the Museo de la Luz, where both children and adults play with and learn from a wide variety of objects that explain the different light phenomena.

★★④ MADERO AND SURROUNDINGS
Ⓜ *line 2 – Bellas Artes*

One of the city's most ancient and legendary streets, Calle Madero received its current name in 1914, in honor of Francisco I. Madero-father of the Mexican Revolution. Before that, the street's 16C appellation, **San Francisco**, referred to the enormous Franciscan monastery *(see below)* that once covered several blocks bordering this street. A century later, the street was renamed **Plateros** (Silversmiths) to allude to the jewelers and silversmiths who set up business here.

Torre Latinoamericana – *Eje Central (Lázaro Cárdenas) 2. Open year-round daily 9:30am–10:30pm. P$30.* ✖ ☏ *55-21-08-44* Built in 1956 and designed by architects Manuel de la Colina and Augusto H. Álvarez, this tower was, for several decades, the tallest structure in all of Latin America. Its foundation system, created by Leandro Zeevaert and based on hydraulic suspension, has allowed this 182m/600ft skyscraper to withstand the marshy ground on which it sits as well as two earthquakes (1957 and 1985). Forty-seven stories—three of which are located underground—comprise the tower. While the 38th floor houses an aquarium *(open daily 10am–10pm; P$21)*, the lookouts on the 42nd–44th floors offer a breathtaking **view**★★ of the city when pollution levels are low.

★**Casa de los Azulejos** – *Madero, 4 (Sanborns store and restaurant). Open year-round daily 7am–1am.* ✖ ☏ *55-12-78-24.* The House of Tiles once functioned as the palace of the Counts of the Valley of Orizaba. In 1737 the fifth countess ordered the reconstruction of the original building, giving it its present appearance. The **tiles** that cover the exterior and interior were brought here from Puebla. In 1881 the house became a gathering place for the *Jockey Club*, whose members included celebrities of the Porfirista era, such as the writer Manuel Gutiérrez Nájera. Sanborns, a company with a significant tradition and history in Mexico, acquired the building in 1900 and transformed it into Mexico's first US-style drugstore. On the landing of the staircase, *Omnisciencia* (1925)—a **mural** by José Clemente Orozco—lends an aesthetic touch.

■ Callejón de la Condesa

Located beside the Casa de los Azulejos. According to legend, during the colonial era, two noblemen rode their carriages into this alleyway, heading in opposite directions. However, the road's narrowness impeded the simultaneous passage of both men. Given that neither one was willing to give up the right of way, they both remained here for several days and nights until the mayor arrived and ordered them to exit through the same end through which they had entered.

★**Templo y Ex Convento de San Francisco** – *Madero, 7. Open year-round daily 7am–8:30pm.* This building was part of the monastery of the same name, founded in 1525 by Fray **Pedro de Gante**. The religious complex originally consisted of a small church, to which was annexed the first open-air chapel for the indigenous peoples. By the 19C, numerous offices, cloisters and chapels had been added to the monastery, which then covered more than 3,000sq km/1,860sq mi. In 1856, after several friars were accused of sedition, the authorities took preventive measures against further insubordination and partitioned and reduced the building to a fourth of its size, selling it to private citizens. Enforcement of the Reform Laws eventually further reduced most of what had been left to the friars.

The present-day entrance leads to a chapel dedicated to the Virgin of Guadalupe, formerly the chapel of Balvanera. In 1868 Episcopalians stripped the Baroque **portal**★ of its sculptures; then in 1949, the interior underwent total remodeling when the church fell under Franciscan supervision. The adjacent church occupies the site where once stood the chapel of La Purísima Concepción (The Most Pure Conception). On Calle de Gante, inside the Methodist church, part of the original main **cloister**★ remains visible.

★★**Palacio de Iturbide (Offices of the National Bank of Mexico – Banamex)** – *Madero, 17. Can be visited only during temporary exhibitions; call for schedules.* ☏ *52-25-02-47.* Designed by architect Francisco Guerrero Torres, this fine example of 18C architecture was completed in 1785 by order of the Marquis de Jaral de Berrio who offered it to his daughter as a wedding present. According to legend, the cost of the building equaled the exact amount of the dowry, as the marquis preferred to invest his money rather than seeing it squandered by his son-in-law, Count Pedro de Moncada.

Agustín de Iturbide resided here from 1821 to 1822 until he was proclaimed emperor. In 1890 Emilio Dondé converted the building into a hotel, which operated until 1928. Banamex purchased it in 1966 and had it remodeled by the famous Mexican architect Ricardo Legorreta.

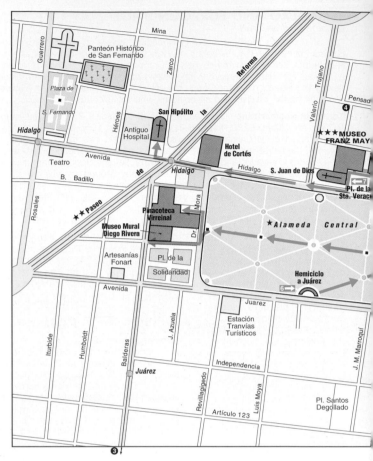

1 **Víctor Artes Populares Mexicanas**
Av. Madero, 8–10, 3rd floor, 305, Centro Histórico. Open Mon–Fri 12:30pm–7pm. ☎ *55-12-12-63.* With over 50 years of experience, this hidden shop sells native Mexican jewelry, textiles, popular antiques and handicrafts related to the celebration of the *Día de Muertos* (Day of the Dead), held Nov 1–2

Close by on the next street lies the **Bazar de Fotografía Casasola** *(on the 2nd floor of No. 26; open year-round Mon–Fri 10am–7pm, Sat 10am–3pm; closed national holidays;* ☎ *55-21-51-92),* which sells and exhibits old photographs dating from the late 19C to the 1940s. Directly across from this building, on the corner of Madero and Bolívar, stands the former mansion of Don José de la Borda, a famous Taxco miner. Further ahead, the Vips *(No. 30; open daily 7am–11pm)* houses Miguel Covarrubia's **mural**, *Una tarde de domingo en Xochimilco* (A Sunday afternoon at Xochimilco, 1947).

Across the street, the **Museo Serfín de Indumentaria Indígena** *(open year-round Tue–Sun 10am–6pm; closed Jan 1, Sept 16 and Dec 25;* ☎ *55-18-15-55)* displays a collection of typical native costumes.

★**Templo de La Profesa** – *Isabel la Católica, 21. Open year-round daily 7:30am–8pm.* Originally under Jesuit supervision, the church was remodeled in 1720 by Pedro Arrieta. Soon after the expulsion of the Jesuits from Mexico, it fell under the direction of the St. Philip Neri order. In 1802 Manuel Tolsá transformed the Baroque decor into Neoclassical and built the high altar. From 1926 to 1932, the church enjoyed "cathedral" rank.

To the right of the main altar, the vestibule of the sacristy features a **sculpture** of the *Rey de Burlas* (The King of the Mockeries)—an excellent example of the *Cristos Sangrantes* (Bleeding Christs), a genre popular in Mexico during the 18C. The upper floor houses a **gallery** *(pinacoteca)* containing a splendid **collection★** of paintings from the colonial era *(reached by a flight of stairs behind the vestibule; open only on Sundays noon–2pm).*

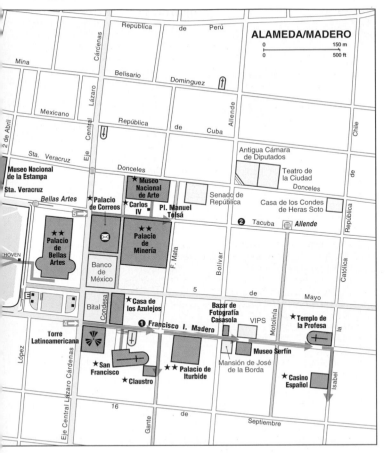

★**Casino Español** – *Isabel la Católica, 29. Open year-round Mon–Fri 10am–6pm, Sat 10am–3pm. Closed national holidays.* ☎ *55-12-08-93.* Emilio González Campo completed construction on this social club in 1903, as a place where families of Spanish origin living in Mexico and members of Mexican high society could inter-mingle. Its stone **facade** is eclectic in style, as is the rest of the building. Of particular interest in the **interior**★ an elaborate **staircase** displays the coat of arms of Charles V. Mariano Denlliure's sculpture, *Agonía de Cristóbal Colón*, found on the landing, portrays Christopher Columbus on his deathbed. The second floor features the **salón de los reyes**★★ (Hall of the Kings), noteworthy for its stained-glass windows and cof-fered ceiling.

★★⑤ PLAZA MANUEL TOLSÁ AND SURROUNDINGS
Ⓜ *line 2 – Bellas Artes*

Surrounded by historic buildings, this plaza was named in 1982 in honor of the famous Valencian architect and sculptor Manuel Tolsá (1757–1816). Two of his greatest works, examples of Mexican Neoclassical style, are found on the plaza: on the south side, the Palacio de Minería; and in the center, the **Estatua Ecuestre de Carlos IV**★ (Equestrian Statue of King Charles IV), better known as *El caballito* (The Little Horse). The statue was crafted in plaster in 1796 and cast in bronze in 1803. Until finding its present home, *El caballito* originally stood in the Zócalo, then moved to the Old University courtyard, and later to the *glorieta* (traffic circle) where Paseo de la Reforma and Bucareli converge.

★**Palacio de Correos** – *Tacuba, 1. Open year-round Mon–Fri 9am–5pm, Sat–Sun & holidays 10am–2pm. Closed Jan 1, Sept 16 and Dec 25.* ☎ *55-10-29-99.* In 1907 Italian architect Adamo Boari completed construction on this refined two-story building. Its carved, white quarry-stone facade and the interior's harmonious blend of white and black marble create an eclectic and distinctive look. The noteworthy **main staircase**★ features on its screens, windows and frames wrought-iron work made in Florence, Italy. Upstairs you will find the Post Office Library and the Philatelic Museum. On the lower level, at window No. 45, one can buy, sell and exchange stamps.

2 Café de Tacuba
*Tacuba, 28, Centro
Histórico.* ☎ *55-18-49-50.*
This traditional cafe, which
dates from 1912 and still
preserves its provincial air
and friendly service, is
recommended for a break
amid the bustle of the city's
Historic Center.

★★Palacio de Minería – *Illustration p 39.
Tacuba, 5. Open year-round Mon–Fri
9am–6pm. Closed national holidays.*
☎ *55-21-40-23.* Built between 1797 and
1813, this imposing structure serves as
one of the best examples of Neoclassical
architecture in Mexico City. It formerly
housed the Real Seminario de Minas
(Royal Seminary of Mines), and presently
belongs to the Universidad Nacional
Autónoma de México (UNAM, Mexico's giant national university). An International
Book Fair is held here annually.

The main entrance consists of three arches separated by Doric columns topped by
a balcony and triangular pediment that was used as an observatory. Inside, the
main courtyard and the staircase merit attention. The chapel preserves its original
decoration: mural paintings by the Spaniard Rafael Ximeno y Planes.
The door on the east side of the building leads to the **Museo de Sitio Manuel Tolsá**
(entrance by way of Tacuba; open year-round daily 11am–7pm), where one can
appreciate diverse objects of his era.

★Museo Nacional de Arte (MUNAL) – *Tacuba, 8. Open year-round Tue–Sun
10am–5:30pm; Closed national holidays. P$20.* ☎ *55-12-32-24.* A notable exam-
ple of Porfiriato-style architecture, the National Museum of Art, completed in 1911
by Silvio Contri, originally housed the Palace of Communications and Public Works.
Its facade blends Renaissance and French Classical styles. Inside, note the iron work
on the handsome **marble staircase** as well as the ceilings of the entrance and reception hall by Carlo Coppdé.
The **museum** illustrates the development of fine arts in Mexico from the 16C to 1950
and contains a splendid **collection★★** of 19C and 20C works.

★★⑥ ALAMEDA CENTRAL AND SURROUNDINGS
Ⓜ *line 2 – Bellas Artes*

★Alameda Central – *Between Av. Juárez and Av. Hidalgo.* Mexico's central park,
the oldest in the city, dates from the late 16C. Its name comes from *álamos,* or
poplars, which, together with other species of trees, were planted in swampland
on what was then the edge of Mexico City.
During colonial times it was the most important promenade of the society of New
Spain and the site of love duels. It reached its present size in the 18C by embracing
what had been la Plaza del Quemadero (Plaza of the Burning Site), the place where
heretics would meet their fate at the hands of the Inquisition. Presently, the latter
is located in front of the Pinacoteca Virreinal (Colonial Art Gallery). In 1868 the
wrought-iron fence that surrounded it was removed. The 1910 festivities for the
centennial celebration of Independence prompted the addition of the **Hemiciclo a
Juárez** monument, and in 1921 the German colony in Mexico donated another in

Alameda Park and Latin American Tower

honor of **Beethoven**. Today the Alameda garden serves as the four-centuries-old inspiration of famous artists, the strolling place of hundreds of ordinary citizens, a lovers' lane and a diverse and colorful fairgrounds on holidays and festivals. This eclectic setting has prompted the Mexican poet Carlos Pellicer to ask: "What has not occurred or who has never strolled through the Alameda?"

★★**Palacio de Bellas Artes** – *Av. Juárez and Eje Central (Lázaro Cárdenas). Open year-round Tue–Sun 10am–6pm. Closed May 1. P$20, free Sun.* ✗ ▣ ☎ *55-21-92-51 ext. 154.* This last palace built in Mexico City now houses its most important cultural shows. In 1904 Italian architect Adamo Boari designed and began constructing this majestic building made almost entirely of Carrara marble. Sinking (1.8m/5.9ft in seven years) of the structure, and the 1910 outbreak of the Mexican Revolution, put a halt to construction. Building recommenced in 1932, this time under the direction of architect Federico Mariscal. Hence the two different styles: outside, Boari's Art Nouveau; inside, Mariscal's Art Deco. Nevertheless, both architects used pre-Hispanic motifs, such as eagle and jaguar warrior masks, Maya deities and serpents, to create cohesion between the two styles.

In the **Main Theater** hangs the extraordinary **crystal curtain**★ (1910) from Tiffany's with an original design by Mexican landscape artist Gerardo Murillo (Dr. Atl), depicting the Popocatépetl and Iztaccíhuatl volcanoes. The *Cortina de cristal* can be seen only before performances, including the **Ballet Folklórico de México**★ *(Wed 8:30pm & Sun 9:30am & 8:30pm; P$175, P$265, & P$315;* ☎ *55-21-92-51 ext. 224)* when a skillful play of lights recreates sunrise and sunset in the Valley of Mexico.

★★**Murals** – Rufino Tamayo's *México de hoy* (Mexico Today, 1953) and *Nacimiento de la nacionalidad* (1952) are on display on the second level; the third level features Diego Rivera's controversial *El hombre controlador del universo* (Man, the Controller of the Universe, 1934) the original version of which, destined for New York's Rockefeller Center, was destroyed because it included an image of the communist Lenin. Orozco's *La Katharsis* (1935) and Siqueiros' *Nueva democracia* (New Democracy, 1945) and *Apoteosis y resurrección de Cuauhtémoc* (Apotheosis and Resurrection of Cuauhtémoc, 1951) are also on display. Begin the tour from the opposite corridor to appreciate the multiple-angle perspective.

Museo Mural Diego Rivera – *Corner of Balderas and Colón. Open year-round Tue–Sun 10am–6pm. Closed national holidays. P$10.* ☎ *55-12-07-54.* The building was designed specifically to exhibit what many consider one of Diego Rivera's greatest works, his 1947 **mural**★★, *Sueño de una tarde dominical en la Alameda Central* (Dream of a Sunday Afternoon on the Alameda). This mural originally hung in the lobby of the Hotel del Prado and was salvaged when the hotel suffered structural damage during the 1985 earthquake. Rivera portrays various figures from Mexican history strolling in the Alameda, including the painter himself, at nine years of age, alongside Frida Kahlo.

Daily *(11am & 5pm)* a light and sound explanation of the mural describes and documents its history.

Pinacoteca Virreinal de San Diego – *Dr. Mora, 7, west side of the Alameda. Open year-round Tue–Sun 9am–5pm. Closed Jan 1, May 1, July 21 & Dec 25. P$10.* ☎ *55-10-27-93.* This colonial art gallery is located in what was originally the church (1591) and part of the monastery of the San Diego friars. The church was open for worship until 1934, when it was expropriated. In 1946 the building became the property of the Instituto Nacional de Bellas Artes (National Institute of Fine Arts), and in 1964, by decree of President López Mateos, the Pinacoteca Virreinal was founded. Its **collection**★ of colonial paintings includes ancient altarpieces that had been selected and preserved by Don José Bernardo Couto and previously kept in the Academia de San Carlos. The art gallery boasts 360 works of art created in Mexico during the colonial period, from the 16C to the first quarter of the 19C, by famous masters such as Andrés de la Concha (1579); Baltasar de Echave Orio (1600); and painters such as José Juárez (1650), considered the greatest of the colonial painters, Cristóbal de Villalpando (1700), Miguel Cabrera (1750) and Rafael Ximeno y Planes (1800), an artist from the Independence period.

> **③ Mercado de Artesanías de la Ciudadela**
> *Plaza de la Ciudadela, 1* Ⓜ *lines 1 & 3 – Balderas. Entrance by way of Plaza de la Ciudadela or Balderas. Open daily 10am–7pm.* ✗ ▣ ☎ *55-10-18-28.* Located on one side of Plaza de la Ciudadela, this large market with over 300 shops is one of the city's most recommended centers for purchasing art works and handicrafts from all over Mexico.

Kitchen with Talavera Ceramic Tiles from Puebla (18C)

⑦ PLAZA DE LA SANTA VERACRUZ AND SURROUNDINGS
Ⓜ *line 2 – Hidalgo or Bellas Artes*

Plaza de la Santa Veracruz – *Av. Hidalgo (between Eje Central and Reforma, beside the Alameda).* This small sunken plaza lies between two handsome colonial churches and two important museums. Locals recognize it as a quiet and pleasant refuge from the daily bustle of the Historic Center of downtown Mexico City.

Templo de la Santa Veracruz – *2 de Abril, 6, intersection with Av. Hidalgo (southeast of the Plaza). Open year-round Mon–Sat 9:30am–1:30pm & 4–8pm, Sun 9:30am–2pm & 4–8pm.* Built in 1527 by the Archicofradía de la Santa Veracruz, an association founded a year earlier by Hernán Cortés, the Church of the Holy Cross' original construction lasted for over two centuries. It was replaced in 1764 by the present structure. The new church, with pilasters in the Baroque *estípite* style, fell under the patronage of San Blas. Following the War of Independence, it was turned over to the Ciudadanos de la Santa Veracruz, whose rector was Emperor Agustín de Iturbide. Today the Opus Dei Catholic movement serves as administrator.
The interior was completely destroyed in the 20C, leaving only the *Cristo de los siete velos* (16C), a Christ of popular devotion donated to the confraternity by King Charles V. The **remains of Manuel Tolsá** lie at rest under the main altar. In Our Lady of Guadalupe's chapel, one can appreciate several paintings by Miguel Cabrera, as well as a supposed relic of the True Cross, adorned with rubies.

Museo Nacional de la Estampa – *Av. Hidalgo, 39 (northeast of the Plaza). Open year-round Tue–Sun 10am–6pm. Closed national holidays. P$10. ☎ 55-21-22-44.* The National Museum of Engravings, located in a Neoclassical 19C building, displays the historical evolution of engraving in Mexico from pre-Hispanic times to the 20C. Due to the large quantity of materials involved and the frequency of temporary exhibitions, the museum rotates its collection.

★★★**Museo Franz Mayer** – *Av. Hidalgo, 45. Open year-round Tue–Sun 10am–5pm. Closed Nov 20 & Dec 25. P$15. ✗ ☎ 55-18-22-65.* Standing on the site of the former San Juan de Dios hospital (16C) for mestizos, blacks and mulattos, the museum was restored in 1980, to house a collection of decorative arts. Donated by Franz Mayer (1882–1975), the **collection** covers four centuries (16–19C) of Mexican artistic creations, as well as European and Asian works that served as models or in some way influenced Mexican artistic production.

Lower Level – Exhibits on this floor, displayed in four large rooms, present a general overview of the applied arts in daily and functional objects. The halls featuring Mexican colonial **sculpture** and **silverwork**★★ merit the most attention.

Upper Level – An excellent collection of European paintings and a series of chests decorated with exquisite techniques comprise this gallery. Continue to the end of the section and bear right to reach the room of **Talavera-style ceramics**★, from Puebla, and the room of textiles. On the left is the collection of Mexican paintings. The tour ends with an extensive display of 17C and 19C artifacts from various countries.

Surrounding the cloister, on the ground floor, four rooms from colonial times have been replicated. The upper floor includes a small site museum, a room of temporary exhibitions and a specialized library.

Templo de San Juan de Dios – *Av. Hidalgo, 51 (western edge of the plaza). Open year-round daily 10am–2pm & 4–6pm.* This unique church was founded in the 18C by the order of San Juan de Dios, who also directed the hospital of the same name (now the Franz Mayer Museum). The exquisitely beautiful **portal**, besides being the oldest in the city, possesses other unique innovations: its concave shape, the decoration of sculptured niches, and wavy-shaped pilasters. Due to the excellent acoustics, this space was used during the colonial era to stage *autos sacramentales* (church pageants with Biblical themes). An 18C fire destroyed the original altarpieces.

Hotel de Cortés – *Av. Hidalgo, 85.* Built in the second half of the 17C to accommodate the Augustinian Friars, who were passing through the city, the building has operated as a hotel since 1943. A deteriorated sculpture of Santo Tomás de Villanueva, added to the facade in 1780, welcomes visitors. The interior **courtyard** now serves as a restaurant.

Templo de San Hipólito – *Av. Hidalgo and Reforma. Open year-round daily 7am–9pm.* This site originally was occupied by a 16C hermitage built in honor of the Spanish soldiers who died during the conquistadors' worst defeat, known as the Noche Triste (Sad Night). Later, the church was dedicated to San Hipólito to commemorate his feast day, August 13, the day of Tenochtitlán's fall. Today, the church attracts scores of devotees of St. Jude Thaddeus.

On the corner of Hidalgo and Zarco, on the outside wall, one can discover a 19C relief with a **depiction** of Moctezuma II's dream foretelling the Conquest.

> **4 Salón México**
> *2nd alley on San Juan de Dios, 25, corner of Pensador Mexicano, Col. Guerrero. Open Fri & Sat 9pm–3am; Sun 2pm–8pm.* ☎ *55-18-09-31.* This famous dance hall was popular from the 1920s to the end of the 1950s, and reopened in 1993 as a restaurant remodeled in the shape of the electric relay station that used to stand here. The hall is ideal for dancing the *danzón* and other tropical tunes to the sound of some of the best orchestras.

ADDITIONAL SIGHT *Map p 67*

Archivo General de la Nación (Antigua Penitenciaría) (CX) – *Eduardo Molina and Albañiles.* Ⓜ *line 4 – Morelos. Open year-round daily 8:15am–3pm. Closed national holidays & during UNAM's winter break. Prearranged guided visits are recommended.* ▤ ☎ *57-95-73-11.* An impressive Neoclassical stone building, the General Archives, a former penitentiary inaugurated in 1900 by Porfirio Díaz, boasts robust ornamentation, high towers and merlons that create the impression of an unassailable fortress. The divergence of seven corridors from one central watchtower produces a remarkable visual effect; presently a great dome covers the central area, creating an ample circular space ideal for temporary exhibitions. Popularly known as "El Palacio Negro de Lecumberri" (The Black Palace of Lecumberri) because during its first 75 years it served as a prison, the building became the home of the National Archives in 1977, responsible for the preservation of Mexico's historical documents dating from the 16C to the present. The most popular archives include a collection of photographs with over 5 million negatives, the Inquisition Archives and those of the Revolution.

Addresses, telephone numbers, opening hours and prices published in this guide are accurate at press time. We apologize for any inconvenience resulting from outdated information, and we welcome corrections and suggestions that may assist us in preparing the next edition. Please send us your comments:

Michelin Travel Publications
Editorial Department
P. O. Box 19001
Greenville, SC 29602-9001
TheGreenGuide-us@us.michelin.com

BOSQUE DE CHAPULTEPEC★★★

🚃 line 1 – Chapultepec
Maps p 66 **(ABY)** and below

Located in a vast zone comprising 730ha/1,800 acres, this historical forest, planted with tall and ancient trees, has stood as a silent witness to the traditions and events that have occurred here since pre-Hispanic times, when Lake Texcoco separated this area from Tenochtitlán.

After their long migration from legendary Aztlán, the Mexicas first settled at present-day Chapultepec Park, with permission from the Tecpanecs. In the Codex Boturini, which narrates the journeys of the Nahuatl tribes, the symbol of a *chapulín* (large grasshopper) on a hill, testifies to the area's abundance of locusts and their importance as a food source. Later, the forest became the residence of the Aztec nobility. "Chapultepec" also alludes to an ancient totemic deity in the mythology of the Mexicas.

During the colonial era, the legendary Castillo de Chapultepec was built (1784–86) atop the locust hill. In 1847 during one of the most memorable Mexican battles against the United States invasion, several young cadets from the Military Academy lost their lives defending Chapultepec Castle; their bravery is recognized in the **Monumento a los Niños Héroes (1)**, dedicated in 1952.

Chapultepec's rich springs supplied the city with water until the end of the 19C. During the Porfiriato, the park underwent major development, and later two more sections were added to create an important ecological area, which serves as the city's lungs. Also an outstanding recreational and cultural center, Chapultepec contains some of Mexico City's most important museums and recreational facilities such as lakes, an amusement park and a zoo.

Visit – *Open year-round Tue–Sun 5am–5pm;* ☎ 55-15-26-97.

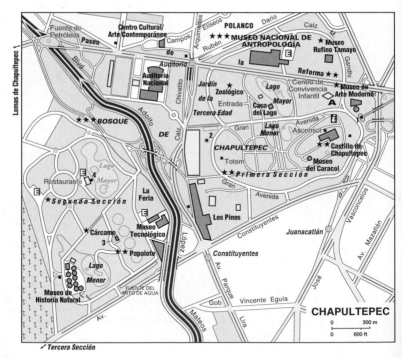

★★FIRST SECTION OF CHAPULTEPEC PARK

In this most ancient part of the woods, one can walk on various trails and enjoy the shade of ancient trees—some of which are older than the city itself. From early morning, the park fills with people exercising and playing sports, families enjoying the outdoors, and groups of students and couples in love, all of whom attract peddlers, photographers and caricaturists with colorful products.

Between the Monumento a los Niños Héroes and the road that leads to the Castle lies the starting point of the **scenic train (A)** *(open year-round Tue–Sun 9am–4:30pm; round trip 20min; live narration; P$8;* ☎ *52-30-21-36)*. The tour winds through several of the historic and attractive sights found along the hidden walkways. Its only stop is the zoo, where people can disembark, but they can not board the train. Rowboats can be rented at the nearby **Lago Mayor**, a large recreational lake. From the end of February through the beginning of April, the National Dance Company stages open-air **night performances** of the ballet *Swan Lake* on the **Lago Menor** islet. Located on the edge of the lake, the **Casa del Lago Mayor**, an early-20C French-style house, hosts cultural activities throughout the year.

★**Zoo** – *Open year-round Tue–Sun 9am–4:30pm. Closed Jan 1 & Dec 25.* ✗ ☎ *55-53-62-63.* Over 270 species of animals from around the world reside in areas that simulate natural habitats. Some endangered species, such as the panda bears, have successfully reproduced here. Unique animals in the zoo include two species indigenous to Mexico, the *teporingo* (a large rodent) and the Mexican wolf, as well as the white rhinoceros. Behind the zoo, near the Calzada Chivatito, the **Jardín de la Tercera Edad** offers a pleasant setting for senior citizens, as well as a botanical garden and an orchid house.

Fuente de Nezahualcóyotl (2) – *On the southern edge of the zoo.* Luis Ortiz Monasterio created this monumental fountain in 1956 as a tribute to the ancient Aztec king-poet, Nezahualcóyotl. Several events of his life are represented in bas-relief. A few steps away stands the oldest fountain in Chapultepec Park, the **Fuente de las Ranas** (Frog Fountain).

★★★ **Museo Nacional de Antropología** – *Paseo de la Reforma and Gandhi. Description p 90.*

★**Museo Rufino Tamayo** – *Paseo de la Reforma and Gandhi, just past Reforma. Open year-round Tue–Sun 10am–6pm. Closed Jan 1, May 1 & Dec 25. P$15.* ☎ *52-86-58-39 or* www.cnca.gob.mx/espacios/tamayo/obtamayo.html. Surrounded by forest, this modern **building**★ designed in 1981 by Abraham Zabludowsky and Teodoro González de León recalls Mexico's pre-Hispanic building traditions. The museum houses an international contemporary art **collection** donated by Mexican painter Rufino Tamayo and his wife Olga, and features works by Picasso, Miró, Fernando Botero, Francisco Toledo and Robert Motherwell, among others. Occasionally this collection is put aside partially or entirely to make room for **temporary exhibitions**. The museum also hosts concerts, dance and theater performances.

★**Museo de Arte Moderno** – *Paseo de la Reforma and Gandhi. Open year-round Tue–Sun 10am–6pm. Closed Jan 1 & Dec 25. P$15.* ☎ *52-11-83-31 or* www.arts-history.mx/museos/mam/home.html. The Museum of Modern Art offers an overview of the visual arts in the 20C, with special emphasis on the works of painters and sculptors, both from Mexico and abroad, of the caliber of Rufino Tamayo, Carlos Mérida, Gerardo Murillo (Dr. Atl), José Clemente Orozco and Gunther Gerzso, among others. It also features works by Diego Rivera and David Alfaro Siqueiros. The female artists' collection includes works by Frida Kahlo, Olga Costa, María Izquierdo, Remedios Varo and Leonora Carrington. Be sure to stroll through the gardens to discover beautiful sculptures.

Museo del Caracol (Galería de Historia) – *Access ramp to the Castle of Chapultepec. Open year-round daily 9am–5:30pm. Closed Jan 1, Dec 12 & 25. P$16.* ☎ *55-53-62-85.* Named El Caracol (The Snail) because of its downward spiraling shape, the History Gallery opened to the public in 1960. Its 12 halls provide an overview of Mexican history and illustrate its most significant events and important characters. The chronological journey ends at the **Recinto de la Constitución**, which exalts the national flag and a reproduction of the 1917 Constitution. José Chávez Morado crafted the hall and bronze entrance door.

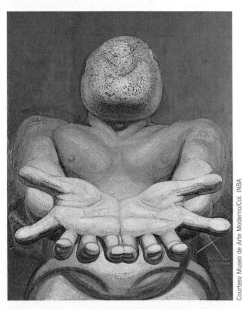

Nuestra imagen actual (1947) by David Alfaro Siqueiros

Courtesy Museo de Arte Moderno/Col. INBA

★★CASTILLO DE CHAPULTEPEC

Commissioned by Viceroy Gálvez and designed by the Catalonian architect Agustín Mascaró, the imposing Neoclassical **palace** (1787) became the Military Academy in 1842. A few years later, Chapultepec Castle witnessed the death of several brave young cadets, remembered as the **Niños Héroes**, who lost their lives during the storming of the castle by US troops.

Maximilian of Hapsburg took up residence here after the old building was remodeled and the Alcázar fortress was added.

During his second term of office as president (1884–1917), Porfirio Díaz used the castle as the presidential residence. It continued functioning in this capacity and housed several Mexican presidents until 1939, when Lázaro Cárdenas designated it as the site for the National Museum of History.

The entrance to the castle can be accessed on foot, by way of a ramp, or by train *(departs every 10min; P$3 round trip)* whose point of departure lies directly across from an elevator that is currently out of service.

Castillo de Chapultepec

Museo Nacional de Historia – *Open year-round Tue–Sun 9am–5pm, Dec 24, 25 & 31 9am–3pm. Closed Jan 1. P$20.* ✗ ☎ *52-86-99-20 or* www.arts-history.mx/museos/castillo. Exhibits of paintings and objects of daily use, from the colonial period to the 1910 Revolution illustrate Mexico's customs, and political and economic organization. Noteworthy are the **murals** by Juan O'Gorman, José Clemente Orozco and David Alfaro Siqueiros. The upper level displays cultural and artistic creations from Mexico's War of Independence to the Revolution. The museum also addresses issues from the end of the 19C.

The Alcázar – *Same times and charges as the aforementioned museum.* The fortress preserves paintings, furniture and porcelain objects offered as a gift by the empress of China in 1910 on the occasion of the hundredth anniversary of Mexico's Independence, as well as the sumptuous quarters of Carlota, Maximilian's wife. Porfirio Díaz' residence, located in the upper corridors, features *Bacchantes*, Pompeii-style paintings created by Santiago Rebull. Díaz commissioned the Galería de Emplomados to be created in France.

★SECOND SECTION OF CHAPULTEPEC PARK
Ⓜ *line 7 – Constituyentes.*

Wide avenues embellished with numerous **fountains** and modern sculptures lead to museums, lakes, restaurants and an amusement park. Locals and tourists alike enjoy the attractive setting when jogging, cycling or roller-skating.

La Feria (Amusement Park) – *Open Holy Week, July, Aug & Dec, daily 9am–9pm; rest of the year Tue–Fri 11am–7pm, Sat–Sun 10am–9pm. P$15 (30 rides) & P$75 (all rides, all times, restrictions apply).* ✗ 🄴 ☎ *52-30-21-21.* A traditional amusement park with over fifty attractions for all ages. La Feria's most impressive mechanical attraction is the famous **roller coaster** that provides riders with a glimpse of Chapultepec Park from above, just before experiencing the vertigo of plunging downward. A variety of live performances can also be enjoyed.

Museo Tecnológico – *Open year-round daily 9am–5pm. Closed Dec 25–Jan 1.* ☏ *55-16-09-64.* The Technological Museum demonstrates different aspects of energy generation, transmission and use. Also, by means of miniature reproductions and original vehicles, it recounts the evolution of the different means of transportation devised throughout history. Hands-on displays allow visitors to test physical phenomena.

★★**Papalote, Museo del Niño** – *Open year-round Mon–Wed, Fri 9am–1pm & 2–6pm, Thu 9am–1pm, 2–6pm & 7–11pm, Sat–Sun 10am–2pm & 3–7pm. P$40 (museum and IMAX P$60). We recommend reserving tickets for the museum and the giant screen.* ✕ ☏ *52-24-12-60. Ticketmaster* ☏ *53-25-90-00.* This children's museum contains over 350 interactive exhibits for children and adults of all ages to play and learn about a variety of subjects. The *prohibido no tocar* (forbidden not to touch, i.e. hands-on) halls are those devoted to communications, the human body, the conscience and expressions. The museum also offers workshops and temporary exhibitions. The **Megapantalla** *(daily 10:30am every hour until 7:30pm, Thu until 9:30pm; P$30;* ☏ *51-60-60-60)* shows IMAX movies with digital sound; the effects can produce dizziness. Just south of the Papalote museum you will find the long fountain, **Fuente del Mito de Agua** (Fountain of the Myth of Water).

★**Cárcamo** – This small building, surmounted by a cupola, formerly collected the waters from the springs of Lake Lerma, once the principal water source for the higher elevations of Mexico City. Diego Rivera's mural *El agua, origen de la vida* (Water, source of life, 1951), meant to be viewed from underwater, is on display; a complex restoration process begun in the 1990s put a halt to this unique form of presentation. Rivera also created the exterior Fountain of Tláloc, a complex interpretation of the rain god, called **Fuente de Tláloc Totopamitl**★**(3)**. The figure and the bottom of the fountain are made from volcanic rock with Mexican onyx and pieces of tile. This fountain was meant to be appreciated from an aerial view.

Museo de Historia Natural – *Open year-round Tue–Sun 10am–5pm. Closed Jan 1 & Dec 25. P$10.* ☏ *55-15-63-04 or* www.arts-history.mx/hnatural.html. The Museum of Natural History illustrates the origin and evolution of the natural species. Though under partial renovation, it has remained open to continue presenting new attractions and interesting temporary exhibits.

Beside the museum, the **Tren Escénico** *(open year-round Tue–Sun 10am–4:30pm; round trip 10min; P$2;* ☏ *55-15-26-97)* makes a short tour around the **Lago Menor** and surrounding areas. At this "small lake" there are boats for hire. In the middle of the **Lago Mayor**, inhabited by ducks and fish, the mighty **Fuente monumental (4)** shoots 50m/155ft into the air, and is illuminated at night. Inviting restaurants can be found along the banks of both lakes.

Sights described in this guide are rated:
   ★★★   *Worth the trip*
   ★★   *Worth a detour*
   ★   *Interesting*

MUSEO NACIONAL DE ANTROPOLOGÍA ★★★

Paseo de la Reforma and Gandhi. ⓜ line 1 – Chapultepec
Floor Plan below 🅸 ☎ 55-53-63-86

Inaugurated in 1964, this remarkable project, directed by Mexican architect Pedro
Ramírez Vázquez, covers almost 70,000sq m/229,600sq ft, with exhibition halls
occupying approximately 30,000sq m/98,400sq ft.

The building – *Located within the first section of Chapultepec Park.* The museum
consists of 23 permanent exhibition halls, laid out around an enormous **courtyard**
inspired by the open spaces of pre-Hispanic cities. Part of the esplanade is protected
by a large, aluminum roof supported by a very tall **column** wrapped in bronze bas-
reliefs shielded by a water curtain. This sculpture, called **El Paraguas** (The Umbrella)
is the work of the brothers José and Tomás Chávez Morado. In the background, a
pond with lake vegetation replicates the swampland where the Mexicas settled, while
a bronze snail on the final platform invokes the pre-Hispanic snail symbol.

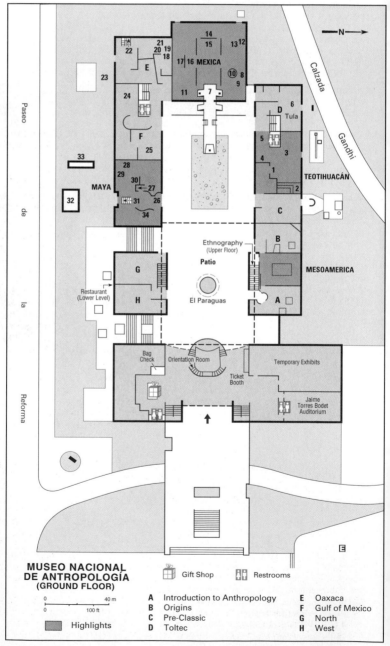

**MUSEO NACIONAL
DE ANTROPOLOGÍA
(GROUND FLOOR)**

	🎁 Gift Shop	🚻 Restrooms

0 ____ 40 m
0 ____ 100 ft

Highlights

A	Introduction to Anthropology	E	Oaxaca
B	Origins	F	Gulf of Mexico
C	Pre-Classic	G	North
D	Toltec	H	West

The museum – *Open year-round Tue–Sun 9am–7pm. P$25, free Sun & holidays.*
✕ 🄴 ✆ *55-53-63-86.* The left wing of the vestibule contains a shop and other
services; to the right of the main entrance lies the hall of temporary exhibits embellished with a mural by Rufino Tamayo, *La oscuridad y la luz* (Darkness and Light).
Opposite the ticket booth, the orientation room provides a multimedia overview of
pre-Hispanic cultures *(shows: Tue–Sat 10am, noon, 2:30pm, 3:30pm; Sun 11am,
noon, 2pm and 3pm)*. The ground floor comprises twelve halls devoted to archaeology, starting with a brief introduction to archaeology and spanning the period
from the first settlement of the American continent to the major achievements of
Mesoamerican cultures. Each exhibition hall stems from the main courtyard and
opens onto an outside garden displaying artifacts, most of which are reproductions. The second floor houses 11 halls on ethnography, illustrating various aspects
of the social and cultural life of Mexico's present-day indigenous groups.

VISIT

*The tour begins at the first door on the right. Start on the first floor before going
to the second.*

Introduction to Anthropology (A) – This hall briefly explains the object of anthropology through four main themes: physical anthropology, archaeology, ethnology
and linguistics. A mural by Jorge González Camarena decorates the entrance.

Mesoamerica – A mural map at the entrance shows the various cultural regions
of Mesoamerica with their characteristic elements. The adjoining chronological
chart points out the different eras of pre-Hispanic cultures in the order they appear
in the museum. Artifacts and models illustrate their common features. José Chávez
Morado created the mural located on the upper wall.

Origins (B) – From the arrival of the first inhabitants of the American continent to
their existence as farmers, these exhibits show the progression from nomadic to
sedentary life.

Pre-Classic (C) – The period 1500 BC to AD 100 marks the consolidation, and the
social, political and cultural development of the first Mesoamerican civilizations.
Some of the most ancient figurines and ceramic artifacts are on display here.
Carefully reconstructed burials discovered at Tlatilco, Mexico state, demonstrate
the importance of funeral rites.

Teotihuacán – One of the most richly illustrated presentations in the museum, this
hall effectively exhibits the artistic and cultural expressions of this period, using a
variety of media: archaeological artifacts, videos, photo-murals, models and excellent reproductions. Of the latter, the most outstanding are the copy of the **Tlalocan
mural (1)**, and the life-size reproduction of part of the **Templo de Quetzalcóatl (2)** from
the original at the Teotihuacán archaeological site. Opposite the temple reproduction stands the immense monolithic sculpture of **Chalchiuhtlicue (3)**, goddess of water,
taken from the site's Plaza de la Luna. Near the end of the hall a showcase holds
a collection of **funeral masks (4)**, which were placed over the faces of the deceased
in order to protect them on their voyage to the netherworld. The last sculpture,
found at the Plaza del Sol at Teotihuacán, probably represents the dead Sun or
Mictlantecuhtli (5), god of death.

Toltec (D) – For a long time, the Toltecs were considered the predominant culture
of the Central Highland Plateau during the post-Classic period. However, other cultures such as the Xochicalco, Teotenango and Tenayuca developed before, during
and after their time. This hall testifies to the importance of these other cultures.
In the area devoted to Tula, the Toltec capital, do not miss the example of the
enormous cilindrical columns shaped like warriors, called **atlantes (6)** *(photo p 156)*,
used to support large roofs.

Mexica – The most astonishing and important hall of all is that of the Mexicas.
Also called Aztecs, they founded the great city of Tenochtitlán in AD 1325. By the
time the Spaniards landed in 1519, the Aztecs had consolidated the biggest empire
in Mesoamerica. The clash of the two empires ended with the defeat of the Aztecs
in 1521. At the entrance stands the stunning sculpture of an **ocelote (7)** carrying a
cuauhxicalli (basin) on its back containing an offering of human hearts to be sacrificed to the Sun. The relief of the **Piedra de los Guerreros (8)** (Stone of the Warriors)
shows two rows of warriors preparing to pierce their earlobes with a prickly-pear
thorn as a sign of self-sacrifice. On the right wing, a copy of the Codex Boturini,
also called the **Tira de Peregrinación (9)**, narrates the Mexicas' pilgrimage to the spot
where they founded Tenochtitlán. The **Piedra de Tizoc (10)** (Stone of Tizoc) records
the conquests of this ruler (the seventh Tlatoani).
The next section contains a large **mural of Tenochtitlán (11)** *(photo p 60)*, a city that
covered 13sq km/8sq mi and supported over 300,000 inhabitants. In front a **scale
model (12)** recreates the original layout of the Templo Mayor, originally located in
the center of the Aztec city before its destruction by the Spaniards in the 16C. Two

© Robert Frerck/Odyssey

Aztec Calendar

twin shrines are clearly recognizable in the model: the blue one to Tláloc, the rain god; and the red one to Huitzilopóchtli, god of the sun and of war. A diorama of the **Mercado de Tlatelolco (13)** shows the great variety of items traded and the presence of different social classes. Usually, items such as cocoa grains or quills filled with gold dust served as currency.

The famous **Aztec Calendar (14)** or **Piedra del Sol** (Sun Stone), weighing 24 tons and measuring 3.6m/11.8ft in diameter, stands on a platform in the center of the room. To the right of the original calendar lies a smaller reproduction, a version in its original colors, featuring the face of Tonatiuh, the Sun, in the center, with his tongue hanging out as an obsidian knife; beside his face, his claw-like hands grasp the human hearts he devours. The four rectangles around the face symbolize the dates on which the four previous worlds of the Mexicas were destroyed. Twenty hieroglyphics representing the days of the month in the 260-day Aztec religious calendar form the next circle. Circling the perimeter are two fiery serpents, called Xiuhcóatl, from whose jaws emerge the heads of the gods of east and west that guide the Sun on its heavenly journey.

An imposing **Coatlicue (15)** *(photo p 94)*, "she with the skirt of serpents", goddess of the earth and of death, reigns over the last section of the room. The sculpture portrays a beheaded woman with two serpents emerging from her neck. Her dress represents blood, life, and death. She wears a necklace of hands and hearts, earrings of skulls, a skirt of braided serpents; her hands, too, are serpent heads and her feet, eagle claws. Near the exit, a glass case displays the controversial **Penacho de Moctezuma (16)** (Moctezuma's headdress). Supposedly given as a gift by Hernán Cortés to King Charles V of Spain, the original, in fact, remains in Vienna, inciting a great controversy over its return to Mexico. The **Mausoleo de los Siglos (17)**, or skull altar, symbolizes the tomb of time; through its top opening Xiuhmolpilli, or "the knotted cord" symbol of the 52-year ancient time-cycle, climbs inside.

Oaxaca (E) – This hall contains elements of Zapotec (800 BC–AD 1000) and Mixtec (AD 100–1521) cultures, which evolved in the present state of Oaxaca. Monte Albán, the principal Zapotec city, contains outstanding reproductions of bas-reliefs depicting **dancers (18)**, **funeral urns (19)**, the **great jaguar (20)**, and, most precious of all, the **jade mask (21)**. Replicas of **tomb 104 (22)** and **tomb 7 (23)** contain examples of offerings and illustrate Zapotec burial customs.

The Mixtec section features several examples of Mitla's decoration and architecture; various gold and decorated ceramic objects complement the display.

Gulf of Mexico (F) – These three sections correspond chronologically with the three cultures that emerged on the edges of the Gulf of Mexico: first, the Olmec (1200–600 BC), to the south; then the Totonac (AD 100–900), in the center; and finally the Huastec (AD 900–1521), to the north. The monumental **heads** at the entrance and **el luchador (24)** (the wrestler) constitute the most representative examples of Olmec culture. The *caritas sonrientes* (smiling faces) and *juguetes con ruedas* (toys on wheels) represent Totonac culture. In the last section, stylized sculptures, painted ceramics and the **Tamuín adolescent (25)** represent Huastec culture.

Maya – Maya culture evolved from 600 BC until the arrival of the Spaniards. Their territory stretched from the south of Mexico to neighboring Central American countries. The Maya's precise and complex knowledge of mathematics, astronomy, and their calendar continue to astound modern scientists. Moreover, the Maya created their own hieroglyphic writing with an intricate deciphering code, and a number system built on zero, centuries before Europeans discovered it.

A **model (26)** with a relief map shows the extent of Maya territory. The lights indicate major archaeological sites. To the right of the entrance lies the fascinating **lintel 26 (27)** from Yaxchilán depicting a couple just before an important ceremony: the male figure, representing the governor, Shield-Jaguar, carries a knife for self-sacrifice; the female, his wife, her clothing denoting her hierarchy, with ritual scars on

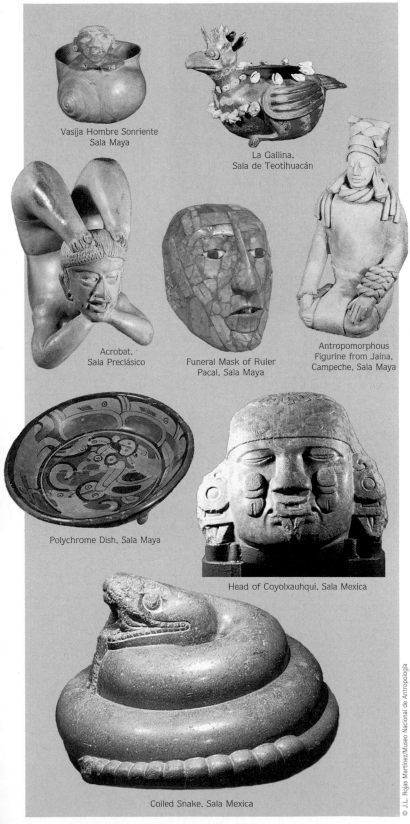

Vasija Hombre Sonriente
Sala Maya

La Gallina.
Sala de Teotihuacán

Acrobat.
Sala Preclásico

Funeral Mask of Ruler
Pacal, Sala Maya

Antropomorphous
Figurine from Jaina,
Campeche, Sala Maya

Polychrome Dish, Sala Maya

Head of Coyolxauhqui, Sala Mexica

Coiled Snake, Sala Mexica

Coatlicue, Sala Mexica

her face, bears a jaguar head-dress and the governor's shield. The glass cases in the following section show general aspects of Maya culture: phys-ical features, social organiza-tion, utensils and other arti-facts that prove this people's extraordinary store of knowl-edge. Most of the lintels and stelae adorning the hall were found at Yaxchilán.

The following section features a **large mask (28)** set in the wall, found in southern Campeche; to the left lies the **disco de Chinkultic (29)** depicting a ballplayer just as he is about to strike the ball with his hip. Nearby are the **tableros de la Cruz Foliada de Palenque (30)** de-picting two figures that flank a maize plant in the shape of a cross. The central staircase leads to an excellent replica of the **Tumba Real (31)** (Royal Tomb) from the Temple of the Inscriptions at Palenque, ac-companied by the original jade treasure.

Life-size models of some Maya temples occupy the exterior courtyard: **temple 2 from Hochob (32)**, Campeche, and the Bonampak **templo de las pinturas (33)** are particularly noteworthy.

The final section, with artifacts from the post-Classic period, is highlighted by jewels from the Sacred Cenote and the **Chac-mool (34)**, or messenger of the gods, both from Chichén Itzá.

North (G) – The *sala norte*, devoted to those pre-Hispanic cultures that inhabited the north of Mexico, is divided into three groups: the desert and plains' peoples, who inhabited parts of the deserts of northern Mexico and the southern United States, living as pre-historic hunter-gatherers with a nomadic life-style; the mar-ginal-Mesoamerica peoples, living in the north and part of central Mexico, practicing farming and living a sedentary life-style; and thirdly, the farming cul-tures, called Oasis-America, whose settlements grew in unorthodox ways, as is the case with the Paquimé.

West (H) – Most of the cultures that settled in western Mexico developed during the pre-Classic, Classic and post-Classic periods. They did not leave traces of major urban settlements, but their ceramic creations constitute the most realistic and artistic in all of Mexico. Noteworthy are the figures found in the **tumbas de tiro** (tombs), and some Tarasc artifacts like the **Chac-mool**.

Ethnography Halls – *Upper level*. Some 10 million indigenous peoples live in Mexico and, after 500 years of change still manage to preserve some of their ancient cultural features. This section attempts to show the diversity of Mexico's present-day ethnic groups: their life-style and homelands, their dress, customs, tra-ditions and crafts. The subjects covered include an introduction to indigenous peoples, as well as exhibits on the Coras and Huichols, and the Purépechas and Otomis. Next, the ethnic groups are presented according to the region they inhabit: the Sierra Madre Occidental; Oaxaca, the Gulf of Mexico, Chiapas, Tabasco and Yucatán; Highland and Lowland Maya; northwestern Mexico and, finally, the Nahua Hall.

Admission prices and hours published in this guide are accurate at press time. We apologize for any inconvenience resulting from outdated information.

■ Markets of Mexico City

The markets of **Xochimilco** *(p 108)*, **La Merced**, **La Lagunilla** and **Jamaica**, the city's oldest, date back to the pre-colonial period when the city was a confederation of towns connected by canals. At that time, each community had its own **tianguis**—a place where goods were traded and sold. Natives would transport products in little boats called **trajineras**. Ancient narrators tell what a marvelous sight it was to watch them steering their canoes: the astonishing effect of the bright colorful costumes, their bronzed faces, and the variety of their products as they glided across the waters against the amazing background of the lake city.

Centuries later, although Mexico City has undergone a complete transformation, these markets have survived and now serve as platforms of exchange for Mexico's ancient beliefs, realities and traditions. Here one can find an infinite variety of products: from aphrodisiac herbs, pre-Hispanic flowers and medicines, to amulets and magical powders from faraway places, miraculous statues of saints and virgins, healers who cure the "evil eye," and unique characters who know more about spells and potions than all the witches in the world. There are, of course, food stands to satisfy more immediate needs.

It should be noted that these are not conventional "markets" that specialize in Mexican handicrafts. More typical markets include the **FONART** stores, **La Ciudadela** *(p 83)* and **Bazar Sábado** *(p 105)*.

Brigitta L. House

PASEO DE LA REFORMA★★

Map pp 66-67 (ABCY) – Map p 86

5 **Mercado de Artesanías de Insurgentes**
Entrance through Londres, 154, and Liverpool, 44, Zona Rosa. Daily 9am–8pm (Sun until 5pm). ✕ ☎ *55-25-64-98.* Silver, typical costumes, leather, ceramics and other curios converge on this great space of 237 stalls linked by small aisles. The Insurgentes crafts market has been open to the public since 1955.

6 **Fonda "El Refugio"**
Liverpool, 166, Zona Rosa (opposite the handicraft market). ▣ ☎ *52-07-27-32 (reservations recommended).* "El Refugio," famous for first-class, authentic traditional Mexican cuisine, serves dishes from a different region of Mexico each day of the week.

The trees of this beautiful bustling avenue, whether providing shade from the blistering sun or decked with lights at Christmas time, stand guard along one of the city's most historical and longest (15km/9.3mi) thoroughfares. Its oldest section goes from Bucareli circle to the entrance to Chapultepec Park. Maximilian of Hapsburg ordered its construction around 1864 so that he could have a direct link between Chapultepec Castle, where he resided, and the National Palace. Hence its original name, **Paseo del Emperador** (Emperor's Promenade).

Over the years, Paseo de la Reforma has been further embellished. Besides its modern buildings, several *glorietas* (traffic circles) have been added, some of them adorned with fountains and important monuments. The nearby **Zona Rosa**, with its concentration of hotels, art galleries, elegant boutiques, lively restaurants and sidewalk cafes, adds to the animation of downtown Mexico City, especially at night. The second stretch, running from the entrance to Chapultepec to the Fuente de Petróleos, is bordered by part of the woods, great museums, and the **Polanco** district that boasts attractive hotels and famous restaurants. Located on the other side of Reforma, the **Auditorio Nacional** *(open only for performances;* ☎ *52-80-92-50),* rebuilt in 1991 by architects Abraham Zabludowsky and Teodoro González de León, hosts shows and social events. **Los Pinos,** the official residence of Mexico's president, stands protected by the Campo Marte section of the park.

© Robert Frerck/Odyssey

Fuente de la Diana Cazadora

The last stretch of Paseo de la Reforma ends at the Toluca Exit near **Lomas de Chapultepec** (Chapultepec Hills), one of the most exclusive residential areas in the city.

SIGHTS

Traveling north on Paseo de la Reforma from the National Museum of Anthropology.

★**Fuente de la Diana Cazadora** – This splendid bronze statue and fountain (1942) depicts the Roman goddess, Diana the Huntress. The sculptor, Mexican Juan F. Olaguíbel, affectionately called his work "the archer."

★★**Monumento a la Independencia** – Symbolizing Mexico City, this monument to the War of Independence consists of a great column 36m/118ft high, crowned by a winged victory known as **El Ángel** (The Angel). The impressive work of architect Antonio Rivas Mercado

© Bob Schalkwijk

Monumento a la Independencia

and French sculptor Enrique Alciati was inaugurated on September 16, 1910 to commemorate the Centennial of Mexican Independence and to pay tribute to its leaders, whose white marble sculptures stand around it. Their remains—including those of the father of independence, Miguel Hidalgo y Costilla—are kept inside the monument *(open year-round daily 9am–6pm)*.

Monumento a Cuauhtémoc – This bronze sculpture by Miguel Noreña (1843–94) portrays the last of the Aztec emperors shooting an arrow into the air. The elegant and energetic style gives a remarkably expressive look to the work, making it a masterpiece of the Mexican academy. On its base, dramatic **reliefs** depict the capture and torture suffered by this great Mexican chief at the hands of Hernán Cortés.

Monumento a Cristóbal Colón – Created in France by Charles Cordier (19C), this sculpture features Christopher Columbus at the top, accompanied by four religious figures symbolizing the evangelization of the New World.

SAN COSME *Map p 66* (BX). 🚇 *line 2 – Revolución.*

Monumento a la Revolución – *Plaza de la República.* Originally conceived during Porfirio Díaz's regime to house the Legislative Palace, the construction of the building was interrupted due to the outbreak of the 1910 Revolution. In 1933 architect Obregón Santacilia transformed the structure that was going to be the large cupola into the present Monument to the Revolution.
The statues on the upper corners are the work of Oliverio Martínez. Each one of the four supports contains the remains of the revolutionary leaders: Francisco I. Madero, Venustiano Carranza, Plutarco Elías Calles, Francisco Villa and Lázaro Cárdenas.

Museo Nacional de la Revolución Mexicana (National Museum of the Mexican Revolution) – *Located in the basement of the Monument to the Revolution. Open year-round Tue–Sat 9am–5pm, Sun 9am–3pm. Closed national holidays. P$6. ☎ 55-46-21-15.* This hidden museum illustrates the periods of the Revolution in three carefully designed halls focusing on economic, political and social development. Photographs, original documents and objects explain 50 years of Mexican history, from the Proclamation of the Liberal Republic in 1867 to the Mexican Constitution of 1917.

★**Museo de San Carlos** (M') – *Puente de Alvarado, 50. Open year-round Wed–Mon 10am–6pm. Closed national holidays. P$20. ☎ 55-66-83-42.* In the early 19C, Manuel Tolsá created the elegant and sober Neoclassical **mansion**★★ of palatial dimensions for the Conde de Buenavista, who died before the work was completed. Once owned by the Condes de Regla and Antonio López de Santa Anna, it later housed Tabacalera Mexicana (Mexican Tobaccos) and the National Preparatory School.
Some of its collections belonged to the **Antigua Academia de San Carlos** (Ancient Academy of St. Charles). They contain a treasure trove of Spanish Gothic panels, along with works of Renaissance, Mannerist, Baroque, Neoclassical, Romantic, Symbolist and other 19C schools. It boasts one of the best collections of 16–20C European paintings in Latin America with works by Ingres, Ribera, Rubens, Sorolla, Titian, Tintoretto, Zurbarán and Goya.

Museo Universitario del Chopo (M²) – *Enrique González Martínez, 10. Open year-round Tue–Sun 10am–2pm and 3–7pm. Closed national holidays and during UNAM's summer & winter breaks. P$6.* ⚒ ☎ *55-35-22-88.* This construction of iron, prefabricated walls and glass was imported from Germany in the early 20C to house industrial exhibitions. In 1910 the Japanese Pavilion was installed here during the Independence Centennial celebrations. Explore the examples of early-20C, French-influenced Mexican architecture in the Santa María de la Ribera district that surrounds the museum.

After serving as the National Museum of Natural History, in 1975, the Palacio de Cristal became a cultural center and an outlet for artistic expressions of both new and well-known artists. The center caters to everything from visual arts exhibitions to rock concerts, plays, workshops and cultural conferences.

TLATELOLCO AND VILLA DE GUADALUPE *Map p 67* (CX)

Tlatelolco Ⓜ *line 3 – Tlatelolco*

Founded in AD 1331, this ancient and noble pre-Hispanic village served as the second capital of the Aztec Empire and purportedly boasted the best-stocked market of all Mesoamerica. Its inhabitants, together with the Tenochcas, were part of a single ethnic group, the Mexicas, who originated in legendary Aztlán. They then separated from the latter to settle the northern part of the city.

Frequently called the "twin cities," Tlatelolco and Tenochtitlán both possessed as their main building an enormous double pyramid with temples dedicated to the principal gods, Huitzilopóchtli and Tláloc.

★**Plaza de las Tres Culturas** – *Visit to the ruins daily 6:30am–9pm.* In the impressive Plaza of the Three Cultures, three great eras converge: pre-Hispanic ruins stand alongside religious edifices of the colonial period and **modern buildings** for public housing designed by architect Mario Pani. Going back to pre-Hispanic times, the square has witnessed great turbulence, from its position as the last redoubt of the Aztecs, to the 1968 student uprising when hundreds of Mexican youths were killed by government forces. In 1985 Tlatelolco was one of the areas most affected by the earthquake that convulsed Mexico City.

Templo de Santiago – *Open year-round daily 7:30am–1pm & 4–7:45pm.* Built on the foundations of a pyramid with materials from ancient pre-Hispanic temples, the Church of Santiago was finished in 1609 under the direction of Fray Juan de Torquemada. Pale Mannerist facades brighten the *tezontle* exterior walls while modern restoration has lent an austere air to the **interior**★ enhanced by its blue **stained-glass windows**. The rather plain altar contains a 16C **relief** of the original altarpiece that depicts St. James struggling with *Ocelotl* (jaguar) warriors. Above, in the triangles formed by the arches, the Four Evangelists appear, and in the upper part of the side door, the monumental figure of **St. Christopher** comes to life.

The remodeled building adjoining the church formerly housed the **Colegio de la Santa Cruz** (School of the Holy Cross), founded in 1536 by Fray Pedro de Gante as the first and only school for indigenous children. Here, in 1564, Fray Bernardino de Sahagún finished his *Historia de las cosas de la Nueva España* (History of New Spain). The cloister, built in 1660 as a home for the Franciscan friars, later operated as a military prison and barracks during the Porfiriato. It is currently home to the Department of Archives, Library and Publications of the Secretariat of Foreign Relations.

Tecpan – *Behind the Templo de Santiago, 400m/438yd east along Almacenes. Open year-round daily 9am–5pm.* ☎ *55-83-02-95.* Meaning "palace" in the native Náhuatl language, the site of Cuauhtémoc's Governing Palace also served as a vantage point from which to oversee trade at the great Tlatelolco open-air market. A dramatic **mural** (1944) by Siqueiros, *Cuauhtémoc contra el mito* (Cuauhtémoc Against the Myth), adorns the north room. The depiction of the last Aztec emperor regaining power over Mesoamerica, symbolized by the lance that pierces the Spanish conquistador represented as a centaur bearing the arms of conquest, provides an example of Siqueiros' techniques of foreshortening and three-dimensional perspective.

From here take the **Calzada de los Misterios**, one of the city's oldest highways, north to the Villa de Guadalupe shrine. Since pre-Hispanic times, this route has linked Tlatelolco with the ancient sanctuary of Tonantzin, in the Tepeyac neighborhood, and was the only land entrance to Tenochtitlán from the north. "The Way of the Mysteries" highway derives its present name from the 15 little monuments built in the 17C representing the mysteries of the rosary.

★VILLA DE GUADALUPE ⑩ line 6 – La Villa

According to tradition the **Virgin of Guadalupe**, by far Mexico's most important religious symbol, appeared on three different occasions to **Juan Diego** here in 1531. Today, as a sign of their devotion and gratitude, thousands of pilgrims from all over Mexico flock to this shrine at the top of Tepeyac Hill to sing *Las mañanitas* (birthday greetings) to Our Lady on December 12.

Antigua Basílica – *To one side of the Nueva Basílica.* Very ample dimensions and four corner towers distinguish the "old" basilica, completed in 1709 under the direction of Pedro de Arrieta. The main entry features a central relief depicting the culminating episode of the Guadalupe tradition: the image of the Virgin Mary appearing on Juan Diego's *tilma* (rough-hewn cape) as he opens it before the astonished gaze of Bishop Fray Juan de Zumárraga. On the left stands the Neoclassical convent of the Capuchin nuns. Due to structural damage resulting from sinking, this building is closed to the public.

Nueva Basílica – *On the left side of the plaza. Open year-round daily 6am–9pm.* A splendid creation of architects Pedro Ramírez Vázquez and José Luis Benlliure, the new basilica was finished in 1976. Its immense roof represents a great cloak spreading out to shelter the faithful. The design of the circular interior, with nine altar-boxes for private masses and a capacity of 10,000, affords all worshipers a view of the original picture of the **Virgin of Guadalupe** *(behind the main altar)*. A front escalator, just below altar level, facilitates the constant movement of pilgrims paying homage to the Patroness of Mexico and Latin America.

Museo de la Basílica de Guadalupe – *Annex behind the old basilica. Open year-round Tue–Sun 10am–6pm (Dec 11 open until 2am) Closed Dec 26. P$3.* ☎ 55-77-60-22 ext. 37. **Votive offerings★**, dating from as far back as the mid 19C cover the walls of the entrance passage. Largely thin metal painted plaques, true expressions of popular art, full of color and naïveté, express the faithfuls' gratitude to the Virgin for favors received or desired. The museum displays an interesting **collection★** of colonial canvases by painters of the caliber of Juan Correa, Nicolás Rodríguez Juárez, Baltasar Echave Ibía and Cristóbal Villalpando. Art from the 19C and 20C can also be viewed. Noteworthy are the carved choir stalls, the atrium cross (16C) in the courtyard, and, in the upper rooms, two gilded altarpieces, one of them from the 17C with paintings by Miguel Cabrera of the four apparitions of Our Lady.

Capilla del Cerrito – *At the top of Cerro del Tepeyac. Open year-round daily 8am–6pm.* Climb to the top of Tepeyac hill—which offers a stunning **view** of Mexico City—to visit the exact place of the three apparitions of the Virgin (associated by the natives with Tonantzin, the mother of the gods). The present church, including the facade, was rebuilt in 1930 in imitation 18C Baroque style. Inside, six large murals by Fernando Leal tell the story of the apparitions. According to tradition, it was here that Juan Diego gathered the miraculous roses that he took to bishop Fray Juan de Zumárraga as proof of the Virgin's visit.

★★Capilla del Pocito – *At the bottom of Cerro del Tepeyac, east of the Basilica. Open year-round daily 8am–1:30pm and 4:30–7pm.* The location of the Chapel of the Little Well outside the Calzada de los Misterios, at that time the colonial city's boundary

La Ofrenda, Basilica of Guadalupe

Brian McGilloway © 1966

99

line, allowed architect Francisco de Guerrero y Torres more latitude in his design. The chapel is uniquely round; the outside walls an interplay of straight and curved lines, finished in a variety of rich, local typical materials-*tezontle*, quarry stone and tiles. The interior consists of three circular spaces: the vestibule where the miraculous well is located; the sacristy *(closed to public)*; and the nave, surrounded by four small chapels, each with paintings of the apparitions.

★**AVENIDA INSURGENTES**   *Map p 66* **(BYZ)**. *Recommended by car.*

Mexico City's second most important avenue, named in memory of the insurgent leaders of Mexican Independence (1810), is considered by some the longest avenue in the world (30.4km/18.9mi). Insurgentes traverses the city from north to south, from the exit to the Pachuca highway, on the northern end, to the junction of the Cuernavaca, Morelos highway on the southern end. The section that crosses the city center—from **Paseo de la Reforma** to **Ciudad Universitaria**—is full of businesses, stores, movie theaters, restaurants and galleries. Day and night this stretch of the famous avenue bustles with people, traffic and activity. Insurgentes crosses the gigantic traffic circle called **Glorieta de Insurgentes** leading to the **Zona Rosa**, while farther south it cuts through old residential neighborhoods with mansions built between 1920 and 1940. One of these, the **Colonia Roma** district, still survives despite the devastation of the 1985 earthquake; here visitors will find a replica of Michelangelo's *David* in the center of **Plaza Río de Janeiro**, and a multitude of cultural sites and cafes along Avenida Álvaro Obregón. The same is true for the **Colonia Condesa** neighborhood and its growing gourmet scene. French-style outdoor cafes and restaurants decorate many of its streets.
Past these two districts rises the **World Trade Center** *(open year-round daily 10am–7pm;* ✗ ☎ *56-28-83-00)*, a modern building with a revolving restaurant on the 43rd floor that offers a panoramic view of the whole city. Beside it stands the **Poliforum Cultural Siqueiros** *(open year-round daily 10am–7pm; P$10;* ☎ *55-36-45-20)* embellished by wonderful murals by David Alfaro Siqueiros.
Farther south, Insurgentes reaches the **Parque Hundido G. Urbina** with its pleasant garden, then moves on to the San Ángel district, featuring the Álvaro Obregón monument. Finally, the long avenue comes to the Ciudad Universitaria (University City), the archaeological site of Cuicuilco, the **Parque Ecológico Peña Pobre** (Peña Pobre Ecological Park) and the **Bosque de Tlalpan** (Tlalpan Forest)-after Chapultepec, Mexico City's second most important pair of lungs.

■ Speaking Walls: The Marvelous Murals of Mexico City

The members of the Mexican school of mural painting, founded by Diego Rivera, covered the walls of government buildings with powerful stylized Revolutionary art. Mexico City's treasures include works by the three greatest muralists, Diego Rivera, José Clemente Orozco and David Alfaro Siqueiros as well as a host of other masters of the art such as Rufino Tamayo, Juan O'Gorman, Alva de la Canal, Fernando Leal and Fermín Revueltas.

Palacio Nacional – On the walls of the main staircase, Diego Rivera painted, between 1929 and 1935, **La epopeya de México**★★★, a pictorial recount of the most important events in the history of the nation.

Iglesia de Jesús de Nazareno – On the ceiling above the choir, the **mural**★ *Apocalypse* (1942–44), by José Clemente Orozco, depicts the horrors of Wold War II.

Museo Nacional de las Culturas – Rufino Tamayo's 1938 mural of the Mexican Revolution adorns the entrance.

Secretaría de Educación Pública (SEP) – Diego Rivera decorated nearly 200 panels and these **murals**★★ are his first major commission on returning from his extended stay in Europe.

Antiguo Colegio de San Ildefonso – Three of the inner courtyards are adorned with beautiful **mural paintings**★★★ by David Alfaro Siqueiros, José Clemente Orozco, Fermín Revueltas, Ramon de Alva de la Canal, Jean Charlot and Fernando Leal.

Casa de los Azulejos – *Omnisciencia* (José Clemente Orozco, 1925).

Vips – *A Sunday afternoon at Xochimilco* (Miguel Covarrubias, 1947).

Palacio de Bellas Artes – This lavish building's decor includes several **murals**★★ by Rufino Tamayo (*Mexico Today*, 1953), Diego Rivera (*Man, the Controller of the Universe*, 1934), José Clemente Orozco *(La Katharsis*, 1935) and David Alfaro Siqueiros *(New Democracy*, 1945).

Museo Mural Diego Rivera – The building was commissioned to exhibit what many consider to be Diego Rivera's greatest work, his 1947 **mural**★★, *Dream of a Sunday Afternoon on the Alameda*. This work is unique as it portrays the painter himself, aged 9, and Frida Kahlo.

Museo Nacional de Historia – More murals by Juan O'Gorman, José Clemente Orozco and David Alfaro Siqueiros.

Tecpan – David Alfaro Siqueiros' dramatic *Cuauhtémoc Against the Myth* (1944).

Rectoría – From Avenida Insurgentes, motorists can see two huge colored-glass **murals**★★ by David Alfaro Siqueiros-*The People for the University* and *The University for the People*. A smaller mural located on the back of the building features the university emblems-the eagle and the condor.

Biblioteca Central – Juan O'Gorman created four **exterior murals**★★ using tiny natural, colored mosaics on paper and reinforced concrete.

Auditorio Alfonso Caso – Crystal mosaic and vinyl **murals**★ by José Chávez Morado.

Facultad de Medicina – Glass-mosaic **mural**★ by Francisco Eppens representing the four pre-Hispanic suns: air, fire, water and earth.

Estadio Olímpico – Diego Rivera's 1950's **mural**★ depicting sport from pre-Hispanic times to the present day.

Museo Dolores Olmedo Patiño – This museum exhibits the world's biggest and most important **private collection**★★★ of works by Diego Rivera and Frida Kahlo.

ZONA SUR

Map pp 66-67 **(BCZ)**

At one time villages linked to the city center by canals, many neighborhoods of the Zona Sur, though engulfed by urban sprawl, try to conserve a small-town atmosphere. Residents cling to their traditions by fighting to save their open spaces and their characteristic buildings as well as working to preserve their cobblestone streets and lanes, small family-owned stores, churches and markets.

★★COYOACÁN AND SURROUNDINGS

Map below. Ⓜ *line 3 – Coyoacán or Viveros.*

Uniquely traditional and picturesque, the historic center of Coyoacán is one of the favorite spots of Mexico City's inhabitants. On weekends, locals congregate to enjoy the many amenities the double central square and its environs offer. Take a stroll down the narrow winding streets of this ancient area accompanied by a good historian or storyteller to become familiar with its fascinating legends.

Coyoacán's rich history begins well before the Spaniards arrived, when it served as the seat of the Tepanecs, a tribe that paid tribute to the Mexicas. Lord of Coyoacán, Ixtolinque, offered his support to Hernán Cortés, allowing the Conquistador to establish the *Segundo Ayuntamiento* (Second City Council) in New Spain here in 1524.

Attracted by its combination of colonial architecture, ancient homes of Spanish conquistadors, and the provincial colors of its enclaves, artists, intellectuals and historical figures, both from Mexico and around the world have lived in Coyoacán. Cultural icons, such as Diego Rivera, Frida Kahlo and Leon Trotsky, had homes here that now operate as museums.

★**Avenida Francisco Sosa** – *Approach from Av. Universidad.* Enter Coyoacán along this avenue, beginning with the tiny 18C **Capilla de Panzacola** and the 1763 romantic **bridge** of the same name. One of the most typical and elegant avenues, Francisco Sosa is lined with handsome houses like the 18C **Casa de Alvarado**—located on the corner of Salvador Novo and erroneously attributed to one of Cortés' captains and restful nooks like the 18C **Plaza** and **Capilla de Santa Catarina**. Close by, the **Casa de la Cultura** invites visitors to roam its spacious gardens. At the end of the street, another misidentified building, the 18C **Casa de Ordaz**, shows off its Mudejar geometric designs.

★**Museo Nacional de la Acuarela Mexicana** – *Salvador Novo, 88 (half a block from Francisco Sosa), in the Barrio de Santa Catarina. Open year-round Tue–Sun 11am–6pm. Closed national holidays. Donations accepted.* ☎ *55-54-18-01.* Located on the grounds of a former private residence and surrounded by flower and sculpture gardens, the National Mexican Watercolor Museum exhibits magnificent works by great Mexican watercolorists. The permanent collection was a gift of its founder, Alfredo Guati, whose works are exhibited on the ground floor. A temporary exhibition gallery and a concert and conference auditorium lie at the end of the garden.

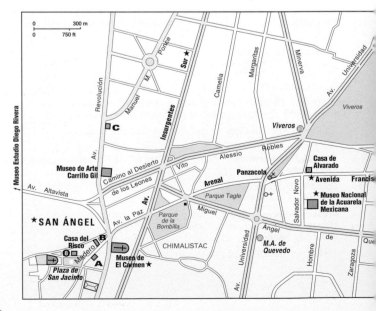

★**Jardín del Centenario** – *Plaza Central de Coyoacán between Calle Carrillo Puerto and Calle Centenario.* Named to commemorate the one hundredth anniversary of Mexican Independence, the lively central square in Coyoacán was originally the atrium of the Parroquia de San Juan Bautista. Its numerous restaurants, cafes, bookstores, ancient colonial buildings, and the **fuente** de los coyotes—a fountain that is the symbol of Coyoacán—create a charming environment.

7 Los Danzantes
Plaza Jardín Centenario, 12, Coyoacán. ☎ *56-58-64-51. (Reservations suggested).* In the small-town atmosphere of the busy Plaza de Coyoacán, this restaurant-bar featuring Mexican Nouveau Cuisine tempts the most demanding gourmets with its exotic menu.

Jardín Hidalgo – *Between Calles Hidalgo, Allende and Carrillo Puerto.* The bronze statue of Independence leader Father Miguel Hidalgo reigns over this garden that, together with Jardín Centenario, makes up the central square, or Zócalo, of Coyoacán. Important cultural and civic events take place regularly on the French-style bandstand, a permanent shelter for local pigeons.

Templo de San Juan Bautista – *Jardín Hidalgo, 8. Open year-round daily 6am–8pm.* Begun as part of a Dominican monastery built in the 16C, the church's facade, the pilgrim's archway, and the unusual Baroque arch (on the left side) are all that remain from the original. The rest of this structure was gradually trans-formed and almost completely rebuilt in the early 20C. The **interior**★ preserves remarkable colorful paintings and a lovely decorated cupola. The even more appealing **Capilla del Rosario** boasts an extraordinary Baroque 18C **altarpiece**★.

Delegación de Coyoacán (Palacio de Cortés) – *Jardín Hidalgo, 1.* ☎ *56-59-22-56 ext. 181.* Coyoacán's Municipal Hall is an outstanding 18C construction erroneously attributed to Hernán Cortés. Behind its terracotta facade, this notable example of colonial architecture has housed various government organizations.

Museo Nacional de Culturas Populares – *Av. Hidalgo, 289, half a block from Jardín Hidalgo. Open year-round Tue–Thu 10am–6pm, Fri–Sun 10am–8pm. Closed national holidays.* ✗ ☎ *55-54-50-30.* Housed in an old mansion, the National Museum of Popular Cultures was created to promote, through temporary exhibits, the vision and initiative of popular culture throughout Mexico. Special attractions consist of stagings of particular **events** that highlight Mexico's deepest traditions, such as the celebration of Day of the Dead and Christmas.

Plaza de la Conchita – *Bordered by Calles Vallarta, Presidente Carranza, Fernández Leal and Arturo Ibáñez.* Named for the vernacular of Concepción, "Conchita" refers to the **Capilla de la Purísima Concepción** (Chapel of the Immaculate Conception). The chapel, a small and popular Baroque jewel, sits amid tall trees and pretty gardens.

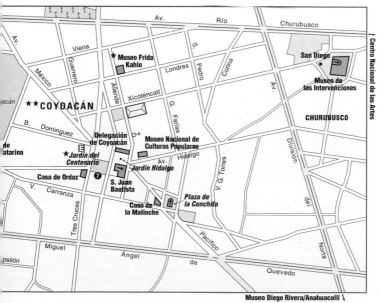

Museo Diego Rivera/Anahuacalli \

Zócalo of Coyoacán

Handsome old houses constitute the surrounding neighborhood, most especially the home associated with **la Malinche**, Cortés' lover and interpreter, though its construction dates from the 18C, two centuries after she lived.

★**Museo Frida Kahlo** – *Londres, 247, corner of Allende. Open year-round Tue–Sun 10am–5:45pm. Closed national holidays. P$10.* ✕ ☎ *55-54-59-99. No photographs allowed.* The "Blue House," where one of contemporary Mexico's most complex artistic personalities was born, grew up and died, now serves as a museum in her memory, with rooms maintained in the same arrangement and style as when the painter died. Frida Kahlo and Diego Rivera lived here from 1929 to 1954. Several of their works and those of their contemporaries, their belongings, letters, clothes and photographs give visitors a look into their everyday life, tastes and ideals. One can also gain insight into Frida's evolving personality during different stages of her life: from her rediscovery of the color and magic of popular traditions, her surrealism and her contact with the Communist Party, to the terrible pain caused by the accident that confined her to a wheelchair.

Barrio de Churubusco – *Map p 103.* Ⓜ *line 2 – General Anaya.* In this area of southern Mexico City lies the **Museo de las Intervenciones** or **Ex Convento de Churubusco** *(corner of 20 de Agosto and General Anaya; open year-round Tue–Sun 9am–6pm; P$16;* ☎ *56-04-06-99)* which holds paintings, lithographs, weapons, flags and other objects related to foreign interventions in Mexico from the 19C through the early 20C. Beside the museum stands the **Templo de San Diego** *(open year-round Mon–Fri 7am–1pm, Sat–Sun 7am–9pm)* which formed part of the Churubusco monastery and was founded in 1524. A restrained Baroque portal highlights the chapel of San Antonio, with its richly adorned tiles.

The **Centro Nacional de las Artes** *(on the corner of Av. Río Churubusco and Tlalpan; open year-round daily 8am–10pm;* ☎ *54-20-44-00)* was created as an interdisciplinary research center for the arts. Each school was specifically designed to suit the respective students' needs. The "José Limón Dance School," the Research Center, and the National School of Painting, Sculpture and Engraving rate as the most ingeniously designed buildings.

★**Museo Diego Rivera/Anahuacalli** – *Map p 67* (CZ). *Calle del Museo, 150, on the corner of Moctezuma. Take División del Norte heading south and turn right onto Árbol del Fuego; at the next light turn right. Open year-round Tue–Sun 10am–6pm. Closed national holidays. P$10.* ☎ *56-17-37-97.* This robust edifice, inspired by pre-Hispanic temples, consists of volcanic rock and onyx. Conceived by Diego Rivera to serve as his study, the building has been transformed into a museum that exhibits part of the artist's **collection** of pre-Hispanic artifacts from all over Mesoamerica.

★**SAN ÁNGEL** *Map p 102.*

The growth of this peaceful and elegant suburb, called Tenanitla by the pre-Hispanic inhabitants, stems from the establishment of the San Ángel Carmelite monastery here in the 17C. Its abundant rivers, tributaries of the Río Magdaleno, facilitated economic development in the 19C, turning it into a prosperous industrial area. Today, San Ángel is the hub of vigorous and quite sophisticated, cultural activities, thanks to the influence of centers like **Centro Cultural San Ángel (A)**, **Biblioteca de la Revolución Mexicana (B)**, and **Centro Cultural Helénico (C)**.

Enter by way of Calle **Arenal** to enjoy the rustic atmosphere of San Ángel, then stroll along its romantic cobblestone lanes to recapture images of bygone eras. Its flower-decked plazas, beckoning nooks, crosses and arches create an overall sensation of colonial grandiosity.

★**Museo de El Carmen** – *Av. Revolución, 4 and 6. Open year-round Tue–Sun 10am–4:45pm. Closed national holidays. P$16.* ☎ *55-50-48-96.* This museum is located in what was originally a monastery founded by the Discalced Carmelite priests in the 17C. The former monastery stands out for its exceptionally colorful **cupolas** and **chapels** finished in Talavera tile. The museum adjoins the church in the old cloister, and houses magnificent colonial art with noteworthy paintings by Villalpando and Correa. Areas that have preserved their original exquisite decoration include the **sacristy**, **sacristy vestibule** and **crypts** where the mummified bodies of friar benefactors are laid to rest.

Plaza de San Jacinto – *From Av. Revolución, go up either Calle Madero or Calle Amargura.* Named for its 16C **church**, the plaza comes to life on Saturdays when a multitude of artists and artisans converge for the **Bazar Sábado**. Around the plaza several restaurants offer a variety of special dishes.

Casa del Risco – *Plaza de San Jacinto, 15. Open year-round Tue–Sun 10am–5pm. Closed national holidays.* ☎ *56-16-27-11.* This attractive 18C residence boasts an exuberant Baroque **fountain**★, attached to the courtyard wall, and made from pieces of Chinese porcelain imported through the Philippines (in the famous ship, the *Manila Galleon*). Climb the stairs to see the magnificent **collection** of paintings from the Flemish, Italian, French, English and Neo-Hispanic schools of the 15C to 19C, as well as Mexican paintings from the 19C and 20C, Baroque sculptures and applied arts of European, Asian, Middle-Eastern and Mexican origin.

> **8 Bazar Sábado**
> *Plaza de San Jacinto, 11, San Ángel. Open Sat only 10am–7pm.* ✗ ☎ *56-16-00-82.* Located in an appealing 17C mansion restored by architect Manuel Parra, this crafts center gave rise to the **jardín del arte**, located in the square. Once a week since 1960, this area, set in the rich and beautiful San Ángel community, welcomes artists and artisans from Mexico and tourists from all over the world. Traditional and contemporary handicrafts of excellent quality are sold here.

Museo Estudio Diego Rivera – *On the corner of Diego Rivera and Altavista. Open year-round Tue–Sun 10am–6pm. Closed national holidays. P$10.* ☎ *55-50-15-18.* The museum-studio, built in 1931 by Juan O'Gorman, became the home of Diego Rivera and Frida Kahlo and exhibits various personal items of Rivera.

Museo de Arte Carrillo Gil – *Ave. Revolución, 1608 on the corner of Altavista, San Ángel. Open year-round Tue–Sun 10am–6pm. Closed national holidays. P$10.* ✗ ☎ *55-50-12-54.* This four-story modern edifice holds a permanent collection of some of Mexico's best contemporary visual artists, such as Rivera, Orozco and Siqueiros among others. It frequently hosts interesting temporary exhibits.

Return to Av. Revolución and head south (10min walk). On the corner of Eje 10 Sur and Revolución lies the Plaza Loreto.

Museo Soumaya – *Plaza Loreto, Av. Revolución and Río Magdalena. Open year-round Wed–Mon 10:30am–6:30pm. Guided tours, Sat 4pm & Sun 2pm. Closed Jan 1 and Good Friday. P$10.* ☎ *56-16-37-31.* This museum boasts a splendid collection of Mexican portraits dating from the 18C and 19C. Of special note are *Retrato de una señora*, by Juan Cordero, and *Retrato de un sacerdote*, by Hermenegildo Bustos. In the room dedicated to Neo-Hispanic art, the most outstanding works include *Meleagro y Atlanta*, by Miguel Cabrera, and *Los cuatro continentes*, by Juan Correa. The museum also exhibits one of the world's three greatest **collections**, and the first in Latin America, of works by the famous French sculptor Auguste Rodin, which includes works from all the projects and stages of his artistic production, such as *The Thinker* and *The Kiss*. This section also displays pieces by other artists from the 19C and 20C, such as Camille Claudel, Emile-Antoine Bourdelle, Degas and Honoré Daumier.

The museum's temporary exhibits room is located in the Plaza Cuicuilco, next to the archaeological site *(Plaza Cuicuilco. Insurgentes Sur, 3500. Open year-round Thu–Tue 10:30am–6:30pm. Closed Jan 1 & Good Friday.* ☎ *52-23-17-46).*

★CIUDAD UNIVERSITARIA AND SURROUNDINGS

Map p 66 **(ABZ)**. Ⓜ *Line 3 – Universidad.*

On January 25, 1553, by decree of King Charles V of Spain, the University of Mexico was founded with an annual endowment of one thousand pesos in pure gold. In 1910, thanks to the efforts of Justo Sierra, it became the National University of Mexico. From then on it was housed in a variety of places throughout the city. In 1929, after the Revolution, during the presidency of Portes Gil, the university achieved its autonomy (hence its full name, National Autonomous University of Mexico, or UNAM, the Spanish acronym). On May 20, 1952, the campus was finally inaugurated in an area called "Pedregal de San Ángel" on the lava of Xitle volcano, close to the Cuicuilco archaeological site.

Rectoría (Administration) (A) – *On Insurgentes Sur, going north.* The northern, southern and eastern facades of this remarkable building are embellished with colored-glass murals created by David Alfaro Siqueiros. Two of these **murals**★★, *El Pueblo a la Universidad y la Universidad al Pueblo* (The People for the University and the University for the People), in large-scale relief, were made expressly to be viewed by motorists traveling along Avenida Insurgentes.

Behind the building, at the fifth story level, a smaller mural covers the University Council area, featuring the eagle and the condor, the university emblems.

Biblioteca Central (Central Library) (B) – North side of the Torre de Rectoría (Administration Tower). Juan O'Gorman made four **exterior murals**★★ using tiny 1sq cm/0.4sq in natural, colored mosaics on paper and reinforced concrete. The south-

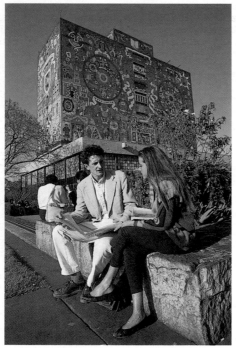

Biblioteca Central, Ciudad Universitaria

ern mural over the entrance portrays the influence of the western world, including the Spanish Conquest and Ptolemy's view of the universe. The northern mural portrays the pre-Hispanic world, the foundation of Tenochtitlán, and the gods of life and death. On the eastern facade, the artist depicts the Mexican Revolution and the modern world: the struggle of Francisco Villa, Emiliano Zapata and the Mexican peasants. The university emblem decorates the western side.

O'Gorman also created two **high reliefs** featuring pre-Hispanic motifs on the wall that separates the library building level from the rest of the campus.

Museo Universitario Contemporáneo de Arte (MUCA) (C) – *Across from the Central Library, beside the Torre de Rectoría. Open year-round Mon–Fri 10am–8pm, Sat–Sun 10am–6pm. Closed national holidays.* ☎ *56-22-04-00.* This museum, one of the first constructions of the Ciudad Universitaria, comprises seven halls of paintings, sculptures, multimedia, and various types of artistic expression-both national and international.

Auditorio Alfonso Caso (D) – *East of Torre de Rectoría, right after crossing the esplanade.* Artist José Chávez Morado embellished this building with three exterior murals: one with crystal mosaic and two in vinyl that, unfortunately, has been erased almost completely with the passing of time. The **front mural**★ presents the conquest of energy, from the discovery of fire to atomic fission. Originally, the other two vinyl murals portrayed the construction of the Ciudad Universitaria, together with Mexican scientists.

Toward the south side of the auditorium, past the Graduate School and inside the School of Industrial Design, a third mural by Chávez Morado, **El retorno de Quetzalcóatl**★ *(open Mon–Fri 8am–9pm; closed during UNAM's summer and winter* breaks; ☎ 56-22-08-35) portrays this pre-Hispanic god traveling in a ship with representatives of scientific endeavors from other cultures, including Greek and Arabic.

Facultad de Medicina (School of Medicine) (E) – *Eastern area of the Ciudad Universitaria, past the Alfonso Caso Auditorium.* Attached to the wall of the School of Medicine, Francisco Eppens created a glass mosaic **mural★** depicting the elements of nature, the four pre-Hispanic suns: air, fire, water and earth. It portrays three faces: the Spanish father, the indigenous mother, and the mestizo son.

To its left, in the courtyard across from the school's entrance, another mural, by Eppens, represents human progress through intelligence, spirit and culture.

Estadio Olímpico – *Opposite the Torre de la Rectoría, on the other side of Av. Insurgentes.* The Olympic Stadium, built in the 1950s, boasts an **exterior mural★** by Diego Rivera. Composed of pieces of colored stone, its images include the university emblem and the development of sport from pre-Hispanic times to the year of its creation.

One of the sites for the 1968 Olympic Games, the stadium has a capacity for 80,000 seated spectators. Its 42 wide tunnels allow it to empty in twenty minutes.

★**Jardín Botánico** – *On the outer beltway (Circuito Exterior) of the Ciudad Universitaria, beside the Olympic Stadium. Open daily 9am–4:30pm. Closed Jan 1, Maundy Thursday, Good Friday, Dec 25 and during UNAM's summer and winter breaks.* ☎ 56-22-90-63. The pleasant 7ha/17.3 acres that compose the ecological park are divided into five zones: dry, temperate, warm-humid, useful plants, and ecological reserve. Toward the arboretum, a small path on the right leads to the **invernadero Manuel Ruiz Oronoz★**, a greenhouse that contains plant varieties from the warm-humid zone. The **Faustino Miranda★ (F)** greenhouse *(same times & charges as the Jardín Botánico,* ☎ *56-22-90-47)* possesses a variety of tropical plants, which makes it unique in Mexico *(located in the eastern sector of the University, inside the inner beltway, Circuito Interior).*

★★**Centro Cultural Universitario** – *In the university's cultural zone, beside the Av. de la Imán.* Toward the end of the 1970s construction began on this modern architectural-cultural group of buildings, which contains almost every kind of artistic expression. It provides rooms for music, dance, cinema, live theater and research. The Cultural Center houses the **Biblioteca y Hemeroteca Nacional** (National Newspaper and Periodicals Library) *(open Mon–Fri 9am–8pm; closed national holidays and during UNAM's summer and winter breaks;* ☎ *56-22-68-13)*, which has a metal Tyrannosaurus rex hanging from the ceiling. Around the building, the **Espacio Escultórico** *(open year-round daily 9am–6pm;* ☎ *56-22-70-13)*, an open-air sculpture gallery features several interesting works-note especially, the creation in the form of a volcano **crater**.

Other notable artistic works include a replica of the Great Wall of China in volcanic stone, and a red metal sculpture that appears to break into four parts.

South of this area stands the **Sala de Conciertos Nezahualcóyotl** *(open only during performances;* ☎ *56-22-71-25)*, a concert hall built with textured concrete, glass and steel. Its layout of five horseshoe-shaped tiers surrounding the orchestra pit makes for an ample space with remarkable acoustics.

★★**Museo Universum** – *Within the "zona cultural" circuit of Ciudad Universitaria. Open year-round Mon–Fri 9am–5pm, Sat–Sun 10am–5pm. Closed Jan 1 and Dec 25. P$20.* ✗ ☎ *56-22-72-99.* Inaugurated in 1992, this "museum" is an interactive learning center spread over three buildings and 12 thematic halls. Topics cover the structure of matter, through chemistry and ecology, to human biology. It also offers workshops for children and adults, stages plays and shows movies and videos.

Cuicuilco – *Av. Insurgentes sur, south-north direction, close to intersection with Periférico. Open year-round daily 9am–5pm.* ☎ *56-06-97-58.* A four-layer circular pyramid, with a base 135m/443ft in diameter and a height of 20m/65.6ft, dominates this archaeological site. Considered the first monument constructed in the Valley of Mexico, it was discovered in 1922 by workers who were excavating volcanic stone from an explosion of the Xitle Volcano. The primitive culture that existed here belongs to the pre-Classic era, which reached its peak between the years 600 and 200 BC. The top of the pyramid contains an interior altar.

Site museum – This museum displays artifacts found during the excavations that unearthed Cuicuilco, as well as photographs of the excavations dating from 1922 onward. One of the walls features a mural by González Camarena depicting the explosion of Xitle.

The archaeological site is located inside the ecological reserve, allowing visitors to appreciate the flora.

TLALPAN AND XOCHIMILCO *Map p 66* (ABZ)

Tlalpan – *Approach on Calzada de Tlalpan toward the Cuernavaca exit; after San Fernando, turn right on Hidalgo (half a block from the Old Hacienda de Tlalpan restaurant).* During colonial times and even after Independence the festivals of Tlalpan, which included gambling, cockfights, and casinos supposedly attracted historic figures as famous as General Antonio López de Santa Anna. Presently, most of its expensive villas, now transformed into schools or research centers, still conserve the provincial atmosphere that characterizes this neighborhood. Close to the **Plaza de la Constitución** stands the 16C austere Baroque **Parroquia de San Agustín**. Located behind the Antiguo Palacio Municipal, the **market** constructed in the *Porfiriato* style now serves as an administrative building for the *delegación* (urban district) of Tlalpan. The pretty **Casa Chata** (Flat House) *(on the corner of Hidalgo and Matamoros),* with its rose-stone octagonal doorway, hosts a study center. The 18C **Casa de la Moneda**, or Mint *(corner of Moneda and Juárez),* housed the State Government Palace when Tlalpan was the capital of all of Mexico. From 1828 to 1830 the mint produced 203,544 gold pesos and 959,116 silver pesos. On the main facade, note the carved rose stone and the inverted arches that end in merlons.

> **9** **Antigua Hacienda de Tlalpan**
> *Calzada de Tlalpan, 4619.*
> 🅴 ☎ *56-55-78-88.*
> *(Reservations recommended).* During the first decade of the 20C, Porfirio Díaz used this attractive 18C construction as a place to relax. At present the old hacienda, nestled amid beautiful colonial-style gardens, prepares a wonderful menu of Mexican and international fine cuisine. Live music makes it a total pleasure for the senses.

Barrio de Xochimilco – This district, whose Náhuatl name means "on sown land of flowers", was originally an island, but during the pre-Hispanic period its inhabitants were able to link it to the mainland by means of mud causeways and a successful planting method called *chinampa*. Today, this method is still used to produce a wide variety of fruits, vegetables and, especially, flowers and plants. Xochimilco's inhabitants strive to keep their traditions alive through celebrations such as the Día de la Calendaria (Candlemas Day, Feb 2), when the villagers bless the baby Jesus, as well as the Flower Fair (Tue during Holy Week). The preferred meeting place for these festivities is the downtown area. Here, one finds the **Parroquia de San Bernardino** *(corner of 16 de Septiembre and Nuevo León; open year-round daily 7am–1pm & 4:30–8pm),* an austere, fortress-style monastic edifice built in 1590. The unusual side portal, in Plateresque style with indigenous influence, deserves careful attention. Inside, the 16C Baroque **altarpieces**, of gold-plated wood, should not be missed. Most outstanding is the **main altarpiece★**, which depicts scenes from the Passion of Christ and from the life of the Virgin Mary. A **mural painting** of St. Christopher decorates the section above the side arch.

Barges in Xochimilco

© Robert Frerck/Odyssey

Upon crossing the plaza across from the church, one finds, to the left, the **Capilla del Rosario** (*corner of José María Morelos and Fco. I. Madero; open year-round, Tue–Sun 9am–6pm*), which boasts intricate lacelike exterior work in stucco. Opposite the chapel, the bustling **Mercado de Xochimilco** attracts shoppers with a large selection of plants at reasonable prices every day of the week.

Xochimilco's downtown area is still surrounded by water avenues. The **trip along the canals**★ is most enjoyable, because not only does it provide an idea of Mexico's lacustrine origins, but it also takes place aboard the colorful and traditional **trajineras** (small barges). These navigate alongside other boats that offer refreshments and live Mexican music.

Jetties – *Open year-round Mon–Fri 9am–7pm, Sat–Sun 8am–8pm; P$5 (collective ride), P$50 (4 people), P$60 (6 people), P$80 (12 people) and P$100 (18 people) per barge per hour; night rides also available.* ✗ ▣ ☎ *56-76-08-10.* The most famous jetties are those of Cuemanco, whose main canal measures 1.2km/0.7mi and is used as an international rowing strip, and that of Nuevo Nativitas, complete with tourist services, restaurants and a handicraft market.

Behind the Parroquia de San Bernardino, the jetties of Salitre and Caltongo offer collective rides to Nuevo Nativitas.

★★ **Museo Dolores Olmedo Patiño** – *Av. México, 5843. No photographs allowed inside. Open year-round Tue–Sun 10am–6pm. Closed Jan 1, May 1, Sept 16 & Dec 25. P$20.* ✗ ☎ *55-55-08-91 or* www.arts-history.mx/museos/mdo/home.html. A few minutes from downtown Xochimilco lies this marvelous museum that bears the name of an enthusiastic art collector friend of Diego Rivera. It contains the world's largest and most important private **collection**★★★ of works by Diego Rivera and Frida Kahlo. The museum also displays paintings by Angeline Beloff-a Russian painter and first wife of Rivera-a collection of more than 600 pre-Hispanic artifacts-belonging to the Olmec, Mixtec, Zapotec, Totonac, Tarascan and Maya cultures-and a sampler of Mexican popular art.

This museum is located in the former, late-17C **Hacienda La Noria**, whose surface area totals 32sq km/19.8sq mi. Its gardens are home to a great variety of trees and plants native to Mexico, as well as peacocks and *xoloitzcuintles* (an endangered canine species), animals of pre-Hispanic origin.

Diego Rivera's collection includes *La tehuana*, a portrait of Dolores Olmedo, and *Las sandías*, the last work painted and signed by Rivera prior to his death. Also noteworthy are some of his pieces created during his sojourn in France, such as *Paisaje de Midi*, the *Retrato de Alberto J. Pani* and *El matemático*. From his Cubist period, the most outstanding work is the last one he created in this genre, *Cuchillo y fruta frente a la ventana*.

The room devoted to Frida Kahlo boasts some of the masterpieces of this controversial artist, such as *Mi nana y yo*, *La columna rota*, *Autoretrato con changuito* and *Unos cuantos piquetitos*, in which Frida portrays her cruel reality by means of different symbols.

The ✗ symbol indicates that eating facilities can be found on the premises of the sight.

EXCURSIONS FROM MEXICO CITY
Map pp 114-115

Universidad Autónoma de Chapingo

Mexico state. 40km/25mi east of Mexico City on the federal highway to Puebla, take the Texcoco exit and 700m/765yd past the road to Huexotla take the left turn into Chapingo.

In 1923, the **Escuela Nacional de Agricultura** (National School of Agriculture) took up residence at this prestigious hacienda in the Texcoco region *(museum open year-round Mon–Fri 9am–3pm; Sat–Sun 10am–5pm; chapel open year–round daily 10am–5pm; P\$8 for Mexicans & P\$25 for foreigners; ☎ 595-4-23-66 ext. 5189).* Invited to paint the walls of the ancient chapel in 1926, Diego Rivera transformed the space into the present day **Salón de Actos** (auditorium), creating a series of marvelous **murals★★★** where he illustrated his conception of land and labor. Upon entering, visitors may be taken aback by the picture of a naked pregnant woman, symbolizing the *Tierra fecundada* (Fertilized soil), hanging over the main altar. Along the side walls *(on the right)* he has depicted *La evolución natural del hombre* (The Natural Evolution of Man), *La germinación* (second panel) and *La floración* (Blossoming). On the way out, under the choir loft the *Tierra virgen* (Virgin Soil) continues the fertility of the land theme with a woman bearing a flowering seed in her hand. Rivera decorated the vault lunettes with male nudes. His female models included the photographer Tina Modotti for *Tierra virgen* and his then wife, Lupe Marín, for *Tierra fecundada.*

Near Chapingo lies **Chiconcuac** *(5km/3mi northeast along Carr. 142; passing San Miguel market take the unnamed street on the left for 1.5km/0.9mi),* popular in winter for its woolen clothes' market; its sweaters and warm jackets are very famous, as well as its *sarapes* (blanket-like shawl usually worn by men) and rugs.

Ex Convento de Azcapotzalco

Av. Azcapotzalco, east of Jardín Hidalgo. Open year-round daily 7am–1pm & 4:30–8pm. ☎ 55-61-04-53.

Built around 1565 under the direction of Fray Lorenzo de la Asunción, this Dominican monastery lies nestled in the heart of the ancient Tepanec capital, the leading settlement in the Valley of Mexico before the Aztecs. Remnants of its original decoration include coffered ceilings and paintings in the cloister, and an illustration of Dominican saints on the entrance gate. The church was partially remodeled with elegant Baroque decorations in the 18C, as can be seen on its front portal. A 17C altarpiece dedicated to Santa Rosa de Lima adorned with **paintings** by Villalpando embellishes the right side of the interior.

Four large gilded altarpieces and two exceptional 18C corner altarpieces adorn the **Capilla del Rosario**, located on the left side of the nave. The chapel contains an outstanding central altarpiece, dedicated in 1779 to Our Lady of the Rosary. Its ultra-Baroque ornamentation, in which the columns melt away into decorative motifs, complements its exquisite burnished sculptures. **Paintings** by Juan Correa (1674–1739) decorate the right transept consecrated to the Virgin Mary.

Parque Nacional Desierto de los Leones

D.F. 20km/12.5mi west on Carr. 15 toward Toluca; or by Periférico Sur, 23km/14.3mi on Calzada del Desierto de los Leones. Open year-round daily 6am–5pm. ▣ ✗.

A favorite of the locals because of its proximity to Mexico City, this national ecological park is usually frequented by families for weekend picnics and excursions. Here, imaginations take flight and curiosity leads visitors to venture along pine and oak-lined enchanted paths, through hills and hollows to sights such as the former **Convento Carmelita** *(open year-round Tue–Sun 10am–5pm; open Mon during university vacations; closed national holidays; P\$2, by car P\$10; ✗ ☎ 55-70-31-58).* The 17C rambling, rugged stone edifice with sections arranged around a series of labyrinthine inner courts and **gardens** allowed the friars of the Carmelite monastery to lead lives dedicated to meditation. Its eastern courtyard allows access to the cold dark cellars that served as the monastery's foundations and water system. Outside, at the end of the garden, lies the **Capilla de los Secretos** (Chapel of Secrets) so called, perhaps, because secrets cannot be kept there: a whisper in one corner can be heard clearly in the other three.

Teotihuacán★★★

Mexico state. 46km/28.5mi. Go northeast on Carr. 130D toward Pachuca and later take the exit for México-Pirámides. Description p 142.

Museo Nacional del Virreinato
de Tepotzotlán★★★

Mexico state. 41km/25.5mi. Go north on Carr. 57D México-Querétaro, and after 38km/23.5mi take a right-hand turn (before the tollbooth) toward Tepotzotlán. Description p 146.

Xochicalco★★

Morelos state. 127km/79mi. Go south on Carr. 95D toward Cuernavaca; after 38km/23.5mi on Autopista del Sol, turn off at Alpuyeca and continue another 15km/9.3mi. Description p 157.

Malinalco★

Mexico state. 105km/65mi. Go southwest on Carr. 15D to Toluca (64km/40mi); then take Carr. 55D south toward Ixtapan de la Sal; at Tenancingo take a left and continue 14km/8.7mi to Malinalco. Description p 123.

Cuernavaca★

Morelos state. 89km/55.3mi. Go south on Carr. 95D. Description p 119.

Tula

Hidalgo state. 98 km/61mi. Take the Querétaro highway; at km69.5/mi43 on toll highway 57D take a right toward Tepeji del Río and continue 25km/15.5 to Tula. Description p 155.

SEVEN DAYS IN MEXICO CITY

Day 1

Centro Histórico – Tour ⒈ Plaza de la Constitución and surroundings *(p 68)*.

Day 2

Centro Histórico – Tour ⒉ Templo Mayor and surroundings *(p 74)*.

Day 3

Excursion – Teotihuacán *(p 142)*.

Day 4

Museo Nacional de Antropología – *(p 90)*.

Day 5

Centro Histórico – Tour ⒊ Santo Domingo and surroundings;

Tour ⒋ Madero and surroundings *(pp 76 & 79)*.

Day 6

Excursion – Museo Nacional del Virreinato in Tepotzotlán *(p 146)*.

Day 7

Zona Sur – Ciudad Universitaria, Coyoacán or Xochimilco *(p 102)*.

CENTRAL MEXICO

Land of Aztecs, Monasteries, Haciendas and Colonial Cities

Handicrafts and Food, p 49. Recognized as the cradle of power of the Aztecs and home to several of the most significant indigenous cultures of present-day central Mexico, the region also possesses a great number of cities established during the colonial period. Many of these cities still preserve their Spanish-style architecture, through structures built by indigenous hands.

The imposing pyramids of Teotihuacán, the beautiful sloping walls and vertical panels of Xochicalco and Yohualichan, nestled in the lush Puebla mountain range enchant and entice visitors to explore the region's magical mysteries.

Each state in central Mexico has its own particular character: Puebla, extraordinary Talavera ceramics; Morelos, clay pottery and wood cottages; Querétaro, a monumental aqueduct; Tlaxcala and Hidalgo, polychrome woodwork; and Mexico state, colorful textiles.

Typical delicacies include *cecina* (jerked meat), *empanadas* (fruit or meat pastries), *chiles en nogada* (peppers in sauce of pounded walnuts and spice), *mole poblano* (chili sauce with chocolate and peanuts), and a wide variety of sweets and candies.

The festivities of *Día de Muertos* (Day of the Dead), *Carnaval* and Holy Week, and other national celebrations highlight the region's jubilant calendar of events.

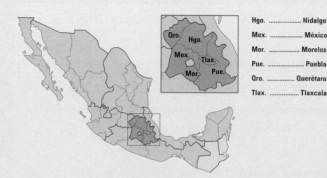

Hgo.	Hidalgo
Mex.	México
Mor.	Morelos
Pue.	Puebla
Qro.	Querétaro
Tlax.	Tlaxcala

Templo de la Virgen de los Remedios and Popocatépetl, Cholula

CACAXTLA-XOCHITÉCATL

Tlaxcala

Map of Principal Sights – Map p 151

🛈 ☎ (2) 462-0952

These two archaeological sites lie atop two hills less than 2km/1.3mi apart. Over 2,300 years old, Xochitécatl, "the place from which flowers descend," began to develop in 600 BC, before Cacaxtla, which was built around AD 550. More than 1,000 years ago, at the end of the Classic period, these two centers held sway over the neighboring farming villages.

CACAXTLA

Head toward the southwest of Tlaxcala via Carr. 119; from the University take a right toward Nativitas; after 18km/11.2mi, passing Nativitas, take a right and climb 1.5km/0.9mi to reach the Cacaxtla site parking area; continue on foot another 1km/0.6mi. Open year-round daily 10am–5pm. P\$14. ✕ ☎ (2) 462-0952.

A **site museum** at the entrance briefly describes the region's ancient history. Apparently from Campeche, Xicalanc-Olmec culture reached its peak during the Late Classic period (AD 600–900), and held sway over the entire Puebla-Tlaxcala valley. Located on a major commercial route, the region reflects influences left by Teotihuacán, Mixtec-Zapotec, Totonac and Maya traders.

Located on a hill protected by natural ravines, the site's broad earth foundation measures 200m/656ft x 110m/360ft, and 25m/82ft high. A metal roof protects the ruins of structures and palaces built around a central plaza. Among the vestiges can be found mural paintings, whose discovery-the fortunate outcome of a 1975 robbery—is considered one of the most important archaeological finds of Mesoamerica in the 20C.

★★★ **Mural paintings** – Executed in tempera with vegetable and animal pigments that include deep cochineal red and a complex blue, called *Maya blue* composed of indigo, these mural paintings are considered the largest in Mesoamerica and are surprisingly well preserved. *(Beginning tour around the corridors of the archaeological site, the paintings are in the following order.)*

113

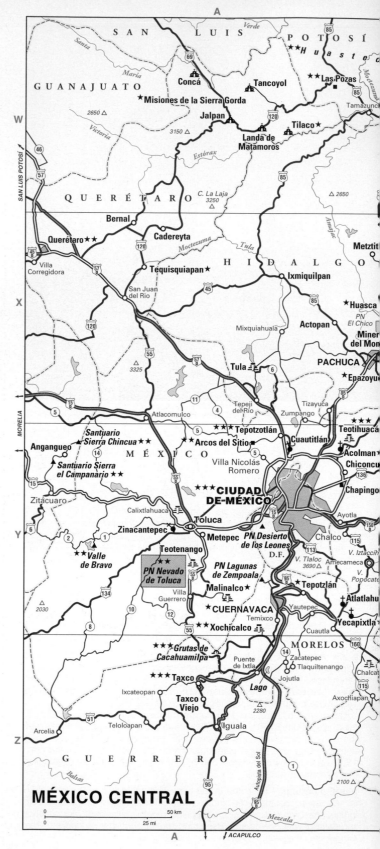

MÉXICO CENTRAL

0 ____ 50 km
0 ____ 25 mi

114

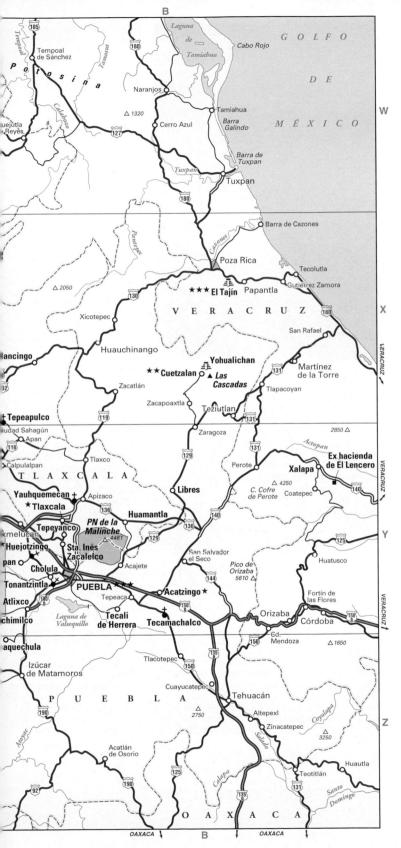

115

Bird Man, detail

© Bob Schalkwijk

Templo de Venus – *From the west corridor.* Two paintings on columns represent human figures, their bodies painted blue, the color of Tláloc, the rain god. Around the female figure, a series of white stars, split in half, refer to the planet Venus. The male figure wears a mask with protruding eyes while the yellow shape of a scorpion, the death symbol, appears between his legs.

Templo Rojo – Named for the predominant red of the painting beside the stairway, the temple presents a representation of a corn plant with human heads instead of corncobs. Under the plant runs a stream with a variety of sea creatures and a blue toad, a cacao tree, an unidentified tropical bird, and a lavishly dressed elder, considered a trader because of the load he carries. His number and glyph designate him as *Señor 4 Perro* (Lord 4 Dog).

El Mural de la Batalla – *Located in front of the central plaza.* The 22m/72ft-long Battle Mural, painted between AD 650 and 700, describes the battle between the jaguar-warriors and the bird-warriors. One interpretation suggests it portrays the conflict between two tribes that joined forces, thus giving birth to the Olmecs-Xicalancas.

Pórtico "A" – Beyond the Battle Mural, two murals appear in what was the first excavation site: **jaguar man** on the left, and **bird man** on the right holding a blue, serpent-shaped ceremonial stick. On one of the jambs, a rough, red stucco relief reveals—as do the other paintings—a marked influence of the Maya and Teotihuacán cultures.

XOCHITÉCATL

From Cacaxtla, return to the road and go west 2.5km/1.6mi; at San Miguel village take a right and climb 1.5km/.9mi to Xochitécatl. Same times and charges as Cacaxtla.

At the summit of the highest hill in the Puebla-Tlaxcala valley rest the recently discovered ruins of Xochitécatl, a site probably dedicated to the worship of Xóchitl, goddess of flowers and fertility. Archaeologists have successfully reconstructed three structures and a platform that divides two plazas. Dedicated to Ehácatl the wind god, the **spiral building**, a circular structure so named because researchers believe a spiral staircase winding around the exterior provided the means for reaching the top, was probably used as an astronomical observatory. Across from the **volcanic base**, which constitutes the great central square, stands the **Pirámide de las Flores**, the largest pyramid at this site and the fourth largest in all of Mexico. Inside, the remains of 30 children and one adult were found, as well as two huge stone monoliths. At the top remains part of a doorway that may have belonged to a temple that crowned the pyramid.

The buildings were constructed in 650 BC and remained occupied until the post-Classic era. During the Late Classic period this site was a contemporary of Cacaxtla; thus, they shared the same architectural and ceramic features.

The ▣ *symbol indicates that on-site parking is available.*

CHOLULA

Puebla
Population 45,872
Map of Principal Sights – Map p 115 **(BY)**
🏛 4 Poniente, 103 ☎ (2) 247-3393

A center of religious worship since pre-Hispanic times, Cholula lies at the foot of an enormous pyramid crowned by a church, a symbol of the region's cultural syncretism and Spanish domination. According to legend, when Hernán Cortés arrived here during the Conquest he thought he saw a great number of towers and domes and exclaimed with astonishment to have seen "as many as the days in a year." Hence, the myth that Cholula had 365 churches, when in reality, it possesses only 39.

Historical Notes – Founded by immigrant Toltecs fleeing from Tula, Cholula, whose Náhuatl name means "place of flight," became one of Mesoamerica's principal religious centers. After 25 centuries of continuous occupation, this city, now the oldest in Mexico, has endured as a sacred place despite events such as the 1519 massacre and pillaging ordered by Cortés.

Due to the damages caused by the earthquake of June 1999, many of Cholula's churches may not have been repaired yet or may have closed indefinitely.

SIGHTS

Plaza Principal – This extensive square boasts a 47-arch arcade and the city hall to its west, to the northwest the Parish Church of St. Peter, founded by Bishop Palafox in the 17C, and to the southeast the 16C Monastery of St. Gabriel. Local families and visitors enjoy the plaza's convivial atmosphere on Sundays.

Convento de San Gabriel – *2 Sur, between Av. Morelos and 4 poniente. Open year-round daily 8am–3pm & 5–8pm.* Founded by the Franciscan friars in 1529, the Monastery of St. Gabriel was erected between 1549 and 1552 on top of a temple to the Aztec god, Quetzalcóatl. Inside, the church displays its remarkable Gothic ribs, adapted later to reflect the influence of 19C Neoclassicism, while the battlements of its exterior reflect monastic-military characteristics.

★★Capilla Abierta (Capilla Real) – *East of the Monastery of St. Gabriel. Open year-round daily 7am–1:30pm & 4–8pm.* This 16C open-air chapel with the regal connotation "Royal Chapel," also called the "Chapel of Indians," boasts 64 columns and 49 cupolas, as well as nine arches, of which only three are still accessible. Reminiscent of Arab mosques built in Spain, the chapel preserves an ample atrium shaded by ancient trees.

Archaeological site – *Photo p 113. South of the main plaza. Follow signs for "zona arqueológica." Open year-round daily 10am–5pm. P$14.* At the time of the Conquest, Cholula was an important trading hub and center for the worship of Quetzalcóatl. The various stages of its construction can be observed through tunnels designed by archaeologists. The last stage, measuring 400m/1,312ft wide and 65m/213ft high, is crowned by the **Templo de la Virgen de los Remedios** (Our Lady of Remedies), a church symbolizing colonial religious syncretism. To the south lies the **Plaza de los Altares**, a space surrounded by *taludes* (sloping walls) surmounted by *tableros* (vertical panels), and dotted with remarkable altar-plaques. The site dates from 4–6C AD. Opposite this square a Mexica offering with human remains and 15C pottery are on display. From the top of the pyramid, there is a splendid view of the surroundings.

EXCURSIONS

★Iglesia de Tonantzintla – *3km/1.8mi southwest of Cholula; take Av. Miguel Alemán and continue on the highway until you reach Tonantzintla. Open year-round daily 7am–6pm.* This quaint church, dedicated to the Immaculate Conception of the Virgin Mary, is one of the jewels of Mexican ornate Baroque. Affectionately called "our dear little mother" by the locals, the church possesses a beautiful **facade★** of brick and tile. Note the impressive decorative work on the columns that support the towers, as well as the polychrome sculptures that appear to be squatting in the niches. The **interior★★★**, an incredible blend of architectural styles, is a veritable syncretistic sampler of Spanish ideas, Christian beliefs, and indigenous color, produced by the artful hands of native builders. On the vault and walls, an elaborate foliage design on gilt stucco weaves images of angels, saints, and plant motifs into a depiction of the Immaculate Conception. The canopy over the Virgin is extraordinarily beautiful, as are the carved and gilded wooden altarpieces.

© Bob Schalkwijk

Iglesia de San Francisco Acatepec, detail

Iglesia de San Francisco Acatepec – *1km/0.6mi south of Tonantzintla. Open year-round daily 9am–6pm.* This late-18C church presents a multicolor Talavera tile **facade★★** with Solomonic (spiral) columns and fluted cornices that lend movement to the tower. The exquisite craftsmanship makes it unique among all Mexican Baroque creations and the greatest achievement of Puebla artisans.

The interior has plasterwork similar to Tonantzintla's, but without the excess of colors. Baroque altarpieces adorn the transept, and Solomonic columns wreathed in angels and plants grace the apse.

Iglesia de Tlaxcalancingo – *3km/1.9mi south of Acatepec on Carr. 19 towards Puebla. Open year-round daily 6am–9pm.* This church possesses a lovely **facade★** decorated with Talavera tiles in a diamond arrangement combined with red brick in a geometric design. The tower, composed of pale Corinthian columns and blue and yellow tiles, enlivens its relative austerity.

★★Ex Convento Franciscano, Huejotzingo – *15km/9.3mi northwest on Carr. 190. Open year-round Tue–Sun 10am–5pm. P$17.* One of the best examples of 16C monastic architecture in Mexico, the monastery of St. Francis was built by the local indigenous people under the direction of Fray Juan de Alameda and completed in 1570. Its height may betray the fact that the monastery was built on top of a pyramid base.

The **main facade** combines several styles: Gothic, the flattened arch of the entrance; Mudejar, the panel of the choir window; and Renaissance, the remainder of the structure. The side portal, called *porciúncula*, is one of the most appealing parts of the building.

Inside, the thick walls and limited openings of translucent *tecali* stone allow in just enough light to bathe the altarpiece in an amber light, creating a mystical ambiance reminiscent of medieval Romanesque cathedrals. A 16C **gilded wooden altarpiece★★**, one of the few remaining in Mexico, and paintings by the Flemish painter Simon Pereyns decorate the interior. The walls contain traces of mural paintings.

The **cloister**, now a museum, features mural paintings in several rooms; note especially those located in the *De profundis* hall with portraits of the first twelve friars and scenes from the life of Saint Francis of Assisi. On the lower level, the refectory and kitchen offer a glimpse of the friars' daily life, while upstairs the cells or dormitories of the monks, a collection of sculptures once dispersed throughout the cloister, and a photo collage describing Franciscan expansion in the region testify to their spiritual and administrative activities.

The **corner chapels★★**, on which the Blessed Sacrament rested during processions, figure among the most beautiful in Mexico. They are richly embellished with reliefs of angels, each one carrying a symbol that depicts a scene from the Passion of Christ.

Calpan – *11km/6.8mi southwest of Huejotzingo along a road bordered by a verdant landscape.* Calpan, a diminutive town, is located at the foot of the Popocatépetl and Iztaccíhuatl volcanoes. The **Ex Convento de San Andrés Calpan** *(open year-round Mon–Fri 5pm–8pm; Sat–Sun 9am–8pm; if closed, inquire within)*, a primitive construction built in 1548, features one of the most handsome facades in the state of Puebla. Note the two angels holding the Franciscan coat of arms, the mullion window, and the columns crowned by flowering maguey. Its **corner chapels★★** *(photo p 37)* display a variety of motifs, such as the *Virgen de los Dolores* (Our Lady of Sorrows), the *Anunciación*, and *Cristo Juez* (Christ Triumphant) bringing the dead back to life at the sound of angelic trumpets.

Consult the practical information section at the end of the guide for details on annual events, sports, recreation, restaurants, shopping and entertainment.

CUERNAVACA★

Morelos
Population 316,782
Map of Principal Sights – Map p 114 (AY)
🖪 Av. Morelos Sur, 187, Col. Las Palmas ☎ (7) 314-3872

Traversed by steep and narrow streets, the "city of eternal spring" has long been the favorite destination of great numbers of Mexican and foreign tourists who come to enjoy its exotic flowers, warm climate and colonial flavor. The favorite summer residence of Hernán Cortés, Cuernavaca became the site of his principal country estate in Morelos *(El Palacio de Cortés)* when he was named the Marquis of the Oaxaca Valley.

The irregularly designed city now boasts modern public services, magnificent residences surrounded by carefully landscaped gardens, and even a small archaeological site, **Teopanzolco**, the home of an ancient Tlahuic settlement.

Historical Notes – In pre-Hispanic times, the Náhuatl tribe of Tlahuics, coming from the legendary Aztlán, called this city **Cuauhnahuac**, meaning "beside the grove." The Spanish changed its name to "Cuernavaca." After serving as the administrative center of the Marquisate of the Valley of Oaxaca during colonial times, in 1834 it received the title of city. Cuernavaca fleetingly became capital of Mexico in 1855, and presently is capital of the state of Morelos. This proud region was also the cradle of the Mexican Revolution led by Emiliano Zapata in the early 20C.

MONASTERY COMPLEX AND SURROUNDINGS

Conjunto Conventual (Ex Convento Franciscano) – *On the corner of Hidalgo, 17 and Av. Morelos. Open year-round daily 7am–2pm & 4–7pm.* A leafy atrium with a crenellated wall encloses the monastery complex; most noteworthy is the ample **open-air chapel**, with a continuous, half-barrel vaulted dome and flying buttresses.

Catedral de la Asunción de María – *Open year-round daily 7am–2pm & 4–7pm. P$10 (to climb the tower; Wed–Mon 8am–2pm & 4–7pm).* Completed in 1552 as the fifth Franciscan building complex in New Spain, this monastery church, now Cuernavaca cathedral, exemplifies a successful remodeling (1957): the sober original elements of the building harmoniously combine with the modern. In the **interior★**, gilded altars, discrete architectural lines and simple stained-glass windows in warm colors create a pleasant atmosphere. Delicately painted **murals★** describing the crucifixion in Japan of the 16C Mexican saint, San Felipe de Jesús, and the 26 martyrs are the principal liturgical motif. The main facade is devoid of ornamentation, and a simple portal adorns the **side entrance**.

The **ex claustro** (cloister), a plain 16C building, consists of two floors in which elaborate red and black mural paintings have been preserved. Its corridors contain a series of frescoes. The portals of the 18C Baroque **Capilla de la Tercera Orden** (Chapel of the Third Order of Saint Francis), revealing popular influence, possess a fine mortarwork finish. Even more remarkable, the **side portal** displays a beautiful arched entryway. Inside, an admirable Churrigueresque gilded **altarpiece**, with exquisite sculptures, merits attention.

★**Museo Robert Brady (Casa de la Torre)** – *Nezahualcóyotl, 4, beside the cathedral. Open year-round Tue–Sun 10am–6pm. Closed national holidays. P$20.* ✗ ☎ *(7) 318-8554.* Housed in part of the monastery complex that by the end of the 19C became the bishop's residence, this colorful museum exhibits **paintings**, sculptures, tapestries, ceramics and furniture from a variety of periods and cultures. The artist Robert Brady combined similar elements to adorn this impeccable house-museum achieving unusual combinations; for example, glass-bead Huichol doves accompany a glass-bead table from Cameroon.

Jardín Borda – *Av. Morelos, 271, opposite the cathedral. Open year-round Tue–Sun 10am–6pm. P$5.* ✗ ☎ *(7) 312-9237.* This peaceful wooded refuge was inherited in the 18C by Don Manuel de la Borda, the son of a rich Spanish Taxco miner, who turned it into a botanical garden and recreation park. In the 19C Emperor Maximilian and his wife, Carlota, made it their country home. Decorated with a series of canvases by Tarazona bearing witness to its imperial history, the house currently hosts important cultural activities as headquarters of the Morelos Cultural Institute. In the Juárez section, the site museum presents aspects of the historic panorama of Morelos and exhibits temporary art shows.

Museo Regional Cuauhnáhuac (Palacio de Cortés) – *Opposite the main plaza (Zócalo). Open year-round Tue–Sun 10am–5pm. P$14.* ☎ *(7) 312-8171.* Built over a pre-Hispanic structure, this colossal **work★** of 16C secular architecture at one time belonged to Cortés, hence its former name of *Palacio de Cortés*. The greatly altered palace now houses a museum with interesting archaeological material, documents, armor, furniture and other objects that illustrate the major phases of Morelo's history. On the upper-level's rear terrace hangs a **mural**★ (1927–30) by Diego Rivera, recounting Mexican history from the time of the Conquest to the Mexican Revolution in which the figures of Cortés, Emiliano Zapata and Morelos predominate. Beside the museum, a *tianguis*, an open-air street market of Mexican handicrafts, entices prospective shoppers.

ADDITIONAL SIGHTS

Jardín Etnobotánico and Museo de Medicina Tradicional – *Matamoros, 14, Col. Acapatzingo. Opposite the church of San Miguel de Acapatzingo. Open year-round daily 9am–4:30pm (museum 9am–3pm).* ☎ *(7) 312-5955.* Once Emperor Maximilian's country estate, this large villa is now used by the INAH-Morelos (local branch of the Mexican National Institute of Anthropology and History).

The small **museum** occupies what was originally the **Casa de la India Bonita** (House of the Pretty Indian Girl), home of one of the emperor's supposed paramours. Its enormous **garden** possesses the most important collection of medicinal plants in Latin America, with each specimen classified by name and use.

La Tallera Casa Estudio de David Alfaro Siqueiros (Studio of Siqueiros) – *Venus, 52, Col. Jardines de Cuernavaca. Open year-round Tue–Sun 10am–5pm. P$5.* ☎ *(7) 315-1115.* The famous muralist created his last works here, his residence during the last ten years of his life. Documents, murals and artists' tools have been preserved, along with photo portraits of the maestro. All his personal belongings have been kept as they were at the moment of his death.

Santuario de Tlaltenango – *Av. Emiliano Zapata, 302, Barrio de Tlaltenango. Open year-round Mon–Fri 9am–2pm, Sat–Sun 9am–1pm.* Two churches comprise the Shrine of Tlaltenango: San Jerónimo, completed in 1523 and considered to be the first chapel built on the American continent, and Nuestra Señora de los Milagros (Our Lady of the Miracles) distinguished by its Baroque facade.

The *fiesta de Tlaltenango*, the biggest in the state of Morelos, takes place on the grounds around these two churches.

Jungla Mágica (Magical Jungle) – *Bajada de Chapultepec, 27, Col. Chapultepec. Open Jul–Aug daily 11am–7pm; the rest of the year Thu–Sun 11am–7pm. P$14.* ✗ ☎ *(7) 315-8411.* The former Chapultepec Park welcomes visitors to its leafy walks and the soothing murmur of its stream. A dolphin pool, a bird theater and other amusements also provide enjoyment.

EXCURSIONS

Lagunas de Zempoala – *25km/15.5mi. Go north from Cuernavaca on Carr. 95 toward Mexico City and after 11km/6.8mi take a left, continue 4km/2.5mi to Huitzilac and go across the town; turn left, continue 10km/6.2mi west on the highway toward Santa Marta, until you reach Zempoala Lagoons National Park. The entrance is on the left of the highway.* "The place of many waters," Zempoala consists of six lagoons, two of which are permanent, the others, closed basins that flood in the rainy season. The **journey** itself to Zempoala offers beautiful, partial views of the Valley of Cuernavaca and provides charming sites for outings.

In this beautiful area, covered by the **Parque Nacional Lagunas de Zempoala**, the majesty of the Sierra Chichinautzin, the turquoise colors of the lagoons, and the shades of green of the surrounding woods make for fascinating vistas.

★★**Xochicalco** – *42km/26mi southwest. Description p 157.*

Ex Hacienda de San José Vista Hermosa and Lago de Tequesquitengo – *Go south from Cuernavaca 20km/12.5mi on toll road 95D toward Acapulco and take the Tequesquitengo–Alpuyeca Exit; continue 4km/2.5mi toward Tequesquitengo, bear right and go 5km/3mi toward Tequesquitengo; take a right on the gravel road and go 1km/0.6mi to the entrance of the Hacienda de San José Vista Hermosa.*

★**Ex Hacienda de San José Vista Hermosa** – *Open year-round daily 24hrs.* ✗ ▤ ☎ *(7) 345-5361.* Built in 1529 by Hernán Cortés, this prosperous hacienda was later inherited by his son, Martín, who spent long periods here. It has served many other purposes—as a rice plantation, a monastery, and a sugar plantation. During the Mexican Revolution, Zapata divided it among the peasants. The **homestead** *(casco)* still preserves its great chimneys, dungeons, and rooms with traces of mural paintings, as reminders of its golden days. One of the rooms houses a permanent exhibit of old carriages and two large canvases. Today, the hacienda operates as a hotel with pretty gardens, appealing nooks and a rodeo ring called a *lienzo charro*.

Lago de Tequesquitengo – *From Hacienda San José return to the highway and turn right; after 5km/3mi you will reach Lake Tequesquitengo.* Bordered by handsome houses and recreation centers for water sports, the lake challenges experienced skin-divers to battle its currents and murky waters as they discover the old town church that was covered by floods in the 19C and lies at its bottom.

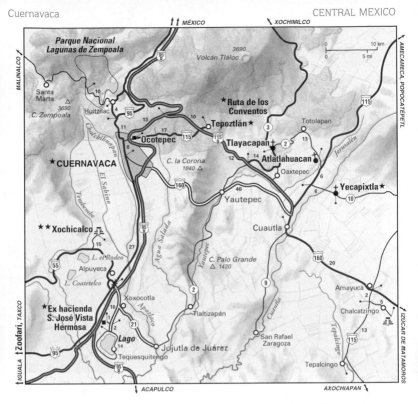

Zoofari – *55km/34mi. Go south from Cuernavaca on Carr. 95 toward Taxco. Open year-round daily 9am–5pm. P$50.* ✗ ▣ ☎ *(7) 320-9794.* From the safety of the car, observe more than 1,000 animals from 150 species at this entertaining zoo.

Cementerio de Ocotepec – *From the city center, go 8km/5mi northwest on old Carr. 115 toward Tepoztlán. Open year-round daily 24hrs.* ☎ *(7) 314-3872.* In this picturesque place, death turns merry as the majority of tombs display different versions of miniature churches painted in bright colors and covered with multicolored mosaics—an example of popular funerary art. The celebration of the **feast** of Día de los Muertos (Day of the Dead, Nov 1–2) can be a very lively occasion.

★**Tepoztlán** – *Take the old Tepoztlán Carr. 115 for 26km/16mi.* Tepoztlán is a delightful little town situated at the foot of an enormous **sierra**★★ of unusual geological formation. The region's temperate climate creates a favorable habitat for bright red *colorín* trees, poincianas, plum trees and jacarandas that fill the town's quiet cobbled streets with a blaze of color. The famed Tepoztlán **carnival**★ (held between Feb and March) includes games such as the *danzas de brinco de los chinelos* (hop dance). The original inhabitants were related to the Xochimilc race and were forced into submission by the Spaniards in 1521, just before the fall of Tenochtitlán. North of the town, at the top of Tepozteco hill, in memory of a local god of the ancient inhabitants, sits the fascinating archaeological site of **Tepozteco** *(open year-round daily 9am–6pm, P$14; free Sun and national holidays;* ☎ *7-312-5955).* Tepoztlán owed its development to the production of paper made from the *amate* tree, which is still sold on Sundays in its famous *tianguis* (open-air market) held in the city center.

The 16C fortress-like **Ex Convento de la Natividad de la Virgen María**★ located in the city center *(open year-round Tue–Sun 10am–5pm)* was declared a World Heritage Site in 1994. Its ample atrium and the vestiges of its **corner chapels** blend Gothic and Renaissance influences. The ingenious layout of the *posa* on the left of the church facade allows it to function both as a chapel and as a monastery gatehouse. To the right lie the remains of an open-air chapel, laid out in the shape of a trapezoid. The **church** entrance features a lovely rose-colored stone-carved **facade** and a lavishly decorated arch; its triangular pediment depicts the *Virgen con el Niño* flanked by St. Dominic and St. Catherine of Sienna. Salient elements of the **interior** include the arch of the lower choir and the groined vaults of the chancel, as well as the colorful murals on the apse. Interesting Renaissance architectural forms characterize the massive **monastery**; a considerable area of its stout walls preserves the original **paintings** and wall finish with contrasting red and black

121

Tepoztlán

colors. Beautiful proportions prevail throughout the building. Its attractive upper cloister has a wonderful **vantagepoint**, which offers a panoramic **view** of the Valley of Tepoztlán.

To the rear of the monastery lies the **Museo de Arte Prehispánico Carlos Pellicer** *(open year-round Tue–Sun 10am–6pm; P$6;* ☎ *7-395-1098)*, a small archaeological museum located in the monastery's old granary. Carlos Pellicer, the famous Tabasco-born poet who actually lived in Tepoztlán for nearly 40 years, donated the varied collection of pre-Hispanic pieces that are on display.

★**Ruta de los Conventos** – *74km/46mi. From Tepoztlán take Carr. de cuota 115D for 9km/5.6mi toward Cuautla; after the second toll booth, exit toward Oaxtepec; continue 14km/8.7mi on Carr. 142 toward Xochimilco until reaching Tlayacapan.* Within a relatively small perimeter lie the ruins of several 16C fortress-type monasteries that attest to the apostolic zeal of the Spanish friars in this indigenous region. Tepoztlán, Tlayacapan, Atlatlahucan, Yecapixtla, Ocuituco, Oaxtepec, Tetela del Volcán and Hueyapan make up the most historically and artistically significant monasteries.

Tlayacapan – This charming village surrounded by towering mountains preserves several 16C chapels built in various neighborhoods by the Augustinian friars, most notably those of Santiago, La Concepción and San Miguel. In the main plaza, facing the monastery, stand the remains of the famous Pantitlán sugar plantation manor house. A rich selection of the region's varied pottery lends a dash of color to the village streets. To the left side of the rather plain church reigns the **Ex Convento de San Juan Bautista** *(enter by Juárez on the left and turn onto Calle Justo Sierra; open year-round daily 10:30am–6pm; closed national holidays; P$5)*, one of the largest Augustinian structures in Morelos state. Using photos and memorabilia, an exhibit in the sacristy provides an overview of the region's history, from pre-Hispanic times to the present. Do not miss the 17C and early-18C **mummies** discovered in 1982 during renovation of the church floor.

Ex Convento de San Mateo, Atlatlahucan – *From Tlayacapan continue east on Carr. 2 toward Totolapan (8km/5mi); continue 15km/9.3mi to reach Atlatlahucan. Enter by the new H. Galeana road, go four blocks, turn left and continue to the corner of Hidalgo. Open year-round daily 8am–8pm.* Built by the Augustinians, San Mateo possesses almost all the elements of the 16C fortress-type monasteries, with a noteworthy processional passage and an open-air chapel of trapezoidal design. Three arches topped by a small bell gable mark the entrance. The mystical blue-shaded church provides access to the cloister, into which women traditionally enter with their heads covered.

★**Ex Convento de San Juan Bautista, Yecapixtla** – *From Atlatlahucan continue south on Carr. 2 and at 2km/1.2mi turn right; go 4km/2.4mi on Carr. 160 toward Cuautla; then turn left and continue 6km/3.7mi on Carr. 10 to Yecapixtla. Calle No Reelección. Open year-round daily 7am–9pm.* Now a World Heritage Site, this Augustinian edifice's enchanting Plateresque **facade** with Gothic influences possesses a remarkable carved **rose window**. The interior's unusual one-story cloister with ogee arches lends it a medieval air. In town, the local fare, *cecina* or cured meat, awaits the hungry traveler.

MALINALCO★

Mexico

Map of Principal Sights – Map p 114 (**AY**)

🛈 ☎ (01-800) 903-9200

Malinalco, "the place of the grass-blossom," possesses perfectly preserved vestiges of its colonial past, making it one of the most beautiful towns in the state of Mexico. During the pre-Hispanic era, the Matlatzingas inhabited the region. Remnants of a ceremonial center testify to occupation by the Aztecs, who conquered the area in 1476.

ARCHAEOLOGICAL SITE

Malinalco lies 105km/65.2mi from Mexico City. Go southwest on Carr. 15D to Toluca (64km/39.7mi), take Carr. 55D south toward Ixtapan de la Sal and in Tenancingo turn left and continue 14k/8.7mi to the archaeological site of Malinalco. Open year-round Tue–Sun 9am–5pm. P$16.

Resting on a terrace carved out of the Cerro de los Ídolos (Hill of the Idols), the architectural complex—six monuments hewn from volcanic rock—balances on the edge of a 125m/410ft high precipice.

Take the street along the south side of the main plaza and follow the signs to the Church of Santa Mónica. Pass by the left side of the church and go through the narrow passageway.

Stairway – A long ramplike flight of 423 steps skirts the hill that leads to the ruins. At midpoint, a pre-Hispanic construction at the bottom of the cliff can be seen, marking the source of the ancient inhabitants' water supply. Remains of rooms, as well as a stone stairway leading to the mouth of a cave, probably a shrine to Oxtoctéotl (Lord of the Cave), a Matlatzinga god, or to Tláloc (the rain god) can also be distinguished.

Main Temple – This large monolithic structure possesses a truncated pyramid facade with a central staircase bordered by ramps. On either side rest two partially destroyed sculptures of seated jaguars. At the center sits a human figure.

Climb the stairs to the right of the temple.

At the top, on each side of the entrance stand two composite figures. On the left, a type of drum covered with jaguar skin, and, above this, the remains of a jaguar or eagle warrior; on the right, a serpent holds the remains of an eagle lord in his jaws. The portal opening simulates the open jaws of a serpent; the surrounding reliefs represent its eyes and fangs, while its forked tongue spreads across the floor. Dedicated to the eagle warriors *(cuauhtli)* and tigers (or jaguars, *ocelotl*), quasi divinities in Aztec society, the temple also served as a site for sun worship ceremonies.

★★**Interior** – The interior preserves a most extraordinary example of stone carving— a circular shrine 3m/10ft in diameter. A semicircular bench on the back wall contains three sculptures: in the center, the stretched skin of a jaguar, complete with head, claws and tail; beside the jaguar, the skins of eagles; and on the floor, the relief sculpture of another eagle facing the door. Behind the eagle lies a small rock-carved basin used to receive the hearts of sacrificial victims.

By looking over the wall behind the staircase, one can see examples of ancient construction techniques. Small holes carved into the rock were filled with wooden wedges; when the wood was soaked in water, the swelling caused the rock to crack. Temples of simple construction can be seen throughout the rest of the site. Note the circular structure to the right of the Main Temple. The rectangular structure beside the hill originally had painted walls.

ADDITIONAL SIGHT

★**Ex Convento de Malinalco** – *Av. Juárez, on the main plaza. Open year-round Tue–Sun 10am–5pm.* Founded by the Augustinians in 1540, the cloister of this monumental monastery preserves a large part of its original **frescoes★** on the walls of both floors and on the stairway.

PACHUCA
Hidalgo
Population 220,488
Map of Principal Sights – Map p 114 **(ABX)**
🚹 Plaza Independencia (Reloj Monumental) ☎ (7) 718-3937
and (01-800) 715-6800

Amidst a changing landscape of mountains and deserts stands this once wealthy mining city, known in Mexico as "la bella airosa." A play on the words for "beautiful" and "breezy," the title refers to the cool winds from the mountains that blow through the city's streets. Pachuca, the state capital's name, comes from the Náhuatl **Pachoacán** "narrow place," or from **Patlachiuhacan** "place of gold and silver." Stubbornly independent, it did not become part of the Aztec Empire until 1450 and did not succumb to the Spanish conquistadors until 1528.

Here, Neoclassical and modern styles of architecture predominate. A stroll along its narrow, winding streets leads to picturesque little plazas and pleasant parks. Close by, magnificent, 16C ecclesiastical buildings testify to the evangelization carried out by the Augustinian and Franciscan missionaries. The town offers visitors pre-Hispanic style dishes and drinks, such as *barbacoa* (barbecue), *escamoles* (ant eggs), *mixiotes* (spicy meat or chicken wrapped in maguey leaves), *pulque* (a fermented cactus drink), as well as the now traditional *pastes*, a type of bread roll introduced by English miners in the 19C.

Mining – The rich mines of this area have been exploited since pre-Hispanic times. During the colonial period mining expanded greatly, owing to the new system of amalgamation discovered by Bartolomé de Medina. It reached its peak in the 18C. Pedro Romero de Terreros, first Count of Regla, promoted mining in Pachuca and nearby Real del Monte as well as in other cities and owned the most important mines in New Spain. The veins of gold, silver and vanadium have been depleted on several occasions, but new ones are constantly being discovered. Pachuca continues to be one of the most important mining centers in the country, which fosters its flourishing goldsmith industry.

SIGHTS

★**Reloj Monumental (Monumental Clock)** – *Plaza Independencia.* The symbol of Pachuca, this attractive Neoclassical stone tower, 40m/131ft high, stands guard in the central square. Created by Tomás Cordero, it was inaugurated to celebrate the centennial of the beginning of the War of Independence. The carillon at the top was made in the same factory as London's Big Ben. Tourist information is available in the tower's lower level.

Centro Cultural de Hidalgo – *Between Arista and Casasola, five blocks east of the Plaza Independencia. Open year-round Tue–Sun 10am–6pm.* This imposing Franciscan monastery *(Ex Convento de San Francisco)*, built between 1596 and 1660 in the fortress style, presently houses Hidalgo state's most important cultural center composed of the Teatro de la Ciudad (City Theater) and Escuela de Artes (Art School), as well as museums, exhibition halls, auditoriums and offices. Graceful gardens and plazas, which replaced the former atrium and orchard, surround the enormous architectural complex.

Templo de San Francisco – *Open year-round Mon–Fri 10am–1pm, Sat by appointment, Sun 10am–noon.* Despite undergoing several modifications, this ancient church begun in 1596 still preserves Baroque elements such as its crisscrossed windows. In a chapel to the right of the main altar lies the mummified body, purportedly of St. Columba, a virgin and martyr put to death in France in AD 273 under Emperor Aurelian. The body was donated to the church in the 18C by the Marquise of San Francisco, daughter of the Count of Regla. In the antesacristy stands an immense washbasin featuring two carved stones and six, pretty Talavera tiles from Puebla. Behind the church stands the **Capilla de Nuestra Señora de la Luz** *(open year-round Mon–Sat, 10am–1pm, Sun by appointment)*, which features four large oil paintings of the Stations of the Cross and an attractive 18C Churrigueresque altarpiece.

★**Museo de la Fotografía** – *Top floor of the cloister. Open year-round Tue–Sun 10am–6pm. Closed national holidays.* ☎ *(7) 714-3653.* Various instruments and processes familiarize visitors with the methods that have been used to create photographic images over the years. Its finest holdings, the core of its **photographic archive**★★★, begin with the Casasola collection, an extensive photography collection covering the Revolutionary era in Mexico. Gradually enriched by works of great photographers such as Manuel Álvarez Bravo, Nacho López, Tina Modotti, Teobert Maler and C.B. Waite, its present store of historical and aesthetic materials makes it one of the largest photographic archives in the world. The archive, Fototeca Nacional del INAH in Pachuca, offers reproduction services of its collection *(Mon–Fri 8am–2pm, by appointment).*

EXCURSIONS

★**Huasca** – *Go northwest on Carr. 105 toward Tampico; at 21km/13mi turn right and continue 8km/5mi to reach Huasca.* A picturesque town of cobblestone streets and pretty white houses with pitched metal roofs, the village of Huasca reflects the influence of the nearby 18C metal-processing haciendas owned by Pedro Romero de Terreros, first Count of Regla. In the animated center of the main plaza stands the **Templo de San Juan Bautista** with its Plateresque entrance. The workers making pottery and traditional products in the surrounding arcades add to its provincial atmosphere. Built in the 18C by the first Count of Regla, the magnificent **Ex Hacienda de San Miguel Regla** mining facility *(2.5km/1.6mi northwest of Huasca; open year-round daily 9am–4pm;* ✗ ◗ ☎ *7-792-0102),* now operating as a hotel, still preserves its silver ore furnaces. The surrounding area offers a variety of diversions from woods and trout-fishing lakes to trails for horseback riding, biking and motorcycling. Known for its basalt formations, which resemble symmetrically arranged columns, the impressive gorge of **Prismas Basálticos de Santa María Regla★** (Basalt Prisms; △ ✗ ◗), 3km/1.9mi northwest of San Miguel Regla, reaches a depth of 50m/164ft. One of only three formations in the world, the unique result of the retraction of the basalt's crystalline components occurs when the volcanic lava undergoes rapid cooling as it comes into contact with air. At both ends of the gorge lie beautiful waterfalls created by the San Antonio dam. Close by *(1km/0.6mi on a dirt road)* the **Ex Hacienda de Santa María Regla★** *(open year-round daily 8am–6pm; P$5;* ✗ ◗ △ ☎ *7-718-4449)* offers a look into Mexico's first and biggest metal-processing hacienda constructed by the Count of Regla.

Mineral del Monte – *Return 8km/5mi to Carr. 105 and go toward Pachuca; after 10km/6.2mi, take the left turn that leads to the town center.* Nestled in the mountains that sheltered the richest mines in Mexico, this pretty village, locally known as Real del Monte, features steep cobblestone streets flanked by colorful houses, a barbershop and *cantina* restored to their 19C appearance. The mines attracted the English during the mid 19C, who in turn left a heritage of *pastes,* known in Cornwall as pasties (a type of turnover made of wheat flour and filled with something salty, such as meat or cheese, or with something sweet), steam engines and a quaint cemetery in the woods. Popular legend says Mexico's first soccer game took place here.

Metztitlán – *From Huasca head west and at 8km/5mi take Carr. 105 toward Tampico; at 41km/25.5mi take a left turn and continue another 23km/14mi to Metztitlán.* Abundant vegetation and imposing mountains surround this picturesque town enriched by a pretty plaza and quaint cobblestone streets. The Augustinian monastery of the **Ex Convento de los Santos Reyes★** *(open year-round daily 8am–6pm)* was constructed on the highest point of the town, with a commanding **view★** of the fertile valley. Possessing peculiar features uncommon in 16C neo-Hispanic monasteries, the fortress-style building boasts a double open-air chapel and a corner chapel placed directly across from the church portal. Its rich Plateresque **portal** finished off by a pretty bell gable with seven bays distinguishes the exterior. The **interior** contains valuable gilded **altarpieces★** with splendid sculptures. Paintings and **frescoes** created by indigenous artists make a striking impression. The paintings on the **staircase** exemplify the didactic themes that pervade the monastery's artwork.

★**Ex Convento de San Andrés, Epazoyucan** – *21km/13mi. From Pachuca go southeast on Carr. 130 toward Tulancingo; at 17km/10.5mi turn right and continue for 4km/2.5mi. Open year-round daily 9am–5pm. P$12.* An impressive Augustinian fortress-style monastery begun in 1540, Saint Andrew's features an ascending stairway that leads to a huge atrium, which still preserves its four corner chapels and small cemeteries from the late 19C. The Renaissance **portal** of the **Templo de San Andrés,** flanked by the open-air chapel, is outstanding. Ruins of arches mark the monastery's entrance. In the lower level of the **cloister,** a series of five magnificent **frescoes★★★** of Florentine influence attributed to Juan Jersón (1556), are considered the most important 16C frescoes on the American continent.

Arcos del Padre Tembleque y Tepeapulco – *Tour: 52km/32mi. Go southeast from Pachuca on the road to Ciudad Sahagún; at 32km/20mi, past El Barrio, turn right and after 1km/0.6mi take a left.*

★**Arcos del Padre Tembleque** – Fray Francisco Tembleque, a Franciscan, built this monumental aqueduct around 1545 to carry water to this region. Its 64 arches span three deep ravines between Cerro del Tecajete and Otumba.

Ex Convento de San Francisco, Tepeapulco – *From Arcos del Padre Tembleque, return to the road to Ciudad Sahagún; at 11km/6.8mi turn left and continue 9km/5.6 to Tepeapulco. Av. Hidalgo. Open year-round daily 8am–3pm.* Fray **Bernardino de Sahagún** began his groundbreaking work *Historia de las Cosas de la Nueva España* (History of Events in New Spain) in this 16C monastery constructed on top of the preexisting *teocalli* (temple). The church has retained its marvelous facade decorated by native hands and distinguished by a remarkable **atrial cross**, adorned with symbols of the Passion of Christ. In the lower cloister a small **exhibit room** features archaeological objects from different cultures, the majority of which were found in the vicinity of the Tecolote pyramid north of Tepeapulco. East of the monastery stands the **Caja de Agua** (reservoir), a picturesque 16C Franciscan structure marking the end of the aqueduct that provided the town with water. For centuries, the lion-shaped spouts have been carrying water to the pool's public washbasins.

Actopan and Ixmiquilpan – *Go northwest from Pachuca on Carr. 85 toward Nuevo Laredo, continue 35km/21.7mi to Actopan.*

Actopan – The main arcade surrounding this village's large plaza leads to the atrium of the former monastery **Ex Convento de San Nicolás Tolentino★** *(open year-round daily 9am–6pm; P$17)*. A monumental 16C Augustinian complex, the structure harmoniously combines the Gothic style of the church's vaults and lower cloister, the Mudejar lines of its high **tower**, the facade's rich Plateresque design and Renaissance-style upper cloister. Inside the **church**, two depressed arches connect the sacristy to the spacious **baptistery**, framed by walls decorated with frescoes and a groined vault. A large monolithic stone-carved baptismal font stands in the middle, its round wooden cover decorated with an attractive small sculpted figure of Saint John the Baptist.

Several cells display paintings, sculptures and altar fragments of the period. Perfectly preserved murals decorate the monastery; the stairway **frescoes★★★**, depicting saints and important personages of the Augustinian order studying in their cells are particularly noteworthy. Its **open-air chapel★★**, to the church's left, claims to be one of the largest in New Spain. The vault, decorated with appealing fresco-painted coffers, and its three walls representing biblical scenes, such as the Creation of Man and the Last Judgment, mix European models with pre-Hispanic inspiration.

Ixmiquilpan – *From Actopan, return to Carr. 85 and continue 40km/25mi to Ixmiquilpan.* This large village, in the heart of the Valle de Mezquital, is an important enclave of the Otomís. Three thermal baths with waters at about 100°F (nearly 40°C) line the road into the city. A replica of the Diana the ·Huntress statue in Mexico City embellishes its central square. Just as the monastery at Actopan, the **Ex Convento de San Miguel Arcángel** *(open year-round daily 9am–4pm; P$12, free Sun)*, on the edge of the main plaza, was built by Fray Andrés de Mata. The enormous church with its Plateresque facade possesses a Moorish-style tower that separates the church from the monastery's portico. The portico's arches and the cloisters reflect Gothic influences. An outstanding frieze, decorated with **frescoes** of mythological and battle scenes, a mixture of European and pre-Hispanic motifs, graces the **interior**. This work, executed in vivid colors by indigenous artists, is considered to be the last pre-Hispanic codex or the first Mexican mural painting. The sacristy preserves a valuable series of **frescoes** on the life of Christ.

★★★Teotihuacán – *70km/43mi south of Pachuca. Description p 142.*

Tula – *100km/62mi west of Pachuca. Description p 155.*

Consult the practical information section at the end of the guide for travel tips, useful addresses and phone numbers, and a wealth of details on recreation and annual events.

PUEBLA★★★

Puebla
Population 1,222,569
Map of Principal Sights – Map p 115 **(BXYZ)**
🏢 5 Oriente, 3, and Palacio Municipal, City Center ☎ (2) 246-2044

One of Mexico's best-preserved colonial cities, Puebla lies in a natural hollow surrounded by the volcanoes Popocatépetl, Iztaccíhuatl, Citlaltépetl-better known as Pico de Orizaba-*(photo p 16)*, and La Malinche. Besides its historical and cultural significance, Puebla is also home to some of Mexico's most famous culinary specialties, such as the delicious *mole poblano* (chili sauce with bitter chocolate and peanuts), *chiles en nogada* (peppers in a sauce of pounded walnuts and spice), and *dulce de camote* (sweet-potato candy). Its gorgeous Talavera ceramics and tiles *(photo p 49)* and the corner balconies on so many downtown buildings contribute to Puebla's unique atmosphere. Mexican folklore and tradition are also reflected in the Puebla horse-woman's *(china poblana)* ruffled dress that includes the eagle and the colors of the Mexican flag, a symbol of racial mixture *(mestizaje)* combining European and indigenous influences. It comes as no surprise that Puebla was declared a World Heritage Site in 1987.

Historical Notes

City of Angels – In the place called **Cuetlaxcoapan**, Náhuatl for "in the snake's skin," the first Renaissance city of New Spain was founded on April 16, 1531. Puebla, unlike many other colonial cities, was not built on the ruins of a native village. Because of the symmetry of its streets, the city's layout is said to have been drawn by angels. Fray Julián Garcés envisioned it thus in his dreams when he chose this stunning valley to build the city. At the request of Juan de Salmerón, Queen Isabella of Spain originally named it "City of Angels." It is presently known as *Puebla de los Ángeles* (Puebla of the Angels).

Colonial Era – Purposely located on the Mexico-Veracruz trade route, Puebla was the only 16C city specifically designed as a settlement for Spanish farmers. It soon began producing not only wheat and flour but also textiles, and by the 18C had become the most important industrial city in Mexico. Another important industry, sheep ranching, met the high demand for wool required by the textile industry, which became the backbone of the Mexican economy. This led to many spin-off industries, such as the production of natural dyes, including cochineal red.

Struggles and Battles – When the House of Bourbon came to power in Spain, Puebla was made an intendance and was granted its own municipal autonomy. During this period, the administration of Count Manuel de Flon was particularly noteworthy. In the early 19C, the city was the setting for the proclamation of the Plan of Ayala, which consummated Mexican independence from Spain. During this turbulent century, a bloody struggle to defend Mexican sovereignty took place in the City of Angels. Puebla offered heroic resistance against a French invasion on May 5, 1862, when General Ignacio de Zaragoza beat back the enemy. As a result of this victory, Puebla became known as "Puebla de Zaragoza" for a short period. Despite Zaragoza's victorious Cinco de Mayo Battle of Puebla, in 1863 the French general, Forey, captured the city and occupied it for over a year. In early 20C revolutionary times, the City of Angels would once more witness bloodshed, this time the assassination of the Serdán brothers during a turbulent ten-day period in 1913, known in Mexican history as *La Decena Trágica* (The Tragic Ten Days).

Due to the damages caused by the earthquake of June 1999, many of Puebla's historic monuments and churches may not have been repaired yet or may have closed indefinitely.

★★★CITY CENTER *Map p 129.*

Plaza Principal and Surroundings

★★**Plaza Principal** – *Av. Juan de Palafox y Mendoza, between 2 Sur and 16 de Septiembre.* Shaded by leafy trees, the main plaza is flanked by the majestic cathedral and the Municipal Palace-designed by English architect Charles S. Hall-as well as other colonial buildings. In the center stands a monument to the patron saint of Puebla, the Fountain of the Archangel Michael, created in the 18C by Antonio Santa María de Incháurregui.

Palacio Municipal – *Portal Hidalgo, 14, opposite the Plaza Principal. Open year-round daily 8:30am–8pm.* ☎ *(2) 232-0357.* Among the buildings bordering the plaza, the Municipal Palace, or City Hall, is remarkable for its quarried stone and beautiful Carrara marble interior staircase. The handsome **Salón de Cabildos** preserves the original Act for the Founding of Puebla (1531).

Museo Universitario – *2 Norte, 2. Open year-round Tue–Sun 10am–5pm. Closed Jan 1 & Dec 25. P$5.* ☎ *(2) 246-2899.* The present day University Museum is housed in what used to be called the **Antigua Casa de los Muñecos** (House of Dolls).

Cathedral

Nobody knows for sure what these Puebla-style male figures on the facade really mean. Some believe they represent Hercules' 12 tasks, while others say it is a mockery of city aldermen who were opposed to building a third floor. Now it houses a museum of ancient scientific equipment and a vast **collection**★ of colonial paintings, the most noteworthy of which are the works of the Talavera brothers, Manuel Caro and Pascual Pérez.

★**Museo Poblano de Arte Virreinal** – *4 Norte, 203, between 2 Oriente and 4 Oriente. Open year-round Tue–Sun 10am–5pm. P$15, free Sun.* ☏ *(2) 246-6618.* Inaugurated in January 1999, this spacious and handsome building-an example of Puebla's traditional architecture-served as the Hospital de San Pedro from the 16C to the beginning of the 20C. The second floor houses a room for permanent exhibits. Here, diverse models, maps, paintings, sculptures, and even the replica of an old drugstore, recreate the development of this edifice and pay homage to the former hospital as one of the most outstanding medical institutions during the colonial period. Next to this room lies a space dedicated to interesting temporary exhibits focusing on Puebla's colonial art.

Templo de la Compañía de Jesús – *Corner of 4 Sur and Av. Juan de Palafox y Mendoza. Open year-round daily 8am–1:30pm & 5–8pm.* The mortar finish of this very elaborate Baroque **facade**★ provides a nice contrast to the austere facade of the neighboring Jesuit church. From one of its arches hung the head of Antonio Benavides, executed by the Inquisition for posing as an inspector. Inside the church lie the remains of Catarina de San Juan, supposedly the original **China poblana**, the lavishly dressed horsewoman of Mexican folklore.

Casa del que Mató al Animal – *3 Oriente, 201, corner of 2 Sur.* Though scholars do not agree as to the origin of the reliefs on the front of this building, the varying interpretations concede that they tell of the courage of a man who faced a monster (a dragon to some, a serpent to others) that had killed several townspeople. Whatever the origin, the house with the unusual name (House of the man who killed the animal) is graced by a pair of jambs in the Plateresque style, embellished with graceful **reliefs**★ that portray a man with mastiffs devouring deer and rabbits.

★★**Catedral** – *16 de Septiembre, corner of 3 Oriente. Open year-round daily 8am–12:30pm & 4:30–7pm.* Although construction of this, the first Herreran-style building in New Spain, began in 1575 under the direction of Francisco de Becerra and Juan de Cigorondo, the cathedral was not finished until the 17C, thanks to the efforts of Juan de Palafox y Mendoza, a resident bishop-viceroy from the province of Navarra, Spain. Its slender towers rise 70m/230ft into the sky, and a wrought-iron fence embellished with figures of angels and cherubs, symbols of the city, surrounds its ample atrium.

The majestic interior boasts the **ciprés** (cypress) by Manuel Tolsá, and the **Altar de los Reyes**★-attributed to Sevillian artist Juan Martínez Montañez-where Cristóbal de Villalpando painted *La Gloria*, an oil **mural** on the vault of the cupola. Fourteen chapels with artistic treasures from different periods flank the side naves, while the **choir stalls** in the finest Puebla marquetry occupy the center of the cathedral. Also noteworthy are Miguel Cabrera's paintings of the Way of the Cross, and the works of José de Ibarra, Miguel Jerónimo de Zendejas and Juan Rodríguez Juárez.

To visit the following four sections, permission is required from the ecclesiastical authorities in charge of the cathedral.

Sacristy – Built between the 16C and the 17C, the sacristy boasts majestic canvases by Baltazar Echave Rioja and Luis Berruecos. It is noteworthy for its furnishings and for the beauty of its austere design.

Salón de los Gobelinos – Preserves wonderful tapestries from the colonial period, which were brought here from Europe.

Capilla del Ochavo – Houses delightful feather embroidery and miniature figurines attributed to Villalpando and Tinoco.

Sala Capitular – Holds portraits of Puebla's bishops and archbishops. Of particular interest are those of Palafox and his predecessors, works by Juan García de Ferrer.

Museo de Arte José Luis Bello y González – *3 Poniente, 302. Guided tour (1hr), year-round Tue–Sun & holidays 10am–5pm. Closed Jan 1 & Dec 25. P$11.* ☎ *(2) 232-9475.* With a rich and varied selection of Mexican, European and Asian works, the Museum of Art collection also includes Chinese, Japanese and European porcelain, as well as paintings by the local (Puebla-Tlaxcala) artist Agustín Arrieta. The first floor holds an important collection of Puebla Talavera-style **ceramics**; on the next floor ancient musical instruments are on display, including a 17C **pipe organ**★ and a vertical harp-shaped **piano**★. Also noteworthy for its variety and artistic taste, the **furniture** placed throughout the museum features examples of Puebla-style inlaid wood.

Casa del Deán – *16 de Septiembre, 5, corner of 7 Poniente. Open year-round Tue–Sun 10am–5pm.* The Dean's House was built in the 16C by order of Don Tomás de la Plaza, then Dean of the Cathedral. It holds two magnificent **mural paintings**★★, one portraying *El desfile de la sinagoga y las Sibilas*, the twelve pagan priestesses who predicted passages of Christ's life—the other, Petrarch's *Triumphs*. Note the frame of the Sibyls, embellished with an abundance of indigenous motifs, such as little monkeys *(ozomatlis)* which, in Mexican folklore, symbolize pleasure and happiness.

★★ **Biblioteca Palafoxiana (Casa de la Cultura)** – *5 Oriente, 5. Open year-round Tue–Sun 10am 5pm. P$10.* Housed on the upper floor of the original Colegio de San Juan, the Palafoxiana Library was named after its benefactor, Bishop-viceroy Juan de Palafox y Mendoza, who donated his personal collection in 1646. A century later, the library's collection was further enriched by Bishop Fabián y Fuero and other benefactors. Inaugurated in 1773, in a hall decked with Baroque bookshelves crowned with an elaborate altarpiece, it presently holds approximately 43,000 volumes, among which it is possible to find some incunabula, thus making it the most important collection of its kind in Latin America.

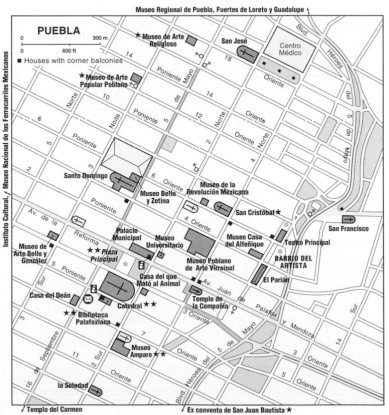

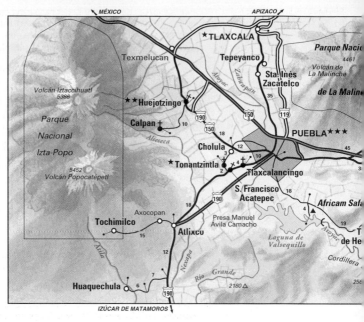

★★ Museo Amparo – *2 Sur, 708. Open year-round Wed–Mon 10am–6pm. P$16, free Mon. Free (1hr) guided tour Sun at noon. ✗ ☎ (2) 246-4210 or www.giga.com/~amparo.* Housed in two important 17C and 18C buildings known as the *Hospitalito* (little hospital), this modern museum is named after Amparo Rugarcía, wife of the Mexican millionaire Manuel Espinosa Yglesias. Its seven halls, equipped with user-friendly CD-ROMs, exhibit a large **collection★** of pre-Hispanic pieces. These culminate in a special hall with remarkable objects, such as the **Pensador** (Thinker)-a sculpture from Las Bocas, Puebla, a **Mayan altar**, and Mexica and Huastec sculptures. Eleven halls are devoted to colonial art: **furniture**, paintings, and various objects from the 17C and 18C, from Europe and the Americas. It also contains a respectable collection of Mexican art, including works by Diego Rivera and Gerardo Murillo (Dr. Atl).

Templo de la Soledad – *2 Sur and 13 Oriente. Open year-round daily 8am–1pm & 4:30–8pm.* This church-dedicated to Our Lady of Solitude, whose statue was brought here from Spain in the 18C-features an enormous cupola adorned with black and white tiles. Seventeen years after completion, the church became part of a Carmelite convent (1748), during which time the nuns took on the responsibility of safeguarding the image. Enhanced by beautiful Baroque *estípite*-style **altarpieces★★** in the transept, La Soledad boasts a marvelous onyx pulpit by José Medina, who also crafted the pulpit in the cathedral.

Templo del Carmen – *16 de Septiembre and 17 Oriente. Open year-round Mon–Sat 7am–1pm & 4–7:30pm, Sun 7am–2pm & 6:30–8:30pm.* Surrounded by an atrium shaded by cypress trees, this Carmelite church in classical Puebla style displays a typical brick and tile facade. The interior preserves lovely colonial paintings, most noteworthy of which is a Villalpando. Remarkable also are the semi-oval design of the **side chapel** and a beautiful wooden inlaid **chest of drawers★**.

Templo de Santo Domingo and Surroundings

Templo de Santo Domingo – *4 Poniente and 5 de Mayo. Open year-round daily 8am–9pm.* On one side of the main entrance stand the remains of a restrained Baroque gate adorned with reliefs. The austere exterior contrasts with the splendor of the interior with its exquisite main altarpiece of carved wooden figures, transept altarpieces, and the pulpit finished in black and white tiles to match the colors of the Dominican order. The left transept leads through a somber entrance into the Chapel of Nuestra Señora del Rosario. It was here, in the 16C, that the Sevillian poet Gutierre de Cetina, renowned for his madrigal *Ojos Claros, Serenos*, was mortally wounded.

★★★ Capilla del Rosario – At the time of its completion in 1690, this exquisite Baroque masterpiece became known as the eighth wonder of the world, most notably for the ornate gilded plasterwork that decorates the interior; children, saints and angels strike playful poses amidst intricate foliage. Dogmas of the faith and virtues

★★Cuetzalan, Libres, Cantona

0   10 km
0   5 mi

129

XALAPA

San Salvador
el Seco

Acajete

140

★ Acatzingo

Tepeaca

150

Cuapiaxtla

10   22

ORIZABA

Tecamachalco

Canal   Principal

Tetzoyacan   150

TEHUACÁN

inscribed on oval-shaped medallions adorn the cupola. The image of a beautiful cypress bush, mystically illuminated by the cupola's windows, represents the venerable Lady of the Rosary. Higher up, the Holy Spirit is symbolized in a dove surrounded by eight Graces: holy virgins and martyrs. A frieze of very fine 18C tiles, with small reliefs of foliage and geometric designs, winds its way around the chapel.

Museo Bello y Zetina – *5 de Mayo, 409. Open year-round Tue–Sun 10am–3:45pm. ☎ (2) 232-4720.* This museum contains a rich collection of European paintings, including a drawing by Goya, a torso by Gericault and a St. Peter by Zurbarán. Among the Mexican works exhibited are an 18C painting by Miguel Cabrera, miniature figurines by Francisco Morales, and 17C watercolors on parchment and gold leaf by Luis Lagarto. The collection includes furniture, ivory, sculptures, porcelain and crystal from different eras.

★**Museo de Arte Popular Poblano (Ex Convento de Santa Rosa)** – *14 Poniente, 305. Open year-round daily 10am–5pm. Closed Sept 1 & 16, Oct 12, Nov 20, Dec 12 & 25. P$10. ☎ (2) 246-4526.* Confiscated under the 19C Reform Laws, this former convent (1690) was later used for public housing, then was eventually returned to public use to house the museum. Seven main halls-one for every region in the state of Puebla-exhibit collections of local handicrafts, fine wooden furniture★ inlaid with mother of pearl, bone and veneer, as well as the famous and beautiful tiled **Puebla kitchen**★★ where Sor Andrea of the Assumption is said to have prepared the original delicious *mole poblano* sauce. The museum preserves its 18C main patio-decorated in 1740 Puebla style, with bricks and tiles.

★**Museo de Arte Religioso** – *18 Poniente, 103. Open year-round Tue–Sun 10am–5pm. P$7.* The former Convent of Santa Mónica possesses an impressive courtyard with brick and tile archways constructed in the best Puebla tradition. This building was founded by Bishop Fernández Cruz, in 1682, for a community of cloistered nuns. Presently, the Museum of Religious Art houses a magnificent **collection** of colonial paintings, including five large paintings on velvet by Rafael Morante, as well as works by Miguel Jerónimo de Zendejas, Antonio de Santander, Nicolás Rodríguez Juárez, Juan Correa, Juan de Villalobos, Pascual Pérez, and Miguel Cabrera. On the third floor, an altar-style memorial preserves the heart of the founding bishop.

Parroquia de San José – *2 Norte, 1803, between 18 Oriente and 20 Oriente. Open year-round daily 7am–1pm & 5–8pm.* Begun as a modest chapel in 1595 to implore the protection of St. Joseph against lightning storms, the Church of St. Joseph was expanded at the end of the 17C to become this quite imposing structure. The original chapel now serves as the vestibule of the larger church, which contains works by Pascual Pérez, most notably the representation of St. Sebastian. Magnificent Baroque and Churrigueresque altarpieces from the 17C and 18C decorate the interior. The Capilla del Calvario (Calvary Chapel) is adorned with paintings by Miguel Jerónimo de Zendejas, while the stone-carved columns depicting foliage and angel motifs, and a painting by José Manzo y Jaramillo make the Capilla de Jesús de Nazareno a veritable jewel.

San Francisco and Surroundings

Templo de San Francisco – *Blvd. Héroes del 5 de Mayo and 14 Oriente. Open year-round daily 6:30am–8pm.* Polychrome tiles, quarried stone, *estípite*-style columns, niches and sculptures combine to create a **facade**★★ of force and grandeur. The side portal, presumably the city's oldest, dates from the 16C. Gothic style ribbed vaults frame the interior, while remarkable paintings by Zendejas decorate the walls. To the left of the main altar stands the **Capilla de la Conquistadora**, the virgin who accompanied Hernán Cortés in his battles. Inside this chapel, the faithful venerate the miraculously preserved body of Fray Sebastián de Aparicio-Hispanic patron saint of travelers to whom were attributed many miracles. The monument on the main entrance steps pays homage to the horse-drawn cart introduced in Mexico by Fray Sebastián de Aparicio.

Barrio del Artista – *8 Norte, between 4 Oriente and 6 Oriente.* Founded in 1941 by Doctor Gonzalo Bautista, this district offers visitors a chance to watch Puebla artists at work and perhaps purchase their handicrafts. A few steps away *(on 6 Norte and 8 Oriente)* lies the 1613 **Teatro Principal**-the first theater to be built on mainland America-which since then has continuously offered performances. A block away from the Artists' Quarter stands **El Parián** *(open year-round daily 10am–8pm; ☎ 2-242-4029)*, a colorful market specializing in Puebla *talavera* and other local handicrafts.

Museo Casa del Alfeñique – *4 Oriente, 416. Open year-round Tue–Fri 10am–4pm. ☎ (2) 232-4296.* Baroque designs flow down the walls from the frieze of this remarkable **facade**★★ distinguishable as the work of local craftsmen. Attributed to Antonio Santa María de Incháurregui, this facade is a noteworthy example of Puebla's distinctive Churrigueresque style.

★**Templo de San Cristóbal** – *4 Norte, corner of 6 Oriente. Open year-round daily 8am–noon & 4–8pm.* Two tall towers emphasize the vertical lines of this splendid church with a stone facade. Dating from 1676 and built under the direction of the architect Carlos García Durango, it is considered the culminating example of Puebla Baroque style. The cupola is covered in fine **plasterwork**★, as are the 16 niches with representations of kings and the heavenly choir surrounding the Virgin Mary. Inside, note the statue of St. Christopher carved in wood.

Museo Regional de la Revolución Mexicana (Casa de los Hermanos Serdán) – *6 Oriente, 206. Open year-round Tue–Sun 10am–4:30pm. P$10.* In this house, home to the Serdán brothers, the plot to launch the Mexican Revolution was discovered, triggering a spate of killings known in Mexican history as *La Decena Trágica* (The Tragic Ten Days). Carmen, the revolutionaries' sister, managed to survive the assault by Federal forces. The interior preserves a mirror full of bullet holes, as well as photos of the revolutionary leaders and other objects that document these events.

ADDITIONAL SIGHTS

Instituto Cultural (Antigua Penitenciaría del Estado) – *Reforma, 1305, corner with 13 Sur. Open year-round Mon–Fri 9am–3pm & 5–8pm.* ✕ ☎ *(2) 232-0462.* Originally designed in the 19C as a penitentiary by architect José Manzo y Jaramillo, the building was damaged during the assault of French troops. Further damage during an 1864 earthquake led to its eventual closure in 1884. Seven years later, President Porfirio Díaz inaugurated the restored premises as a cultural center, where today the young people of Puebla meet for art classes. The Institute preserves its impressive fortress-like towers, as well as its original stone and brickwork. Rehearsals and recreation take place in the octagonal courtyard where prisoners used to exercise.

Fuertes de Loreto y Guadalupe – The walls of the fortresses that defended the city against the French Invasion on May 5, 1862 still stand guard atop the hills surrounding Puebla.

Fuerte de Loreto – *Av. Ejército de Oriente. Centro Cívico 5 de Mayo. Open year-round Tue–Sun 10am–5pm. P$10.* Originally a 17C hermitage dedicated to Our Lady of Loreto, the building was renovated at the end of the same century to meet the requirements of the Loreto Order. Nearly half a century later, in 1815, a fortification was built that would help General Berriozábal and his troops defend the city in the Battle of Cinco de Mayo. Presently the chapel houses a museum that exhibits objects, drawings and uniforms of the era.

Fuerte de Guadalupe – *Av. Ejército de Oriente Centro Cívico 5 de Mayo. Open year-round Tue–Sun 10am–5pm. P$10.* Today the austere ruin of a former church, this structure at one time acted as a fortress to defend the city against Napoleon III's troops. The Mexican hero, General Ignacio Zaragoza, led the resistance.

Museo Regional de Puebla – *Calzada Ejército de Oriente, Centro Cívico 5 de Mayo. Open year-round Tue–Sun 10am–5pm. P$10. ☎ (2) 235-9720.* Pre-Hispanic and colonial artifacts, and historical objects from Mexican Independence through the Revolution comprise the collection of this regional museum. A colossal 17C **sculpture**★★ of Saint Christopher, in burnished polychrome wood, and a **painting** by Miguel Jerónimo de Zendejas on a pharmacy cupboard door highlight the exhibit. **Covered crosses**—wooden crosses adorned with flowers-and the particular and elegant fashion of preparing coffins for funeral services provide good insight into local customs and folklore.

Museo Nacional de los Ferrocarriles Mexicanos – *11 Norte, 1005, between 10 and 18 Poniente, main entrance via Calle 10 Poniente. Open year-round Tue–Sun 10am–5pm. Closed national holidays.* ▣ ☎ *(2) 232-7848.* On September 16,

1869, Benito Juárez inaugurated Puebla's first train station in this austere, Neoclassical structure. Today, the building houses interesting temporary exhibits that recount the history of Mexico's trains. Unique in Latin America, this museum allows visitors to view, on the exterior railway platform, ancient wagons and locomotives that still preserve their original furnishings.

EXCURSIONS   Maps p 115 (BXYZ) and pp 130-131.

Cholula – *7km/4.3mi west of Puebla on Carr. libre 150/190 to Huejotzingo. Description p 117.*

From Atlixco to Huaquechula – *87km/62mi. Go southwest from Puebla on Carr. 190 toward Atlixco.*

Atlixco – Called Villa de Carrión during colonial times, Atlixco became a dukedom during the Bourbon era. Because it is surrounded by nurseries and green houses, this ancient city is now known as the "city of flowers." Equally renowned, its medicinal waters from the spring at Axocopan have been compared to those of Vichy, France. The **Convento Franciscano de Santa María de Jesús** *(open year-round Tue–Sat 9am–5pm, Sun 9am–1pm; monastery Sun noon–2pm)* erected atop St. Michael's hill (Cerro San Miguel), a superb stone mass, can be seen for several miles. Dating back to early colonial times, the monastery preserves original altarpieces in the church and the remains of some mural paintings in the cloister. The **Capilla de la Tercera Orden** *(three blocks west of the Plaza de Armas; open year-round daily 10am–2pm)*, a gem of popular art, boasts mortarwork that is repainted every year in vivid colors. Atlixco proudly possesses one of the few hospitals of the colonial period still a working hospital: **Hospital Municipal de San Juan de Dios** *(five blocks west of the Plaza de Armas, on Calle 11 sur turn left and go one block; open year-round Mon, Wed–Fri & Sun 9am–3pm, Sat 9am–2pm; ☎ 2-445-0021).* The Saint John of God Municipal Hospital possesses a handsome patio, and upstairs, a museum with good examples of colonial paintings.

Tochimilco – *From Atlixco head south until reaching the intersection with Carr. 21, turn right (west) to access the road to Metepec; past Puente del Obispo turn left toward Axocopan (3km/1.9mi), cross the town and continue 11km/6.8mi on Carr. 425.* Nestled on the slopes of the Popocatépetl Volcano, Tochimilco enjoys a privileged close-up view, making the "Popo" seem just an arm's length away. Of special note on the 16C octagonal fountain, found in the main plaza, are a spout in the shape of a lion's head and inscriptions in Náhuatl. Water arrived here through a series of aqueducts, of which several arches have been preserved. An austere Renaissance portal and Mudéjar window crowned with battlements distinguish the **Ex Convento Franciscano** *(one block northwest of the Plaza; open year-round daily 6am–6pm; if closed, inquire within).* Its single-nave interior features several altarpieces from the 17C and 18C, with beautiful colonial paintings.

Huaquechula – *From Tochimilco, return to Atlixco and head south. Continue for 12km/7.4mi on Carr. 190, towards Izúcar de Matamoros; turn right and continue straight on for another 12km/7.4mi.* Several pre-Hispanic monoliths with calendar reliefs and a 16C stone cross that was originally in the atrium of the monastery have been preserved in the main square of this small town. The **Ex Convento Franciscano** *(on the east side of the plaza; church open year-round daily 9am–6pm; monastery open Tue–Sun 10am–5pm; if closed, inquire within; P$7)* is an impressive stone monument built in the 16C. Its elaborate portal combines Elizabethan Gothic elements with Plateresque shapes. The **side portal★★** has an exceptional medieval feel; its jambs feature the images of St. Peter and St. Paul, and above, one sees Christ, the Almighty, surrounded by angels announcing the Last Judgment. Inside, the church preserves several altarpieces and Baroque paintings-most noteworthy of which are those by Cristóbal de Villalpando-as well as a medieval-style carved stone pulpit. Facing into the atrium, the open-air chapel possesses a magnificently elaborate pointed vault.

★**Ex Convento de San Juan Bautista, Cuauhtinchán** – *57km/35mi. From Puebla head southeast on Blvd. Valsequillo and take Carr. 528 towards Valsequillo. After 44km/27.3mi, exit left and take Carr. 527 towards Tecali; 7km/4.3mi later bear left at the bifurcation and continue 6km/3.7mi to reach Cuauhtinchán. Open year-round Tue–Sun 10:30am–2pm & 3–6:30pm. P$5.* This imposing fortress-like complex, of the late 16C, includes all the elements of a monastery: an atrium, a church, a pilgrim's portico, an open chapel (partly destroyed), a cloister, wells and an orchard. Most notable in its exterior are the remaining walls of the open-air chapel, which depict scenes of Franciscans that were assassinated during the Evangelization. The interior is accessed through the church, which boasts a 17C, Plateresque **main altarpiece**. The south wall of the cloister is decorated with a unique **mural painting** of a lintel whose theme is the dialogue between an eagle and a jaguar, a symbol of the town's pre-Conquest martial heritage.

Don't miss the **Museo de Arte Religioso** *(located only steps away from the monastery, in what used to be a parish church; open Sun 10am–5pm, other days through appointment with Father Pedro Torija; P$5;* ☎ *2-275-0807)*. The Religious Art Museum features a fine 16C altarpiece and impeccable, ornamented wooden sculptures, as well as historic documents on the development of Cuauhtinchán.

Africam Safari and Tecali de Herrera – *45km/28mi. Go south from Puebla on the Carr. Estatal toward Tecali and after 18km/11mi turn right; 2km/1.2mi ahead lies Africam Safari.*

Africam Safari – *Open year-round daily 10am–5pm. P$45.* ✗ 🅴 ⚠ ☎ *(2) 236-1212.* This open-air zoo covers 34ha/84 acres bordering the Manuel Ávila Camacho Dam, better known as Laguna de Valsequillo. Either from your car or from one of the zoo buses, observe the free-roaming animals. Boat trips available at the first stop meander through the waterways ornamented with water lilies.

Votive Offerings

Tecali de Herrera – *From Africam Safari, return to the Carr. Estatal and continue 19km/11.8mi to Tecali de Herrera.* Onyx, alabaster and marble figures are preserved in the pleasant square of this small town. The now roofless basilica, **Ex Convento de San Francisco★** *(east of the plaza; open year-round daily 10am–5pm; P$7)*, an imposing ruin with a lovely facade, grass floor and sky-blue vaults, was built in the purest Renaissance style by the Franciscan friars who evangelized the region in the 16C. The three-aisle interior preserves a double row of Tuscan columns and round arches that used to support a pitched roof. The cloister still houses the remains of mural paintings and an exquisite gray stone baptismal font from the 16C. The **Parroquia de Tecali** *(north of the plaza; open year-round daily 8am–7pm)* possesses magnificent 18C gilded altarpieces, most crafted in the Baroque *estípite* style. Note the exception on the right, which is composed of oil paintings. Two 16C carved stone stoups and a pair of 17C fonts, one of which has an inscription in Náhuatl, lend a unique appearance to the interior.

Ex Convento de Tecamachalco – *Go east from Puebla on Carr. 150 toward Tehuacán to Tecamachalco (60km/37mi). Open year-round, daily 9am–6pm. Monastery Tue–Sun 10am–5pm. P$7.* The town's unimposing 16C **Franciscan monastery** possesses some of the most important **mural paintings★★** of the era. Created in 1562 by Juan Gersón and painted on *amate*, or ficus bark, paper and then glued on the lower choir ribbing, the paintings were inspired by Old Testament themes copied from European Bibles. Also noteworthy is the 16C baptismal font sculpted with archangels and foliage designs. A striking relief of an eagle with a *copilli* (headdress) decorates the base of the tower.

Cantona – *From Puebla head east and take the carr. federal libre (federal freeway) to Amozoc; after 18km/11mi exit left and continue 62km/38.4mi to reach the town of Oriental. Continue on the same road, which from here on becomes a dirt road and, after 10km/6.2mi, exit left. Continue 18km/11mi, following the signs to the archaeological site of Cantona. Open year-round daily 10am–5pm. P$16, free Sun and national holidays.* Over basaltic grounds rises the city of Cantona, considered the most urbanized of pre-Hispanic Mexico. This is reflected in its multiple interconnected avenues, which together create a vast network of communication among the diverse structures. To this day, archaeologists have only explored 1% of the site, which includes 15 buildings. Three spacious units make up this settlement: the largest, with a surface of 5sq km/3sq mi is located on the southern end; the ones in the center and on the northern end have similar proportions, each one 3.5sq km/2.2sq mi in magnitude. The site's numerous ball courts and religious plazas are indicative of the importance of rituals and religious ceremonies for its ancient inhabitants.

According to archaeological research, Cantona's occupation began during the Late Classic period, at a time when other great cities in central Mexico, such as Teotihuacán and Cholula, were coming to an end. During its apogee in the Epi Classic period (between AD 700 and 950), its inhabitants were distributed in

© Robert Frerck/Odyssey

residential courtyards. They established a system to control the flow of traffic and built avenues, alleyways, ball courts and structures in the architectural style that distinguishes Cantona: stones laid one over the other, without mortar or any material holding them together.

★ **Acatzingo** – *Go northeast from Puebla on Carr. 150D toward Orizaba 45km/28mi, turn left and continue 2km/1.2mi northeast on Carr. 140 toward Xalapa.* On Tuesdays, the town's main square holds one of the most important vegetable and fruit markets, selling lettuce, turnips, radishes, cabbage and other produce, in an incomparable feast of colors and scents. On the south side stands a long 19C arcade. An **Ex Convento Franciscano** *(east of the plaza; open year-round Fri 5pm–8pm, Sun 8am–5pm)* preserves vestiges of altarpieces and a few paintings. Its 16C, stone-carved holy water font is of exceptional quality. The parish church *(north of the plaza; open year-round daily 7am–8pm)*, **Parroquia de Acatzingo**, is set in an atrium embellished with a fountain decorated with pre-Hispanic emblems of Acatzingo. In the Latin-cross interior, two paintings by Miguel Jerónimo Zendejas adorn the main altar. On the left side, the **Capilla de la Virgen de los Dolores**★ *(same times and charges as the parish church)* boasts three elegant Baroque altarpieces with sculptures and paintings by the same artist; in addition, a band of beautiful tiles extends around the walls. The silver facade of the altar (1761) also merits attention. The Capilla de la Soledad (Chapel of Our Lady of Solitude), in the atrium, features additional works by Zendejas.

Libres – *94km/58mi. From Puebla head east 19km/12mi on Carr. 150D. At the tollbooth take the exit for Amozoc and continue on Carr. 129 toward Oriental (62km/38.5mi) and Libres (75km/46.6mi).* Formerly called San Juan de los Llanos (St. John of the Plains), this town's jewel-a set of magnificent altarpieces, made of carved and gilded wood and decorated with paintings-lies in the interior of the **parish church** *(open year-round daily 6am–2pm & 4–8pm)*. The **main altarpiece**★★ features burnished gold figures carved so delicately they resemble filigree. Worth noting are the caryatid columns and corresponding capitals of the third section and the right altarpiece.

★★ **Cuetzalan** – *Follow directions to Libres. From Libres, head 41km/25.5mi north on Carr. 129 to the Zacapoaxtla and Cuetzalan connection (Carr. 207); continue 15km/9.3mi to the Cuetzalan by-pass (libramiento), take a right (Carr. 201) and go another 36km/22.3mi to Cuetzalan.* This enchanting city lies nestled between thickly wooded mountain slopes. Its tropical climate prompted the construction of tile-covered pitched roofs with eaves that sometimes hang more than halfway across the street. A daily presence of Totonacs and Nahuas, the men in their traditional cotton shirts and pants, the women in their sparkling white **huipil** gowns, balancing multi-colored headdresses over .45m/1.9ft high, enlivens the town. Locals dress in all their finery especially for the Fourth of October **fiestas**★★ in honor of Saint Francis of Assisi, and during the Feria del Café (Coffee Fair) celebrating Cuetzalan's excellent coffee bean. Interesting sights include: **Parroquia de San Francisco de Asís** *(Plaza Principal; open year-round Mon–Sat 8am–7pm, Sun 8am–9pm)*, a 19C parish church with a basilican layout in the Renaissance style with Doric and Romanesque features; the **Museo Regional Calmahuiztic** *(2 de Abril, 1; open year-round Thu–Mon 10:30am–2pm & 3:30–5pm;* ☎ *233-100-04)* a regional museum

135

featuring dancers' costumes, musical instruments, ceremonial offerings to the dead, masks, fossils, indigenous costumes and some handicrafts; and the **Santuario de Nuestra Señora de Guadalupe** (*Calzada de Guadalupe, in the cemetery; open year-round daily 7:30am–6pm*) that commands a superb view of the city and surrounding hills. Familiarly known as the **Iglesia de los Jarritos** (Church of the Jars), its spire is decorated along the edges with the images of small clay jars. Cuetzalan is a good starting point for the following two excursions.

Yohualichan – *8km/5mi north of Cuetzalan along a paved road. Open year-round Tue–Sun 10am–5pm. P$7.* ☎ *(2) 331-0004.* Amid lush vegetation, discover the ceremonial mounds of this Totonac center, similar to those at El Tajín. Three pyramids, with a plaza in front, were raised on terraces to correct the unevenness of the terrain. To the south of the central plaza lie the ball court and *la tumba* (the tomb), a small underground vault.

Las Cascadas – *5km/3mi east along a dirt road and gully trail. A guide is recommended.* Of the natural swimming places created by the falls of the Cuixiatl River, Las Brisas is the most famous. Others include El Salto, Atempatahua and Las Hamacas. In these exotic surroundings of coffee bushes and tropical vegetation, swimmers can glide between smooth and mossy boulders.

QUERÉTARO★★

Querétaro

Population 559,222

Map of Principal Sights – Map p 114 **(AX)**

🄸 Pasteur, 4 Norte, Centro ☎ (4) 212-1004

Strategic in the country's development, this state capital is situated in the low-lying Bajío, one of the most fertile regions of Mexico. From a distance, visitors can enjoy a fine view of this attractively designed colonial city, neatly framed by its monumental aqueduct. Its narrow streets are flanked by palaces, old monasteries, luxurious residences and simple houses where time has left its patina on quarried stone buildings and on beautiful, intricately wrought ironwork. In spite of modern influences, the city has maintained its provincial and colonial air, best appreciated when strolling its peaceful walkways. No wonder the historic city center was added to UNESCO's list of World Heritage Sites in 1996. Querétaro is a crossroads: having witnessed important historic events due to its privileged location it continues to be at the center of the region's rapid growth and industrialization.

Historical Notes

The Founding of Querétaro on July 25, 1531 is attributed to the Otomí, Kho-ni (hispanicized as Conín), who took the Christian name Fernando de Tapia. Originally inhabited by a great indigenous majority, by the 17C Querétaro was ranked as the third city of New Spain, with the title **Muy Noble y Leal Ciudad de Santiago de Querétaro** (Very Noble and Loyal City of St. James of Querétaro) thanks to the prosperity derived from its fertile soil. In the 18C, the city reached its economic, social and artistic peak. At the dawning of the 19C, Querétaro became the scene of important events in the history of Mexico. In 1808, under the cover of literary meetings, leaders such as **Josefa Ortiz de Domínguez**, wife of the royally-appointed mayor, therefore called *La Corregidora*, organized the **Querétaro Conspiracy** against Spanish domination. Despite the fact that the conspiracy was discovered and its leaders placed under arrest, the Independence Movement was proclaimed not far from here, in Dolores, Hidalgo, on September 16, 1810.

Querétaro continued to play a prominent role in Mexican history. From 1847 to 1848, the city was the provisional capital of Mexico. The Treaty of Guadalupe Hidalgo that terminated the war with the United States was ratified here. In 1867 on the nearby hill, **Cerro de las Campanas**, Emperor Maximilian of Hapsburg was executed by a firing squad with Mexican generals Miguel Miramón and Tomás Mejía, thus putting an end to a period known as the *Segundo Imperio* (Second Empire). Half a century later, between 1916 and 1917, for the second time Querétaro became the provisional capital of Mexico according to a decision by Venustiano Carranza, when he promulgated from Querétaro the Constitution that still rules Mexico.

★★CITY CENTER *Map, p 137. 222km/138mi from Mexico City.*

Jardín Zenea – *Av. Corregidora, corner Av. Madero.* Also called Jardín General Obregón and built on the site of the former Plaza de los Escombros (Square of the Ruins), this central, shaded garden preserves its original design ordered by Governor Benito Zenea in 1874. At its center stands a fountain dedicated to the goddess Hebe with matching characteristic bandstand and lamps. East of this garden lies the **Templo de San Francisco** with a relief of the Apostle James on its facade. Admire the beautiful cupola in its quiet Neoclassical interior.

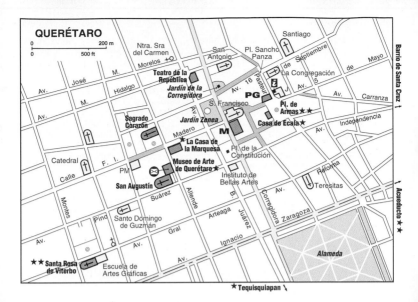

Museo Regional de Querétaro (Ex Convento de San Francisco) (M) – *Av. Corregidora, 3 South, east of the garden. Open year-round Tue–Sun 10am–7pm. Closed national holidays. P$16.* ☎ *(4) 212-2031* This museum presents a survey of Querétaro state's history. Beginning in 1540 as the St. Francis Monastery, the site had become the center of Querétaro's life and activities by the 18C. As liberal troops destroyed most of the immense monastery in the 19C, today only the two-story section around the **main courtyard** and the pleasant **orange grove** remain.

Lower level – This collection of artifacts from state archaeological sites reflects Querétaro's geographical location on the border between Mesoamerica and the Arid Zone inhabited primarily by nomadic tribes. One hall explains the development of the indigenous groups that have lived in the state from pre-Hispanic times to the present: the Pames and Otomis.

Upper level – The **main hall** contains several valuable pieces. These include 18C richly carved wardrobes, an enormous 17C wooden door, beautiful 18C polychrome inlaid statues of saints, such as Our Lady of Sorrows in its original colors, a burnished wood table and oil paintings by Juan Correa and José de Ibarra, also from the 18C.

★★Plaza de Armas (Plaza de la Independencia) – *Av. Pasteur, corner of 5 de Mayo.* Leafy Indian laurels ornament the main plaza, considered one of the most beautiful in Latin America. In the center, note the statue of the Marquis de la Villa del Villar del Águila, who built the aqueduct that brought water to Querétaro. Bordering this attractive square, graceful well-preserved ancient buildings now house appealing restaurants, the **Casa Queretana de Artesanías** handicraft store *(Andador Libertad, 52; open year-round Tue–Thu 11am–2pm & 4–8pm, Fri 11am–2pm & 4–9pm, Sat 11am–9pm and Sun 10am–5pm; closed Jan 1 & Dec 25;* ✗ ☎ *4-214-1235).* An elegant hotel occupies an 18C **building**.

Palacio de Gobierno (Antiguas Casas Reales, Cárcel y Palacio de la Corregidora) (PG) – *On the Plaza's north.* This beautiful, 18C government palace once housed the treasury and prison before becoming the residence of *La Corregidora*, **Josefa Ortiz de Domínguez**. The tall sturdy walls of this solid two-story building harbored the furtive meetings that launched Independence. When the conspiracy was discovered, *La Corregidora* was placed under house arrest. With the help of the mayor, Ignacio Pérez, she was able to alert Miguel Hidalgo, the priest in the nearby parish of Dolores, that the conspiracy had been discovered.

★Casa de Ecala (Oficinas del Desarrollo Integral de la Familia-DIF) – *West side of the Plaza.* This handsome, 18C two-story palace is now the headquarters of the government-sponsored Comprehensive Development of the Family Program. The Baroque **facade★** of this stately house is striking for the sumptuous elegance of its wrought-iron balconies. In the top section, a cord carved in stone separates the quarried stone work from the blue and white Talavera tiles.

Jardín de la Corregidora – *Av. Corregidora and Andador 16 de Septiembre.* In this peaceful spot, the romantic **monument★** to Doña Josefa Ortiz de Domínguez and the **Árbol de la Amistad** (Friendship Tree) endure in harmony. Restaurants and cafes surrounding the garden offer a variety of dining opportunities.

Teatro de la República – *Av. Juárez, 22, corner of Av. Ángela Peralta. One block east of Jardín de la Corregidora.* A historic edifice built in the mid 19C, the theater, originally named after General Iturbide, opened its doors in 1852. Maximilian of

Hapsburg was sentenced to death here by a war tribunal in 1867, and the current Mexican Constitution was signed in this building in 1917. In recent years, the theater has hosted outstanding national and international cultural figures, and is presently used exclusively for important cultural and civic events.

Templo del Sagrado Corazón de Jesús (Santa Clara) – *Francisco I. Madero, corner Ignacio Allende. Open year-round daily 10am–1pm & 5–7pm.* This plain, 17C building was erected thanks to a donation from Diego de Tapia, descendant of Fernando de Tapia (Conín), the Founder of Querétaro. The front garden, formerly the convent orchard, contains a **fountain** with a sculpture of Neptune by the Mexican artist, Francisco Eduardo Tresguerras (1759–1833). The severe construction of the exterior does not match the richly ornamented 18C **altarpieces** that are preserved in the **interior★★** of the single-nave church, now dedicated to the Sacred Heart of Jesus. Noteworthy are the elaborately decorated pulpit and a choir screen that partially conceals the organ. On September 15, 1810, Josefa Ortiz de Domínguez, *La Corregidora*, was held in one of these convent cells after the discovery of the conspiracy of Independence.

★**La Casa de la Marquesa** – *Madero, 41, corner Ignacio Allende (across from the Santa Clara church). Visit by appointment only.* ☎ *(4) 212-0092.* The Marquise de la Villa del Villar del Águila lived in this stately Baroque house, completed in 1756, with a distinguished stone facade and a lovely, carved wooden gate. The mansion possesses a *zaguán* (large entranceway) and a pretty Mudejar interior **courtyard★** with Moorish arches. Remodeled in 1995, La Casa de la Marquesa now operates as a luxury hotel.

★**Museo de Arte de Querétaro (Ex Convento de San Agustín)** – *Ignacio Allende, 14, Sur. Open year-round Tue–Sun 10am–6pm. Closed Jan 1 & Dec 25. P$10, free Tue.* ☎ *(4) 212-2357.* Built in the 18C by the local architect, Ignacio Mariano de las Casas, the Querétaro Art Museum presently contains an important historical retrospective of national and European art. The gallery also boasts a rich collection of colonial paintings, from 17C Mannerist to 17C and 18C Baroque. A series of oil paintings by Cristóbal de Villalpando on the *apostolado* (apostolate) merits special attention. The museum is located in the monastery's magnificent Baroque **cloister★**, richly adorned with remarkable stonework including **caryatid columns**, bird and floral decorations.

Templo de San Agustín – *Ignacio Allende, corner Pino Suárez. Open year-round daily 11am–1pm & 5–8:30pm.* This handsome 18C church, attributed to Fray Luis Martínez Lucio, was erected atop a large stepped platform. Its truncated tower was never finished, and the great tile-covered **cupola** appears to be supported by a band of musician angels. The **facade★** recalls the structure of an altarpiece, framed by spiraling Solomonic columns that guard the sculptures of Augustinian saints. A great stonework **crucifix★** rises above, supported by a warrior angel.

★★**Templo de Santa Rosa de Viterbo** – *Arteaga, corner Ezequiel Montes. Open year-round daily 6:30am–8pm.* The Church of Santa Rosa de Viterbo is the crowning achievement for Ignacio Mariano de las Casas, an architect who left a profound mark throughout Querétaro. This tall and stately 18C structure inspires respect and at the same time stimulates the viewer's fantasy with its Mudejar influence, apparent in the cupola and the slim tower, and with its unusual upward thrusting **flying buttresses**. These odd inverted buttresses, each one decorated with an impish mask that is sticking out its tongue, have become the symbol of Querétaro.

Interior – Dedicated to the Virgin of Guadalupe and other saints, the six gilded 18C altarpieces constitute veritable jewels of Baroque art. An outstanding altarpiece covers the upper and lower choir, crowned with a golden fan, while the lower choir is decorated with medallions depicting Christ and the Apostles. Below, the venerable image of *Santo Cristo del Llanto* (The Crying Christ) attracts the devotion of the faithful. Behind the lower choir's double grille hides the church's Baroque organ, built in 1759 and still in use. On the right, do not miss the **pulpit★** inlaid with silver, ebony and ivory.

The **minor sacristy** preserves an anonymous 18C **portrait★** of the beautiful Sor Anna María de San Francisco, a convent student.

The vast **sacristy** hall houses an enormous painting of an orchard representing the history and traditions of the convent. Note the sculptures of Christ and the Twelve Apostles, which belonged to the original main altar, the 18C octagonal burnished carved-wood table, the stoup and a set of gilded wooden towel-holders.

BARRIO DE SANTA CRUZ

800m/875yd east of the City Center along Calle Independencia.

Set on Sangremal Hill, this district offers a splendid panorama of the colonial city with its impressive aqueduct. Fernando de Tapia defeated the indigenous diehards here who continued to defy Spanish authority, thus establishing the Villa de Santiago de Querétaro. According to local tradition, the apparition of Saint James on horseback helped sway the battle in Tapia's favor. Begun in 1609, the **Convento**

de la Santa Cruz *(Independencia, corner of Felipe Luna; 25min guided visit, year-round Tue–Fri 9am–2pm & 4–6pm, Sat–Sun & holidays 9am–4:30pm; donations accepted)* by the end of the 17C housed the Colegio Apostólico de Propaganda Fide (Apostolic School for the Propagation of the Faith), the first catholic, missionary school in the American continent. This learning center would spawn many generations of great missionaries who brought the Christian faith and Western culture to northern Mexico and to Central America. Within the convent, a graceful patio surrounded by stone walls proudly preserves the popular **thorn trees** *(árboles de espina)*, so called because their branches fill with cross-shaped thorns that, according to legend, descend from the cane belonging to Fray Margil de Jesús, a dedicated evangelizer of saintly reputation.

★★ AQUEDUCT *Calzada de los Arcos.*

This imposing construction was begun in 1726 and finished in 1736, thanks to Juan Antonio de Urrutia y Arana, Marquis of the Villa del Villar del Águila. Symbol of Querétaro, the aqueduct has been considered one of the most admirable works of civil engineering on the American continent. It combines aesthetic and technical skills in a monumental 74-arch stretch 1,280m/1,400yd long, which reaches a height of 23m/76ft. The aqueduct facilitated the construction of many public and private fountains in the city.

© Gustavo Gatto

Aqueduct

EXCURSIONS

Bernal – *58km/36mi. Exit the city of Querétaro heading east on Carr. 57 Querétaro-México, after 17km/10.5mi, take the exit to Cadereyta and continue straight on to reach the town of Bernal.* The main attraction in this charming town with colorful streets is its giant rock monolith (reaching an altitude of approx. 300m/984ft) known as the **Peña de Bernal**. It stands out in the desert-like landscape for a 100km/62mi radius. A source of inspiration, the monolith was considered sacred by the ancient Chichimec tribes that inhabited this region. In the downtown area, one can also purchase the traditional and delicious *dulces de leche* (milk sugar candy), regional handicrafts and minerals, such as opals and quartz.

★**Tequisquiapan** – *51km/31.7mi. Go southeast from Querétaro on Carr. 57D; after 47km/29mi, take the left exit and continue 22km/13.7mi.* Stone paved streets adorned with colorful bougainvillea grace this pleasant town, famous for its thermal springs, which supposedly possess medicinal and soothing qualities. While the town's attractive **plaza** is dominated by the late-19C, Neoclassic Parroquia de Santa María de la Asunción, it is also surrounded by **pedestrian walkways** and archways lined by restaurants, handicraft shops and candy stores. Nearby **markets** offer regional handicrafts, such as wicker baskets, rattan furniture and hand-woven textiles. According to calculations made in the early 20C, Tequisquiapan is the geographical center of Mexico. Just 3km/1.9mi southeast of the downtown area, amid the silence of cactus plants, lies the **Bernal railway station**, an early-20C construction that commands an excellent **view** of the surrounding valley.

Cadereyta – *43km/26.7mi. Exit Tequisquiapan heading north and take Carr. 120 to Cadereyta.* The colorful houses and churches in this serene village invite one to discover more of the picturesque spots in the state of Querétaro. Particularly appealing is a visit to the greenhouses and nurseries in "Quinta Fernando Schmoll" *(Calle del Pilancón, Barrio de Fuentes and Pueblo Nuevo; open year-round daily 9am–5pm; ☏ 4-276-0256),* where its owners have spent decades reproducing and caring for over 200 species of cacti and succulent plants.

Misiones de la SIERRA GORDA★

Querétaro
Map of Principal Sights – Map p 114 **(AW)**
🛈 Pasteur, 4 Norte, Centro ☏ (4) 212-1287

These five interesting evangelizing missions lie in a setting of extensive valleys and wild mountain ranges that give them an unforgettable charm. Known as the Sierra Gorda, this mountain range extends to the east of the Sierra Madre Oriental, which spans the states of Querétaro, Hidalgo, Guanajuato and San Luis Potosí. The rich and varied countryside possesses lush vegetation, valuable minerals hidden in arid zones, lofty pine-covered mountains and fertile lands irrigated by the Moctezuma, Jalpan and Concá rivers. For many years, the roads leading to the missions were accessible only during the dry season, until they were paved around the mid 20C.

Historical Notes

The indomitable nature of the numerous ancient settlements of Chichimec hunters and gatherers, as well as conflicts between the different missionary orders hampered the early evangelization of this region. The Franciscan order at the Colegio Franciscano de San Fernando (in Mexico City), in favor of a more gentle approach, took charge of the existing missions and established new ones. The famous Franciscan missionary, **Fray Junípero Serra**, arrived in the region in 1750 and settled down in Jalpan. Together with Fray Francisco Palou, he accomplished great evangelizing work and promoted the economic and agricultural development of the region. The Franciscans gradually gained the trust of the natives who subsequently accepted the sedentary life and settled in five communities that correspond to the mid-18C mission outposts.

VISIT

Although vestiges of missions founded since the 16C abound in the Sierra, the five most important-Jalpan, Concá, Landa, Tilaco and Tancoyol-were founded and constructed between 1744 and 1768. Possessing specific characteristics that make the buildings unique examples of Mexican Baroque architecture, these missions preserve elements of 16C architecture and integrate other elements, such as Florentine ornamentation. Indigenous craftsmanship, apparent in the elaborate polychrome facades over stone mortar, presents Christian and Franciscan symbols with a clear didactic intent. All five missions share similarities in their design and towers; their interiors follow a Latin cross layout and display precarious ornamentation, as well as "porthole"-shaped choir windows.

Misión de Jalpan – *174km/108mi northeast of Tequisquiapan on Carr. 120. Open year-round daily 7am–8pm. ☏ (4) 212-1004.* This enchanting mission, the first and largest of the five, dedicated to the Apostle James, was built by **Fray Junípero Serra**. Its **facade★**, adorned in red and yellow painted mortarwork, presents an interesting combination of plant motifs, Franciscan symbols and a double-headed eagle (a Hapsburg emblem) devouring a serpent; peculiar figures are also present in the side streets. The second row of niches holds both the Mexican Virgin of Guadalupe and the Spanish Virgin of the Pillar.

Opposite the church, the **Museo Histórico de la Sierra Gorda** *(Fray Junípero Serra, 1; open year-round Mon–Fri 8am–7pm, Sat 8am–3pm, Sun 9am–1pm; closed national holidays; P$5; ☏ 4-296-0165)* occupies the space where once stood a 16C fort. Through its collection, visitors can delve into the historic development of the missions, as well as into the life and works of Fray Junípero Serra.

Misión de Concá – *Leave Jalpan on Carr. 69 toward Río Verde; after 35km/21.7mi turn left and continue 1km/.6mi on a stone-paved road. Open year-round daily 8am–8pm. ☏ (4) 212-1412.* Crossing a modern bridge over the Santa María and Ayutla Rivers-characterized for having different colored waters due to their various temperatures-visitors arrive at the smallest of the mission churches, located in a town with the same name.

Concá possesses a stunning bright red **facade★** and an imposing Franciscan coat of arms. The second section boasts four spiraling columns hung with grapes, flanking the figures–in curved arched niches–of St. Louis King and St. Roque with his loyal dog. Above, the Archangel St. Michael, the mission's patron, steps on the devil while raising his sword in victory.

Misión de Landa – *Go east from Jalpan on Carr. 120 toward Xilitla; continue 22km/13.6mi, then turn left for 300m/328yd on a stone-paved road. Open year-round daily 7am–6pm.* ☎ *(4) 212-1004.* The church's regal **facade★★** honors the Immaculate Conception of Landa de Matamoros. In the first section, four *estípite* pilasters forming curved-arch niches hold the figures of St. Jacob of La Marca, St. Bernardino of Sienna, St. John of Capistran and St. Albert of Sarzana, 5C evangelizing preachers who were also reformers of the Franciscan order. While a niche with the Blessed Virgin crowns the door, striking images of Juan Duns Escoto and Sor María de Agreda, defenders of the Blessed Virgin's purity, depicted in a writing pose, flank the choir windows.

The third section contains two medallions representing passages from the life of Christ: the Entry into Jerusalem and the Flagellation. Just as at Concá, St. Michael triumphantly presides over the building.

★**Misión de Tilaco** – *Exit Landa heading northeast on Carr. 120 toward Xilitla, after 10km/6.2mi turn right and continue 16km/10mi. Open year-round daily 7am–5pm.* ☎ *(4) 212-1412.* Tilaco consists of a church, a convent and an open-air chapel. Its unusual two-level atrium preserves the corner chapels and a wrought-iron cross in the center. On the third section of the **facade★**, flanked by *estípite* pilasters, St. Francis of Assisi-to whom this mission is dedicated-contemplates the marvelous **view** of the valley from his balcony. Four angel musicians surround the saint—one plays the violin, another the guitar and the other two appear to be singing while opening the curtains. A tiny well stands in the middle of the small lancet-arch cloister.

Misión de Tancoyol – *From Tilaco, return to Carr. 120 and turn right heading toward Xilitla; after 7km/4.3mi, turn left and continue 21.6km/13.4mi. Open year-round daily 7am–5pm.* ☎ *(4) 212-1004.* Dedicated to Our Lady of Light, this mission arises from a beautiful and fertile valley surrounded by mountains covered in thick vegetation. Located in front of a broad atrium, the Tancoyol complex has preserved the remains of its corner chapels, and the pedestal of the atrial cross. In the second section of the church's **facade★** a bas-relief depicts the appearance of Christ's wounds on St. Francis' skin. In the third section, two angels with incense holders flank a slender cross, while, directly above them, two smaller angels pull back the curtains.

EXCURSION

★★**Las Pozas (Casa del Inglés)** – *83km/51.5mi, located in the town of Xilitla. Description p 215.*

Mexico

Map of Principal Sights – Map p 114 **(AY)**

🖪 ☎ (5) 956-0052 or www.archaeology.la.asu.edu/teo

For a variety of reasons, Teotihuacán was clearly the most important city in Mesoamerica during the Classic period. Presently, it rates as the most important archaeological site of the Mexican High Plateau, not only for its historical value but also for its size, monumental constructions, and perfect urban design. Precursor of a large portion of Mexican mythology, the sacred site celebrated the meeting of the gods, the heavens, the earth and humanity.

Historical Notes

Teotihuacán appeared at the beginning of the present era and bloomed between AD 300 and 600, during which period it held its greatest economic sway over all of Mesoamerica's people and innumerable buildings were constructed. The city eventually covered an area of 20sq km/7.7sq mi and supported a population of 200,000. Around AD 600 the center began its decline due to an exhaustion of natural resources, social conflict and the crisis of centralized political power. Scholars believe that between AD 600 and 750 during a terrible fire the city was looted and partially destroyed.

After the fall of Teotihuacán (AD 700–750), the region was occupied by Toltec tribes and, finally, by the Aztecs (around 1325), who used it as a ceremonial center until the arrival of the Spanish. The name Teotihuacán, "place of the gods or where men were transformed into gods", was given by the Aztecs.

ARCHAEOLOGICAL SITE *Map opposite.*

At km46/mi28.5 on the Carr. México-Pirámides (highway to Pachuca). Open year-round daily 7am–6:30pm. P$20. ✗ 🖪 ☎ (5) 956-0052. The site has five entrance doors. Enter by Door 1. Through the vestibule, the Calzada de los Muertos begins on the left; facing the vestibule exit stands la Ciudadela.

La Ciudadela – Upon seeing this enormous plaza (400m/1,312ft on each side) and the four platforms flanking it topped by small temples, the Spaniards assumed it was a military structure; hence, the name, "the citadel" for what was, in fact, Teotihuacán's governmental palace.

Templo de Quetzalcóatl y Tláloc – *Walk along the passageway behind the first structure.* One of the most fascinating buildings of the complex, this temple best exemplifies the expressive force behind Teotihuacán's sculptures. Serpent heads decorate the temple's stairway walls, while slithering plumed serpents, surrounded by seashells, adorn the ramps. On the vertical panels with aquatic motifs, several heads of Quetzalcóatl, the plumed serpent, seem to emerge from flowers. This snake deity, representing the constant duality between the material and the immaterial, alternates with Tláloc, the rain god, depicted in the form of a deity with large ringed eyes.

Calzada de los Muertos – The city's main thoroughfare, named "Avenue of the Dead" because of the tomblike mounds flanking it, was originally 4km/2.5mi long and ran from the Citadel to the Plaza of the Moon. Up to now only a small portion (2km/1.2mi) of this grand street has been explored. A few yards farther on, a canal traverses the avenue. Originally a stream that supplied the city with water through a complex underground system, it marks the border between north and south.

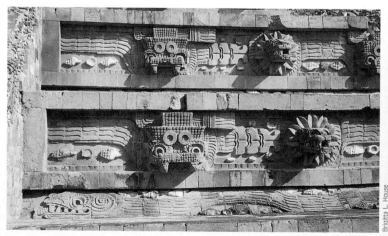

Templo de Quetzalcóatl, detail

Brigitta L. House

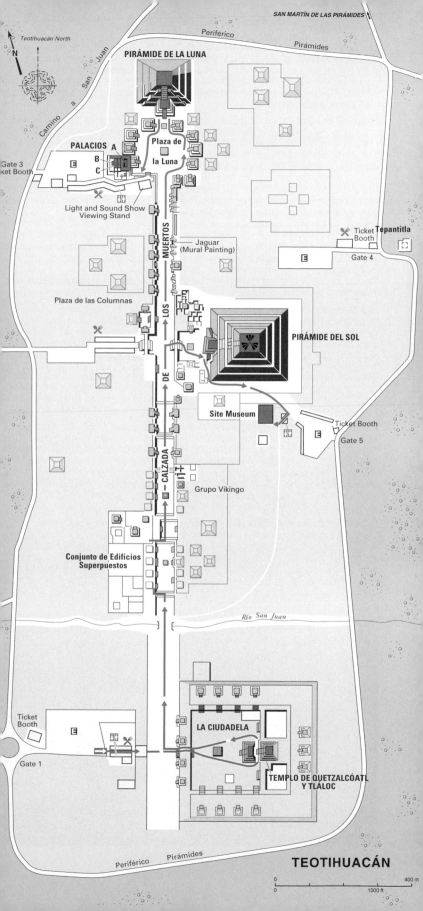

Conjunto de los Edificios Superpuestos – Located on the left side of the Avenue of the Dead, these buildings housed the priestly classes. So as not to damage the outer structures, exploration was carried out through a system of tunnels, revealing the manner in which the design of the ceremonial center was altered in different periods. The intriguing remains of staircases, floors and mural paintings can be seen in the passageways.

Pirámide del Sol – One of the most astonishing structures of the pre-Hispanic world, the Pyramid of the Sun embodies the sum of the astronomical knowledge possessed by the inhabitants of the fabulous ancient city. The remarkable precision of its design continues to astound archaeologists and scientists. Constructed along the Avenue of the Dead, the pyramid faces west, aligned with a point on the horizon where the sun sets on May 19 and July 25—the two days of the year in which the sun sits exactly over the peak of the pyramid at noon uniting the zenith of the heavens with the center of the world. This special orientation explains the 17-degree deviation of the north-south Avenue of the Dead.

The impressive Pyramid of the Sun, 225m/737ft on each side and 65m/213ft high, was constructed with five successive layers of mud, covered with blocks of stone, thus producing five tiers. Many scholars suggest that there was probably a temple atop the pyramid. In spite of its gigantic proportions, the structure is strikingly well balanced.

The ascent—242 stairs with narrow steps and high risers—rewards visitors with a **view**★★ of the site's grandeur.

Site Museum – *On the south side of the Sun Pyramid, through door 5.* Designed by architect Pedro Ramírez Vázquez and inaugurated in 1994, this modern building contains an excellent collection of artifacts found on the site, as well as a large, scale model that explains Teotihuacán's design and the layout of its buildings.

Return to the Avenue of the Dead and walk to the northern end.

Plaza de la Luna – Symmetrical temples bordering this intriguing plaza create a striking aesthetic ensemble. All the lower facades display the typical Teotihuacán *talud-tablero* (sloping panel) structure. Archaeologists believe that this smaller plaza was used for specialized ceremonies.

Pirámide de la Luna – *North end of Avenue of the Dead.* With a base measuring approximately 42m/138ft high and 150m/492ft on each side, the Pyramid of the Moon boasts a summit the same height as the Pyramid of the Sun because it stands on the site's highest point. The structure is four-tiered with sloping sides. The lower section's facade presents the Teotihuacán talud-tablero structure with a central stairway flanked by ramps. From the top platform, looking toward the south, visitors can admire the impressive layout of the complex, as well as its harmonious integration with the surrounding **landscape**.

Palacio de Quetzalpapálotl (A) – *Southwestern corner of the Plaza of the Moon.* The Palace of the Butterfly-bird (from the Náhuatl, *quetzal*, bird, and *papálotl*, butterfly), once part of the priests' residential complex, has been completely restored. A staircase leads to a rectangular chamber on the right, a sort of small vestibule with square columns. These pillars still bear the original reliefs symbolizing the butterfly-bird. It is thought that the eye sockets were inlaid with obsidian and that the birds were painted red.

View from Pirámide de la Luna

Palacio de los Jaguares (B) – *On the left, west of the Quetzalpapálotl Palace.*
Sitting on a level lower than the adjacent building, the Palace of the Jaguars consists of a series of porticos connected to a square courtyard. On the east side of
the courtyard, a small staircase leads to the temple entrance. In the back and on
the left, the exterior walls of the chambers feature paintings representing enormous, beautifully stylized jaguars. Wearing feathered headdresses, they blow into
a sea conch grasped with one paw, from which emerges a sign that symbolizes
the sound produced. Glyphs abound, referring to dates and to Tláloc, the rain god,
while most of the jaguar figures allude to rain and fertility.

Templo de los Caracoles Emplumados (C) – *Follow the passageway to the right
of the wall painting, entering the building to the west.* Containing several different
facades and situated directly below the Quetzalpapálotl Palace, the Temple of the
Plumed Snails belongs to the oldest substructure on the site. On the right, note
the masterfully decorated facade with bas-reliefs of plumed snails that gives the
temple its name; there are also well-preserved paintings of colorful birds.

Additional Sights

Taking the route around the site, visitors can reach other Teotihuacán complexes
that still preserve traces of mural paintings.

Tepantitla – *Opposite Door 4, 100m/109yd from the route.* Do not miss the
intriguing features of the various mural paintings contained in these ruins, most
notably the interpretation of the elements comprising the *Tlalocan*, or paradise of
the god Tláloc. On the upper part, the god himself is portrayed reigning in heaven.
The Museo Nacional de Antropología in Mexico City displays an excellent reproduction of this mural in the Teotihuacán hall.

Tetitla – *Between Doors 2 and 3 (follow the signs).* Approximately 120 walls
painted with different figures related to jaguars, serpents, birds and aquatic elements grace this complex labyrinth of priestly courtyards and corridors.

Atetelco – *700m/766yd east (Take the path opposite the exit).* Note in one of the
courtyards a small pyramid built to scale, with its stairway and sections in a talud-
tablero configuration.

Conjuntos de Zacuala y Yayahuala – *Returning toward Tetitla, take the left path.*
At the **Zacuala** site, a residential structure, observe the representations of Tláloc.
Yayahuala, a complex of rooms, preserves vestiges of mural painting on its walls.

EXCURSION

★★**Convento de Acolman** – *On the Carretera México-Pirámides toward Mexico City,
9km/5.6mi from Teotihuacán. Calle de los Agustinos, Acolman. Open year-round
Tue–Sun 10am–5pm. P$14.* This notable Augustinian monastery, built in 1571,
has preserved its original layout despite having been rebuilt and remodeled several
times over the centuries following flood damages. One of the few examples of
Plateresque style in Mexico, it blends features of the iconography and crafts of the
neighboring indigenous communities.
Inside the church, on the first section of the left wall, the mural painting of a
Churrigueresque altarpiece merits attention.
The **main cloister**, designed in the Renaissance style, features columns accented with
plant motifs crafted with indigenous artistry. Note the lovely fresco paintings in
several monastery passageways and copies of European engravings on the door-
frames.
Across the road from the atrium's main door stands a fascinating 16C **atrial cross**
of indigenous workmanship with symbols of the Passion of Christ carved in stone.

*Unless otherwise indicated, distances given after each stop on an itinerary are
calculated from the previous town or sight described.*

Museo Nacional del Virreinato
in TEPOTZOTLÁN★★★

Mexico
Map of Principal Sights – Map p 114 **(AY)**
🖪 Plaza Hidalgo, 99, Downtown ☎ (5) 876-2771

The majestic architectural complex of the **Ex Colegio Jesuita de Tepotzotlán** (Tepotzotlán Seminary), now housing the National Colonial Museum, dominates the small town of Tepotzotlán. The rich facade of the church, the tree-lined atrium and the enormous orchard bear witness to the wealth of the Jesuit seminary of St. Martin and St. Francis Xavier whose beautiful interior can still inspire a sense of awe.

Historical Notes

Although the first evangelists of this Otomí town were Franciscans, at the end of the 16C Tepotzotlán was given to the Jesuit order with the mission of converting the children of the local indigenous chiefs (at St. Martin Seminary) and later forming new generations of Jesuits (at the Novitiate of St. Francis Xavier). In 1591 the novitiate was transferred to Puebla, but in 1606 it returned to Tepotzotlán, thanks to a generous gift willed by the rich merchant, Pedro Ruiz de Ahumada. The Jesuits used the money to build three seminary schools—the third a language institute where the members could learn Náhuatl, Otomí and Mazahua—and to buy lands that would become productive haciendas.

After the Jesuits' expulsion in 1767, the building stood vacant for years, until it was given to the secular clergy for the Royal College Training Seminary (Real Colegio Seminario de Instrucción), which continued until the 19C. After their return, the Jesuits reoccupied the seminary until 1914, when they finally left as a result of the turmoil caused by the Mexican Revolution.

VISIT

Go north from Mexico City on the road to Querétaro; after 38km/23.5mi, take the right exit for Tepotzotlán and cross over the highway; continue 3km/1.9mi to Plaza Hidalgo.

Plaza Hidalgo – This square consists of the walled atrium of San Pedro church and a large esplanade facing the Iglesia de San Francisco Javier which boasts a solitary stone-carved **atrial cross** with the symbols of the Passion of Christ.

Iglesia de San Francisco Javier – Construction of this church lasted from 1670 until the mid 18C. In 1760 the rector, Pedro Reales, ordered the facade, tower and altarpieces remodeled. The splendid **facade★★** carved in stone is considered one of the most outstanding examples of the Baroque *estípite* style in Mexico. It sets off a marvelous play of light and shadow that produces different tonalities in the stone. Jesuit iconography and rich ornamentation on the outside are echoed in the altarpieces on the inside. Lavishly decorated double *estípite* pilasters and intricate ironwork grace the tower.

★★★**Museo Nacional del Virreinato** – *The museum entrance is reached through the tree-filled atrium. Open year-round Tue 10am–5pm, Wed–Sun 9am–6pm. Closed Jan 1 & Dec 25. P$16. ✗.* This museum contains a priceless **collection★** of arts that flourished during colonial times: silver instruments, liturgical robes, statues, ivory figures and portraits of crowned nuns that were part of a private collection donated to the museum. The southern side of the building opens onto a wide overlook.

Claustro de los Aljibes – The austere Cloister of the Cisterns, ornamented with a series of **paintings★** by Cristóbal de Villalpando (1649–1714) depicting scenes from the life of St. Ignatius of Loyola, founder of the Jesuits, greets visitors at the entrance to the museum. In the central **patio**, note the ingenious play of cornices in descending order that guide falling rain into the large cisterns.

Sacristy – *Descending one side of the Claustro de los Aljibes.* This colorful sacristy preserves **paintings** by Miguel Cabrera, as well as flowing **floral motif** decorations on borders and friezes in tempera.

★★★**Church's Interior** – *Beside the sacristy.* Inside, the gilded altarpieces glistening in the light coming through the openings in the dome, and the vivid red carpets and illuminated pilasters create an indelible impression. Eleven *estípite* altarpieces of remarkable craftsmanship embellished with beautiful sculptures decorate the church walls. The high altar is dedicated to St. Francis Xavier, the church's patron saint. Two monumental paintings by Miguel Cabrera: *Alegoría de la Sangre de Cristo* (The Allegory of the Blood of Christ) and *El Patrocinio de la Virgen María a la Compañía de Jesús* (Patronage of the Virgin Mary to the Jesuit Order) grace the walls of the lower choir.

★★★ **Camarín de la Virgen** – *Access through the Capilla de la Virgen de Loreto*. The dressing room, used to change the robes on the statue of Our Lady before processions, is a jewel of Mexican Baroque. In this small space, the walls of which are completely covered with polychrome mortarwork, classical Baroque features combine with local elements such as mirrors, caryatids with indigenous traits and rich coloring. Beside the chapel, the **Relicario de San José★** preserves a precious, richly adorned altarpiece.

★ **Capilla Doméstica** – *Between the two cloisters*. This chapel, containing a striking altarpiece gaily decorated with mirrors, relics and paintings, was reserved for Jesuit novices in training. Small paste figures now replace the original ivory.

Cocinas – *Lower level, beside the Orange Cloister*. Near the patio, which has an unusual water spigot, take time to appreciate the layout of the seminary's old kitchen, with its cellar, pantry and cold room.

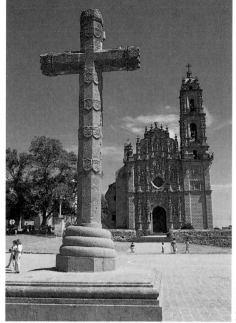

© Gustavo Gatto

Iglesia de San Francisco Javier

Claustro de los Naranjos – A recreation and leisure area for the order's novices, the Cloister of the Orange Trees consists of an attractive stone-carved fountain amid inviting orange trees surrounded by a graceful arcade. A small, picturesque chapel in the large and shady orchard nearby offered a place for quiet prayer.

EXCURSION

★ **Arcos del Sitio** – *Go 26km/16.2mi west from Tepotzotlán toward Fraccionamiento Cabañas*. This majestic 18C **aqueduct**, almost 60m/197ft high at midpoint, consists of 56 arches on several different levels. Considered one of the tallest in Latin America, it carried water from the prosperous Jesuit Hacienda de Xalpa to the seminary.

TLAXCALA★

Tlaxcala
Population 63,423
Map of Principal Sights – Map p 115 **(BY)**
🚻 Av. Juárez, 18, corner of Lardizabal ☎ (2) 462-0027

A charming and pleasant city, Tlaxcala maintains its colonial atmosphere through the preservation of its original city plan and the 16C buildings that border its shaded plazas. Capital of Mexico's smallest state, it is also one of the richest in history, culture, religious architecture, handicrafts and culinary art. The area's diversified economy centers on the agricultural produce from the fertile valleys of Huamantla, the fierce bulls from the wild zones of Terrenate and Tlaxco, and traditional textile manufactures from the region of Santa Ana Chiautempan. Because of Tlaxcala's proximity to Puebla, local architecture has been widely influenced by the Puebla Baroque style, as evidenced in the elaborate facades covered with brick, tiles and mortarwork and the church interiors decorated with plasterwork. Large numbers of fine Baroque altarpieces, found even in the most modest villages, attest to the strong religious devotion of the inhabitants.

Historical Notes

Upon the arrival of the Spaniards, Tlaxcala consisted of four dominions: Tepeticpac, Ocotelulco, Quiahuiztlán and Tizatlán, north of the present capital. These territories maintained a strong rivalry with México-Tenochtitlán, which led the Tlaxcaltecs to establish a military alliance with the Conquistadors. Their chieftain, **Xicohténcatl**, who first fought against the Spaniards, eventually assisted them in capturing the capital of the Aztec Empire. Later, the Tlaxcaltecs helped the Spaniards conquer northern Mexico and Central America. The city of Tlaxcala, as such, was founded on October 3, 1525 by the Spaniards, who did not consider the locations of the ancient pre-Hispanic domains adequate. Because of its rapid growth, Tlaxcala received from King Charles V of Spain the title of Loyal City, as well as a coat of arms, on April 22, 1535.

CITY CENTER

115km/71.4mi from Mexico City and 32km/20mi from Puebla.

★ **Plaza de la Constitución** – Tlaxcala's most significant buildings border this broad, shady plaza. The square itself has several interesting features: in the center, a bandstand of brick, stone and Talavera tiles from the mid 19C; the octagonal fountain (1646), a gift from Spain's King, Philip IV; and four more fountains, of modern manufacture, representing the Four Dominions that ruled ancient Tlaxcala. **Los portales** (the arcade) has served as a meeting place for traders since the 16C. Today, several cafes and restaurants under the arches offer tasty food and a nice view of the plaza.

Palacio de Gobierno – *North side of the plaza. Open year-round daily 8am–8pm.* ✕ ☎ *(2) 462-5307.* This building originally served as the seat of the Viceroyalty and of the city government. Its lower facade, the portals of which are delicately carved in gray stone, dates from 1545, the time of its original construction. The structure has been modified as a result of destruction by a fire started during a native rebellion in 1692 and an earthquake in 1711.
Inside, Desiderio Hernández Xochitiotzin, a contemporary local artist, has created a series of **murals★**. Begun in 1957, and covering just over 450sq m/492sq yd, they recount the history of the Tlaxcaltec people from their original settlements to the 19C.

Palacio de Justicia (Antigua Capilla Real) – *West side of the plaza.* At the base of the stone mortar Baroque facade of this 18C building, two handsome bas-reliefs attract the visitor's attention: one represents the coat of arms of the Kingdoms of Castille and Leon; the other, the Royal House of Austria's coat of arms, features a two-headed eagle.

Parroquia de San José – *Northwest corner of the square, across the street. Open year-round daily 6am–8pm.* A former cathedral, this enormous church, painted in bright colors to complement its cupolas decorated with Talavera tiles, was built in stages between 1526 and 1864. Two monolithic, stone holy water fonts mark the entrance. The left-hand stoup bears the Spanish royal coat of arms on its base; the right hand font, a representation of Camaxtli, the Tlaxcaltec god of war. A series of 18C **altarpieces** adorn the walls, while an ebony and ivory **cross★** on a sumptuous embossed silver stand graces the main altar. To the left of the main altar lies the 18C Baroque **chapel of expiation★**, dedicated to the Virgin of Guadalupe and the Virgin of the Rosary.

★ **Ex Convento de San Francisco (Antiguo Convento Franciscano de Nuestra Señora de la Asunción)** – *To the southeast of Plaza de la Constitución, across Plaza Xicohténcatl. Open year-round daily 7am–2pm & 3–8pm, holidays 6am–9pm.* This 16C Franciscan monastery stands on the edge of a large atrium with two access ramps. On the north side of the entrance rises a free-standing tower that was probably used as a watchtower. The atrium still preserves a corner chapel from which you can watch the bullfights in the **Plaza de Toros** below, built in the 19C.

★ **Museo Regional de Tlaxcala** – *Open year-round Tue–Sun 10am–5pm. P$7.* ☎ *(2) 462-0262.* Housed in the former cloister, this museum exhibits artifacts pertaining to Tlaxcaltec history: archaeological objects from Cacaxtla-Xochitécatl and a hall related to the Four Dominions of Tlaxcala, as well as the blending of races and cultures following the Conquest. The upper cloister contains a collection of 17C and 18C oil paintings and a room devoted to spiritual conquest.

Catedral de Nuestra Señora de la Asunción – *Open year-round daily 7am–8pm.* Preserving its fine **ceiling** in Mudejar-style coffered wood, the 16C Renaissance Cathedral of Our Lady of the Assumption underwent modifications in the 18C and 19C. It gained the status of Cathedral of Tlaxcala in the 20C. Historically significant, the **Capilla de la Tercera Orden** (Chapel of the Third Order of St. Francis), to the right of the chancel, richly adorned with Baroque **altarpieces**, contains the font where the Four Chieftains of Tlaxcala were baptized, as well as the first pulpit of New Spain.

★ **Capilla Abierta** – *Enter by the staircase across from the facade.* Because of its design, this open-air chapel is considered one of the most original in the world. Built in the Gothic style in 1539, it features three ogee arches rising above a hexagonal floor.

★Museo de Artes y Tradiciones Populares – *Av. Emilio Sánchez Piedras, 1; three blocks west of the main plaza. Open year-round Tue–Sun 10am–6pm. Closed Jan 1, May 1 & Dec 25. P$6. ✗ ☎ (2) 462-2337.* Indigenous people from Tlaxcala's diverse regions act as guides in this unique museum. The tour includes an explanation of their lifestyle and how they make handicrafts. A model of a typical Otomí house, and samples of the textiles woven by Otomí women highlight the collection; a workshop further explains different styles of textile manufacture, and the complex and delicate production of *pulque*, made from fermented cactus sap, is demonstrated. A selection of *carnival* wardrobes from several towns throughout the area is also on display. In the **Fonda del Museo** (Museum Inn), locals prepare and serve their traditional dishes.

★★★SANTUARIO DE LA VIRGEN DE OCOTLÁN

From Plaza de la Constitución, go two blocks north along Av. Juárez to Av. Guridi y Alcocer; at this point, turn right and climb 1km/.6mi. Open year-round daily 7am–7:30pm (respect religious ceremonies underway).

Standing at the top of a hill that affords a marvelous view of Tlaxcala, this magnificent 17–18C shrine, representative of the Puebla-Tlaxcalan Baroque architecture, was erected in honor of the Blessed Virgin who, according to legend, appeared here to Juan Diego Bernardino in 1541.

The **facade★** appears very tall, thanks to its slender white towers decorated in delicate mortarwork, while the lovely arched entrance bears images of the Virgin Mary, Saint Francis and the archangels.

Six oil paintings telling the story of the Virgin of Ocotlán's apparitions adorn the **interior** transept. The chancel virtually swirls with golden glints from the 18C **altarpieces★★** made by **Francisco Miguel Tlayoltehuanitzin**. Containing an effigy of Our Lady of Ocotlán, the central urn is a fine example of the goldsmith's craft. The same fine craftsmanship extends to the tabernacle at her feet, the altar table and the lamps. Depicting Christ's Passion, six large canvases by Jose Joaquín (18C) grace the **sacristy**. An octagonal chamber used to change the robes on the statue of the Virgin for important ceremonies, the **dressing room★★** displays lavish Baroque **decoration** on the walls and the cupola. This 25-year labor of love, begun in 1715 by Francisco Miguel Tlayoltehuanitzin, portrays figures of angels and saints skillfully intertwined with garlands. Complementing the decoration, a series of seven paintings by Juan de Villalobos (18C) depicts scenes from the Virgin's life.

© Mario Mutschlechner

Santuario de la Virgen de Ocotlán, interior

149

EXCURSIONS *Map opposite*

Cacaxtla-Xochitécatl – *19km/11.8mi west of Tlaxcala. Description p 113.*

Tepeyanco and Santa Inés Zacatelco – *Total distance 12km/7.5mi. Go south from Tlaxcala on Carr. 119 toward Puebla; Tepeyanco is 7km/4.3mi away.*

Tepeyanco de las Flores – The majestic ruins of the 16C **Franciscan monastery** stand guard over the quiet and simple village of Tepeyanco. To the left of the church lies an open-air chapel. **San Francisco parish church** *(open year-round daily 7am–7:30pm)*, built to the southwest of the monastery in the 17C, possesses a facade reminiscent of the colorful Puebla churches with the characteristic combination of tiles, brick and mortarwork, decorated with images of saints and executed in Talavera ceramics. Inside, a series of **altarpieces★** (17–18C) depicts scenes from the lives of Christ and the Blessed Virgin.

Santa Inés Zacatelco – *From Tepeyanco, continue 5km/3mi south to Santa Inés Zacatelco.* Facing the main square of this small trading town is the interesting **Parroquia de Santa Inés** *(open year-round daily 7am–7pm)*, built in the 18C on the ruins of the original 16C structure, the remains of which are visible on the right. Inside, the single-piece **holy water stoup** *(left side of the nave)* and the huge (18C) **main altarpiece★** devoted to its patron saint, Santa Inés (St. Agnes), characterized by robust columns decorated with paintings of archangels testify to the locals' devotion to their saint.

La Trinidad and Santa Cruz, Tlaxcala – *Total distance, 16km/9.9mi. Go east from Tlaxcala on Carr. 117 toward Apizaco; at 10km/6.2mi exit right and continue 5.4km/3.6mi to Trinidad.*

Centro Vacacional IMSS-Trinidad – *Open year-round daily 9am–5pm. P$16.* ⚠ ✗ 🖻 ☎ *(2) 461-0700 and (01-800) 711-0614.* This vacation spot occupies the premises of an old textile factory in operation until 1967; its large turbine once produced power for the factory *(door opened on request)*. Remodeled cottages that formerly housed the workers now offer accommodations for travelers in a modern resort with swimming pools, playing fields, horses and all-terrain vehicles.

Parroquia de Santa Cruz Tlaxcala – *1km/.6mi south of the Vacation Center. Open year-round daily 6:30am–noon & 4–7pm.* Inside, the church contains a rich collection of gilded **altarpieces**, one of which includes an exceptional depiction of the souls in purgatory that shows indigenous peoples participating in the ceremonies for the dead. On the main altar hangs an unusual 17C **painting★**: Adam and Eve are shown almost life size, half naked and surrounded by medallions representing the capital sins, with inscriptions in Náhuatl.

Parroquia de Santa Isabel, Xiloxoxtla – *7.5km/4.7mi from Tlaxcala. Go southwest on Independencia and take Carr. 119 toward Puebla; at 3km/1.9mi from Tlaxcala center, past the Acuitlapilco church, exit left; pass Atlahapa and continue 2.5km/1.6mi to Xiloxoxtla. Open year-round Fri 5am–7pm, Sun 10:30am–noon, holidays 8am–noon.* Fine lacelike **plasterwork** covers the vaults and even the walls of the nave of this church making its **interior★** one of the loveliest in Tlaxcala. The main **altarpiece★★** (18C), an extraordinary example of the Solomonic Baroque style, holds in its central niche a graceful burnished gold **sculpture**, showing the visitation of the Virgin Mary to her cousin St. Elizabeth.

Atlihuetzía and Yauhquemecan – *17km/10.6mi. Leaving Tlaxcala, take Carr. 117 toward Apizaco; at 9km/5.6mi exit right, toward the Hotel Misión Tlaxcala.*

★**Atlihuetzía** – The pretty **waterfall** that gives this quaint town its name—in Náhuatl, the "place where water falls"—can be seen from a distance of 1km/0.6mi. *(The waterfall is on the grounds of the Hotel Misión Tlaxcala.)* The thick walls of the imposing, 16C Franciscan monastery church reveal three stages of construction: pre-Hispanic cut-stone, volcanic rock, and brick. Its **interior**, with its high roofless walls, seems to dwarf visitors. A graveyard borders the church where the cloister used to stand. North of the monastery lies the **Parroquia de la Inmaculada Concepción★** *(open year-round Mon–Sat 4–6pm, Sun 9:30–11am)* which preserves two **paintings** (18–19C) depicting an important moment in the region's religious history. These illustrate the martyrdom of a number of Tlaxcaltec children who were sacrificed for practicing the Catholic religion and burning pre-Hispanic idols during the early years (1527 and 1529) of the colonial period; Cristobalito, a child from Atlihuetzía, is given special importance. Note the 17–18C **altarpieces★**, most especially the central fixture with its delicate burnished gold sculptures and a statue of Our Lady of the Immaculate Conception brought from the Philippines.

Parroquia de San Dionisio, Yauhquemecan – *From Atlihuetzía, return to Carr. 117 and after 3km/1.9mi turn right onto Carr. 136 toward Calpulalpan; at 2km/1.2mi turn right and go 1km/.6mi to Yauhquemecan. Open year-round daily 9am–6pm,* *holidays 6am–8pm*. A large carved wooden door leads to the interior which houses a splendid 18C **main altarpiece**★ that obscures the apse with a profusion of gilded, wood plant motifs and burnished gold statues. An outstanding embossed silver monstrance holds an image of Christ, while the sacristy displays an 18C painting of the Last Supper by Cayetano Pérez.

Parque Nacional de la Malinche and Huamantla – *Total distance 63km/39mi. Go northwest from Tlaxcala on Carr. 117; at 11km/6.8mi turn right onto Carr. 136 to Apizaco (6km/3.7mi), go through Apizaco and continue east on Carr. 136 toward Veracruz; after 13km/8mi turn right; continue 4km/2.5mi and in Teacalco, turn left and go another 8km/5mi to the Centro Vacacional Malintzi.*

Parque Nacional de la Malinche – By a road that winds up the gentle slope of **La Malinche Volcano** (4,462m/13,596ft), visitors enter these richly varied pine woods, the only wooded area in the state. The volcano and park honor the memory of the maiden, La Malinche (Náhuatl, *Malintzin*), who became Cortés' interpreter and lover. Along the road pleasant spots for outings and excellent views of the Apizaco region abound. At the end of the ride awaits the **Centro Vacacional la Malintzi** *(3,333m/10,936ft; open year-round daily 9am–6pm; P$16;* ✗ ⊟ ☎ *2-462-4098),* a starting point for the ascent to the volcano's summit, which takes four hours with proper equipment. Legend states that after Doña Malinche died in Mexico City, a group of Tlaxcaltec leaders from the Letrán district claimed her body and buried it at the top of this volcano.

Huamantla – *From La Malinche, return to Carr. 136 toward Veracruz; continue 13km/8mi to reach Huamantla.* An otherwise quiet town with an enchanting plaza, Huamantla is famous for its August **fair**★. On the evening of August 14, about 2km/1.2mi of the main streets exhibit their showy flower and sawdust carpets that are destroyed when the midnight procession of Our Lady of Charity passes over them. Also in mid-August, during the Huamantlada Fiesta, bulls to be used in the afternoon's bullfight are set loose in the town's streets. The **Parroquia de San Luis Obispo** *(northwest corner of Jardín Juárez; open year-round Tue–Sat 7am–8pm, Sun 6:30am–8pm),* an old 17C Baroque structure in honor of the Bishop of St. Louis, features carved alabaster statues on its facade. Inside, it preserves three 18C altarpieces, the most noteworthy being the main altarpiece (c. 1780), in Churrigueresque and rococo style, for its refined carving and burnished sculptures. A puppet museum, the **Museo Nacional del Títere Rosete Aranda** *(Parque Juárez, 15; open year-round Tue–Sun 10am–2pm & 4–7pm; P$10;* ☎ *2-472-1033),* grew out of the Rosete Aranda family's private puppet collection. From 1835 until the mid 20C, the family collected 5,040 puppets from classical drama and from their own works based on social issues and popular customs. Puppets made by Mexican and foreign artists from different eras complement the collection. It also hosts an International Puppet Festival every August.

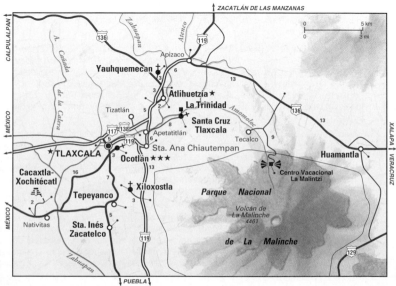

TOLUCA
Mexico
Population 564,476
Map of Principal Sights – Map p 114 **(AY)**
🛈 Centro de Servicios Administrativos, Av. Urawa, 100, corner of Paseo Tollocan, Puerta 110, Izcalli Ipiem ☏ (7) 212-6048

Located in the nation's highest elevation point, Toluca, capital of the state of Mexico, can be reached from Mexico City in only 30 minutes thanks to a modern highway with breathtaking vistas. During the trip, two gastronomic stops are recommended: one, at the Parque Nacional Miguel Hidalgo, also known as "La Marquesa," at 33km/20.5mi, to admire the landscape and sample the regional food; the other at Lerma, 16km/9.9mi farther on, to savor the area's famous sausage. Soon after reaching the beltway circling the city, the highway becomes Avenida Tollocán. Presently considered one of the most important industrial corridors in Mexico, Toluca is surrounded by excellent handicraft production centers.

Historical Notes

During pre-Hispanic times Otomí, Mazahua and Matlazinc groups settled in Toluca and left important ceremonial centers throughout the state before being overrun by the Aztecs. The name Toluca, given by the Aztecs, comes from the Náhuatl **Toloche** or **Tolocan**, "where the god Tolo dwells." In 1521, the Spaniards recognized this city, then "Toluca de San José," as part of the Marquisate of the Valley granted to Hernán Cortés. To this day many of the monasteries built during colonial times for the purpose of evangelizing the natives still survive, as well as haciendas from the large farm and livestock ranches. A strong insurrectionist movement jolted the area in 1800. La Conjura de los Machetes (The Machete Plot) led the way to participation of the masses in the 1810 fight for Independence. Toluca was officially made state capital in 1830, and in 1861 took the name "Toluca de Lerdo," in honor of the 19C patriot, Miguel Lerdo de Tejada.

HISTORIC CENTER

Plaza Cívica or Plaza de los Mártires – *Bordered by Calles Independencia, Riva Palacio, Lerdo de Tejada and Nicolás Bravo*. The name, Plaza of the Martyrs, refers to the 99 indigenous prisoners put to death here on October 19, 1811. It is surrounded by the buildings that represent the main seats of power: the Government Palace, the Palace of Justice, the State Chamber of Deputies (State Legislature), the Municipal Palace, and the cathedral whose structure is composed of the old facade of Saint Francis' Church.

Portales – *Av. Hidalgo, behind the Cathedral*. One of the most traditional places in Toluca, this arcade, Mexico's most extensive, spans 580m/634yd and consists of a series of 118 arches that date from 1832. It now shelters stalls selling typical foods such as sausages, dairy products, sweets and the famous *mosquitos* drink, made of spirituous liquor and orange liqueur.
Off to one side of the arcade, the **Plaza González Arratia** provides a perfect setting for enjoying a stroll, as well as open-air theater performances and diverse cultural and artistic events.
Return by way of Nicolás Bravo (west of Portales) to Lerdo de Tejada, to find a series of museums.

★**Museo José María Velasco** – *Av. Lerdo de Tejada Pte. (west), 400. Open year-round Tue–Sun 10am–6pm, holidays 10am–3pm. Closed Jan 1, Good Friday and Dec 25.* ✗ ☏ *(7) 213-2814*. This museum houses an extraordinary collection of paintings by the famous Mexican landscape artist José María Velasco (1840–1912), a disciple of Pelegrín Clavé, Eugenio Landesio and Santiago Rebull during his studies at the San Carlos Fine Arts Academy. Several drawings from Velasco's student days are also on display.

★**Museo Felipe S. Gutiérrez** – *Nicolás Bravo Nte. (north), 303. Open year-round Tue–Sun 10am–6pm. Closed Jan 1, Good Friday, Dec 25.* ✗ ☏ *(7) 213-2647*. A splendid collection by Felipe Gutiérrez (1824–1904), another alumnus of the San Carlos Academy, can be appreciated at this museum. Born in Mexico and educated in Rome and New York, Gutiérrez became one of the most important exponents of *costumbrismo*, a genre dealing with local customs. He later went on to found the Academia de Bogotá, Colombia.

Museo-Taller Luis Nishizawa – *Nicolás Bravo Nte. (north), 305. Open year-round Tue–Sun 10am–6pm, national holidays 10am–3pm. Closed Jan 1, Good Friday, Sept 16 & Dec 25.* ☏ *(7) 215-7465*. Nishizawa, a native of the state of Mexico, is one of the best-known contemporary fine-arts masters on the international scene. The master himself teaches at the museum, which is also a *taller*, or workshop, as well as a gallery that exhibits a magnificent collection of Nishizawa's works.

Museo de Bellas Artes – *Santos Degollado Pte. (west), 102. Open year-round Tue–Sun 10am–6pm. Closed national holidays. P$2.* ☎ *(7) 215-5329.* This fine arts museum, with a permanent collection consisting of 16C to 18C works, is housed in the Convento de la Purísima Concepción (old Convent of the Immaculate Conception) founded by the Discalced Carmelite nuns. The ground floor features an impressive 18C catafalque, together with several 18C paintings, including works by Villalpando and Cabrera. On the upper level, works from the San Carlos Academy are on display, including outstanding paintings by Pelegrín Clavé and Manuel Villar. Adjoining the museum stands the **Templo del Carmen** (Carmelite Church), one of the few examples of colonial architecture preserved in Toluca.

Walk toward the east end of the plaza

★**Cosmovitral and Jardín Botánico** – *Av. Lerdo de Tejada, corner of Juárez. Open year-round Tue–Sun 9am–5pm. P$5.* ☎ *(7) 214-6785.* Formerly the site of a popular market, Mercado 16 de Septiembre, from 1933 to 1975, this large Art Nouveau iron structure (1909) presently displays the biggest stained-glass construction in the world. The curtain wall, with a surface of 3,000sq m/3,280sq yd, was created between 1978 and 1980 by the Mexico state artist Leopoldo Flores. Composed of 71 panels and 28 different colors, the curtain expresses a theme of universal duality. A short distance away, the botanical garden cultivates over 450 plant species.

★★CENTRO CULTURAL MEXIQUENSE

Ex Hacienda La Pila, Camino a San Buenaventura. 8km/5mi from the city center. Take Av. Las Torres Solidaridad west, and go left on Reyes Heroles. Open year-round, Tue–Sun 10am–6pm. National holidays 10am–3pm. Closed Jan 1 & Dec 25. P$10 (all-museum pass) P$5 (each museum). ☎ *(7) 274-1200 ext. 309.*

Wide green areas and quiet paths characterize this impressive cultural complex, built on the spacious property of La Pila ranch. Modern architecture blends with the vestiges of the old hacienda, while cultural treasure troves enrich the open landscape.

Museo de Arte Moderno – *First building on the left.* Occupying an unfinished planetarium that was remodeled and modernized in 1987, this museum houses an excellent collection of Mexican paintings. Luis Nishizawa created a mural in volcanic rock for the vestibule. Works by Mexico's most famous modern painters-Tamayo, Zalce, Mérida, Montenegro, Orozco, Toledo and many others-make up the permanent **collection**★.

Museo de Culturas Populares – *Second building on the right.* This former hacienda contains the most representative collection of the state's handicrafts. In the indoor patio, a model **pulquería**, or traditional drinking house, has been reconstructed in an old wooden granary. The last section, devoted to the art of Mexican horse riding *(charrería)*, displays a series of popular cowboy sayings painted on the walls. The tour ends at the Patio de las Palomas (Dove Courtyard), which still preserves original dovecotes along the hacienda walls.

Museo de Antropología e Historia del Estado de México – *Building located at the back of the complex.* A series of five rooms, with background music for children, explain the most relevant geographical data and socio-historical events of the state of Mexico from pre-Hispanic times to the present. Extraordinary finds such as the Ehécatl wind-god stone **statue** found in Calixtlahuaca, and a ceremonial **drum** from Malinalco, enrich the archaeological exhibit.

World-renowned Mexican architect, Pedro Ramírez Vázquez designed the museum complex that also embraces the State Archives and the Public Library. Nishizawa's fascinating glazed clay mural with pre-Hispanic motifs adorns the library vestibule.

EXCURSIONS *Map p 154*

Metepec – *Total distance: 15km/9.3mi. Take Carr. 55 toward Ixtapan de la Sal; the historical sites are 8km/5mi from Toluca. Public transportation is available.* A typical 16C **Franciscan monastery** in the main square characterizes this small, lively city that preserves its deep-rooted pottery tradition. Family workshops, where talented potters work and sell their products, line its narrow streets that use small clay tablets for signs *(ask for Altamirano St.)*. Recognized as the cradle of some of Mexico's most famous pottery, Metepec produces the **Trees of Life** *(Árboles de la Vida)* and pots for cooking *mole*. On Mondays, market day, many varieties of handicrafts fill the main plaza with color. In October the Festival Internacional de Quimera allows for the exhibition and sale of a vast array of cultural expressions and artistic endeavors.

Zoológico de Zacango – *From Metepec, continue 7km/4.4mi on Carr. 55; take the exit to the zoo. Public transportation is available. Open year-round daily 10am–5pm. P$15.* ✗ ☎ *(7) 298-0631.* In the natural setting of an immense 34ha/84 acre,

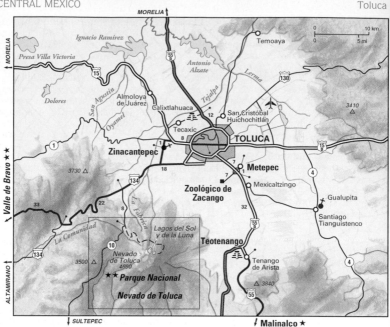

pre-Revolutionary hacienda, live 205 species of animals, amounting to 1,500 specimens, from all over the world. The zoo comprises a special section recreating the natural habitat of certain species and houses an interactive educational center and a children's playground called *Cri-Cri*. Francisco Gabilondo Soler, popularly known as *Cri-Cri*, a gifted and beloved 20C Mexican musician, composed an amusing series of children's animal songs. This section provides an ideal setting for the daily children's activities organized by zoo personnel.

Teotenango – *25km/15.6mi. Go south on Carr. 55 toward Ixtapan de la Sal until reaching Tenango del Valle (or de Arista). Open year-round Tue–Sun 9am–4:30pm. Holidays (Feb 5, March 2 & 21, May 1 & 5, Sept 16, Nov 2 & 20) 10am–3pm. Closed Jan 1, Good Friday & Dec 25. P$6. ☎ (7) 144-1344.* Located on **Tetépetl** hill, this Matlatzinc settlement flourished between AD 900 and 1200 before it was conquered by the Aztecs. Teotenango, "place of the sacred wall," derives its name from the western wall—2km/1.3mi long and 10m/32.8ft high. The **Museo Arqueológico del Estado de México, Dr. Román Piña Chán** exhibits a comprehensive collection of pre-Hispanic artifacts from the entire Valley of Toluca and from as far away as the Valley of Mexico.

Plaza del Jaguar, a broad esplanade named after the relief situated halfway up the stairway on the left, was used as a vestibule or entrance to the ceremonial center. The **Monolito del Jaguar**, a relief depicting a jaguar devouring a flower or a heart, allegorically represents an eclipse: the animal symbolizes the earth or the moon, while the flower or heart denotes the sun. *(From the Jaguar monolith, climb the stairway to the plaza and continue up to the right.)* The **Temascal** was a type of ritual or therapeutic steam bath, probably made with adobe walls and a wooden roof. On both sides, rectangular rooms may have been used as living quarters. The enclosed I-shaped sunken **ball court**, measuring 53m/174ft in length, was equipped with mid-court upper level stone rings through which players were to pass the ball. The 120m/394ft-long **Basamento de la Serpiente** *(crossing the ball court, climb the next platform and turn right)* owes its name to the snake carved on one of the corners of the base of the structure; it is crowned by an altar.

At the end of the archaeological site extends **Calle de la Rana**, a road named for a figure of a frog carved in stone. La Plaza del Durazno adjoins Basamento de la Serpiente.

Ixtapan de la Sal – *79km/49mi to the south on Carr. 55. At the exit located approximately 3km/1.9mi before the town of Tenango, take the toll highway to Ixtapan de la Sal. Plaza San Gaspar. Open year-round daily 7am–7pm (bathing resort and spa), 10am–6pm (aquatic park). Boat rides P$10. ☎ (7) 143-0878.* Nestled in the Sierra Madre, at an elevation of 1,981m/6,500ft, this small town is famous for its popular thermal waters, purported for their powers to cure arthritis and rheumatism. The various relaxation and reflexology massages, as well as beauty treatments and weight reduction packages offered at the **Hotel Spa Ixtapan** attract both national and international visitors. In addition, the bathing resort includes an amusement park with swimming pools, water slides and boat rides.

In the lovely village of **Tonatico** *(5km/3mi south, on Carr. 55)*, one can enjoy a less frequented bathing resort of thermal waters and explore the grottoes known as **Grutas de la Estrella** *(11km/6.8mi south, on Carr. 55).*

★**Malinalco** – *64km/39.8mi Go south from Toluca on Carr. 55D toward Ixtapan de la Sal; in Tenancingo turn left and continue 14km/8.7mi to the archaeological site. Description p 123.*

Ex Convento de Zinacantepec (Museo Virreinal) – *8km/5mi west of Toluca on Carr. 15, towards Valle de Bravo. Open year-round Tue–Sat 10am–4pm, Sun & holidays 10am–3pm. Closed Jan 1, Feb 5, Good Friday, May 1 & Dec 25. P$2.* ☎ *(7) 218-2593.* Designed to welcome pilgrims, the portals of this late-16C Franciscan structure preserve an altarpiece sketch from the 17C. On the sides remain several frescos with scenes from the life of St. Francis. At one end, the baptistery contains a monolithic 16C baptismal **font★** that combines indigenous iconography with European Christian motifs. An 18C oil painting of St. John the Baptist graces the interior. The museum attempts to recreate ancient monastic life, remaining faithful to the original use of the rooms. A number of walls preserve portions of the original frescoes.

★★**Parque Nacional Nevado de Toluca** – *44km/27.3mi from Toluca on Carr. 130 towards Valle de Bravo. Take Sultepec-Nevado Exit. Go 8km/5mi and turn left; continue 18km/11.2mi to the park. Bus service is available. During inclement weather or heavy snowfall, the summit is only accessible on foot. Open year-round daily 24hrs. P$5.* ☎ *(01-800) 849-1333.* Pico del Fraile (Friar's Peak), the highest point of the Xinantécatl—better known as Nevado de Toluca (The Snow Peak of Toluca)—rises to a height of 4,630m/14,325ft. Xinantécatl, "naked man," appears to have separate peaks because of the giant crater's nine jagged edges. Two crater lakes named after the sun and moon have diameters of approximately 400m/1,312ft and 200m/656ft respectively. Offerings and vessels of different forms recovered from the lakes indicate the site was used for pre-Hispanic religious worship.

★★**Valle de Bravo** – *107km/66.5mi from Toluca. Go southwest from Toluca on Carr. 130; after 40km/24.9mi, turn right and continue 33km/20.5mi. Buses are available from Toluca and Mexico City.* Despite strong tourist development in the area in recent years, Valle de Bravo has been able to preserve its rural ambiance, expressed in its red slate roofs and stone-paved streets. Woods, cascades, rivers and a large artificial lake for sailing, fishing and water-skiing offer a variety of diversions. Originally part of Presa Miguel Alemán hydroelectric system and presently part of the Cutzamala system, the lake supplies Mexico City with drinking water. To admire Valle de Bravo from a birds-eye view, thrill-seekers can engage in a hang-gliding adventure.

On the southern part of town beckons Avándaro, a luxury residential area with a golf club.

TULA

Hidalgo
Map of Principal Sights – Map p 114 **(AX)**
🅱 ☎ (7) 732-0705

On a dry plain rich in limestone, magueys, prickly pears and cacti stand the vestiges of the capital of the Toltecs, principal heirs to the knowledge and traditions of legendary Teotihuacán. Widening its frontiers by conquering neighboring peoples, the Toltecs exacted high tributes and exploited their work force for the extraction of obsidian, a black volcanic glass used for making knives, arrowheads and other instruments.

Historical Notes

At the beginning of the 10C AD, the inhabitants of the area were conquered by the son of Chimalma and Mixcóatl, a Toltec hero bearing the name of one of the principal gods, the plumed serpent, Ce Ácatl Topiltzin Quetzalcóatl. By justifying religious warfare and promoting cults that required human sacrifices, this powerful ruler created a climate of tension that ultimately unleashed a confrontation with his neighbors to the north. These semi-nomadic groups set Tula's temples and palaces on fire, forcing the Toltecs to emigrate south in 1168. According to legend, a representative of Tezcatlipoca, god of war, tempted and deceived Quetzalcóatl into getting drunk on *pulque* and committing incest. Full of shame for this crime, Quetzalcóatl fled Tula in the late 10C AD and traveled southward to the land of the Maya.

The dominion of Toltec civilization in Chichén Itzá and the admiration they enjoyed among the Aztecs led the Aztecs to mistake the arrival of Cortés for the second coming of Quetzalcóatl.

ARCHAEOLOGICAL SITE

100km/62mi west of Pachuca via Ajacuba. 98km/61mi from Mexico City. Leave Mexico City toward Querétaro on Hwy. 57D; after 69.5km/42.4mi, take a right toward Tepeji del Río; continue 25km/15.5mi to Tula. Open year-round daily 9am–5pm. P$20. ✗ 🄴 ☎ *(7) 732-0705.*

Museum – The **ceramics** and **sculptures** gathered at the site are on display in this modern building. Most striking is the reclining figure of Chac-mool, the intermediary between the gods and humans, holding a vessel in his hands to receive offerings.
Continue along the path.

Coatepantli – Erected to protect the ceremonial center, this wall fragment with matching side decorations was crowned with battlements representing fragmented snail shells, symbols of Quetzalcóatl portrayed as the planet Venus. Rattlesnakes devouring fleshless human faces appear on the central frieze.

Templo de Tlahuizcalpan-tecuhtli – Immediately behind the wall stands this five-tiered temple with protruding stones. A number of these slabs still bear bas-reliefs on the north and east sides depicting buzzards and eagles devouring hearts, as well as walking jaguars and coyotes. Such mystical animals were associated with the planet Venus, a manifestation of Quetzalcóatl.

Atlantes

Four monumental columns in the shape of warriors, known as **atlantes**★, stand on the summit. The column at the extreme left is a replica, replacing the original, which is on exhibit in the National Museum of Anthropology in Mexico City. Each one weighs 8.5 tons and consists of four stone blocks assembled by the tongue and groove system. The warriors wear feathers and butterfly-shaped breastplates and, on their backs, a large circular brooch in the form of a sun. In their right hand they carry dart-throwers and in their left, resin bags. A panoramic **view** from this point encompasses the hills and plains once populated by as many as 85,000 Toltecs, and is now obstructed by tall chimneys of oil refineries.

Palacio Quemado (Burned Palace) – *East of the Templo de Tlahuizcalpan-tecuhtli.* Composed of a series of vestibules with numerous pillars that supported roofs made of perishable materials, the palace preserves the remains of benches set in the walls and adorned with bas-reliefs of processions of warriors in their original colors. Scholars believe that this area was used for the most important religious ceremonies or for bustling markets, where traders brought cotton, cacao and feathers from tropical regions, precious shells and snails from the coasts, and fruit and resins from the colder areas. The Chac-mool now displayed in the museum was found here.

Templo del Sol – *Opposite the Central Plaza.* Originally, this structure was decorated with slabs with bas-reliefs like those on the Temple of Venus. Apparently, this main religious edifice was deliberately destroyed in pre-Hispanic times. It too may have been crowned by warrior columns. Beside the stairway lies a mound built during Aztec occupation.
In the middle of the main plaza stands a shrine similar to that of the Temple of the Eagles in Chichén Itzá.

XOCHICALCO★★

Morelos

Built atop the hill called *Xochicalco*, Náhuatl for "place of the house of flowers," this civic and religious center flourished between AD 700 and 900. In order to accommodate construction, the inhabitants had to modify the natural slope of the terrain with terraces. Evidence points to a well-fortified city, not only because of the outer defense walls, but also for the staircases, ramps, trenches and moats strategically placed inside. Scholars suggest that internal strife probably caused a fire leading to an exodus from the ceremonial center.

ARCHAEOLOGICAL SITE

On the Autopista del Sol heading toward Acapulco, 38km/23.6mi from Cuernavaca. Bus services are available. Open year-round daily 10am–5pm. P$14. ✗ ☎ (7) 312-5955.

While the lower portion of the city was open to the general public, the upper area was reserved for the ruling classes. The architecture blends the salient Mesoamerican styles of the time, namely Teotihuacán, Zapotec and Maya.

Site Museum – Reconstructing the site's history, the museum's six halls illustrate a particular aspect of daily life in Xochicalco society. Especially significant are the *Señor de Rojo* (Lord in Red) in Room 2, representing the sun god, and the east ball-game ring with relief figures of toucans and bats representing day and night. The museum boasts eco-friendly facilities: natural lighting; a cistern system to gather and circulate water; and architectural designs that allow the passage of natural air currents, dispensing with artificial air-conditioning.

Plaza de la Estela de los Dos Glifos – Designed for large public meetings, this plaza contains two glyphs adorning the central shrine stela denoting the date (10 sugarcane and 9 reptile eye).

Continue along the path to the right of the Great Pyramid, north of the plaza.

Rampa de Animales – *At the top, on the right.* Unique in Mesoamerica, this structure consists of 255 slabs, each one decorated with an animal design.

Juego de Pelota Este – Every ball game involved its own particular ritual. Here, the ceremony of day and night was performed, as evidenced by the ring on display in the site museum. Farther on, the **Juego de Pelota Norte** (Northern Ball Court) is dedicated to rain and drought.

Go down the stairs and continue left. Turn left at the end of the path.

Observatory – *Visitors need a caretaker or at least a flashlight to access this area.* Used to observe the sun, this artificial cave is accessed by a tunnel on the left leading to a hexagonal opening. From April 30 to August 15, at midday, the sun's rays enter through the hexagon creating a design on the floor. (The phenomenon is best observed on May 14 & 15 and on July 28 & 29.)

Go up the stairs and continue.

Cistern – Such an enormous city required a very elaborate system of water gathering, storage, and distribution. Cisterns such as this were indispensable; once full of rainwater, the plug was pulled and water flowed to storage areas.

Temascal (Steam baths) – In this structure, four pillars supported a flat roof. A passageway leads to a tub where water sprinkled onto the previously warmed stones produced steam.

Go up the stairs on the left side.

Plaza Principal – Dedicated to political, military and religious uses, this esplanade was considered a reserved area. On the west side, climb the **Acrópolis**, residence of the governing class, to enjoy a wonderful **view★**.

Pirámide de la Serpiente Emplumada (Pyramid of the Plumed Serpent) – This, the most significant structure of Xochicalco, consists of a lower tier of sloped walls and vertical panels *(talud-tablero)*. Attractive **ornamentation★** includes eight feathered serpents, and on the panels, various seated persons with Maya traits, as well as the constant repetition of the *9 reptile eye* glyph with a symbol of new fire. On the top rests a small temple. South of the plaza lies the **Pirámide de las Estelas** (Pyramid of the Stelae), the residential area of the ruling classes, where three carved stelae were found.

At the end of the plaza, go down the right side.

Staircases and Porticos – Possessing decorated stair beams, this structure limited access to the Main Plaza. It appears that the pillars belonged to porticos that acted as crowd-control buffers.

The view from the **Plaza de la Estela de los Dos Glifos** includes the Southern Ball Court, the Malinche complex and the Laguna del Rodeo.

Region 3

CENTRAL WEST

Land of tequila, mariachis, beaches and Huichols

Handicrafts and Food, p 50. Due to its diverse ecosystems, ranging from temperate forests to semiarid zones, this magnificent region constitutes a fascinating tourist destination.

The mixture between indigenous races and Spaniards is obvious in this geographical area, whose popular traditions clearly represent the classical images of Mexico. They include Jalisco with its tequila and mariachi music; Guanajuato with its beautiful colonial cities, a product of the wealth found in its mines, which today still figure among the world's primary areas of silver production; and Aguascalientes with its textile industry, renowned and recognized throughout Mexico. Moreover, all these states share a religious fervor that is present throughout their celebrations and customs.

The states of Jalisco, Nayarit and Colima share the beauty of wonderful beaches along the Pacific Coast, lined by tourist resorts that take advantage of Mexico's vast natural resources to attract its visitors. One common denominator prevails among these states: the strong presence of western indigenous cultures. While dancing clay dogs characterize Colima, Jalisco is famous for its fertility dolls. Nayarit boasts the most colorful appearance due to the **Huichols**, who preserve their ancestral traditions far removed from civilization, high up on the mountain range where they recount their lives through their beautiful yarn creations known as the **Eyes of God**, a symbol of divinity in their festivities.

For all these reasons, the region is a showcase of color and celebration embedded in the fabulous mosaic of cultures that make up the marvelous country that is Mexico.

Ags. ..... Aguascalientes
Col. .... Colima
Gto. .... Guanajuato
Jal. .... Jalisco
Nay. .... Nayarit

City of Guanajuato

AGUASCALIENTES★

Aguascalientes
Population 582,827
Map of Principal Sights – City Map p 161
🅑 Palacio de Gobierno ☎ (4) 915-1155

Both the state and the capital city of Aguascalientes owe their name to the thermal springs found in this small region of Mexico, once inhabited by Chichimec tribes. When the Spaniards arrived here, they initiated their expeditions to the north. Shortly thereafter, on October 22, 1575, King Philip II of Spain founded the Villa de Nuestra Señora de La Asunción de las Aguas Calientes (Village of Our Lady of Assumption of Hot Springs), which belonged to the territory of Nueva Galicia.

Aside from its cultural effervescence and the activity of its textile industry, Aguascalientes is famous for its spectacular sunsets.

Initiated on April 25, 1604, the state's most important annual event, the **National Fair of San Marcos**, is the oldest state fair in all of Mexico. This festive celebration includes a *palenque* (where cockfights are staged), bullfights, fireworks, a casino and cultural events.

★PLAZA DE LA PATRIA AND SURROUNDINGS

Catedral Basílica de Nuestra Señora de la Asunción – *West side of Plaza de la Patria. Open year-round daily 7am–2pm & 5–9pm.* One of Aguascalientes' oldest buildings, the church obtained its status as a cathedral in 1899. Its rose quarry-stone facade, in Solomonic Baroque style, boasts four sculptures of the mitered saints of the Roman Catholic Church: St. Gregory the Great, St. Ambrose of Milan, St. Augustine and St. Jerome. The basilica's floor plan contains the **Capilla del Sagrario**, with a beautiful German altar from the 19C. Paintings by Miguel Cabrera, Andrés López, Juan Correa and José de Alcíbar decorate the walls.

Exedra (1) – *Central point of Plaza de la Patria.* Erected in 1808 in honor of King Charles IV of Spain, the Ionic column is surrounded by a stone balustrade. At its apex the column boasts a bronze sculpture of an eagle devouring a serpent, a creation by Jesús Contreras.

★**Palacio de Gobierno** – *Southern side of Plaza de la Patria. Open year-round Mon–Fri 8am–9pm, weekends & holidays 8am–6pm.* The 17C estate was inherited by Ciénega del Rincón's eldest son and has housed the offices of the state government since 1856. The reddish volcanic rock used to build its remarkable facade contrasts with the quarry stone of the balconies.

Its interior consists of 111 arches surrounding two courtyards that are separated by a monumental central **staircase**. Decorating both floor plans, murals by Chilean artist Osvaldo Barra Cunningham depict the history of Aguascalientes, as well as the most traditional scenes from the Fair of San Marcos.

Museo Regional de Historia – *V. Carranza, 118 on the west side of Plaza de la Patria. Open year-round Mon–Sat 10am–2pm & 5–8:30pm. P$10.* ☎ *(4) 915-5228.* Renowned architect Refugio Reyes Rivas built this charming house at the beginning of the 20C. Its rooms recount the historical development of Aguascalientes and include a map of the city. One of the rooms narrates and illustrates the life of one of Aguascalientes' most endearing artists, musician Manuel M. Ponce.

★**Jardín de San Marcos** – *At the entrance of V. Carranza, on the west side of Plaza de la Patria.* Locals favor this placid garden as a recreational spot, surrounded by a magnificent balustrade with arches that welcome visitors from all four corners of the garden.

Templo de San Marcos – *Beside the Jardín de San Marcos, on the west side of Plaza de la Patria. Open year-round Mon–Fri 7am–2pm & 4–9pm, weekends 7am–9pm.* Built by the ancient Tlaxcaltecs, who once inhabited the area, the 18C edifice displays a humble portal. The sacristy features a marvelous painting by José de Alcíbar (1751–1800), which represents the Adoration of the Magi.

Santuario de Nuestra Señora de Guadalupe – *Guadalupe, 213, Downtown. Open year-round daily 7am–1:30pm & 5–9pm.* With an elaborate Baroque facade, the 18C church boasts an interior with intricate ornamental carvings on stone, also Baroque.

★**Museo de Aguascalientes (Ex Escuela Normal del Estado)** – *Zaragoza, 505, Downtown. Open year-round Tue–Sun 11am–6pm. Closed national holidays. P$5.* ☎ *(4) 918-6901.* Built by Refugio Reyes Rivas, the Neoclassical palace consists of a stone facade, Doric columns and Ionic capitals, all dating from the beginning of the 20C. Although the building originally housed the state's Normal (Teachers') School, today it is considered the best place in the city to become acquainted with Aguascalientes' fine artwork. The museum features masterpieces of the state's most prominent artists, as well as of other national artists of great influence during the contemporary movement that occurred in Mexico from 1910 to 1950. Of particular interest is the nationalistic work of **Saturnino Herrán**.

★**Templo de San Antonio** – *On the corner of Pedro Parga and Zaragoza. Open year-round daily 6:30am–1pm & 6:30–8:30pm.* Completed in 1908, this church represents the most unique of the architectural works by self-taught architect Refugio Reyes Rivas. It stands out in its urban surroundings for its unusual composition, a fusion of various architectural structures made of rose and yellow stone. Its surprisingly colorful **interior** includes a Latin cruciform floor plan crowned at the cross vault by a magnificent cupola with twin stained-glass windows. Beautiful enormous medallions, painted by Candelario Rivas, decorate the walls and recount several of St. Anthony's miracles.

Museo de Arte Contemporáneo – *Juan de Montoro, 222, Downtown. Open year-round Tue–Sun 10am–6pm. Closed national holidays. P$5* ☎ *(4) 918-6901.* Inaugurated in 1991, the Museum of Contemporary Art offers the best of the Encuentro Nacional de Arte Joven (National Meeting of Contemporary Art),

Bullfight, National Fair of San Marcos

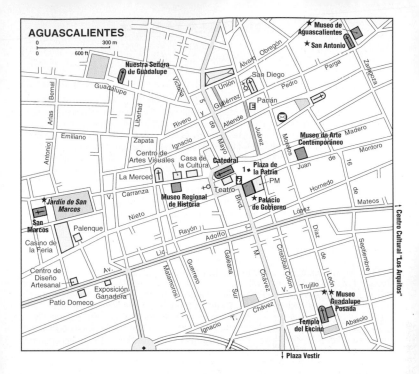

considered the event with the oldest tradition of its kind in all of Mexico, as it has been held annually in Aguascalientes since 1966. It displays traveling exhibits of contemporary fine art, both national and international.

★★**Museo José Guadalupe Posada** – *Jardín del Encino, in old Barrio de Triana. Open year-round Tue–Sun 10am–6pm. P$5. ☎ (4) 915-4556.* This museum boasts a wonderful example of the work of José Guadalupe Posada, a marvelous innovator of popular prints, who with his playful critique of the politics of Porfirio Díaz significantly influenced the conscience of the people. Of special interest are his **skulls**, in which caricatures express both life and death. The museum also holds a splendid collection of etchings by Manuel Munilla.

Templo del Encino – *Jardín del Encino, in old Barrio de Triana. Open year-round daily 6:30am–1pm & 4:30–9pm.* Located in the city's oldest sector (the Barrio de Triana), this church displays an elegant, Baroque portal. It venerates the miraculous Señor del Encino, a black Christ who is the subject of many fantastic legends and anecdotes.

ADDITIONAL SIGHTS

Plaza Vestir – *10km/6.2mi south via Rte. 45, heading toward Lagos de Moreno Blvd. José María Chávez, Industrial City.* Most of the state's manufacturers of clothing and linens are concentrated in this mall. The famous and traditional pulled-thread handwork and embroideries are sold here at unbeatable prices and quality.

Centro Cultural "Los Arquitos" – *Alameda and Héroe de Nacozari, on the east side of the city. Open year-round Mon–Fri 9am–9pm, Sat–Sun & holidays 9am–8pm. Closed Dec 15–31. ☎ (4) 916-9201.* Part of the *patrimonio nacional* (the official national registry of sites that comprise Mexico's heritage), "Los Arquitos" houses the ruins of a spa that operated from 1821 to 1973 and whose thermal spring waters came from Ojo Caliente, located to the east of Aguascalientes. The site museum illustrates its history.

Consult the practical information section at the end of the guide for travel tips, useful addresses and phone numbers, and a wealth of details on recreation and annual events.

GUADALAJARA★★

Jalisco

Population 3,279,424

Map of Principal Sights – City Map p 165

🅱 Morelos, 102, Plaza Tapatía ☎ (3) 658-2222 and (01-800) 363-2200

Known as "the city of roses" *("la ciudad de las rosas")* or "the pearl of Jalisco" *("la perla tapatía")*, the capital of the state of Jalisco ranks among Mexico's three major cities. Despite its rapid growth in recent years, this modern metropolis still retains much of its colonial charm in the historic center. The outlying religious center of Zapopan, and handicraft villages of Tonalá and Tlaquepaque also merit a visit. Guadalajara is synonymous with festivals and women with big beautiful eyes. According to a popular Mexican song, no eyes are more beautiful than those of the women of Jalisco. The state is to be credited for the symbols considered characteristically Mexican: **mariachis** and **tequila**. Both the music of the **jarabe tapatío** (Mexican hat dance) and the strong taste of tequila transport us to Guadalajara, which offers a wide variety of entertainment, including its famous **October Festival**, the **Mariachi Festival**, and the traditional rides in horse-drawn buggies.

Historical Notes

Prior to the arrival of the Spaniards, the region was part of the Tarasc (or Michoacán) Empire (14–16C). The city owes its name to its founder, Nuño de Guzmán, a native of the Spanish province of Guadalajara, baptized by the Arabs as **Wad-al-hidjara** ("river of stones") during their rule over Spain. Nuño de Guzmán overcame local Tarascan resistance by annihilating the indigenous peoples, from Michoacán to Sinaloa. The conquistador was named governor of the city that was to be called Nueva Galicia, which was moved to the current site of Guadalajara in 1542 and maintained a certain degree of autonomy from the rest of New Spain until 1786.

During the War of Independence, Father Miguel Hidalgo y Costilla abolished slavery. Following the *coup d'état* led by Comonfort in 1858, President Benito Juárez and part of his administration were forced to take refuge in Guadalajara during the **Three Years' War**. In the 20C the city witnessed multiple revolutionary events and, from 1926 to 1932, supported the *Rebelión Cristera*, a revolt of militant Catholics against President Calles' anticlerical clauses of the 1917 Constitution. Since the 1950s, Guadalajara has become an important industrial, agricultural and handicraft center.

HISTORIC CENTER

★The Four Plazas

Plaza Guadalajara (Plaza de los Laureles) – *Av. Alcalde and Hidalgo, facing the cathedral.* Commemorating the founding of the city, a bronze representation of Guadalajara's coat of arms rises at the center of the circular fountain. On the north side stand the **Templo de la Merced** (1721) with its Baroque facade and the neo-Colonial **Palacio Municipal** *(open year-round Mon–Fri 8am–7:30pm)*, completed in 1952. Its main staircase displays **murals** (1964) by Gabriel Flores.

Cathedral (A) – *Av. Alcalde, between Hidalgo and Morelos. Open year-round daily 8am–7:30pm.* The vast shape of the Colonial cathedral dominates the center of Guadalajara. The twin spires, now a symbol of the city, were added three centuries after the construction of the cathedral had begun in 1561. A bas-relief of the Assumption of the Virgin extends over the three **portals** of the main facade. The **interior** consists of three naves with ribbed vaults and twelve altars. Oil paintings by Cabrera, Alcíbar, Castro and Páez, as well as a painting of the Immaculate Conception-attributed to the Spanish painter Murillo-adorn the walls of the sacristy.

Plaza de Armas – *Av. 16 de Sept, between Morelos and Pedro Moreno.* The elegance of this attractive square carries through to its Art Nouveau **kiosk/bandstand★**, cast in Paris in 1910 and supported by eight caryatids holding different musical instruments. Every Tuesday, Thursday and Sunday, starting at 6:30pm, the state band presents free, open-air concerts.

★ **Palacio de Gobierno** – *Corona, between Moreno and Morelos, opposite the Plaza de Armas. Open year-round daily 9am–8pm.* ☎ *(3) 614-5414.* The Government Palace was initiated in the mid 17C and completed in 1790. Canon-shaped gargoyles and warriors' torsos guard the Baroque facade.

José Clemente Orozco's Murals – The main staircase boasts a **mural★★★** created between 1937 and 1939 by José Clemente Orozco, world-renowned painter from Jalisco. Covering three sections of the central vault, the mural, known as Lucha Social (Social Struggle), depicts Hidalgo, who, flaming torch in hand, appears to advance toward the viewer. To the right of the mural, the caricature of factions of different government systems is named Circo político (Political Circus). To the left, Las

Practical Information ....Area Code: 3

Getting There – **Guadalajara International Airport:** 25km/15.5mi south of the city. Transportation to the city: Transportes Terrestres ☎ 688-5890 and Transportes Amarillos ☎ 688-5925.. The airport offers **car rental** agencies. **Bus Terminal:** Junction of the freeway to Zapotlanejo and the highway to Tonalá.

Getting Around – **Gray Buses** *(P$2.50).* **Línea Tour** ☎ 634-2220. One-way trip to Tonalá P$5, round trip P$7. For info. & reservations on 1st and 2nd class bus trips to Tequila: **Servicios Coordinados,** ☎ 679-0433. **Public Parking:** (24hrs) lower level of Plaza Tapatía ☎ 614-6090 *(P$5).* **Taxi Station** (24hrs) ☎ 630-0050.

Tourist Information – **Tourism Board of the Government of the State of Jalisco** and **Tourist Information Desk (1)**, Morelos, 102, Plaza Tapatía, C.P. 44100 ☎ 668-1601 and (01-800) 363-2200. **Tourist Information Desk (2)**, Palacio de Gobierno, Planta Baja, calle Corona y Pedro Moreno (Mon–Fri 10am–3pm & 4–8pm, Sat 10am–1pm). **Convention and Visitors Office, Guadalajara Metropolitan Area**, Av. Vallarta, 4095, Fracc. Camino Real, C.P. 45000 ☎ 122-8707 and (01-800) 719-3545. These offices provide free information on sights and tourist services, as well as maps and brochures. **Tourist Aid** (Angeles Verdes) ☎ 668-1800 ext. 1489.
The US Consulate *(open Mon–Fri 8am–4:30pm;* ☎ *825-2700)* and the Canadian Consulate *(open Mon–Fri 10am–1pm;* ☎ *625-3434)* provide assistance to their citizens through the Consular Services offices.

Accommodations – The **Tourist Information Desk** and the **Convention and Visitors Office** *(above)* offer general information on hotels. Hotel rates range from deluxe hotels *(P$1,700)*, moderate *(P$500)* and budget *(P$200)*. *These average rates are per day for a double room and are subject to change.*

Guided Tours – Tours of the city's Historic Center: Panoramex, Av. Federalismo Sur, 944 ☎ 810-5109; Viajes Copenhagen, Av. J. Cloutier, 152, Col. Prados Vallarta ☎ 629-4758.

Entertainment – **Charreadas** (Rodeos): Lienzo Charro Jalisco ☎ 619-0315 *(year-round Sun noon–2:30pm; P$20).* **Bullfights:** "El Nuevo Progreso" Bullring ☎ 637-9982 *(Oct–Dec & Apr–May only).* **Mariachis:** Plaza de los Mariachis *(daily starting at 6pm)*; **Folkloric Ballet, Mariachis and trio:** Hotel Francés, Calle Maestranza, 35, City Center ☎ 613-1190 *(Fridays starting at 7pm).*

Handicrafts – "Agua Azul" House of Handicrafts, Calz. González Gallo, 20 ☎ 619-4664 and Mercado Libertad; shop for textiles, leather and blown glass in Tlaquepaque, and for ceramics, clay, wrought iron, pottery and wood in Tonalá.

Fiestas – **Mariachi Encounter:** Aug 26–Sept 5 (exact dates may vary). **October Festivals:** inaugural parade in the city center followed by a month of fairs in the Auditorio Benito Juárez, P$20, foods, handicrafts, rides, folkloric dances, palenque and various artists.

Plaza de Armas and Palacio de Gobierno

Hidalgo Mural by José Clemente Orozco, detail

fuerzas tenebrosas (The Brutal Forces) represents the relationship between the clergy and the army; it is considered one of the greatest of all the Mexican mural paintings. On the ceiling of the former chamber of the State Congress, located on the upper level, another of Orozco's murals represents the liberation of the slaves and portrays figures of Hidalgo, Morelos, Juárez, Carranza and Zapata. Here, in the Government Palace, Hidalgo abolished slavery on December 6, 1810, and Juárez survived an assassination attempt in 1858.

Museo Regional de Guadalajara (M¹) – *Liceo, 60, beside the cathedral. Open year-round Tue–Sat 9am–5:45pm, Sun 9am–3pm. Closed national holidays. P$20, free Tue & Sun.* ☎ *(3) 614-9957.* This building with a Baroque facade was built in the early 18C as a theological seminary. In 1918 it opened its doors as a museum. The paleontology section showcases a nearly intact skeleton of a **mammoth** found in 1962, in Zacoalco. The ornamented **doorway** in the northeastern corner of the cloister leads to ethnographic displays about indigenous groups (1550 BC to AD 1500). The upper level displays colonial paintings from the 17C and 18C, and Mexican paintings from the 19C.

Across from the museum is the **Rotonda de los Hombres Ilustres de Jalisco**, a departure point for *calandria* (horse-drawn buggy) rides around the city.

Plaza de la Liberación – *Behind the cathedral and opposite the Teatro Degollado.* This plaza is also known as the Plaza de los Tres Poderes (Plaza of the Three Powers) or Plaza de Dos Copas (Plaza of the Two Goblets)—for its two enormous fountains. Its name is reflected in the sculpture of Miguel Hidalgo, whose open hands hold fragments of chains. The Palacio Legislativo, the **Palacio de Gobierno** and the Templo de San Agustín surround the plaza.

★**Teatro Degollado (B)** – *Calle Belén, between Morelos and Hidalgo. Open year-round Mon–Sat 10am–1pm. Closed national holidays.* ☎ *(3) 614-4773.* During the mid 19C, Santos Degollado, governor of Jalisco and martyr of the Reform, commissioned this building. It was completed in 1964 with the addition of a portico supported by 16 Corinthian columns and a triangular pediment adorned by a relief representing the nine muses. A **fresco★** created by architect Gálvez and Gerardo Suárez crowns the elegant, U-shaped **concert hall**. The fresco depicts the scene of the Fourth Canto in Dante Alighieri's *Divine Comedy*. Every Sunday at 10am, the Folkloric Ballet from the University of Guadalajara performs here.

Plaza Tapatía – *Between the Degollado Theater and the Instituto Cultural Cabañas.* Considered Guadalajara's most important commercial, cultural and recreational center, the plaza consists of several esplanades, adorned with fountains, monuments and gardens. The tourist office is located in the legendary Rincón del Diablo (Devil's Corner). The fountain behind the Degollado Theater commemorates the founding of the city (1539). Farther ahead stands a beautiful bronze sculpture representing Guadalajara's heraldic coat of arms granted by Charles V. The main esplanade boasts an enormous sculpture that symbolizes the flame of new fire, surrounded by heron-serpents personifying Aztlán and Quetzalcóatl. In the background stands the majestic Instituto Cultural Cabañas, whose entrance is graced by Alejandro Colunga's **Sala de Los Magos** (Magicians' Room). A stroll through the Plaza Tapatía concludes with a visit to the Plaza López Portillo y Weber, to see **La Estampida**, a sculpture that won the National Sculpture Prize in 1982.

Instituto Cultural Cabañas and Surroundings

★★ **Instituto Cultural Cabañas (Antiguo Hospicio Cabañas)** – *Plaza Tapatía. Open year-round Tue–Sat 10:15am–5:45pm, Sun 10:15am–2:45pm. Closed Jan 1, May 1 & Dec 25. P$8. ✗ ◻ ☎ (3) 617-4322.* In 1810 Archbishop Juan Cruz R. de Cabañas y Crespo founded the institute as La Casa de la Caridad y la Misericordia (The House of Charity and Mercy). Designed and built by Manuel Tolsá, José Gutiérrez and Manuel Gómez Ibarra, this magnificent architectural masterpiece is one of Mexico's most noteworthy examples of the Neoclassical style. The building, with its 23 beautiful courtyards, has served as an asylum, school, prison, barracks and orphanage. In 1983 it became a cultural institute, reserving a very special place for works by the renowned muralist José Clemente Orozco, who decorated the Main Chapel between 1938 and 1939. In December 1997 UNESCO recognized the institute as a World Heritage Site.

Capilla Mayor – Orozco's **murals★★**, whose central theme is the Conquest of Mexico, reflect the painter's social critique through strong images that represent the clash between indigenous and Spanish cultures, their history and consequences. The artist also depicts the tragic result of certain political regimes, as well as the terrible dehumanization of mankind. Beneath the cupola, **El hombre en llamas** (The Man in Flames) symbolizes a person who is elevated by the flame of his own torch. Other rooms in the institute also display drawings by Orozco.

Barrio de San Juan de Dios – *Beside the Instituto Cultural Cabañas.* One of Guadalajara's most popular districts, the neighborhood of San Juan de Dios hosts the huge **Mercado Libertad★** *(open year-round Mon–Sat 8am–8pm, Sun 8am–6pm; ☎ 01-800-363-2200)* where vendors peddle almost everything imaginable-from medicinal herbs, white magic and witchcraft, typical foods and regional crafts to imported goods. A footbridge connects the market to what remains of the 18C Church of San Juan de Dios *(corner of Independencia Sur and Javier Mina)*, whose chapel is dedicated to the Holy Cross. Beside the church in the **Plaza de los Mariachis**, *birria*, *sopes* and enchiladas, accompanied by *tepache* (a beverage made of pulque, water, pineapple and cloves), and tequila are served in the evening to the unmistakable sounds of mariachi music.

San Francisco

In the 16C the Franciscans built a religious complex that includes the San Francisco convent and a series of chapels surrounding the church's atrium. Most of the buildings were demolished in 1861. At present only the temple and the chapel of Aránzazu remain standing. The plot formerly occupied by the convent and atrium was transformed into the **Jardín de San Francisco**, a pleasant spot with flowers, fountains and shade trees, as well as a few vestiges of what once constituted the enormous Franciscan complex.

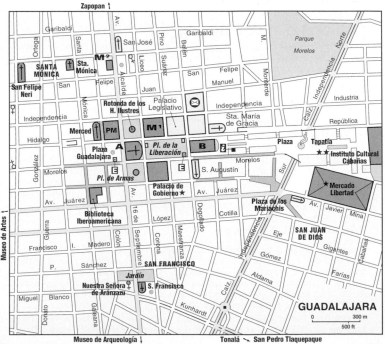

Templo de San Francisco – *Av. 16 de Septiembre and Av. Héroes. Open year-round daily 7am–2pm & 4–8:30pm.* Although the original construction (1554) has been modified several times over the centuries, today this church represents a prime example of restrained Baroque architecture. Between the main facade's Solomonic columns and ornamentation with plant motifs, stands an open-winged eagle perched on a prickly pear cactus—the national emblem found on the Mexican flag and most coins.

Capilla de Nuestra Señora de Aránzazu – *Av. 16 de Septiembre. Open year-round daily 10am–2pm & 4–7pm.* Completed in 1752, the chapel features Churrigueresque **altarpieces★**, highly ornamented with gilded wooden carvings, unique to the state of Jalisco. Note how this style contrasts with the Baroque portal.

Biblioteca Iberoamericana "Octavio Paz" – *At the corner of Pedro Moreno and Colón. Plaza Universidad. Open year-round Mon–Fri 9am–9pm, Sat 9am–5pm. Closed national holidays, Holy Week & Easter (15 days) & Dec 15–31. ☏ (3) 658-3256.* Originally the Church of St. Thomas of Aquinas (17C), which formed part of the Jesuit seminary, it became the first seat of the Royal University of Guadalajara in 1792. During the 19C various state government offices were housed here. In 1986 the building was returned to the university and restored to establish the present-day library. Its current Greco-Roman facade was added during the mid 19C, shortly after the original towers and altars were demolished. Of particular interest is the mural by David Alfaro Siqueiros and Amado de la Cueva, completed in 1926, the theme of which centers on agriculture and the Mexican Revolution. On the main door, various reliefs, designed by Siqueiros and carved by Juan Hernández, represent revolutionary characters and symbols.

Santa Mónica

Iglesia de Santa Mónica – *Santa Mónica, 250, corner with San Felipe. Open year-round daily 10am–12:30pm & 5–7:30pm.* Considered the city's most beautiful church, it was completed in 1733 as the chapel of the Augustinian nuns' convent. The building boasts a **twin portico★★** elegantly adorned with Solomonic columns entwined by grapevine motifs. The base of the church's second section displays carvings of leaves, bouquets and angel faces, as well as a papal tiara.

Templo de San Felipe Neri – *San Felipe, 558, corner with Contreras Medellín. Open year-round Mon–Sat 7am–2pm & 5–7pm, Sun 7am–8pm.* Guadalajara's masterpiece construction, this 18C church with majestic tower features a restrained Baroque portal, with a semicircular arch and reliefs with plant motifs, as well as Corinthian columns. Note St. Philip's coat of arms beneath the choir window and the red-stone sculpture of the Assumption of the Virgin above it.

Five streets east of the church, on Av. Fray Antonio Alcalde, the "Casa de los Perros"—where the city's first printing house was inaugurated in 1792—houses the unique **Museo del Periodismo y las Artes Gráficas (M²)** *(open year-round Tue–Sat 10am–6pm, Sun 10:30am–3pm, closed national holidays; P$5; ☏ 3-613-9286).*

SAN PEDRO TLAQUEPAQUE

8km/5mi southeast of Guadalajara, in the metropolitan area. Take Av. Revolución to reach the Plaza de la Bandera; then, take Ejército and turn onto Gral. Marcelino García Barragán to reach Tlaquepaque.

San Pedro Tlaquepaque which means "place on high hills" is famous for its pottery-making and craftsmanship (blown glass, jewelry, tin, papier-mâché, wood, clay and leather). The central plaza, **El Parián**, once the local marketplace (completed in 1883), today constitutes a major center where locals and visitors alike can enjoy the cheerful music of the mariachis and savor a typical Jaliscan meal.

Museo Regional de la Cerámica (Casa del Burro de Oro) – *Independencia, 237. Open year-round Tue–Sat 10am–6pm, Sun 10am–3pm. ☏ (3) 635-5404.* The small museum is located in a 19C mansion that belonged to J.F. Velarde, one of Santa Anna's generals. The objects on display are representative of the local craftsmanship, such as polished clay, ceramic, tiles, blown glass and miniature figurines. Another highlight is the Mexican kitchen featuring typical utensils.

ADDITIONAL SIGHTS

Museo de Artes – *Av. Juárez, 975. Open year-round Tue–Fri 10am–8pm. P$5. ☏ 3-826-6114.* The French-style building completed at the beginning of the 20C, once seat to the University of Guadalajara, is now a museum exhibiting works by natives of Jalisco. two of José Clemente Orozco's **murals★**, *El hombre principio y fin de todas las cosas* (Man, Beginning and End of All Things) and *El pueblo y los falsos líderes* (The People and False Leaders), grace the auditorium.

Do not miss the beautiful stained-glass windows in the Gothic Revival **Templo del Expiatorio** located behind the museum *(open year-round daily 5:30am–10pm).*

© Robert Frerck/Odyssey

■ Mariachis

Originating in Jalisco, mariachis, like tequila, are symbols of Mexican culture and fascinate locals and visitors alike. Both are inseparable friends, essential at any Mexican festivity nationwide.

The mariachi image known around the world was born in the 1930s. At that time, various musical groups—native of Cocula, Jalisco but based in Mexico City—decided to transform the style of the **sones** (a mixture of folk music from Spain, Mexico and Africa). Thus, they altered the original instrumentation—consisting of four violins, a harp, guitar, *vihuela* (a 5-string guitar) and bass—by eliminating the harp, replacing the vihuela with a different guitar and adopting the **trumpet**, now indispensable in any mariachi group.

Although initially the repertory of songs included only *sones*, today it encompasses a wide range that covers almost any musical genre, including classical music. However, the mariachi is associated above all with the **ranchera** song, considered almost a national hymn. Those who pride themselves on being Mexican know by heart at least two lines to a *ranchera*.

Museo de Arqueología del Occidente de México – *16 de Sept. 889, opposite the Agua Azul Park. Open year-round Tue–Sun 10am–7pm. P$3. ☎ (3) 619-0104.* Here the pre-Hispanic past of the states of Jalisco, Nayarit, Sinaloa, Michoacán and Colima, as well as part of Guanajuato and Guerrero, comes to life through works of great beauty. They include the **mujer cubierta de niños** (woman covered by children), **vasija del acróbata** (acrobat's vessel), **hombre meditabundo** (pensive man), **perros de Colima** (Colima's dogs) and a clay figure of Tláloc, all of them representative of western Mexico's cultures.

Zapopan – *8km/5mi from downtown Guadalajara, accessed from Alcalde and Ávila Camacho Aves. heading northwest.* Founded shortly after Guadalajara, this suburb of the capital is home to the **Basílica de Nuestra Señora de la Expectación de Zapopan** *(open year-round Mon–Sat 6:30am–9pm, Sun 5:30am–10pm).* The basílica boasts an effigy of the "miraculous" **Virgin of Zapopan**, whose annual pilgrimage on October 12, from Guadalajara's cathedral to its home in Zapopan, has drawn nearly two million devoted followers.

Adjacent to the basílica, the **Museo Huichol** *(open year-round Mon–Sat 10am–1pm & 4–7pm; closed Jan 1, May 1, Oct 12, Dec 12 & 25; ☎ 3-636-4430)* displays an interesting collection of artifacts made by Huichols, Coras and Tepehuans.

Tonalá – *14km/8.7mi from the center of Guadalajara, accessed via Av. Revolución and Calle Río Nilo, heading southeast. We recommend Thursday or Sunday visits.* This village constitutes one of Jalisco's most important handicraft centers. Visitors can find a wide variety of **handicrafts★★** elaborated from ceramic, clay, wrought iron and wood. Tonalá's world-renowned, pottery-making tradition is enhanced by modern sophisticated techniques.

EXCURSIONS

Tequila – *58km/36mi northwest of Guadalajara, accessed via Carr. libre 15, heading toward Tepic. We recommend arriving before noon.* This region of blue agave plants is appropriately named for the distilled liquor that has brought international fame to Mexico. Some of the **factories★** in the city, such as **Tequila Cuervo** *(1hr guided tour, year-round Mon–Sat 9am–2pm; closed national holidays; reservations recommended; ☎ 3-742-0050),* offer visitors a chance to observe first-hand the tequila-making process.

The nearby town of Amatitlán produces **Tequila Herradura** *(2hr guided tour, year-round Mon–Thu 9am–1pm; closed national holidays; reservations required; P$25; ☎ 3-745-0011 and 17).*

Ajijic – *57km/35mi south of Guadalajara and 7km/4mi west of Chapala.* Famous for its moderate climate, this picturesque site of the riverbanks of Chapala is the center of activity of one of Mexico's largest colonies of foreigners. Over the last ten years, the town has witnessed a proliferation of art galleries. Of special note, the **Billy Moon★** art gallery *(open year-round daily 10am–6pm; ☎ 3-766-1000)* offers diverse types of crafts of the utmost originality and quality.

★ Mazamitla – *132km/82mi south of Guadalajara. 98km/61mi from Ajijic.* Nestled in the foothills of the Sierra del Tigre, amid a forest that seems to have emerged from a book of fairy tales, appears this charming village with houses built of lime-stone and trimmed with dark wood ornamentation. Typical of Mazamitla are its delicious milk products, jellies and fruit liqueurs. This magical place offers nature's touch and tranquillity.

■ Tequila Express

Washington Train Station, Av. 16 de Sept and Calzada Independencia, Sur, near the Parque Agua Azul. Year-round, Sat 10:30am. P$400 (includes unlimited tequila tasting and lunch). ✗. For more information and reservations, contact the Cámara de Comercio, Av. Vallarta, 4095, Fracc. Camino Real, Zapopan, Jalisco ☎ (3) 122-8626. Well before leaving the train station, one begins to breathe the ambiance of Jalisco, set by the mariachi music. In spacious comfortable wagons, the "Tequila Express" takes its passengers to a town that bears the same name as the national drink that enjoys worldwide fame-tequila. Upon arriving, visitors are greeted with a demonstration of the jima (the art of cutting the agave plant to obtain its heart), followed by a performance of folkloric dances, mariachis, singers and rope tricks.

The **excursion★** includes admission to the Museo Francisco Javier Sauza Mora-a tribute to the owner of one of Mexico's most important tequila companies-as well as a visit to a former tequila workshop. The visit ends in a hacienda, where one can savor typical dishes from the state of Jalisco, accompanied by diverse shows. During the return trip to Guadalajara, passengers enjoy more music and, of course, more tequila.

■ Tequila Production

The production process begins with the selection of 8–10 year-old **blue agave** plants. The *piñas*, or cores, of the plants are split open and steamed in giant ovens in 24 hours. Then, they pass through a mill where they are squeezed to extract a concentrated juice that is fermented for six days. During the process of fermentation, the yeast transforms the sugar into alcohol. Afterward, the alcohol is distilled several times until it reaches its pure state. The result is, of course, the indispensable alcoholic beverage known as tequila.

Unless otherwise indicated, distances given after each stop on an itinerary are calculated from the previous town or sight described.

GUANAJUATO★★★

Guanajuato
Population 128,171
Map of Principal Sights – City Map pp 170-171
🖪 Plaza de la Paz, 14 ☎ (4) 732-1982

The allure of Guanajuato *(photo p 159)*, included in UNESCO's list of World Heritage Sites, resides in its exquisite architecture, as well as in its unique urban plan.
Nestled at the foot of **Cerro del Cubilete**, the capital of the state of Guanajuato, a former mining center, today owes the extravagance of its architecture to the silver mines still in production. Due to its economic power, Guanajuato flourished, mastering mountains and rivers that are now contained by a dam built in the 1960s. Such is the case of the ancient Belauzarán River, the riverbed of which has been transformed into one of the magnificent underground streets or **tunnels** that improve driving through the city.
Today this state capital is also a lively cultural and educational center. Its streets, theaters, churches and plazas are also home to the annual **Festival Internacional Cervantino** (International Cervantes Festival).
Also representative of Guanajuato are its **estudiantinas** (groups of student musicians). On Fridays and Saturdays, dressed in colonial attire, they conduct their **callejoneadas**, or strolls through the city's small plazas and alleys, singing alongside the locals who join them.

Historical Notes

Beginnings – The name *Guanajuato* comes from the Purépecha word **Quanaxhuato**, which means "hill of frogs." According to legend, the hill-populated by the city's first settlers—resembled this amphibian. The **Chichimecs** inhabited the city prior to the arrival of the Spaniards. In 1530 Nuño de Guzmán set foot on the territory today known as the state of Guanajuato, while the Spaniards were dividing among themselves the rest of the country. In 1546 Rodrigo Vázquez was granted a license to establish a cattle ranch in the vicinity of what today is known as the city of Guanajuato. Given the Chichimecs' refusal to work for the Spanish, Vázquez was forced to bring in manual laborers from other regions, including mestizos, blacks and indigenous peoples.

Mining Bonanza and Independence – During the construction of a safe route from Mexico City to Zacatecas, through Querétaro, abundant silver was found in Guanajuato. This discovery attracted a multitude of adventurers in search of wealth. One of the first mines to be worked was **Mina de Rayas**.
After nearly three centuries of domination, Spanish rule was threatened by the Insurgents, whose first armed uprising took place here in Guanajuato, in 1810. This event marked the beginning of the War of Independence.

Nineteenth and Twentieth Centuries – In 1858, during the Reform, Benito Juárez declared Guanajuato the capital of the new Republic and relocated here, but remained only a month. At the beginning of the 20C, Guanajuato was still an important mining center, and following the sale of the mines to foreign companies, prosperity returned to the city. It has flourished as a lively and picturesque cultural and educational center.

★★★HISTORIC CENTER

Through narrow cobblestone streets, visitors may explore this wonderful colonial city, which has been well preserved.

From Alhóndiga to the Templo de la Compañía

★Alhóndiga de Granaditas (Regional Museum) – *Mendizábal, 6. Open year-round Tue–Sat 10am–1:30pm & 4–5:30pm, Sun 10am–2:30pm. Closed national holidays. P$20.* ☎ *(4) 732-1180.* Completed in 1809 under the direction of José del Mazo y Avilés, the simple Neoclassical fortress originally served as a granary. Only a year after its completion, on September 28, 1810, the Alhóndiga was the site of one of Mexico's first struggles for Independence, in which Miguel Hidalgo y Costilla participated. Of special note is the outstanding statue of miner Juan José Martínez de los Reyes.

■ El Pípila

During the battle of 1810 at the Alhóndiga, miner Juan José Martínez de los Reyes—nicknamed **El Pípila**—managed to crawl through enemy fire, shielded by a slab of stone tied to his back, until he reached the main door and set it ablaze. Due to his bravery, the Insurgents were able to seize the warehouse, which had been transformed into a seemingly impregnable fortress.

In 1811 the leaders of the Insurgency movement—Hidalgo, Allende, Aldama and Jiménez—were executed and their decapitated heads were hung in metal cages at each corner of the Alhóndiga and left there for 10 years.

Main Staircase and Upper Level – The main staircase is adorned with a mural by José Chávez Morado, illustrating the War of Independence and the abolition of slavery. The first floor features a collection of more than 3,500 pre-Hispanic seals. The second room displays Mesoamerican art, followed by a narration of the state's history, from the War of Independence to the Republic. The mural *Canto a Guanajuato*, also by Chávez Morado, decorates a second staircase.

Lower Level – This floor features busts of Aldama, Morelos and Hidalgo, as well as a votive lamp in their honor. The lower level includes one room dedicated to the arts and customs of the state of Guanajuato.

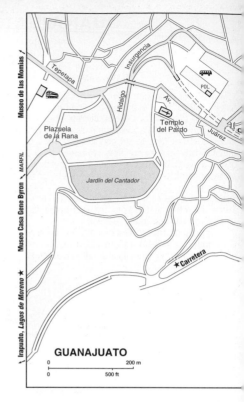

GUANAJUATO

★**Museo Casa Diego Rivera** – *Pocitos, 47. Open year-round daily 10am–6:30pm. Closed national holidays. P$8.* ☎ *(4) 732-1197.* The Neoclassical building was the birthplace and home of muralist Diego Rivera. In 1973 it was inaugurated as a museum. The **first level** displays momentoes of the Rivera family and 19C furnishings. The **second level** exhibits many of Diego Rivera's paintings and drawings, including preliminary sketches of his murals and works from his Cubist period. Subsequent levels feature additional works by Rivera, as well as a variety of paintings by other renowned artists.

Museo del Pueblo (M) – *Pocitos, 7. Open year-round Tue–Sat 10am–7pm, Sun 9am–3pm. Closed national holidays. P$8.* ☎ *(4) 732-2990.* The elegant colonial mansion was once part of an estate which belonged first to the Marquises de Rayas and then to Don José Manuel de Sardaneta, one of the signers of Mexico's Declaration of Independence.
Today it houses a museum. The **mezzanine** displays secular and religious paintings from the 17C and 19C, sacred and profane objects, wooden sculptures and other crafts of the period. The **intermediate level** features the personal collections of Olga Costa and José Chávez Morado. Of note on the **second floor** are the former chapel and a beautiful Churrigueresque portal, graced by one of José Chávez Morado's murals, *El estípite fracturado* (The Fractured Pilaster), depicting the foundation and history of the city of Guanajuato.

★**University** – *Lascuráin de Retana, 5. Open year-round Mon–Fri 7am–9pm, Sat 7am–4pm. Closed national holidays.* ☎ *(4) 732-2770.* Although architect Vicente Urquiaga constructed this outstanding Neoclassical building with green quarry stone in 1955, the university dates back to 1732, when a group of benefactors from Guanajuato donated the funds necessary for founding a Jesuit seminary. The university's coat of arms—including two frogs, a beehive, honeycomb, bees and torch—adorns the facade. The frogs represent the city of Guanajuato. The beehive refers to the legend of the site—once the home of Doña Teresa de Busto y Moya. When Doña Teresa left her home, she took the beehive with her, but the bees returned to their old home. Inside the monumental structure, accessed from Calle Lascuráin, the School of Industrial Relations (Facultad de Relaciones Industriales) possesses a courtyard, a Baroque chapel and, on an upper level, the **portal** of the former parish church from Marfil.

★**Templo de la Compañía** – *Plaza de la Compañía, near the corner of Calle Hidalgo. Open year-round Mon–Sat 7:30am–9pm, Sun 7am–2pm & 6–9pm. Closed national holidays.* Constructed on a promontory and completed in 1765, this stone church has an impressive main portal in Churrigueresque style. A sun carved by indige-

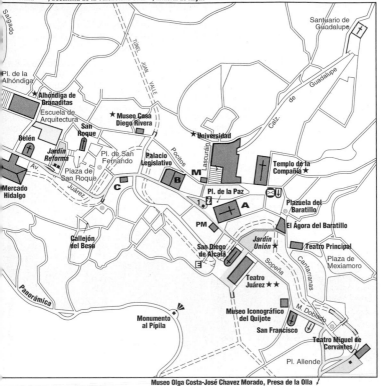

Museo Olga Costa-José Chavez Morado, Presa de la Olla

nous hands hovers above the door. Inside, the Neoclassical main cupola replaced the original one, which collapsed in 1808. Various 18C paintings by Jesús Cabrera decorate the walls, while an **art gallery** located to the left of the presbytery houses other 18C works.

Plazuela del Baratillo – *By the final apex of the Jardín Unión.* This site formerly served as a marketplace where vendors would peddle their inexpensive merchandise, hence the name *baratillo* (bargain sales). The center of the plaza holds a replica of the Florentine fountain that stood in the Plaza de la Paz in the 19C. In front of the plaza stands **El Ágora del Baratillo** (Bargain Sales Marketplace) through which visitors may access the Jardín Unión.

From the Jardín Unión to the Basilica of Guanajuato

★**Jardín Unión** – *Where Calles Sopeña and Cruz Verde (extension of the Plaza de la Paz) run parallel to each other.* Rows of laurel trees joined at the crown mark the boundaries to this delightful triangle-shaped garden. In the 18C it was the atrium of the **Templo de San Diego de Alcalá**. In 1842 it was transformed into a garden; 41 years later the people of Guanajuato celebrated a welcome addition—a charming bandstand where the state band plays on Tuesdays, Thursdays and Sundays.
At present, various shops and restaurants surround the garden, a gathering place favored by locals and visitors alike.

Teatro Principal – *Calle Hidalgo. (before Calle Cantarranas), at the corner with the Callejón de Ánimas. Open only for performances.* In 1788 this site was home to Guanajuato's Coliseo Principal (Main Coliseum), which was abandoned during Mexico's War of Independence. In 1826 the coliseum was reinaugurated only to be consumed by flames a hundred years later. The present theater was built during the mid 20C and today also houses a movie theater.

Teatro Miguel de Cervantes – *In the Plaza Allende. Open only for performances.* Prior to its inauguration as a theater in 1979, the building functioned as a smelting then as an ore-processing plant. Today it faces a small plaza that features a sculpture of Don Quixote and his loyal friend Sancho Panza, appropriate figures for a city that hosts the International Cervantes Festival.

Iglesia de San Francisco – *In the Plaza Manuel Doblado. Open year-round daily 7am–2pm & 4–8pm.* Built on the site of a former monastery, the church was completed in 1792. A series of Baroque carvings on the facade depicts the image of

171

Christ above the arch and that of St. Francis of Assisi, the temple's patron saint, above the choir window. The interior boasts seven Neoclassical altarpieces and 18C paintings.

Museo Iconográfico del Quijote – *Manuel Doblado, 1. Open year-round Tue–Sat 10am–6:30pm, Sun 10am–3pm* ☏ *(4) 732-6721.* The beautiful green mansion possesses an inner courtyard displaying a collection of paintings and sculptures, as well as a variety of objects with the central theme, the "Man of La Mancha."
Other works include those by artists such as Raúl Anguiano, Alberto Gironella, Martha Palau, José Luis Cuevas, Pedro Coronel and Manuel Felguérez, as well as a **collection★** of original sketches and paintings by Salvador Dalí also inspired by Spain's literary classic, *Don Quixote.*

Teatro Juárez

★★Teatro Juárez – *Calle de Sopeña, in front of the Union Garden. Open year-round Tue–Sun 9am–1:45pm & 5–7:45pm. P$5.* ☏ *(4) 732-1542.* Considered one of Guanajuato's architectural masterpieces and characterized by a Neoclassical facade crowned by eight sculptures representing the muses, the theater was built by the architect José Noriega on the site of the Convento de San Pedro de Alcántara. Although work began in 1872, the theater was not completed until 1903, when it was inaugurated by Porfirio Díaz. Its splendid horseshoe-shaped interior includes four levels, featuring decorative ironwork balconies and a Moorish decor.

Templo de San Diego de Alcalá – *Calle de Sopeña, 7, across from the Union Garden. Open year-round daily 7am–9pm.* Formerly part of a convent, the church is characterized by a beautiful Baroque **facade★** with a hint of Churrigueresque. Although the convent originally consisted of several levels, today only the second level can be visited. Paintings from the 18C decorate the interior. Of particular interest is the chapel in honor of *El Señor de Burgos,* whose portrait was sent to Veracruz by King Charles III in 1785 and reached its present destination in 1789.

Palacio Municipal (PM) – *Luis González Obregón, 12.* Built in 1707, the mansion has witnessed numerous historical events, as it was seat to the three powers of the Mexican State when Independence was achieved. It also served as Benito Juárez's residence at the beginning of the Reform War, during which time Guanajuato was the capital of the Republic. Moreover, from the end of the 19C to the beginning of the 20C, it housed the legislative and judicial bodies.

Plaza de la Paz – *Calle de la Paz, by Av. Juárez.* Several avenues converge in this triangle-shaped space whose center boasts the **Monumento a la Paz (1)**, a female figure crowned with laurels. Created by Jesús Contreras in 1898, this sculpture, popularly known as *La Mona,* also provides a favorite gathering place for students and locals.

From the Basílica to the Hidalgo Marketplace

★Basílica Colegiata de Nuestra Señora de Guanajuato (A) – *On Plaza de la Paz. Open year-round daily 7am–9pm.* Completed in 1696, Guanajuato's largest building was granted basilica status in 1957. Its striking Baroque **portal** contrasts vividly with the plain yellow walls. The interior shimmers with gold, a legacy of the city's mining wealth, highlighting the magnificent altar, enormous chandeliers and columns. According to local lore, the polychrome wooden statue of the Virgin Mary, in the main altar, was a gift from King Charles V and his son Philip II.

Tribunal Colegiado de Distrito (Mansión del Conde Rul) (B) – *Plaza de la Paz, 75. Open year-round Mon–Fri 7am–2pm. Closed national holidays.* Completed in 1803 by architect Francisco Eduardo Tresguerras, this rose quarrystone building is considered one of the purest examples of Neoclassical architecture in Mexico.

Palacio Legislativo – *Plaza de la Paz, 77. Open year-round Mon–Fri 7am–9pm. Closed national holidays.* Under the direction of architect Cecilio Luis Long, this beautiful Neoclassical structure, with green quarry stone, was completed in 1900 and inaugurated by Porfirio Díaz himself. Of particular interest in the **interior** is the Congressional Sessions Room, located on the second floor, elegantly paneled in wood and decorated with paintings by José Escudero, an artist from the Porfiriato era.

■ A Mexican Romeo and Juliet

Located beside the Plaza de los Ángeles, the 0.7m/2ft-wide **Callejón del Beso** (Alley of the Kiss) is overlooked by a pair of flower-covered balconies belonging to two different houses. It owes its fame to the legend about two adolescents who were neighbors and became lovers against the wishes of the girl's father. The latter decided to send her to a convent and drive away her beau. Different endings conclude the tale—from the one where the father kills the young man, to the one where he murders his own daughter. According to local lore, any couple who walks by the two balconies could fall victim to a seven-year curse if they do not kiss on the third step of the stairway.

Casa Real de Ensaye (Oficinas de Banca Serfín) (C) – *Av. Juárez, 16.* The Baroque facade boasts the coat of arms of the Marquis of San Clemente, Guanajuato's first titled citizen, as well as a plaque alluding to the building's original function as the Royal House of Assaying from the mid 17C until 1824.

Templo de San Roque – *Plaza de San Roque, 1. Enter from the Plaza de San Fernando, which connects to the Plaza de San Roque. Open year-round daily 7am–9pm.* This church was commissioned in 1726. Its restrained Baroque facade is built of rose quarry stone. Inside, frescoes of the four evangelists decorate the cupola's pendentives, and ancient paintings of the Passion of Christ and the Last Supper adorn the walls.

The Plaza de San Roque serves as the stage for open-air theater performances of Cervantes' **Entremeses** (interludes) during the International Cervantes Festival.

Jardín Reforma – *Av. Juárez.* A round arch flanked by Ionic columns, remnants of the Mercado Reforma, marks the entrance to the garden, which is surrounded by splendid mansions dating from the 16C to the 19C. Shade trees create a peaceful setting in which visitors may rest and relax.

Templo de Belén (Parroquia del Inmaculado Corazón de María) – *Av. Juárez, 2. Open year-round daily 6:30am–1:30pm and 4:30–9:30pm.* Completed in 1775, the Church of Belén, with its restrained Baroque facade, merits a visit for its unusual floor of mosaic tiles imported from Rome.

★**Mercado Hidalgo** – *Av. Juárez. Open year-round daily 7am–9pm.* The cast-iron market building, designed by architect Ernesto Brunel, was inaugurated by Porfirio Díaz in 1910. The bustling market offers all kinds of sweets, ready-to-eat foods and handicrafts, which vie with one another for their bright colors.

★PANORAMIC ROAD

Museo de las Momias (Panteón Municipal) – *Pantheon's Esplanade. Open year-round daily 9am–6pm. P$15.* ☏ *(4) 732-0639.* The unique museum exhibits 108 mummified human corpses and four skulls. Most of the bodies came from the municipal cemetery, and they were exhumed after the concession had expired. A chemical in the local soil halted their complete decomposition. For an extra P$5, one can visit the museum's recent addition: a hall dedicated to death-related elements, holograms and torture instruments.

★★**Templo de San Cayetano de la Valenciana** – *Km 5 on the Carr. Panorámica to Dolores. Open year-round Tue–Sun 9am–7pm. Photos of the interior are not allowed.* Completed in 1788 by architects Andrés de la Riva and Jorge Archundia, this church features a Churrigueresque facade. Its interior is decorated with 19C paintings by Luis Monroy and boasts an extraordinary **pulpit**★ with inlays of ivory, tortoiseshell, bone and precious woods. Also of interest are the Churrigueresque altarpieces and the organ, still played to this day.

Templo de San Cayetano de la Valenciana

Bocamina de la Valenciana (Mina de San Cayetano de la Valenciana) – *Km 5 on the Carr. Panorámica to Dolores. Open year-round daily 10am–6pm. P$8.* ☎ *(4) 732-0570.* This passageway served as the main entrance to Guanajuato's richest mine, the Valenciana, which was in operation from 1558 to 1810. During the 16C, the mine yielded one-fifth of the world's total production of gold and silver. Today, visitors may take a tour that descends to a depth of 50m/165ft.

★Templo de Cata – *Carr. Panorámica to Dolores. Open year-round daily 7am–9pm.* Completed at the end of the 18C, this lovely church features a Baroque facade made of pink quarry stone, with medallions in relief depicting biblical scenes. The shrine was dedicated to the Christ of Villaseca, whose effigy was imported from Spain in 1618 and is part of the main altar. Like the Valenciana, this church is the epitome of neo-Hispanic art in the region. The interior includes an elaborate wooden pulpit and two beautiful gilded altarpieces. Most outstanding is the **Chapel of Our Lady of Sorrows★**, inlaid with tiny quartz stones from nearby mines.

Mineral de Rayas – *Carr. Panorámica to Dolores, heading east on the Cata-Sanctuary route.* Named after Juan de Rayas, a muleteer who discovered the mine in 1550, the Rayas is one of Guanajuato's three mines still in operation. Visible from the esplanade are the mine shaft and a panoramic view of the city.
Located just up the hill, the village of Mellado is home to the Templo de la Merced, constructed at the end of the 17C. To the southern side, in the valley, lie the ruins of what is believed to have been the cloister.

Presa de la Olla – *At the end of Paseo de la Presa.* Although the reservoir was completed in 1749 to alleviate the problem of drought, it only began to supply the city with water in 1832. Surrounded by ash, eucalyptus and jacaranda trees, this is the setting for St. John's Festival, celebrated annually from June 18–24, as well as the opening of the floodgates, which takes place on the first Monday in July. From the Paseo de la Presa Ave., some of the city's 20C buildings of unique beauty—such as the **Escuela Normal**, on the left side of the avenue, and the **Palacio de Gobierno**, opposite the Plazuela Antonia del Moral—can be admired.

Monumento al Pípila – *Follow the Panoramic Road toward the south of the city.* Atop the hill of San Miguel rises a monument erected in 1939 in memory of this hero of Independence. This site offers a panoramic view of the city.

EXCURSIONS

★Ex Hacienda de San Gabriel de la Barrera – *Old road to Marfil, at Km 2.5. Open year-round daily 9am–6pm. Closed Jan 1 & Dec 25. P$10* ✗ ☎ *(4) 732-0619.* The ore-processing hacienda, where silver and gold were refined, belonged to the brothers Juan and Gabriel de la Barrera. It boasts 16 wonderfully maintained gardens.
Located on the upper level of the hacienda's former residential area, a small museum features 17C and 18C furniture imported from China, England and Italy. Across from this area stands a chapel with a Spanish Gothic **altarpiece**, originally from the Cathedral of Jaen, Spain. Three different kinds of gold and three stained-glass windows, one of which dates back to the 15C, ornament this magnificent work of art.

Museo Casa Gene Byron – *Old road to Marfil. Open year-round Tue–Sat 10am–3pm. P$8. ☎ (4) 733-1029.* Formerly the home of painter Gene Byron, this beautiful house today holds a permanent collection of Byron's furniture and paintings.

Museo Olga Costa-José Chávez Morado – *Pastita, 158, Barrio de Pastita. Torre del Arco. Open year-round Tue–Sat 10am–4:30pm, Sun 9am–3pm. P$8. ☎ (4) 731-0977.* Once the private residence of Olga Costa and José Chávez Morado, this museum now displays furniture, handicrafts and archaeological artifacts belonging to the two painters, who constantly exhibit their works here. From time to time, the master painters' collection is set aside temporarily to feature the talent of young artists.

León – *66km/41mi. Coming from Guanajuato, on Carr. 110 to Mexico, take the exit to León by Carr. 45.* The state's largest city is a burgeoning industrial center specializing in the production of shoes and leather goods. For this reason it is highly frequented by tourists. The Neoclassical **cathedral**★★ *(at the corner of Álvaro Obregón and Hidalgo)*, was built by the Franciscans in the mid 18C. The Neoclassical **Palacio Municipal**, with three levels, and the **Parroquia del Sagrario**, with a mannerist-style facade and an 18C Baroque tower, surround the **Plaza de los Mártires** *(Downtown)*. Other buildings of interest include the **Teatro Doblado** *(on the corner of Pedro Moreno and Hermanos Aldama)*, with a Neoclassical facade, and the **Templo del Expiatorio**★ *(Madero, 722)*, an impressive Gothic Revival building, begun in 1921.

★**Lagos de Moreno** – *(State of Jalisco) 94km/58.3mi. Exit Guanajuato heading southwest on Carr. 110. Turn right at the junction with Carr. 45D, go past León (66km/41mi) and continue on Carr. 45. At the junction with Carr. 80, turn left.* Located in the eastern part of the state of Jalisco, Lagos de Moreno is considered the region's most important city, known as Los Altos de Jalisco. It was the birth-place of musician Juventino Rosas, poet Juan de Dios Peza and writer Mariano Azuela. Visitors can step back to the colonial era in this classical city. The symbol of the city, the **Parroquia de la Asunción** *(Av. Hidalgo, across from the main plaza)* was constructed during the 18C. Its facade and side portals display fine carvings in Baroque style with a touch of Churrigueresque. Behind the parish church stands the **Teatro Rosas Moreno** *(Calle José Rosas Moreno)*, in French Neoclassical style. Begun in 1857, the building was inaugurated in 1907 with Verdi's *Aida*. The **Rinconada de las Capuchinas** *(from the main plaza walk one street south on Miguel Leandro Guerra and turn left onto Mariano Azuela)* consists of a garden plaza sur-rounded by magnificent structures. Located off to one side, the museum-gallery was once the House of Agustín Rivera, a local priest and writer. Adjacent to the museum, the church and former convent of the Capuchin nuns now houses the Cultural Center, opposite the Miguel Leandro Guerra Arts School. Behind the Rinconada, visitors may access the **Paseo de la Rivera**, a pleasant street lined by the huge walls in the back of the church. The path runs parallel to the Rio Lagos and ends at the Puente Grande, a Renaissance bridge.

★★**San Miguel de Allende** – *92km/57mi. Exit Guanajuato heading north on Carr. 110 toward Dolores Hidalgo (54km/33.5mi). Continue east on Carr. 51 until reaching San Miguel de Allende (38km/23.5mi). Description p 179.*

Irapuato – *53km/33mi. From Guanajuato head north on Carr. 110. At the junc-tion with Carr. 45D, turn left (south) and continue for 17km/10.5mi.* This industrial city, a center of agricultural and commercial activity, is best known for its pro-duction of strawberries, broccoli and asparagus. Visitors may enjoy a tour of its Historic Center, beginning with the **Jardín Hidalgo** *(on Calle Juárez, between Calles Ramón Corona and Fernando Dávila)*. On this small but lively square stands the **Templo del Convento** (or Church of St. Francis) with a Baroque portal. The **Templo del Hospitalito** *(on the corner of Berriozábal and Fernando Dávila)* boasts a beautiful Baroque facade, with stone carvings of the sun and the moon. Southeast of down-town Irapuato lies the frequented **Plaza Hidalgo**. On the western edge of the square stand **La Parroquia**, with a Baroque facade and imposing columns, and the **Templo de San José**, displaying a wonderful hand-carved portal.

★★**Ex Convento de San Agustín de Yuriria** – *70km/43.4mi southeast of Irapuato. Take Carr. 45 to Salamanca, then Carr. 43 to Morelia, until reaching the exit to Yuriria. Open year-round daily 9:30am–4:45pm. P$7. ☎ (4) 168-2036.* The Augustinian order is to be credited for this monumental building, as well as for the Church of San Pablo Yuriria. Initiated in 1540, the monastery in time gained recognition as a liberal arts seminary. It was declared a Historical Monument in 1932.

Facade – This exquisite facade has been compared to that of **Acolman** in the state of Mexico. The **main portal**, in Plateresque style, is divided into three sections that are elegantly decorated with various motifs of flowers and fruits, as well as cherubs and sculptures. The first section contains two effigies, flanked by two pairs of intri-cately carved columns. To the right stands the statue of St. Peter, the church's patron saint, identifiable by his book and sword. A figure of St. Augustine appears on the upper level.

Interior – The convent's interior displays a mixture of Renaissance and Gothic elements, characteristic of the 16C Mexican Plateresque style. While the presbytery and the transept possess vaults reminiscent of the Gothic style, the nave shows Renaissance influence with its coffered barrel vault.

Cloister – To the left of the temple, a portal with four splendid archways leads into the former convent, today transformed into the Colonial Museum. Originally, the museum's rooms served as a refectory, a kitchen and a *de profundis* room. On the lower level, note the vaults with Gothic ribs and the remains of decorative paintings on the walls. A staircase with a double vault, also reminiscent of the Gothic style, leads to the upper level, which formerly housed the cells, sleeping quarters and library.

MANZANILLO★
Colima
Population 108,584
Map of Principal Sights
🚹 Blvd. Miguel de la Madrid, 1033, Fraccionamiento Playa Azul
☎ (3) 333-2277

Known as "the World's Capital of the Sailfish," due to the multiple fishing tournaments held here throughout the year, Manzanillo is recognized as one of Mexico's most important commercial and tourist ports. It is shaped by two major bays: **Santiago** and **Manzanillo**, both divided by the famous **Península de Santiago**. These bays possess many beautiful beaches that span 20km/12.4mi and offer a great variety of aquatic recreational activities. The most noteworthy beaches, from southeast to northwest (on the way to the airport) include Playa Ventanas, El Majo, El Malecón (in downtown Manzanillo), San Pedrito, Las Brisas, Playa Azul and Salagua. Some of the country's most luxurious hotels and most beautiful beaches—such as El Tesoro, Las Hadas, Playa Escondida and La Audiencia—can be found on the Península de Santiago. Farther ahead lie Playa Santiago, Olas Altas, Miramar and La Boquita. For swimming, the beaches of **San Pedrito, Playa Azul, La Audiencia, Miramar** and **La Boquita** are recommended. Located on the campus of the University of Colima, in the San Pedrito area, the **Museo Universitario de Arqueología** *(open year-round Tue–Sat 10am–2pm and 5–8pm, Sun 10am–1pm; P$10 ☎ 3-332-2256)* holds an impressive collection of pre-Hispanic objects belonging to Colima and other Mexican states. Of particular interest is a life-size replica of a tomb.

EXCURSIONS

★**Barra de Navidad** – *In Jalisco, 64km/39.7mi northwest of Manzanillo on Carr. 200. On-going departures from the bus terminal.* Jalisco's southern coast, known as the **Costalegre**, begins with this lovely fishing town. In addition to a 2km/1.2mi-long beach, ideal for surfing and other water sports, Barra de Navidad boasts a beautiful lagoon, spectacular for its mangroves and diverse bird species. Across from the lagoon lies the Isla de Navidad (Christmas Island) home to a luxurious tourist resort, and Colimilla, famous for its fine restaurants. Every year Barra de

Las Hadas, Santiago Peninsula

Navidad is the seat to various, international fishing tournaments. Several **beaches**★ can be found along the Costalegre. Located on the northern end of the bay, the peaceful beach of **San Patricio Melaque** offers a full range of tourist services. Even more beaches can be found on the way to Puerto Vallarta. Some of them are private and accessible only to guests of luxury hotels, such as **El Tamarindo** and **Bel-Air Careyes**. However, several worthwhile destinations can be reached by car. They include the secluded beach of **El Tecuán** and its freshwater lagoon; **Tenacatita**, an ecological reserve perfect for scuba diving, swimming and fishing; and **Chamela**, with calm waves, offering excursions to the nearby islands inhabited by a wide variety of marine birds.

Cuyutlán – *42km/26mi southeast, on the Carretera Colima-Guadalajara. It may also be accessed by the freeway that runs along the Cuyutlán Lagoon, where salt mines can be seen. At the bus terminal, board a bus heading to Tecomán, get off at Armería and take a second bus to Cuyutlán.* Annually, hundreds of visitors flock to this village's beach to witness firsthand the spectacular **ola verde**★ (green wave), which reaches up to 8m/26ft in height and occurs from April through June. Independent of this phenomenon, the seaside town, with its long waterfront, continues attracting tourists during the rest of the year due to its ambiance and natural beauty. The endless list of visitors who have become enamored of Cuyutlán includes Mexican filmmaker Emilio "el Indio" Fernández, who has filmed two of his movies at this location. One street away from the central plaza, the **Museo Comunitario de la Sal** *(open year-round Tue–Sun 10am–6pm; donations accepted;* ☎ *3-322-0564)*, unique in all of America, recounts the history of Cuyutlán and its importance as a producer of salt mines from pre-Hispanic to modern times. Just 3km/2mi away, the **Centro de Desarrollo Productivo, Recreativo y Ecológico "Miguel Álvarez del Toro"** *(open year-round daily 10am–6pm; P$5;* ⚠ ◳ ☎ *3-322-0564)*, a turtle camp, invites people to participate in the collection of turtle eggs, as well as in freeing the young turtles.

Colima – *96km/59.5mi northeast of Manzanillo (48km/29.8mi from Cuyutlán) on the Carretera Guadalajara-Manzanillo.* The "City of Palm Trees" is protected by the **Nevado de Colima** (4,335m/14,219ft) and the **Volcán de Fuego** (3,960m/12,989ft). In the center of the state's capital, the rhythm of life oscillates between modernity and the tranquillity of the countryside. Its ancient inhabitants were known as **Colimotes**. Although Colima does not possess architectural vestiges of the ceremonial centers of its ancestors, some of Mexico's most beautiful and artistic pre-Hispanic sculptures have been found here. The majority of the objects have been rescued from the so-called **tumbas de tiro**, tombs used in western Mesoamerica and northwestern South America. The figure of the *xoloitzcuintle* dogs has become the symbol of both the city and the state not only for its beauty, but also for the importance that the Colimotes granted to this animal. These dogs served as their loyal companions during their existence on earth as well as during their voyage to the next world.

Dedicated to the exhibit of archaeological stones, the ground floor of the **Museo Regional de Historia** *(Portal Morelos, 1, Plaza Principal; open year-round Tue–Sat 9am–6pm, Sun 5–8pm; P$17;* ☎ *3-312-9228)* features in Room 4 an exact, life-size **replica**★ of a *tumba de tiro*. The **Museo Universitario de Artes Populares "María Teresa Pomar Aguilar"** *(on the corner of Gabino Barreda and Manuel Gallardo. Cross the plaza and walk down Constitución for seven streets. Turn right onto Calle M. Gallardo and continue straight on until reaching the corner with Gabino Barreda; open year-round Tue–Sat 10am–2pm & 5–8pm, Sun 10am–1pm;* ☎ *3-312-6869)* displays an admirable collection of folkloric and popular art.

A must-see destination, the **Museo de las Culturas de Occidente "María Ahumada de Gómez" de la Secretaría de Cultura**★★ *(Calz. Galván Norte; corner with Ejército Nacional; taxi ride recommended; open year-round Tue–Sun 9am–6:30pm; P$15;* ☎ *3-312-3155)* exhibits objects of great archaeological and aesthetic value. Visitors are greeted by the symbolic figure of the **perros bailarines** (dancing dogs), located in the vestibule. The rooms on the lower level explain in chronological order the various compounds in which pre-Hispanic life unfolded. The stained-glass windows in the upper level depict a variety of subjects related to the daily life and culture of the ancient Colimotes.

Nogueras – *6km/3.7mi north of Colima via Carr. 16. Accessed by bus or taxi.* The Nogueras hacienda is now home to the **Museo Alejandro Rangel Hidalgo** *(open year-round Tue–Sun 10am–2pm & 4:30–7:30pm, holidays 10am–6pm; closed Jan 1, May 1 & Dec 25; P$10;* ✗ ◳ ☎ *3-315-5280)*, named after the renowned painter and native of Colima. In addition to a sample of Rangel's works, the museum features an excellent **collection**★ of pre-Hispanic ceramics of high anthropological and aesthetic value, donated by Rangel. All the figures were found in Nogueras and its surroundings.

PUERTO VALLARTA★★

Jalisco
Population 149,876
Map of Principal Sights
🅱 ☎ (3) 222-0242 or www.puertovallarta.net

The famous tourist center is located in the middle of the **Bay of Banderas**-Mexico's second most developed and one of the world's longest bays-and surrounded by the Sierra Madre Occidental, whose mountains are covered with an exuberant jungle vegetation. In 1851 Guadalupe Sánchez founded Puerto Las Peñas as a center for distributing salt to the nearby mine of Real de Cuale. In 1918 the town was renamed Puerto Vallarta in memory of Ignacio Luis Vallarta, governor of Jalisco from 1871 to 1875.

More than sun and sand, Puerto Vallarta embodies a typical Mexican town, including cobblestone streets and white buildings with red-tile roofs. Several art galleries line its waterfront, while **Isla Cuale** houses a museum, with a small sampling of pre-Hispanic artifacts from western Mexico. In this picturesque island, earth, heaven and sea combine to create an authentic paradise.

ACTIVITIES IN PUERTO VALLARTA

Various companies offer boat excursions around the Bay of Banderas or to Islas Marietas, as well as to Arcos Yelapa and Quimixto, where one can enjoy snorkeling and kayaking. Options available include morning boat trips, such as those provided by *Day Off (☎ 3-221-0657)* and *Marigalante (☎ 3-223-0309)*, or sunset excursions, such as those aboard the *Marigalante, Rhythm of the Night (☎ 3-221-0657)* or *Princesa Vallarta (☎ 3-224-4777)*, which also depart in the morning.

For those who prefer to remain on land, Puerto Vallarta offers horseback rides in the foothills of the Sierra Madre Occidental. These expeditions are guided by experts and vary in duration from three hours to seven days. Consult the specialized agencies *(Rancho Ojo de Agua: ☎ 3-224-0607 and Rancho El Charro: ☎ 3-224-0114)*, or a travel agency. In addition, one can explore the area on bike or motorcycle *(Bike Mex: ☎ 3-223-1680 and Moto River Tour: ☎ 3-221-2716)*, as well as from a plane *(Open Air Expeditions: ☎ 3-222-3310)*, or simply hike the Sierra Madre and discover its numerous springs of volcanic origin *(Viva Tours: ☎ 3-224-0410)*.

SIGHTS

Beaches – Playa Olas Altas (High Surf Beach) and Playa de los Muertos (Beach of the Dead) are located in downtown Puerto Vallarta. On the outskirts of the port, toward the south, lie the most popular beaches: **Mismaloya** and **Boca de Tomatlán**, a departure point for boat rides to **Las Ánimas, Quimixto** and **Yelapa**. While these beaches are not extensive, they are nestled at the foot of several mountain streams, which occasionally form waterfalls of great beauty that highlight the dense vegetation growing on steep and rugged rocks.

Restaurants – *On carr. 200, 21km south of Puerto Vallarta.* Several restaurants line the banks of the river known as Los Horcones. Here, one can sample delicious regional dishes and seafood. *Avoid swimming in the river during the rainy season.*

EXCURSIONS

Nuevo Vallarta – *17km/10.5mi. From Puerto Vallarta head north on Carr. 200, following the signs to Nuevo Vallarta.* Located in the Bay of Banderas and part of the state of Nayarit, the nautical/tourist development includes a modern marina, hotels, condominiums and a residential zone with private docks on the navigable channels that connect to the sea. One can explore the inlets and islands of the Ameca River, inhabited by diverse species of birds.

Toward the northern edge of the bay, Punta Mita (El Anclote, Nuevo Corral de Risco) serves as a departure point for boat trips to the **Marietas Islands**, a marvelous spot that constitutes a natural sanctuary for marine birds, such as the red-footed booby bird. In addition, its underwater caves and tunnels are ideal for diving and spotting dolphins, gigantic manta rays and humpback whales, which visit these coasts during the winter to mate and give birth.

Rincón de Guayabitos and Peñita de Jaltemba – *75km/46.5mi north via Carr. 200 heading toward Tepic.* **Playa de Guayabitos★**, with its charming colonial town, and **Playa de Ayala** are located on the southern coast of Nayarit, on the Jaltemba Cove. The breathtaking landscape of the Sierra de Vallejo frames these two beaches. Their calm waters allow for a wide variety of water sports. Visitors may enjoy excursions on glass-bottom boats to the islands of El Cangrejo (The Crab) and El Coral. Approximately 2km/1mi to the north, the coastal town of **Peñita de Jaltemba** offers attractive marine panoramas.

Guanajuato
Population 118,769
Map of Principal Sights – City Map p 180
🅱 Plaza Allende ☎ (4) 152-6565 and (01-800) 902-3200
or www.unisono.net.mx/sanmiguel/index.html

San Miguel de Allende was named after Ignacio de Allende, one of its natives and a hero of the War of Independence, and Fray Juan de San Miguel, who together with a group of Purépechas and Otomís, founded the city in 1542 and named it Itzcuinapan. While quintessentially colonial, oddly enough the city is represented by a church in Gothic Revival style.

Abounding in trees and benches, the main plaza, crowded on Tuesdays and Sundays, is favored by the city's community of foreigners for relaxation, recreation and cultural activities. Art comes to life in San Miguel's galleries, shops and cobblestone streets, which offer views of wonderful landscapes.

Historical Notes

Fray Juan de San Miguel, Michoacán's Franciscan evangelizer, founded San Miguel in 1542. Shortly thereafter the settlement was transferred to Itzcuinapan, whose spring still provides its people with water.

In 1555 Viceroy Don Luis de Velasco founded the village of San Miguel el Grande (St. Michael the Great). In the 18C Father Benito Díaz de Gamarra taught Cartesian philosophy—for the first time in America—in the school of San Francisco de Sales, thus revolutionizing education. Not surprisingly, Allende, Aldama and Father Luis Felipe Neri de Alfaro—builder of the Sanctuary of Atotonilco—attended this school.

Toward the 18C, with the flourishing of industry and commerce, particularly cattle ranching and craftsmanship, San Miguel el Grande became an important mercantile center. The 19C brought about conspiracy meetings, which led to the Grito de Independencia (Cry for Independence) in 1810. Sixteen years later, the city acquired the name of one of its Insurgents, thus becoming San Miguel de Allende.

CITY CENTER

Plaza Allende – *Between Canal and Umarán.* Heart of the city's social life, this plaza was erected on a quadrangular platform, adorned by well pruned laurel trees that offer shade to a multitude of visitors. Every angle of the city affords a view of the elegant colonial buildings—as well as the Gothic Revival church, San Miguel's icon.

Parroquia de San Miguel Arcángel – *Opposite the Jardín Principal (Main Garden) or Plaza Allende. Open year-round daily 6am–2pm & 4–8pm.* The original building, constructed in 1542, functioned as a Franciscan mission founded by Fray Juan de San Miguel. In 1564 Don Vasco de Quiroga converted it into a parish church. The present church, begun in 1683, was remodeled at the end of the 19C when Zeferino Gutiérrez Muñoz headed the construction of the Gothic Revival **facade** and fashioned it after a French Gothic cathedral he had seen on a postcard. Its cruciform **interior** preserves a collection of paintings by Juan Rodríguez Juárez.

Museo Histórico de San Miguel de Allende (Museo Local) – *Cuna de Allende, 1. Open year-round Tue–Sun 10am–4pm. Closed national holidays.* ☎ *(4) 152-2499.* Formerly the private residence of Ignacio Allende, the museum is now recognized as one of the best examples of 18C secular architecture influenced by the Baroque style. At present it houses a series of exhibits on the history and culture of San Miguel. It also offers an overview of Mexico's pre-Hispanic culture.

Casa de los Condes de la Canal (Oficinas del Banco Nacional de México) (A) – *Corner of Hidalgo and Calle de la Canal.* Narciso Loreto de la Canal y Landeta built this

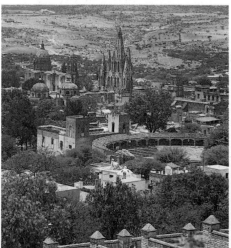

San Miguel de Allende

© Bob Schalkwijk

magnificent Neoclassical mansion in the late 18C. Its most impressive feature, a marvelous **gate★** overlooking Calle de la Canal 4, is carved in wood with high reliefs, some of which display plant motifs, and crowned by an eagle. The second level portrays the Virgin of Loreto, flanked by two columns on either side.

Templo de San Francisco – *On the corner of Calles San Francisco & Benito Juárez. Open year-round daily 7:15am–8pm.* Completed in the late 18C, this church features a beautiful Churrigueresque portal, with pilasters grouped in threes on both sides of the entrance. A Neoclassical tower, created by architect Eduardo Tresguerras, crowns the church. Its interior, also Neoclassical, houses a sacristy with grand paintings by Juan Rodríguez Juárez and Juan Correa.

Templo de Nuestra Señora de la Salud (B) – *Between Colegio & Papellanos. Open year-round daily 7am–2pm & 5–8pm.* ☎ *415-265-65.* Built in 1735, the church originally served as the chapel of the San Francisco de Sales School. Its Churrigueresque facade is characterized by an enormous conch-shaped **molding**, which shelters the niches of five saints. The church faces the tranquil **Plaza Cívica Allende**, guarded by the sculpture of its namesake hero.

★**Oratorio de San Felipe Neri** – *On the eastern side of the Plaza Cívica Ignacio Allende. Open year-round daily 6am 8:45pm.* Completed in 1712, the building originally housed the Hermandad de Mulatos (Brotherhood of Mulattos). The Philippians recreated the **facade** of the original structure in a Baroque style using rose-colored, quarry stone. The Cross of Lorena (or Carvaca), finely carved in stone, crowns both the side wall and the oratory, which houses a linen cloth of the Virgin of Guadalupe.

★**Santa Casa de Loreto** – *Open year-round daily 8am–noon.* The left transept of the oratory preserves a magnificent **portal★★** with golden Solomonic columns, which leads to this beautiful chapel dedicated to the Virgin of Loreto. A fervent devotee, Manuel Tomás de la Canal founded the chapel. Statues of de la Canal and his wife guard the sculpture of the virgin.

A reproduction of the Holy House of the Virgin in Loreto, Italy, the chapel is decorated with various types of tiles from China, Valencia (Spain) and Puebla. The paintings on the exterior walls depict various biblical scenes.

★★★**Camarín (Alcove)** – *Same times and charges as those for the Casa de Loreto.* The extraordinary, octagonal Baroque enclosure impresses visitors with three remarkable altarpieces and its crossed-arch roof with Mudejar influences. Dedicated to the Virgin of Loreto, this dressing room is the culmination of the Santa Casa de Loreto.

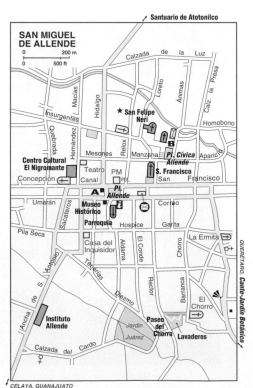

Centro Cultural El Nigromante (Ex Convento de la Concepción "Las Monjas") – *Hernández Macías, 75. Open year-round Mon–Sat 9am–8pm, Sun 10am–2pm.* ✗ ☎ *(4) 152-0289.* The Necromancer Cultural Center, formerly the "Nuns" Convent of the Conception, was built with the inheritance money received by María Josefa Lina de la Canal, eldest daughter of Manuel Tomás, the benefactor of the Santa Casa de Loreto. Although the main building was completed in 1754, the tower and enormous cupola of the church—today adjacent to a lively cultural center and school of arts and crafts—were completed during the 19C.

The highlights of the center are its vast, tree-shaded courtyard, with a central fountain that runs uninterruptedly, and an unfinished mural by David Alfaro Siqueiros, titled *Vida y obra de Ignacio Allende* (initiated in 1948).

ADDITIONAL SIGHTS

Instituto Allende (Casa Solariega de Tomás de la Canal and Bueno de Baeza) – *Ancha de San Antonio, 20. Open year-round Mon–Fri 8am–6pm, Sat 9am–1pm.* ✗ ☎ *(4) 152-0190.* The huge 18C Allende Institute possesses an interior courtyard with an arcade, shade trees and a fountain, as well as two more courtyards, one of which offers a breathtaking **view** of the city.
Located on the southern side of the building, its chapel still preserves frescoes and an effigy of Christ. At present the institute serves as a school where Spanish, arts and literature are taught.

Paseo del Chorro – *Runs from Calle Santa Elena to Recreo.* The interesting walkway begins at the Parque Juárez and offers a view of beautiful houses, some of which still preserve their colonial appearance. The stroll ends at **los lavaderos**, a quadrangular small plaza with 19 washbasins.

Jardín Botánico (Cante) – *On the exit to Querétaro, past the Plaza Real del Conde, take the gravel road and follow the signs. Open year-round daily 8am–6:30pm.* △ ▣ ☎ *(4) 152-2990.* This natural reserve, whose name means "water that gives life," includes a conservatory of succulent Mexican plants. Visitors may stroll among the wide variety of Cactaceae, while enjoying a **view** of the canyon and the city. In addition, visitors can legally purchase cacti here for exportation; restrictions apply as to the quantity.

EXCURSION

Santuario de Atotonilco – *10km/6mi north of San Miguel de Allende by way of the road to Dolores Hidalgo; at the beach resort turn left and continue on the dirt road for 2km/1.2mi. Open year-round daily 7am–8pm.* For the past 200 years, the locals have practiced San Ignacio de Loyola's spiritual exercises in this religious citadel, set against an arid landscape. The fortress was initiated in 1746 by order of Luis Felipe Neri de Alfaro.
The architectural compound features a sanctuary in which, beginning with the **partition**★★ at the entrance, visitors can appreciate wooden slate paintings by Miguel Antonio Martínez Pocasangre that depict scenes of vices, virtues, punishments and rewards.
Similar images decorate both the vault and walls, in **mural paintings**★★ that portray scenes of Christ's life. Just beyond the vestibule, to the left, rises a huge, polychrome sculpture of St. Christopher carved in wood. To the right of the altar, the chapel dedicated to Our Lady of the Rosary displays 18C glass paintings.
The sanctuary's effigy of the Virgin of Guadalupe inspired Hidalgo to design the Insurgents' banner. In addition, Ignacio Allende was wed in this very sanctuary in 1802.

TEPIC

Nayarit
Population 292,780
Map of Principal Sights
🅱 Av. México and Ejército Nacional, Ex Convento de la Cruz
☎ (3) 214-8071 to 73

Capital of the state of Nayarit, Tepic is nestled in the valley of Matatipac between the spurs of the Sierra Madre Occidental and the Pacific Ocean, in the neovolcanic mountain range. Meaning "place between the hills," Tepic rests among the Sangangüey Volcano and the San Juan, Molcajete and Cruz hills.

Historical Notes – At the beginning of the 16C, Nuño Beltrán de Guzmán founded the city and named it Santiago de Compostela, capital of the province of Nueva Galicia. Two centuries later it was renamed Tepic and served as a strategic site for the conquest of northwestern New Spain, as well as the departure point for the colonization and evangelization of the Peninsula of Baja California-an expedition headed by Fray Junípero Serra in 1768.

SIGHTS

Museo Regional de Nayarit – *From the main plaza, head south on Av. México for two streets to reach 91 North, between José María Morelos and Emiliano Zapata. Open year-round Mon–Fri & holidays 9am–7pm, Sat 9am–3pm. Closed Dec 25 & Jan 1.* ☎ *(3) 212-1900.* The 18C house belonged to the Counts Miravalle. Its interior features various pre-Hispanic objects found in Jalisco, Colima and Nayarit. Most noteworthy are the ethnographic room, detailing the cultures of the Coras and Huichols, and an art gallery with paintings from the 17C to the 19C.

Templo y Ex Convento de la Cruz – *From the main plaza, take Av. México and head south for 2km/1.2mi. Open year-round Mon–Fri 9am–8pm, Sat–Sun 9am–2pm. Closed national holidays.* The monastery was built at the end of the 18C and restored in the 20C to house Nayarit's Offices of Tourism. It is famous due to its legendary straw cross, whose formation is deemed a miracle, as it has kept its shape since 1540. Another historical event that took place here involves Fray Junípero Serra's sojourn from 1767 to 1768 in preparation for his trip to found missions in the Peninsula of Baja California.

★**Museo de Cultura Popular** – *From the main plaza, take Av. México southbound; turn left onto Calle Hidalgo and continue one more street. Open year-round Mon–Fri 9am–2pm & 4–7pm, Sat 10am–2pm. Closed national holidays.* ☎ (3) *212-1705.* Also known as the Casa de los Cuatro Pueblos (House of the Four Towns), this museum illustrates in detail the strong indigenous presence in the state, through a look at the customs and traditions of the Huichols, Coras, Tepehuans and Mexicaneros.

EXCURSIONS

Santa Cruz to the Bay of Matanchén – *126km/78mi trek. From Tepic head west on Carr. 66, toward Santa Cruz. From there head north, following the signs to San Blas.*

From Tepic to Ensenada de los Cocos – *51km/31.6mi.* The attraction of this excursion resides in the wonderful landscape that can be appreciated from the road. In a very short distance, one passes from oak tree forests, characteristic of a temperate climate, to medium-size tropical jungles. The trip offers spectacular **views**, ranging from the intense green of the mountain range to the alluring blue of the Pacific Ocean at Ensenada de los Cocos (Coconut Cove).

★**From Ensenada de los Cocos to the Bay of Matanchén** – *12km/7.4mi. In the afternoons, protection against the jején (gnat), a tiny mosquito with a bothersome bite, is advised.* The cove features low-surf beaches that span several miles. Located south of Playa los Cocos, the small beach of **Miramar** offers panoramic views of the bay. Visitors may also enjoy the beaches of Santa Cruz.

Another 12km/7.4mi to the north lies Matanchén. It is believed that Fray Junípero Serra departed from here on the ship, the *Purísima Concepción*, on March 12, 1768, on a mission to colonize and evangelize the Californias. To reach the beach of **Las Islitas**, consisting of several small coves separated by rock formations, one must cover 3km/1.9mi on a dirt road. Be sure to enjoy fresh seafood and surf the famous long wave that extends from this beach to that of Matanchén.

★**Puerto de San Blas** – *138km/85.6mi trek. Exit Tepic and head west on Carr. 66, following the signs to San Blas, or take Carr. 64 to arrive via Carr. Fed. 15.* During the Conquest of America, San Blas constituted one of the Spanish Crown's most important ports, serving as the home of ships destined for California and Sonora. A few vestiges of the buildings constructed during that era are still preserved— for example, the Church of Our Lady of the Rosary, "La Marinera," and the Contaduría (accountancy) offices, a building located high atop its namesake hill and guarded by an enormous wall, which served to ward off pirate attacks. Subsequently, in the 18C, José María Mercado sought shelter on this hill, also known as the "Basilio," to combat foreign invaders. San Blas has become immortalized in Longfellow's world-renowned poem *The Bells of San Blas*, which he wrote a few days before his death in 1882.

★★**La Tovara** – *Early arrival is recommended to fully enjoy the area's birds and animals.* Located by the entrance to the village of San Blas, at the foot of the Contaduría Hill, La Tovara boasts a vast network of crystalline, freshwater channels that lead through aquatic ferns and mangroves. These form tunnels that impede the passage of sunlight. The fabulous excursion ends at a water spring that has been converted into a natural bathing resort where one can swim among the fish and turtles. A small restaurant is located at the foot of the spring. Also of interest at this site is the crocodile breeding grounds.

Laguna de Santa María del Oro and Los Toriles – *240km/149mi trek. Exit Tepic heading toward Guadalajara, after 32km/19.8mi turn left at the exit to Santa María del Oro and continue straight on for 20km/12.4mi to the lagoon.* The excursion through the lagoon offers a landscape of volcanic cones, including the Sangangüey Volcano with its peculiar round rocky massif at its highest point, and the **Ceboruco Volcano**, covered by a stony basaltic overflow.

Laguna de Santa María del Oro – On the way to the lagoon, from the **Jacarandas Overlook**, admire the marvelous view of the lagoon and the mountain range. Approximately 2km/1.2mi in diameter, this peaceful body of crystalline water, whose color ranges from gray to turquoise blue, is ideal for engaging in a variety of water sports.

Los Toriles – *From Santa María del Oro, return to Carr. 15, turn left and continue straight on for 55km/34mi until reaching Ixtlán del Río. Continue on the same road for another 2km/1.2mi to the archaeological site. Open year-round daily 8am–5pm, holidays 8am–3pm. P$12.* ☎ *(3) 216-2038.* Also known as the archaeological site of Ixtlán, "place of the obsidian," Los Toriles was named after the ranch where it was found. One of the few architectural vestiges of Mesoamerica's western region, its development began in the Classic period, around AD 400, and continued up until the post-Classic period. The ceremonial center, with stone structures that form both religious and secular plazas, features a circular temple dedicated to Ehécatl-Quetzalcóatl, god of wind.

Recipe for one of Nayarit's typical dishes: Guinea Hen with Mango Sauce

Ingredients:

6 small Guinea hens (1.65lbs/.75kg each)
1 tablespoon of freshly ground black pepper
1 clove of garlic
2 teaspoons of salt
1/4 cup (60ml) of water
6 tablespoons of melted butter

Sauce:

3/4 cup (200g) of canned mangoes, drained
1 1/2 cups (375ml) of mango syrup
1 tablespoon of butter
1 tablespoon of brown sugar

Instructions:

Remove the Guinea hens' entrails, then season the hens with pepper.

In a food processor, grind the garlic clove with salt and water, then pour over the hens and allow them to marinate in the refrigerator for 2 hours.

To prepare the sauce, make a purée with the mangoes and syrup. In a small pan, melt the butter, add the purée and brown sugar, mix well. When it begins to boil, remove from the burner.

Approximately one hour before serving, preheat the oven at 500°F/260°C; place the hens, breast down, in a greased baking dish. Baste them with the melted butter and bake for 15 minutes. Flip over the hens and leave them in the oven for another 15 minutes, frequently basting them using pan drippings. Lower the temperature to 375°F/190°C. Flip over the hens once again, drain the baking dish and add the pan drippings to the mango sauce.

Arrange the hens, breast up, and cover them with the mango sauce. Bake for another 5 to 7 minutes, or until golden. Serve immediately and garnish with slices of mango.

Serves 6 people.

Source: Editorial Patria. *El libro de la cocina mexicana*. México: Editorial Patria, S.A. de C.V., 1992.

Region 4

NORTHWEST

Land of the Tarahumaras, Majestic Gorges and Birthplace of Pancho Villa

Handicrafts and Food, p 52. Four states in the Sierra Madre Occidental best represent the spirit of Mexico's North, and four items—the bass drum, *norteña* music, the scent of *carne asada* and flour tortillas—best express this spirit. Ranching and agriculture have made northwestern Mexico prosperous. More modern than traditional, its cities today are great industrial and commercial centers. Called the province of Nueva Vizcaya during the colonial era, the land was originally inhabited by nomadic **Chichimecs**, who were especially resistant to colonization. The old legend of the Seven Golden Cities of Cibola also originated in this region and attracted the Conquest's first explorers, though the famed treasures were never found. In the 17C, Jesuit missionaries brought Christianity to northern Mexico. In the early 18C, the growth of Chihuahua, Sonora, Durango and Sinaloa centered around mining, which continues to the present day.

The Mexican Revolution—the great social struggle that would transform the country—began formally in the north, in Chihuahua. Though vestiges of indigenous cultures remain throughout the northwest, the largest communities are still found in Chihuahua and Sonora, two of the largest states in Mexico. The **Tarahumaras** inhabit the magnificent Copper Canyon, braving hunger and harsh weather, while on the northern coast of Sonora, the **Seris** subsist near their ancestral lands. The **Yaquis** resisted persecution by Porfirio Díaz only to be annihilated in the Mexican Revolution. Though they left their mark on Sonoran culture, today this indigenous group is difficult to distinguish from the rest of the population.

The United States influences the entire region, as is apparent in city infrastructure, as well as in the presence of foreign products. Along the border, the cultural exchange between the US and Mexico is especially evident, due to the affluence of North American tourists and the passage of Mexican immigrants toward the "Land of Opportunity."

Chih. .... Chihuahua
Dgo. .... Durango
Sin. .... Sinaloa
Son. .... Sonora

184

Tarahumara Rulers from Huahuacherare, Sierra Tarahumara

CHIHUAHUA ★

Chihuahua
Population 627,662
Map of Principal Sights
ℹ ☎ (1) 429-3421 or (01-800) 849-5200

Today the capital of Mexico's largest state is an important industrial, ranching, and commercial center. The city's architecture is marked by contrasts, as colonial and modern buildings intermingle.

Historical Notes

This capital city was once a mining village founded on October 12, 1709 as El Real de San Francisco de Cuéllar. In 1718, it was given the status of *Villa* and named San Felipe El Real de Chihuahua. *Chihuahua* was adapted from the Tarahumara name **Xicuaga**, which means "sandy and dry area." On July 19, 1823, it gained the rank of *City* and the name Chihuahua, and was designated capital of the province that bears the same name. A year later, Chihuahua was decreed State of the Federation.

Toward the end of the 19C, tensions mounted as economic and political power was concentrated in the hands of a few families. General unrest and the appearance of popular *caudillos*—a Spanish word for "leader"-preceded the beginning of the Mexican Revolution in 1910.

One of the most powerful armies of the revolutionary movement came from Chihuahua-the famous *División del Norte* (Division of the North)-commanded by Francisco Villa. A man with an extraordinary gift for organization, Villa was highly efficient in combat. Also known as the "Centaur of the North," he is one of the most famous figures of Mexican history.

SIGHTS

Cathedral – *South of the Plaza de Armas. City Center. Open year-round daily 6am–8pm.* A reminder of the mining boom, this magnificent Baroque cathedral was constructed between 1725 and 1757. The **portals**★ of quarry stone are adorned with ornamental foliage, while columns and sculptures of the 12 apostles with their respective symbols grace the **main facade**★★.

185

Inside, the Baroque main altar fashioned out of quarry stone dates from 1790. It is hidden by a Neoclassical altar finished in 1920, made of Carrara marble. The chapel of **Cristo de Mapimí★**, with its 18C *estípite* Baroque altarpiece, is located under the left tower.

The **Museo de Arte Sacro** (Museum of Religious Art) is located in the basement of the cathedral's right atrium *(open year–round Mon–Fri 10am–2pm & 4–6pm; closed Thu–Sat during Holy Week. P$9.)* and preserves sacred objects and religious paintings by important 18C Mexican artists.

Calabozo de Miguel Hidalgo – *Av. Juárez, between Av. J. Neri Santos and V. Carranza. Open year-round Tue–Sun 9am–7pm. P$3.* Previously the site of the Colegio de Loreto de la Compañía de Jesús, the Dungeon of Miguel Hidalgo is located behind the Palacio Federal. Considered by Mexicans as "Father" of their nation, Miguel Hidalgo was imprisoned here from April 23 to July 30, 1811, before being executed by firing squad. Inside, the verses he dedicated to his jailer are inscribed on a bronze plaque.

Palacio de Gobierno – *Av. Aldama, between Av. J. Neri Santos and V. Carranza. Open year-round Mon–Fri 7am–7pm, Sat–Sun 9am–2pm.* After a fire destroyed everything except the main entrance, this 19C Neoclassical building had to be completely restored in 1941. The Government Palace also contains the Altar de la Patria and its eternal flame, which marks the exact spot where Miguel Hidalgo was executed. Murals by Aarón Piña Mora depict Chihuahua's history.

Centro Cultural Universitario (Quinta Gameros) – *Paseo Bolívar, 401, corner of Calle 4. Open year-round Tue–Sun 11am–2pm & 4–7pm. Closed Jan 1 & Dec 25. P$20, guided tours P$20. ☎ (1) 416-6684. No photos or videos allowed.* For its elegance and similarity to classic French castles, this **house★** is considered one of the most beautiful in Chihuahua. Inside, the decorations and furnishings are pure Art Nouveau.

Begun in 1907 by Julio Latorre and Manuel Gameros, the home features an exquisite display of carved and polychrome wood **furniture** designed by Pedro Fossas Requena. A picture gallery, with the latest works of Chihuahua's artists, occupies the upper level.

★Museo Histórico de la Revolución Mexicana (Casa de Pancho Villa) – *Calle 10, 3010, corner of Calle Méndez, east of the city. Open year-round Tue–Sat 9am–1pm & 3–7pm, Sun 9am–5pm. Closed national holidays. P$10. ☎ (1) 416-2958.* When Doña Luz Corral de Villa, wife of Pancho Villa, died in 1981, the original "Quinta Luz" was enlarged and renovated. The house and barracks were converted into the Historic Museum of the Mexican Revolution and preserve some of Pancho Villa's personal items. Pictures, furniture, documents and weapons recall his life and legend, as well as the bloody episodes of the revolutionary movement. The courtyard behind the museum displays the automobile in which General Villa and his companions were assassinated in Parral, Chihuahua.

EXCURSIONS

Mennonite Grounds – *Guided tour recommended.* The **Mennonites**, a sect of German origin that arrived in Mexico in 1922, inhabit nearby Ciudad Cuauhtémoc. Makers of the famous Chihuahua cheese, they wear typical dress, live in characteristic homes and have unique customs.

★★Cascada de Basaseáchi – *276km/171mi. From Chihuahua, go southwest on Carr. 16. After 147km/91mi, at La Junta turn left on the road to Tomochic. After 56km/38mi, turn left in the direction of San Juanito, continue 2km/1.2mi, turn right at the entrance of the National Park of Basaseáchi. Continue 4km/2.5mi to the overlook. Tours depart from the city of Chihuahua and from Creel.* This attractive drive meanders through meadows, fertile pastures and apple orchards. Later, the road traverses mountains and pine and evergreen oak forests before arriving at the National Park, home to the Barranca de Candameña, one of the most breathtaking gorges in America. The 1,640m/5,381ft gorge features spectacular overlooks, as the canyon's vertical walls plunge to depths of more than a kilometer. Do not miss the impressive overlook located directly in front of the 246m/807ft **waterfall**, second highest in Mexico. A footpath descends 1,830m/2,001yd to La Ventana overlook and continues 2.2km/1.4mi to the bottom of the gorge. This area also boasts Mexico's tallest waterfall, **Piedra Volada**, with a height of approximately 453m/1,486ft (accessible only to experienced mountain climbers).

★Hidalgo del Parral – *225km/140mi. From Chihuahua, go southwest on Carr. 16. After 36km/22mi, turn left on Carr. 24 and continue 189km/117mi.* This city preserves its old mining atmosphere and several colonial buildings. Tall, striking,

Romanesque Revival towers distinguish the **Catedral de Nuestra Señora de Guadalupe** *(Av. General Maclovio Herrera and Pedro Gómez)*. The **Templo de San Juan de Dios** boasts a well-preserved, 18C *estípite* Baroque altarpiece *(west of the Plaza Guillermo Baca; open year-round Mon 10am–11am & 3:30–6:30pm, Tue–Sat 9am–1pm & 3:30–6:30pm, Sun 9am–1pm & 4–8pm)*. With its sumptuous neo-Baroque **portal★**, the Neoclassical **Palacio de Alvarado** *(one street west of Plaza Guillermo Baca)* is reminiscent of the Italian palaces of the Renaissance. The 17C **Parroquia de San José** houses a Baroque altar and a presbytery containing the remains of Parral's founder, Juan Rangel Viezma *(Calle Francisco Moreno, corner of General Benítez, north of the main plaza; open year-round Mon–Fri 10am–1pm & 3:30–7pm, Sat 6pm–8pm, Sun 6am–1pm & 4–9pm)*. This *parroquia* is the only parish church still containing its original pulpit, crafted of quarry stone. The **Museum-Library**, site from which General Francisco Villa was assassinated on July 20, 1923, merits a visit.

★★★ Ferrocarril Chihuahua-Pacífico (Copper Canyon) – *Train station at Calle Méndez and Calle 24, 2km/1.2mi southwest of the Plaza de Armas. Description p 188.*

★★ Paquimé – *292km/181mi. Go 104km/65mi northwest on Carr. 45, take the exit to Ricardo Flores Magón (44km/27mi), turn left, take Carr. 10 towards Nuevo Casas Grandes (136km/84mi) and take the exit for Casas Grandes (15km/9mi southwest). Description p 195.*

■ Pancho Villa

Doroteo Arango Arámbula, commonly known as Francisco "Pancho" Villa, was born in San Juan del Río, in 1876. During his adolescence, he declared himself independent from his parents and initiated his life as a bandit in the states of Chihuahua and Durango.

At the age of 34, Pancho Villa joined Francisco I. Madero's followers in a democratic campaign against Porfirio Díaz's reelection. His guerilla activities in the Revolution of 1910–11 contributed to Madero's triumph. However, victory was short-lived; in February 1913, Victoriano Huerta betrayed Madero and signed the Ciudadela pact. Under Venustiano Carranza's leadership, Villa joined the Constitutionalists in the armed struggle against Huerta, and headed the cavalry *Los Dorados*, whose success in the brilliant battles against the federal army in northern Mexico served as a catalyst for Huerta's resignation from the presidency in July 1914.

Subsequently, partly due to the animosity between Villa and Carranza, there was a separation of powers, in which Alvaro Obregón teamed with Carranza and Emiliano Zapata with Villa. At the head of the *División del Norte* (Division of the North), Villa, together with Zapata, occupied Mexico City from December 1914 to January 1915. A few months later, they were defeated by Obregón's armed forces, and were forced to return to the north.

The fact that US President Wilson recognized Carranza as president of Mexico, in October 1915, infuriated Villa. In January 1916 a group of Mexican bandits assassinated several US citizens in Chihuahua, and, in March of that same year, a group of Pancho Villa's men invaded the town of Columbus, New Mexico and murdered some of its residents. Although there is no certainty as to whether Villa was involved in these killings, the whole world held him responsible. In March 1916, Wilson ordered his capture. At the command of General Pershing, the US army searched for Villa for a period of 11 months, without success.

Until the last days of Carranza's administration, Villa continued his revolutionary activities in northern Mexico. In 1920 Congress named Adolfo de la Huerta provisional president of the Triumphant Revolution. In view of the national reconstruction labor initiated by de la Huerta, Villa called a truce with the Mexican government. Three years later, in 1923, he was assassinated in his ranch, in Hidalgo del Parral, Chihuahua. Nonetheless, the image of this controversial, legendary figure, idolized by the masses and converted into a type of Robin Hood, lives on in innumerable short stories and ballads.

Ferrocarril CHIHUAHUA-PACÍFICO
Copper Canyon★★★
Chihuahua
Map of Principal Sights — Map below
🛈 ☏ (1) 429-3421 and (01-800) 849-5200

The railroad trip through the Barranca del Cobre (Copper Canyon) is one of the most spectacular excursions in Mexico, while the railroad itself is one of the world's most amazing engineering feats. Begun in 1898-owing to Arthur Stilwell's vision-and inaugurated by the Mexican Government on November 24, 1961, the railroad from Chihuahua to the Pacific was built to promote the development of the Sierra Tarahumara and furnish an outlet to the ocean through Sinaloa.

The Copper Canyon gets its name from the copper mine found in the village of Tejabán and is often used to refer to this whole section of the Sierra Madre Occidental and its series of beautiful and majestic gorges. The **Barranca del Cobre** joins the canyon of Tararécua and the **Barranca de Urique**, while the **Barranca de Batopilas** merges with the canyon of the Bufa and the canyon of Muneráchi. The **Barranca de Sinforosa**, the **Barranca de Chínipas**, the **Barranca de Oteros**, and the **Barranca de Candameña** complete the list. Rising to more than 3,000m/9,840ft in altitude, this mountainous massif originated some 30 million years ago; today it is the most impressive geological system of gorges and canyons in the world.

TRAIN TRIP
653km/406mi. One-way trip: 14hrs by train, subject to changes or delays.

Begin the trip in the city of Chihuahua or in Los Mochis, Sinaloa and disembark in Creel, Divisadero, Bahuichivo, El Fuerte, etc., to make excursions into the sierra.

The train climbs through wide meadows and cultivated fields as it leaves the city of Chihuahua before meandering through the mountains connected by 39 bridges and 86 tunnels. Later, it passes through pine and evergreen oak forests and by winding streams and imposing rock formations, which contrast to the semi-desertic landscape of organ-pipe *nopales* (prickly pear) and other types of plains cactus, seen as the train descends through Sinaloa. The train stops in small villages like Creel, Divisadero and Bahuichivo, excellent places for excursions.

EXCURSIONS

Creel – Founded in 1907, this wood-producing village was named in honor of engineer Enrique C. Creel, one of the railroad's principal promoters and builders. The town boasts the area's best tourist services and is the point of entry and departure for the most interesting trips into the sierra. It is also the suggested place to buy

Practical Information...Area Code 1

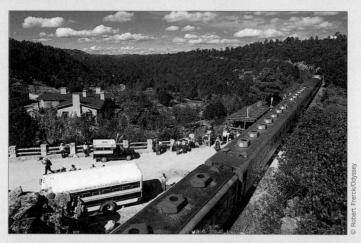

Chihuahua-Pacific Railroad

When to Go – The best season to visit the attractions of the Sierra Tarahumara is from August to December.

Getting There – **By train:** Departures from the city of Chihuahua (Calle Méndez and Calle 24): First class year-round daily at 6am; P$850. Second class: Mon, Wed & Fri at 7am; P$118. Reservations recommended. ☏ 415-7756. Because the train does not provide a dining service, we suggest you take food provisions with you.
Departures from Los Mochis (the train station's location is well known): First class: year-round daily at 6am; P$850. Second class: Tue, Thu, & Sat at 7am. P$118. Reservations recommended. ☏ (6) 812-0853.
If traveling from the city of Chihuahua to Los Mochis, request a seat on the left side of the train and vice versa.
By Bus: Several paved roads, in good condition, connect the city of Chihuahua with Cuauhtémoc, Creel and Divisadero. Estrella Blanca ☏ 429-0249 offers daily transfers to these sites, as well as to Ciudad Juárez, Basaseáchi and Nuevo Casas Grandes, Paquimé.

Accommodations – The tourist information office in the city of Chihuahua *(open year-round Mon–Fri 8:30am–6:30pm, Sat–Sun 10:30am–5pm; ☏ 429-3421 & 01-800-849-5200)* provides brochures and information on lodging in the Sierra Tarahumara and on agencies that offer transportation and guides for excursions.

Time Zone – The Sierra Tarahumara, which crosses the states of Chihuahua and Sinaloa, is in the Pacific time zone: turn the clock forward one hour the first Sunday in April and backward one hour the last Sunday in October. *Time Zones p 399.*

Sightseeing – A guided tour is recommended to visit the Mennonite grounds; David Friesen offers guided tours in Spanish and English *(Agencia de Viajes Cumbres Friesen, Calle 3ª, 466, Cd. Cuauhtémoc, Chihuahua. ☏ 582-5457 & 582-3064).* DIVITUR travel agency *(Francisco de Cuéllar and Poniente, 5, Col. San Felipe, Chihuahua. ☏ 414-6046)* offers excursions to Cascada de Basaseáchi, including transfers, accommodations and hikes around the area. To explore Creel's surroundings and the attractions of the Sierra Tarahumara, including Cascada de Basaseáchi, contact Tarahumara Tours *(Plaza Central, Creel; ☏ 456-0065)* or UMARIKE EXPEDICIONES. Most of the hotels in this location offer assistance in planning these trips. For excursions and hikes in Divisadero, contact Hotel Divisadero Barrancas www.hoteldivisadero.com.mx. In Cerocahui, the Hotel Paraíso del Oso *(Batechi, 443, Cd. Chihuahua; ☏ 421-3372)* organizes excursions and horseback rides.

Tarahumara arts and handicrafts. Located west of the main plaza, the **Casa de las Artesanías del Estado de Chihuahua** *(open year-round Tue–Sat 9am–1pm & 3–7pm, Sun 9am–1pm; P$5; ☏ 1-456-0080),* in addition to selling handicrafts, has an interesting display on the people of the Sierra and their way of life.
Attractions near **Arareko** include the Jesuit mission of **San Ignacio**, the **Valle de los Hongos** (Mushroom Valley), the **Valle de las Ranas** (Frog Valley), **Bisabírachi★**—better known

as the **Valle de los Monjes** (Valley of the Monks)—and the charming **Lago de Arareko★**. This beautiful and tranquil lake has a small pier with boat rentals. Only 25km/15.5mi ahead, on the Gran Visión road, are the **village** and **Cascada de Cusárare★** *(walk 3km/1.9mi on a dirt road to reach the waterfall)*. Another point of interest is the mining town of **Batopilas**, one of the loveliest and most picturesque of the Sierra Tarahumara. Nearby lie the remains of the old mining hacienda of Alexander Shepherd, built at the end of the 19C, the striking early-18C church of Satevó, and a large community of Tarahumaras. *(Visits during the months of June, July and August are not recommended, as hotels close due to the torrential rains.)* The Creel-Batopilas trip, one of the Sierra's longest and most exciting, includes the Doble Herradura overlooks, the bridge of Humirá-from which the Urique River can be seen-and the Cañón de la Bufa overlook.

Divisadero – The train stops at Divisadero station, 58km/36mi beyond Creel with just enough time (10–15min) to admire the **view★★** of the confluence of the Copper, Tararécua and Urique canyons.

The town offers accommodations and is an ideal excursion center for hikes to the surroundings and for enjoying the confluence of the various gorges found here. An overnight stay is highly recommended. Divisadero can also be reached by road from Creel.

Estación Bahuichivo-Cerocahui – *Accommodations and excursions on foot or by horse available.* From this stop, visitors can take a break from the trip and go 18km/11mi down a dirt road to the town of **Cerocahui**. Set in a beautiful valley, this little town possesses a 1680 mission, which is frequented by the local Tarahumaras. Located only a few miles away from this village, The Barranca de Urique is visible from the **Cerro El Gallego** overlook, which affords one of the area's best **views★★**. From here, the old mining town of **Urique** is seen in the distance on the other side of the river.

■ The Tarahumaras

© Robert Frerck/Odyssey

When the Spanish arrived, the Tarahumaras occupied a large part of the present-day state of Chihuahua. As colonization advanced, they were forced to retreat to the mountains to avoid forced labor in haciendas and mines. Today, approximately 100,000 Tarahumaras live in ranching settlements and villages in the gorges of the **Sierra Tarahumara**.

The word **Tarahumara** is a Hispanization of **Rarámuri**, an indigenous word for "fast-running sole" (as in the soles of the feet). In a broader sense, it means "those of nimble feet," a reference to the ancestral tradition of running.

Like many other indigenous groups in the Americas, the Rarámuri consider their culture, spiritual values and love of nature to be their most cherished inheritance. Thousands of years of social struggle have given them an exemplary zest for living, way of life and social harmony, as well as harmony with the environment. While most Tarahumara live in houses made from pine trees; some live in insulated caves to protect themselves from the cold. Others even live a semi-nomadic existence and move to the Baja Tarahumara in winter, in search of warmer temperatures.

DURANGO★

Durango
Population 464,566
Map of Principal Sights
🏛 Calle Hidalgo, 408, south, City Center ☎ (1) 811-2139

Drawn by the splendor of precious metals, those who founded the Villa of Durango on July 8, 1563, crossed the Sierra Madre Occidental and chose the Valley of Guadiana to build this capital city.

Today, Durango is a thriving city with a modern feel, much like the none-too-distant American cities. The architectural landmarks of the past cluster around Avenida 20 de Noviembre in the historic Downtown. Arts and crafts are sold in the conveniently located **Mercado F. Gómez Palacio**. Many of these objects include a representation of the scorpion, a native arachnid of the region, which is especially visible in periods of hot weather.

Since the 1960s, American filmmaking companies have built their movie sets a few kilometers north of the city of Durango. The rough country has set the backdrop for dozens of old westerns, and with a little luck, visitors may catch one in action.

SIGHTS

★**Cathedral** – *Av. 20 de Noviembre, across from the Plaza de Armas, in the City Center. Open year-round daily 8am–9pm.* Built between 1695 and 1787 the church's interior was modified in 1844. An air of mystery surrounds the church, and its tall majestic towers reign over the panorama of the Plaza de Armas and surrounding buildings. Admire the **facade**★★ from every angle; it beckons for a stroll around the building. Inside, the presbytery boasts gorgeous **choir stalls**★★, while the back of the cathedral houses a tenebrae hearse—a ceremonial furnishing of Asian origin inlayed with ebony wood and bone. The sacristy preserves elaborately decorated Baroque mahogany chests of drawers and four 18C canvases by Juan Correa and others by José de Ibarra.

Palacio de Gobierno – *Av. 5 de Febrero, facing the Plaza del IV Centenario, between Bruno Martínez and Zaragoza, in the City Center. Open year-round Mon–Fri 8am–8pm, Sat–Sun & holidays 10am–6pm. P$3.* ☎ *(1) 813-1094.* The rich landowner José de Zambrano commissioned this mansion in 1795, which then served as his private residence and boasted a small theater that today is called the Teatro Victoria. A remnant of the colonial era, the Government Palace rises over an extraordinary series of arches, and inside, colorful murals depict incidents from the history of Mexico.

Casa del Conde del Valle de Súchil (Banco Banamex) – *Av. 5 de Febrero, corner of Francisco I. Madero, in the City Center. Open year-round Mon–Fri 9am–5pm. Closed national holidays.* ☎ *(1) 811-1107. No photographs allowed.* An architectural jewel of the city, this 18C house originally belonged to Count Juan José del Campo Soberón y Larrea. Made of quarry stone, the Baroque facade is a perfect fit in an eight-sided recess and divided in two sections—the first very austere, the second lavishly decorated with St. Joseph in his niche. Inside, richly decorated arches merit attention, and striated columns create a dizzying sensation.

★**Museo Regional de la Universidad Juárez del Estado de Durango** – *Calle Victoria, 100, Sur, corner of Aquiles Serdán, in the City Center. Open year-round Tue–Sat 9am–3:40pm, Sun 10am–2:30pm. Closed national holidays. P$3.* ☎ *(1) 813-1094.* Popularly known as "El Aguacate" for the avocado tree that grows in the outside gardens, this building houses the city's best museum of regional history. The picture gallery with oil paintings by Miguel Cabrera (1695–1768), the archaeology room with displays of cave paintings and mummies, and the room dedicated to the Mexican Revolution, with a giant photograph of General Porfirio Díaz, highlight the collection.

Museo de Culturas Populares – *Juárez, 302, Norte, corner of Gabino Barreda, in the City Center. Open year-round Tue–Sat 9am–6pm, Sun 10am–8pm. Closed national holidays. P$1.* ☎ *(1) 811-1107.* This small museum shows off the artistic talent and inventiveness of the people of the state of Durango. Displays of textiles, basket weaving and pottery, as well as other forms of popular art, acquaint visitors with handicrafts produced in various parts of the state. Cultural events are often sponsored in the afternoon.

EXCURSIONS

Parque Natural El Tecuán (El Tecuán Nature Park) – *57km/35mi southwest of the city, via Carr. 40 (Durango-Mazatlán). Open year-round daily 8am–8pm. Cabins P$150.* △ 🏛 ☎ *(1) 817-2764.* A path winds through mountains covered with vegetation before arriving at a thick forest perfumed by pines, evergreen oaks and madrone trees. With its small group of cabins, El Tecuán makes the perfect spot for a day in the country.

Sombrerete – *In the state of Zacatecas. 125km/78mi southeast via Carr. 45. Description p 233.*

HERMOSILLO

Sonora
Population 559,154
Map of Principal Sights
🎫 Edificio Estatal, fourth floor, Calle Comonfort and Paseo del Canal,
☎ (6) 217-0076 and (01-800) 716-2555

The capital of Sonora—the state where mountains, ocean and desert unite—extends along the arid, coastal plain of the Pacific. With 250 years of history, Hermosillo preserves its Neoclassical 19C buildings, even as recent architecture fosters the image of a new and modern city. Today, Hermosillo is a distinguished center of commerce, manufacturing, agriculture and ranching.

Historical Notes – Before the Spanish arrived in present-day Sonora, two different cultures inhabited the area: hunter/gatherers such as the Seris and farmers like the Cahitas, Pimas and Opatas. Despite a very old agricultural tradition, no group in Sonora managed to establish grand, permanent settlements.

Originally a Seri ranching settlement called Pitic, it was given the status of city in 1828, and the name was changed to Hermosillo in honor of a Jaliscan general named José María González de Hermosillo.

SIGHTS

Museo de Sonora (Old Penitentiary of Hermosillo) – *End of Jesús García and Esteban Sarmiento. Open year-round Tue–Sat 10am–5pm, Sun & holidays 9am–4pm. P$10.* ☎ *(6) 217-2580.* Begun in 1897, this building is credited to the Polish engineer Arthur F. Wrotnowsky, who was inspired by the palaces of the Italian Renaissance. The rock used in construction was quarried from the Cerro de la Campana, located next to the museum. Prisoners already lived in the penitentiary in 1905; the majority of which were Yaquis who were forced to construct the building. Inaugurated in 1908; the building functioned as a penitentiary until 1979. Its 18 rooms outline Sonora's general history. Solitary confinement cells are preserved in the basement.

Centro Ecológico de Sonora – *2km/1.2mi south of Hermosillo via Carr. 15, in the direction of Guaymas. Open Apr–Oct, Wed–Sun & holidays 8am–7pm; Nov–Mar, Wed–Sun & holidays 8am–5pm. P$10.* 🍴 ☎ *(6) 250-1034.* Set in the central Sonoran semi-desert, this ecological center is dedicated to the research and greater understanding of the region's different ecosystems: the rugged mountains, productive meadow, arid desert and warm Gulf of California. About 250 animal and 300 plant species, both typical of the region and exotic, can be viewed during the pleasant stroll through the grounds, which also boast an astronomical observatory and play area.

EXCURSIONS

Bahía Kino – *116km/72mi southwest of Hermosillo on Carr. 16.* Two towns are located around this bay across the arid coastal plain from Hermosillo. Kino Viejo is a simple town dependent on the sea for its livelihood, as well as on handicrafts made from the wood of the Palo Fierro tree, while Kino Nuevo has modern tourist services and ample beaches that still have the feel of barely explored land. Today, the Bahía Kino area is one of Mexico's most productive farming regions. Tiburón Island, a Seri refuge, watches over Kino Nuevo.

A small **museum** *(open year-round Wed–Sun 9am–6pm; ☎ 6-217-0076)* familiarizes visitors with Seri culture.

Guaymas – *Go 138km/86mi south on Carr. 15 to Guaymas.* Surrounded by rich mineral deposits, this important fishing town has witnessed a turbulent history. For more than 200 years, war characterized the region-clashes against the Yaquis and Mayos, skirmishes during the War for Independence and the Reforma, and raids by adventurers and pirates who wanted to conquer these lands.

Caressed by the blue waters of the Gulf of California, Guaymas' port is famous for its wonderful seafood and great sailing in the **Bahía de San Carlos**, also known for its excellent beach, Playa de los Algodones. It offers excellent opportunities for sport fishing and diving, as well as yacht excursions.

★★**Álamos** – *394km/245mi. Go south on Carr. 15 to Navojoa (332km/206mi), turn left on Carr. 162 and continue 53km/33mi.* Carved into the foothills of the Sierra Madre Occidental, this picturesque village is a National Historical Monument. An elegant and prosperous colonial city, Álamos was built toward the end of the 17C, when the silver mines were founded, and it still preserves the harmony of the elegant 18C and 19C buildings constructed around flower-filled courtyards. This city is also the world capital of the Mexican jumping bean *(frijol saltarín)*. When the small seed is implanted with a larva during the rainy season, it jumps about for three to six months until the larva bursts out of the skin as a small butterfly. The early-19C, restrained Baroque **Iglesia de la Inmaculada Concepción** dominates the Plaza de Armas. The **Palacio Municipal**, reminiscent of medieval, Spanish fortresses, also guards the plaza. The **Museo Costumbrista de Sonora** is located east of the plaza *(open Jul–Aug, Wed–Sat 9am–3pm, Sun 9am–6pm; rest of the year Wed–Sun 9am–6pm. P$2; ☎ 6-428-0053)*. Situated in an old 19C home, the museum covers the regional history, traditions, habits and customs of Álamos.

MAZATLÁN★★

Sinaloa
Population 357,619
Map of Principal Sights
🄳 Edificio Banrural, 4º piso, Av. Camarón Sábalo, corner of Calle Tiburón
☎ (6) 916-5160 to 65 or www.mazatlan.com

Famed for beautiful sunsets, this city is bathed by the ocean and surrounded by islands and beaches of golden sand. Combined with the friendliness of its inhabitants, Mazatlán offers an ideal beach experience.
Today, Mazatlán's huge fishing and shrimping fleet has made the port one of the largest and most important on the Mexican Pacific Coast. One of Mexico's greatest tourist destinations since the 1960s, the city boasts a sun-drenched panorama and pleasant temperatures year-round. The wildest display of happiness and raucousness is unleashed in February during **Carnival**, one of Mexico's best known. Mazatlán, or "the land of deer," also offers many forms of recreation such as fishing tournaments where marlin, sailfish and *dorado* (a large fish resembling a dolphin) are the prize.

SIGHTS

Beaches – *Av. Camarón Sábalo, in the Zona Dorada*. Three popular beaches with fine sand and medium surf are found north of the port at the foot of the largest and most luxurious hotels. Visitors prefer **Playa Gaviotas**, **Playa Sábalo** and **Playa Cerritos** for sunbathing, walking, engaging in water sports or simply contemplating the pleasant seascape of three **islands**: Isla de Pájaros, Isla de Venados and Isla de Lobos (Chivos).

★**Paseo del Malecón** – *Av. del Mar, south of the Zona Dorada*. The solitary and almost untouched Playa Norte, one of the largest oceanfront promenades on the Mexican coasts, extends south of Punta Camarón on the Malecón. This long stretch of bay offers attractive views and sensational sunsets.

★**Paseo Claussen (Panoramic Drive)** – *Paseo Claussen, Av. Olas Altas and Paseo Centenario. It is recommended to take a taxi*. A series of **overlooks**, following one after the other, extends along a very winding section of Paseo Claussen, south of the Fuerte 31 de Marzo. At the overlooks, monuments dedicated to the city contrast with the intense blue of the ocean.
Panoramic **views** atop the cliffs facing the sea, especially between the **Nevería** rocks and the **Cerro del Vigía**, show the contrast of old and new Mazatlán. The city's best overlook is found atop the Cerro del Vigía *(accessed by way of the Paseo del Centenario)*, once a strategic point of defense of the port. Visible are Mazatlán's main pier and the **Cerro del Crestón**-a natural formation rising 157m/515ft over the ocean to sustain the world's highest natural lighthouse in operation.

© Robert Frerck/Odyssey

Sábalo Beach

Acuario Mazatlán – *Av. de los Deportes, 111, a few steps from the Av. del Mar. Open year-round daily 9:30am–6pm. Closed Sept 13. P$30.* ✗ ☎ *(6) 981-7817.* This hexagon-shaped building contains a large aquarium with a few varieties of sharks. Other rooms boast smaller aquariums, with more than 100 marine and freshwater species. A sea museum displays regional techniques and equipment used in the different types of fishing, in addition to reproductions of other marine species. The botanical garden, aviary, crocodile exhibits, freshwater turtle exhibit and ponds for sea lions are outside the aquarium. Every day the aquarium's staff presents diving shows, sea lion shows and bird shows.

Museo Arqueológico de Mazatlán – *Calle Sixto Osuna, 76, in Old Mazatlán. Open year-round Tue–Sun 10am–1pm & 4–7pm. Closed national holidays. P$6.* ☎ *(6) 985-3502.* This small museum possesses a collection of archaeological remains of pre-Hispanic cultures that once inhabited Sinaloa, and provides visitors with an overview of the development and customs of the native inhabitants. The first room depicts the region's geography through the use of maps.

EXCURSIONS

Concordia and Copala – *Total trip: 67km/42mi from Mazatlán to Copala. Go south from Mazatlán on Carr. 15 and continue to Villa Unión. Turn left and take Carr. 40 to Durango, arriving at Concordia after 20km/12mi.*

Concordia – Little white houses with red-tiled roofs surround the small central plaza and the parish church of San Sebastián. An interesting example of 18C Baroque architecture, the church's facade, made of quarry stone, is carved with harmonious detail. Concordia is famous for its arts and crafts, such as fine, richly carved ebony and cedar furniture and cracked clay pottery.

Copala – *From Concordia, continue another 24km/15mi east on Carr. 40 until reaching the exit for Copala. Then continue 1km/0.6mi on the dirt road.* An old mining settlement, this picturesque village practically hangs from the slopes of the Sierra Madre Occidental. Copala's narrow cobblestone streets, multicolor building facades, and ironwork balconies and windows delight lovers of old Mexico. The charm of lush vegetation such as palm and *tabachine* trees—evidence of the warm semi-tropical climate—adds to this rustic ambiance. On the tiny central plaza stands the parish church, offering lovely views of the verdant landscape.

La Paz – *Access by ferry or plane. Description p 210.*

PAQUIMÉ**

This labyrinthine city is found in the Valley of Casas Grandes, next to a river of the same name. It was called *Paquimé* by the native inhabitants and *Casas Grandes* (Big Houses) by the Spanish and considered to be the most important urban, commercial and religious center of northern Mexico. Politically and economically, it dominated a huge region, which included the territory of Gran Chichimeca and encompassed the entire width of the Sierra Madre. The area of Arizona, New Mexico, Utah and Colorado in the US, and portions of Sonora and Durango would have been under Paquimé's zone of influence. Mineral products, precious stones (turquoise in particular), wood and foodstuffs were obtained from this vast area, then traded with the Mesoamerican states. This culture enjoyed its peak during the Paquimé phase, between 1300 and 1450.

VISIT

Located 292km/181mi from Chihuahua. Go 104km/65mi northwest on Carr. 45, take the exit to Ricardo Flores Magón and go 44km/27mi. Turn left and take Carr. 10 for 136km/85mi, in the direction of Nuevo Casas Grandes. Then go 15km/9.3mi southwest and take the exit to Casas Grandes. Continue south for 0.6km/0.4mi. Located 309km/192mi from Ciudad Juárez. Go south on Carr. 45. After 20km/12mi, go west on Carr. 2 to Janos for 232km/144mi, take the exit and go southeast on Carr. 10 to Casas Grandes, about 57km/35mi. Continue south for 0.6km/0.4mi.
Open year-round Tue–Sun 10am–5pm. P$12. The area is closed during periods of heavy rain.

Communal Housing Units

Pedro Urbina-Martin

★Museo de las Culturas del Norte (Centro Cultural Paquimé) – This modern museum is located to one side of the archaeological site. It displays over 800 exhibits of large animal fossils, Paquimé pottery, scale models, textiles and other regional objects, representing the most important cultures of northern Mexico. Landscaped and designed to integrate into the environment, the building was inspired by Paquimé's ceremonial mound. Upstairs, the site and its natural surroundings are visible from an overlooking terrace.

Archaeological Site – Paquimé differs from the rest of Mexico's pre-Hispanic archaeological sites, thanks to the earthen constructions. This urban center's buildings were both secular and religious in function and were oriented from southwest to northwest. Some structures show a clearly Mesoamerican influence, as in the ball court (one to the northwest, the other in the southern part of the city) and the Casa de la Serpiente (Serpent's House) to the southwest. There is a **Central Plaza**, as well as remains of **Unidades Habitacionales Comunales** (Communal Housing Units). These units were supplied with running water via subterranean waterways and boasted multiple courtyards and rooms of up to six levels in height. The

T-shaped entryways are also noteworthy, as they might have served as a defensive tactic and insulation for interior rooms during windy and cold spells. North of the housing units, the **Montículo de la Cruz** (Hill of the Cross) can be seen. This earthen mound has an astronomical orientation and was probably related to Paquimé's agriculture, which developed by a system of terraces. Special attention was also given to breeding tropical birds, perhaps to use their feathers for ornamentation. In the courtyards of the **Casa de las Guacamayas** (House of the Macaws), southwest of the central plaza, a series of small cages is attached to the walls.

This culture's sensitivity was expressed through **pottery**, which was originally monochromatic but later displayed geometric designs of combinations of black and red over cream and white.

Around 1450, before the arrival of the Spanish to the area, the city was abandoned. Circumstances may have already been aggravated by changes in climate or permanent drought when a probable enemy attack and subsequent fire finished off the city.

EXCURSION

Ciudad Juárez – *303km/188mi. Go north on Carr. 10 in the direction of Janos (70km/43mi). Take a right onto Carr. 2 to Ciudad Juárez.* During the 16C, travelers journeying through northern Mexico crossed the Rio Grande and often stopped to rest at a ford in the river, called Paso del Norte. In the 17C, Franciscan friars founded a mission at the same place; it would later become Ciudad Juárez. Today a dynamic frontier city, Ciudad Juárez is the most important center of *maquiladoras* in Mexico. The city is located in a fertile valley that contrasts with the desert environment around it. Classic desert dunes, like the **Médanos de Samalayuca**, are found nearby.

Tourists flock to Ciudad Juárez for its lively nightlife, complete with shows, nightclubs, gambling houses and bullfights. The **Misión de Nuestra Señora de Guadalupe** is the highlight of the cultural attractions; richly decorated beams support the mission's magnificent ceiling *(open year-round Mon–Thu & Sun 7:30am–7:30pm, Fri 7:30am–6:45pm, Sat 9–11am & noon–3pm; ☎ 1-615-5562)*. Other interesting places to visit are the Museum of Art in the commercial area of PRONAF, the Museum of Anthropology and History, located in the old border customs building, and the Parque Chamizal.

List of archaeological sites

Mexico

Mexico City
Cuicuilco (D.F.)
Templo Mayor (D.F.)
Central Mexico
Cacaxtla-Xochitécatl (Tlaxcala)
Cantona (Puebla)
Cholula (Puebla)
Malinalco★ (México)
Teopanzolco (Morelos)
Teotenango (Mexico)
Teotihuacán★★★ (Mexico)
Tepozteco (Morelos)
Tula (Hidalgo)
Xochicalco★★ (Morelos)
Yohualichan (Puebla)
Central West
Los Toriles (Nayarit)
Northwest
Paquimé★★ (Chihuahua)
Northeast
Alta Vista★ (Zacatecas)
Boca de Potrerillos (Nuevo León)
El Consuelo (San Luis Potosí)
La Quemada★ (Zacatecas)
Gulf of Mexico
Cempoala★ (Veracruz)
Comalcalco★ (Tabasco)
El Tajín★★★ (Veracruz)
Pacific Coast
Chinkultic (Chiapas)
Dainzú (Oaxaca)
Lambityeco (Oaxaca)

Pacific Coast (cont.)
Mitla★★ (Oaxaca)
Monte Albán★★★ (Oaxaca)
Palenque★★★ (Chiapas)
Tenam Puente (Chiapas)
Toniná★★ (Chiapas)
Yácatas★ (Michoacán)
Yagul★ (Oaxaca)
Yaxchilán★★ (Chiapas)
Yucatán Peninsula
Becán★ (Campeche)
Bonampak (Chiapas)
Cobá★ (Quintana Roo)
Chicanná (Campeche)
Chichén Itzá★★★ (Yucatán)
Dzibanché (Quintana Roo)
Dzibilchaltún (Yucatán)
Edzná★ (Campeche)
El Rey (Quintana Roo)
Kabah (Yucatán)
Kinichná (Quintana Roo)
Kohunlich★ (Campeche)
Labná★ (Yucatán)
Mayapán★ (Yucatán)
Muyil (Quintana Roo)
San Gervasio (Quintana Roo)
Sayil (Yucatán)
Tulum★★ (Quintana Roo)
Uxmal★★★ (Yucatán)
Xel-Ha (Quintana Roo)
Xlapak (Yucatán)
Xpuhil (Campeche)

Guatemala

Abaj Takalik★
Ceibal
Copán★★★ (Honduras)
El Baúl
La Democracia
Quiriguá★
Tikal★★★
Uaxactún

Belize

Altun Ha★
Cahal Pech
Caracol★★
Cerros★
La Milpa
Lamanai★★★
Lubaantun★
Nim Li Punit★
Santa Rita
Xunantunich★★

Baja California Peninsula

Mythical Land of Missions, Whales and Beaches

Handicrafts and Food, p 52. Embraced by the Pacific Ocean and the Gulf of California (also known as the Sea of Cortés, named after its discoverer Hernán Cortés), Baja California is the world's largest **peninsula★★**, measuring 1,200km/745mi in length. Baja was separated from the continental landmass millions of years ago, and much of its charm is a result of this relative isolation. It is one of the driest places on earth, and its climate is extreme.

BC .... Baja California (Norte)
BCS .... Baja California Sur

Mexico's least populated region, the peninsula has not been fully explored and at times seems like another country. Though Mexican by culture, thanks to immigration from other Mexican states the peninsula has been greatly influenced by its northern neighbor, as purchases are made in US dollars and English is spoken frequently.

Completed in 1973, Carretera 1 (1,645km/1,022mi long) runs the length of the peninsula. To travel it is to delve into Baja's enigmatic interiors, discern the ocean's many shades of blue and witness the contrasts between deserts and rugged, cacti-speckled mountains sculpted by the San Andreas Fault. The mountain ranges, uninhabited islands and coves offer a variety of attractions and delicacies, from fertile agricultural valleys and exquisite beaches, minerals and pearls, diverse animal species and cave paintings, to wines and seafood. For more than 450 years, these distinctive features have attracted colonizers, adventurers and travelers in search of their dreams.

Historical Notes — The Cochimís once inhabited the northern and central areas of the peninsula, while the Pericúes and Guaycuras lived in the south. Due to disease, these nomadic groups almost vanished during colonization. The first colonizers imagined Baja was the heavenly island of California, home of the mythical queen Califia, mentioned in Garci Ordóñez de Montalvo's popular novel *Las Sergas de Esplandián* (*The Exploits of Esplandian*). After Baja's discovery in 1532, every attempt to colonize the area failed. The Jesuit missionaries arrived in 1697 and spent 80 years trying to convert the indigenous peoples to Christianity. In the end their efforts, and later those of the Franciscans and Dominicans, accomplished what weapons of war could not. The missionary era, Spain's last major territorial expansion in America, ended in 1834. When the US claimed the peninsula after the Mexican-American War of 1847, Mexico refused to cede it. Later, Baja California was divided into northern and southern states along the 28th Parallel.

Natural Arch, Cabo San Lucas

BAJA CALIFORNIA (NORTH)

Population 2,112,140
Map of Principal Sights
🅱 Av. Revolución, 711, corner of Calle Primera, Tijuana
☎ (6) 688-0555

Northern Baja California's climate is distinctly different from the dry climate of the rest of the peninsula. Rains falling in the northwest aid in the cultivation of grapes, cotton and wheat in fertile valleys like that of Guadalupe, famous for its wines. Pine and evergreen oak forests blanket the slopes of the **Sierra de San Pedro Mártir** (3,078m/10,099ft), snow-capped in winter and the site of the National Astronomical Observatory. Auto racing, cycling, fishing, surfing and **whale watching** are some possible activities among nearly 300 events held during the year throughout the state. Hidden **cave paintings** and **missions**—many of them in ruins and founded for the most part by Dominicans—are also scattered around the state. The **trek from Tijuana to Los Cabos★★**, on Carretera 1, enjoys international fame due to its natural beauty and numerous attractions. A minimum of 19 days is suggested for covering the 2,308km and reaching the main sights found along this route.

TIJUANA

Tijuana is known as "the city of possibilities" due to the great number of Mexican immigrants who attempt to cross the increasingly patrolled and brightly lit, 5km/3mi-long border, in search of work in the US. Located only 30 minutes from San Diego, the city has become the fourth largest in Mexico. Tijuana receives millions of US citizens who cross the border to shop and visit restaurants and lively nightclubs on the famous **Avenida Revolución**, as well as to attend bullfights, greyhound races in the Hipódromo de Agua Caliente and games of Jai Alai—a high-speed ball game from the Spanish Basque country.

★Centro Cultural de Tijuana – *Paseo de los Héroes and Mina, in the Zona Río; open year-round Tue–Sun 10am–8pm;* ✗ ☎ *(6) 687-9600 P$20.* Tijuana's Cultural Center houses the **Museo de las Californias**, which offers a historic journey through the region and hosts temporary exhibitions that reflect border art and culture. The adjacent multi-theater **Omnimax** *(showings Tue–Fri 2–9pm, weekends & holidays 11am–9pm, every hour on the hour; P$44)* projects **films** onto a 180° screen.

Cava L.A. Cetto – *Cañón Johnson, 2108, between Constitución and Calle Diez. Open year-round, visit by guided tour only, Tue–Fri 10am–5:30pm, Sat 10am–4:30pm.* ☒ ☏ *(6) 685-3031.* During the wine cellar tour, visitors learn about the process of wine aging, followed by a wine tasting session *(P$20).*

Excursion

Playas de Rosarito – *37km/23mi south of Tijuana on Carr. 1.* Popular among Californians, this tourist center is lined with grand hotels and restaurants. Here, Puerto Nuevo-style lobster, one of the area's culinary delights, is served with butter, beans and tortillas. Besides its lively nightlife, Rosarito offers a museum that exhibits objects from *Titanic*, which was actually filmed in the nearby **Fox Baja Studios** *(7km/4.3mi south, via the freeway; visit by guided tour only, Fri–Sun 10am–6pm; P$50; reservations required;* ☏ *6-614-0110).* The **Museo Wa-Kuatay** *(next to the Hotel Rosarito Beach; open year-round Wed–Mon 10am–4pm)* displays indigenous artifacts and provides information on the history of this growing town.

MEXICALI   *189km/117mi east of Tijuana via Carr. 2.*

Capital of Baja California Norte, this border city saw its economy boom at the beginning of the 20C when the Colorado River was first used to irrigate the valley. Today, Mexicali is considered one of the most important industrial and agricultural centers in Mexico.
Due to the great number of Chinese immigrants who arrived here in the mid 19C, Chinese restaurants abound in Mexicali.

Museo Universitario – *Reforma and Calle L. Open year-round Mon–Fri 9am–6pm, Sat–Sun 10am–4pm. Closed Jan 1 & Dec 24.* ☏ *(6) 552-5715.* The University Museum presents information on regional history, indigenous groups and geography. A separate section is reserved for temporary exhibits *(P$7).*

Museo Sol del Niño – *Av. Alfonso Esquer Sandez, half a block from Blvd. López Mateos. Open year-round Mon–Fri 9am–6pm, Sat–Sun 10am–7pm. P$25.* ✗ ☏ *(6) 554-9393.* This family-geared educational center offers fun ways for children to learn about physical and natural phenomena, as well as the development of certain professional activities and careers.

Excursions

El Vallecito – *From Mexicali take the toll road, heading towards Tijuana. After 75km/46.5mi, take the exit to the town of Rumorosa; 7km/4.3mi later, turn right and continue 3km/1.9mi. Open year-round Wed–Sun 8am–5pm. P$12.* ⚠ ☏ *(6) 566-1116.* After crossing the imposing **Sierra la Rumorosa★**, one arrives at this semidesertic area, the boulders of which are engraved with cave paintings. During the winter solstice (Dec 21), in the morning, the sun's rays shine directly on the eyes of a red human figure, known as *el diablito* ("the little devil").

San Felipe – *215km/133mi south of Mexicali via Carr. 5.* Tucked between the Gulf of California and the desert, this fishing village is surrounded by majestic rocky mountains. Especially fascinating are the **tides★★**, which every six hours move the tranquil waters of the Sea of Cortés, across a distance of up to 300m/328yd, turning the beach into a shipyard.

★**Valle de los Gigantes** – *Exit San Felipe, heading south; after 26km/16mi, turn right (get directions from the gatekeeper) and continue 2.5km/1.6mi.* At the foot of the **Sierra de San Pedro Mártir**, dozens of imposing **cardones★** (giant cacti) rise above this mystic desert valley. Autochthonous of this region, the *cardón* is the Earth's tallest and heaviest cactus. It can reach a height of more than 20m/65ft and can weigh up to 10 tons. Moreover, it can withstand droughts of up to 8 years and can live more than 200 years.

ENSENADA   *108km/67mi south of Tijuana via Carr. 1.*

Cut into the Bahía de Todos Santos, the deep-water port of this inviting city is the oldest and most important on the peninsula. Juan Rodríguez Cabrillo, a Portuguese navigator, founded Ensenada, which means "cove" in Spanish, in 1542; 60 years later, the Spaniard Sebastián Vizcaíno christened it **Ensenada de Todos los Santos** (All Saint's Cove).

A *calandria* (horse-drawn buggy) ride *(departures from Blvd. Costero, at the corner of Calle Madero; daily 9am–6pm)* offers a great opportunity to explore the waterfront from a comfortable vantagepoint.

Centro Social, Cívico y Cultural Riviera de Ensenada (Ex Casino Riviera del Pacífico) – *Blvd. Costera Lázaro Cárdenas and Av. Riviera. Open year-round daily 8am–6pm;* ☏ *(6) 176-4310.* Inaugurated in 1930, this renowned hotel and casino was frequented by famous artists of the past until it was shut down eight years later, when gambling was outlawed. The building has some characteristics of Andalusian architecture, and part of it now houses the **Museo de Historia de Ensenada** *(open Jun–Aug Tue–Sun & holidays 9am–5pm, Sept–May Tue–Sun & holidays 10am–5pm; closed Jan 1, May 1 & Dec 25; P$5; ☎ 6-177-0594).*

Cantina Hussong's – *Av. Ruiz, 113. Open year-round daily 10am–3am. ☎ (6) 178-3210.* Founded in 1892, Hussong's is the oldest cantina on the peninsula. Both locals and tourists frequent this bar for its great atmosphere. Diverse artists and celebrities occasionally make a guest appearance.

Bodegas de Santo Tomás – *Av. Miramar, 666. Open year-round, visit by guided tour only, daily 11am, 1pm & 3pm. P$20; ☒ ☎ (6) 178-2509.* The city's oldest wine cellar, this place offers a taste of the wines produced in Baja California's vineyards.

Excursions

★**Vineyards** – Not far from Ensenada, the Valley of Guadalupe extends to the north and the Valley of Santo Tomás to the south. These regions are famous for their vineyards and wineries. *(For further information, contact Vinos L.A. Cetto ☎ 6-155-2264, Monte Xanic ☎ 6-174-6769 or Domecq ☎ 6-155-2249.)*

Isla de Todos Santos – *27 nautical miles from Ensenada. Boat trips depart from the dock. 8hr excursion: from USD$200–$300 for 8 people.* Popular among surfers, this small island also lends itself for fishing and diving. During whale season *(Dec–Feb)* this marvelous mammal can be spotted on the way to the island.

La Bufadora – *36km/22mi from Ensenada. Go south on Carr. 1 for 16km/10mi to Maneadero. Then go west for 20km/12mi on the road to Punta Banda.* Here the mountains plunge perpendicularly into the ocean, forming a cavity at the base of a cliff. After water pushes into the cave, it blasts out with unusual force, reaching heights of 20m/66ft and producing a unique sound.

Bahía de San Quintín – *191km/119mi south of Ensenada via Carr. 1.* Shaped like a horseshoe, this bay is protected by a chain of small volcanoes making it a good place for sport fishing. Nearby are the **remains** of an English colony, the English Land Company, established in this agricultural zone in 1880.

Between San Quintín and Guerrero Negro, fill the tank at every gas station. Canned gasoline is sold in Cataviña and Bahía de los Ángeles.

Cataviña – *197km/122mi south of San Quintín, on Carr. 1.* To reach this isolated town, one must travel on a winding road with an attractive **desert panorama**★, where rock formations and giant and saguaro cacti abound. Here stands the only hotel within a 200km/124mi radius. Just 4km/2.5mi north, Not too far from the road, lies a group of **cave paintings**.

★**Bahía de los Ángeles** – *Exit Cataviña, heading south on Carr. 1; after 109km/67.6mi, turn left and continue 69km/42.8mi.* ⚠ ☒. Protected by **Ángel de la Guarda** (Guardian Angel) island, which extends along 70km/43.4mi, this pretty bay offers the chance to practice diverse recreational activities on its various islands. Along the way, it is common to see dolphins and, with luck, one of the 11 species of **whales** found here.

In the mountains and cannons that surround the bay, one can explore the **Misión de San Borja** *(accessible only to four-wheel-drive vehicles)*, a few places with cave paintings and ancient mines.

In addition, the town has four hotels, a sea turtle observation and research center and the **Museo de Historia Natural y Cultura** *(open year-round Mon–Fri 9am–noon; donations accepted).*

After crossing the 28th Parallel—the frontier between Baja California and Baja California Sur—move watches ahead one hour.

PRACTICAL INFORMATION

Getting There – By plane: AeroCalifornia ☎ (800) 237-6225 (US) or (6) 684-2100, **Alaska Airlines** ☎ (800) 426-0333, **Aeromexico** ☎ (800) 237-6639 (US) or ☎ (01-800) 909-99, **Mexicana Airlines** ☎ (800) 531-7921 (US) or ☎ (01-800) 502-20 offer daily flights to major cities. US airlines offer connections through Los Angeles, San Francisco and Dallas. International flights connect through Mexico City. Taxi service and car rental agencies are available at all airports.

By bus: Regular bus service connects the peninsula's main cities. Buses leave from the Central Bus Terminal; check with local terminals for schedules. **Autotransportes de Baja California** provides service between Tijuana and La Paz *(one way USD$56;* ☎ *6-626-1701)*. **Greyhound Bus Lines** provides service from Los Angeles and San Diego to Tijuana *(for information & schedules in the US* ☎ *619-239-3266)*.

By car: Visitors to the Baja area do not need a tourist card but should purchase Mexican car insurance at the border. Carretera 1 connects Tijuana with Cabo San Lucas (1,600km/1,000mi). A four-lane highway runs between Tijuana and Ensenada (toll). Gas stations are sparse along some stretches of highway. Major roads are paved and in good condition, but driving at night is not recommended.

By boat: Grupo SEMATUR operates a regularly scheduled ferry service (cars & passengers) connecting the peninsula with the Mexican mainland (Mazatlán to La Paz, Topolobambo to La Paz, Guaymas to Santa Rosalía). Year-round service; departures vary according to season. Advance reservations (1 week) required. Mazatlán to La Paz *(departs Sun–Fri 3pm; arrives La Paz 9am; one-way trip P$215–$856; return to Mazatlán, same hours)*; Topolobambo to La Paz *(departs daily 10pm, arrives La Paz 8am; P$144–$569; return to Topolobambo, same hours)*; Guaymas to Santa Rosalía *(departs Tue & Fri 9am, arrives in Santa Rosalía 4:30pm; P$144; return to Guaymas Tue & Fri 11pm, arrives at 8am)*. For information, tickets & reservations: La Paz ☎ (1) 125-3833; Mazatlán ☎ (01-800) 696-9600; Mar de Cortés (Cabo San Lucas) ☎ (1) 143-3717, Festival Tours (Los Mochis) ☎ (6) 818-3986. Advance reservations (2 weeks) recommended.

Tourist Information – For more information on hotels, a list of travel agencies and tour operators, as well as maps and brochures contact the tourist offices below, *www.bajalife.com* or*www.bcs-tourism.com*.

Ensenada Tourist Office, Blvd. Lázaro Cárdenas, 1477, corner of Calle Las Rocas, Ensenada C.P. 22830 ☎ (6) 172-3022

La Paz Tourist Information Office, Paseo Álvaro Obregón, corner of 16 de Septiembre, La Paz C.P. 23000 ☎ (1) 122-5939

Loreto Tourist Information Office, Madero and Salvatierra, Loreto, C.P. 23880; ☎ (1) 155-0411

Los Cabos Tourist Information Office, Zaragoza, corner of Blvd. Mijares, San José del Cabo, C.P. 23400; ☎ (1) 142-2960

Tijuana Tourist Office INFOTUR, Av. Revolución, 711, corner of Calle 1a, Tijuana C.P. 22000 ☎ (6) 688-0555

Mexicali Tourist Information Office, Blvd. Benito Juárez and Francisco L. Montejano, 2nd floor, Mexicali C.P. 21260, ☎ (6) 566-1116

San Felipe Tourist Information Office, Av. Mar de Cortés and Manzanillo, San Felipe, C.P. 21850, ☎ (6) 577-1155

Accommodations – Major hotel chains are found in Tijuana, Ensenada, Mexicali, La Paz and Los Cabos. Reservations recommended, especially during high season *(Dec–Apr)*. **La Pinta Hotels** offer lodging throughout Baja ☎ (01-800) 026-3605; for condos, hotels & resorts contact **Mexico Accommodations** ☎ (800) 262-4500 (US) and ☎ (800) 654-5543 (Canada). Small hotels and guesthouses can be found throughout Baja. **RV Parks** are located near most larger towns and along beaches.

Water Sports and Ecotourism – Most beaches are safe for **swimming** but bathers should be aware of strong currents. Camping along beaches is permitted. Most hotels can arrange excursions for a myriad of activities. **Snorkeling, scuba diving** *(Apr–Nov)* and **kayaking** *(Nov–Apr)* can be practiced on various points of the peninsula. In Loreto, **sport fishing, boating, scuba diving** and **snorkeling** are popular. It is advisable to book fishing trips well in advance during the season *(Mar–Nov)*; a fishing license is required. A wide variety of excursions, such as sea kayaking, exploration of caves and natural reserves, scuba diving and **whale-watching** *(Jan–March)*, depart from La Paz.

For guided **horseback riding** and **mountain bike** tours to beaches and desert areas, and **bird-watching** contact Las Parras Tours, Loreto ☎ (1) 135-1010. In Mulegé, Ecomundo ☎ (1) 153-0409 also offers bird watching.

Ecotourism and Adventure Travel

Servicios Turísticos Mar de Cortés Pacífico	Av. Mar de Cortés y Zona Estero, San Felipe, BC ☎ (6) 577-1164
Bajarama de México	Virgilio Uribe 496C, Ensenada, BC ☎ (6) 178-3512
Cali-Baja Tours	Macheros y Blvd. Costero, Ensenada, BC ☎ (6) 178-1641 or www.sdro.com/calibaja
Expediciones de Turismo Ecológico y de Aventura	Blvd. Costero 1094-14, Ensenada, BC ☎ (6) 178-3704
Off Road Adventure	Balandra, La Paz, BCS ☎ (1) 128-0504 or www.offroadadventure.com.mx
Ecomundo	Hotel Las Casitas and Km111 Bahía Concepción, Mulegé, BCS ☎ (1) 153-0409
Baja Adventure Tours	Hotel Vieja Hacienda, Mulegé, BCS ☎ (1) 153-0021
Vámonos Tours	Hotel La Concha, La Paz, BCS ☎ (1) 121-6161
Katun Adventure in Baja	16 de Septiembre y A. Obregón, 460, Local 204, La Paz, BCS ☎ (1) 123-4888

Whale watching

Enchanted Island Excursions	Fracc. Marysol 50, San Felipe, BC ☎ (6) 577-1431
Malarrimo Ecotours	Blvd. Emiliano Zapata, Guerrero Negro, BCS ☎ (1) 157-0100 or www.malarrimo.com
Laguna Tours	Blvd. Emiliano Zapata, Guerrero Negro, BCS ☎ (1) 157-0050 or www.bajalaguna.com
Ecoturismo Kuyima	Dom. Conocido, San Ignacio, BCS
Antonio's Whale Tours	R.V. Park El Padrino, San Ignacio, BCS ☎ (1) 154-0089
Las Parras Tours	Francisco I Madero, Loreto, BCS ☎ (1) 135-1010 or www.tourbaja.com/lasparras.html
The Loreto Center	Hidalgo y Pino Suárez, Loreto, BCS ☎ (1) 135-0798 or www.loretocenter.com
Brennan's y Asociados	Puerto San Carlos, Bahía Magdalena, BCS ☎ (1) 136-0288
Viajes Mar y Arena	Puerto San Carlos, Bahía Magdalena, BCS ☎ (1) 136-0076
Baja Expeditions	San Diego, CA ☎ (619) 843-6967 or Sonora 585, La Paz, BCS ☎ (1) 125-3828 or www.bajaex.com
Baja Outdoor Activities	A. Obregón 25, La Paz, BCS ☎ (1) 125-5636 or www.kayactivities.com
Mar y Aventura	Topete 564, La Paz, BCS ☎ (1) 122-7039
Off Road Adventure	Balandra, La Paz, BCS ☎ (1) 128-0504 or www.offroadadventure.com.mx
Cabo Acuadeportes	Hotel Hacienda, Cabo San Lucas, BCS ☎ (1) 143-0117 or www.allaboutcabo.com/cadactivities.htm
Aerocalafia	Plaza Las Glorias 4-A, Cabo San Lucas, BCS ☎ (1) 143-4307 or www.caboland.com/aerocalafia
Baja's Water Sports	Revolución y Madero, Cabo San Lucas, BCS ☎ (1) 143-2050

Scuba Diving and Snorkeling

Dale's La Bufadora Dive Shop	Rancho La Bufadora, Punta Banda, Ensenada, BC ☎ (6) 154-2092
Cortez Explorers	Moctezuma 75-A, Mulegé, BCS ☎ (1) 153-0500 or www.cortez-explorer.com
The Loreto Center	Hidalgo y Pino Suárez, Loreto, BCS ☎ (1) 135-0798 or www.loretocenter.com
Loreto Diver	Int. Hotel Las Trojes, Loreto, BCS ☎ (1) 135-1106
Cortez Club	Hotel La Concha, La Paz, BCS ☎ (1) 121-6120 or www.cortezclub.com
Baja Quest	Sonora 174, La Paz, BCS ☎ (1) 123-5320
Baja Expeditions	San Diego, CA ☎ (619) 843-6967 or Sonora 585, La Paz, BCS ☎ (1) 125-3828 or www.bajaex.com

Scu-Baja	Nicolás Bravo y Álvaro Obregón, La Paz, BCS ☎ (1) 122-7423 or *www.scubaja.com*
Baja Diving & Service	A. Obregón Int. Plaza Cerralvo, La Paz, BCS ☎ (1) 122-1826
Mar y Aventura	Topete 564, La Paz, BCS ☎ (1) 122-7039
Land's End Divers	Blvd. Marina Int. Plaza Las Glorias, Cabo San Lucas, ☎ (1) 143-2200 *www.mexonline.com/landsend.htm*
Amigos del Mar	Blvd. Marina y Av. Solmar, Cabo San Lucas, BCS ☎ (1) 143-0505 or *www.mexonline.com/amigos-delmar.htm*
Pacific Coast Adventure	Blvd. Marina Int. Plaza Las Glorias, Cabo San Lucas, BCS ☎ (1) 143-1070
Cabo Acuadeportes	Hotel Hacienda, Cabo San Lucas, BCS ☎ (1) 143-0117 or *www.allaboutcabo.com/cadactivities.htm*
Andrómeda Divers y Más	Playa El Médano, Cabo San Lucas, BCS ☎ (1) 143-2765
Aerocalafia	Plaza Las Glorias 4-A, Cabo San Lucas, BCS ☎ (1) 143-4307 or *www.caboland.com/ aerocalafia*
Baja's Water Sports	Revolución y Madero, Cabo San Lucas, BCS ☎ (1) 143-2050
Tío Sports Adventure & Nature	Hotel Melia Cabo San Lucas, BCS ☎ (1) 143-2986 or *www.tiosports.com*
Vista Sea Sport	A.P. 42, Buena Vista, Cabo del Este, BCS ☎ (1) 141-0031 or *www.vistaseasport.com*
Pepe's Dive Center	Cabo Pulmo, BCS ☎ (1) 141-0001

Kayaking

Ecomundo	Hotel Las Casitas and Km111 Bahía Concepción, Mulegé, BCS ☎ (1) 153-0409
Cortez Club	Hotel La Concha, La Paz, BCS ☎ (1) 121-6120 or *www.cortezclub.com*
Baja Quest	Sonora 174, La Paz, BCS ☎ (1) 123-5320
Baja Expeditions	San Diego, CA ☎ (619) 843-6967 or Sonora 585, La Paz, BCS ☎ (1) 125-3828 or *www.bajaex.com*
Baja Outdoor Activities	A. Obregón 25, La Paz, BCS ☎ (1) 125-5636 or *www.kayactivities.com*
Aerocalafia	Plaza Las Glorias 4-A, Cabo San Lucas, BCS ☎ (1) 143-4307 or *www.caboland.com/aerocalafia*
Baja's Water Sports	Revolución y Madero, Cabo San Lucas, BCS ☎ (1) 143-2050
Tío Sports Adventure & Nature	Hotel Melia Cabo San Lucas, BCS ☎ (1) 143-2986 or *www.tiosports.com*

Sailing and Windsurfing

Cortez Club	Hotel La Concha, La Paz, BCS ☎ (1) 121-6120 or *www.cortezclub.com*
Cabo Acuadeportes	Hotel Hacienda, Cabo San Lucas, BCS ☎ (1) 143-0117 or *www.allaboutcabo.com/cadactivities.htm*

Sportfishing

Sergio's Sportfishing Center	Malecón, Ensenada, BC ☎ (6) 178-2185
Tony Reyes & Longfin Sportfishing	Av. Mar Bermejo, 130, San Felipe, BC ☎ (6) 577-1120
Aqua Sports de Loreto	Club de Playa Hotel Eden, Loreto, BC ☎ (1) 135-0560
Cortez Club	Hotel La Concha, La Paz, BCS ☎ (1) 121-6120 or *www.cortezclub.com*
Pesca Deportiva Solmar	Blvd. Marina, Cabo San Lucas, BCS ☎ (1) 143-0646 or *www.solmar.com*
Flota Hotel Palmas de Cortés	Los Barriles, Cabo del Este, BCS ☎ (1) 141-0050
Flota Buena Vista Beach	Buena Vista, Cabo del Este, BCS ☎ (1) 141-0033
Flota Punta Colorada	Buena Vista, Cabo del Este, BCS ☎ (1) 141-0208

With hundreds of miles of prime coastline bordering the Pacific Ocean and the Sea of Cortés, the Baja California Peninsula offers visitors of all ages the opportunity to practice a multitude of water sports. Snorkeling, kayaking and surfing equipment can be rented at some of the local beaches.

Kayaking in Playa Posada, Bahía Concepción

Selected Beaches	swimming	scuba/snorkeling	surfing	fishing	camping
Rosarito	●		●	●	●
Ensenada				●	
Isla Espíritu Santo	●	●	●	●	●
San Miguel				●	
La Bufadora		●			
San Felipe	●			●	
Bahía de San Quintín				●	
Bahía de los Ángeles	●	●		●	●
Mulegé / Bahía Concepción	●	●		●	●
Santispac	●				●
Posada Concepción	●				●
El Burro	●				●
BuenaVentura	●				
El Requesón	●				●
Loreto and nearby islands	●	●		●	
La Paz	●	●		●	●
El Tesoro	●				
Pichilingue	●				●
Balandra	●				
Tecolote	●				●
Isla Espíritu Santo	●	●			●
Todos Santos					
Punta Lobos				●	
San Pedrito			●		●
Los Cerritos	●		●	●	●
Cabo San Lucas					
El Médano y Finisterra	●	●		●	
Cabeza Ballena (5.5 km from Cabo San Lucas)	●				
El Faro y Barco Varado (10 km)	●				
Bahía Santa María (12.5 km)	●	●			
El Chileno (14.5 km)	●	●			
Costa Azul/Acapulquito (28 km)			●		
San José del Cabo	●			●	
Cabo del Este	●	●		●	
Cabo Pulmo	●	●			

The symbols on the above chart indicate ≊ swimming, ◣ scuba/snorkeling, ⏏ surfing, ✎ fishing and △ camping.

BAJA CALIFORNIA SUR★★

Population 375,494
Map of Principal Sights
🛈 Edificio Fidepaz, on Carretera al Norte, km 5.5
☎ (1) 124-0100 and
16 de Septiembre and Obregón, La Paz ☎ (1) 122-5939

Attractions ranging from cave paintings to nature reserves dot the entire southern part of the peninsula. Baja California Sur was made a Mexican state in 1974, year in which the Transpeninsular Highway was completed. Off this main route, diverse excursions, the majority of which require special guides, await the adventure traveler.

South of the 28th Parallel, the **Reserva de la Biosfera del Desierto de Vizcaíno** extends all the way to the south of San Ignacio and constitutes Mexico's largest protected area. This reserve is home to **coastal lagoons**, where, in addition to the gray whale, hundreds of thousands of migratory birds arrive each year. For a more rugged landscape, one can turn to the Vizcaíno Desert's plains and sand dunes, whose *cardones* (giant cacti) and *cirios* (saguaro cacti) are only found in Baja California and Sonora. The reserve's mountain ranges, such as the **Sierra de San Francisco**, are home to numerous endangered species, including the golden eagle and the agile, big-horned wild sheep.

From Santa Rosalía to Loreto, the highway wanders between the ocean and jagged mountainous terrain, such as the imposing **Sierra de la Giganta**. Accessible by mule or mountain bike from Loreto, the sierra's **missions** and fertile ranches, established by the Jesuits some three centuries ago, merit a visit. A wildlife reserve for species endemic to the region, the **Reserva de la Biosfera Sierra de La Laguna**, located south of La Paz in the direction of Los Cabos, offers hikes through canyons, conifer forests and exuberant vegetation. The sierra's summit (2,200m/7,216ft) rewards hikers with a panoramic **view★** of both the Pacific Ocean and the Gulf of California, where the adventure continues.

GUERRERO NEGRO

250km/155mi from Cataviña, 141km/87.4mi from the exit to Bahía de los Ángeles and 7km/4.3mi from the 28th Parallel on Carr. 1.

Guerrero Negro is home to the world's largest salt flat. At the Ojo de Liebre lagoons *(9km/5.6mi south of Guerrero Negro by highway, 20km/12mi further by dirt road)* and Guerrero Negro, one finds good **observation points★★★** for sighting **gray whales** in

© Fernando García Aguinaco

■ The Gray Whale

For thousands of years, the **gray whale** *(Eschrictius robustus)* has initiated in December, at 9km/h (5.6mph), its annual trek of 10,000km/6,200mi-from the Arctic seas of Alaska and Russia's Chuckchi Peninsula to the Pacific coasts of Baja California Sur-to calve after a 13-month gestation period. During this marvelous **spectacle★★★**, these gigantic whales weighing 40 tons can be seen accompanied by their newly born calves. At the end of March, the gray whales return to the Arctic, where they feed to reinitiate, when the cold weather sets in, the longest migration ever registered for any mammal.

Cave Paintings, Sierra de San Francisco

winter. *Whale-watching expeditions depart from Guerrero Negro, Dec 15–Mar daily at 8am & 11am; round trip. Reservations recommended. P$200 (90min trip from docks at Ojo de Liebre) and P$400 (3hrs). For more information and to make reservations contact Ecotours Malarrimo ☎ (1) 157-0100 or Tours Laguna ☎ (1) 157-0050.* From Guerrero Negro, one can also join an excursion to see the **cave paintings** of the **Sierra de San Francisco** and the **missions** of San Borja and Santa Gertrudis.

Excursion

Sierra de San Francisco – *103km/63.9mi south of Guerrero Negro, by way of Carr. 1, lies the 37km/23mi dirt road that leads to the sierra's cave paintings. Guided tours last one, three or six days (for excursions lasting several days, it is necessary to rent mules and camp out). Visitors must request permission at San Ignacio's local museum (Calle Valdivia, San Ignacio, BCS, C.P. 23930; ☎ 1-154-0222) and hire the services of specialized guides.* This **sierra** of abrupt canyons and breathtaking landscapes is home to the famous **cave paintings★★**, designated as a World Heritage Site in 1993. These drawings, which possibly date back to 8000 BC, represent deer, whales, manta rays and human figures. The most interesting paintings lie beyond the territory covered by the one-day excursion.

★SAN IGNACIO *150km/93mi from Guerrero Negro.*

With its tall date palms, this village resembles an oasis in the middle of the desert. Strolling through San Ignacio, one encounters fine views of the river flowing past the steep banks. In 1728 the Jesuit Juan Bautista Luyando founded the mission of San Ignacio Kadacaamán, when the place was inhabited by no more than 200 Cochimís.

Church – *Open year-round daily 6am–7pm. ☎ (1) 154-0222.* Built by the Dominicans in volcanic rock, this church was completed in 1786 and remains almost unchanged. Featuring a Latin cross layout, the church boasts elaborate gilded Baroque altars.

Museo Local – *Open Oct–May Tue–Sat 8am–6pm; Jun–Sept Tue–Sat 10am–3pm. ☎ (1) 154-0222.* Located beside the church, San Ignacio's local museum provides information on the nearby **cave paintings★★**.

Excursion

Laguna de San Ignacio – *60km/37.2mi from San Ignacio, by way of a dirt road.* Season permitting, this lagoon constitutes a fine **observation point★★★** for sighting the **gray whale** *(departures Dec 15–Apr 15, daily; P$350 from the lagoon; transportation from San Ignacio: USD$120 for 1 to 10 people; all-inclusive excursions lasting several days: USD$150/day; reservations recommended; Kuyima ☎ 1-154-0070).*

SANTA ROSALÍA *76km/47mi from San Ignacio.*

Facing the Gulf of California, this village built at the end of the 19C preserves its original wood structures, designed in French-Californian style and constructed by the French mining company, El Boleo. *Boleo,* or "bowling," in English refers to the spherical shape of the copper mined in the area. A stroll through the **Mesa Francia** area, which includes the **Museo Histórico Minero** *(open Mon–Fri 9am–3pm; P$10)*, and along the main street, home to the 100-year-old bakery **El Boleo** *(open year-round Mon–Sat 9am–9pm;* ✆ *1-152-0310)*, transports visitors back to another era.

Iglesia de Santa Bárbara – *Open year-round daily 6am–8pm.* ✆ *(1) 152-0008.* Made of light metal plates, this building was one of the world's first prefabricated constructions. The church was designed in 1884 by the Frenchman Gustave Eiffel, creator of the famous tower in Paris, and assembled in Santa Rosalía in 1897.

MULEGÉ *61km/38mi from Santa Rosalía.*

Founded as a mission in 1705, Mulegé (a Cochimí word meaning "great gorge with the white mouth") spreads across a broad valley. Surrounded by lofty palms and orchards, the town is bisected by a river that flows through the **estuary** before emptying into Bahía Concepción.

*★***Iglesia de la Misión de Santa Rosalía** – *Open year-round Mon–Fri 8am–3pm, weekends only during mass.* ✆ *(1) 124-0100.* Completed in 1766, this church graces the crest of a hill and is distinguished by an unusual, square-shaped ground floor. Abandoned in 1828 and later restored, the building preserves its simple, original facade.
Nearby, to the west, a small overlook offers a great **view** of the date palms and the mountains where the sun sets.

Museo Comunitario – *Open Oct–Apr Mon–Sat 9am–3pm; Apr–Sept Mon–Sat 9am–1pm. Guided tours in Spanish and English.* Located in what served as the **local prison** from 1906 to 1975, this museum, inaugurated in 1994, today exhibits historic objects of the region. During its prison days, the cellmates followed an unusual "open-door" policy, wherein they would set out to labor in the fields and return at 6pm when they were summoned back with the sound of a conch shell.

Excursions

Cueva Trinidad – *33km/20.5mi from Mulegé, in the Sierra San Borjita. P$400 (transportation and lunch included) 4 people minimum; for more information, inquire at your hotel.* The excursion to see the cave paintings at this site enjoys a great deal of popularity. To reach the cave, one must swim across natural pools of water found amidst narrow canyons. The company of a guide is strongly recommended to avoid getting lost on the way there.

*★★***Bahía Concepción** – *South of Mulegé.* ⚠. With a length of 50km/31mi, this bay possesses irresistible, almost untouched beaches. Camping is allowed in all of them. *The fee for a tent or palapa (thatched-roof) shelter ranges from P$30–$60.* Although some of these beaches do not provide any services, others offer lodging. Most popular is **Santispac★** *(22km/14mi from Mulegé).* **Posada Concepción** *(23.5km/14.6mi away)* features kayak rentals and excursions *(for more information*

El Requesón, Bahía Concepción

Sierra de la Giganta

© Fernando García Aguinaco

inquire at the Hotel Casitas in Mulegé or call ☎ 1-153-0409), while **El Burro★** *(26.5km/16.4mi away)* is ideal for snorkeling. Of all the beaches in this bay, the most beautiful is **El Requesón★★** *(45km/28mi from Mulegé),* a narrow strip of sand leading to a small island.

LORETO *136km/84mi from Mulegé.*

This tranquil, seaside village is also known as **Concho**, an indigenous term meaning "Red Mangrove."

Misión de Nuestra Señora de Loreto – *Open year-round daily 7am–1pm & 4–8pm. ☎ (1) 135-0005.* In 1697 Juan María de Salvatierra founded the Mission of Our Lady of Loreto in this spot, from which the first attempts to colonize California originated. In fact, the church's facade reads "capital and mother of all Californian missions." This Renaissance edifice was rebuilt after damages by earthquakes and hurricanes. The tower (1947) does not follow the same architectural style of the original cupola. Inside, the main altar, *estípite* style, displays the image of the Virgin of Our Lady of Loreto, patroness of the spiritual conversion of Baja California, in addition to oil paintings of the Jesuit saints.

★**Museo de las Misiones** – *Beside the church. Open year-round Tue–Sun 9am–1pm & 1:45–6pm. P$17. ☎ (1) 135-0441.* Situated in an 18C building made of stone and mesquite wood, the Museum of the Missions focuses on Baja California's colonization and exhibits religious art, weapons and household objects, the majority of them 18C. A typical ranching settlement of Baja California Sur, part of the Jesuits' legacy, is also reproduced. The **cross** in the central courtyard was carved by nature itself.

Excursions

Bahía de Loreto – Several islands dot this lovely bay, which has been declared a National Park. Excursions to **Isla del Carmen** and **Coronado** are popular among divers, snorkelers and fishermen.

★**Misión de San Francisco Javier** – *38km/23.6mi from Loreto. Open year-round daily 9am–1pm & 1:30–4pm. ☎ (1) 135-0411.* By way of a dirt road that crosses the abrupt and panoramic **Sierra de la Giganta★**, one arrives at the Mission of St. Francis Xavier, the second oldest mission of the Californias, founded in 1699. The church, the area's most beautiful and best preserved, still possesses its original Baroque altar.

Bahía Magdalena – *207km/128.3mi southwest of Loreto, via Ciudad Insurgentes and Puerto Adolfo López Mateos (excursions Jan–March; 3hr boat trip: USD$40; ☎ 1-131-5171); and 260km/161.2mi northeast of La Paz, via Ciudad Constitución and Puerto San Carlos (excursions Jan–March; 3hr boat trip: USD$40; ☎ 1-136-0288). Reservations recommended. One–day excursions from Loreto (USD$99; ☎ 1-135-1010) and La Paz (USD$100 & USD$120; ☎ 1-121-6120 and 121-6161 ext. 1414) are also available.* Protected by islands and connected to the Pacific Ocean by means of narrow channels, this bay offers another **observation point★★★** for sighting the gray whale.

Oceanfront Promenade, La Paz

LA PAZ *359km/222.6mi from Loreto.*

A state capital famous for its pretty sunsets, this friendly city extends around the still waters of **Bahía de la Paz**. Although Captain Sebastián Vizcaíno named it La Paz (Peace) in 1596, the hostile environment and lack of provisions prevented the establishment of a permanent settlement until 1811, nearly three centuries after Hernán Cortés founded the city in 1535 as the port and bay of Santa Cruz.

Beaches – For peace and quiet, go north of the seafront promenade to enjoy one of the inviting beaches: **El Tesoro** *(13km/8mi)*, **Pichilingue★** *(17km/11mi)*, near the ferry terminal, **Balandra** *(23km/14mi)*, formed by eight small bays, and **El Tecolote** *(26km/16mi)*. Boats depart from El Tecolote for **Isla Espíritu Santo★**, an island where visitors can snorkel alongside sea lions, kayak or just enjoy the peaceful coves. *(departures year-round daily before 10:30am; 4hr round trip; P$380–$500/person; ☎ 1-122-8885 & 121-6120)*. La Paz serves as a convenient point of departure for diving, fishing and whale-watching excursions.

Museo Regional de Antropología e Historia – *Altamirano and 5 de Mayo. Open year-round Mon–Fri 8am–7pm, Sat 9am–2pm; closed Dec 25 & Jan 1. ☎ (1) 125-6424.* The Regional Museum of Anthropology and History has informative exhibits on 1,000-year-old fossils, cave paintings, indigenous groups and area missions.

★LOS CABOS

Todos Santos – *79km/49mi south of La Paz and 73km/45.3mi north of Cabo San Lucas, via Carr. 19.* Located on a fertile plateau on the shore of the Pacific Ocean, this tranquil village prospered due to the cultivation of sugarcane, which lasted a century, from 1850 to 1950. Today, it provides refuge to artists and surfers, who enjoy the waves on the nearby beaches of **San Pedrito** and **Los Cerritos**. Not far from the downtown area, the ranches of "La Borrera," "Las Piedritas" and "San Martín" serve as departure points for excursions to the **Reserva de la Biosfera Sierra de la Laguna** *(open year-round daily, 24hrs; ⚠ ☎ 1-122-6890)*. The reserve's summit can be reached on foot *(19km/11.8mi)* or by mule.

★**Cabo San Lucas** – *73km/45.3mi south of Todos Santos, 152km/94mi from La Paz, via Carr. 19.* Located in a protected cove at land's end where pirates such as Sir Francis Drake (1578) once hid in ambush, this great resort, famous for its sport fishing, was only opened in 1974.
Surrounded by steep cliffs of igneous rock, the golden **Playa del Amor★** (Beach of Love) flirts between the Pacific Ocean and the Gulf of California. Next to it is the Cueva de San Andrés (St. Andrew's Cave), where, according to a saying, "two go in and three come out." Formed by fissures connected to the San Andreas Fault, the famous **Arco Natural★** is located at the very tip of the peninsula *(photo pp 198-199)*. Various embarkations offer excursions that include both attractions *(from USD$10; for more information inquire at the dock or in your hotel)*. At six different points in the surroundings, divers can explore the marine life and underwater landscapes.

Lively bars and a wide variety of shops and eateries abound in and around the marina. In the **glass factory** *(1km/0.6mi northwest of Av. Lázaro Cárdenas, on Carr. 19, follow the signs to "Fábrica de Vidrio"; open year-round Mon–Sat 7am–2pm; guided tour; donations accepted;* ☎ *1-143-0255)* visitors can observe workers as they create wonderful, blown-glass objects and figurines.

White sand beaches and crystalline waters, excellent for snorkeling, fill in the 33km/20mi corridor that connects Cabo San Lucas to its neighbor San José del Cabo. **Playa Santa María★** and **El Chileno** stand out for their striking beauty.

San José del Cabo – *33km/20mi from Cabo San Lucas, 183km/114mi from La Paz, via Carr. 1.* Founded as a mission in 1730, the church of San José del Cabo was built in the old mission style and is located near the central plaza surrounded by stores and inviting restaurants. Next to the ample **beach** and its large hotels lies an **estuary**. Inhabited by 150 species of birds, it is considered the only bird sanctuary in the entire peninsula.

Cabo del Este – *Los Barriles is located 80km/49.6mi north of San José del Cabo and 103km/63.9mi south of La Paz, via Carr. 1.* Both **Los Barriles** and **Buena Vista** are small fishing villages that opened up to tourism in the 1950s. Despite the increasing popularity of Bahía de Palmas and its surroundings, as a peaceful getaway spot and excellent sport-fishing destination, the "marlin capital" has managed to retain its relaxed and tranquil ambiance.

The various inlets around the southeastern tip of the peninsula lead to different points of interest. **Cabo Pulmo** *(45km/27.9mi south of Los Barriles and 25km/15.5mi south of La Ribera; offers lodging in cabins, from USD$65, as well as scuba diving excursions;* ☎ *1-141-0001)* is home to the only coral reef in North America's western coast. Declared a National Marine Park in 1995, this area possesses 14 dive sites and is inhabited by more than 200 species of tropical fish.

■ Aquarium of the World

In contrast with the rough waves of the Pacific Ocean, the tranquil Gulf of California, also known as the Sea of Cortés, bathes the peninsula's eastern coast. Its seductive waters, rich in nutrients stimulated by the entry of cold water currents into the Gulf, are home to 3,000 marine species, 900 of which are diverse species of fish and marine mammals. From Mulegé to Los Cabos, scuba divers can observe a wide variety of marine life, from a small sea horse to an enormous blue whale, as well as coral reefs and underwater sandfalls, and swim with curious, yet territorial, **sea lions**. In the summer, the pelagics swim into the Gulf of California; thus, with luck, it is possible to dive alongside a whale shark, caress a giant manta ray, or see a school of hammerhead sharks. That is why the famous oceanographer Jacques Yves Cousteau nicknamed the Sea of Cortés the "aquarium of the world."

© Bob Schalkwijk

Sea Lions

NORTHEAST

Land of lofty peaks, vast plains and white sombreros

Handicrafts and Food, p 52. Shaped by the arid terrain and bustling US-Mexican border, this region of contrasts began to develop more than 450 years ago, when rich silver deposits were first discovered in Zacatecas. Today, the city of Monterrey and its exacting industrial layout reflect the modernity of the 20C. The nomadic **Chichimecs**, who originally inhabited the region, opted to fight rather than submit to the Spanish empire, which was attracted to the region for its valuable gold and silver deposits. Here began the Spaniards' efforts to spread Christianity to the northern reaches of the Viceroyalty of New Spain. The Northeast's development was delayed by the great distances, scarce population, pirate raids on the coast of Tamaulipas, and attacks by the Chichimecs, Apache and Comanche, which continued into the 19C. Since the 16C, people of different origins have colonized this part of Mexico: Tlaxcaltecs in search of land and privilege, Spanish immigrants seeking converts and silver, and Europeans and Arabs hoping to find peace and opportunity. This area is also known for its brave heroes who were willing to risk their lives in the wars and military invasions of the 19C. The climate is arid, but oases, such as the unexpected swamps of Coahuila, are scattered about the desert. Because of its proximity to the US, it is one of the most industrialized sections of the country and boasts numerous *maquiladoras*. Northeastern Mexico is known for roasted meat, *dulces de leche* (milk sugar candy) and honest, hard-working and friendly folk.

Coah. .... Coahuila
NL .... Nuevo Léon
SLP .... San Luis Potosí
Tamps. .... Tamaulipas
Zac. .... Zacatecas

Catedral de Zacatecas, detail

La HUASTECA POTOSINA★★

San Luis Potosí
Map of Principal Sights – Map p 114 **(ABW)**
🔲 Carr. Mexico Laredo Sur km1 CP 79060

The Huasteca Potosina is one of the richest regions in San Luis Potosí. Owing to the abundance of natural resources and attractions, this area enjoys nationwide fame in Mexico and ranks as an excellent option for ecotourism and adventure sports. Located on the southeastern part of the state, the Huasteca Potosina is a productive agricultural and cattle raising region. The area owes its name to the **Huastecs**, an indigenous group that spread out evenly among the states of Tamaulipas, Veracruz, Hidalgo and, according to the latest anthropological research, also in some parts of the states of Querétaro and Puebla.

To initiate your visit to the region, the warm **Ciudad Valles**–the state's second most important city-known as "the gateway to the Huasteca," is the most convenient departure point to access the principal sights. Ciudad Valles offers a good tourist infrastructure, with diverse hotels, restaurants and services.

Historical Notes

The present-day Huasteca Potosina encompasses part of the territory inhabited by the Huastecs during pre-Hispanic times. They settled along the Gulf Coast and enjoyed a cultural development contemporary with that of other indigenous groups in Mesoamerica. Although the Huastecs initially shared similarities with various peoples in southern Mexico, the Huastec culture defined its own characteristics during the Classic period, between AD 200 and 800. This becomes evident in the originality of the archaeological vestiges of ceramics, sculptures and, especially, architecture, with a notable manifestation of round shapes in multiple structures and buildings. In the 16C, the Huastecs became allied with the Spanish conquistadors in order to defend themselves against Aztec attacks that had been occurring for over a century. Nevertheless, Governor Nuño Beltrán de Guzmán-who founded Ciudad Valles in 1533-dedicated himself to trading Huastec slaves, thus nearly wiping out the region's indigenous population during the colonial period. Today, various Huastec communities live in the surroundings of Aquismón, Axtla, Tamazunchale, Tancahuitz and Tanquián. During religious festivals, they practice ancient rituals and traditions, such as the "dance of the flying stick" and the "dance of the sparrow hawk," similar to those conducted by the famous flying men of Papantla.

213

PRACTICAL INFORMATION ON EXCURSIONS

Before organizing an excursion from Cd. Valles or renting a vehicle to access the diverse sights in the Huasteca Potosina, it is advisable to contact one of the city's tourist agencies, such as **Promotora Turística de la Huasteca** *(Escontría, 17, Centro, Cd. Valles; Attention: Martha Santos; ☎ 1-381-1888)*. The **Tourist Information Office** in Cd. Valles provides information about guide services for excursions around the Huasteca. **Turismo Pirasol** *(Carr. México-Laredo Sur, corner of 3ra Avenida; Attention: Juan Pérez Ríos; ☎ 1-382-2533)* rents buses and cars, with or without chauffeur service. The latter is recommended for transporting groups of tourists, but does not offer specialized guide services.

SIGHTS

El Consuelo – *35km/21.7mi. From Cd. Valles head east on Carr. 70 towards Tampico; 28km/17.4mi later, after passing the town of Tamuín, turn right. Head south for 6km/3.7mi, then turn right and continue 1km/0.6mi to reach the archaeological site. Open year-round Tue–Sun 10am–6pm. Closed national holidays.* One of the most explored, accessible and important archaeological sites of Huastec architecture, El Consuelo dates back to AD 800, approximately. Two **tombs**, where deformed head skulls were found, stand out among several rectangular ceremonial platforms. The paintings on the tombs' walls remain nearly intact. It was here that archaeologists found the extraordinary sculpture known as "the adolescent of Tamuín," currently exhibited at the National Museum of Anthropology in Mexico City.

★★**Cascada de Tamul** – *47km/29mi. From Cd. Valles head southwest on Carr. 70 towards Río Verde; 25km/15.5mi later, turn left and continue 20km/12.4mi on a dirt road to the town of Tanchachín and another 2km/1.2mi to reach the Santa María River (also known as the Tampaón).* Of crystal-clear waters with celestial blue tones, the Tamul waterfall is considered the most beautiful aquatic jewel of the numerous ones found in the state of San Luis Potosí. Formed by the Gallinas River that descends over the Santa María River from a height of 105m/344ft, this spectacular waterfall can reach a width of more than 300m/984ft during the rainy season. To access the waterfall by boat *(the trip lasts a little over 2hrs upstream and 1hr downstream)* depart from the outskirts of Tanchachín. On the way there, it is possible to make a stop and hike up a hill to visit the unique **Cueva del Agua**, a tranquil cave with a natural pool of sapphire-blue waters that flow into the river. At several points along the way, one can enjoy swimming, rappelling, whitewater rafting or kayaking. *Due to torrential rains, it is not advisable to visit the waterfall during the months of August and September; the best time to appreciate the waterfall in all its splendor is from November to April.*

Cascadas de Tamasopo – *66km/40.9mi. From Cd. Valles head southwest on Carr. 70 towards Río Verde; 57km/35.3mi later turn right and continue 7km/4.3mi to the main avenue in the town of Tamasopo. Turn right onto Calle Juárez and continue 2km/1.2mi to reach "Las Cascadas". Open year-round daily 7am–9pm. P$6/pers. and P$6/car. △ ※ ▣ We recommend visiting on weekdays.* Fed by the Tamasopo River, these three waterfalls, each approximately 20m/66ft in height, form natural pools of emerald-green waters, which are enjoyed by numerous bathers. For a birds-eye view of the park and all its natural beauty, hike up to the spring of the waterfalls.

★★**Puente de Dios** – *5km/3mi from Tamasopo waterfalls. Return to the main avenue and after passing the cathedral, turn right onto Calle Hidalgo; 0.5km/0.3mi later, exit to the right and continue on a dirt road, following the signs to "El Cafetal". The trail to the site is located just beyond the railroad tracks. ※* Inside "El Cafetal" lies this paradisiacal spot, which can be reached after descending down a relatively steep trail. The place owes its name to a natural bridge, whose rocks were sculpted by the waters of the Tamasopo River. The most torrential waterfall at this site originates from a grotto and descends from a height of some 20m/66ft. While swimming in this heavenly place, keep in mind that the currents can be quite strong.

★**Cascadas de Micos** – *25km/15.5mi. From Cd. Valles head southwest on Carr. 70 towards Río Verde; 7km/4.3mi later, turn right and continue 18km/11.2mi to reach the waterfalls. We recommend visiting between 9am and 5pm. ※ ▣.* An evocative natural environment creates the perfect setting for this series of seven waterfalls, named Cascadas de Micos due to the monkeys that previously inhabited the area. Here, magnificent Sabine trees line the riverbanks. Micos, popularly known as Pago-Pago, guarantees fun for every level of kayaker, from novice to expert. Those less inclined to engaging in adventure tourism can explore the waterfalls up close, during a 15min excursion in a small boat led by a "guide" *(donations accepted)*.

★Sótano de las Golondrinas – *59km/36.6mi. From Cd. Valles head southwest on Carr. 85; 48km/29.8mi later take the exit to Aquismón and continue 4km/2.5mi to reach the town. The site lies 7km/4.3mi southwest of Aquismón. It is advisable to hire the services of a guide recommended by the Tourist Information Office in Cd. Valles.* A veritable spelunker's paradise, this cavity enjoys international fame due to its 512m/1,680ft depth, its 376m/1,233ft free fall-ranking as the world's sixth vertical fall-and a mouth whose diameter measures 60m/197ft. Those who do not practice spelunking can admire the marvelous sight of thousands of swallows that arrive here every day, both at dawn and dusk.

★Xilitla – *76km/47mi. Exit Cd. Valles heading south on Carr. 105; just beyond Huichihuayán, after 62km/38.4mi, exit right heading towards Xilitla on Carr. 120 and continue 14km/8.7mi.* Nestled in the Sierra Madre Oriental, this coffee town with a semi-tropical climate has been a source of inspiration and joy for its inhabitants and visitors. In addition to the provincial flavor of the Huasteca, the area offers multiple natural treasures, such as the Cueva del Salitre *(guide recommended)* where waves of green parakeets arrive towards sunset. In the popular Sunday *tianguis* (market), located across from the Ex Convento de San Agustín, in the central plaza, one finds all types of regional products from surrounding villages. The town's most important festival takes place at the end of August, during which time locals celebrate the Coffee Fair and the Annual Festival of the Huapango, a musical expression native to this region.

★★Las Pozas (Casa del Inglés) – *1km/0.6mi from the town of Xilitla. Open year-round daily 9am–6pm. P$10. ✗ ☎ (1) 365-0082.* Located beside a waterfall, this surrealistic sculpture garden was designed by British poet Edward James (1907–84) descendant of King Edward VIII. Among James' friends who frequented this place are famous exponents of avant-garde art, such as Salvador Dalí and Pablo Picasso. Blending harmoniously into the tropical rain forest, this architectural project was begun in 1949 and, after 30 years of construction, still remains unfinished. It consists of tall columns and lintels that do not support anything, walls without roofs, and staircases winding into magical spaces.

MONTERREY
Nuevo León
Population 2,900,000
Map of Principal Sights – City Map p 216
🏛 Av. Hidalgo, 441 Ote. (across from the Gran Hotel Ancira)
☎ (8) 345-0870 and (01-800) 832-2200 or www.monterrey-mexico.com

Carved into a broad valley at the foot of the Sierra Madre Oriental, the state capital is surrounded by imposing rock formations, justifying the saying, "there are no mountains like those of Monterrey." The **Cerro de las Mitras**, the **"M"** of Chipinque, and the symbol of the city, **Cerro de la Silla** (Saddle Mountain) are the backdrop for the second largest industrial zone in Mexico.

Although noted for its extreme semi-arid climate, the area also suffers from severe flooding, like the inundation caused by Hurricane Gilbert in 1988. Nevertheless, the upper reaches of the mountains along Monterrey's southern edge possess abundant vegetation and moderate temperatures that serve as a refuge during the hottest months.

Monterrey's inhabitants, known as *Regiomontanos*, are proud of their prosperity and tout their city as the "industrial capital of Mexico." Because industry was established by a small number of families, it is not surprising that today last names like Garza, Sada and García predominate in the names given to streets and public places, as well as among people with high administrative or governmental posts.

Historical Notes

Beginnings and Unification – The Metropolitan City of Our Lady of Monterrey was founded on September 20, 1596 near the Santa Lucía spring by Diego de Montemayor and a group of 12 families. Named in honor of the then Viceroy of New Spain, Gaspar de Zúñiga Acevedo, Count of Monterrey, the city later fell into a long period of inactivity, broken by the **US invasion** in 1846. The signing of the Treaty of Guadalupe liberated Monterrey in 1848. Years later, the **French Intervention** posed a new threat. **Mariano Escobedo**, head of the Mexican troops, expelled the invaders, thus aiding the government of President Benito Juárez.

Industrial Powerhouse – The well-known industrialization that revitalized the city was launched at the end of the 19C. The establishment of the **brewery** in 1890 led to the opening of a **glassworks** in 1909, to produce beer bottles. About the same time, a **foundry** opened its doors to supply metal bottle caps. The Fundidora Monterrey (Monterrey Foundry), which opened in 1900, became the first iron and steel company in Latin America. Nationalized by the Mexican government in 1976, it declared bankruptcy in 1986. The smelting industry's importance to Nuevo León is reflected in the state's emblem, which depicts the chimneys of the Foundry's Furnace No. 2.

All three of these industries have been the base of the city's growth and economic power. Today, thanks to its proximity to the United States, Monterrey commands a strategic role in the regional economy.

★GRAN PLAZA (MACROPLAZA) AND SURROUNDINGS

The plaza is bordered on the north by 5 de Mayo, on the south by Av. Constitución, on the west by Av. Zaragoza and on the east by Dr. Coss (Colonia Centro).

Sharp contrasts mark this large and controversial plaza, an icon of the city. Modern buildings intermingle with old churches and open spaces, designed so citizens can enjoy the view of the mountains. Constructed in the 1980s, the plaza, popularly known as the **Macroplaza**, is composed of monuments, fountains, shopping centers, buildings and museums, all built over the site of Old Monterrey. This reflects the focus of the people of Monterrey, who look to the future instead of the past.

At 6:30pm classical music starts to pour from the speakers set up in the plaza inviting people—especially couples—to gather in its open spaces. On Sundays, men out for a stroll proudly don their white sombreros, which look out of place amid the concrete, glass and light from the laser beam atop the Beacon of Commerce. The Teatro de la Ciudad (City Theater), Biblioteca Central (Central Library), Congreso del Estado (State Legislature), Tribunal Superior de Justicia (Supreme Court) and Parque Hundido (Sunken Park) are all found in this plaza. Built at the end of the 18C, the tiny **Capilla de los Dulces Nombres** (Chapel of Sweet Tender Names) sits next to the theater *(Dr. Coss, corner of Matamoros; open year-round Tue–Sun 8:30am–12:30pm & 3–6pm, weekends until 7pm)*. The chapel's name refers to the Holy Family of Jesus, Mary and Joseph, featured in the altar painting. In front of a modern government building that houses the offices of Infonavit (the National Agency of Housing for Workers), stands the **Fuente de la Vida** (Fountain of Life, 1994), designed by Luis Anguino. A striking sculpture of Neptune graces the fountain.

Finished in 1908, the two-storied, Neoclassical **Palacio de Gobierno** *(on 5 de Mayo, between Zuazua and Zaragoza)* sits at the northern end of the plaza facing the **Explanada de los Héroes** (Esplanade of the Heroes). Six leaded, stained-glass windows, depicting famous figures, adorn the Government Palace's main facade.

Across Calle Zuazua, on the left side of the plaza, lies the monument dedicated to the workers of Nuevo León, titled **A los obreros de Nuevo León (1)** (1985), by Cuauhtémoc Zamudio.

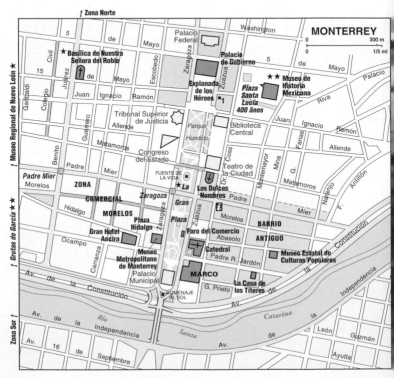

On the southern end of the Macroplaza *(on Av. Constitución)* is the monument paying homage to the sun, **Homenaje al sol**, by Rufino Tamayo.

Faro del Comercio – Built in 1984 by architect **Luis Barragán**, this bright orange beacon of commerce, a 70m/230ft column, provides great contrast to the yellow walls of the cathedral. At night, the tower emits a laser beam that illuminates different parts of the city.

Catedral Metropolitana – *General Zuazua, 1100, near the corner of Raymundo Jardón. Open year-round daily 7am–8pm.* In 1994 Monterrey was granted Mexico's third cardinalship. The cathedral's construction lasted from 1600 to 1750. In the 19C the interior, originally Baroque, was expanded and renovated in a Neoclassical style, when the clock tower was added. The Art Nouveau **murals★** (1942–45) In the apse were painted by Durango-born artist, Ángel Zárraga. The

Faro del Comercio

© Bob Schalkwijk

altar's image represents Our Lady of Monterrey with her papal tiara, received in 1996. In 1951, medallions of Saint Peter and Saint Paul were added to the silver, 18C altar covering.

Museo de Arte Contemporáneo (MARCO) – *General Zuazua, corner of Padre Raymundo Jardón. Open year-round Tue, Thu–Sat 11am–7pm, Wed & Sun 11am–9pm. P$20, free Wed.* ✗ ☎ *(8) 342-4820.* Architect **Ricardo Legorreta** was responsible for the design of this spacious building, today the site of the Museum of Contemporary Art. Founded in 1991, the museum hosts interesting temporary exhibits, some of them traveling exhibitions from other countries. A cafeteria, restaurant and bookstore offer refreshments and shopping opportunities. The statue **La Paloma** (The Dove) by **Juan Soriano** welcomes visitors at the entrance.

★★Museo de Historia Mexicana – *Dr. Coss, 445 Sur, in the Plaza Santa Lucía 400 años. Open year-round Tue–Thu 11am–7pm, Fri–Sun 11am–8pm. P$10.* ✗ ☎ *(8) 345-9898.* This enormous and imposing museum was founded in 1994. Upstairs, the permanent collection of original artifacts, interactive video screens, games and models narrate the history of Mexico from the pre-Hispanic era to the 20C. Temporary exhibits, as well as an audiovisual room with related films, are located downstairs. The building also houses an auditorium, library, video-library, cafeteria and store.

The museum is located on the **Plaza Santa Lucía 400 años**, inaugurated in 1994 in honor of the founding site of Monterrey. The plaza includes a manmade river flanked by a few restaurants.

Museo Metropolitano de Monterrey (formerly, Municipal Palace) – *Av. Zaragoza, between Hidalgo and Corregidora. Open year-round daily 8am–8pm. Closed Jan 1, May 1 and Dec 25.* ☎ *(8) 342-4820.* Built for the city council in 1612 and reconstructed in 1845, this building houses the Metropolitan Museum of Monterrey. There are two floors of temporary exhibits related to the city, nicknamed "the Sultan of the North." The rear of the building opens onto the **Plaza Hidalgo**, a peaceful haven in the middle of the bustling **Zona Comercial Morelos** where shops, hotels and restaurants abound. Built in 1901, the elegant Neoclassical **Gran Hotel Ancira** rises above one side of this inviting plaza.

Barrio Antiguo – *Bordered by Calle Dr. Coss on the west, General Matamoros on the north and Av. Constitución on the south and east. Calles Abasolo, Morelos and Fray Servando are closed to cars Thu–Sat after 6:30pm.* The majority of the homes in this attractive district, which covers 15 city blocks, were constructed or remodeled in the 19C. Today, many of them have been converted into galleries, cafes or antique shops. Others open their doors at night as bars or discos. The fascinating **Casa de los Títeres** boasts a collection of puppets from around the world *(Padre*

R. Jardón, 968; open year-round Mon–Fri 2–6pm, Sun noon–6pm; closed national holidays; P$5; ☎ 8-343-0604). The **Museo Estatal de Culturas Populares** (State Museum of Popular Culture), also known as **La Casa del Campesino** (Farmer's House), is located in Monterrey's oldest home (1769) *(Abasolo, 1024, between Mina and Naranjo; open year-round Tue–Sun 10am–6pm; closed Jan 1, May 1 and Dec 25; ☎ ☎ 8-345-6504).* A **mural★** by Crescenciano Garza Rivera (1938) adorns the ceiling and walls of La Capilla (Chapel) and depicts the history of Mexico from the Conquest to the early 20C.

CITY CENTER

★**Basilica de Nuestra Señora del Roble** – *Av. B. Juárez and 15 de mayo. Open year-round Mon–Fri 8:30am–noon & 3:30–8pm, Sat 8am–8pm, Sun 8am–1pm and 3:30–8pm.* This Romanesque basilica is the fourth religious edifice dedicated to the patron saint of Monterrey. Images related to the Virgin adorn the facade, such as a mosaic mural, as well as other depictions on the bronze entryways. According to legend, the Virgin appeared in 1592 in the hollow of an oak. Shortly after Monterrey was founded, a shepherdess was out walking when she heard voices. As she neared the oak, she encountered an effigy of the Virgin bathed in light and surrounded by a sweet aroma. The statue was carried to the parish church, only to reappear in the oak the next day. After the event occurred three times, the church was built at the location of the oak. Today the original statue is kept in a niche of the high altar. The basilica's **stained-glass windows** and marble columns are remarkable.

★**Museo Regional de Nuevo León** (Ex Obispado) – *Obispo Rafael José Verger. Open year-round Tue–Sun 10am–5pm. P$20, free Sun & holidays. ☎ (8) 333-9588.* Bishop Rafael José Verger lived in this palace until his death in 1790. Completed in 1787, the edifice is built on a hill called Loma de la Vera. It served as a fortress during the US invasion of 1846. Noteworthy is the chapel's Baroque **facade**.

On exhibit are personal belongings and historical items reflecting the state's history from its founding to the Revolution. Also featured in the museum's collection are the printing press, brought by Fray Servando Teresa de Mier to Nuevo León in 1817, a machine used to make bullets, and a variety of religious art, including 18C oil paintings by Antonio Vallejo and Miguel Zendejas.

ZONA NORTE

Cervecería Cuauhtémoc – *Av. Alfonso Reyes, 2202 Norte. Open year-round Mon–Fri 9am–5pm, Sat 9am–2pm. Closed national holidays. ☎ (8) 328-5355.* This brewery offers numerous attractions, such as the guided tour that outlines the factory's history and introduces visitors to the manufacturing process, during which up to 1,200 bottles per minute are produced. Guests can quench their thirst in the garden by sampling free Carta Blanca beer, the pride of the Regiomontanos. The **Salón de la Fama del Béisbol Profesional de México**, also located in the gardens, is Mexico's version of a baseball hall-of-fame. Personal items belonging to national well-known players and the stories of how these men rose to fame are the focus of the exhibit *(open year-round Tue–Fri 9:30am–5:30pm, Sat–Sun 10:30am–6pm; closed national holidays; ☎ 8-328-5815).*

★★**Museo de Monterrey** – *Located in the gardens of the Cervecería Cuauhtémoc, Av. Alfonso Reyes, 2202, Norte. Open year-round Tue, Thu–Sun 11am–8pm, Wed 10am–8pm. Closed Jan 1, Dec 25. ✗ ☎ (8) 328-6060.* Since 1977, important exhibitions have been held in what was a brewery until 1930. Today, this museum displays a valuable permanent collection of modern and contemporary Latin American art, with the emphasis on Mexican works. From the third floor, there is a great view of the wrought-iron stairs, as well as a display of antique vats, once used to brew beer. The museum also possesses a bookstore and a mediateque that allows the public to conduct art research and studies by means of multimedia and electronic resources, such as the Internet.

★**Pinacoteca de Nuevo León** – *Av. Alfonso Reyes, in the Parque Niños Héroes. Open year-round Tue–Sun 10am–6pm. Closed Jan 1, Dec 25. ☎ (8) 331-5472.* This permanent collection of paintings and sculptures introduces visitors to the history of fine arts in Nuevo León since the end of the 19C. The chronological tour passes through two floors of pioneering works of art by Eligio Fernández and Ignacio Martínez Rendón, engravings by Manuel Durón, and paintings by Gerardo Cantú and Guillermo Ceniceros, among others. Sculptures like **La Ola** (The Wave) by Fidias Elizondo and works by Federico Cantú are also worthy of note. The second building features temporary exhibits of sculptures and paintings of national and international stature.

The art gallery is located in the **Parque Niños Héroes** *(open year-round daily 9am–7pm. P$3; boat rentals P$5; fishing P$15 for fishing pole; ✗ 🅴 ☎ 8-351-2817).* This park boasts a botanical garden, aviary, small lake and children's playground and is also the site of La Casa de la Tecnología (House of Technology), Museo del Automóvil (Museum of the Automobile) and the **Museo de la Fauna y Ciencias Naturales** (Museum of Fauna and Natural Sciences).

★**Museo del Vidrio** – *Zaragoza and Magallanes, 517, in the Vidriera Monterrey. Open year-round Fri–Wed 9am–6pm. Closed Jan 1, May 1, Dec 24 & 25.* ☏ *(8) 329-1000 or www.museovidrio.vto.com.* Opened in 1992 inside the former office buildings of the Monterrey glassworks, the Museum of Glass begins its collection on the first floor with the history of glass and continues on the second floor, emphasizing the value of glass to handicrafts and industry. Among the highlights are "La Nacional," a mid-19C pharmacy brought here from Teotihuacán, the old glass-making workshop from the Casa Pellandini-Marco, and other displays that narrate the history of the Vidriera Monterrey.

Farther ahead, another building houses a gallery with temporary exhibits and a gift store with a wide variety of glass objects.

ZONA SUR

★**Planetario Alfa** – *Av. Roberto Garza Sada, 1000. Take Av. Gómez Morín. Open year-round Tue–Fri 3–9pm, Sat 2–9pm, Sun noon–9pm. Closed Dec 24 & 31. P$25 (P$43 with movie).* ✗ ☏ *(8) 356-5696 or www.planetarioalfa.org.mx.* The profile of the main building resembles a telescope pointed at the sky. Upon entering, visitors are greeted by six huge aquariums with freshwater species. The interior consists of five levels-the first two dedicated to art, science and technology. On the third floor, interactive games and presentations explore various phenomena related to physics, chemistry and optics. On the fourth level, children and adults alike can test their knowledge of the principles of physics. The exhibit of eight different Mesoamerican cultures on the fifth floor consists of a **collection**★★ of archaeological pieces, details of the indigenous peoples' lives prior to the arrival of the Spanish, and videos of related topics. Located in the center of the complex, the multi-theater **Omnimax** seats 300 people and boasts a hemispheric projection screen with a diameter of 24m/79ft *(showings Tue–Fri 4pm, 5:30pm, 7pm & 8:30pm; Sat each hr 2:30–9pm; Sun each hr 12:30–9pm).* The planetarium also has gardens-devoted to scientific and pre-Hispanic themes-and an aviary, home to approximately 200 birds, representing 15 different species. The modern **Pabellón El Universo** shelters the only **stained-glass window**★ ever conceived by artist **Rufino Tamayo**. Made of laminated glass, this work depicts the creation of the universe and was produced in Mexico by the Dutch company Van Tetterode.

★★**Parque Ecológico Chipinque** – *17km/11mi south of Monterrey on Av. Gómez Morín. Be aware of oncoming traffic while driving up the narrow road. Open year-round daily 6am–8pm. P$5.* ✗ ☏ *(8) 303-0000.* This 1,625ha/4,015-acre forest, located at the foot of the Cerro de la "M," boasts trails and open spaces, ideal for jogging or cycling. The ecological park is also home to woodpeckers and opossums. The Chipinque meseta (1,270m/4,167ft), located about 7km/4mi away, is the highest point reachable by car. Overlooks along the road to the summit offer lovely **views**★ of the city of Monterrey.

EXCURSIONS

★★**Grutas de García** – *Located in central Nuevo León. From Monterrey, take Carretera. fed. 40 toward Saltillo. After 23km/14mi, take the exit to the municipality of Villas de García and continue 25km/16mi. The entrance to the grottoes is located 9km/6mi from the center of town. Open year-round daily 9am–5pm. Closed Dec 12. P$30.* ✗ Situated beneath a peak called the "Indian's Head," the spectacular formations of García's Grottoes were created over a period of 50 million years by stalactites and stalagmites. The opening to the grottoes is reached by a cable car that ascends a steep 750m/2,461ft trajectory. Fairylike figures, located throughout the 2km/1.2mi circuit, have sparked the imagination of visitors since 1843, when the grottoes were first discovered by Father Juan Antonio de Sobrevilla. Among the most notable phenomena is the "Eighth Wonder of the World," a surprising union of a stalactite and a stalagmite.

★**Cascada Cola de Caballo** – *The waterfall is located in southern Nuevo León, 44km/27mi from Monterrey on Carr. 85 toward Linares. Shortly after Santiago, turn right and continue 6km/4mi to the entrance.* From the banks of the stream, a trail traverses lush vegetation to the famous cascade, which issues from a spring-fed water deposit. The cascade has a height of 25m/82ft and resembles a horse's tail, and is especially frothy in periods of heavy rain.

In Santiago, across the highway, is the **Presa de la Boca** (La Boca Dam), where visitors can practice water sports and savor fresh seafood.

■ The Towns of Nuevo León

Map of Principal Sights. The small towns of Nuevo León are scattered over roads coursing the heart of the Sierra Madre Oriental. In this area of semi-desert plains and enormous orange groves, American music is heard as often as the cadences of the Huastecs. Simple, thick-walled homes constructed of adobe populate these communities, which also boast video clubs, 24-hour Oxxo stores and cars bearing American license plates. The atmosphere in these towns is unique.

Linares is the birthplace of the tasty *glorias*, scorched milk and sugar confections. In addition to its traditional breads, **Bustamante** offers visitors nearby grottoes and spring-fed ponds, called *ojos de agua*, which are dispersed throughout the area. Also nearby is the **Parque Nacional Cumbres de Monterrey**, the largest national park in Mexico with 246,500ha/609,102 acres. The town of **Mina** has **Boca de Potrerillos**, an archaeological site with approximately 3,000 petroglyphs *(57km/36mi northwest of Monterrey; open year-round Tue–Sun 9am–6pm).* Near the settlement of **Zuazua** stands the **Hacienda de San Pedro★★** *(32km/20mi north of Monterrey; open year-round Mon–Fri 9am–2pm; ☎ 8-247-0510),* which dates back to the 17C and houses the Regional History Information Center.

The people of Nuevo León are religious and spirited. Many wear white sombreros with pride and brag about being *neoleonenses* and Mexicans, in that order. A phrase inscribed on a sign found at the edge of **Iturbide**, a small town set in the mountains of southern Nuevo León, says it best: "One hand braced to God, the other on the hoe."

SALTILLO

Coahuila
Population 527,979
Map of Principal Sights
🅱 Blvd. Echeverría, 1560, Edificio Torre Saltillo, piso 11
☎ (8) 415-7936 and (01-800) 718-4220

This tranquil city, surrounded by the arid mountains of the Sierra Madre Oriental, was founded in 1577 by Captain Alberto del Canto. The founding site lies next to a waterfall, for which the city was named. In 1591 the Villa de San Esteban de la Nueva Tlaxcala was founded nearby and inhabited by Tlaxcaltec families from central Mexico in order to thwart attacks by the Rayados, Borrados and Guachichiles that were disrupting the development of the city. When Texas proclaimed its independence in 1836, Saltillo became the capital of Coahuila. Since the 19C, the city has been called the "Athens of Northern Mexico" thanks to the quality and quantity of its educational institutions. Saltillo is also famous for multicolor sarapes.

SIGHTS

★★Catedral de Santiago – *Juárez and Hidalgo, facing the Plaza de Armas. Zona Centro. Open year-round daily 8am–1pm & 4–8pm.* Considered one of Mexico's most beautiful cathedrals, this building was constructed between 1745 and 1800, next to the Capilla del Santo Cristo (Chapel of Christ the Saint) which dates from 1762. The Baroque **main facade★** bears Solomonic columns in the first section and *estípite* in the second. Thick columns adorned with the image of the Virgin of Zapopan flank both sections. The characteristic shell located above the central door is repeated on the exterior as well as the interior.

Interior – The cathedral's layout is a Latin cross, and the central altar is graced with the image of St. James the Apostle, patron of the city. On the cupola, an iconographical history of the salvation is depicted in colorful relief, culminating in the image of Christ at the top. The right side of the cathedral shelters the **Altar de San José** (St. Joseph's Altar). Golden in color, the Baroque-Solomonic altarpiece is adorned with a painting of the **Sacred Family** by José de Alcíbar, who also completed some of the works in the central nave. The silver **frontal★**, located at the foot of the altar, was engraved in the middle of the 18C and is widely considered a masterpiece of sacred art of this type. The **pulpit** with gold overlay in the central nave also merits attention.

Museo Rubén Herrera – *Bravo, Norte. 342. Open year-round Mon–Fri 4:30pm–8pm, Sat–Sun 10am–1pm & 3–8pm. If the museum is closed, inquire within. ☎ (8) 412-5939.* The residence of the renowned artist Rubén Herrera (1888–1933), founder of Saltillo's Academy of Painting, opened as a museum in 1971 and exhibits approximately 125 of his works. Portraits and paintings of the human figure predominate in the collection.

★**Museo de las Aves de México** – *Hidalgo and Bolívar. Zona Centro. Open year-round Tue–Sat 10am–6pm, Sun 11am–6pm. P$10.* ✗ 🄴 🕾 *(8) 414-0167.* Built in the middle of the 19C, this building, today devoted to the birds of Mexico, was once the Colegio de San Juan (School of St. John). Open since 1993, the museum has a collection of 2,100 preserved specimens, representing 75% of the birds in Mexico. The quetzal and harpy eagle, both in danger of extinction, highlight the exhibit.

Alameda Zaragoza – *Calles Cuauhtémoc, Aldama, Purcell and Ramos, 0.5km/0.3mi from the Plaza de Armas.* Shaded by poplars and ash trees, this park is adorned with eight monuments, one of which is dedicated to **Ignacio Zaragoza**, the general who defeated the French at Puebla on May 5, 1862. The tiny **Lago de la República** was thus named because the lake's shape resembles that of Mexico. Considered one of the most beautiful parks in the country, it attracts joggers and students from nearby schools. The grounds also contain two libraries.

Ateneo Fuente – *Blvd. Venustiano Carranza and Av. Universidad. Open Jul–Aug daily 9am–3pm. Rest of the year Mon–Fri 9am–3pm.* 🕾 *(8) 415-7513.* Constructed in 1933, this beautiful Art Deco building is home to the Ateneo Fuente institution, founded in the 19C as Mexico's first senior high school. The name combines Saltillo's nickname of "Athens of Northern Mexico" with the last name of Don Juan Antonio de la Fuente, a government minister under president Benito Juárez. The school still operates today.

In the building's north wing, the **art gallery**★ *(open year-round Mon–Fri 9am–1pm; closed Dec 20–Jan 6;* 🕾 *8-415-7572 ext. 22)* displays a collection of paintings, spanning the 17C to 1920. The 19C works were completed in the Academy of San Carlos. Worthy of note are the *Leyenda de los volcanes* (Legend of the Volcanoes) (1910) by Saturnino Herrán, *San Pedro* (St. Peter) by Juan Rodríguez Juárez, as well as a copy of *The Flight of Lot* by Peter Paul Rubens. On the first floor of the south wing is the **Museo de Historia Natural** *(same times and charges as the Ateneo Fuente)*. This museum of natural history shows preserved animals, rocks and fossils. On the fourth floor, the **Salon of Colonial Art Artemio de Valle Arizpe** exhibits colonial furniture from the 17C to the 18C, the majority of which belonged to De Valle Arizpe, a writer from Coahuila *(same times and charges as the Ateneo Fuente; if the room is closed, inquire at the museum)*.

EXCURSIONS

Parras de la Fuente – *Located 157km/97mi from Saltillo. Go 129km/80mi on Carr. 40, then exit left and continue 28km/17mi to the town.* The greenness of this pleasant town greatly contrasts its desert-like surroundings. Due to the favorable climate, grapes were cultivated in this fertile valley, called the "Oasis of Coahuila," long before the town's founding in 1598. In the 19C, local wine production was the most important in Mexico. Highlights of Parras include the white-walled **Hacienda de San Lorenzo**★ *(7km/4mi north of Parras on the road to La Paila; open year-round daily 9am–5pm;* 🕾 *8-422-0111),* which Lorenzo García established in 1597 as the continent's first winery. The late-16C **Templo de San Ignacio de Loyola** (Church of St. Ignatius of Loyola) is furnished with an 18C Baroque altarpiece *(Madero and Treviño, beside the Plaza Hidalgo; open year-round daily 10am–6pm).* The **Museo María y Matheo** located inside the church displays documents, books and old paintings *(open year-round daily 10am–1pm and 4–6pm; if closed, ask the custodian to open it).* Finally, the **Santuario de Guadalupe** (Sanctuary of Guadalupe) bears an austere facade and houses pretty Baroque and Neoclassical altarpieces, as well as 16–18C paintings *(Viesca and Ocampo; open year-round daily 7am–5pm).*

Torreón – *Located 278km/173mi from Saltillo on Carr. 40 or 162km/101mi from Parras de la Fuente.* Situated in the busy Comarca Lagunera (Lake District), Torreón was founded in 1883 and acquired the rank of city in 1907. During the Revolution, in 1914, rebel and outlaw Pancho Villa captured the city after demolishing the federal army of Dictator Victoriano Huerta. Noteworthy attractions include the **Teatro Isauro Martínez** *(Matamoros, corner of Galeana; when there are no performances in the theater, the entrance is at Galeana, 73, Sur; open year-round Mon–Fri 10am–2pm and 4–8pm; closed Holy Week and the last two weeks in Dec;* 🕾 *1-716-6261).* Because of its **interior**★★, this theater is considered the second most beautiful in Mexico. Valencian artist Salvador Tarazona created its mural paintings and stuccowork, inspired by oriental themes. The front stage boasts a diadem of stucco sculptures, which are illuminated from behind. Above and on either side of these, huge paintings depict street festivals, dramatic effects and Asian motives, especially from India. Abundant plasterwork adorns the columns, box seating and the **central ceiling**.

Bilbao Dunes

★ **Dunas de Bilbao** – *55km/34mi from Torreón. Take Carr. 40 toward Saltillo and go 45km/28mi to the town of Emiliano Zapata, then take the exit to Viesca. Continue 10km/6mi to the entrance to the dunes.* Covered with spectacular sand dunes formed by erosion, this desert has been the setting for numerous films, as it conjures images of an exotic African landscape.

★ **Puente de Ojuela** – *70km/43mi from Torreón. Take Carr. 49 toward the city of Chihuahua. Take the exit in Bermejillo and go left on Carr. 30 toward Mapimí. Continue 21.5km/13mi to the entrance to the road leading to the bridge and then another 7km/4mi to the bridge itself.* Constructed in 1892, this bridge is the longest in Mexico, suspended 315m/1,034ft in length. It was built over a gorge, with a depth of 95m/312ft, to facilitate local silver production and connect the mine with the production plant. Nearby, the ruins of a ghost town, once home to 2,000 miners, provide a magnificent **view**★ of the valley.

★ **Zona del Silencio** – *Go 128km/79mi west on Carr. 49, toward the city of Chihuahua until reaching Ceballos. From this town, a road through a gap leads to the Zone of Silence, still 50km/30mi away. This region extends between the Vértice de Trino, where the states of Coahuila, Durango and Chihuahua intersect, and the Valley of Allende. Visitors should be accompanied by a guide. An overnight stay is recommended, as well as carrying a compass, a portable radio preset to an AM station, and a magnet for recovering micrometeorites.* So named because in certain parts of this mysterious desert the transmission of radio waves is obstructed, the legendary Zone of Silence was declared a Biosphere Reserve in 1975. Marine species like the turtle have adapted well to this ecological niche. High levels of ultraviolet rays in the area have caused mutations in the genes of local plants and animals; for example, the unique turtle has yellow eyes and triangular markings on its body, while the prickly-pear cactus is violet instead of green. Large numbers of micrometeorites and magnetic rocks can be found here as well as metalized marine fossils that date back to the Lower Cretaceous period. The night sky bursts with a myriad of stars, satellites and constellations. During certain times of the year, static electricity produces light phenomena, and for people sensitive to the frequency, their hair can sometimes stand on end.

★★ **Pozas de Cuatro Ciénegas** – *277km/172mi from Saltillo, 252km/156mi from Torreón or 82km/51mi from Monclova via Carr. 30.* The Valley of Cuatro Ciénegas (Four Marshes) is home to approximately 60 endemic species of plants and animals that live near the more than 200 *pozas*, unique spring-fed water deposits scattered about the desert. These transparent pools issue from subterranean sources of water, containing high levels of minerals. Surrounded by gorgeous mountain scenery, the *pozas* acquire a turquoise-blue color, unimaginable in the midst of this arid valley. When Cuatro Ciénegas was decreed a protected area for wild animal and plant life, access to many of the *pozas* was no longer permitted. In addition, the physical terrain prevents easy access to others. **Azul**★, **La Becerra**★, **Las Playitas**★ and **Balneario Río Los Mezquites** rank among the most popular.

SAN LUIS POTOSÍ★

San Luis Potosí
Population 625,466
Map of Principal Sights – City Map below
🏛 Álvaro Obregón, 520, Downtown, ☎ (4) 812-9939

The warmth of its people characterizes this state capital. Declared a Historic Landmark in 1990, its rich Baroque structures carved from quarry stone survive amid the elegant but severe Neoclassical downtown area.

Historical Notes

Drawn by the deposits of gold and silver of the nearby Cerro de San Pedro, Fray Diego de la Magdalena, Juan de Oñate and Captain Miguel Caldera founded this city in 1592. It was given the name San Luis in honor of King Louis XIV of France, and Potosí because of its comparison to the splendid Bolivian mines of Cerro de Potosí. The city was laid out in grids like a chessboard to provide access to the religious buildings that surround it. By 1631 San Luis Potosí was already the third most important city of the Viceroyalty. Benito Juárez moved the state capital here in 1863 and, again, in 1867, when he refused to accept the government of Maximilian of Hapsburg and instead attempted to restore the Republic. In 1910, after his imprisonment in the city, Francisco I. Madero proclaimed the Plan de San Luis, which denounced the reelection of Porfirio Díaz and launched the Mexican Revolution. Today, the city is an industrial powerhouse marked by democratic activity, reflected in recent years by the efforts of Salvador Nava Martínez.

★★CITY CENTER

★★**Plaza de los Fundadores (Plazuela de la Compañía)** – *Av. Álvaro Obregón, Av. Damián Carmona and Av. Venustiano Carranza.* The land for the Plaza of the Founders, the birthplace of the city, was ceded to the Society of Jesus (Jesuits) in 1621. Construction of the Neoclassical **Templo de la Compañía** was completed during the 18C. It stands north of the plaza next to the lovely **Capilla de Loreto**, which has a Baroque portal. A **building** belonging to the Autonomous University of San Luis Potosí (UASLP) stands beside the chapel. Its central courtyard preserves the vestiges of the Jesuit school once located here *(open year-round Mon–Fri 8am–8pm;* ☎ *4-812-2357).*

The **Edificio Ipiña** rises on the west side of the plaza. This Neoclassical edifice was constructed between 1906 and 1912 from quarry rock. Vendors set up shop under the building's pedestrian arcade.

Plaza de Armas (Jardín Hidalgo) – *Allende and Hidalgo.* Adorned with a central pavilion, this tree-shaded plaza pays homage to eight Mexican musicians. On the northern part of the plaza stands the **Casa de la Virreyna (A)**. Built in 1736, this house is considered the oldest in the city and was the former residence of Doña Francisca de la Gándora, the only Mexican woman to hold the title of vicereine, female equivalent of viceroy. Today, the complex includes a restaurant, **Posada del Virrey**. The pedestrian zone **Calle de Hidalgo**, an important commercial street since the early 19C, extends from one side of the house. On the same street, near the plaza, stands the Neoclassical **Palacio de Cristal (B)** (1909, Guindon).

Palacio de Gobierno (PG) – *Jardín Hidalgo, 11. Open year-round daily 9am–3pm and 6–9pm.* ☎ *(4) 812-9480.* Begun at the end of the 18C, this austere Neoclassical building was constructed as the site of the new Casas Reales (Royal Houses). The second floor contains a depiction of the meeting between Benito Juárez and Princess Salm-Salm on June 18, 1867, when

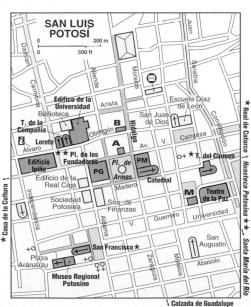

Juárez denied her request to pardon Maximilian of Hapsburg and had him executed the next day. One may also visit the Sala Hidalgo (Hidalgo Room) and the Reception Room.

Palacio Municipal (PM) – *Jardín Hidalgo, 5. Open year-round Mon–Fri 8am–3pm.* ☎ *(4) 814-4142.* This 19C edifice was built over the remains of the former Royal Houses, which were partially destroyed in the revolt following the expulsion of the Jesuits, ordered by Charles III of Spain in 1767. Its **interior** features a forked staircase, from which visitors can appreciate a **stained-glass window** with the city's emblem. Oil paintings by Italian artist Erulo Eroli decorate the **ceiling** in the council room located on the second floor.

Cathedral – *Jardín Hidalgo. Open year-round daily 9am–2pm & 4–7pm.* Head of the Guanajuato and Querétaro diocese, this cathedral was begun in 1670 and consecrated in 1730. The Baroque **facade★** features Solomonic columns, *estípite* pilasters and two large, smooth buttresses. Also adorning the facade are sculptures of the Apostles, which were carved from Carrara marble as smaller copies of the sculptures at the Basilica of St. John Lateran in Rome. The structure is designed like a basilica with three naves. The church was granted cathedral status in the mid 19C. During the same period, the current Neoclassical altars were added to the **interior**. In 1896 Bishop Montes de Oca redecorated it in the Byzantine style. A few paintings from the colonial era by José Paez and Morlete Ruíz, as well as a gigantic 19C pipe organ, are also preserved. The main altar venerates Our Lady of Expectation, patron saint of the city.

★Templo del Carmen – *Plaza del Carmen. Open year-round daily 9:30am–1:30pm & 4–8:30pm.* Built in the mid 18C, the impressive Baroque Church of the Carmelites faces a beautiful and tranquil plaza. The **main portal★★** is designed in the Churrigueresque style with Solomonic columns and contains a detailed stone carving of six angels supporting a curtain that appears to cascade over the figure of the Lord. A statue of the Virgin of Carmen resides in a niche below.

© Fernando García Aguinaco

Templo del Carmen

Interior – The church's single nave is adorned with sumptuous Churrigueresque altarpieces. Two golden altars, carved from stone, stand near the transept. To the left of the transept is the **Capilla del Santísimo** (Chapel of the Most Holy) and its **portal★** decorated with several colorful figures of saints and angels. In the interior a gilded altar, remodeled in the 20C, shelters the Virgin of Carmen. A huge conch shell extends over the altar. To the right of the transept, the **sacristy** boasts nine large canvases (1764) by Francisco Vallejo, which represent the life of St. Elias.

Teatro de la Paz – *Segunda de Villerías, Jardín del Carmen. Open year-round Tue–Sun 10am–2pm & 5–8pm. Closed national holidays.* ☎ *(4) 812-2698.* The Theater of Peace, an elegant Neoclassical building made of quarry stone, was designed by architect José Noriega. The prose and verses of the poet Manuel José Othón enhanced its inauguration in 1894. Rebuilt in the mid 20C, the theater has kept its original layout. The facade's frontispiece rests on a cornice supported by slender columns. Its U-shaped **interior** seats 1,500 spectators. Murals designed by Fernando Leal and executed in mosaic by Ramón Sánchez decorate the stairways.

★Museo Nacional de la Máscara (M) – *Villerías, 2. Open year-round Tue–Fri 10am–2pm & 4–6pm, Sat–Sun 10am–2pm. Closed national holidays (except Holy Week). P$2.* ☎ *(4) 812-3025.* This French Neoclassical structure boasts wrought-iron decorations in its interior. Completed in 1898, it originally served as the residence of Spanish landowner Don Ramón Martí. In 1904 it was sold to the Mexican government. Since 1982 the museum has exhibited a collection of approximately 750 masks, accompanied by excellent displays regarding the largely ceremonial role that masks have played throughout the country and during different periods of Mexican history.

★**Templo de San Francisco** – *Plaza San Francisco. Open year-round daily 7am–1:30pm & 4:30–8pm.* Completed in the early 18C, the Church of St. Francis boasts a Baroque facade carved from pink quarry stone and adorned with sculptures of saints and Franciscan emblems. The building's **interior** is laid out in the shape of a Latin cross and decorated with paintings by Antonio Torres and Francisco Martínez. An enormous chandelier hangs from the dome above the nave. Legend describes how the chandelier, which is shaped like a ship, was given as a votive offering by a survivor of a wreck at sea.

★**Sacristy** – This large room features paintings by Martínez, Torres and Miguel Cabrera. A stone **relief** covered with polychrome depicts an episode of St. Francis' life and adorns the door splays opening onto the **Sala de Profundis**. This large room contains a reproduction of the old main altar, designed in the Baroque *estípite* fashion.

Museo Regional Potosino – *Plaza Aránzazu. Open year-round Tue–Sat 10am–7pm, Sun 10am–5pm. P$10.* ✗ ☎ *(4) 814-3572.* This regional museum is located inside the former Monastery of St. Francis, which was shut down and divided up in 1859. Since 1952, the museum has exhibited archaeological pieces of several different Mesoamerican cultures. This collection includes items found at the Laguna de la Media Luna, belonging to the Guachichile, who are associated with the Pame culture. The Huastec room features a replica of the adolescent from Tamuín. Representing a young Quetzalcóatl or "plumed serpent," the original piece was discovered at the archaeological site of El Consuelo *(description p 226)*. This room also displays sculptures related to the cult of fertility. In fact, many likenesses of the goddess of fertility, Tlazolteotl, have been found in the area. The anthropomorphic sculptures, characteristic of the Huastec region, are tied to the cult of the phallus. The upper level displays a collection of wrought-iron pieces, made between the 16C and 20C, as well as the original act of the foundation of the city.

★**Capilla de Aránzazu** – This once private chapel of the Franciscan monks was built between 1750 and 1758 and is considered a significant architectural landmark of northern Mexico. The chapel is noteworthy for its odd placement on the upper floor of the building, for its covered atrium and for the triple *estípite* pilasters, divided into five sections; 18C paintings by Miguel Cabrera and Pedro López Calderón grace the interior. The left transept leads to the damaged sacristy and a small chamber with a 2m/6.5ft, 17C Christ made of corn stalks.

CALZADA DE GUADALUPE

Along Av. Benito Juárez between the historic center and the Sanctuary of Guadalupe.

Several interesting structures—such as a **penitentiary**, built in 1904, where revolutionary leader Francisco I. Madero was imprisoned—flank this pleasant, tree-lined roadway. The **Caja de Agua**★ (Water Box), symbol of the city and one of the most beautiful Neoclassical structures in Mexico, stands a street away from the Mercado Tangamanga. It was built at the beginning of the 19C and designed by José María Guerrero y Solachi. The people of San Luis Potosí were supplied with water—guarded like a treasure—that issued from the Cañada del Lobo (Wolf Ravine). The roadway ends at the **Santuario de Guadalupe**★ *(open year-round Mon–Sat & holidays 6:30am–11pm, Sun 5:30am–11pm).* The 18C sanctuary, of mixed Baroque and Neoclassical styles, stands next to the city's oldest building, a hermitage built in 1656. In the sanctuary's elegant and dignified interior, in the shape of a Latin cross, the Neoclassical high altar features a painting of the Virgin of Guadalupe by Jesús Corral. As in the Church of St. Francis, a votive offering, made of glass and molded like a ship, suspends from the ceiling.

ADDITIONAL SIGHT

★**Casa de la Cultura** – *Av. Venustiano Carranza, 1815. West of the historic center. Open year-round Tue–Fri 10am–2pm & 4–6pm, Sat 10am–2pm & 6–8pm, Sun 10am–2pm. P$5.* ☎ *(4) 813-2247.* This elegant mansion was designed in an English Neoclassical style and rebuilt at the beginning of the 20C. It was then the country residence of Don Gerardi Meade Lewis. Inside are Huastec archaeological pieces, as well as fascinating objects of religious art, ranging from European to Mexican from the 16C to the present. The Italian Gothic Revival **altar** dates from the end of the 19C. Also of note are the 18C corn-stalk Christ figures, antique furnishings, *rebozos* (shawls) from the town of Santa María del Río, and paintings by José María Velasco and Claudio José Vernet. Recitals, conferences and film festivals are held in this building, which also has an auditorium and library.

EXCURSIONS

Santa María del Río – *Some 50km/31mi south of San Luis Potosí. Head south on Carr. 57, towards Querétaro; 50km/31mi later, turn right to enter the town.* Considered "the world capital of the *rebozo*," Santa María del Río has a long tradition of handcrafting one of the most representative articles of a Mexican woman's folkloric attire: the *rebozo* (a long and narrow stole or shawl). While these are made in private homes throughout town, it is possible to see the entire process in the artisan schools, located around the central plaza, and to purchase one of these colorful shawls. The **Escuela de Artesanías** *(Jardín Hidalgo, 5; open year-round Mon–Sat 9am–7pm & Sun 10am–1pm; closed national holidays; ☎ 4-853-0568)*, was inaugurated in 1953.

*★**Real de Catorce** – *260km/161mi north of San Luis Potosí. Go north on Carr. 57. Continue through Matehuala (202km/125mi) and take Carr. 62, toward Cedral. After 30km/18mi, take a left onto the gravel road that continues 23km/14mi to the entrance of Real de Catorce.* Practically a ghost town, this village is reached via the famous **Ogarrio Tunnel**, built at the end of the 19C as part of a local mine. Founded in 1778, Real de Catorce was once one of the most prosperous mining towns in New Spain. The origin of its name is steeped in two legends, which recount the story of either 14 robbers or soldiers who were murdered in this mountain range. Despite difficult access and high altitude (2,756m/9,042ft), sumptuous buildings-vestiges of which still remain-were erected in this magical setting. At its peak, Real de Catorce had a population of 30,000. In the early 20C, however, the town was slowly abandoned as a result of the Revolution, the decline in silver prices and the flooding of the mines.

The town's attractions include the **Casa de Moneda** (Mint). This large structure was opened as a mint in 1863, but only functioned for three years, which explains why the minted coins are so prized by collectors. Other sights include the 18C **Templo de la Purísima Concepción**; the **Museo Parroquial**; the well-preserved **Palenque de Gallos★** (Cockfight Arena) with excellent acoustics; and the **Templo de Guadalupe**. A monumental stone wall surrounds this church and the **Panteón de Guadalupe** (Guadalupe Cemetery). Across from the Church of Guadalupe, which only holds worship services three times a year, stand the **Alameda** and the **Plaza de Toros**, with a marvelous **view** of the ravine and valley.

■ Pilgrimage to Real de Catorce

Each year, following the October festival in honor of the beloved St. Francis of Assisi, the Huichol initiate a three-day (550km/342mi-long) pilgrimage from Nayarit to **Wirikuta**-as they call the sacred grounds of nearby Cerro del Quemado. Upon arriving at this hill, the center of their world, they leave offerings-such as Huichol textiles, deer antlers and children's drawings-and prepare to celebrate their ritual "hunt" for the hallucinogen *peyote-venado*.

Peyote is a small underground cactus, the tip of which surfaces above ground. The search for the blue deer *(venado)*-a sacred animal which the Huichol associate with the peyote-is initiated by a spiritual guide, or *marakame*, who begins digging at a spot where only he can see the blue deer. He then uncovers a treasure of peyotes and shares them with the rest of the group.

Ironically, this centuries-old tradition may soon come to an end due to a growing number of tourists drawn to these sacred grounds in search of a free drug, whose nine alkaloids produce a trance that may liberate them from a material world and temporal constraints. As a result, peyote is becoming increasingly difficult to find.

---

*★★**Huasteca Potosina** – *Accessed through Ciudad Valles, located 264km/164mi east of San Luis Potosí. Description p 213.*

TAMPICO

Tamaulipas
Population 278,933
Map of Principal Sights
🛈 20 de Noviembre, 218 Norte, City Center
☏ (1) 212-0007 and (01-800) 715-7100

With nearby Ciudad Madero, this port city forms a metropolitan area at the mouth of the Pánuco River and also marks the border of the states of Tamaulipas and Veracruz. The importance of petroleum in Tampico has converted the port into one of the most important in Mexico.

The development of the city was disrupted by attacks from the Chichimecs in the 16C and pirate raids in the 17C, as well as the attempted Spanish Reconquista (Reconquest) in 1829 and other 19C wars.

Sport fishing for shad in the **Laguna de Chairel** and marlin in the Gulf of Mexico has brought worldwide fame to this port. Art Nouveau buildings surrounding the renovated **Plaza de la Libertad** evoke the second half of the 19C, when New Orleans-style architecture with wrought-iron balconies and supporting iron columns flourished in the city. A lovely example of this architectural style is the dockside **Aduana** (Customs) building, constructed in 1902.

SIGHTS

Laguna del Carpintero (Carpenter's Lagoon) – *Blvd. Fidel Velázquez.* Visitors can take pleasant boat rides on the lagoon, situated only six streets from the city center, to observe turtles, iguanas, lizards, cranes and ducks. Visible from the park is the 1,500m/4,922ft **Puente de Tampico**, a bridge that can withstand winds of up to 300km/186mi per hour. A streetcar departs from the park and takes a 30-minute trip through the city center. Because of the calm waters, this lagoon is considered a great track for speedboat racing and is often the site for international competitions.

Museo de la Cultura Huasteca – *Av. 1 de Mayo and Sor Juana in the Instituto Tecnológico de Madero (Technological Institute of Madero). Take Blvd. López Mateos. At Ejército Nacional, turn right and continue to Sarabia. Then turn left at Av. Del Maestro and continue to 1 de Mayo. Open year-round Mon–Sat 10am–5pm.* ✕ ☏ *(1) 210-2217.* This small museum exhibits an interesting collection of archaeological artifacts from the nomadic Huastec culture, such as obsidian arrowheads that date back to 1000 BC, clay figurines and pre-Hispanic pottery. A replica of the Adolescent from Tamuín and samples of contemporary clothing worn by local indigenous women also hold particular interest. In another exhibit, visitors learn that the Huastecs and Totonacs had already discovered crude petroleum or tar, which they used for painting.

Playa Miramar – *15km/9mi from Tampico. Take Blvd. López Mateos. Cross the train tracks and continue straight ahead. Alternate access is provided on Calle Obregón.* This ample 10km/6mi-long beach boasts fine, fine sand and warm waters. All along the beach, vendors sell figures made from seashells. A pier extends south of the beach near the mouth of the Pánuco River, where visitors can observe dolphins or watch the fishing boats and cargo ships from all over the world as they leave the port. Also visible is a 15-ton breakwater torn from the base of the pier by Hurricane Gilbert in 1988.

EXCURSION

★★**Huasteca Potosina** – *Accessible from Ciudad Valles, 138km/86mi west of Tampico. Description p 213.*

Planning a trip to the United States?
Don't forget to take along the Michelin Road Map (No. 930).

ZACATECAS★★★

Zacatecas
Population 118,742
Map of Principal Sights – City Map opposite
🆔 Av. Hidalgo, 403 ☎ (4) 924-4047 and 922-3426

At an altitude of 2,496m/8,187ft, this state capital stands out for the friendliness of its people and the striking contrast between its blue sky and red earth. Its magnificence is reflected in the well-preserved colonial architecture carved from pink quarry stone. Zacatecas was founded in 1546 by the Spanish conquistadors Juan de Tolosa, Baltazar Termiño de Bañuelos, Cristóbal de Oñate and Diego de Ibarra.

Historical Notes

Origins and Colonial Era – Originally inhabited by the Zacatec, Caxcan, Guachichil, Tecuex and Irritila, this region is blessed with rich mineral deposits. Located at the foot of the Cerro de la Bufa, the city was nicknamed the "Evangelist of the North," due to the fact that mendicant orders began the construction of their churches during the 16C with the help of rich, Spanish miners. Also in the 16C, Philip II of Spain gave the city the title of Very Noble and Very Loyal City of Our Lady of Zacatecas—due to its rich silver deposit—and granted it a coat of arms.

The Twentieth Century – The celebrated "Capture of Zacatecas" occurred in 1914, when rebel soldiers led by Pancho Villa defeated the federal forces of Victoriano Huerta, in an important triumph for the Revolution. The proudly preserved, historic city center, restored in the late 20C was declared a World Heritage Site in 1993.

★★CATHEDRAL AND SURROUNDINGS

★**Cathedral** – *Av. Hidalgo, beside the Plaza de Armas. Open year-round Mon–Sat 6:30am–1:30pm & 4:30–9pm, Sun 6:30am–1:30pm & 4:30–10pm.* Begun in 1729, this cathedral is considered a masterpiece of both Mexican Baroque and Hispanic-American architecture. Although the structure was dedicated in 1752, the bell tower was not completed until 1782. It was declared a cathedral in 1863 and basilica in 1959.

★★★**Facade** – *Photo p 212-213.* Resembling a papal tiara, the facade merits contemplation to appreciate the lavishness of its decorations. The center of attention is the rose window and its depiction of cherubs, infant angels and animals, as well as the sculptures of four giants of Latin priesthood—St. Gregory the Pope, St. Jerome, St. Augustine of Hipona and St. Ambrose of Milan. A statue of Christ the King, bearing a globe of the earth in His left hand and making a gesture of blessing with His right, as well as the figures of the 12 Apostles surrounded by angels playing instruments, also decorate the front of the cathedral. A statue of Mary the Immaculate, adorning the keystone of the main doorway's mixtilinear arch, welcomes visitors. Displaying a more restrained Baroque style, the **south facade** is dedicated to Our Lady of Zacatecas. The Churrigueresque **north facade** features an effigy of the crucified Christ, an example of indigenous craftsmanship.

Interior – The soft aroma of burning incense used in mass accentuates the restrained architectural style. In the central nave, the keystones of the arches represent popes, evangelists, martyrs and confessors. The keystones in the south nave, dedicated to Our Lady of the Zacatecans, depict allegories related to the Virgin Mary, while in the north nave, they recount the Passion of Christ.

Galería Episcopal – *In the building next to the cathedral's south facade. Open year-round Tue–Sun 10am–6pm. P$10.* ☎ *(4) 924-4307.* This gallery was inaugurated in 1998 with the objective of creating a forum to exhibit religious art and educate visitors with respect to the role of the Catholic Church. Formerly part of the cathedral, the museum's collection consists of sacred ornaments, liturgical books and religious paintings, including works by Miguel Cabrera's school.

■ Callejoneadas

Any stroll through the city on a Friday or Saturday will likely lead to one of these street parties. Traditional drums and metal instruments mark the rhythm of two-step dances, as this festive procession navigates the city's winding streets and unexpected alleyways and pays homage to the legends, customs and traditions of this bizarre capital, as Zacatecan poet Ramón López Velarde once described it. Shots of Huitzil *mezcal* are used to banish the chill; in fact, a mule bearing this delicious liquor often leads the playful march. The *callejoneadas* usually begin in the Alameda. Some of the hotels organize these activities and finish, as custom dictates, with a mouthwatering taco dinner.

Palacio de Gobierno (PG) – *Av. Hidalgo, 604, southeast of the Plaza de Armas. Open year-round daily 8am–8pm.* ☏ *(4) 922-1211.* This 18C house was the residence of the first and second Count of the Laguna. A lovely representation of the Zacatecas coat of arms decorates the bell tower. The mural inside by Antonio Rodríguez was completed in 1970 and narrates the history of the state. In 1867, Benito Juárez inhabited the present-day reception room. The facade of the house next door, under which passes the Callejón de las Campanas (Alley of the Bells), is adorned with 14 dogs, which according to legend, killed the lady of the house for buying stolen jewels that belonged to the Virgin of Patronage.

Callejón de Veyna and Cathedral

© Gustavo Gatto

Palacio de la Justicia (Palacio de la Mala Noche) (A) – *Av. Hidalgo, 669, facing the Plaza de Armas.* This old white mansion, nicknamed the "Palace of the Bad Night," was built near the end of the 18C by Don Manuel Rétegui. The story goes that Don Rétegui had invested every penny he had in a mine, and finding himself in a state of dire poverty, contemplated suicide. But as he wrote the suicide letter, shouts of joy in the street heralded the news that the mine had at last yielded the anticipated vein. Thus the mine and this house, built with money from the recovered fortune, were christened "Bad Night." A **false door** still opens onto Callejón de Veyna, where the miner could enter and leave the house unnoticed with his treasures, which he would one day use to overlay the cathedral's cross with silver in honor of his daughter's baptism.

Mercado González Ortega – *Hidalgo, beside the Plaza Goitia. Open year-round daily 9am–8pm.* ✗ ☏ *(4) 922-0033.* Inaugurated in 1889 this Neoclassical building served as the city's central market. Now remodeled, since 1982 it has boasted a shopping center with two levels of restaurants and stores like the **Centro Platero** (Silver Center), as well as wine, clothing and sweets shops. Artistic activities are often presented in the Plaza Goitia.

Teatro Calderón – *Av. Hidalgo, 501, facing the Plaza Goitia. Open year-round daily 10am–2pm & 4–8pm.* ☏ *(4) 922-8620.* The Neoclassical Calderón Theater was inaugurated in 1897. Today, it is the setting of major cultural events.

★Templo de Santo Domingo – *Plaza de Santo Domingo, 601. Open year-round daily 7am–1pm and 3–10pm.* In 1749 the Jesuits completed this building in a restrained Baroque style. After Charles III of Spain expelled the Jesuits in 1767, the Dominicans took possession of the church. Eight Churrigueresque altarpieces of gilded wood make this shrine the most lavish in the city. The eight-sided **sacristy** is adorned with eight, mid-18C paintings by Francisco Martínez Sánchez.

★★★ Museo Pedro Coronel – *Plaza de Santo Domingo. Open year-round Fri–Wed 10am–5pm. Closed national holidays. P$15.*

☎ *(4) 922-8021*. This 18C fortress was once the site of the Jesuit school of San Luis Gonzaga and later served as a jail, hospital and boarding house. Restoration began in 1970, and Zacatecan painter Pedro Coronel (1922–85) donated his vast collection, making this museum unique in Mexico and Latin America. The Elías Amador **library**, located near the entrance, boasts a 16C collection of approximately 20,000 books. One onyx sculpture and three basaltic sculptures by Pedro Coronel are exhibited in the arcades of the central courtyard, which is planted with orange trees. Especially powerful is the **Venus Negra** (Black Venus, 1978). An exhibit on international art, dating back to the 16C BC, also called "The Universe of Pedro Coronel," is found on the second floor. Among the items featured are an array of **pre-Hispanic art★★** and a select sample of Mexican masks. The colonial art room displays 17C Zacatecan Christs, the earliest exhibits in the collection. The greatest acquisition, however, has been a series of **etchings★** by Francisco de Goya y Lucientes, called *Tauromaquía* (Bullfighting) and *Los Proverbios* (The Proverbs), placed near the remains of Pedro Coronel. The collection also includes works by William Hogarth, Giovanni Piranessi, Picasso, Miró, Chagall, Dalí, Wifredo Lam, Alexander Calder and Victor Vasarely, among others. Oriental and Ancient Greek pieces, as well as a fantastic selection of **African masks**, complete the collection.

Museo Zacatecano – *Dr. Hierro, 301. Open year-round Wed–Mon 10am–5pm. P$10.* ☎ *(4) 922-6580*. This museum is located on the second floor of the old Mint, Mexico's second most important mint during the 19C. Its three collections feature 169 Huichol pieces of embroidery with magical and religious symbols, shaman chairs, wooden figures and Huichol instruments. Various pieces of colonial wrought iron and 196 religious paintings (16–19C) are also displayed.

Antiguo Templo de San Agustín – *Plazuela Miguel Auza. Open year-round Tue–Sun 10am–7pm.* Dedicated in 1782, this church and monastery was built by the Augustinians over the foundation of a Franciscan hospice. During the second half of the 19C, the church passed into the hands of Presbyterians, who used it for storage. The magnificent Churrigueresque relief on the **side portal★★**, depicting the conversion of St. Augustine, is the only reminder of the original church, which was salvaged in the mid 20C. At present, the interior contains temporary exhibits.

★Mesón de Jobito – *Jardín Juárez, 143*. This inviting building was used as an inn in the 19C for travelers, who no doubt found peace and quiet in the pretty plaza lined with wrought-iron balconies—evoking images of carriages full of merchandise, bustling down the streets. In 1993 it opened its doors as a hotel, including a restaurant-El Mesonero-and a handicraft shop. In front of the inn, the beautiful, tree-shaded Jardín Juárez provides a perfect setting for another restaurant and art gallery.

MINA EL EDEN AND SURROUNDINGS

Mina El Edén – *Antonio Dovalí. From Av. Hidalgo, go to Av. Juárez and walk northwest on the Alameda. Behind the IMSS (Instituto Mexicano del Seguro Social) building is Calle Antonio Dovalí. Visit by guided tour (1hr) only, open year-round daily 11am–6pm P$15.* ☎ *(4) 922-3002*. Exploited from 1586 to 1960, this mine is located 320m/1,050ft below the summit of Cerro del Grillo. The 1km/0.6mi-trip begins in the Socavón de la Esperanza (Hope Cavern), where a little train covers 600m/1,969ft of its length. Visitors continue the next 400m/1,312ft on foot. Only four of the seven levels are open, because the lower three are flooded. The greenish-blue color of the water is caused by minerals and prolonged stagnation. At night, part of the mine becomes the discotheque "El Malacate." *We recommend exiting by the elevator, which covers 36m/118ft, and walking about 200m/656ft through the Socavón del Grillo (Cricket Cavern). The entrance to the cable car is 100m/328ft away.*

Teleférico – *Cerro del Grillo Station, points of departure are Cerro del Grillo and Cerro de la Bufa; Apr, Jul, Aug & Dec, daily 10am–7pm; rest of the year daily 10am–6pm. P$10.* ☎ *(4) 922-5694*. Reaching a maximum height of 85m/279ft over the city, the cable car connects Cerro del Grillo with Cerro de la Bufa in a 650m/2,133ft trajectory. The trip takes seven minutes, during which the conductor narrates the history of the city and of Cerro de la Bufa.

Cerro de la Bufa – *This mountain can also be reached by car.* A symbol of the city, this giant crest of exposed rock is named for its resemblance to a pig's bladder. Zacatecan poet Ramón López Velarde also likened it to an angry steed. Crowning the mountain is the **Santuario de Nuestra Señora de Patrocinio** (Sanctuary of Our Lady of Patronage) *(open year-round daily 7am–8pm)*. Since 1728, the sanctuary's chapel has revered the patron saint of the city. Images of the Sun and Moon grace the facade, which combined with the Virgin, the Cerro de la Bufa and the figures of the four founders, constitute Zacatecas' five symbols-depicted in the coat of arms that Philip II of Spain granted the city in 1588.

The **Museo Toma de Zacatecas** (Museum of the Capture of Zacatecas), also located atop the mountain *(open year-round Tue–Sun 10am–5pm; closed Dec 25; P$10;* ☎ *4-922-8066)* recounts the capture of Zacatecas and exhibits reproductions of newspapers, weapons and photographs related to this momentous battle of the Mexican Revolution, which took place on June 23, 1914. The rebel army was led by Francisco Villa, General Felipe Ángeles and Pánfilo Natera, whose large **statues** adorn the mountain. Behind the statues, at the top of the peak, stands the Mausoleo de los Hombres Ilustres de Zacatecas, which guards the remains of illustrious Zacatecan men. A nearby meteorological station offers a sweeping **view★★** of the city.

ADDITIONAL SIGHTS

★★★**Museo Rafael Coronel** – *Former Monastery of St. Francis. 0.5km/0.3mi northeast of the city on Hidalgo and Juan de Tolosa. Open year-round Thu–Tue & holidays 10am–5pm. P$15.* ✕ ☎ *(4) 922-8116*. The Baroque structure (16–18C) was home to the Franciscans until their expulsion in 1857. The outstanding restoration of the museum began in 1987. The collection features objects of art donated by painter Rafael Coronel, brother of Pedro Coronel and son-in-law of renowned Mexican artist, Diego Rivera.

The Chapel of St. Anthony is annexed to what was once the monastery's church. Today, the beautiful Zacatecan sky serves as the chapel's roof. The temporary exhibition room displays, on a permanent basis, the **Mortaja** (The Shroud), a painting by Rafael Coronel, depicting the death of St. Francis of Assisi. The Virgin's banner, the coat of arms and the title of "Very Noble and Very Loyal," granted to the city in the 16C, are displayed in what was once the sacristy.

Past the gardens and more ruins of the convent is the Rostro de México (Face of Mexico), displaying approximately 3,000 of the 5,000 **masks★★★** donated by Rafael Coronel—the world's largest collection. These "popular works of art with ceremonial purpose" are accompanied by descriptions of their corresponding regional dances. The Ruth Rivera room boasts a collection of drawings by Diego Rivera, and the "Tandas de Rosete" room exhibits a collection of **puppets★★**, predominately from Rosete Aranda's company, begun in 1835. Marionettes are showcased as if in a real puppet show. A selection of pre-Hispanic vessels and terracotta figurines, a popular form of colonial art, complete the exhibition.

Museo Rafael Coronel, Masks

© Robert Frerck/Odyssey

★**Museo de Arte Abstracto "Manuel Felguérez"** – *Corner of Cristóbal Colón and 1a del Seminario. Open year-round Wed–Mon 10am–5pm. P$15.* ☎ *(4) 924-3705*. After functioning originally as a Diocesan Seminary in the 19C and then as a prison, from 1964 to 1995, this building was renovated for its inauguration as a museum of abstract art, in September 1998. Thanks to the initiative of the distinguished Zacatecan artist, Manuel Felguérez (b. 1928), "Illustrious Citizen of Zacatecas" who donated an important collection of his works to the state government, the building now boasts a modern display of over 100 paintings and sculptures, representative of four decades of Felguérez labor, as well as works by other abstract artists. One of the pioneers of the abstract art movement that emerged in Mexico in the 1950s, Felguérez has been recognized both nationally and internationally. The museum also houses a library specializing in abstract art.

★**Museo Francisco Goitia** – *General Enrique Estrada, 102, across from the Parque Enrique Estrada. Open year-round Tue–Sun 10am–5pm. Closed Jan 1 and Dec 25. P$15.* ☎ *(4) 922-0211*. Located in a mid-20C house, this museum focuses on the works of painter Francisco Goitia. His oil paintings **Caballo famélico** (Starving Horse), **Paisaje de Santa Mónica** (Landscape of Santa Monica), and **Cabeza de ahorcado** (Head of a Hanged Man), as well as the famous self-portraits, merit attention. A copy of the renowned painting **Tata Jesucristo** (Papa Jesus Christ), considered a masterpiece of 20C Mexican painting, is also displayed, along with more than 100 years of contemporary Zacatecan fine arts. Other noteworthy works include the *Retrato de un señor* (Portrait of a Man) by Julio Ruelas, dating to 1894; a painting by Pedro Coronel, completed in 1985, the year of his death; and sculptures by José Kuri Breña, Manuel Felguérez and Rafael Coronel. Located behind the museum, the Gothic Revival tower belonging to the **Parroquia de Nuestra Señora de Fátima**, begun in 1950, is visible from various points of the city.

★**Hotel Quinta Real** – *Av. González Ortega near the aqueduct*. This beautiful hotel is located in what was the bullring of San Pedro, from 1876 to 1975. Since 1989, it has operated as a hotel, the only one in the world built around a bullring. Surrounded by art galleries, handicraft shops, travel agencies and a restaurant, the ring provides an unusual and dramatic setting for enjoying a scrumptious meal, occasionally served here. On Saturdays, Quinta Real organizes the festive *callejoneadas (p 228)*.

Outside the hotel, visitors can admire the **Acueducto del Cubo**, which supplies water to the southern part of the city.

EXCURSIONS

Ex Convento de Guadalupe – *7km/4mi southeast of Zacatecas on Blvd. López Portillo, across from the Plaza Principal de Guadalupe. Open year-round daily 7am–1pm & 4–8pm. Closed Jan 1, Dec 25. P$10.* ☎ *(4) 923-2501.* Located in the outskirts of Zacatecas, this monastery was founded in 1707 and once housed the Colegio Franciscano de Propaganda (FIDE), responsible for evangelizing northern New Spain. From this school, which administered to all within a range of 25sq km/15sq mi, more than 30 missions were established. Declared a Historic Monument in 1919, the monastery features the Museo de Guadalupe, the Templo de Guadalupe and the Capilla de Nápoles, located inside.

★★★**Museo de Guadalupe** – *Jardín Juárez Ote. Enter by the gatehouse. Open year-round daily 10am–4:30pm. Closed Jan 1, Dec 25. P$20.* ☎ *(4) 923-2386.* This museum is blessed with one of Mexico's finest collections of colonial art. While the **lower cloister** is adorned with 25 large canvases depicting the life of St. Francis, the main stairway is graced by *La Virgen del Apocalipsis* by Miguel Cabrera. Climb the stairs to see the gigantic painting *San Cristóbal* by Nicolás Rodríguez Juárez. Works by Cristóbal de Villalpando, Juan Patricio Morlet de Ruiz, Antonio de Torres, José de Ibarra and Juan Correa are also to be admired. Correa painted *Nuestra Señora del Patrocinio de los Zacatecos* (Patron Saint of the Zacatecans), which adorns the infirmary chapel. A series of paintings, noted for their strong color and contrast, by Gabriel José Ovalle narrates the *Passion of Christ*. The **choir stalls** are furnished with carved chairs and an expressive representation of St. Francis, who appears to preside over the same ceremonies that the Franciscans observed here. The Passion of Christ is again depicted in giant canvases decorating the **high cloister**, an area where time has stopped. Works of decorative feather art and 16C Christ figures, made of corn stalk paste or marble, are displayed in this enormous space. Of special interest are the **library** and objects of glass and Talavera pottery used in the monastery. The annex building exhibits a collection of **vehicles** and **carriages**.

★★**Capilla de Nápoles** – Upon entering the Church of Guadalupe, bear left to reach this chapel (1877), which boasts rich decorations of laminated gold over quarry stone. Its decorative elements correspond to a late Baroque architecture. The mesquite-wood floor bears a compass design, while the exterior of the tall, richly adorned cupola is covered with Talavera plasterwork ornamentation. A revered figure of the Most Pure Immaculate Conception, brought from Naples, is also displayed in this pretty chapel.

★**La Quemada** – *Go 56km/35mi southwest of Zacatecas on Carr. 54 heading toward Guadalajara. Exit the highway and continue on a 1km/0.6mi road to the archaeological site. Open year-round daily 10am–5pm. P$16.* ✗ ☎ *(4) 922-5085.* From AD 100 to 900, this site functioned as a ceremonial center of the Mesoamerican culture whose nucleus was the city of Teotihuacán. The center fell into a period of deterioration in AD 900 and suffered a huge fire in AD 1000, which left scars on the stones still visible today. The **Salón de las Columnas** bore walls which might have been as thick as 5m/16ft. Also worthy of a visit is the **Pirámide Votiva** (Votive Pyramid), found in the structure called **El Palacio**. More than 200 sites, as well as a 170km/106mi-long system of highways, have been discovered. This system is said to be the legendary Chicomostoc, where the Aztecs spent nine years on their voyage to Anáhuac. The **site museum**★ is built with the same style and materials as other nearby structures. On exhibit are pieces found at La Quemada and Alta Vista-Zacatecas' other large pre-Hispanic site.

Sombrerete – *167km/104mi from Zacatecas on Carr. 45 toward Durango.* In the 16C, at the foot of the Cerro del Sombreretillo, the Villa de San Juan Bautista de Llerena was founded. Today, the town of Sombrerete retains the splendor of its mining days. Among the most interesting colonial buildings are the 18C **Templo de San Francisco** and its annex, the **Capilla de la Tercera Orden** (Chapel of the Third Order), unique in Mexico for its elliptical layout *(open year-round daily 6:30am–8pm, holidays 6am–9pm)*. Remarkable caryatid columns, shaped like women, adorn the facades of the Baroque **Templo de Santo Domingo**, the **Templo de la Soledad** and its chapel, the **Capilla de la Santa Veracruz**. Beside the **Parroquia de San Juan Bautista**, a mass of quarry rock that suffered an explosion during the Revolution, stands the house where Thomas Alva Edison is said to have lived.

★**Alta Vista** – *From Sombrerete, take Carr. 11 toward Jiménez de Teul and continue 50km/31mi to the town of Chalchihuites. Go 6km/4mi west of town on a dirt road and cross the Colorado River. The archaeological site is located on a hill. Open year-round daily 10am–5pm. P$10. ☎ (4) 922-5085.* This site features the interesting ruins of the Chalchihuites' main ceremonial center. These indigenous people are considered an intermediary group between the sedentary Mesoamericans and the Chichimecs of the arid North. Straddling the Tropic of Cancer, the center was built sometime between AD 450 and 850. More than 750 pre-Columbian mines have been discovered around what was a principal distribution center of precious stones. The city was designed in such a way that the corners of the main structures coincide with the cardinal points. During the equinox, the sun rises over the crest of a mountain located at the far end of the Colorado River Valley; its first rays appear between two walls of **El Laberinto** (The Labyrinth). Also noteworthy are the **Salón de las Columnas** (Hall of Columns), possibly dedicated to the cult of Tezcatlipoca, the **Pirámide del Sol** (Pyramid of the Sun) and the **Templo de las Calaveras** (Temple of Skulls).

★★**Sierra de Órganos** – *From Sombrerete, take Carr. 45 toward Durango. After 22km/14mi, exit and follow a dirt road for 10km/6mi to the sierra.* This mountain range offers an inspiring view of seven gorges with fantastic basaltic formations. **El Cáliz** (The Chalice), **Los Frailes** (The Friars) and **El Campanario** (The Bell Tower) rank among the best known. The 35,000-year-old landscape resembles an ageless prehistoric setting, unaltered by the passage of time. The film *El cavernícola (The Caveman)*, starring Ringo Starr, is one of the more than 60 films produced in the area. Ideal for camping, the sierra also boasts a series of canyons to challenge mountain climbers.

When planning your trip, consult the Practical Information section
for travel tips, useful addresses and phone numbers, and information on sports
and recreation, and annual events.

GULF OF MEXICO

Cradle of Mesoamerica and Port of the Spanish Conquest

Handicrafts and Food, p 53. Some of Mexico's most important cultural and historical events have occurred in the present-day Gulf Coast states of Tabasco and Veracruz. The **Olmecs** established the first Mesoamerican civilization here around 1800 BC. Given the Mexica name for "the inhabitants of the rubber country," the Olmecs ruled a territory that extended from the southern part of the present-day state of Veracruz to the western part of Tabasco.

The **Huastecs** in the north and the **Totonacs** in the central part of the state were other mighty civilizations that rose to power in Veracruz. For its design and architecture, the Totonac city of El Tajín was one of the most intriguing and fascinating cities of the pre-Hispanic world. Many battles and alliances between the conquistadors and the indigenous cultures unfolded in the Gulf Coast, a point of entry for the Spanish during the Conquest. In one of the Tabascan ports, the notorious traitoress—La Malinche—was given to Hernán Cortés, who founded the Villa Rica de la Vera Cruz (Rich City of the True Cross)—the first colonial settlement on the American continent. Later, he would set off with his army from Veracruz to conquer the great Aztec city of Tenochtitlán, heart of the Aztec Empire. The region also served as an important crossroads for travelers and commerce between Europe and Mexico during the colonial era. Boasting a variable and extreme climate and extending from the Gulf of Mexico to the heights of the Sierra Madre Oriental, the region functions as a pillar of the Mexican economy, partly due to its abundant crops (sugar, coffee, bananas and citrus fruits, among many others), but primarily because the majority of Mexico's oil fields and refineries lie along the Gulf coast.

Tab. .... Tabasco
Ver. .... Veracruz

© Robert Frerck/Odyssey

Plaza de Armas, Tlacotalpan, Veracruz

EL TAJÍN★★★

Veracruz

Map of Principal Sights – Map p 114 (BX)

ℹ ☎ (2) 932-1999 and (01-800) 712-6666

El Tajín, the "sacred city of the god of thunder" bears traces of human occupation dating back to the 2C AD. It is believed that in the 6C El Tajín benefited from Teotihuacán's cultural influence. During its peak period, from AD 800 to 1150, El Tajín constituted one of Mesoamerica's most important urban, political and religious centers *(Gulf of Mexico, p 32)*, with a population that reached an estimated 25,000 inhabitants. El Tajín sustained itself economically with the tributes paid by neighboring towns in services and products. As a result of continual wars, sociopolitical disorganization and the disruption of trade, El Tajín was abandoned sometime in the 12C.

Today, due to the strong Totonac presence in the region, El Tajín has always been considered a Totonac city. Nonetheless, the most recent findings indicate that the only certainty is that this city was the cultural center of El Tajín.

According to the most recent count, more than 168 buildings make up the 1.5sq km/1sq mi site. Niches decorated with frets set El Tajín's architecture apart from other archaeological sites. The city boasts a total of 17 ball courts and exuberant tropical vegetation. Two sections comprise the site; most of the structures are found in the ceremonial section, located in a flat area between two creeks. On a mound separated by a retaining wall stands Tajín Chico, which once housed the rulers and priests of El Tajín.

ARCHAEOLOGICAL SITE *Map p 238.*

Flights and buses from Mexico City arrive in nearby Poza Rica. From Veracruz, go north approximately 223km/138mi on Carr. 180 to Papantla. Then continue 16km/10mi to the archaeological site. Be prepared for rainy weather. Open year-round daily 8am–6pm. P$25. ✗ 🅔 ☎ *(2) 932-1999.*

Beginning at noon, the **Voladores de Papantla** (Flying Men of Papantla) give ongoing performances on the esplanade at the entrance to the site. These "flyers" come from the nearby town of Papantla, located only 13km/8mi away and renowned for its traditional customs, production of vanilla and the celebration of the festival of **Corpus Christi** held in early June. Accompanied by drum beats and flute music, the flyers, who are positioned on top of a very tall pole, try to summon the god of sun and the winds of the four cardinal points through a ritual dance. One of the five dancers remains standing on top of the pole and continues to dance and play the flute and drum, while the other four, seated on a giant spool-like construction just below, bind their feet with rope and let themselves fall backward into the air. As the ropes loosen, each of the four flyers spins 13 times in the descent. Added up, this equals 52—the number of years corresponding to the arrival of the new sun.

Site Museum – *Located beside the ticket office.* The site museum features outstanding discoveries such as the fragments of stone drums taken from the columns of the Edificio de las Columnas (Building of the Columns), a building not yet open to the public, where it is believed resided El Tajín's main ruler. The museum also displays a scale model of El Tajín.

Grupo Plaza del Arroyo – The Plaza of the Creek and its structures are designed along the classic Mesoamerican style of four buildings framing a rectangular esplanade. The one important difference is that no altar adorns the center, which indicates that this square may have served as a monumental market. Rows of niches, a recurring characteristic of El Tajín's architecture, punctuate the surface of the three-story building on the northern side of the plaza. The function of these niches seems to have been purely decorative. Four ball courts-three on the left and one on the right-mark the plaza's exits.

Turn left and enter the last and largest ball court.

Juego de Pelota Sur – The South Ball Court differs from the other ball courts for its *talud* (a trapezoidal-shaped side panel characteristic of Mesoamerican architecture). Typical of most courts, the *talud* here is unique because it contains bleacher-like seats for spectators. **Six carved tableros** also adorn the sides of the court and depict various scenes related to this ritual game, which usually culminated in the decapitation of one or more of the players. The sequence begins with the two *tableros* on the far left, continues with the two on the far right, jumps to the center right and ends with the center left.

Tablero [1] portrays a player preparing for a game, while the god of death rises out of a clay pot in the corner. **Tablero [2]** depicts two people, one shaking a rattle and the other playing on a tortoise shell. It also portrays a man dressed as an eagle-perhaps a priest perched over a player who is lying face down-most probably in preparation for a sacrifice. In **Tablero [3]**, two players talk to one another, possibly the captains of the two teams of ball players. While one bears a knife, the god of death observes them from the background. **Tablero [4]** shows a player who is to be decapitated and eviscerated. The upper portion of **Tablero [5]** portrays the gods of rain and thunder as a one-headed god with two bodies. From above, the god watches a man carrying a clay pot. In the last panel, **Tablero [6]**, the god of rain sacrifices his own genitals, spilling his blood over the earth to make it fertile. Another person, wearing a fish-shaped headdress, collects this precious liquid.

Upon exiting the South Ball Court, notice the small temple (10), the staircase of which has been partly removed to reveal another staircase underneath. This proves that the architects of El Tajín, as in other areas of Mesoamerica, built

Ball Court and Pirámide de los Nichos

temples on top of each other, probably every 52 years at the end of a solar cycle. The structure to the right, with a straw roof, forms part of another ball court. Pass through this ball court and Temple 10 to reach Temple 12.

Temple 12 – The characteristic fret-lined niches found on many other buildings also decorate this structure. The frets have been associated with a snail's spiral, the movement of the ocean, and the geometric representation of the serpent, also called **xicalcoliuhqui**. Framed by small, carved columns, these frets also symbolize the endlessness of life cycles, with neither a beginning nor an end. Across from this building lies Ball Court 11.

Return to the South Ball Court and turn left. Edificio 15 stands on the right. Marked by larger niches, this building was originally painted red. Today it is believed that all the structures were painted at one time. Edificio 5 is on the left.

Edificio 5 – Constructed on a large platform, this building resembles a truncated pyramid decorated with niches, the upper ones adorned with the same fret design. A great sculpture representing a deity, perhaps the god Tajín, stands on the platform. In front of this pyramid stands an altar, where dances and other ceremonies were held in honor of this god.

Continue farther ahead to the small esplanade.

Pirámide de los Nichos – Symbol of El Tajín, the spectacular, seven-story Pyramid of the Niches was discovered in 1785 by Diego Ruiz, a Spanish soldier in search of clandestine tobacco plantations. A total of 365 niches mark the pyramid's surface, the same as the number of days in a solar year. Tablero panels and friezes from this pyramid are displayed in the site museum.

Farther on lies a large plaza with another ball court, whose six tablero panels depict mythical and historical figures. This plaza is bordered on two sides by a retaining wall, which originally separated the ceremonial center from the residential area. Home of the rulers and priests, this exclusive neighborhood was known as **Tajín Chico** *(climb the retaining wall to reach the plaza).*

© Robert Frerck/Odyssey

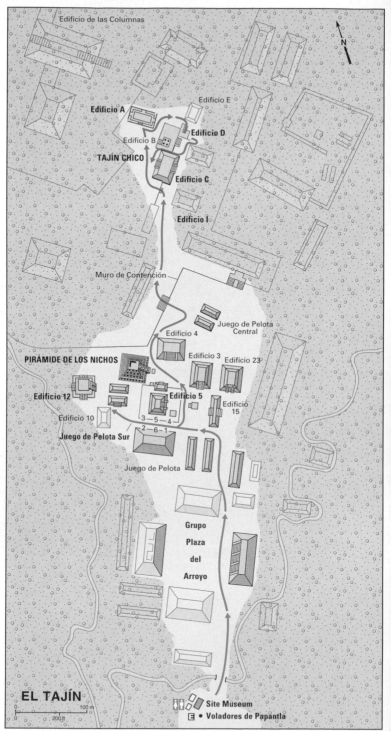

Tajín Chico – During excavation, archaeologists discovered that the roofs on the homes in this area were made of lime, seashells and sand, and mixed with ground-up pumice and bits of pottery. Once cast, the mixture produced the same effect as cement.

All the structures at Tajín Chico are identified with letters. Ascending Tajín Chico, one sees the imposing **Edificio C**, with two rows of intricately carved frets. Stylized representations of the feathered serpent Quetzalcóatl, these frets attest to

Teotihuacán's cultural influence. To the left, northwest of this group, stands **Edificio A**, important for its vast number of rooms. A staircase covered by an arch, possibly Mayan, and flanked by frets leads to the entrance. To the right, a great residential structure known as **Edificio B** still boasts the pillars that originally sustained its roof. A small pathway behind this building leads to **Edificio D**, rising over the carved walls of a terrace. There, a staircase descends to a tunnel that may have been used by the priests of El Tajín to access the ceremonial area below. Great, intertwined rhombuses adorn the upper level of the entrance to Edificio D.

Return to the entrance of the plaza and continue along the border.

The leaf and cane-pole roof of **Edificio I** shelters the remains of painted murals, all bearing religious symbols.

EXCURSIONS

Playa de Tuxpan – *From the entrance to El Tajín, bear right until you reach Poza Rica (16km/10mi). Then, turn left onto Carr. 180 north. At the outskirts of Poza Rica turn right to access Carr. 130 & 132 to Tuxpan. Immediately after crossing the Pantepec River bridge, turn right and follow the Playa ("Beach") signs for 8km/5mi to the oceanfront.* Here, one can kick back and enjoy fresh seafood in *palapa* (thatched-roof) restaurants. Showers and bathrooms are readily available.

Playa de Tecolutla – *From the entrance to El Tajín, turn right and continue straight on until you reach Poza Rica (16km/10mi). Then, take Carr. 180 south and drive 53km/33mi to the town of Gutiérrez Zamora. Here, turn left and follow the signs to Tecolutla (10km/6mi).* This peaceful village has a tang of the sea. While the downtown area consists of a few small hotels and several handicraft shops, the beach abounds with thatched-roof restaurants, showers, bathrooms, beach umbrellas and peddlers.

VERACRUZ★

Veracruz
Population 425,140
Map of Principal Sights – City Map p 240
🏛 Palacio Municipal, Zaragoza and Independencia ☎ (2) 932-1999

Famous for its tradition of good food and music, this delightful tropical city offers visitors warm hospitality, soft ocean breezes and relaxing walks along the ocean. The raucous, lively side of Veracruz surfaces in a variety of places. Dine at a traditional restaurant on the Plaza de Armas, practice the **danzón** (a dance held after dark several times a week, to the sounds of a live orchestra), sip the obligatory *café con leche* (coffee with milk) at the port-side cafe, **La Parroquia**, or revel in the famous **carnival★** in February.

Among the port's other attractions, its more adventurous activities include rafting, kayaking, eco-archaeology, scuba diving, trekking and *temascal* (indigenous steam-bath therapy).

■ El Danzón

Created by Miguel Faílde y Pérez in Cuba in 1879, the *danzón* is one of the most cherished Mexican dances. The term *danzón* refers both to the music and the choreography, which are inseparable. Though the music of the *danzón* was originally foreign (*contra dance*), new choreography has made it distinctly Mexican.

Shortly after its invention, the *danzón* was introduced on the Gulf coast where the inhabitants adopted it as their own, gradually infusing it with the flavor and rhythm of tropical Mexico.

At the beginning of the 20C, the *danzón* craze arrived in Mexico City and created the same sensation as it had on the coast. Innumerable dance halls sprang up as early as 1908, and the *danzón* eventually became another national legend. The dance halls seemed removed from the real world; here the ritual of the dance, being a good dancer, and having the best partner became the sole concerns of participants.

Though today this dance has spread throughout Mexico, the *danzón* enjoys a special place in the hearts of the people of Veracruz and Mérida. Two or three times a week, the young and old come together to attend the dances energized by the sounds of live orchestras.

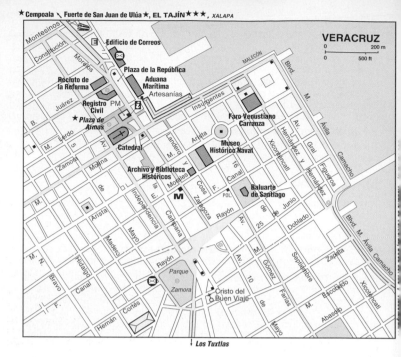

Historical Notes

Sixteenth Century – On June 24, 1518, Spanish conquistadors Juan de Grijalva, Francisco Montejo and Pedro de Alvarado embarked on an expedition from Cuba to the banks of the Coatzacoalcos River continuing along the Papaloapan River to the two islands at its mouth, named Sacrificios (Island of Sacrifices) and San Juan de Ulúa. Hernán Cortés dropped anchor here on April 21, 1519 and later founded the Villa Rica de la Vera Cruz to honor the day of his arrival, Good Friday, or the Day of the True Cross. From that day on, Veracruz served as a way station for conquistadors and as a launching point for expeditions—including Cortés' famous journey to Tenochtitlán, heart of the Aztec Empire. Merchandise bound for the Old World entered and left this port, making it a great center of trade. For this reason, Veracruz was the object of frequent pirate attacks. Fortified walls and the fortress of San Juan de Ulúa testify to these recurrent threats to the city

Four times heroic – Toward the end of the colonial era, Veracruz, together with Havana, was considered one of the most important ports of Spanish America. Nicknamed "four times heroic," the city experienced several momentous events: the last battle against the Spanish at the Fort of San Juan de Ulúa in 1825, its defense against French occupation in 1838 during the Guerra de los Pasteles (Pastry War), and invasions by the United States in 1847 and 1914.

After the proclamation of the Constitution in 1857, Benito Juárez chose Veracruz as the seat of his government, as did Venustiano Carranza in 1914. When Porfirio Díaz was sent into exile in 1911, the ship carrying him, the *Ypiranga*, set out from this city's port.

CITY CENTER

★**Plaza de Armas** – *Located between Calles Zaragoza, Independencia, M. Lerdo and Zamora, beside the Palacio Municipal.* A wide variety of local dishes are sold in the arcades of this small plaza where vendors and musicians entice visitors to dance and partake of the local cuisine and where the national flag is ceremonially hoisted and lowered. The **danzón**★ is held here three times a week *(Tue, Fri & Sat 8pm–10pm)*. On the southwest corner of the plaza stands the **cathedral** *(open year-round Mon–Fri & Sun 6am–10pm, Sat 6am–1pm & 4–10pm)*, which boasts four candelabra that originated in Baccarat, France and supposedly, belonged to Maximilian of Hapsburg and his wife Carlota.

Plaza de la República – *Marina Mercante*. A rectangular plaza bordered by palms, benches and flower-filled planters, the Plaza of the Republic adjoins a smaller plaza dedicated to Benito Juárez that is surrounded by 16 monoliths, carved with the

Leyes de Reforma (Reform Laws). Nearby, the foyer of the **Registro Civil** (Mexican Civil Registry) *(open year-round Mon–Fri 8am–4pm; closed national holidays)* preserves a replica of the civil registry's first birth certificate, dated October 10, 1860, belonging to Jerónima Francisca Juárez, daughter of Benito Juárez and Margarita Maza de Juárez. The **Recinto de la Reforma** *(open year-round Tue–Sun 8am–8pm; closed national holidays)* is distinguished by the first lighthouse to illuminate the port. Sculptures of Benito Juárez and other illustrious men of the Reforma stand guard in the Sanctuary. Other important buildings on the plaza include the monumental **Telégrafos y Correos** (Telegraph and Post Office) and a building with the name of **Aduana Marítima** (which currently houses the offices of the Secretaría de la Hacienda). All of these buildings reflect the architectural style common during the *Porfiriato*-period when Porfirio Díaz ruled over Mexico.

★FUERTE DE SAN JUAN DE ULÚA

Leave the city center in the direction of Cardel. Take exit for San Juan de Ulúa–Aduanas and continue to the end of the road. Open year-round Tue–Sun 9am–4:30pm. P$16, free Sun and national holidays. ☎ (2) 938-5151.

Initiated in 1535 to better protect the sea routes and the port from pirate attacks, the fort saw the beginning and end of Spanish domination of Mexico. The use of rock dredged from the coral reefs to construct the fort explains the extreme dampness of the walls.

The Holy Inquisition used the fort as a prison for the people judged in its courts—including some of the greatest figures in Mexican history. Generally considered the cruelest prison the country has ever known, it was here that governmental troublemakers Fray Servando Teresa de Mier, Fray Melchor de Talamantes and Benito Juárez all served time, as did the legendary **Mulata de Córdoba**, and **Chucho el Roto**.

Various forms of torture took place in cells filled with seawater, called *tinajas*. Several of these "vats" were christened *Purgatory, Glory* and *Hell*, according to the "comforts" each room offered in the way of lodging.

By order of Venustiano Carranza, the fort ceased to function as a prison in 1915. Today, the fort's **museum** displays the military armaments used repeatedly to defend the port from foreign invasions, most notably those headed by Sir John Hawkins and Sir Francis Drake (1568) and Laurent De Graf—better known as *Lorenzillo* (1683).

ADDITIONAL SIGHTS

Baluarte de Santiago – *F. Canal, corner of Vicente Gómez Farías. Open year-round Tue–Sun 10am–4:30pm. P$16. ☎ (2) 931-1059.* Completed in 1635, St. James' Bastion remains as the last vestige of the walls erected to defend the port from pirate attacks. Its high, thick walls and restricted entryways are characteristic of military architecture. The fort consists of three stories. Gunpowder was stored on the lower level where a drawbridge helped protect the entrance of the

Fuerte de San Juan de Ulúa

© Robert Frerck/Odyssey

■ Legendary Figures of Veracruz

Popular lore describes how the **Mulata de Córdoba**–a woman of mixed African and European ancestry–was accused of sorcery and sentenced to San Juan de Ulúa by the Inquisition. Once inside, she asked her jailer to give her a piece of coal so she could draw. Once her wish was granted, she drew a boat on the cell wall and used it to free herself from her miserable imprisonment.

Jesús Arriaga–alias **Chucho el Roto**, a robber in the style of Robin Hood–stole from the rich and gave to the poor. Eagerly pursued by the authorities, he was imprisoned in Ulúa, but was set free by a friend and escaped in a boat, for at that time, the fort was built on an island and was not connected to the port. Chucho was unfortunately caught again and forced to endure horrifying waterdrop torture where a prisoner is tied to a wall underneath one of the fort's many water leaks. Drops of water would fall upon the prisoner's head driving him to madness.

---

pentagonally-shaped ground floor. Artillery was mounted upstairs. A small museum displays 40 gold pieces rescued from the ocean floor by a fisherman in 1976, veritable works of art by pre-Hispanic goldsmiths. A second room exhibits interesting maps and documents from previous centuries, as well as projectile heads, iron bullets and a howitzer.

Museo de la Ciudad (M) – *Zaragoza, 397, corner of E. Morales. Open year-round Tue–Sun 10am–8pm. Closed national holidays.* ☎ *(2) 931-8410.* This early-20C Neoclassical building features exhibits on the culture, history and folklore of the port of Veracruz. Here, visitors can appreciate not only the Spanish and indigenous heritage in the history of Veracruz, but also the cultural influence from Africa, resulting from several centuries of slave trade. Outside the museum, stone mosaics-reproductions of codices-narrate the history of the clash between the indigenous and Spanish cultures.

Museo Histórico Naval – *Calle Arista, between Landero y Coss and Av. Gómez Farías. Open year-round Tue–Sun 9am–5pm.* ☎ *(2) 931-4078.* The Naval Historic Museum was inaugurated in 1997 in what formerly served as the Naval Military School. On the first floor, one finds models of all kinds of boats from different cultures and eras, ancient instruments of navigation, maps from the 15C and 16C showing the maritime explorations of Columbus, Magellan and others, and a large collection of maritime armaments. The galleries on the second floor feature exhibits on the colonial period, the various maritime invasions of Veracruz and the history of the Military Naval School.

Archivo y Biblioteca Históricos – *Landero y Coss, corner of E. Morales. Open year-round Mon–Fri 8am–3pm. Closed national holidays, Dec 20–Jan 2.* ☎ *(2) 931-2754.* Constructed from rock dredged from coral reefs, the Historical Archives and Library now preserves the archives and historical documents relating to Veracruz and San Juan de Ulúa. The collection also includes reproductions of items in the General Archives of Simancas and the West Indies. Its 19C library was previously housed in the Monastery of San Francisco.

Faro Venustiano Carranza – *Paseo del Malecón, corner of Xicohténcatl. Open year-round Tue–Sun 9am–3pm.* ☎ *(2) 932-1864.* Photographs and documents relating to Venustiano Carranza, as well as furniture he used during his 11-month stay in Veracruz comprise the collection. While revolution rocked Mexico, Carranza set up his government in Veracruz. After infighting with other revolutionary armies, he eventually gained control of the country in 1916. Of particular interest are his death certificate, dated May 22, 1922 in Puebla, and the 25-centavo bill signed by Francisco "Pancho" Villa.

★**Acuario de Veracruz** – *Blvd. Ávila Camacho, Playón de Hornos. Open year-round Mon–Thu 10am–7pm; Fri–Sun 10am–7:30pm. P$15.* ✗ ☎ *(2) 932-7984.* Opened in 1992, this aquarium is one of the port's greatest attractions and home to a huge variety of marine life. In the spectacular **ocean gallery** sharks and other large species intermingle. A touch-tank exhibits mollusks, snails and shark jaws.

EXCURSIONS

★**Tlacotalpan** – *From Veracruz, head south for 100km/62mi on Carr. 180 (along the banks of the Papaloapan) towards Alvarado. Take the exit to Tlacotalpan, 13km/8mi away.* An impressive bridge that extends over the wide Papaloapan River leads to Tlacotalpan, which means "surrounded by water." In the 16C the Spanish chose the town as the seat of the local government. Due to its role as a port and to the rich sugar crops in the region, it prospered during the colonial era. Today, countryside tranquillity reigns in this colorful village, which boasts attractions such as the Plaza de Armas *(photo p 235)* with its Mudejar pavilion. The Iglesia de la Virgen de la Candelaria honors its patron saint during a great festival, which includes the **Encuentro de Jaraneros** (Reveller's Night), a *pamplonada* (bull festival) and the procession of the Virgin, which takes place on February 2. The **Museo Salvador Ferrando** *(Manuel M. Alegre, 6; open year-round Tue–Sun 10am–5pm. P$10; ☎ 2-812-8500 ext. 130)* exhibits paintings by the local artist, as well as 19C furniture, appliances and photos, and some pre-Hispanic artifacts from the region. Fresh seafood, accompanied by the music of the *jaraneros*, is served in the numerous restaurants that line the banks of the Papaloapan River.

Boca del Río – *Bordering the port of Veracruz.* Hotels, discos, Mocambo Beach and excellent restaurants lining the banks of the river enliven this district. **Mandinga** *(located at km 5.5 on Carr. 180 in the direction of Alvarado)* offers the best dishes in Veracruz, accompanied with music and *jarocho* dances.

★**Cempoala** – *Go 35km/22mi northwest of Veracruz via Carr. 180. Pass the toll-booth in Cardel and follow the signs for Poza Rica. Take the exit to Cempoala and follow signs to the "Zona Arqueológica." Open year-round daily 9am–6pm. P$17, free Sun. ☎ (2) 938-5151.* This Totonac city dates back to AD 1027–1600. Cempoala means "Place of Twenty Days," perhaps a reference to trading that took place here every 20 days, according to the 18-month calendar of 20 days. When the Spanish arrived in 1519, the Totonacs entered into the first Spanish-Indian alliance, in hopes that the Spanish would liberate them from Aztec rule. Both Totonacs and Tlaxcaltecs assisted in the 1521 conquest of México-Tenochtitlán. Eleven walled areas preserve the remains of the archaeological complex. As the Totonacs were a peaceful people, these walls did not protect against possible attacks, but rather against frequent floods. The site visit takes us to System 4, the only one completely restored. It consists of four plazas-one for religious ceremonies and three for markets. Most impressive is the ceremonial plaza. Especially note-worthy are the **Templo Mayor** (Great Temple), which the Totonacs believed was inhabited by their gods, and the **Templo de las Chimeneas** (Temple of the Chimneys), so named because the columns had a wooden nucleus, which upon disintegrating left a hollow interior that resembles a chimney. A small altar, where it is believed animal sacrifices were held, faces both temples.

In the same area rise two circular structures. It is known that one of these served as an altar, where a great ceremonial fire was built at the beginning of each 52-year cycle. In a small hearth nearby, the fire was kept burning constantly during the 52 years. Legend claims that once the fire ceased, the world would end. Hence, the sacred firewood was probably kept dry in the hollow columns of the Temple of the Chimneys. An interesting sound effect is produced in the circular structure known as the "Circle of Gladiators." Whoever speaks from the center of the circle towards the north will perceive a microphone-like resonance. It is believed that gladiatorial combats were enacted here, especially after 1469, year in which the Aztecs conquered Cempoala.

Antigua – *14km/8.7mi north of Veracruz, on Carr. 180 (heading towards Cempoala). Pass the tollbooth and take the first road to the left; continue straight on for 2km/1.2mi.* Not to be confused with the actual city of Veracruz, the first **Villa Rica de la Vera Cruz** was established in this small town. Overgrown fig trees have helped preserve the remains of Hernán Cortés' house, found to the left of the main plaza. Cortés lived here for almost a year, in 1520, while preparing for his final expedition against Tenochtitlán. Built in 1519, the small church on Av. Independencia is considered the first church in continental America. Two blocks away, one can enjoy seafood or a boat excursion along the Antigua River.

Los Tuxtlas – *144km/89mi. Go south on Carr. 180 (on the banks of the Papaloapan River) to Santiago Tuxtla. San Andrés Tuxtla is 15km/9mi east; Catemaco, 27km/17mi.* The fertile lands of the verdant, mountainous and rainy sierra of Los Tuxtlas create the perfect environment for cattle ranching and the harvesting of corn, beans, sugarcane and tobacco. The Volcano of San Martín (1,700m/5,578ft) crowns the sierra; it is believed that from here the Olmecs quar-ried the rocks they used to build the famous colossal heads.

The trip begins with the picturesque town of **Santiago Tuxtla**★ *(26km/16mi away from Catemaco, via Carr. 180)*. Due to the abundant vegetation, the Spanish built sugar mills and livestock farms shortly after the Conquest. The largest **Olmec head** found to date, called the Head of Cobata—the only head with closed eyes—sits to one side of the **Parque Juárez**. The **Museo Regional Tuxteco** *(open year-round Mon–Sat 9am–6pm, Sun & holidays 9am–3pm; P$10; ☎ 2-947-0196)* is located nearby. **San Andrés Tuxtla** *(14km/9mi from Santiago Tuxtla)* operates as the commercial center of the area with a primary focus on the tobacco industry.

★Salto de Eyipantla – *From San Andrés Tuxtla, take Carr. 180 heading towards Catemaco. After 5km/3mi, turn right in Sihuapan and continue 8km/5mi south.* This impressive waterfall, one of Mexico's largest (approx. 50m/164ft long by 40m/131ft wide) and most beautiful, forms part of the natural drainage of the Catemaco Lagoon. Eyipantla, meaning "Three Waterfalls," has been the setting for several movies. Descend to the riverbank to view it in all its splendor.

Catemaco – *12km/7mi from San Andrés Tuxtla.* This village lies on the shores of one of Mexico's most beautiful and largest natural lagoons. Traditions of the mystic Olmecs, influenced by their miscegenation with Negro slaves brought to work the plantations, and contact with the Western world combine to create an enchanting ambiance where witch doctors practice a mixture of magic, invocation of the spirits and medicinal herbal cures. In fact, a national annual convention of healers, witch doctors and shamans is held here on the first Friday of March.

Catemaco Lagoon, Veracruz

For its variety of herbs and medicinal plants, this immense **lagoon★** ranks among the world's richest. Thousands of birds migrate here during the winter. For an up-close tour of the lagoon, join one of the boat excursions, which take visitors to small islands where mandrills can be spotted in their natural habitats.

★★Parque Ecológico Educativo Nanciyaga – *7km/4mi from Catemaco. Located on the road to Coyame; accessed by car or boat; open year-round daily 8am–6pm; P$15; (cabins P$220, mud bath and use of kayaks included).* △ ✗ ▣ ☎ *(2) 943-0808.* Nanciyaga, meaning happiness, ranks as the ecological park with the most northerly tropical rain forest on Earth. It is an ideal spot to go for a stroll, observe local plants and animals, take a medicinal plant bath or mud bath, or enjoy a dip in the mineral springs. Visitors can make an appointment to see a *curandero*, or native healer, and experience the ceremony of *temascal*, a sweat bath of pre-Hispanic origins with curative powers. An ecotourist's paradise, the park served as the setting for the film *The Medicine Man*, starring Sean Connery.

Consult the legend on page 9 for an explanation of symbols and colors appearing on maps throughout this guide.

VILLAHERMOSA

Tabasco
Population 465,449
Map of Principal Sights
⚑ Av. de los ríos, corner of Calle 13, Complejo Tabasco 2000
☎ (9) 316-5122

The state capital of Villahermosa reflects the economic success that agriculture, ranching, fishing, commerce and most especially the petroleum industry have brought to Tabasco. Numerous mighty rivers crossing the state generate a third of the hydraulic power in Mexico. Three rivers, the most important being the Grijalva, surround the city, practically making it an island. Villahermosa lacks Colonial architecture, because Tabasco did not possess good local building stone or precious metals, common in other centers of colonial Mexico. Nevertheless, modern construction and design begun after the recent economic boom have more than made up for the previous building deficit. The remains of the pre-Hispanic Olmec and Maya cultures are the city's chief attraction.

Friendliness, warmth and hospitality describe the atmosphere of Villahermosa. Here, one can admire a great variety of flora and fauna native of the state. This perhaps contributes to the city's unique cuisine. Try dishes such as *pejelagarto*, a prehistoric animal, half-fish, half-lizard; *piguas*, a type of prawn, *chipilín*, a seasoning herb; *chorote*, a cacao and corn drink; and *oreja de mico*, a dessert made of small papayas and *piloncillo*, a sweet substance derived from sugarcane.

LAGUNA DE LAS ILUSIONES AND SURROUNDINGS

North of the city. Visitors can take trips on small rowboats across this enormous and beautiful natural lagoon. Taxis are recommended for touring the principal sights. On the banks of this lagoon lies the Parque Museo La Venta.

★★**Parque Museo La Venta** – *Av. Adolfo Ruiz Cortines. Open year-round daily 9am–5pm. Closed Jan 1, Dec 25. P$15. ✗ ☎ (9) 314-1652. Bring insect repellent, especially in May, June and July.* Located 4km/2.5mi east of the Tonalá River in the municipality of Huamanguillo, which borders the state of Veracruz, the **Olmec** ruins at **La Venta** nearly faced obliteration when the construction of a refinery altered the environment and destroyed several pre-Hispanic ruins. Discovered in 1940 by Matthew Stirling, the site appeared doomed until the renowned Tabascan poet, Carlos Pellicer built the park in the 1950s, in an attempt to recreate the Olmec site, and brought here the most representative pieces.

An introductory room displays a scale model of La Venta and describes the development of Olmec culture. Accented by tropical trees and free-roaming friendly animals, 7ha/17 acres of trails wind around the mighty Olmec heads. Pellicer's footprints mark the recommended path through the museum grounds. Although the exhibits are not in chronological order, scholars determined that the sculptures were carved over a period of 600 years. One of the great mysteries of the Olmecs centers around the fact that the stone used for the giant sculptures is not local. One theory claims that the material came from a nearby region, which raises the still unanswered question: How were they transported from so far away? For their monumental size and facial features, the **Olmec Heads**★★★, as well as **La Inconclusa** (10), **El Altar de los Niños** (12), **El Altar Triunfal** (23) and **La Estela del Rey** (25), constitute the most impressive of the 33 pieces on display.

Located at the end of the visit, the **zoo** *(same times and charges as the museum, except that it closes on Monday)* features local plants, jaguars, pumas, panthers, wildcats, monkeys, crocodiles, macaws, parrots and other birds. The collection is enriched by an aviary, a reptile room and a nocturnal animals room.

Museo de Historia Natural – *Across from the park. Open year-round Tue–Sun 9am–4:30pm. P$15. ☎ (9) 315-2889.* This modern museum displays exhibits on the flora, fauna and geology of Tabasco. Of special note is a presentation on the formation of petroleum, vital in the history and economy of the region.

Beside the museum, a trail leads to the Laguna de las Ilusiones, bordered by the Parque Tomás Garrido Canabal.

Parque Tomás Garrido Canabal – *Av. Adolfo Ruiz Cortines, at the intersection with Paseo Tabasco.* In 1930 Tomás Garrido Canabal, twice governor of Tabasco from 1923 to 1926 and from 1931 to 1934, inaugurated this park as the original site of the state fair. In honor of the former governor, the park was renamed in 1965. Inspired by the architecture of **Comalcalco** *(p 247)*, architect Teodoro González de León later remodeled the park. Reinaugurated in 1985, it boasts wide recreational spaces, a theater, and exhibit areas for art and other cultural events. The lovely sculpture *El Toro* (The Bull) by Juan Soriano, the *Cuadrángulo de los Arcos* (Quadrangle of the Arches), which symbolizes the fusion of Maya and Spanish culture, and the *Mirador de las águilas* (Eagle Lookout) complement the park's natural beauty.

Olmec Head, Parque Museo La Venta

MALECÓN *Southeast of the city.*

The downtown pedestrian zone borders to the west with the Malecón Carlos A. Madrazo, or waterfront promenade. From the latter, take the wide pedestrian bridge that crosses the Grijalva River. Across the bridge, turn right and continue down the other promenade to the CICOM (Research Center of Maya and Olmec Cultures). Captain Beuló's **restaurant-boat** docks here and sails the Grijalva River for dinner *(open year-round Tue–Sat, two departures: 3:30pm & 9:30pm; Sun, two departures: 1:30pm & 3:30pm; reservations recommended. Minimum consumption: P$50. ☎ 9-312-9209).* Landmarks visible from the boat include the **Biblioteca Pública José Maria Pino Suárez**, a public library designed by Teodoro González de León and Francisco Serrano which earned acclaim from the International Academy of Architecture in the late 1980s. Farther ahead note the **Teatro Esperanza Iris**–a theater named for the renowned Tabascan actress-the restaurant Los Tulipanes and the Museo Regional, one of the city's best museums.

★Museo Regional de Antropología "Carlos Pellicer Cámara" – *Av. Carlos Pellicer, 511. Open year-round Tue–Sun 9am–7pm. Closed Jan 1 & Dec 25. P$10.* ✗ ☎ *(9) 312-6344.* Donations from the INAH, part of the state's permanent collection, and Carlos Pellicer's own acquisitions, exhibited for 26 years in its entirety in the old Museum of Tabasco, make up the Regional Museum of Anthropology. Under the initiative of Pellicer, with the objective of housing more pieces, the museum was inaugurated in 1980, three years after his death.

The visit begins on the third floor, with an overview of the pre-Classic, Classic and post-Classic periods in Mesoamerica. Olmec and Mayan objects, originating from various parts of Tabasco and the Mayan area, are on display on the second floor. The **bricks** carved in high relief from **Comalcalco** and the **urns** from Teapa and Tacotalpa are the highlights of a fascinating collection. The urns of Tapijulapa are rare, as they have a partial coating of lime carbonate, which formed while they lay hidden in caves for hundreds of years. Two short, limestone *telamones* (columns shaped like men) from Chichén Itzá and handsome, earthen figurines from the Isla de Jaina, Campeche, complete the collection.

The ground floor houses the **Cabeza Colosal 2★★★** from La Venta (the best preserved of the four heads found in Tabasco), in addition to a room of monumental sculptures, which feature representations of jaguars and Maya stelae. The **Mezzanine★★** exhibits select pieces.

ADDITIONAL SIGHTS

Museo de Cultura Popular – *Zaragoza, 810. Open year-round Tue–Sat 10am–5pm, Sun 10am–4pm. Closed Jan 1, Dec 25.* ☎ *(9) 312-1117.* Three rooms of permanent exhibits comprise the Museum of Popular Culture. A collection of women's clothing from southeastern Mexico occupies the first room, while the second room, devoted to regional dance, displays tortoiseshell instruments, flutes and drums. A form of cultural expression still popular to this date, better known dances include the Dance of the Pochó, relating to Carnival, and the Dance of the

Little White Horse, symbolizing the impact the conquistadors' horses had upon the Aztecs. The last room displays artifacts such as typical Chontal household items and ritual utensils. A reproduction of a Chontal hut stands in the inner courtyard.

Museo de Historia de Tabasco (Casa de los Azulejos) – *Benito Juárez, corner of 27 de Febrero. Open year-round Tue–Sat & holidays 9am–8pm, Sun 10am–5pm. Closed Jan 1 & Dec 25. P$5.* 🍴 ☎ *(9) 316-5143.* This magnificent **House of Tiles★** belonged to José María Graham MacGregor, a businessman and book collector originally from Campeche. The only example of late-19C aristocratic Tabascan architecture, the house boasts a wide variety of Arabic, Gothic, Baroque and Renaissance elements and decoration. The walls' multicolor tiles were imported from Barcelona. Today the museum offers a journey through the state's history.

EXCURSIONS

★**Comalcalco** – *Go 51km/32mi northwest on the road Villahermosa-Comalcalco. Buses connect to Comalcalco from Villahermosa. Taxi service to the archaeological site is available in Comalcalco. Open year-round daily 10am–5pm. P$20.* 🍴 ☎ *(9) 316-5143.* A Maya-Chontal site, Comalcalco, or "place of the comal house," referring to the earthenware dish used for baking tortillas, experienced its heyday from AD 800–1250. The lack of suitable, building stone forced the inhabitants to construct their buildings from bricks—made from a mixture of sand, mud and burnt, ground-up seashells, and then baked in the open air. The bricks crafted through this process form the foundation for Comalcalco's architecture, unique among pre-Hispanic sites. Located at the entrance, the **site museum** exhibits a few of these bricks, and the most important artifacts found during the excavations. A short path provides access to the site. The first group of buildings, called the **Plaza Norte** *(accessed from the southeastern end)* consists of Templos I, II, III and IV and borders the northern edge of an enormous esplanade. To the east lies an unexplored platform. To its left, modern red stairs lead to the **Gran Acrópolis**, a series of temples, courtyards and residential buildings. From the top of this staircase, one can see on the immediate right the **Templo del Mascarón**, thus named for the stucco mask displayed there. This mask represents the sun god *Kinich Ahau*. To the left, various figures carved in relief embellish the **Templo de los Personajes Sedentes** (Temple of the Seated People). Returning to the main path and following the directional arrows, one reaches the **Templo IX**, also called the **Templo de los Bolontikú**, which houses the **Tumba de los Nueve Personajes** (Tomb of Nine People). Nine figures modeled in stucco adorn its walls. Here, human remains, vestiges of columns, and necklaces made of red-dyed shells were discovered. Next, an ascending pathway on the left leads to Temples IV and V. Turn left once again to access **El Palacio**, whose interior boasts a sunken courtyard and a complex system of waterworks. The system's earthenware pipes connect with drainage ditches. The summit of this great complex offers a sweeping **view** of the site.

★**YUMKA'** (Center of Interpretation and Coexistence with Nature) – *16km/10mi. From Villahermosa, take the highway to the airport. Shortly before arriving, turn right and continue on a small road for 4km/2.5mi to the site. Open year-round daily 9am–5pm. P$20.* 🍴 ☎ *(9) 356-0107. Bring insect repellent.* Yumka', Maya–Chontal for "the elf who cares for the jungle," aptly describes this splendid recreational park created for the enjoyment and study of the environment. More than 100ha/247 acres preserve the three Tabascan ecosystems: jungle, savanna and lagoon. Excursions on foot, by car or by panoramic boat offer a look at over 200 species of local fauna in its natural habitats, 32 animal species-including zebras, giraffes, rhinoceroses, elephants and Bengali tigers-and over 250 kinds of plants. The boat excursion *(P$10),* may be canceled during the dry season.

Michelin covers the USA with maps 491 Northeastern USA/ Eastern Canada, 492 Southeastern USA and 493 Western USA/ Western Canada.

XALAPA

Veracruz
Population 336,632
Map of Principal Sights – Map p 115 **(BY)**
🚹 Callejón de Rojas, 10, next to the Palacio Municipal
☎ (2) 818-6622 and (01-800) 712-6666 or www.xalapa.net

Xalapa, derived from the Náhuatl **Xallpan**, means "in the water of the quicksand." Nestled among mountains, the state capital and oldest city in Veracruz, Xalapa reached its apogee in the 18C, thanks to the increase in the commerce of maritime products yielding a building boom of neighborhoods, including the Neoclassical buildings that grace the heart of the city. Featuring a world-class symphony, Xalapa, site of the University of Veracruz, today boasts a lively cultural atmosphere, spanning every area of art. The city offers numerous cafes and bars with live folkloric music, jazz and *trova latina* (troubadour music).

★★★MUSEO DE ANTROPOLOGIA DE XALAPA

Av. Xalapa. Unless traveling by car, it is advisable to take a taxi to the museum.

This modern museum of anthropology *(open year-round daily 9am–5pm; closed national holidays; P$15.. ✗ ☎ 2-815-0920)* displays some 3,000 archaeological finds from the state of Veracruz, corresponding to the three great civilizations that occupied the region for 30 centuries before the Conquest-the Huastecs, the Totonacs and the Olmecs. The highlight is the collection of colossal **Olmec heads★★★**. Of the 17 heads discovered thus far, seven reside in this museum, all seven from San Lorenzo. These heads are said to personify different Olmec rulers. While the headdresses differ, the faces have very similar features: a flat nose, thick lips and cross eyes. Theories differ as to whether the Olmecs originated from Asia or Africa, but as yet no conclusive evidence prevails.

Vestibule – Two of the heads are on dispaly in the vestibule: one (8) sporting a headdress of jaguar paws, and farther back a second (5) with a jaguar-skin head-dress and eagle claws, possibly representative of the earth-sky duality.

First Section – *Two rooms and one courtyard.* Olmec artifacts from the pre-Classic period (1300–400 BC). The largest, weighing 18–20 tons, and most imposing **head★★★** (1) dominates the first courtyard. The adjacent room has other Olmec heads, including the only smiling one (9), as well as a variety of stelae, thrones, altars, heads and diverse anthropomorphic figures. Noteworthy in the second room are the **Sacerdote de las Limas**, bearing a jaguar-like infant in his arms; the jade masks, offerings to the god of water; and huge, post-Olmec stelae.

Second Section – *Three rooms and two courtyards.* This collection features objects from various ceremonial sites in central Veracruz. Although smaller than the Olmec artifacts, the clay figurines from the Classic period (3–9C AD) are more elaboratè, diverse and realistic. The first room boasts a splendid sculpture of Mictlantecuhtli, Lord of the Kingdom of the Dead, and small, ceramic smiling faces, probably Totonac. The next room exhibits several ball-game relics and bas–reliefs, primarily from El Tajín, as well as mural paintings from Las Higueras and female clay fig-urines from El Zapotal, a sanctuary of the *Cihuateteo*, women exalted for having died in childbirth.

Last Section – *One room.* The simpler design of these Huastec objects from the post-Classic period distinguishes them from those of the preceding cultures. Highlights include various male figures, with cone-shaped headdresses, and other figures dedicated to the Sun, Earth and Moon.

CITY CENTER

Located in the heart of Xalapa, the flower-filled **Parque Juárez** merits its reputation as a favorite resting stop. From the park's overlooks, the mountains of Pico de Orizaba, Cofre de Perote and Cerro de San Marcos can be seen in the distance on clear days. Three 18C buildings surround the plaza: the **Palacio de Gobierno** on the east side, the **Palacio Municipal** on the north side, and next to it the **cathedral**.

Descend the stairs on the west side of Parque Juárez (in front of the Desarrollo Agropecuario y Pesquero building) to reach the Pinacoteca Diego Rivera.

Pinacoteca Diego Rivera – *Open year-round Tue–Sun 10am–6pm. Guided tours Tue–Fri every 30min starting at 10:30am.* ☎ *(2) 818-1819.* This art gallery boasts a collection of 36 works by the famous Mexican painter **Diego Rivera**, who donated them to the state of Veracruz. Most notable are the *Retrato de la madre del pintor* (Portrait of the Painter's Mother, 1904), *Niño con pollito* (Child with Chick, 1935) and *Desnudo con girasoles* (Nude with Sunflowers, 1946).

Next to the cathedral, Calle Dr. Rafael Lucio climbs up to **Xallitic**, one of Xalapa's oldest neighborhoods. The bridge overlooks a small plaza and its early 19C **washbasins**, still in use to this day. Downtown's main avenue—which passes in front

248

of the cathedral—once called Calle Real (Royal St.), is known today as Juan de la Luz Enríquez. To explore this area, walk from the cathedral to the Church of San José *(facing the front of the cathedral, go right)*. The first little street on the left, once named **Callejón de El Diamante** (Diamond Alley) and today called Antonio M. de Rivera, serves as a gathering place for artisans and locals. Farther on, bear left when the street divides into Xalapeños Ilustres. One of the most beautiful areas in Xalapa lies a few streets away on **Callejón de Jesús te Ampare** (Alley of May Jesus Protect You), today called Cuauhtémoc, almost directly across the Church of St. Joseph. For a snack at one of the numerous cafes, return to Calle Zamora.

★**Museo de Ciencias y Tecnología de Veracruz** – *Av. Rafael Murillo Vidal. From the city center, follow Av. Murillo Vidal until you nearly reach its easternmost point, where it merges with Carr. 140. The museum is on the right. Open year-round Tue–Fri 9am–6pm, Sat–Sun 10am–7pm. P$24.* ✕ ☎ *(2) 812-5088.* This attractive and spacious museum of science and technology, inaugurated in 1992, features interactive displays and models that educate and entertain children of all ages. Visitors can see a simulated cave, the center of the Earth, or a real space capsule. Documentary films are projected on the enormous IMAX screen.

EXCURSIONS

★**Ex Hacienda de El Lencero** – *10km/6mi. From Xalapa, go southeast on Carr. 140 to Veracruz. After 9km/5.6mi, turn right in front of the military fields and continue 1.4km/0.9mi. Open year-round Tue–Sun 10am–5pm. P$10, free Tue.* ✕ ☎ *(2) 812-8500.* This unique, early-16C hacienda sits on top of a low hill, blanketed with a forest of fragrant laurel trees. The hacienda was named for its first owner, Juan Lencero, a soldier of Hernán Cortés. Lencero converted the hacienda into a modest inn for travelers. **Antonio López de Santa Anna**, eleven times president of Mexico, purchased the hacienda in 1842 and, two years later, was married in the chapel. With the cattle he raised here, Santa Anna fed the soldiers who fought in the war against the US. A splendid **collection**★ of 19C furniture, most of them European, graces the interior. In the backyard rises an enormous fig tree, over 500 years old, under whose canopy Santa Anna held periodic cockfights.

★**Jardín Botánico Francisco Javier Clavijero** – *Go 2.5km/1.6mi south of Xalapa on the old road to Coatepec. Open year-round daily 9am–5pm. Closed Jan 1, Dec 25. P$3.* ☎ *(2) 812-1827.* Dedicated to the maintenance, diffusion and study of the flora of Xalapa and its surroundings, this botanical garden exhibits over 1,500 plants, ranging from jungle to conifer forest, which attest to the great botanical diversity of Veracruz. The 8ha/20 acre grounds also include a decorative flower garden, a man-made estuary for aquatic plants and a traditional vegetable garden.

★**Coatepec** – *From Xalapa, head south for 8km/5mi on Carr. estatal 7. Once you reach the traffic circle at the entrance to Coatepec, continue on the same path, bearing slightly to the right, for another km/0.6mi to reach the old city center. Turn right onto Calle Jiménez del Campillo (the first paved street) to access the main plaza.* Coatepec, or "hill of serpents," is renowned for its exquisite coffee and annual Coffee Fair (April–May), as well as for its fine Colonial architecture. This small picturesque city, with its cobblestone streets and red-roofed houses, gives a feel of the past and is best discovered on foot. Start in the main plaza, with one of the famous ices *(nieves)* from the kiosk in the center. On the east side of the plaza stands the Church of San Jerónimo, built by the Franciscans shortly after they evangelized the area in 1560. It faces the Neoclassical city hall.

★**Xico (Cascadas de Texolo)** – *Once you reach Coatepec from Xalapa, take the main road (Cuauhtémoc) to Calle Juárez. There, turn left and follow the signs to Xico (6km/3.7mi). In Xico, turn left when you see a small, hand-painted sign with the word Cascada. Continue another km/0.6mi on an unkempt dirt road and another 2km/1.2mi on a cobblestone road.* ✕. The Texolo waterfall is a spectacular sight as it crashes down the cliff face. No wonder Hollywood chose this setting to film *Romancing the Stone*. One can admire the waterfall from above, via a hanging bridge across the face of the cliff, or from the riverbanks below (350 steps). Every July the village of Xico holds a *pamplonada*, or bull festival.

★★★**El Tajín** – *217km/135mi. From Xalapa, go 36km/22mi north via Carr. 140 to Perote. Turn right and take Carr. 131 to the junction with Carr. 180 (96km/60mi). For an alternate route, go southeast on Carr. 140 for 55km/34mi to Cardel. Then go north on Carr. 180 to Papantla (188km/117mi) and continue 16km/10mi to the archaeological site. Description p 235.*

PACIFIC COAST

Land of Ancient Cultures and Unparalleled Natural Beauty

Handicrafts and Food, p 53. Mexico's Pacific Coast encompasses many of the nation's greatest cultural treasures. This region occupies a diverse landscape, which ranges from vast plains and magnificent beaches to verdant mountain chains and lofty peaks. This area also boasts many of Mexico's most stunning geologic wonders. Fantastic grottoes delight visitors with imaginary and whimsical formations, cascades and lakes bear every shape and color, and mighty cliffs guard images and legends within their walls. The region's flora and fauna, unique in the world, complement all of these natural marvels. Historically, the importance of each of these states relates in some way to this natural wealth.

Chis. .... Chiapas
Gro. .... Guerrero
Mich. .... Michoacán
Oax. .... Oaxaca

During the pre-Hispanic era, some of the most powerful indigenous groups established themselves here, erecting great temples and cities and leaving behind many remains that exist to the present day. Later, the Spanish transformed the majority of these sites into colonial cities. Despite the destruction and changes wrought by the Conquest, indisputably, the Spanish left behind an incredibly rich architectural and artistic legacy. Monumental convents, churches and other buildings of that era form part of the historical and artistic heritage of Mexico, as well as the rest of the world. In addition, the mixture of cultures and races found here provides the key to understanding the complex Mexican identity and helps to explain how Mexico evolves and changes today. The Pacific Coast shelters the majority of the nation's indigenous groups, who keep their traditions, languages and customs alive. In some areas, their influence remains extremely strong; in others, the modern world has prevailed. Without a doubt, the most interesting Mexican states are those where the direct descendants of the ancient civilizations still thrive today.

Though Guerrero, Michoacán, Oaxaca and Chiapas share a common natural, historical and cultural richness, each state possesses distinctive traits that help make it special. The languages, customs and cuisine vary so greatly that visitors might envision the states as separate countries. Such magic and charm characterize the region and draw people who visit it solely for its beaches, as well as those thirsting for knowledge in history, archaeology, anthropology and architecture.

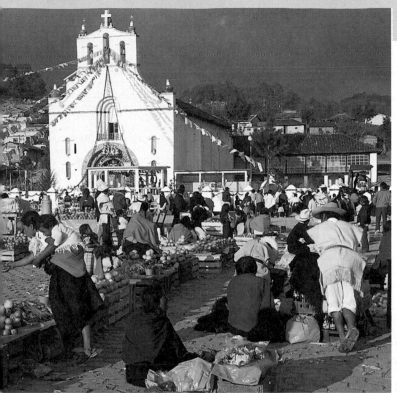

Market, San Juan Chamula, Chiapas

ACAPULCO★★

Guerrero
Population 687,292
Map of Principal Sights – Map p 253
🅱 Costera Miguel Alemán, 4455 (Centro Internacional Acapulco) and 187
☎ (7) 484-4416 and 486-9171

Known as the **Pearl of the Pacific** for the beauty of its beaches and magnificent climate, Acapulco glories in being the most visited vacation spot not only in Mexico, but in all Latin America. Hundreds of domestic and foreign tourists visit this famous port annually, which despite the pace of modern life, still manages to preserve its loveliness and original attractions.

Historical Notes – In the colonial era, Acapulco became the most important center of communication between Europe and Asia, after being founded in 1566 as a stopping point on the commercial route to the Far East. Shortly after the Spanish established the route, the much feared pirates made their appearance and tried to take advantage of this gold mine. To protect its interests, the Spanish Crown ordered the construction of the **Fuerte de San Diego**. The last of the embarkations took place in 1815.

BAHÍA DE ACAPULCO AND COSTERA MIGUEL ALEMÁN

This enormous bay, measuring almost 7km/4mi long, lies at the heart of modern Acapulco. The Costera Miguel Alemán, the city's longest avenue, fringes the port and intersects with the various **beaches** along its route. During the day, the large hotels and restaurants offer every service and convenience to those who flock here to enjoy the sun, sea and sand. In the afternoon, the shopping centers and diverse stores beckon visitors to stroll along the Costera. By night, the scene glitters with the lights of discotheques, yachts and romantic locales. In the **Centro Internacional Acapulco** *(Costera Miguel Alemán, 4455)*, a modern building located on the far, west end of the boulevard, the **Fiesta Mexicana** *(year-round Mon, Wed & Fri starting at 7pm; P$350; includes dinner and one drink; reservations required; ☎ 7-484-7152)* takes place three times a week. This celebration features several regional Mexican dances and the fascinating **Papantla Flyers** from Veracruz.

★ **Museo Histórico de Acapulco (Fuerte de San Diego)** – *Morelos and Hornitos. Open year-round Tue–Sun 9:30am–6:30pm. P$20. ☎ (7) 482-3828.* The Spanish Crown ordered the construction of the original fort in 1615 to protect the famous **Manila**

251

Galleon (also called the *Nao de la China*, or China Ship), which pirates attacked in order to steal cargo arriving from the Far East. After an earthquake destroyed the original fort in 1776, five years passed before the pentagonal stone structure was finished, this time with a moat and multiple new sections. The information the museum provides describes in detail the port's history and focuses on the importance of maritime trade. Among the curiosities is a scale model of the aforementioned galleon and several objects related to trade with the Far East.

Those traveling with children might enjoy a visit to one of Acapulco's recreational parks: **Cici** *(corner of Costera Miguel Alemán and Cristóbal Colón; open year-round daily 10am–6pm; P$50;* ☎ *7-484-1971)* and **Papagayo** *(Gómez Morín, 1; open year-round daily 7am–9pm;* ☎ *7-485-6837).* The first park boasts a huge swimming pool with artificial waves, toboggans, slides and marine animal shows; the second consists of an ecological area that offers rides through man-made lakes, a skating rink and amusement rides, among other forms of entertainment.

ACAPULCO BY SEA

In the western part of the bay, towards the center and along the Costera highway, lie the attractions that made Acapulco famous in the 1940s.

★**Isla Roqueta** – *Opposite Caleta and Caletilla, 1km/0.6mi offshore. The pier sits directly in front of the Mundo Mágico Marino (Magical Marine World).* One of Acapulco's most traditional excursions, the small, glass-bottom boats allow visitors to observe the underwater world live and in full color. The trip takes approximately 45min and includes visits to additional sights before arrival at the island. The tour passes by several of the homes of celebrities like John Wayne and Juan Gabriel, as well as by the mansion where the very entertaining movie *El inocente* (The Innocent One), starring the famous Mexican actors Pedro Infante and Silvia Pinal, was filmed. Next to the tiny island of Yerbabuena, a statue of the **Virgin of Guadalupe** rests underwater at a depth of 7m/23ft. The statue was set in place on December 12, 1959, after being brought from the Basilica of Guadalupe in Mexico City in a highway procession that stopped in each town.

Roqueta offers safe and tranquil beaches. Good services like dining, beach chair and umbrella rentals, and aquatic activities are available at the **Reserva Marina La Roqueta**. This marine reserve is a protected area, and the coral reefs teem with beautiful fish. Another attraction is the **Aca Zoo**, a small zoological park that is home to different local species. Visitors may also follow the path that winds around the island and climbs the trail to **El Faro**, a lighthouse.

★★**Espectáculo de La Quebrada (Cliff Diving)** – *Plazoleta de la Quebrada, Downtown. Year-round daily 12:45pm, 7:30pm, 8:30pm, 9:30pm and 10:30pm. P$12.* ✗ ▣ ☎ *(7) 483-1400.* The breathtaking cliff divers of La Quebrada are known around the world. Beginning the show with an appearance in the small square, the diver then descends the cliff to the water, swims across to a crevice on the facing rock, which he climbs up to a height of 25m/82ft or 35m/115ft, before diving fearlessly into the void. Supposedly, no native has ever lost his life making the dive. Occasionally, the dives become terrifically complex, and the most spectacular is the last one of the day.

Acapulco Bay

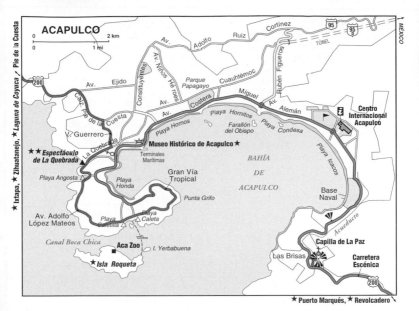

CLEMENTE MEJÍA SCENIC HIGHWAY

An extension of the Costera Miguel Alemán, this scenic highway possesses numerous overlooks with **panoramic views★**. For another place to enjoy the beautiful landscape, check out the **vantage point★** at the **Capilla de la Paz** (Chapel of Peace), located next to the church and inside the Fraccionamiento Las Brisas at Costera Miguel Alemán, 5255.

★**Puerto Marqués** – The bay's beauty resembles that of Acapulco Bay, only on a smaller and less commercial scale. This place once served as the refuge of the insatiable pirates. One of the most famous of these men, Pierre Marqués, who gave his name to the bay, was said to have hidden here. Visitors may choose from several types of activities, ranging from snorkeling and scuba diving to water-skiing and sailing. On the beach, vendors sell delicious seafood dishes and refreshing beverages.

★**Revolcadero** – An ideal place for long strolls or horseback rides, the "Wallow" gets its names from the beach's powerful waves. Authorities do not recommend swimming far from shore, because the beach faces the open sea.

EXCURSIONS

★**Laguna de Coyuca** – *Located on Carr. Fed. 200, toward Ixtapa–Zihuatanejo, 13km/8mi from Acapulco.* This enormous lagoon offers scenery very different from that of Acapulco. The lagoon trip presents an exceptional opportunity to view the flora and fauna of this marvelous jungle filled with estuaries, mangrove swamps and numerous birds that inhabit the trees of the tiny islands. For many years, a jail stood on the **Isla del Presidio**. During this time, fierce crocodiles surrounded the island and impeded the prisoners' escape. Today, the island provides a sanctuary for blackbirds, ducks and quite curiously, an abundance of cats. From the docks, do not miss the archaeological site, thus named for the strange drawings that the tide reveals as it retreats. Lastly, visit **La Montosa** Island for excellent food and rest before starting the return trip.

After disembarking from the boat, a stop at the **Pie de la Cuesta** provides the perfect chance to watch a splendid **sunset★** and end the day with a golden memory. The awesome waves, which reach heights of nearly 4m/13ft, also make this beach memorable.

Ixtapa and Zihuatanejo – *245km/152mi. Head northwest on Carr. 200.*

★**Ixtapa** – This magnificent tourist complex, built to face the open sea, features great luxury hotels, elegant restaurants and exclusive shopping. The **Isla Ixtapa★** and its four small, tranquil beaches are the premier attractions. The waters resemble natural aquariums and boast unrivaled beauty.

★**Zihuatanejo** – *7km/4.3mi from Ixtapa.* This city exudes a charming, small town atmosphere. During the day, visitors can enjoy promenades and aquatic activities offered on the bay's three tranquil beaches—La Madera, La Ropa and Las Gatas—

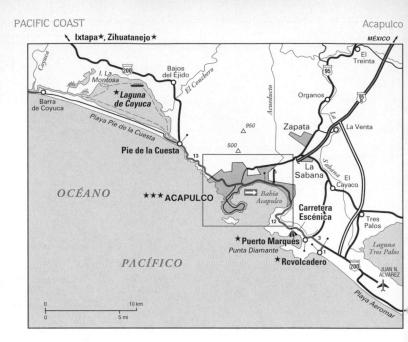

as well as the main pier. When the sun sets, the markets and shops turn into pleasant meeting places. In the evening, the restaurants located on the main beach offer fine dining.

The city boasts the **Museo Arqueológico de la Costa Grande** (Archaeology Museum of the Costa Grande), which explores the region's history *(open year-round Tue–Sun 9am–7pm; closed Jan 1 and Dec 25; P$4; ☎ 7-554-7552).*

Bahías de HUATULCO★★

Oaxaca
Map of Principal Sights
🅱 Av. Chahué, Bahías de Huatulco ☎ (9) 587-0090

Huatulco Bay is without doubt one of the most beautiful areas on the Pacific Coast. The stunning consecutive placement of nine marvelous bays gave rise in the 1980s to the construction of an elegant tourist complex, which helped to develop this splendid corner of Oaxaca. Before the government decided to build the resort, Huatulco was a small fishing town with a population of 500. In return for their lands, the villagers received housing, money and the concession of public transport. The push for tourism development sparked a rise in migration from other parts of Mexico, and many people have found a new way of life here.

★★BOAT TOUR OF THE BAYS

Guided tours depart from the port of Santa Cruz year-round daily 8am–4pm. Reservations recommended. From P$300 to P$1,000 depending on the tour (price per boat for 1–10 people, round trip). 🍴 🅱 ☎ (9) 587-0081.

The general tour includes visits to the nine bays, with the option of anchoring in some of them to enjoy the beaches and tranquillity of the ocean, as well as the opportunity to observe the fantastic natural aquariums visible through the crystalline waters.

Leaving Santa Cruz Bay, the boat stops first at **La Entrega** (The Delivery) Beach, so-named because it was here that authorities took former Mexican president Vicente Guerrero into custody, as he attempted to flee the country, before executing him at Cuilapan de Guerrero, Oaxaca. Later, the tour passes the **Isla de los Pelícanos** (Pelican Island) and **El Bufadero**. The next stop finds **El Órgano**, which owes its name to the organ pipe cacti scattered about this as yet untouched pristine island. Then the tour visits the **Cara de Piedra** (Rock Face), also called the **Cara Olmeca** (Olmec Face), sculpted by nature upon the rocky crag. The nearby bay of **El Maguey** boasts a mild surf and offers water sports as well as delicious seafood. **Cacaluta** Bay features an enormous, still unspoiled beach, which from an aerial view supposedly resembles a heart. This beach's Zapotec name means "place where the blackbird comes to perch." Another Zapotec name, **Chachacual**, means "place where the turtles lay their eggs." A rock formation, which looks like a lion lying down casting its gaze toward the horizon, separates the last two bays, **Riscalillo** and **San Agustín**. A fisherman's beach, San Agustín sells very fresh and delicious seafood. On the other side of Santa Cruz, commercial bays reserved for hotel construction are **Tangolunda**, **Chahué** and **Conejos**.

EXCURSIONS

Zona Aromática – *On the road to Salina Cruz, 45km/28mi into the mountains. An organized tour is recommended.* The regional economy depends upon the production of **pluma coffee** for the Mexican market and exportation. English pirates brought the first coffee plants to the area during the colonial era. Toward the end of the 19C, the Germans gave the coffee industry a great boost, converting this region into one of the most productive. In the middle of the 20C, the German estates were expropriated, and the surrounding towns adapted themselves to this lucrative work. The area boasts totally organic coffee production. The harvest season brings together many of Oaxaca's diverse ethnic groups, among them the Mixes, Zapotecs, Chontals, Huaves and Triquis.

The most frequently visited region consists of more than 50,000ha/123,550 acres. Several of the estates remain very isolated and are accessible only by jeep. The journey is fascinating both for the experience of visiting a coffee plantation and for the natural marvels that unfold en route. The great variety of tropical vegetation switches abruptly to typical mountain scenery.

Puerto Angel – *Carr. 200 heading to Puerto Escondido, 45km/28mi from the Bays of Huatulco.* Puerto Angel's main bay is small but very beautiful. The turquoise blue, crystal-clear water and tranquil surf make this bay an ideal spot for swimming and scuba diving. Also found here is **Playa del Panteón**, a beach named for the cemetery carved into the side of a nearby mountain.

Zipolite, a nudist beach, unfolds a little farther ahead. The entire length of this marvelous beach faces the open sea with plenty of *palapas* (thatched-roof huts) offering inexpensive accommodations.

Centro Mexicano de la Tortuga (Mexican Turtle Center) – *Approximately 10km/6mi from Zipolite, located on Mazunte beach. Visit by guided tour (1hr), year-round Tue–Sun 10am–4:30pm. P$4.* ⚓ ▣ . For three decades, the sale of turtle eggs, meat and shells was a very successful business in the area. This caused the Mexican government to prohibit the capture of the species in 1990. In 1992 the government also inaugurated the turtle center in Mazunte with the hope of contributing to the global effort to prevent the extinction of this species. The center opened to the public in 1994 to help foster environmental awareness; one of the activities is excursions to observe the turtles as they lay their eggs.

Puerto Escondido – *110km/68mi. From Huatulco Bays, head west on Carr. 200.* Formerly known as Punta Escondida, Puerto Escondido boasts ten splendid beaches, located one after the other, spreading from the tiny bay of **Puerto Angelito** to the ample beach of **Zicatela**, whose giant waves peak at 7m/23ft. This beach sponsors two annual surfing competitions, one for amateurs and one for professionals. From the main pier, small boats frequently depart, offering an unforgettable opportunity to observe dolphins and turtles before touring the bay's many beaches. The tourist walkway along the rocks provides a pleasant, meeting place and also offers stunning **views** of the ocean.

Despite the lack of developed tourist services, the natural beauty attracts visitors from around the world, creating an international atmosphere.

★**Parque Nacional Lagunas de Chacahua** (Lagoons of Chacahua National Park) – *Located on Carr. Fed. 200 heading to Acapulco, approximately 70km/43mi from Puerto Escondido. Open year-round, daily 8am–5pm.* ⚓ ▣ ☎ *(9) 516-0123. We recommend joining an escorted tour: minimum of 4 people, P$250/ea. (Turismo Rodimar:* ☎ *9-582-0734).* A visit to the park promises to be one of the most fascinating excursions on the Pacific Coast. The adventure begins on land with the unique natural phenomenon of the "love trees." Once the boat has docked and entered the waters of Pastoría and Chacahua Lagoons, the spirit of adventure increases as the tour passes through a thick jungle inhabited by migratory birds. The highlight of the tour includes face-to-face encounters with ferocious crocodiles that, despite being caged, instill fear. After such excitement, the chance to relax and sample local culinary specialties is a welcome respite.

MITLA★★

Oaxaca
Map of Principal Sights
🖪 ☎ (9) 568-0316

The last religious center of the pre-Hispanic era, where the inhabitants buried only great lords and important figures, rests in the heart of the town of San Pablo Mitla. More than the majesty of the structures, it is the decoration that sets this site apart. Thousands of tiny, perfectly cut and polished stones, assembled without any adhesives and set in clay walls, comprise the fret design that has made Mitla famous. The impeccable geometric designs are related to the ancient gods.

Mitla was founded around AD 100 and is considered to be the last Zapotec city. Because the Mixtecs exercised hegemony over the Zapotecs in later years, its structures reveal a strong Mixtec influence. The name Mitla comes from the Náhuatl **Mictlán**, which means "place of the dead." Though the Zapotecs called it **Liobaá**, it kept the Náhuatl name, as the Aztecs conquered the city in its last days. Mitla was still inhabited when the Spanish arrived in 1521.

ARCHAEOLOGICAL SITE

Located 46.5km/28.8mi from Oaxaca. Head east on Carr. Fed. 190; after 11km/25.4mi, take the exit to Carr. Fed. 175 and continue 5.5km/3.4mi. Open year-round daily 8am–6pm. P$17. ☎ (9) 568-0316.

The archaeological site is comprised by five sections: Iglesia, Columnas, Adobe, Arroyo and Sur. The most important are the first two, and although the remaining areas can be visited, they have been only partially explored.

Grupo de la Iglesia – *Located behind the 17C Church of San Pablo Apóstol (St. Paul the Apostle).* Behind the church, a street leads to a courtyard holding three small structures with fret-decorated lintels over the doors. This courtyard connects to a smaller one. More remains can be seen embedded in the walls of the church, which was built over ruins.

Grupo de las Columnas – This group consists of two large quadrangles that connect at one corner. The two quadrangles are similar in structure, and both possess inner courtyards with small temples in the center and rooms on three sides.

The **Salón de las Columnas** (Hall of Columns), built over a medium-size foundation with stairway, rests in the first complex. The upper section features a 38m/123ft x 7m/23ft hall; two thick columns split the entrance into three sections. Six monolithic columns support the interior. In the right corner, a small doorway leads to **El Palacio** (Patio de las Grecas). The fret design decorating the courtyard contains over 100,000 carved stones. Narrow cubicles, which served as tombs, line the sides.

To enter the second complex, return to the main pathway and walk south.

On the northern side of the courtyard lies a tomb whose entrance opens under the front of the building. A column, popularly known as the "column of life," sustains a portion of the interior ceiling. According to legend, anyone who wraps his arms around the column can ascertain how many more years he will live. One person embraces the column, while another measures the space left between the first person's hands, with his fingers in a vertical position. Each finger counts as two years. Popular lore also claims that once someone sits three times on the enormous rock found here, that person will marry soon thereafter.

Patio de las Grecas, detail

Hierve el Agua, Oaxaca

Museo de Arte Zapoteca de Mitla (Museo Frisell) – *Located at the entrance to Mitla. Open year-round Thu–Tue 10am–5pm. P$10.* ☎ *(9) 516-0123.* This small, late-18C house exhibits approximately 2,000 pre-Hispanic items of Mixtec and Zapotec origin.

EXCURSION

★★**Hierve el Agua** – *28km/17.4mi from Mitla. Head east on the road to Ayutla; after 18km/11.2mi, take the dirt road to the right and continue 10km/6.2mi. Open year-round daily 7am–8pm. P$10.* ✗ ▤ ⚠ ☎ *(9) 562-0922. We recommend avoiding holidays to visit this sight.* Amid a jagged mountain range sits this pre-Hispanic irrigation system, which has produced eye-catching, fossilized formations. Between 700 BC and AD 1350, the springs in this region were used to create a system of 600 terraces and at least 6km/3.7mi of canals that irrigated an approximate area of 17sq km/10.5sq mi.

The saline waters have contributed towards fossilizing this system, resulting in marvelous formations, such as the impressive **cascadas de sal**★, through which water continues flowing. One can also see remnants of pre-Hispanic canals. *(The best way to see these attractions is by way of a 2.3km/1.4mi trail.)* On the upper platform, known as the **Anfiteatro**, visitors can enjoy a unique and refreshing bath in the natural pools, while appreciating a spectacular **view**★ of the mountains.

Hierve el Agua ("Water Boils") was named for the bubbles formed when water emerges from the spring, which resemble boiling water. Ironically, the water temperature is actually ideal for calming the heat found in this zone.

Traveling through the United States? Consult THE GREEN GUIDE USA East and USA West.

MONTE ALBÁN★★★
Oaxaca
Map of Principal Sights – Map p 259
☎ (9) 516-1215

From the heights of this impressive pre-Hispanic center, one may contemplate the beauty of the Oaxacan landscape. Monte Albán's imposing structures guard untold secrets and stories within their walls, including the city's true origin. Despite hundreds of years of abandonment, the site continues to command respect and admiration. The Zapotecs built Monte Albán with their own hands, without the help of animals or machinery. It is enigmatic to determine how they alone could have flattened the terrain and constructed this marvelous site, which was declared a World Heritage Site in 1987.

Historical Notes

Origins – The name is derived from a mixture of the Zapotec word **Danibaá**, which means "Sacred mountain," and the Spanish phrase *Colinas Albanas*, used by conquistadors to describe the site's hilly location. Monte Albán's origin dates back to 500 BC. For almost 1,300 years, the city served as the Zapotec region's chief political, economic and cultural center. Around AD 750 to 800, its inhabitants abandoned the city for unexplained reasons.

Ancient Research Center – Many researchers believe that the inhabitants never intended Monte Albán to be used as an urban center because of the absence of nearby rivers. Here, the Zapotecs could ponder their existential, creationist and scientific philosophies. After being abandoned, Monte Albán came to life again when groups reinhabited the city and used it as a mausoleum and military fortress. The Mixtecs occupied the enclave long after the departure of the Zapotecs. Later, both cultures would use it as military quarters during their struggle for control of the valleys.

Archaeological Exploration – In the lapse of time between the Conquest and the beginning of the 20C, Monte Albán was forgotten. However, when **Leopoldo Batres** first explored the site in 1902, he found that it had been sacked innumerable times. To the present day, the greatest discovery has been **Tomb 7** by **Alfonso Caso**, who explored the site on two occasions, from 1931 to 1949 and again in 1958. Mexico's National Institute of Anthropology and History (INAH) launched a series of new excavations in 1996. Monte Albán, the only hill explored to date, forms part of the four hills comprising the archaeological site. According to the chronological system used to study Mesoamerican cultures, anthropologists have divided the history of Monte Albán into five periods: Period I (500 to 100 BC), Period II (100 BC to AD 250), Period III (AD 250 to 800), Period IV (AD 800 to 1300) and Period V (AD 1300 to 1521).

ARCHAEOLOGICAL SITE

On the new highway to Monte Albán, 10km/6mi southwest of Oaxaca. Open year-round daily 8am–6pm. P$25. ✗ ☲ .

Unidad de Servicios Culturales (Cultural Services Unit) – This small museum, which describes Monte Albán's history and importance, features exhibition rooms that display replicas and original pieces, as well as a bookstore and restaurant. A monument dedicated to the historian and archaeologist Alfonso Caso marks the area between the service unit and site entrance.

Gran Plaza – The esplanade of this ceremonial civic center measures about 200m/656ft wide and 300m/984ft long. The ancient Zapotecs leveled out the terrain as best as they could and then took advantage of natural rocky formations for construction, as was the case in the central buildings and the interior of the outer platforms. To achieve the nearly perfect visual symmetry, because the east side was wider than the west, the Zapotecs decided to construct courtyards and small structures to face the great buildings on the narrow side. Thus, both halves balance each other.
The buildings seen here did have specific functions; yet, they were not houses. The Zapotecs lived on the nearby mountain slopes.
The site tour begins on the Plataforma Norte (North Platform), to the right of the entrance, and continues counterclockwise.

Plataforma Norte – The front section of this ensemble boasts a wide flight of stairs flanked with ample balustrades that measure almost 12m/39ft thick. To the right of the base (the east side), there is a small sanctuary with a carved stone. The stone is framed by drawings, while its sides are covered with reliefs and the top section is decorated with anthropomorphic figures. In front of the stairs is a freestanding stela, bearing figures and glyphs on all four sides. The platform's upper section has remnants of 12 columns, which might have once supported a roof. Around it, there are four small square temples and, in the center, a sunken patio with a sanctuary in the middle.

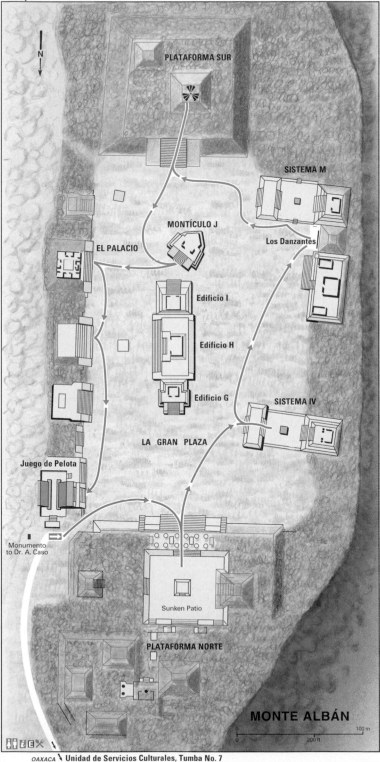

↑ Edificio 7 Venado

N

PLATAFORMA SUR

SISTEMA M

MONTÍCULO J

Los Danzantes

EL PALACIO

Edificio I

Edificio H

Edificio G

SISTEMA IV

LA GRAN PLAZA

Juego de Pelota

Monumento
to Dr. A. Caso

Sunken Patio

PLATAFORMA NORTE

MONTE ALBÁN

100 m

200 ft

OAXACA ↘ Unidad de Servicios Culturales, Tumba No. 7

Sistema IV and Sistema M

Sistema IV – System IV features the **Templo-Patio-Adoratorio** (Temple-Courtyard-Sanctuary), one of the most important innovations of Zapotec architecture. Two foundation-like structures, divided by an intermediary courtyard with a central sanctuary, protrude from the front of the edifice. A building with a stairway rises in the background. This building's upper levels feature the remains of four columns that form a small vestibule.

A 5m/16ft stela, originally much taller, stands to the right of System IV. Calendar glyphs decorate the western face. Some guides call it the **sand clock**, but in reality no one knows exactly what purpose it served.

Los Danzantes – This building is named for the figures on the **reliefs** on the left side of this structure. The figures seem to be performing ritual dances; nevertheless, historians hold varying opinions concerning them. Some say that the figures depict sacrificial victims; others claim they are leaders of neighboring regions. Still others suggest that those depicted represent sick people, or even images belonging to a sex cult. Whatever the case may be, it is indisputable that these "dancers" bear the physical traits of the **Olmecs**, rulers of Mesoamerica's first civilization.

Sistema M – System M mirrors the layout of System IV and provides architectural balance to the west side.

Plataforma Sur – The facade resembles that of the North Platform for the flight of stairs flanked with wide balustrades. This platform has been partially explored. On the outer, lower edges of the base, there are some embedded stelae with decorative carvings. Two small earthen mounds crisscrossed by looters' tunnels rise above the upper level. From here, a marvelous **view★★★** of the plaza and landscape unfolds.

Edificio 7 Venado – *250m/820ft southeast of the plaza. Continue on the trail on the east side of the South Platform.* The Seven Deer Building is composed of four structures grouped around a plaza, each oriented toward a cardinal point. The name 7 Venado comes from the carved inscription on one of the lintels.

Montículo J – The most interesting of the central buildings, Mound J boasts several noteworthy features like the building's southwesterly orientation, its arrowhead design and interior tunnels. These elements lead researchers to believe that the structure functioned as an astronomical observatory. The carved slabs along the sides of the building are related to the conquests by Monte Albán.

El Palacio – Inside this building, the nature of the remains in several rooms grouped around the central patio suggests they belonged to the ruling classes.

Edificios G, H and I – It is believed that these central buildings were constructed over a rocky mound of earth. Visitors can access the upper levels from three sides of the plaza. Two rooms, located on the upper level of Building H, between Buildings G and I, attract attention for the columns on the side walls. The famous bat shaped jade mask, now exhibited at the National Museum of Anthropology in Mexico City, was found in front of the building's main stairway in a small underground temple.

Juego de Pelota – This ball court lacks rings on the sides, as do other ball courts in this region. As was the case with the **Mixtec ball game** common throughout Oaxaca, at the beginning of a game the players bounced the ball against a large stone facade located in the center of the court. A sculpture of a grasshopper is found on the upper portion of the east wall, while two monoliths with calendar glyphs are found on the west side.

In the area surrounding Monte Albán, Alfonso Caso found 170 tombs. Although most of them are Zapotec structures, the offerings found inside them were Mixtec. Archaeologists determined this from the type of ceramic used in the offerings. Tomb 7, located next to the parking lot, merits special attention. Some of the other tombs, though distant from the main plaza, can be visited, while the most interesting ones have been moved to museums.

MORELIA★★

Michoacán
Population 578,061
Map of Principal Sights – City Map pp 262-263
🏛 Nigromante, 79, Palacio Clavijero
☎ (4) 317-2371 and (01-800) 450-2300

At an altitude of 1,950m/6,396ft, the state capital Morelia crowns a slight hillock in the ancient Guayangareo Valley. The layers of sandstone encircling the city have been used to create that majestic and solid appearance that made Morelia worthy of being recognized as a World Heritage Site in 1991.

The colonial flavor permeating the streets combines with a college-town atmosphere, as many of the colonial buildings today form part of the university's facilities. Cultural activities and strong musical tradition bring Morelia great fame. The international festivals of regular as well as pipe organ music figure among the most anticipated annual events.

Historical Notes

Pre-Hispanic and Colonial Era – During the pre-Hispanic era, the state was inhabited by the **Mazahua, Otomí, Nahua, Matlatzinca** and **Michuaca**. This last group, referred to after the Conquest as **Tarascan** or **Purépecha**, dominated the majority of the western territory. Little is known about their origin, but they have been compared to groups from Peru, owing to the similarities in language and culture. The Tarascans were one of the few groups capable of defending themselves successfully against the Mexicas, also known as the Aztecs. The three Tarascan kingdoms were situated in **Pátzcuaro, Tzintzuntzan** and **Ihuatzio**. As a result of the peaceful submission of the indigenous cultures, the Spanish Conquest was not as savage or destructive in this region as it had been in Tenochtitlán (present-day Mexico City). Nevertheless, around 1530, the local Spanish magistrate **Nuño de Guzmán** unleashed a terribly violent war against them, forcing them to flee from their settlements into the mountains as an act of protest. **Vasco de Quiroga**, sent by the Second Audience of New Spain to mediate this conflict and calm the indigenous rebellion, began his pacifying, evangelical work in Tzintzuntzan in 1538, and again in Pátzcuaro a year later. This converted him into the justice-loving protector of the local people, who respectfully called him **Tata Vasco**, as *tata* is the Purépecha word for "father".Some years later, in 1541, Viceroy **Antonio de Mendoza** founded the city of Valladolid where Morelia stands today. The Spanish Crown granted the city the official title and coat of arms in 1546. In 1580, both secular and ecclesiastical authorities moved from Pátzcuaro to Valladolid. During the colonial era, Michoacán flourished culturally and enjoyed excellent economic development thanks to the work of the religious authorities and the natural wealth of the earth.

Nineteenth and Twentieth Centuries – Michoacán played the protagonist in several of the most important events of the war for Mexican Independence. Suffice it to mention the name of José María Morelos y Pavón, native of Morelia, who joined efforts with Father Miguel Hidalgo y Costilla and won great triumphs for the Independence movement, thanks to his great gift for organization and military genius. In addition, Ignacio López Rayón proclaimed the Manifest of the Nation in 1811 in Zitácuaro. In Apatzingán, the Congress of Anáhuac created the First Constitution of Mexico in 1814. In 1824 Michoacán was declared a Free and Sovereign State. Four years later, Valladolid officially adopted the name of Morelia in honor of Morelos.

During the Mexican Revolution, the efforts of Salvador Escalante, Francisco Mújica and Lázaro Cárdenas were also crucial. Today, Cárdenas is considered one of the most beloved and respected figures in Mexico.

★★HISTORIC CENTER

★★**Cathedral** – *Av. Madero. Open year-round daily 6am–8:30pm.* One of the first buildings constructed of pink quarry stone, the cathedral's architecture and style set the model that other buildings would later follow. Built between 1660 and 1774, with the original design by Vicencio Barroso Escaloya, it replaced a cathedral destroyed by a fire in 1640.

Main Facade – Framed by two heavy towers, the restrained Baroque facade atypically faces the street and not the plaza. Three doorways, each one divided into three sections, are designed in a triptych style. Panels with niches and pilasters decorate the surface. The center relief represents the Transfiguration of Christ, while the left relief depicts the Adoration of the Shepherds and the right relief the Adoration of the Three Wise Men. At each of the entrances, the heavy wooden doors conceal smaller, more delicate **doors★** lined with leather and carved in the Cordoba style.

Interior – Natural light filtering through the windows of the transept cupola and upper nave provides wonderful illumination of the three naves. Baroque and Neoclassical combine in the interior decor, culminating in the 18C silver Manifestador on the main altar. A Christ made of sugarcane paste, popularly called the Lord of the Sacristy, which was donated by Spanish King Philip II, enlivens the left side nave. The German pipe organ was placed above the entrance in 1905. This instrument helped begin the **International Festival of the Pipe Organ**, which for more than 30 years has taken place in May. Other noteworthy items in the interior include the pulpit with double access. A regal **font★** made of carved silver, used only on special occasions and christenings, illuminates the **baptistry**, where José María Morelos y Pavón and Agustín de Iturbide were baptized. Lovely paintings decorate the walls of the former monastery, today home to the cathedral's offices.

Plaza de Armas – *Av. Madero, Zócalo.* Morelia is one of the few cities to boast two main plazas, as the cathedral splits the main esplanade into two sections. Plaza Melchor Ocampo spreads to the east, with Plaza de Armas on the west. The latter is also known as the Plaza de los Mártires (Plaza of the Martyrs) in honor of the revolutionaries who were executed here, including José Guadalupe Salto (1812), Mariano Matamoros (1814) and a group of young defenders of liberal ideas (1830).

The Plaza of the Martyrs served as a point of departure for designing the city plan in the 16C. The arcades, where the richest families of the 17–19C built their great **mansions**, surround the plaza. Today these stately homes function as hotels and restaurants. So characteristic of the city, Morelia's elegant arcades unify the spec-

Av. Madero, Cathedral and Plaza de Armas

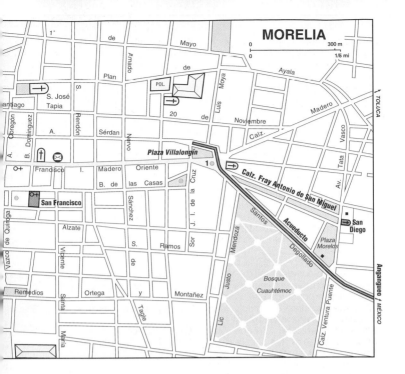

trum of architectural styles. A French pavilion, constructed at the end of the 19C, graces the center of the plaza. Locals enjoy the cool shade trees and savor the snacks and delicious candy made of fruit and sugar cane sold in the plaza. As the shoeshine men do their job, visitors can appreciate the majesty of the cathedral and local street life.

Palacio de Justicia (A) – *Portal Allende, 267. Open year-round Mon–Fri 8am–8pm.* ☎ *(4) 312-1579.* This building dates from the 17C. The interior preserves its handsome colonial style, but the current facade, remodeled in 1883 by Woddon de Sorinne, features Neoclassical and Art Nouveau elements. The exterior boasts numerous noteworthy objects, such as arcades built on pilasters and balcony windows with wrought-iron banisters. The corners of the interior courtyard exemplify the false double arch and lend it an ample, rounded appearance. On the stairwell, murals painted by Agustín Cárdenas in 1976 celebrate the existence of the First Court of Justice.
Before the remodeling, this building housed many offices in different periods, including the Council House, City Hall, the Government Palace and a school.

Museo Regional Michoacano – *Allende, 305. Open year-round Tue–Sat 9am–7pm, Sun 9am–2pm. Closed national holidays.* ☎ *(4) 312-0417.* This elegant 18C stone mansion originally belonged to Don Isidro Huarte, father-in-law of Agustín de Iturbide. In 1886 it opened its doors as a museum of state history, spanning the pre-Hispanic era to the 20C. The exterior features Baroque decorations such as the corner balcony overlooking the Plaza de Armas, fine moldings and other projecting balconies with stone eaves. Inside, the complex is graced by a charming courtyard surrounded by a double arcade. Towards the back, a stairway opens below a double false arch which, instead of a keystone, bears a sculpture of St. Anthony with a tiny, winged cherub beside his feet. The mural *Cuauhtémoc y la Historia*, by Alfredo Zalce, adds color to the stairway. In the Colonial Room, an enormous 18C canvas by an anonymous artist narrates the move by the Dominican nuns from one convent to another *(see Conservatorio de las Rosas, p 264)*.

Colegio de San Nicolás Hidalgo (B) – *Francisco I. Madero, Poniente (west). Open year-round Mon–Fri 7am–9pm, Sat 8am–4pm. Closed national holidays.* ☎ *(4) 312-3191.* This was the first school to open its doors to both indigenous and Spanish students at the same time. It resulted from the fusion of two schools, one called San Nicolás, founded by Vasco de Quiroga in the city of Pátzcuaro, and the other called San Miguel, which was already established at this site. The merger took place in 1580, after the ecclesiastical seat moved from Pátzcuaro to Valladolid, today the city of Morelia. In 1847 the name of Hidalgo was added in honor of the national hero, Miguel Hidalgo y Costilla, who served as a teacher and rector at the school, and taught José María Morelos y Pavón. Today, the school forms part of the University of Michoacán.

Palacio Clavijero (C) – *El Nigromante, 79. Open year-round Mon–Fri 8am–8pm, Sat–Sun and holidays 9am–7pm. Closed Jan 1 and Dec 25.* This gigantic quarry-stone construction dates from the 17C. Originally a church and Jesuit school, the institution received its name in honor of one of the most renowned teachers and historians of this order, Francisco Xavier Clavijero. Today, the building houses various governmental offices including the office of tourism. The space once occupied by the church now houses the handsome library of the University of Michoacán. The entryway to the palace opens on one side of the church. Its restrained Baroque facade merits attention for its imperial eagle emblem, gargoyles and other finishing touches, as well as the tower that connects with the church. Great arches surround the first level of the enormous interior courtyard, graced by a handsome fountain. On the second floor, 28 open windows crowned with valances and gargoyles line up with the arches below.

Conservatorio de las Rosas – *Santiago Tapia, 334. Open year-round Mon–Fri 9am–2pm and 4–7pm, Sat 9am–2pm. Closed national holidays.* ☏ *(4) 312-1469.* The conservatory was the first convent of the Dominican nuns. After nearly 150 years of residence in this complex, due to the building's deterioration, the nuns moved to a new home on Calle Madero, today known as the **Templo de las Monjas** (Church of the Nuns).

After the restoration, in 1743 the convent was converted into the school of Santa Rosa María, established for the daughters of the working class. This school would set a musical precedent, which would persist in all the ecclesiastical schools housed in this building until the 20C. Today, it is the seat of one of the most prestigious music conservatories in Mexico, where the **Niños Cantores de Morelia** (Young Singers of Morelia) study and train.

The church's **facade★** (1757) consists of typical convent elements, such as a twin portal connected with a buttress. Highlights include reliefs of the Sacred Family and Santa Rosa de Lima, as well as gargoyles shaped like crocodiles. The interior boasts a Churrigueresque main altarpiece, complete with miniature angels and complex ornamentation.

To the right of the church lies the entrance to the **convent**. The garden in the one-story cloister features *Danza* (Dance), a sculpture by Alfredo Zalce.

★**Museo del Estado (M¹)** – *Guillermo Prieto, 176. Open year-round Mon–Fri 9am–2pm and 4–8pm, Sat–Sun and holidays 9am–2pm and 4–7pm. Closed Jan 1 and Dec 25.* ☏ *(4) 313-0629. No photographs allowed.* This 18C Baroque mansion was once known as the "Empress's home," because according to popular legend Ana Huarte, the wife of Agustín Iturbide, had lived here. The house was redesigned in the 1980s to exhibit a rich collection of historical items. The entrance features a former **pharmacy★**, founded in 1868, complete with the original furniture and utensils. On the first floor, rock crystal, jade and turquoise jewelry made by the Tarascans highlight the collection. On the second floor, an educational display of mannequins, scale models, clothing and handicrafts helps to explain some of the ecological and cultural characteristics of Michoacán's eight regions.

Museo de Arte Colonial (M²) – *Benito Juárez, 240. Open year-round Tue–Fri 10am–2pm and 5–8pm, Sat–Sun and holidays 9:30am–2pm and 4:30–7pm.* ☏ *(4) 313-9260.* Located in a large 18C house, where the city's first printing press was installed in 1821, the Colonial Art Museum was inaugurated in 1984. It boasts two important collections. The first exhibits an impressive array of effigies of Christ spanning the spectrum of time periods, styles, techniques and materials. Especially interesting are the figures made of corn and sugarcane paste. The second collection exhibits colonial paintings with works by Oaxacan Miguel Cabrera.

Casa de la Cultura (Ex Convento del Carmen Descalzo) – *Av. Morelos Norte, 485. Open year-round Mon–Fri 10am–2pm and 4–8pm, Sat–Sun and holidays 10am–6pm. Closed Jan 1 and Dec 25.* ✕ ☏ *(4) 313-1215 ext. 233.* This building's enormous size is unparalleled in the city. A large section of what was once the Carmelite convent today houses the House of Culture, while small private businesses occupy the rest of the building.

Construction began at the end of the 16C, and the three cupolas were erected in the 16C, 17C and 18C. During these centuries, internal modifications greatly altered the edifice's original space. Nevertheless, many features merit admiration, such as the large central courtyard and the old dining hall, located beside the stairway. This hall preserves its original 16C wooden pulpit, as well as the remains of a fresco of the Sacred Family.

The upper floor and its old rooms and cells, today converted into offices, merit a visit. The **museum** on the ground floor exhibits splendid masks used only in regional dances. Its collection includes most of the Mexican states, with particular emphasis on Michoacán and Guerrero.

Palacio de Gobierno – *Av. Madero, Poniente, 63, open year-round daily 9am–9pm.* ☏ *(4) 312-9182.* Begun in 1732 and completed in 1778, the building originally functioned as the Colegio Seminario Tridentino (Tridentine Seminary).

Here many of the heroes of the War of Independence, such as José María Morelos y Pavón, Ignacio López Rayón, Melchor Ocampo and Agustín de Iturbide, received their education. After the Reform Laws were proclaimed, the building became the state's Government Palace.

Flanked by two unusual, Oriental-style towers, the facade features several wrought-iron balconies and a replica of the **Campana de Dolores** (Bell of Dolores Hidalgo), rung in 1810 to proclaim Independence.

The interior holds three courtyards with two stories of arcades. In 1962 Alfredo Zalce, a renowned painter from Michoacán, decorated the walls on the third floor of the first courtyard, as well as the handsome stairwell leading to it. The murals depict various periods of the state's history, from the pre-Hispanic era to modern day.

Templo and Ex Convento de San Francisco – *Humboldt and Fray Juan de San Miguel. Open year-round daily 9am–3pm & 5–9pm.* Morelia's first religious complex was built by Fray Antonio de Lisboa between 1525 and 1536, before the city received the name of Valladolid. For the next three centuries, the building underwent numerous modifications, wherein Baroque teamed with Plateresque, Renaissance and Gothic elements.

The church's **facade** displays a clear Plateresque influence in the fine columns flanking the arch and choir windows, as well as in the detailed decorations of the entrance arch and the left side door. To the right of the church, five handsome molded arches, linked by fluted columns, form a pleasant entrance to the **monastery**. The two-story **cloister** constitutes the most sublime part of this religious complex. Today, only a fraction remains of the original structure, said to have been quite large.

The **Casa de las Artesanías** (House of Handicrafts) exhibits a large **collection★** of handicrafts from the entire state, as well as workshops, located in the upper level, where visitors can witness the creation of some of these marvels.

PLAZA VILLALONGÍN AND SURROUNDINGS
Madero Oriente and Aquiles Serdán

The hustle and bustle of the modern world seems far away in the peaceful refuge of this plaza, which boasts an attractive garden, shade trees, sidewalks with paving stones and wrought-iron benches. Named for the revolutionary Manuel Villalongín, the plaza is centered around the **Fuente de las Tarascas (1)**, emblem of the sensitivity and tradition of Michoacán, as well as two other amazing urban structures of the old city of Valladolid.

Across from the plaza, the impressive **aqueduct** was commissioned by Bishop Fray Antonio de San Miguel in the 18C, with the aim of supplying water and saving the city from the drought that scorched the region. Both for its historic value and beauty, the aqueduct has become a symbol of the city. Its 253 arches of pink quarry stone span 1.7km/1mi, alongside Cuauhtémoc Forrest.

To the left of the arches, one of Mexico's oldest cobblestone streets, the **Calzada Fray Antonio de San Miguel**, received its name in honor of Bishop Antonio de San Miguel, who not only funded the construction of the aqueduct, but also the street and other public works. The roadway is fringed by stone benches and lovely trees, and flanked by large old houses that have changed little and lend an atmosphere of days gone by.

The roadway ends in front of the 18C **Templo de San Diego** *(open year-round daily 7am–8pm)*. The church's handsome **interior★★** boasts magnificent ornamental work by Joaquín Orta Menchaca. Today, the monastery houses the law school of the University of Michoacán.

EXCURSIONS

Angangueo – *Located 115km/71mi east of Morelia on Carr. 15; take the exit to Ocampo, by way of San Felipe los Alzatí (9km/5.6mi before reaching Zitácuaro). Also accessible from Mexico City (205km/127mi) via the tollroad to Morelia. At the intersection to Maravatío, take the exit to Ciudad Hidalgo and continue to Angangueo by way of Aporo.* Amid forests of pine and oyamel trees, pretty colorful houses, with wooden balconies filled with flowers, rise over the town's steep streets. Since the 18C when minerals were found at a nearby hacienda, Angangueo has developed without a definite layout, open to the vicissitudes of the mines. The town provides easy access to the sanctuaries, where each year millions of Monarch butterflies come to spend the winter.

★★Santuario Sierra el Campanario – *Located 6km/3.7mi south of Angangueo by dirt road. Guided tour lasts 3 1/2hrs, Feb 10–Apr 1, daily 9am–3pm. P$10.* ⚕ ☏ *(7) 156-0044 ext. 22 and (01-800) 450-2300.* Over the entire length of this 2km/1.2mi, marked trail, the vision of countless, colorful butterflies overwhelms visitors. Designed to handle up to 100,000 annual tourists, this sanctuary was the first to open its doors to the public.

★★Santuario Sierra Chincua – *From Angangueo, head northeast for 8km/5mi on the road to San José del Rincón to reach the sanctuary's entrance. Visit by guided tour (3hrs), Dec 15–Mar 30 daily 9am–3pm. P$15. ☎ (7) 156-0044 ext. 22 and (01-800) 450-2300.* A 2.4km/1.5mi hike through a forest leads to the sanctuary. Once reserved exclusively for researchers, today it receives more than 650 daily visitors. To protect the enormous quantity of butterflies that rest on the ground as the sun rises, walking within more than 100m/109yd of the butterfly zone is prohibited.

★★Convento de Cuitzeo Santa María Magdalena – *Located on the Carr. Morelia–Salamanca. 30min. Buses to Cuitzeo depart from the bus station every 15min. Open year-round Mon–Sat 10am–6pm, Sun 10am–5pm. Closed Jan 1, Mar 21, May 1, Sept 16, Nov 20, Dec 12 & 25. P$17.* A magnificent and serene lake of the same name welcomes visitors to the small town of Cuitzeo. Over the main plaza rises one of the most formidable and best-preserved structures of the 16C, the Monastery of Santa María Magdalena. Founded by the Augustinians in 1550, this monumental religious complex resembles a veritable fortress.

Facade – The facade's three sections (entry arch, choir window and upper niche) boast central images flanked by balustrades. The Plateresque decorations reveal a clear influence of indigenous craftsmanship. Several hearts of Jesus—emblems of the Augustine order-as well as cherubs and floral motifs extend over the portal.

Interior – This church lacks a cupola, but has numerous items worthy of admiration. These include the nave, the barrel-vaulted ceiling with its thick columns, the Gothic ribbing tracing the ceiling of the apse, and one of the state's oldest pipe organs.

Cloister – Next to the church, six arches lead to the cloister. Formerly, this portal served as an open-air chapel. Original frescoes with religious themes still adorn the walls. The first courtyard inside the cloister boasts a well in the center. Given the high content of salt in this region's upper rocky layers, the locals used this system to obtain fresh rainwater.

Today, the former refectory houses a small museum that focuses on the history of Mexican engraving, from the 16C to the 19C.

★★Ex Convento de San Agustín de Yuriria – *State of Guanajuato. 64km/40mi. From Morelia, head north on Carr. 43. Description p 175.*

OAXACA★★★

Oaxaca

Population 244,827

Map of Principal Sights – City Map p 268

 Av. Independencia, 607, Downtown; ☎ (9) 516-0123

In this charming, provincial city the remains of majestic, pre-Hispanic cities stand side by side with impressive colonial structures. The beauty of Oaxaca can be described as magical and surreal, thanks to the diversity of its people. Here, the locals go about their daily business alongside the noisy bustle of crowds of visitors. At the same time that visitors succumb to the grandeur of Oaxaca's ancient past, they may be surprised by the innate talent of the hundreds of artists wandering the streets. Some of the greatest stars of the contemporary arts scene were born in the state of Oaxaca. The writer **Andrés Henestrosa** and painters **Rufino Tamayo, Rodolfo Morales** and **Francisco Toledo** are especially renowned. Toledo is one of the most important men in the city today, hard at work at constantly improving Oaxaca's cultural scene. The city was declared a World Heritage Site in 1987.

★★ZÓCALO AND SURROUNDINGS

★Zócalo – A fantastic ring of shade trees surrounds this lovely plaza. In the early evening, the state band and marimba musical groups play in the central pavilion. Inspired by the music, even the most timid onlookers clap to the rhythm, while the more adventurous stop to dance. The restaurants located under the plaza's arcade are a good place to enjoy a beverage and watch the world go by. In the nearby **Alameda**, artisans, booksellers, balloon and snack vendors, and even political propagandists set up shop. Local entertainment, accompanied with traditional music, takes place in the evening and includes everything from ballerinas dressed like gigantic dolls to ritual dances that interpret pre-Hispanic and Christian rites.

Cathedral – *Av. Independencia, 700. Open year-round daily 8am–8:30pm.* Founded in 1535, this cathedral has been reconstructed and repaired on several occasions following damage by earthquakes. In August 1994, the **First Bell Ringing Festival of the American Continent** took place at this cathedral.

Begun in 1702 and completed in 1728, the **main facade** has a lovely relief of the Virgin of the Assumption, to whom the church is dedicated, above the central doorway. This relief is a replica of a painting by Titian, the famous Italian painter of the Renaissance. The south bell tower clock, donated by King Ferdinand VI of Spain in 1752, once graced St. Mark's Cathedral in Venice. One of the peculiarities of this clock is that the Roman number IV appears as IIII.

Interior – The cathedral has a basilica floor plan and a spacious interior. The **central nave** begins with the **Altar del Perdón** (Altar of Forgiveness). A monumental **pipe organ**, made in Germany in the 17C, rises behind and above the altar. At the foot of this instrument, 65 wooden chairs take the place of the **choir**, which connects to the **main altar** via a pathway lined with two wrought-iron banisters. Supported by a pedestal of black Grecian marble, a splendid bronze sculpture, created in Italy by Tadollini, protrudes from the center of the altar. The central nave culminates in the **Altar del Espíritu Santo** (Altar of the Holy Spirit), with its colorful, lead glass windows, also from Italy, which depict St. Peter and St. Paul. The outer naves shelter 13 chapels and the sacristy. The most important paintings are found on the side walls. The outstanding painting of *San Cristóbal* (Marcial de Santaella, 1726) hangs at the left side entrance. Another painting by the same artist called *Los siete arcángeles en gloria* (The Seven Archangels in Glory) faces it on the right side. On the back wall, twelve medallions, by Miguel Cabrera, depict the Apostles.

Palacio de Gobierno (PG) – *Bustamante and Guerrero. Open year-round daily 9am–3pm and 4–8pm.* ☎ *(9) 514-4177.* First built in 1576 and later reconstructed numerous times due to earthquake damages, this edifice has served as the council house for several centuries. The last restoration was carried out during the 1930s, after damage produced by the earthquakes of 1928 and 1931. The interior boasts great murals (1985–87) by master painter Arturo García Bustos, a student of Frida Kahlo.

Iglesia de la Compañía de Jesús – *Flores Magón, corner of Valerio Trujano. Open year-round, daily 7am–12:30pm and 5–8:45pm.* This church was built by the Jesuits around 1579 and formed part of the Colegio Casa Fuerte, where until their

---

Practical Information ....Area Code: 9

Getting There – Xoxocotlán International Airport: 8km/5mi south of the city. Information Booth *(daily 8am–8pm).* Transportation to downtown: Transportes Terrestres TASA (P$15) ☎ 514-4350. **Car rental** agencies located at airport. **Bus station:** Av. Niños Héroes de Chapultepec, 1036.

Getting Around – Transportes Guelatao and Choferes del Sur offer local transportation *(daily 7am–9pm; P$2).* Main taxi station ☎ 515-6575. **Public parking:** Calle Hidalgo, 908B, Downtown ☎ 516-2122 *(P$6/hr).* Most tourist sights are within easy walking distance.

Tourist Information – The **Tourist Development Office**, Av. Independencia, 607, Downtown, C.P. 68000 ☎ 516-0123 *(open year-round daily 8:30am–8pm)* provides free information on services and tourist sights, as well as maps and brochures. **CEPROTUR**, Av. Independencia, 607, C.P. 68000 ☎ 516-0123, offers aid to tourists.
The US Consulate, Macedonio Alcalá 201 *(open Mon–Fri 9am–2pm)* provides assistance to US citizens through the Consular Services office.

Accommodations – The Tourist Development Office *(above)* provides information and guidance regarding hotels. Hotel rates range from deluxe hotels *(P$1,700),* moderate *(P$500)* and budget *(P$200). These average rates are per day for a double room and are subject to change.* In addition, Oaxaca offers nine ecological units (houses) called Tourist Yu'u *(P$50);* for information contact the Tourist Development Office.

Guided Tours – Tour companies offer guided visits of the city year-round led by multilingual guides, as well as excursions to archaeological sites (Mitla, Monte Albán), neighboring towns (San Bartolo Coyotepec, Teotitlán del Valle) and markets (Ocotlán). Turismo El Convento de Oaxaca ☎ 516-1806; Cantera Tours ☎ 516-0512; Viajes Turísticos Mitla ☎ 516-6175. Guides can be hired *(P$5/hr)* for private tours; check with the local tourist office for a list of licensed multilingual guides.

Handicrafts – Shops and galleries offering a variety of handicrafts include La Mano Mágica, Alcalá, 203, Downtown ☎ 516-4275; Artesanías Oaxaca, Plazuela Adolfo C. Gurrión. FONART, a government-run store at Crespo, 114, corner of Morelos, ☎ 516-5764 sells wares at fixed prices; the state-run Artesanías e Industrias Populares (ARIPO), García Vigil, 809 ☎ 514-4030 sells black pottery, rugs and typical local clothing.
Southwest of downtown, the **Mercado de Abatos**, **Mercado Benito Juárez** and **Mercado 20 de Noviembre** street markets are open daily, but busiest on Saturdays when villagers from nearby regions offer their wares in open-air stalls; products range from pottery, woven goods and crafts to produce and livestock. Local craftsmen in nearby towns hold markets on various days of the week. In **Tlacolula** (Sunday – textiles, leather and sombreros); **Teotitlán del Valle** (Monday: rugs and wool looms); **Santa Ana del Valle** (Tuesday: rugs and woolen items); **Etla** (Wednesday: produce); **Zaachila** (Thursday: pottery and jewelry); **Ocotlán** (Friday: textiles and animals).

expulsion in 1767, the Jesuits educated hundreds of youngsters. The school originally occupied the entire block. In 1867 the church was restored along with one of its courtyards, where the Jesuit priests still reside today.

★Benito Juárez and 20 de Noviembre Markets – Oaxaca's markets enjoy widespread fame. Some of the items that every visitor should taste are *mole* (a savory bitter chocolate chili sauce, frequently served over meat), Oaxacan cheese, grasshoppers, beef jerky and **chocolate**. The **Benito Juárez** market *(open year-round daily 8am–8pm)* also offers every type of regional handicraft, from black or green earthenware and embroidery, to tapestries and leather goods. The **20 de Noviembre** market *(open year-round daily 6am–10pm)* doubles as a popular eatery.

Templo de San Agustín – *Corner of Armenta and Guerrero. Open year-round daily 7am–2pm and 5–8:30pm.* The Augustinians built this church between 1699 and 1722. It is one of only a few churches with neither cupola nor bell tower, as a precaution against earthquakes. The main portal epitomizes Oaxacan Baroque. The central **relief★** depicts St. Augustine carrying a church in his left hand and protecting the monks with his robe. Three Baroque **altarpieces** grace the interior.

Iglesia de San Felipe Neri – *Av. Independencia, corner of Tinoco and Palacios. Open year-round daily 7am–2pm and 5–7pm.* The church's Baroque facade dates from 1733. The only statue on the doorway, which resembles an enormous altarpiece, depicts St. Philip Neri. Inside, a handsome Churrigueresque altarpiece features statues of the Virgin of Patronage and St. Philip Neri. Placed throughout the church, a series of eight **altarpieces** display outstanding pictorial works by two 18C artists, Agustín Santaella and José de Paéz. It was in this church that Benito Juárez married Margarita Maza on July 31, 1843.

★Basilica de la Soledad – *Av. Independencia and Galeana. Open year-round daily 6am–8:30pm.* This amazing church is dedicated to Our Lady of Solitude, patron saint of Oaxaca. Pope John XXIII granted the shrine minor basilica status in 1959. Every year, on December 18, thousands of devoted followers arrive from all over the state to carry out bequests, leave gifts and ask for favors during the festival of Our Lady of Solitude.

Long ago, when the ancient Aztecs established the Huayacac garrison on this site, they worshiped a rock, which was the source of a limitless supply of water. During the colonial era, the Spanish built, next to the site, a hermitage dedicated to St. Sebastian. According to the legend, one cold winter night, around 1620, a solitary mule arrived at the entrance to the hermitage, collapsed and died. The animal was carrying a box with pieces of statues of Christ and the Virgin, as well as an inscription that read, "Our Lady of Solitude at the foot of the cross." For many years, the remains of the statue of the Virgin were kept in the church. In 1682 Viceroy Antonio Manrique commissioned the church and monastery and dedicated them to the **Virgen de La Soledad** (Our Lady of Solitude).

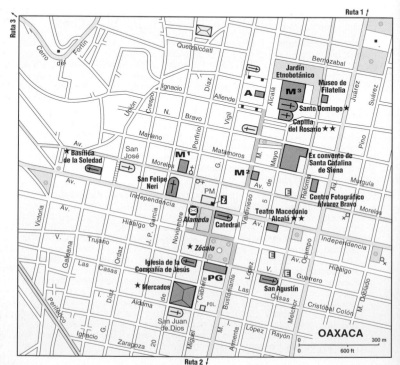

The **facade** is one of the best examples of Baroque architecture of the colonial period. Above the main doorway is the figure of **Our Lady of Solitude** at the foot of the cross, as indicated in the legendary inscription.

Interior – A **sacred stone** stands to the right of the doorway; some believe that this is the slab where the mule collapsed, while others say it represents the stone worshipped by the Aztecs.

★**Museo de Arte Prehispánico Rufino Tamayo (M¹)** – *Morelos, 503. Open Holy Week and Dec 15–31, Mon, Wed–Sat 10am–7pm, Sun 10am–5pm. Rest of the year Mon, Wed–Sat 10am–2pm and 4–7pm, Sun 10am–3pm. Closed Jan 1, Good Friday, May 1, Sept 16, Nov 2 and Dec 25. P$14. ☎ (9) 516-4750.* This museum, located in an 18C house, contains a fascinating **collection**★ of pre-Hispanic pieces from all over Mexico. The artist Rufino Tamayo donated the items in 1974 to highlight the collection's aesthetic rather than archaeological value.

Museo de Arte Contemporáneo de Oaxaca (MACO) (M²) – *Macedonio Alcalá, 202. Open year-round Wed–Mon 10:30am–8pm. Closed national holidays. P$10. ✗ ☎ (9) 514-1055.* The coat of arms above the entrance to this 18C mansion belonged to the first owners. The interior still has its three original courtyards. The museum organizes rotating exhibitions of local, national and international contemporary art.

Macedonio Alcalá is the most visited street in the city, as it is filled with handicraft stores, galleries and restaurants.

★★SANTO DOMINGO AND SURROUNDINGS

★**Templo de Santo Domingo** – *Macedonio Alcalá. Open year-round daily 7am–1pm and 4–8pm (please respect worship hours).* Between 1575 and 1608, the Dominican friars built the Church of St. Dominic, the most impressive colonial structure in Oaxaca. In the mid 19C, following the nationalization of clerical property, the building suffered considerable damage and was eventually converted to serve as a barracks. Successive restorations repaired the damaged altars and altarpieces, and remodeled the atrium. Today, the Dominicans still occupy part of the building, while the other part houses the **Centro Cultural Santo Domingo**.

The restraint and elegance of the **facade** contrast greatly with the rich, exuberant ornamentation of the interior. Above the doorway is a relief of St. Dominic and St. Hypolite, carrying a church with the Holy Spirit perched above it. The finial depicts the emblem of the Dominican order surrounded by the three theological truths. The flanking bell towers rise to a height of 35m/115ft.

★★★**Interior** – *Photo pp. 270–271.* The initial and lasting impression is one of shimmering gold leaf and delicate decoration. In the antechoir, statues of eight cardinals mark the spandrels, while the vaulting is covered with an intricate plasterwork **genealogical tree** of the founder of the Dominican order, Don Domingo de Guzmán. Entwining branches, leaves and fruit link the 30 members of the Guzmán family and top out with the Virgin. The vaulting of the nave is no less decorative, with 36 paintings of scenes related to the Virgin and 20 medallions depicting events in the lives of Jesus and Mary. Eight other paintings portray scenes from the Old Testament.

At the far end of the nave is the magnificent gilded, three-tiered main altarpiece adorned with statues and twisting Solomonic columns. The pulpit, with its canopy and banister, also forms a handsome ensemble. Off the south aisle, the 18C **Capilla del Rosario**★★, decorated in a similar vein to the rest of the church, has a remarkable relief of the Virgin on the vaulting. The main altarpiece pays homage to the Virgin of the Rosary, revered in the October celebration. The statue spends the 31 days of the month of October at the main altar.

★**Centro Cultural Santo Domingo (Ex Convento de Santo Domingo) (M³)** – *Macedonio Alcalá. Open year-round Tue–Sun 10am–8pm. ☎ (9) 516-9741.* Once the army had relinquished the former buildings of the 16C monastery, several years of restoration followed before they were inaugurated in 1998 as a cultural center.

Museo de las Culturas de Oaxaca – *Open year-round, Tue–Sun 10am–8pm. P$20. ☎ (9) 516-2991.* The museum now occupies the rooms on the third floor, where interactive displays present the history and traditions of Oaxaca, from the earliest nomadic peoples to the many indigenous groups of more recent times.

Particularly noteworthy among the fascinating pre-Hispanic artifacts of the Zapotec and Mixtec cultures is an extraordinary **collection**★★ of objects (primarily of Mixtec origin) from Monte Albán's **Tomb 7**. This treasure, with some of the most unique pieces found to date, constitutes an important source of information about the lifestyle of the pre-Hispanic civilizations that once occupied the state of Oaxaca. From the antechoir, situated just beyond room IX, one can get a good view of the **choir**★ of the Templo de Santo Domingo, which depicts reliefs of various martyrs.

Biblioteca "Fray Francisco de Burgoa" – *On the second floor, next to the staircase.* The library occupies the site where once stood the Capilla de la Tercera Orden, and boasts a collection of more than 23,000 volumes, published between 1484 and 1940. It holds 11 incunabula (books printed before the year 1501) and one manuscript by Fray Bartolomé de las Casas. *(Only researchers who present identification have access to this library.)*

Jardín Etnobotánico – *Guided tours Tue–Fri 1pm & 5pm; Sat 1pm; by appointment only, scheduled at the museum's ticket booth.* ☎ *(9) 516-7915.* The former monastic orchard is now a botanical garden with over 1,200 species from the state's seven geographical zones. Oaxaca has one of the richest flora in Mexico.

Instituto de Artes Gráficas de Oaxaca (IAGO) (A) – *Macedonio Alcalá, 507. Open year-round Wed–Mon 9:30am–8pm. Closed Jan 1, Mar 21, May 1, Sept 16, & Nov 2.* 🍴 ☎ *(9) 516-6980.* This cultural center continually exhibits excellent graphic art of national and international stature. The interior boasts a public library with a collection of more than 10,000 books, which master Francisco Toledo allows visitors to enjoy.

Museo de Filatelia – *Reforma, 504. Open year-round, Tue-Sun 9am-7pm.* 🍴 ☎ *(9) 514-2375.* This museum, Mexico's first in philately (stamp collecting), houses a collection of stamps and envelopes from different parts of the world. A charming rear patio provides an enjoyable setting for an on-site restaurant.

Ex Convento de Santa Catalina de Siena (Hotel Camino Real) – *5 de Mayo, 300. Open year-round, daily.* ☎ *(9) 516-0611.* The Discalced Carmelites lived in this 16C convent until the passing of the **Reform Laws**. Later, the building became a jail and even the Municipal Palace, and finally, in 1976, it was converted into a hotel. The chapel and ornate stone **washbasins**★ located in the northwest garden recall the grandeur of the convent.

Centro Fotográfico Álvarez Bravo – *Murguía, 302. Open year-round, Wed–Mon 9:30am–8pm.* ☎ *(9) 514-1933.* This lovely 18C house displays a permanent collection of photographs taken by Manuel Álvarez Bravo. The exhibits include works by important Mexican and foreign photographers.

Genealogical Tree, Templo de Santo Domingo

★★Teatro Macedonio Alcalá – *5 de Mayo and Independencia. Open only during peformances.* ☎ *(9) 516-3387.* This early-20C building bears the name of a well-known Oaxacan musician and composer. The architecture, like that of many of the other structures constructed in the era of President Porfirio Díaz (called the Porfiriato), imitates the classic Parisian style of the 19C. The symmetrical and identical facades open away from the rounded doorway. The rococo interior features a handsome staircase made of white marble.

EXCURSIONS

An infinite number of marvelous places to visit surround the city of Oaxaca, from small towns boasting handicrafts to impressive and majestic pre-Hispanic ruins. Three routes are suggested.

Route 1

Templo de San Andrés, Huayapan – *9km/5.6mi from Oaxaca. Go east on Carr. Fed. 190. After 3km/1.9mi, turn left on Carr. 175 heading to Tuxtepec. Continue 4km/2.5mi and then at the fork in the road, go left and continue 2km/1.2mi. Open year-round daily 9am–2pm and 4–6pm.* With one of the most beautiful Baroque altarpieces of the 17C, the Church of San Andrés also preserves woodwork that stands out as some of the finest ever crafted in Mexico. The side chapel, dedicated to the **Señor de las Aguas del Arroyo**, merits special attention. Uniquely, a large amount of votive offerings, painted by people in gratitude of the favors or miracles granted by saints and virgins, fills this chapel.

© Robert Frerck/Odyssey

271

Guelaguetza Festival

© Bob Schalkwijk

■ Guelaguetza (Lunes del Cerro)

The origin of this festival dates back to the pre-Hispanic period. Two different versions explain the event's origin; both deal with the festivities celebrated on the Cerro del Fortín. Beginning on July 19, in the city of Huayacac, diverse ethnic peoples would gather together to celebrate and honor the "Great Rulers," that is, the Aztecs who once ruled the region. The second version attributes the origin to a Mexica (Aztec) ritual dedicated to **Centeotl**, the goddess of corn, which villagers celebrated on the last two Mondays in July. Whatever the origin, during the colonial era, all indigenous festivities merged with Christian rites, a result of evangelization efforts and construction of the Christian churches on the sites of the ancient pre-Hispanic ceremonial centers. Therefore, until the end of the 19C, the towns celebrated the fiesta of the Virgin of Carmen along with the indigenous fiesta of "Lunes del Cerro."

The tradition of this fiesta resurfaced during the 1930s, renamed as **Guelaguetza**, which the Zapotecs had used to signify activities where cooperation existed among the people of different regions. Dressed in typical customs and eager to share their traditions, music and popular dances, people from all over the state participate in the event.

Santa María el Tule – *11km/6.8mi from Oaxaca. Go east on Carr. Fed. 190. P$2.* Next to the 17C Church of Santa María de la Asunción (St. Mary of the Assumption) rises one of the most surprising marvels of nature. This very ancient **Tule tree★** has witnessed the passage of time, boasting 2,000 years of age. It weighs 636 tons and measures 42m/138ft in height, while the diameter of its trunk is 14m/46ft. The roots of this king of the juniper trees conjure images of an infinite variety of animal shapes, objects, fruits and people. On the second Monday in October, the townspeople celebrate a fiesta with music and dance in honor of the Tule.

Templo y Ex Convento de San Jerónimo, Tlacochahuaya – *21km/13mi from Oaxaca. Go east on Carr. Fed. 190; after 19km/11.8mi, bear right and continue for another 2km/1.2mi. Open year-round daily 10am–2pm & 4–6pm. P$3.* The Dominicans built this religious complex in the early 17C. St. Jerome, St. Augustine and St. Dominic grace the main facade, while an old stone sundial marks the front of the left side entrance. Very simple frescoes of flowers and cherubs, painted by indigenous artists, decorate the especially beautiful **interior★★**. An oil painting of St. Jerome, by the indigenous artist Juan de Aurré, enhances the main altarpiece. Just above the choir is a marvelous 16C **pipe organ**, which began to make music again in 1994 after a long period of silence. In this monastery, during 25 of his 100 years, lived Fray Juan de Córdoba, of whom it is said that he never touched a single coin. This friar is to be credited for the first Zapotec dictionary.

Dainzú – *22.5km/14mi from Oaxaca. Go east on Carr. Fed. 190; after 21.5km/13.3mi, turn right and continue for another km/0.6mi. Open year-round daily 8am–6pm. P$10.* This small Zapotec center was a contemporary of Monte Albán. Its name means "mountain of the pipe organ cactus," and historians believe the village was established around the year 600 BC; it remained inhabited until approximately AD 1200. Construction work continued from the onset until AD 250. The principal characteristics of the site include a system of terraces and open spaces designed to overcome the steep gradient of the mountainside, and the **ball court**, considered one of the oldest in Mesoamerica. **Edificio A** (Building A) claims a staggered-stepped platform structure with three terraces. The bas reliefs exhibited in the lower section depict the ball players in motion and priests and men dressed as jaguars. **Tomb 7**, which unlike the tomb at Monte Albán was completely sacked before its discovery, stands northwest of **Edificio B**. The frame of the entrance door bears the carved figure of a jaguar. The small terrace of **Edificio C** connects to adjacent buildings and is the site of **Tomb 3**, found with its offerings intact. **Edificio D** contains the **ball court** with its reconstructed south end. Of the court's northern edge, only the foundation remains visible. Like all the other Oaxacan ball courts, it lacks the typical stone rings through which the ball passed.

Teotitlán del Valle – *28km/17mi from Oaxaca. Go east on Carr. Fed. 190; after 25km/15.5mi, turn left and continue for another 3km/1.9mi.* The artisans of this town, whose name means "land of the Gods," busily work at their looms to produce traditional **woolen rugs** depicting creations by famous painters or pre-Hispanic drawings, or craft their own beautiful and original designs. Several of the craftsmen preserve the tradition of using natural dyes.

Don't miss the **Museo Comunitario** *(opposite the handicrafts market; open year-round, Tue–Sun 10am–6pm. P$5. ☎ 9-516-5786)*, which provides interesting information about the process of creating textiles and about the town's traditions.

Lambityeco – *29km/18mi from Oaxaca. Go east on Carr. Fed. 190. Open year-round daily 8am–6pm. P$10.* A Zapotec city important for its salt production, Lambityeco, which means "keg mountain" or "hollow hill," rose in importance in 700 BC, but was abandoned by AD 750 due to warring by local peoples. The majority of this city's residents moved to **Yagul** *(p 274)*. Lambityeco reached its heyday with the decline of power in Monte Albán, as one of the royal families, related to Monte Albán's rulers, called Lambityeco home.

Figures of the Lambityeco lords and their wives, next to the symbols of their calendar names, decorate the interior panel of the altar in **Estructura 195**, also known as the "Casa del Coqui" (Great Lord). **Tumba 6** (Tomb 6) stands in front of the altar. The facade displays the faces of *Señor 1 Terremoto* (Lord 1 Earthquake) and *Señora 10 Caña* (Lady 10 Sugar Cane), the city's last rulers and ancestral relatives of *Lord 8 Death* buried in this tomb. **Estructura 190** is also called "Courtyard of the Cosijos" for its two identical masks, which depict Cosijo, the god of rain, thunder and lightning. The masks cover almost the entire face and are crowned with feather adornments and the C glyph. Each of the figures grasps a water vessel in the right hand and thunder and lightning in the left.

Iglesia de Santo Cristo, Tlacolula de Matamoros – *32km/19.8mi from Oaxaca. Go east on Carr. Fed. 190; after 31km/19mi, turn right and continue for another km/0.6mi. Open year-round daily 7am–2pm & 4–8pm, Sat–Sun 7am–8pm.* During

Pipe Organ (16C), Templo de San Jerónimo, Tlacochahuaya

© Bob Schalkwijk

■ **Ecotourism in the Sierra Norte:
A Walk through the Clouds**

*From Oaxaca, head east on Carr. Fed. 190. After 25km/15.5mi, take the
exit to the left and, just beyond Teotitlán, take the steep dirt road and continue 20km/12.4mi to reach Benito Juárez.*

The Sierra Norte, or Sierra Juárez, stands out for its rich biodiversity.
According to the World Wildlife Fund (WWF), this area boasts the world's
richest mixed pine-oak forests. The deeper one ventures into the sierra, the
higher the likelihood of spotting a wild cat or one of the endangered species
found here, such as the spider monkey or the tapir.

Within the sierra, **Benito Juárez**, the village closest to the city of Oaxaca, is
situated at an altitude of 2,800m/9,184ft. Only 2.5km/1.6mi from here,
an overlook offers a panoramic **view★** of the Valley of Oaxaca and, on clear
days, of the Pico de Orizaba, located in Veracruz.

This small town provides accommodations (Tourist Yu'u and cabins), as
well as guided excursions lasting several days, as it is outfitted with mountain bikes and other equipment necessary for camping. In this way, visitors
can explore various villages such as **Ixtlán de Juárez**, the tour of which
includes an impressive waterfall; **Guelatao**, the birthplace of President Benito
Juárez; or participate in different activities in neighboring towns. The community itself manages the ecotourism project, and, as its members affirm,
these treks present a great opportunity for engaging in "a walk through
the clouds."

the construction of this 17C church, the authorities annexed the **side chapel★★** dedicated to the **Lord of Tlacolula**. Known as the **Capilla del Rosario** or the **Capilla de los
Mártires**, this chapel remains one of the most beautiful Baroque structures of the
colonial era. The remarkable interior decorations include gilded plasterwork and
polychrome reliefs. The hand finished wrought iron of the choir grille and pulpit
stand out for their detail. Excellent silverwork graces the handsome banister and
the two candlesticks of the presbytery, as well as the candelabras hanging from
the ceiling. The **Capilla de los Espejos** (Chapel of Mirrors) is another name given to
this chapel, for the great number of mirrors hanging all along the upper part of
the nave.

Yagul – *35.6km/22mi from Oaxaca. Go east on Carr. Fed. 190; after 34km/21mi,
take a left and continue for another 1.6km/1mi. Open year-round daily 8am–5pm.
P$17.* Yagul means "old tree," and these ruins rose to prominence as one of the
family centers after the abandonment of Monte Albán. The absence of a hegemonic
seat of power created a situation of instability and war. For this reason, the inhabitants of several of these centers built fortifications, like the structures in Yagul,
which are divided into four sections.

Archaeologists uncovered a triple tomb—including one decorated with frets and
anthropomorphic figures—in the **Centro Cívico**. The **ball court** is the second largest
in Mesoamerica, the largest being located at Chichén Itzá, Yucatán. The
serpent head, today exhibited at the Museo de las Culturas de Oaxaca *(p 270)*,
was found embedded in the south wall. The **Palacio de los Seis Patios** (Palace of
the Six Courtyards) splits into three sections, each one with two courtyards.
Several of the courtyards contain tombs, affirming the residential nature of the
structure, for the inhabitants, by custom, buried the dead in the doorway of the
house.

Returning to the palace entrance, through a passageway decorated with Mitla-style
frets, a small street connects to the **Sala de Consejo** (Council Room). Two columns
divide this edifice's structure into three sections. The entrance lies to the south.
Authorities held public and administrative activities in this room. Archaeologists
also believe this room served as the model for the main structure of the Group of
Columns at Mitla.

East of the main structures stands **La Fortaleza**, reached after a 5min walk through
a trail. Situated atop the hill, which offers a magnificent **view★** of the Valley of
Oaxaca, this fortification was used as a refuge in case of military attacks during
pre-Hispanic times. Here, one can look at the entrance to a tomb whose lid displays calendar inscriptions. The natural rock formations served to shelter this site.
In 1998 Yagul and its surroundings were declared a Natural Monument in order
to protect the flora and fauna of this region, home to 60 native species of plants
and animals.

★★**Mitla** – *46.5km/28.8mi from Oaxaca. Go east on Carr. Fed. 190; after 41km/25.4mi, take the exit to Carr. Fed. 175. Description p 256.*

★★**Hierve el Agua** – *28km/17.4mi from Mitla. Head east on the road to Ayutla; after 18km, take the dirt road to the right and continue for another 10km/6mi. Description p 257.*

Route 2

★★★**Monte Albán** – *10km/6mi from Oaxaca. Go southwest on the new road to Monte Albán. Description p 258.*

Templo and Ex Convento de Santiago Apóstol, Cuilapan de Guerrero – *12km/7mi from Oaxaca. Go southwest on Carr. Fed. 131. Open year-round daily 10am–6pm. P$10.* The Dominicans initiated this monumental structure in 1555. For reasons unknown, construction was halted in 1560 and despite numerous later attempts was never finished. An open-air chapel stands to the left side, while the pilgrims' portal, composed of nine arches, opens on the right. One of the entrances to the supposed church occupies the center.

The Dominican emblem, located in the second section of the entrance, welcomes visitors to the **open-air chapel**★ with a basilican floorplan. Two rows of thick columns separate the three naves. On the side walls, large open arches still show traces of the original paintings. A replica of an inscription, decorated with Mixtec calendar symbols and the Christian date of 1555, adorns the rear right wall.

■ Oaxaca's Community-Based Museums

Eighteen communities, located primarily in the Valley of Oaxaca and the Mixtec regions, are home to small museums that exhibit objects and provide information on the traditions and history of each town. These museums stand out for their unique archaeological artifacts, such as those in the **Museo de San José el Mogote**, located in a former hacienda; for their explanations of festivities and textile work, such as those in **Santa Ana del Valle** and Teotitlán del Valle; or for their photographs of Mixtec manuscripts, such as those displayed in the village of **San Miguel Tequixtepec**, whose museum is located in an old house of Mixtec style, with an architectural floorplan similar to that seen in certain archaeological sites such as Mitla. Parallel to the inauguration of new museums, this cooperative offers unique excursions where one can experience firsthand the work or festivals of the indigenous towns. Thus, one can observe the labor of weavers, potters, sculptors, bakers, or manufacturers of candles, fireworks and cheese. Visitors can even attempt to learn to use the tools employed by these workers in tasks that require a high degree of skill, such as spinning wool. Another excursion involves a visit to a traditional medicine man or *curandero*.

Spinner, Santa Ana del Valle

© Fernando García Aguinaco

In addition, these communities offer a few treks by bike or on horseback. Reservations are necessary. For more information, contact the Sociedad Cooperativa de Museos Comunitarios del Estado de Oaxaca *(Calle Tinoco y Palacios, 311-12, Centro, Oaxaca, CP 68000.* ☎ *9-516-5786).*

The entrance to the church, also unfinished, opens through the right wall as well. Visitors can see the Gothic ribbing of what would have been the cupola.

The proportions of the **cloister** contrast greatly with the size of the exterior structure. Downstairs, visitors can see what was once the kitchen, dining room, oratory and chapter house. This last room served as the prison of general and former Mexican president **Vicente Guerrero**, just before he was executed. In a courtyard located south of the cloister, in the exact location where Guerrero was shot, stands a monument dedicated to this hero. Also in honor of him, Cuilapan adopted the name of Guerrero. Located upstairs are the friars' former rooms, part of which today belong to a center of history studies.

Route 3: Excursion to the Mixtec Region

This region boasts three of Oaxaca's most handsome Dominican religious centers. Though the sites are distant from the city, the trip in both directions can be accomplished in a day, by car. Transportation service may be arranged through tourist agencies or at hotels.

★**Templo y Ex Convento de Santo Domingo, Yanhuitlán** — *83km/51.5mi from Oaxaca. Head northwest on Carr. de Cuota (toll road) 135D; after 69km/42.8mi, take the exit to Carr. 190, heading towards Huajuapan and continue for another 14km/8.7mi. Open year-round, daily 10am–6pm. P$10.* This was the second most important monastery of the Dominican order. Its construction lasted 25 years, from 1541 to 1566, a relatively short time considering the majestic results. The interior preserves its original paintings and sculptures. The most outstanding objects in the church are the **main altarpiece**, completed in 1570 by Sevillian painter Andrés de la Concha, the **baptismal font** and the craftsmanship on the wood **ceiling**, with Mudejar characteristics. What once served as the **monastery** now functions as a museum of religious sculpture. A gigantic **mural**, depicting St. Christopher, adorns the stairwell to the second floor. The staircase banister, the hallway niches and lintels over the doorways to the cell-like rooms still display many examples of fine, detailed work in stone.

Templo y Ex Convento de San Pedro y San Pablo, Teposcolula — *Located 110km/68mi from Oaxaca or 27km/16.7mi from Yanhuitlán. After Yanhuitlán, continue towards Huajuapan and, 14km/8.7mi later, turn left (south) onto Carr. 125 (towards Tlaxiaco and Pinotepa) and continue 13km/8mi. Open year-round daily 10am–6pm. P$10.* This religious complex, constructed by the Dominicans in the 16C, was declared a Colonial Historic Monument in 1986. The **open-air chapel**★★ commands attention for its beauty and its colossal dimensions with respect to the rest of the complex. The two choirs, one for the singers and one for the musicians, also merit attention. Works by Andrés de la Concha and Simón Pereyns adorn the church's interior. The monastery also features interesting paintings and sculptures of saints and Christ figures.

■ Isthmus of Tehuantepec

Located in the southeastern part of Oaxaca, this isthmus stands apart from the tourism and fast pace of the state capital. Here, traditions and customs totally permeate the way of life. One of the peculiarities of these communities is the power and role of women in the streets and markets. The colors of the typical dress and the people's attitude and manner of expression reflect a society where women have assumed a more powerful role. The majority of women work alongside the men, which has given them a respectable role within the family, as well as social rights in the community. This social tolerance extends to homosexuals, whom the inhabitants treat with respect and dignity.

During the months of May and September, the **Fiesta de las Velas** (Fiesta of Candles), one of the most beautiful and ancient celebrations in Mexico, takes place on the isthmus. Although its origin dates back to the pre-Hispanic period, during the colonial era, the fiesta evolved and acquired new characteristics, which endure to the present day. The celebration consists of a vigil lasting for several days in honor of each town's patron saints. Everyone takes part in the organization of this most important social event of the isthmus' communities. On these days, visitors can witness the regional folklore in all of its splendor, including the music, dances, cuisine and beautiful regional costumes, among which the famous **Tehuana dress** especially shines.

★**Templo y Ex Convento de San Juan Bautista, Coixtlahuaca** – *Located 49km/30.4mi from Teposcolula; return to Carr. Fed. 190 and continue towards Huajuapan; 12.5km/7.8mi later, in the town of Tejupan, turn right and continue 23km/14.3mi. Or, located 105km/65mi from Oaxaca; take toll road 135D; after 102km/63.2mi, take the exit to the right and continue 3km/1.9mi. Open year-round daily 10am–6pm.* This church's facade was completed in 1576. As a unique characteristic of the facade, thirty-two empty niches mark the front sections and surround the center rose window. Historians believe the niches were never intended to hold images, but rather to create the impression of light and dark. Figures of saints and symbols of the Passion of Christ surround the side entrance; this artwork shows a clear indigenous influence. The highlight of the interior is the main altarpiece, which occupies the entire apse. Though it dates back to the 17C, it preserves elements of the original work.

The main arch of the presbytery of the **open-air chapel** features floral decorations and carved friezes on its surfaces. Depictions of dragon or serpent heads with their bodies intertwined, which surround pelican-related emblems, decorate the friezes. In this work, the indigenous artistry resurfaces.

PALENQUE★★★

Chiapas
Map of Principal Sights – Map p 278
🅱 ☎ (9) 678-6570 and (01-800) 280-3500

Considered one of the most extraordinary Maya ruins, the archaeological site of Palenque is a shining example of the wisdom and complexity of this passionate, pre-Hispanic culture. The incomparable architecture of its buildings, the secrets within the walls and the numerous hieroglyphics, which have been deciphered to this day, allow modern visitors the opportunity to uncover part of these ancient mysteries, which have lain in the hidden recesses of the jungle for centuries.

Palenque was founded as an agricultural town around the year 100 BC. The city's golden age reached its apogee between AD 600 and 700, when the majority of the buildings were constructed and the greatest number of conquests took place. Historians believe the fall of Palenque resulted from a social rebellion by lower classes who no longer believed in their gods and rulers. After a long period of internal warfare, the inhabitants deserted the city. With the passage of time, the temples and other structures were slowly overrun by the dense jungle.

The first news of the existence of this ancient city surfaced at the end of the 18C and at the beginning of the 19C, when Spanish captain Antonio del Río sent a report to the local Royal Audience of the Spanish government. Years later, this text was translated into English and illustrated by J. Frederick Waldek. The first organized exploration was carried out by John Lloyd Stephens and Frederick Catherwood, in 1839. Palenque was declared a World Heritage Site in 1987.

ARCHAEOLOGICAL SITE

On the Carr. Ruinas de Palenque, 8km/5mi from the city of Palenque. The site can be accessed from Villahermosa (Tabasco) by car or bus (132km/82mi). From Villahermosa, take Carr. 186 east for 93km/58mi; at the location indicated by the signs, turn right and continue 31km/19mi to reach the town of Palenque. If you are arriving here from San Cristóbal de las Casas (188km/117mi away, approx. 4hrs) we recommend travel by bus due to the winding nature of the roads. Access is also possible from the city of Mérida (Yucatán), by bus or train (8hrs). Open year-round daily 7am–5:45pm. P$25, free Sun and holidays. ☎ (9) 678-6570.

Site Museum – *1km/0.6mi before the site.* The museum exhibits numerous items found during the archaeological excavations. Visitors are enchanted by the carved slabs, stucco and ceramic figures, several incense burners, as well as elegant obsidian, jade and mother-of-pearl jewelry, found with the funeral offerings. The stucco heads embody the Mayan concept of beauty: elongated craniums, almond-shaped eyes, aquiline noses, wide foreheads and small chins.

Templo de la Calavera (Temple of the Skull) – The first structure to the right of the entrance, this small temple displays architecture typical of the entire site, with its Mayan arch (or Korbel arch). It was named for a bas-relief carved in stucco, which depicts the death god wearing big earrings.

A little farther ahead, to the right, rises Palenque's largest temple.

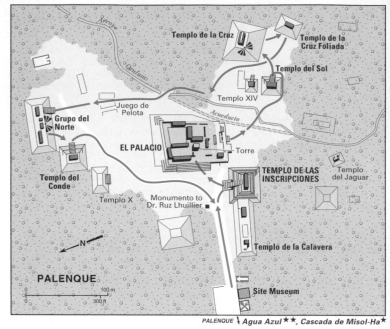

PALENQUE \ *Agua Azul*★★, *Cascada de Misol-Ha*★

Templo de las Inscripciones (Temple of the Inscriptions) – This impressive, eight-level building, with a height of 25m/82ft, was constructed at the end of the 7C AD. Archaeologists have uncovered a treasure trove of information and other findings within its walls. The temple gets its name from the three panels with hieroglyphic inscriptions, carved in fine bas-relief found on the structure's upper level. The stairs in the middle room lead to a **funerary crypt** discovered in 1952 by Mexican archaeologist Alberto Ruz Lhuillier.

El Palacio and Grupo del Norte

The funerary room measures 9m/30ft in length by 4m/13ft in width and is 7m/23ft high. Nine priests who symbolize the netherworld in the Maya concept of creation decorate the walls. A monolithic sarcophagus, weighing 13 tons, rests in the center. The remains of Pakal, famous Palenque ruler from AD 680 to 720, were found inside. The relief on the memorial slab covering the sarcophagus bears an interesting depiction: the mask of the Earth Monster decorates the lower end, while a human figure leaning his torso and head backward adorns the center.

Ruz Lhuillier's interpretation of this design confirms that the bottom section symbolizes death and the upper one represents life and hope. The middle section depicts man, trapped in an ambiguous position between the other two elements. An excellent reproduction of this tomb is found in the National Anthropology Museum in Mexico City.

In 1994 another burial site, with the cadaver of a woman presumed to be the mother of Pakal, was discovered in this same temple near the right side of the main facade.

El Palacio – Built over the course of 400 years to serve as a royal residential complex, this palace remains one of the most beautiful Maya structures. A trapezoidal, staggered-step foundation supports the building, which measures 100m/328ft in length and 80m/262ft in width, and from the plaza to the top of the watchtower reaches 15m/49ft in height. The rooms and small buildings that surround the great tower and four small courtyards feature outstanding architectural and decorative elements: hallways, subterranean galleries, roofed passageways, drainage systems, T-shaped windows (the T-shape was the sign of the wind god), carved walls and panels covered with sculptures and calendar hieroglyphics. To enter the palace, go up the stairway on the west side of the building. In the first courtyard to the right (on the southwest side), a series of small rooms, with low roofs, functioned as steam rooms in ancient times. The openings on the floor served as drains, through which the water flowed to an underground aqueduct. Towards the back of the same courtyard, a great bas-relief portrays King Pakal's mother bestowing on him a huge headdress, symbol of power. Nine impressive, **stone-carved figures**, measuring 3m/10ft in height, mark the northeast courtyard. According to different interpretations, these figures depict either kneeling leaders or hostages. Access to the underground areas, which lead visitors to the outside, opens on the south.

© Bob Schalkwijk

To the southern edge of the site, across the Otolum Creek, lies a grandiose plaza with four sublime temples that seem to extend toward the heavens. Some archaeologists believe that this entire complex, built towards the end of the 7C AD, was the masterpiece of Chan Bahlum, the eldest son of King Pakal. To access this plaza, take the pathway to the right, which climbs through the undergrowth.

Templo del Sol (Temple of the Sun) – The best-preserved temple at the site stands on the western side. Built atop a high foundation, the distinguishing characteristic is the vertical thrust of the edifice, crowned by cresting over 4m/13ft tall. The **Sun Panel**, made of richly carved limestone and considered one of the greatest Maya sculptures, graces the rear wall of the interior of the sanctuary. The center of the panel bears the sun mask, set above two crossed spears in a kind of altar, symbolized by a ceremonial staff with a serpent head on each end and a jaguar mask in the middle. At the sides, King Pakal (on the left) and his son Chan Bahlum (on the right) give offerings to the sun. Four columns of hieroglyphics complete the panel.

Templo de la Cruz – Rising for several tiers, the Temple of the Cross, the tallest structure of the site, stands north of the plaza-built over a pyramid-shaped base. Two carved memorial slabs with representations of two richly dressed men flank the entrance to the sanctuary. While the younger man symbolizes the jaguar-serpent ruler, the older man, who smokes a pipe and wears a headdress made of tobacco leaves, depicts a deity of the netherworld.

This temple's original panel rests in the National Museum of Anthropology. Nevertheless, in the center of the reproduction that remained at the site, the mask of the Earth Monster can be discerned. From the mask, a cruciform figure symbolizing the corn plant leaps forth, while the quetzal or a fantasy bird perches on it. Two priest effigies flank the scene. One makes an offering, while the other stands on either a cranium or a mask.

Templo de la Cruz Foliada (Temple of the Foliated Cross) – Taking advantage of the natural terrain on the east side, the ancient Maya built another temple on top of this hill. The front facade and battlements were completely destroyed. Nevertheless, one of the upper rooms still preserves a carved panel, with a theme similar to the one in the previous temple.

Upon exiting the plaza, cross the river again and walk north. Before arriving at the Northern Group buildings, visitors will pass next to a small ball court.

Grupo del Norte (Northern Group) – Five buildings, constructed on different levels and at different times, yet lined up over the same foundation, comprise the Northern Group. Several of them still contain their original decorations, stone carvings and hieroglyphic inscriptions.

Templo del Conde (The Count's Temple) – This structure rises to the west of the Northern Group and boasts a five-tier foundation. A small temple with the majority of its original architecture still intact, except for the cresting, crowns the apex. It was named in honor of the Neoclassical artist, Count Jean-Frédéric Waldeck, who arrived in Palenque in 1832 and lived in this temple for nearly two years while he explored the site and created his fantastical theories about Palenque. In this building, archaeologists discovered several tombs with their funerary offerings undisturbed.

EXCURSION

★★**Agua Azul** – *64km/40mi from Palenque on the road to Ocosingo. It is not advisable to visit during the rainy season (May–Oct) or at night. P$20/car.* This spectacular waterfall of the Shumulijá River begins its descent from the rocks high above and collects in tiny natural pools; it then plunges downward in white, frothing, curtain-like cascades. During the hottest season, the water radiates a stunning shade of turquoise blue, which contrasts with the verdant vegetation and creates a fantastic and unique sight. The higher you ascend along the riverbanks, the more beautiful this sight becomes. Swimming is possible at the lower elevations.

★**Cascada de Misol-Ha** – *Km. 18, on the road to Ocosingo. Open year-round 24hrs. P$20/car.* ✕ ▤ ☎ *(9) 345-1210.* Located between enormous conifers, this beautiful waterfall plunges into a lagoon of crystal-clear waters. A small trail leads visitors behind the water curtain to the other side of the river, where one can appreciate several springs among the rocks. Continue farther ahead to reach another waterfall located inside a cave *(accessible with a guide and lantern).* The lagoon, underneath the waterfall, beckons visitors to jump in and enjoy a refreshing swim. Misol-Ha park also offers rustic cabins *(P$140/night)* and a restaurant.

PÁTZCUARO★★★

Michoacán
Population 75,264
Map of Principal Sights
▣ Portal Hidalgo, 1, Downtown ☎ (4) 342-0215 ext. 16

Its name in Tarasco, the local dialect, means "seat of the Cúes or temples." The Cúes were a local indigenous group, and the town received this description because its ancient inhabitants believed this place was the gateway to the heavens, through which the gods descended and ascended. The history dates back to AD 1100 when groups apparently coming from the north integrated with groups already established in the area. In all likelihood, Pátzcuaro was founded by the Pahuacume and Hueapani, who mixed with the Cúe.

When the ecclesiastical power shifted to Pátzcuaro, the town received city status and was converted into the capital of the province of Michoacán. This title lasted until 1580 when, by viceregal order, the political and religious powers moved to Valladolid, or present-day Morelia.

Today Pátzcuaro remains a charming city set in the central part of the state. Tourists arrive by the busloads, thanks to the picturesque, red-roofed houses, friendly people, tranquillity and excellent handicrafts, as well as the islands in the lake.

★★CITY CENTER

★ **Plaza Vasco de Quiroga** – *Bordered on the south by Nicolás Romero and Dr. Coss, on the east by Portugal and Quiroga, on the north by Dr. Benito Mendoza, Iturbe and Ahumada, and on the west by Ibarra and Ponce de León. From the bus station, take one of the city buses, nicknamed "combis," marked with "Centro" on the front.* This quadrangular plaza measures 160m/525ft in length by 130m/427ft in width. Apparently, the designers envisioned the plaza as a place to play games during the colonial era. It is noteworthy that around the plaza no church was ever built; instead, it is surrounded by private homes, today converted into businesses and offices. Stone benches around the edge of the plaza provide a place to relax and sample the town's traditional *nieves de pasta* (frozen desserts). Cobblestone streets and red-roofed houses add color to the city. The main fountain features a statue of Vasco de Quiroga—the kind Spanish priest who evangelized this region in the 16C.

La Casa de los 11 Patios (Ex Convento de las Monjas Dominicas) – *Madrigal de las Altas Torres, between Dr. José María Coss and Lerín. From the Plaza Vasco de Quiroga, head south on Dr. José María Coss and turn left on Madrigal de las Altas Torres; continue halfway down the street. Open year-round daily 10am–6pm. ☏ (4) 342-0967 ext. 16.* This lovely convent of the Dominican nuns was completed in 1747 in what was previously the Hospital of Santa Martha, founded by Vasco de Quiroga. Although the original complex had eleven courtyards, it lost six of them after the construction of adjacent streets.
At the end of the entryway stands a mural by José Luis Soto (1979), representing Pátzcuaro's benefactor, **Vasco de Quiroga**.
Upon entering on the left, visitors see one of the courtyards that has been preserved intact, with handsome arcades of Corinthian columns and keystones with plant motifs, as well as a central fountain. On the west side, a round window shaped like the sun illuminates the interior of a **bathroom★**. This room, adorned with two carved figures that allow the water to spout, occupies the hollow of a rock. Exquisite detail covers the Baroque interior doorway. This work is surprising, as rarely in the colonial era was a specific site designed for bathing. The former nuns' quarters today serve as shops for local artisans, who may often be seen at work on site.

El Sagrario – *Lerín, between Madrigal de las Altas Torres and Portugal. From Madrigal de las Altas Torres, go left on Lerín. A few steps away is the entrance to the church. Open year-round daily 7am–6:30pm. ☏ (4) 342-1214.* This fortification-like structure rises above Calle Lerín. A wall of tiny arches, with bell-shaped finials, surrounds the Church of the Shrine. Of modest design, featuring a Neoclassical doorway and interior, the building was completed in the 17C.
The shrine, also named the Sanctuary or Church of Our Lady of Health until her effigy was transferred to the present-day basilica, consists of only one nave and side entrance. Worthy of note in the interior is the side chapel, which holds a Baroque-Churrigueresque **altarpiece★** dedicated to Our Lady of Solitude. This 18C altarpiece features gilded wood and four *estípite* pilasters that frame the statue of the Virgin. Denoted by its inverted pyramid shape with an abbreviated top, an *estípite* is a common element in the architecture of Mexican churches. The altarpiece is the only one of this style preserved in the city of Pátzcuaro.

Templo de la Compañía – *Lerín and Portugal. From Madrigal de las Altas Torres, take a left onto Lerín and continue to Portugal. Open year-round daily 7am–6:30pm.* Vasco de Quiroga commissioned this edifice, which was completed in 1546. The church was assigned to carry out the functions of a cathedral until 1573, when it was turned over to the Jesuits who administered it for nearly two centuries. This building features a pitched roof and restrained Baroque portals. The wooden ceiling inside lengthens in a half-barrel vault. Indigenous nobility and important Jesuits, in addition to Spanish nobles, were buried here. Even the remains of Vasco de Quiroga were kept in the church until they were moved to the present-day basilica. Like many others throughout Mexico, this church was built over a pre-Hispanic base, in this case, a great Tarascan temple. To its right stands the former Jesuit School, today a cultural center.

★ **Museo de Artes e Industrias Populares** – *Enseñanza, corner of Alcantarilla. Take Lerín to where a water tank or fountain marks Calle Alcantarilla. Open year-round Tue–Sat 9am–7pm, Sun 9am–2:30pm. Closed Jan 1 & Dec 25. P$20. ☏ (4) 342-1029.* This building was once the School of St. Nicholas, founded in 1540 by order of Vasco de Quiroga, who set out to make it a school for indigenous priests. It gave way to the current Colegio de San Nicolás de Hidalgo (School of St. Nicholas of Hidalgo), in the city of Morelia.

An interesting feature of the exterior is the eight-sided **portal**, which follows the shape of the corner, over which rises a bell tower with two empty niches and three arches.

A vestibule with two sculptures (one pre-Hispanic, the other colonial) greets visitors at the entrance to the **museum**. Next, ten rooms present a wide **collection**★ of regional handicrafts, such as earthenware and lacquered works, textiles, masks, vessels, wooden basins, kitchen utensils, sculptures and religious paintings, as well as votive offerings and Christ figures made of corn and sugarcane paste.

The room featuring the furniture of a typical **Michoacán dining room**★ also provides access to the rear garden with remnants of a great platform, which once supported a Purépecha ceremonial center.

On Calle de Alcantarilla, a water tank with a sculpture of the Virgin rests on an octagonal pedestal. The locals call it the Fountain of Don Vasco due to the legend surrounding the tank's origin. Because of the lack of water, area residents complained to Don Vasco, who took his pastoral staff, and with several whacks against a rock, made water spout forth.

Basílica de Nuestra Señora de la Salud – *Arciga, corner of La Paz, one street from the museum. Arciga is a continuation of Enseñanza, which is itself an extension of Lerín. Access is also possible via Calle La Paz, which climbs up from Plaza Gertrudis Boca Negra. Open year-round daily 6am–8:30pm.* Begun in the 16C, the basilica was meant to have five naves. Due to the church's opponents, however, only one nave was finished. The shrine became a cathedral upon the arrival of the Jesuits, who were assigned the old cathedral.

Corinthian columns flank its Neoclassical facade. In the 17C and 18C the building underwent modifications and suffered severe damage as a result of earthquakes, which in 1845 forced it to close its doors to its worshipers because the old tower had begun to fall apart and had cracked the church's roof.

A highlight of the interior, also Neoclassical, is the **main altar**★★, dedicated to Our Lady of Health. Above it rises the cupola, which represents the power of the Pope and the figure of Jesus as a crowning symbol of the same power. The sacristy boasts an interesting **collection** of colonial paintings.

The mausoleum of Vasco de Quiroga, the city's bishop and benefactor who had conceived this church as a great cathedral, stands to the left of the entrance. In 1924, four centuries after Don Vasco's death, Pope Pius XI granted the shrine the status of Minor Basilica.

Biblioteca Gertrudis Boca Negra – *Iturbe, facing the Plaza Gertrudis Bocanegra. From the basilica, take Buena Vista and descend on Padre Lloreda to the corner of Títere. Open year-round Mon–Fri 9am–7pm. Closed national holidays, July, Aug and the last 2 weeks in Dec.* Occupying the space where once stood the 16C Church of St. Augustine, this library was built in the 18C. Its highlights include a wooden half-barrel vault, enormous dimensions, and a north wing **mural**★ by Juan O'Gorman. The mural centers on the history of Michoacán, with scenes depicting the arrival of the natives, the Conquest, the War of Independence and the Revolution.

Across from the library lies the Plaza Gertrudis Bocanegra, named in honor of this heroine of Independence. The locals call it **Plaza Chica** (Little Plaza), in comparison to the Plaza Vasco de Quiroga. At the market to the northeast of the plaza, vendors hawk fruits, vegetables, fish, typical regional food, small utensils and handicrafts. On Fridays, commercial activity heightens as a great number of artisans and fishermen come from other areas to sell their products.

ADDITIONAL SIGHTS

Lago de Pátzcuaro – Ten minutes from downtown Pátzcuaro lies this lake of the same name. It is surrounded by diverse towns, in addition to six island villages. One of the best known is **Janitzio**, a Tarascan name meaning "cornsilk," famous for its **Day of the Dead** festivals. Its history dates back to the ancient Tarascan Empire when, according to legend, the kings used the island to hide their treasures of gold and silver. Among the attractions is the enormous 40m/131ft **monument to José María Morelos y Pavón**, created by sculptor Guillermo Ruiz. Inside, murals chronicle the life of this hero of Independence, while outside magnificent views of the lake and the city of Pátzcuaro create a memorable setting. The nearby islands of **Tecuena**, **Pacanda** and **Yunuén** also hold Day of the Dead festivities. Tarascans on the small island of Yunuén own the small tourist center with cabins and restaurants.

★**El Estribo Grande Volcano** – A cobblestone road lined with tall trees leads to a small plaza and pavilion, which offers a great **view**★★ of all of Pátzcuaro and its surroundings, the lake and its islands. A stairway, which some say has 300 steps, climbs farther up to the mouth of the extinct volcano.

© Gustavo Gatto

■ Day of the Dead

Funerary rites in Mexico have played an important cultural role since the pre-Hispanic era. When the Catholic religion was introduced in the area, these celebrations evolved, and death assumed the fearsome symbol of the skull. Toward the end of the 18C, this image began to acquire more human traits. Finally, In the 19C, the celebrated engraver **José Guadalupe Posada** transformed it into a popular and humorous character. Since then, death represents an ordinary figure to the Mexicans, and they have fun and tell jokes about it, creating nicknames like *calaca* (skeleton), *patas de hilo* (deadhead) and *huesuda* (bony one), among others.

This unique conception of death is most strikingly expressed during the traditional Day of the Dead celebration. Mexicans believe that on November 1 and 2 the deceased return from the hereafter to visit with loved ones. The fiesta takes place in cities as well as in the countryside, in cemeteries and homes, and in offices and schools. Altars spring up everywhere and offer the honored one's favorite food and drink during life, as well as traditional dishes. Images of either the deceased or saints, small yellow chrysanthemums, candles, papier-mâché and skull-shaped breads and candy decorate the altars.

Although a national celebration, the activities vary in each region. In some towns, the celebration begins on October 31, when the *Vigil of the Little Angels* takes place to receive the souls of dead children. Among the most beautiful and traditional of the **fiestas★★** are the celebrations in **Mixquic**, near Mexico City; at the **Tzintzuntzan** cemetery and in **Pátzcuaro**, Michoacán.

EXCURSIONS

Villa Escalante (Santa Clara del Cobre) – *16km/10mi to the south on Carr. 120 to Ario de Rosales. Transportation to Santa Clara del Cobre departs from the bus station.* The people of this picturesque, red-roofed town earn their livelihood by creating copper handicrafts. This material even appears in the main plaza's pavilion, where vendors sell an abundance of their wares. Since coppersmithing is the town's principal activity, every house resembles a workshop. Santa Clara was the first town to obtain the National Prize for Popular Art for its hammered coppersmithing, a tradition that dates back to the era of Don Vasco de Quiroga.

★**Museo Nacional del Cobre (National Copper Museum)** – *Av. Morelos, corner of Pino Suárez. One street from the main plaza, on Av. Morelos. Open year-round Tue–Sat and holidays 10am–3pm and 5–7pm, Sun 10am–4pm. Closed Jan 1, May 1 and Dec 25. P$2.* ☏ *(4) 343-0254.* This museum displays the copper artwork that has won recognition in its annual fairs. Several vessels, jars and wash basins show the artisans' skill and great ingenuity in sculpting geometric forms on the surface of the material.

★**Templo de Santiago Caballero, Tupátaro** – *18km/11mi east of Pátzcuaro on Carr. 120. After 15km/9mi, take the exit to Cuanajo and follow the signs. Open year-round daily 9am–6pm.* ◨. Finished in 1725, this small and moderate church merits a visit for its wooden, trapezoidal **ceiling★★**, adorned with impressive poly-chrome paintings, which were completed in 1761 by indigenous artists. Thirty-three angels, one for each year of Jesus' life, greet visitors. Each angel holds up a symbol of the Passion of Christ. The six mysteries of the Virgin Mary, as well as the six mysteries of Jesus Christ, mark the center of the ceiling. Lined with gold leaf, the **main altarpiece★** boasts representations of ears of corn and avocados, as well as 18C oil paintings of scenes of the Passion of Christ and the Adoration of the Three Wise Men. An effigy of Jesus Christ, known as the "Lord of the Little Pine Tree," presides over the ensemble. According to legend, a woodcutter dis-covered the statue in the heart of a pine tree. The locals believe that the 19C Christ, also on exhibit, has grown with the passage of time. Originally measuring 1.5m/5ft, its actual size currently reaches 1.65m/5.4ft. An annexed museum con-tains objects of worship from the 17C to the 19C.

Tzintzuntzan – *17.5km/11mi northwest on Carr. 15 heading toward Morelia. Transportation departs for Quiroga from the bus station.* The Tarascan word *Tzintzuntzan* means "place of the hummingbirds." The center of the pre-Columbian empire in the area until the arrival of the Spaniards, Tzintzuntzan also served as the site for Vasco de Quiroga's initial evangelical work, after he pacified the indigenous rebellions caused by the abuses of the authoritarian Spanish Captain Nuño de Guzmán. Like other towns on the banks of Lake Pátzcuaro, Tzintzuntzan preserves its rustic flavor, as well as the traditional tile roofs. In addition, the town's principal activity is the production and sale of handicrafts, rich in a variety of shapes, colors and materials.

★**Las Yácatas** – *1km/0.6mi south of Pátzcuaro. Take Carr. 15 towards Quiroga, or follow Carr. Fed. 120 Morelia-Pátzcuaro, take the exit to Quiroga and follow signs to Tzintzuntzan. The archaeological site can be accessed from the southeastern end of the town that bears the same name, beside the cemetery. Without a vehicle, the trip must be made on foot as no local transportation is available. From the Church of St. Francis, continue on Av. Las Yácatas, which is adorned with wooden sculptures. Open year-round daily 9am–5pm. P$17. ☎ (4) 312-8838.* This archae-ological site was the capital of the Purépecha or Tarascan Empire. It consists of a foundation, with a length of approximately 400m/1,312ft and a width of 250m/820ft. To this day, the different structures constructed above this base still remain visible; these include the Palace, Edificio E and spaces for administrative and ceremonial activities. This complex is located in the main plaza, east of the *yacatas* (or stacked stones) and encompasses the most notorious buildings. Five structures, made with overlapping layers of rock, form layered sections with mixed shapes, both rectangular and semicircular. Wood and straw temples were built atop these circular sections.

The most accepted chronology for this site corresponds to the last three centuries before the arrival of the Spanish conquistadors. This period was one of maximum expansion for the Purépechas, who shared their hegemony with important ancient cities such as Pátzcuaro and Ihuatzio.

Uruapan – *60km/37mi from Pátzcuaro on Carr. de cuota (toll road) 14-B.* Michoacán's second largest city, Uruapan, spreads along the banks of the Cupatitzio River and in the fertile foothills of the Purépecha plateau. Since the days of the Purépechas, Uruapan has been a center of wealth, which controlled the agriculture of the nearby *tierra caliente* ("hot land") region. Today, the townspeople take pride in having planted over a million avocado trees in the "world capital of the avocado." The **Parque Nacional Eduardo Ruiz★★** *(Calzada Fray Juan San Miguel, 1, eight streets west of the main plaza; open year-round daily 8am–6pm; P$2; ☎ 4-524-0197)* figures among Uruapan's attractions. This national park boasts plenty of lush veg-etation to keep out the sun's rays. Water flows parallel to the cobblestone trails, which meander past views of fountains, springs and bridges steeped in legend. The **Museo Regional de Arte Popular La Huatapera★** *(facing the main plaza, next to the Church of the Immaculate Conception; open year-round Tue–Sun 9:30am–1:30pm & 3:30–6pm; closed national holidays; ☎ 4-524-3434)* also merits a visit. This pretty building consists of white walls, tile roof, dirt floor and a Plateresque facade. Constructed in 1533 by Fray Juan de San Miguel, it served as a hospital and meeting place for locals. Throughout its six rooms, the museum exhibits regional handicrafts and lacquered pieces of special interest, typical of the area.

Cascada Tzaráracua (Tzaráracua Waterfall) – *10km/6mi south of Uruapan on the road to Apatzingán, followed by a 800m/.5mi hike, which makes its descent on approx-imately 700 steps.* △ ✕ ◪. At the end of a gorge, the Cupatitzio River makes a tumultuous plunge of 60m/197ft and then filters through a series of rocks which resemble a sieve—or, in the native language, a **tzaráracua** or "cloth through which water passes."

Angahuan – *37km/23mi from Uruapan. Go north on Carr. 37. After 16km/10mi, turn at the intersection to Los Reyes; 21km/13mi later you will reach Angahuan.* A certain sadness tinges the wooden barns of this old town, while the colorful dresses of the women contrast with the dark layers of gray sand, left by the nearby volcano of Paricutín after its eruption.

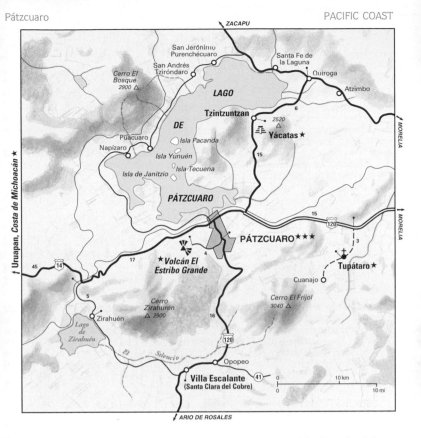

The worthwhile **Templo de Santiago Apóstol** *(open year-round daily 6am–8pm)* faces the main plaza. The Franciscans built the church in a 16C Plateresque style. Both its facade, which displays a richly decorated Mudejar **relief★★**, and the atrial cross exhibit lovely indigenous interpretations. A narration of the eruption of Paricutín hangs on the wooden door of a house beside the church.

Paricutín Volcano and the Ruins of San Juan Parangaricutiro – *1km/0.6mi from Angahuan stand the cabins from which trails depart for the ruins (45min) or via another route to the crater of the volcano (8hrs round trip). The trip takes the same amount of time, whether on foot or horseback. Thick-soled shoes are recommended.* On the morning of February 20, 1943, farmer Dionisio Pulido watched as a fiery hole opened up in one of his pastures. At five in the afternoon, the volcano awoke and began to stir at an alarming rate. A year later, admitting defeat, the inhabitants of **San Juan Parangaricutiro** completely abandoned their 16C town. Today, only the towers and part of the altar of this church, built in 1618, rise over the broken earth left in the wake of the volcanic lava. From here can be seen the 410m/1,345ft volcano, whose crater has a diameter of 250m/820ft. For nine years, eleven days and ten hours, Paricutín erupted lava and ash; it became dormant on March 4, 1952. Today the town of Nuevo Parangaricutiro proudly occupies what once was the Hacienda de los Conejos.

★**Michoacán Coast** – *From Uruapan. Head south on Carr. 37 toward Guacamayas (265km/165mi). The beaches lie to the west along Carr. 200.* ⚠ ✗ ▣. This coast spans nearly 300km/186mi in length between the states of Guerrero and Colima. Numerous beaches stretch from Lázaro Cárdenas to Boca de Apiza, near Colima. Of special note is **Playa Azul**, one of the state's principal tourist attractions. From here, the coastal highway departs to the west. This route offers paradisiacal landscapes, still unexplored beaches, fantastic islands and coves, a great diversity of exotic fauna and an infinite variety of delicious dishes. Among the most attractive places figure **Manzanilla** and **Rangel**, two coves with freshwater springs; the **Caletilla de Mexcalhuacan**, a departure point for sporting expeditions and home of the Pacific's largest coconuts; the **Bahía de Bufadero** (Bufadero Bay), also called the **Caleta de Campos**, an ideal spot for camping and fishing; and finally the **Bahía de Maruata★**, which boasts the region's most beautiful beaches.

From October to March, sea turtles arrive at the coast of Michoacán to lay their eggs on Playa Azul, Boca de Apiza and Cololá.

SAN CRISTÓBAL DE LAS CASAS★★★

Chiapas
Population 116,729
Map of Principal Sights
🛈 Miguel Hidalgo, 2, local 10, ☎ (9) 678-6570
and Palacio Municipal, Plaza 31 de Marzo, ☎ (9) 678-0660 ext. 126

San Cristóbal de las Casas is the most enchanting place in the state of Chiapas. Its charm results from its colonial heritage and the enigmatic magic of old and powerful indigenous traditions. The Mayan past is still deeply rooted here, and the border with Guatemala seems to exist only on maps. The city's name pays homage to **Fray Bartolomé de las Casas**, who despite his short stay in this city always championed and defended the indigenous people. San Cristóbal de las Casas served as the regional capital from the colonial period until 1829. During the 16–18C period, the city changed names several times and formed part of various territories, including the Yucatán and Guatemala.

SIGHTS

San Cristóbal de las Casas is located only 89km/55mi (1 1/2hrs) from Tuxtla Gutiérrez, the capital of Chiapas. The trek from Tuxtla to San Cristóbal follows a winding road with spectacular views of the mountains that surround it. Within the city, there is little need for transportation, as visitors can reach any destination by foot on lovely streets that beckon one to browse.

The heart of the city lies between two plazas that meet on the diagonal. The **Zócalo** *(Calle Guadalupe Victoria and 16 de Septiembre)*, in front of the Cathedral, is a great open space whose center is marked by an enormous wooden cross. Plaza 31 de Marzo *(Calle Guadalupe Victoria and Insurgentes)*, thus named to commemorate the founding of the city on the same date in 1528, is imbued with the full flavor of a provincial town, with its picturesque kiosk and leafy trees. On the west side rises the **Palacio Municipal**; on the north, the side entrance to the cathedral; and on the east side, a colonial arcade.

Cathedral – *Entryway is through the side door. Plaza 31 de Marzo. Open year-round daily 6–7am, 10am–2pm and 4–8pm.* This church was completed in 1533. Seven years later, it became a diocese when Juan de Arteaga was named the first bishop. Later, Fray Bartolomé de las Casas would also serve as bishop. During the following centuries, especially the 17C, the structure underwent several alterations that remodeled the entire edifice in the restrained Baroque style. St. Michael and the four evangelists crown the top of the main facade; below stands St. James, guarded by a pair of double-headed eagles; the Virgin of the Conception crowns the main arch. Inside, at the far end on the left, **paintings★** by **Juan Correa** decorate the altarpiece. In the sacristy, one finds an excellent work by **Miguel Cabrera** (the last painting on the right wall).

Walk in front of the cathedral, along 20 de Noviembre, five streets to the north.

★Templo de Santo Domingo – *20 de Noviembre and Comitán. Open year-round daily 6am–2pm & 4–8pm.* The present-day appearance of this church results from a late-17C reconstruction of the original 16C structure. The mortar facade imitates a Baroque altarpiece, its three sections decorated with plant motifs and Solomonic columns. A striking image of St. Dominic, flanked by a pair of two-headed eagles (which symbolized Spanish power), graces the pediment. Inside, the Capilla del Rosario (Chapel of the Rosary) and the altarpieces of gilded cedar, with excellent pictorial and sculptural works by Guatemalan artists, merit special attention. Without a doubt, the most beautiful piece in the entire church is the carved, gilded wooden **pulpit★**.

The monastery, located on the north side of the church, houses the **Museo de los Altos de Chiapas** *(open year-round Tue–Sun 10am–5pm; P$16; ☎ 9-678-1609)*. The first floor exhibits a few pre-Hispanic artifacts found in the region, most noteworthy of which are the Olmec and Maya figurines and ceramics. The history room on the second floor centers on the 16–19C, with emphasis on the Conquest and domination of the indigenous peoples during the colonial era. Also showcased is a splendid collection of textiles from all the ethnic groups in Chiapas.

★★Mercado Abierto de Artesanías Indígenas – *Near the Church and Monastery of St. Dominic. Open year-round daily 8am–3pm.* Artists and craftsmen from neighboring towns, and even some Guatemalans, use the esplanade of Santo Domingo to sell a great variety of handicrafts, characterized by their fantastic colors and intricate designs. The same products sell in stores at double or triple the price of what these artisans charge. The simple pleasure of walking amid the stalls, browsing and listening to the diverse indigenous dialects is very rewarding.

★Museo Na Bolom (La Casa del Jaguar) – *Av. Vicente Guerrero, 33. Walk nine streets east on Calle de Comitán and turn left. Guided tour in English (1 1/2hrs) daily 4:30pm. P$20. ✗ ☎ (9) 678-1418. With advance reservation, one can spend the* *night here for P$300. The museum organizes tours to the Lacandon jungle as well as trips to Yaxchilán and Bonampak.* Built in 1891, this old mansion belonged to archaeologist Franz Blom (1891–1963) and his wife, the photographer Gertrudis Blom (1901–94), who both dedicated their lives to the study of the Maya culture. Through their work they established a particularly close relationship with the **Lacandons.** With their help, the Bloms initiated a series of cultural and ecological projects, including the reforestation of the Lacandon Jungle. During their lifetime, the house was always open to students and researchers who needed lodging, as was the **library★**, which is now open to the public and contains more than 5,000 books on the Maya culture. Today, guided tours give visitors a chance to see some of the archaeological pieces which Blom found during more than 40 years of work in Chiapas, as well as some of the 50,000 photos taken by Gertrudis and an interesting display on the Lacandons. In the garden behind the house, reforestation work continues to this day.

Practical Information ....Area Code: 9

Getting There – **Base Militar de Terán Airport, Tuxtla Gutiérrez:** 5km/3mi west of Tuxtla and 85km/53mi west of San Cristóbal de las Casas. Transportation to San Cristóbal de las Casas by bus *(2hrs of direct travel on semi-luxury class; P$38):* **Central de Autobuses Cristóbal Colón,** Av. 2a Norte and 2a Poniente, Downtown, ☎ 612-5122 or 612-2624. **Taxis Premier:** ☎ 612-9869 or 611-0777 *(1 1/2hrs of direct travel; P$350).* The airport has **car rental agencies.** We recommend traveling during daylight.

Getting Around – The Bus Station (Central de Autobuses) ☎ 678-0291 and Auto-transportes Tuxtla Gutiérrez ☎ 848-69 offer luxury and first-class service to Palenque (4hrs) and other destinations. **Radio Taxis Ciudad Real** ☎ 868-99. **Public parking:** 5 de Febrero, Plaza Catedral, Downtown ☎ 678-0660 *(P$6/hr).* Most tourist sights are within easy walking distance.

Tourist Information – **State Tourist Office** (Secretaría de Desarrollo Turístico), Región II Altos, Av. Miguel Hidalgo, 1-B, Downtown, C.P. 29200 ☎ 678-6570 *(Mon–Sat 9am–9pm, Sun & holidays 9am–3pm)* and the **Municipal Tourist Office** (Oficina Municipal de Turismo), Palacio de Gobierno, Plaza Central C.P. 29200 ☎ 678-0715 ext.126 *(Mon–Sat 9am–8pm)* provide free information on sights and tourist services, as well as maps and brochures. Due to political unrest, it is advisable to check with these tourist offices before traveling to the region.

Accommodations – The above tourist offices provide information and help with hotel reservations. **Hotels:** *(P$450–$550 in 4 and 5-star hotels; these are average daily rates for a double room and are subject to change.)* Hotel Catedral (has travel agency offices), Calle Guadalupe. Victoria, 21, ☎ 678-1363; Casa Mexicana, Calle 28 de Agosto, 1, ☎ 678-0698; Casa Vieja, Calle María Adelina Flores, 7, ☎ 678-6868; Ciudad Real Teatro, Diagonal Centenario, 32, ☎ 678-4400; Diego de Mazariegos, Calle 5 de Febrero, 1, ☎ 805-13; Flamboyán, Calle 1 de Marzo, 15, ☎ 678-0045; Bonampak, Calzada México, 5, ☎ 678-1621.

Guided Tours – The following agencies in San Cristóbal de las Casas, as well as travel agencies located in major hotels, offer city bus tours, as well as regular and private excursions to nearby archaeological sites (Yaxchilán, Palenque, Toniná and Bonampak), towns (San Juan Chamula and Zinacantán) and natural attractions (Sumidero Canyon, Agua Azul Waterfalls, Montebello Lakes and the San Cristóbal Grottoes). Service includes transportation and narration by multilingual guides. ATC ☎ 678-2550, Viajes Navarra ☎ 678-1143, Pakal Viajes ☎ 678-2818; and Museo Na Bolom *(p 286)* ☎ 678-5586. Private guided tours are available; check with the local tourist office *(above)* for a list of licensed multilingual guides.

Handicrafts and markets – **Textiles:** San Jolobil, Ex Convento de Santo Domingo ☎ 678-2646 *(Mon–Sat 9am–2pm & 4–7pm)*; J'pas Joloviletik at Av. General Utrilla, 43, ☎ 678-2848, *(Mon–Sat 9am–2pm & 4–7pm)*; Casa de las Artesanías, Av. Hidalgo and Niños Héroes, Downtown, ☎ 678-1180 *(daily 10am–2pm & 4–7pm)*. **Artisan workshops:** Kun Kun (mosaics & looms) at Real de Mexicanos, 21, Barrio de Mexicanos ☎ 678-1417; La Albarrada (rugs & leather), Av. de la Juventud, Barrio de María Auxiliadora, ☎ 678-6580, *(Mon–Fri 8am–4pm)*; Plaza de la Calle Real (textiles & jewelry), Real de Guadalupe, 5, Downtown, ☎ 678-0992 *(daily 7am–11pm)*. **Markets:** Mercado de las Artesanías (handmade textiles and leather products), located beside the Church of Santo Domingo *(daily 8am–3pm)*; Mercado de Artesanías de San Juan Chamula *(daily 9am–2pm)*.

EXCURSIONS

★★★ **Parque Nacional del Cañón del Sumidero** – *74km/46mi. From San Cristóbal, go west on Carr. 190 to Chiapa de Corzo (where the trip by boat begins). Description p 295.*

San Juan Chamula and Zinancantán

11km/7mi northwest of San Cristóbal. Next to the municipal market of San Cristóbal, buses frequently depart and return from both of these places. In both towns, photos of the temples' interiors or of religious authorities are not allowed. We recommend visiting Chamula on **holidays**★★ or on Sundays, when the food market takes place *(photo p 251)*. For an explanation of the importance of the traditional dresses, visit the **community museums** in both locales.

★ **San Juan Chamula** – In this small town of **Tzotzil** origin, ancient political, religious and social elements intermingle in such a way that might baffle visitors. The inhabitants still speak their original language and maintain traditional social order, based on hierarchies and reflected in their dress. The ceremonial attire consists of a hat with three colors of ribbons, one for each of the three sections of the town or each of the three protector saints of the Chamulas; the necklace or rosary belt; the **caite** (a type of sandal used daily by the ancient Maya and still in use today); a hand-held rod indicating authority; and the **chuj** (a black wool serape colored with natural dyes). The political-religious authorities, such as town stewards and other officials, don the handkerchief or white turban. Women are excluded from high official positions, but not from religious ones, and they may become **iloles** or healers.

Museo de Etnología – *Located behind the Palacio Municipal. Open year-round daily 9am–5pm. P$5.* The Ethnology Museum displays interesting samples of the traditional dresses in San Juan Chamula, as well as typical handicrafts, musical instruments and household appliances.

★ **Templo de San Juan Bautista** – *Facing the main plaza in San Juan Chamula. To gain admittance to the church, one must acquire a special pass from the Municipal Office of Tourism. Open year-round daily 9am–5pm. P$5, covers admission to both the church and the Ethnology Museum. No photos allowed inside.* This church astounds the senses. Here, amid the odor of incense, the pagan rites of the Maya merge magically with the Catholic religion, abruptly diverging from all the established traditions of western Christianity. Close to 40 statues of saints, covered with adornments that originate from old traditions (such as the colorful ribbons and the mirrors suspended around the neck) hang on the walls. These mirrors symbolize the sacred eye that sees everything with great clarity.

The church has neither priests nor mass. Worshippers may pray to whichever saint they choose. Nevertheless, mainly shamans use the church, for cleansing and healing. These events include unique body movements, prayers of entreaty, and consumption of various types of food and drink. Candles are very important, and the color of each one varies according to the prayer and type of cure. Today, this fusion of beliefs includes the use of Coca-Cola, as the locals believe the gas caused by its ingestion helps to expel the evil spirits of the sick.

Zinancantán – *8km/5mi from San Juan Chamula and 11km/7mi from San Cristóbal. Admission to the temples is paid at the Office of Tourism, located in front of the new Palacio Municipal.* The municipality of San Lorenzo Zinancantán also belongs to the Mayan ethnic group of the Tzotzils. An important commercial center during the pre-Hispanic era, today the city plays a key role in the supply and exportation of floral products. Like the residents of San Juan Chamula and all of the Tzetzal and Tzotzil municipalities of the Chiapan Highlands, the inhabitants of Zinancantán preserve their traditional customs. Everyday wear is distinguished by the rose-colored shirts and shawls of the men, women and even the children. The ceremonial dress of the authorities greatly differs from that of the Chamulas. The **Iglesia de San Lorenzo** and the **Ermita del Señor de Esquipulas** should not be missed during secular and religious festivities *(no photos allowed inside either building)*.

Chinkultic and Tenam Puente – *292km/181mi. We suggest joining a tour organized by a travel agency to visit these archaeological sites. Due to occasional military checkpoints along the way, be prepared to show your passport.*

Chinkultic – *Head southeast for 88km/55mi, on Carr. Panamericana 190, to the municipality of Comitán de Domínguez. From there, continue 49km/30mi south toward Parque Nacional Lagos de Montebello. Open year-round daily 8am–4pm. P$17. ☎ (01-800) 280-3500.* Chinkultic, or "Layered Well," was thus named for the deep cenote that lies at the foot of the site's most important temple. Chinkultic's heyday took place during the Late Classic period (AD 600–900). Not only did it serve as a ceremonial center, but also as a defensive site, due to the strategic placement of the Main Pyramid atop a hill. Shortly before AD 1200, the city was permanently abandoned. Of the 150 structures found thus far, only eight

Tzotzil Weaver, Zinancantán

have been restored partially. The ruins' greatest treasures consist of the **Main Pyramid**, with its spectacular **view**★ from the summit; the **Ball Court**, with a handsome bas-relief depicting a ballplayer (now exhibited in the National Museum of Anthropology); and the **blue cenote**, from which archaeologists have salvaged valuable artifacts that were tossed inside during maiden sacrifices. Excavations have also uncovered numerous objects with hieroglyphics corresponding to the site's golden age, some of which may be viewed during the tour.

Tenam Puente – *59km/37mi from Chinkultic. Return to the municipality of Comitán de Domínguez and take Carr. Panamericana 190 southeast for 10km/6mi. Open year-round daily 8am–4pm. P$17.* ☎ *(01-800) 280-3500.* Here lie the remains of an enormous Maya structure of a civic, residential and religious nature. The splendor of this city occurred during the Classic and early post-Classic periods, after the Maya had abandoned the central region and specifically, the city of Petén. Tenam Puente was strategically constructed over a mountain with a view of the entire plain. This site is impressive for its large scale and numerous buildings more than for its complex architecture.

Grutas del Rancho Nuevo – *8km/5mi from San Cristóbal de las Casas. Head southeast on Carr. Panamericana 190. Open year-round Mon–Fri 9am–4:30pm, Sat–Sun 9am–5:30pm. P$3.* Through a 0.7km/0.5mi–long corridor, visitors can explore these grottoes, formed thousands of years ago by an underground river, and admire stalactites, stalagmites, columns and various other rock formations.

★★**Toniná** – *117km/73mi from San Cristóbal de las Casas. Head east on Carr. Panamericana 190 and turn left (northeast) on Carr. 199 to the municipality of Ocosingo. Then continue 16km/10mi to the east. Open year-round daily 9am–4pm. P$20, free Sun and national holidays. Organized tours are recommended for visiting the archaeological site.* Toniná, whose Tzeltal name means "Stone House," flourished during the Late Classic period (between AD 600 and 900). Toniná stands out as one of the most important archaeological sites of the Maya civilization. The work of laborious excavations, which began in the early 1980s, uncovered an imposing **acropolis** that measures 70m/230ft in height; a **ball court** 72m/236ft in length; and an infinite variety of artifacts, bas-reliefs and sculptures—all of which can be viewed during the tour.

Seven superposed platforms, each one with different structures, comprise the **Great Acropolis**. Characteristic of almost all of the constructions, which connect by means of stairways and narrow passages, is the Mayan arch. The first level features the **Palacio del Inframundo** (Palace of the Netherworld) a complex of labyrinthine passages representing the journey of the ancient Maya to the other world. The second and fourth levels hold palaces with numerous rooms where Toniná's rulers resided. A palace with layered frets that represent Kukulkán, the plumed serpent, stands out on the third level, which also displays painted murals with serpent motifs carved on stucco. The fifth level boasts Toniná's most valuable item: the **Mural de las Cuatro Eras**★★, discovered in its entirety in 1992, measures 4m/13ft in height and 16m/53ft in width. It dates from the time period between AD 790 and 840 and depicts a four-page codex of the principal Maya deities described in the legend of the four suns or eras of creation. This magnificent mural features a smiling skeleton, carved in stucco, whose hand holds the decapitated head of a Maya warrior. The unfortunate figure is Kan-Xul (Yellow Rabbit), the second son of

Pakal, a famous Maya ruler who is buried in Palenque's Templo de las Inscripciones. Kan-Xul ascended to the throne in Palenque in AD 704 and was beheaded in AD 714 by his enemies in Toniná.

The sixth level houses an **altar to the earth god**, as well as a 30m/33yd tunnel where ceramics and offerings have been found. The temple on the seventh level is characterized for its bas-reliefs, which portray captives with yokes around their necks, clear evidence of the warring nature of these people. The summit of the acropolis offers a marvelous panoramic **view**★ of the entire valley.

★★ **Parque Nacional Lagos de Montebello** – *On Carr. Panamericana 190, 140km/87mi from San Cristóbal de las Casas. Open year-round daily 24hrs, but it is advisable to visit during the day, up until 5pm. ☏ (9) 673-9396. It is recommended to use the services of a travel agency. Due to the occasional military checkpoints between Comitán and the entrance to the park, visitors are advised to carry their passports or other means of identification. Visits during the rainy season (May–October) are not advisable.* Situated on the frontier with Guatemala, between thick pine and evergreen oak forests, dense jungle and exotic fauna, this secluded national park contains the most beautiful lake region in all of Mexico. This is reaffirmed by twenty-eight beautiful lakes and lagoons (of which eight are accessible by trails), with tones spanning the entire range of greens and blues. These spectacular deposits of water, vestiges of chains of ancient **cenotes**, have merged over time. The hue of the water varies according to the soil's chemical composition, the vegetation and the refraction of light.

TAXCO★★★

Guerrero
Population 95,144
Map of Principal Sights – Map p 114 **(AZ)**
🛈 Centro de Cultura de Taxco, Av. Plateros, 1 ☏ (7) 622-6616

Nestled in the hillsides of Mt. Atachi, Taxco, which means the "lord of the rains" in reference to the torrential rains that often fall over the area, is surrounded by beautiful churches and chapels. It excels as a colonial city that understands how to preserve its style and traditions. The little white houses with red roofs and the winding cobblestone streets give the city simplicity yet character.

Historical Notes

Old Taxco – The **Tlahuica**, who settled in present-day Old Taxco, inhabited this region during the pre-Hispanic era. In this period, they called it **Tlachco**, the "place of the ball game." Like many others, the Tlahuicas were dominated by the Aztecs, and thanks to the riches of the earth, they could pay their tribute with bars of gold and silver. When the Conquest began, the Spanish decided to explore the area upon learning of its precious minerals. In 1522 they discovered the first mine close to Tlachco, naming it the **Socavón del Rey** (King's Cavern), which Hernán Cortés later owned. A few years later, around 1528, the explorers arrived as far as Tlachco and established a camp before finding a warmer location 12km/7mi north. The new settlement was called **Real de Minas**. Owing to the growing number of laborers needed to work the mines-almost all of them from indigenous groups-new villages continued to form until they finally united in 1570 under the name of Taxco.

Mining Boom – Today called Taxco de Alarcón, as the birthplace of the famous writer **Juan Ruiz de Alarcón**, the city reached its true mining boom in the 18C thanks to **José de la Borda**. A miner of French origin, he encouraged industry and raised the economic level of the entire city. Borda financed many public works and is to be credited for Taxco's greatest attraction, the Santa Prisca and San Sebastián Church, which he built with profits from the Lajuela mine located near Tehuilotepec.

Periods of Crisis – During the first decades of the 19C, Taxco underwent a difficult transition, as the mining industry was shut down completely by the Mexican struggle for independence from the Spanish Crown. During this period, the Spanish destroyed their mines, fearing the revolutionaries would capture them. Thus, when the War for Independence ended, Taxco found itself in dire straits. During this period, the city was the setting for several momentous events. Among these figure the execution of Captain García by José María Morelos y Pavón, Agustín de Iturbide's (Mexico's first emperor's) visit to the city, and the discussion of the Plan de Iguala among the Royalists at the **Monastery of San Bernardino**. At the end of the 19C and the beginning of the 20C, several foreign companies tried to revive the mining industry, but they were halted by the Mexican Revolution.

New Horizons – In 1928 a highway opened connecting Taxco to the capital, fostering new commercial hopes. A year later **William Spratling** moved to Taxco. This American architect revolutionized the way of life for the Taxcans by promoting their artisan silverwork worldwide. In his workshop, **Las Delicias** (The Delights), he instructed many apprentices, who maintain and pass on his teachings to the present day. The result of his efforts brought the entire city innumerable economic benefits.

Today Taxco is a National Monument and one of the most visited cities in Mexico. The mining industry remains its strength, and every day, thousands of kilos of silver, copper and zinc, among other minerals, are extracted and then distributed to various other cities. About 80 percent of Taxco's inhabitants earn their livelihood from silverwork, selling their products not only in Mexico but also abroad.

PLAZA BORDA AND SURROUNDINGS *Map p 292.*

Comfortable shoes with good traction are recommended.

The **Plaza Borda**, named in honor of Don José de la Borda, dominates the heart of Taxco. At this must-see meeting place, the city's architectural beauty mixes with the pulse of street life. Most large local events and important celebrations take place in the plaza. A handsome pavilion occupies the plaza's center. Large shade trees offer solace and tranquillity to weary pedestrians, tireless vendors and young couples in love.

★★★**Parroquia de Santa Prisca y San Sebastián** – *Plaza Borda, 1, Open year-round Mon–Sat 6am–8pm, Sun 5:30am–9pm.* Known popularly as Santa Prisca, this church was commissioned by Don José de la Borda and dedicated to the same patron saint. The church's construction lasted for ten years (1748–58) and left behind one of the most outstanding Baroque shrines of its day. Cayetano de Sigüenza handled the architectural plans; Miguel Custodio Durán and Juan Caballero managed the construction; and Luis and Vicente Balbás made the altarpieces. The last two men were the sons of Jerónimo Balbás, designer of the famous altarpiece of The Kings at the Catedral Metropolitana in Mexico City. Santa Prisca and St. Sebastian, 12C Roman martyrs, were elected to be the church's saints. She was the patron saint of the former church and deemed as a protector against lightning and thunderstorms, common occurrences in Taxco. He protected Christian prisoners and converted pagans. In 1759 Borda's son, a priest, took charge of the church, thus fulfilling the dream of the rich miner who had owned Santa Prisca for many years.

The church's architecture exhibits many unique and novel features, necessitated by the narrowness of the building plot. Observe the compact nature of the cruciform ground floor and the very tall and elongated towers. On the other hand, the adornments and design display the neo-Hispanic style, giving it an appearance different from that of European churches.

Facade – The Solomonic and Classic columns are noteworthy. Sculptures of apostles, virgins and martyrs grace the towers. The left side once led to the old crypts and common ossuary, where a skeleton rests above the door. Two cupolas covered with colorful glazed tiles crown the church. While the larger dome stands above the principal nave, the smaller dome covers the chapel.

Parroquia de Santa Prisca y San Sebastián

Portal – The **Baptism of Christ** recalls the importance of this sacrament. The statues of Santa Prisca and St. Sebastian gesture at the sacrifice of Christ, made for the salvation of humanity, while the effigies of the apostles reinforce the importance of the scriptures and the gospel's oral tradition.

Altarpieces of the Nave – The **nave's** majestic altarpieces, arranged in pairs, stand along the side walls. Each altarpiece faces an identical twin on the opposite wall, though it contains a different illustration. From the main entrance to the altar, the order ascends from lower to higher ecclesiastical hierarchy. San Isidro Labrador, San Juan Nepomuceno and San José altarpieces line the left wall; Santa Lucía, the Virgin of the Pillar and the Virgin of Sorrows altarpieces adorn the right wall.

High Altar – The statue of the Immaculate Conception, seen as a carved Baroque wooden figure accompanied by Santa Prisca and St. Sebastian, is the highlight of this magnificent **altarpiece**. Presently standing in front of the altarpiece, the Manifestador was sawed into pieces in the middle of the 19C. The majority of its pieces remained in the sacristy, though others were left carelessly about the church and some were lost. In 1987, during the exhaustive work of restoration, experts attempted to put the sacred object back together. They found 70 percent of the original pieces and ordered the rest be made using colonial techniques. Then, they refitted the mirrors and the three figures of the theological truths, previously displayed separately in the sacristy. Finally, the Manifestador returned to its original place in 1990, even though the church's restoration was not completed until 1992.

Left Side Chapel – This oratory was originally known as the **Capilla de los Indios**. When Borda built Santa Prisca, part of the land belonged to the natives, who ceded the ground to Borda on the condition that he make a chapel for them. This name disappeared over the years. Today the parishioners call the chapel the **Capilla de Nuestro Padre Jesús de Nazareno**. The central altarpiece honors the souls of Purgatory. The Virgin's altar stands on the right, while the altar of Jesus of Nazareth sits on the left.

Cabrera's Paintings – One of the most famous painters of the 18C, Miguel Angel Cabrera created the majority of the altarpiece paintings and other works at Santa Prisca. From his paintbrush flowed the drawings of the half shells, illuminating the upper section of the side entrance and the area above the entryway to the Chapel of Our Father Jesus of Nazareth. The shells represent the martyrdom of the church's patron saints.

Choir Organ – Made in Spain in the mid 18C, this marvelous object, located above the choir, arrived by donkey from Veracruz.

Museo de la Platería Antonio Pineda – *Plaza Borda, 16. Open year-round daily 10:30am–5pm. P$8.* ✗ ☎ *(7) 622-0658.* Situated within the **Patio de las Artesanías**, the museum belongs to Antonio Pineda, a member of one of Taxco's oldest and most traditional silversmith families. The museum consists of three small rooms,

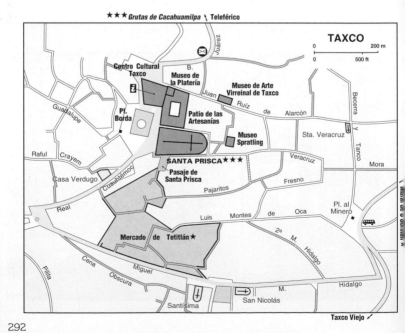

with 55 pieces of various sizes on exhibit, the majority being silverwork and jewelry. Several items have won prizes at the **Feria de la Plata** (Silver Fair), one of the city's most significant annual events.

Centro Cultural Taxco (Antigua Casa Borda) – *Plaza Borda, 14. Open year-round Tue–Sun 10am–3pm and 5–7pm, Sun and holidays 10am–4pm.* ☎ *(7) 622-6617.* Constructed in 1750, the building originally formed part of Don José de la Borda's private residence. When he moved from Taxco to Zacatecas, the property fell into the possession of various individuals for nearly two centuries. In 1992 the current Center of Culture was inaugurated. The center occupies only a portion of the house and boasts a museum with ten rooms. Monthly exhibits feature a variety of mediums of national and international origin: photography, sculpture, painting and handicrafts, among others. From the wide balconies filled with plants, one can admire the inviting Plaza Borda. The ground floor houses the photography room.

Museo de Arte Virreinal de Taxco (Antigua Casa Humboldt) – *Juan Ruiz de Alarcón, 12. Open year-round Tue–Sat 10am–5pm, Sun 9am–3pm. Closed national holidays. P$15.* ☎ *(7) 622-5501.* In this handsome, late-18C mansion, the celebrated German explorer and scientist, Baron Alexander Von Humboldt, stayed for a few days en route from Acapulco to the capital in 1803, after 16 months of research throughout America. The facade still preserves its Mudejar architecture. Inaugurated in 1992, the current museum boasts 14 permanent exhibition rooms. The majority of the items in this collection are sacred works of art from the colonial era and from Taxco's churches, especially Santa Prisca. In one of the terraces, visitors can appreciate an original 18C fountain.

Museo Guillermo Spratling – *Porfirio Delgado, 1 (Plaza Hidalgo). Open year-round Tue–Sun 9am–5pm. P$20.* ☎ *(7) 622-1660.* Built in 1975 in honor of William Spratling, "Taxco's favorite son," this museum exhibits a portion of his enormous collection of pre-Hispanic objects. Spratling donated the majority of the works to Mexico City's Museo Nacional de Antropología.

★**Mercado de Tetitlán** – *Accessed through the Tetitlán district and Plaza Borda. Open year-round daily 9am–8pm.* One of Mexico's prettiest, this multilevel market lies unevenly on the sloping terrain. The layout resembles a storybook labyrinth, complete with every kind of shop, selling fruit, cooked food, vegetables, clothing, accessories, fabric and handicrafts. On the left side of the Plaza Borda and beside the Santa Prisca church, the market connects with the **Pasaje de Santa Prisca** *(open year-round daily 11am–8pm),* where silversmiths offer their wares (especially jewelry) at **wholesale** prices.

ADDITIONAL SIGHTS

★**Mural de O'Gorman a Nuestro Rey y Señor Cuauhtémoc** – *Cerro de la Misión, 32 (on the grounds of the Hotel Posada La Misión).* ✗ 🖻. This mural, also known as *Homenaje a Cuauhtémoc* (Homage to Cuauhtémoc), decorates a wall near the hotel pool. Completed in 1956, the mural was designed by Juan O'Gorman from pieces of naturally colored rocks collected from various parts of the state of Guerrero. In the mural Cuauhtémoc, the last Aztec king, stands upon the heads of two serpents that symbolize Quetzalcóatl. The eagle above Cuauhtémoc's head represents the national emblem. Two citizens of **Tlachco** practice the ball game behind Cuauhtémoc's back. To the right of Cuauhtémoc, the tiger and the moon embody the past and darkness. The figures seen on this side of the mural hail from the pre-Hispanic era: a woman, a warrior, a dancer disguised as a coyote and, lastly, Tláloc, the god of rain. The sun and heron on the left symbolize light and hope. Behind these last figures, the worker, farmer, and country woman with child, followed by Vicente Guerrero and the national flag (symbol of an independent Mexico), represent modern Mexico.

Teleférico (Cable Car) – *To one side of the buildings of UNAM (Universidad Nacional Autónoma de México – National Autonomous University of Mexico). Open year-round daily 8am–7pm. Round trip. P$26.* ☎ *(7) 622-1468.* Access to the cable car is near the entrance to the city, marked off by a series of arches. The Convention Center and the UNAM building, formerly the Hacienda del Chorrillo (16C), can be reached easily nearby. The cable car ascends as far as the luxurious Hotel **Monte Taxco**. Both from the cable car and the hotel terrace, a spectacular **view**★★ of Taxco rewards visitors.

EXCURSIONS

Old Taxco – *Carr. Fed. 95, heading toward Iguala, 13km/8mi from Taxco.* A short and narrow road surrounded by beautiful scenery, wildlife, little houses and an occasional villager leads visitors from the town entrance to the plaza, site of the **Iglesia de San Francisco** *(open year-round daily 7am–6pm),* the earliest church built in this area in the 16C. The bell tower was supposedly the model for the tower at **Santa Prisca**. Constructed around 1543, the **Ex Hacienda de San Juan Bautista** (formerly the Hacienda of St. John the Baptist and today called the University Cultural Center of the Universidad Autónoma de Guerrero – UAG) dominates this tiny, peaceful village. Returning to Taxco, visitors may stop at **Rancho la Cascada** *(open year-round Mon–Fri 9am–1pm and 2–6pm, Sat 9am–1pm; closed Jan 1, Maundy Thursday, Good Friday and Dec 25;* ☎ *7-622-1016; reservations recommended).* The ranch boasts a handicraft store and a handsome workshop where artisans produce silver, gold, copper and brass items. Its owner, the Castillo family, has played a central role in Taxco's silver and handicraft tradition for more than 60 years, as one of its best-known representatives both nationally and internationally.

★★★**Grutas de Cacahuamilpa** – *31km/19mi. From Taxco, head north on Carr. 95, towards Cuernavaca. After 22km/14mi, turn left; 9km/6mi later, turn right and continue straight on to reach the entrance to the grottoes. Visit by guided tour (2hrs), year-round daily every hour 10am–5pm. P$15.* ✗ ☎ *(7) 622-2274.* In 1834 Manuel Sáenz de la Peña, a wealthy local landowner, discovered these grottoes, the largest and most spectacular in Mexico. Other area findings confirm that the ancient, pre-Hispanic inhabitants knew of these caves. The grottoes might have served as a refuge and hiding place during the Independence movement. Locals claim that Porfirio Díaz, Antonio López de Santa Anna, Adolfo López Mateos and Baron Alexander Von Humboldt visited the site.

The grotto's huge opening measures 21m/43ft in height and 42m/138ft in width. The first room lies at a depth of 24m/79ft. Today, 2km/1.2mi of the grottoes feature adequate, artificial lighting and concrete walkways, so visitors may safely tour the caves and admire the impressive stalactite and stalagmite figures of multiple shapes and sizes.

TUXTLA GUTIÉRREZ
Chiapas
Population 386,135
Map of Principal Sights
🛈 Belisario Domínguez, 950, Plaza de las Instituciones Building, PB,
Downtown ☎ (9) 613-9396 to 99 and (01-800) 280-3500

The name of the city of Tuxtla, state capital of Chiapas, comes from the Náhuatl words of either **Tuchtlán** or **Tochtla**, meaning "land of rabbits." During the colonial era, Chiapas and Guatemala formed a single province. At this time, the city was called Villa de San Marcos Tuxtla. During the Independence movement (1810–21), Chiapas declared itself independent of Spain and Guatemala, and joined Mexico. In 1848, in honor of General Joaquín M. Gutiérrez, the outstanding independence-minded politician and ardent supporter of annexation to Mexico, Tuxtla acquired its current name and was granted the official title of city. Since 1892 it has served as the state capital, although for a time it alternated and fought with its rival San Cristóbal de las Casas for the seat of power.

SIGHTS

Tuxtla Gutiérrez is located only 89km/55mi (1 1/2hrs) from San Cristóbal de las Casas.

★★**Zoológico Miguel Álvarez del Toro** – *Callejón Cerro Hueco. Accessed via the Southern Bypass of Tuxtla Gutiérrez, following the "ZOOMAT" signs. Open year-round Tue–Sun 8:30am–5:30pm.* ☎ *(9) 612-3754.* Considered one of the best in Latin America, this zoo displays a collection of exclusively regional fauna. Due to the great diversity of climate in Chiapas, which includes a tropical jungle, the zoo boasts over 220 species and approximately 1,500 animals. The care, respect and treatment of the animals is a surprise to visitors. The majority of animals live in very spacious enclosures, which imitate their natural habitat as much as possible. Pheasants, *chachalacas* (dark colored, pheasant-like birds), iguanas, *guaqueques* (a type of rodent) and the famous howler monkeys, which emit a very strange sound, roam freely about the park. The **aviary**, **reptile room** and **nocturnal animal room** deserve special attention for the diversity of species and the detail of explanatory information. The trails that lead through the zoo cover 2.5km/1.6mi.

★**Museo Regional de Chiapas** – *Calzada de los Hombres Ilustres. Next to the Teatro de la Ciudad, accessible from 5a Ave. Norte. Open year-round Tue–Sun 9am–4pm. P$16.* ☎ *(9) 613-4479.* The archaeology room, located on the ground floor, boasts an interesting collection of original pieces from the pre-Hispanic Olmec and Maya civilizations in the state of Chiapas, from sites such as Palenque, Toniná, Yaxchilán, Bonampak and Chinkultic. Several sculpted ceramic pieces, a stela fragment (the oldest in Mesoamerica), carved bones, textiles and pieces rescued from the Tapesco del Diablo cave highlight the collection. The upper level recounts the

history of Chiapas, from the Conquest to the 1910 Revolution. It includes important information on how the natives were treated over the centuries, as well as on
the autonomous tendencies of the state of Chiapas.

Parque de la Marimba – *Av. Central, between Calles 8 and 9 Poniente.* With its
picturesque kiosk and its leafy trees, this park evokes the full flavor of a provincial town. Every night, from 7pm to 9pm, local bands offer excellent **concerts**★ with
marimbas, the regional instrument of Chiapas.

Casa de las Artesanías de Chiapas y Museo Etnográfico – *Blvd. Belisario
Domínguez, 2035. This blvd. is the western extension of Av. Central, the city's
main road. Open year–round Mon–Fri 10am–3pm, 6–8pm; Sat 10am–3pm.* ☎ *(9)
612-2275.* Inaugurated in 1994, this attractive museum displays the customs, way
of life, typical dresses and traditional handicrafts of the various ethnic groups in
Chiapas. Some of the rooms have successfully recreated the region's natural atmosphere, with lush vegetation. The gift shop offers a wide variety of handicrafts from
Chiapas, at reasonable prices.

EXCURSIONS

Chiapa de Corzo – *15km/9mi east of Tuxtla Gutiérrez on Carr. 190.* An enormous
Mudejar fountain, completed in 1562 and known as **La Pila**★ (The Baptismal Font)
guards the central plaza of this city, founded by the Spanish in the 16C. The fountain's shape resembles the crown of the Catholic Kings.

★★★ **Parque Nacional del Cañón del Sumidero** – *The park can be seen by boat ride or
from the overlooks on the hill. To join a boat tour, take Carr. 190 heading toward
Chiapa de Corzo. Departures from Cahuaré (right after passing the Belisario
Domínguez bridge, 10km/6.2mi from Tuxtla Gutiérrez) and from the wharf in Chiapa
de Corzo (15km/9.3mi from Tuxtla Gutiérrez). Year-round daily 7:30am–5pm. Round
trip. P$60.* ✗ ☎ *(9) 612-1270.* This impressive tectonic fault is one of the greatest
marvels of nature. The gorge's immense rock walls, which soar at certain points to
more than 1,000m/3,281ft in height, overshadow the waters of the Grijalva River.
The boat trip (35km/22mi total) provides a fantastic adventure, as the incomparable scenery and sensations at the bottom of the gorge will astound visitors.
Marvelous Chiapan wildlife, including crocodiles, can be seen throughout the
trip. Admire the stunning phenomena that nature has wrought over the course of
millions of years. With a little luck, the guide may share some old legends. The
best known story relates to the troubles the Spanish had in subduing the Chiapans
who inhabited the region. When they finally accomplished their goal, the natives—
men, women and children—threw themselves over the edge of the canyon, because
they preferred to die rather than succumb to Spanish domination.

The trip ends when the boat docks at the **Presa Manual Moreno Torres**, a dam known
as **Chicoasén**. Because of its proximity to a seismic zone and the regional faults, the
dam boasts a gigantic 260m/853ft retaining wall.

If you make the trek by car from Tuxtla Gutiérrez, take the Carretera del Sumidero
for 5km/3mi to reach the entrance to the National Park *(open year-round daily
6am–5pm)*. The visit covers 17km/10.5mi. Of the five overlooks, the best are the
fourth and fifth. In addition to splendid **views**★★ the park offers a restaurant and
a small handicraft shop.

Cañón del Sumidero

YAXCHILÁN**

Chiapas
Map of Principal Sights
🛈 ☎ (9) 678-6570

Lost in the thick brambles of the **Lacandon jungle**, this city rises above singing birds, screeching howler monkeys and enormous tropical lizards. One of the most influential Maya cities of antiquity, Yaxchilán flourished between AD 350 and 810, with its period of greatest splendor occurring between AD 600 and 800. Accessible only by river, Yaxchilán held close ties with other jungle cities, such as Bonampak, Piedras Negras and Tikal, and, for some time, it served as the most important city in the region. Its name means "city of the green stones."

ARCHAEOLOGICAL SITE

Yaxchilán is located on the banks of the Usumacinta River, on the border with Guatemala. The archaeological site can be accessed by small plane or boat. Airplanes can be contracted from Palenque or San Cristóbal de las Casas (Chiapas), or from Villahermosa (Tabasco); flying time is 1hr. For overland trips, it is recommended to hire the services of a travel agency. One-day excursions departing from Palenque lead visitors to Yaxchilán and Bonampak. From Palenque, the minibus travels 2 1/2hrs southeast (10km/6mi south on Carr. Ocosingo, turning left at the junction, towards Chancala, and continuing on this road) until reaching Frontera Corozal, where one boards a motorboat to initiate a 1hr trek on the Usumacinta River. Two-day excursions are also available from San Cristóbal de las Casas or Palenque. Open year-round daily 8am–4:45pm. ☎ (9) 678-6570.

Access to the ruins, whether by boat or by plane, offers a splendid and unforgettable **panorama**★★. Upon arrival at the site, visitors enter a structure and walk through its narrow **labyrinth** of underground passageways, which lead to tiny rooms. Scholars believe this building was used to simulate a journey to the netherworld during priest initiation rites. In its central area, the site boasts approximately 120 structures distributed among three large complexes: the **Gran Plaza**, located on the lower part parallel to the Usumacinta River, the **Gran Acrópolis** and **Acrópolis Sur** to the south of the Gran Plaza.

Gran Plaza – A small crack in the rock and a narrow staircase provide access to this plaza, which boasts an abundance of structures and **carved stelae** with hieroglyphics and figures. Of special note is **Stela I**, a portrait of Pájaro-Jaguar IV (Bird-Jaguar IV), powerful ruler of Yaxchilán from AD 752 to 772. The left side of the esplanade features **Edificio 14** or the **ball court**, complete with ancient score boards that preserve their inscriptions, and **Estructura 6** or **Templo Rojo** (Red Temple), dedicated to Chac, the rain god. Here, a great number of Lacandon pottery was discovered centuries after the city was abandoned. For some time, the Lacandons came here to carry out ceremonial rites.

A bit farther ahead, next to the river, six wide steps are decorated with 160 glyphs. It is believed that the entrance to a hanging bridge, which connected to present-day Guatemala, once stood on this very same spot. In another section of the plaza, lie the vestiges of a series of structures which comprised a palace similar to the one in Palenque and which today harbor a few stone sculptures with bas-reliefs. At the end of the Gran Plaza lies the enormous **Stela 3**, which depicts ruler Escudo Jaguar ceding power to his son Pájaro-Jaguar III. This stela was lifted by a helicopter in 1964 to be transported to the National Museum of Anthropology, but slipped off at the bank of the river and broke in two. Consequently, the plan to exhibit it in Mexico City was abandoned and the stela was painstakingly moved to its current site.

Right Compound – On the other side of the plaza, several structures with stelae and high-quality **carved lintels**★★ over the doorways flank the stairway of a great platform. The stairway leads to the Great Acropolis.

Gran Acrópolis – This structure of many rooms crowns a tall hill. It features **Edificio** or **Estructura 33**★★, with three exquisite lintels carved in stone that depict various moments in the life of ruler Pájaro-Jaguar IV. Inside, one can appreciate a decapitated sculpture of the same ruler. The Lacandons believe that when the head returns to this site, the world will end.

Acrópolis Sur – A narrow trail through the jungle leads to the South Acropolis, the highest point in Yaxchilán. A series of three buildings with circular altars and sculpted stelae in the vestibules rises majestically above the landscape. Of the three, the building still crowned by a cresting preserves traces of original paint from ancient murals.

The return trip leads to the **West Acropolis**, consisting of two small plazas and a group of structures. Bas-reliefs in an excellent state of preservation enliven the lower face of the lintels of one of the edifices.

★BONAMPAK

Valley of the Lacanhá River. From Palenque, drive 10km/6mi south on Carr. Ocosingo; at the junction, turn left, heading towards Chancala, continue on this road for 145km/90mi until reaching the Bonampak junction. Bear right and take the dirt road for 9km/5.6mi, through the thick jungle undergrowth, to access the archaeological site. For security reasons, we recommend hiring the services of a travel agency. Open year-round daily 8am–5pm. P$25. ☎ (9) 678-6570.

The 1946 discovery of Bonampak amidst this exuberant Lacandon jungle was a key element in the history of research on the Maya culture. The fierce battle scenes painted on the walls of a small temple ruled out the theory that the Maya constituted an utterly peaceful society. The total size of Bonampak (AD 250–792) covers around 4sq km/2.5sq mi. Unfortunately, archaeologists have explored only the small section corresponding to the Great Plaza and Acropolis. For many years, Bonampak remained practically inaccessible to the outside world; now, thanks to a road opened in 1998, one can reach this site without having to undertake long walks through the jungle.

Great Plaza – This site features a **stela** that measures 5m/16ft in height and 2m/7ft in width. An image on the stela depicts one of the most notable city rulers, *Chaan Muan II*. Elegantly dressed, Chaan Muan II grasps a ceremonial lance in the right hand and a shield with the figure of the jaguar god of the netherworld in the left hand. The hieroglyphics of the lower section, as well as the carvings on the stelae, which grace the stairway of the acropolis, trace the genealogy of this character. In the left stela, two women (supposedly his mother and wife) accompany him in a ritual of self-sacrifice. On the right one, Chaan Muan II appears with a bearded character (quite uncommon in pre-Hispanic depictions), kneeling at his feet.

Acrópolis – Three important rooms in the **Templo de las Pinturas★★** (Temple of Paintings), located at the extreme right of the first platform, stand out in this remarkable ensemble. On the lower faces of the lintels that decorate the three entry doors, carved representations narrate the capture of different people. Mural paintings of excellent quality add color to the rooms' interiors. Although the original tones have deteriorated over the years, it is still a thrill to see these paintings in their original setting, as they figure among the most important ever discovered in the entire Maya world. The National Museum of Anthropology boasts faithful, life-size reproductions of these works.

In **Room 1★★** *(first on the left)*, the scenes depict a ceremony with the heir to a ruling family. All along the walls, high-ranking figures appear as they prepare themselves for the event. Musicians with various instruments enliven the mood, while a man carries a small child in his arms. Large masks of deities and religious elements decorate the upper section of the wall. While **Room 2** recounts the events of a fierce battle, **Room 3** depicts the celebration of victory.

Region 9

YUCATÁN PENINSULA

The Maya Route, sparkling beaches and wonderful cuisine

Handicrafts and Food, *p 54*. Known for its sun-baked beaches, transparent waters and magnificent modern resorts, the Yucatán Peninsula, a geographically remote corner of Mexico without elevations or rivers, experienced a far different cultural development from AD 400 to 1200, as it was here that the ancient Maya civilization was established.

The peninsula's geographical and political separation from central Mexico encouraged attempts at secession during the 19C, a period marked both by the cultivation of **henequen**—an agave plant from which rope fiber is extracted—and by the outbreak of the **Caste War** when the Maya rebelled against the oppression of the landowners. Meanwhile the region was divided into three states, where travelers and explorers discovered the rich archaeological legacy of the Maya.

About 900,000 natives that still speak Maya live in this region. The artistic works of their ancestors and the natural riches of the area have reactivated the economic development of one of Mexico's less industrialized regions. Since the mega-development of Cancun in the 1970s, millions of people from all over the world have visited this natural paradise.

Ruins of ancient Maya cities, beaches of fine white sand, islands to the east of the peninsula caressed by transparent waters that nurture the world's second largest coral reef, grottoes, and numerous ecological reserves offer tremendous possibilities for enjoying the region's natural wonders. Franciscan monasteries, ruins of the great henequen haciendas, villages with huts whose design has not changed since the ancient Maya inhabited the region a thousand years ago, and a varied cuisine make the Yucatán Peninsula the ideal place from where to begin touring the magical world of the Maya. *(See the Maya pp 32 and 314.)*

Camp. .... Campeche

Q. Roo .... Quintana Roo

Yuc. .... Yucatán

Cuadrángulo de las Monjas, Casa del Adivino and Ball Court, Uxmal

CAMPECHE
Campeche
Population 204,533
Map of Principal Sights – City Map p 300
🛈 Plaza Moch-Cohuo, Avenida 16 de Septiembre, Downtown ☎ (9) 816-6767

In March 1517, more than two years before Cortés initiated the conquest of Mexico, the first Spaniards headed by Francisco Hernández de Córdoba arrived in Campeche, situated on the edge of the Gulf of Mexico. In 1540 the Spaniard Francisco de Montejo (son) founded the city on the site of the ancient Maya village of **Ah Kin Pech**, "place of the sun," and named it "Villa de San Francisco de Campeche."

The exportation to Europe of precious woods, in particular *Palo de Tinte* dye-wood—also called "Campeche wood"—turned Campeche into the most important port of the Yucatán Peninsula toward the second half of the 16C. Its success as a trading center drew the attacks of corsairs under the patronage of various European governments, as well as pirates, who overran, sacked and burned the city repeatedly until the beginning of the 18C when an elaborate defense system was built. Begun in 1685, with the support of the Spanish Crown, and completed in 1704, this system consisted of a stretch of wall with bastions and gates, forts on the hills and batteries near the sea. The vestiges of that imposing hexagonal fortress today separate the ancient city from the modern state capital. While alongside the waterfront contemporary large hotels and public buildings occupy land recently reclaimed from the sea, the cobblestone streets in the historic center are lined by charming mansions with high roofs-which allow air to circulate-and balconies, wrought-iron gates and lamps, and colorful facades decorated with geometric motifs reminiscent of the colonial period. Thanks to extensive renovations in the 1990s, the old city preserves its attractiveness, with a harmonious palette of colors that enhance the style of the colonial era.

★OLD CITY

Plaza de la Independencia (Plaza Principal) – *Between Calles 55 and 57, 8 and 10.* This lovely park, with shade trees and a picturesque kiosk, is surrounded by colonial buildings. On the north side of the plaza stands the **Cathedral**; the east side is graced by handsome, two-story arcades; 16C and 17C mansions flank the southern side; and the west side boasts the **Baluarte de la Soledad★**, as well as a section of the old **Muralla★** (wall).

From the east side of the plaza, **trolley rides** depart *(year-round Mon–Fri 9:30am, 6pm, 8pm; Sat–Sun 9:30am, 6pm, 7pm, 8pm. P$15.)* to tour the city's historic center. Departing from the same place, additional trolley rides lead to the **Fuerte de San Miguel** *(Tue–Sun 9am and 5pm. P$15)* and the **Reducto de San José El Alto** *(Tue–Sun 10:30am and 6:30pm. P$15).*

Cathedral – *Calle 55, at the corner of Calle 10, opposite Plaza Central. Open year-round daily 6:45am–noon & 3:30–8:45pm.* The pale stone of this beautifully proportioned church-the oldest in the Yucatán Peninsula, built between 1540 and 1705-seems to gain luminescence in the simple facade through a chiaroscuro effect produced by its five niches, which contain sculptures of saints. At the sides are two tall and slender towers, the "Spanish" on the left, and the "Campechana" on the right, ending in graceful little cupolas. Inside, to the left of the chancel, a remarkable wood-carved statue of Christ, with silver inlays, lies in the **Santo Entierro** (Entombment) glass case.

Museo de la Casa Seis – *Calle 57, between Calles 8 and 10 (facing the Plaza Principal). Open year-round daily 9am–9pm, guided tours.* This colonial mansion dating from the 16C was probably inhabited by Francisco Montejo and later by various families belonging to colonial Campeche's high society. Completely renovated in 1998–99 with state funds, the present-day museum boasts beautiful 18C and 19C furnishings in diverse European styles.

★**La Muralla** – In 1686 construction began on this strong belt of stone with a perimeter of 2.5km/1.6mi. The resulting wall had four gates that faced the four cardinal points, of which two remain, as well as eight bastions, of which seven have been preserved. The fragments of wall facing the sea are 6m/20ft tall, and those that face inland are 8m/26ft tall.

Puerta del Mar – *Calle 8, opposite Calle 59.* At one time, this sea gate-the west entrance to the walled city-provided the only means of access to the city by water. In those days, the tide almost reached the gate.

★**Baluarte de la Soledad** – *Calle 8, opposite the Plaza Principal (Plaza de la Independencia). Open year-round Tue–Sat 8am–8pm, Sun 8am–1pm. P$4, free Sun.* For over three decades, this bastion has housed the **Museo de las Estelas**, which displays approximately 50 monoliths finely carved by the ancient Maya and found at several state archaeological sites. After climbing the exterior ramp that leads to the upper level terrace, walk along one side of the parapet for a panoramic view of the Cathedral and the Plaza de la Independencia, and on the other side for a view of the city's modern buildings, the Malecón (sea wall) and the Gulf of Mexico.

Baluarte de Santiago – *Calle 8, at the corner of Calle 49. Open year-round Mon–Fri 8am–2pm & 3–8pm, Sat–Sun 9am–2pm & 3–8pm.* Completed in 1704, this bastion was the last one to be built, thus completing the city's fortification system. Today over 250 varieties of tropical plants are to be found in its **Xmuch'-Haltun** botanical garden.

Baluarte de San Pedro – *NE corner of Circuito Baluartes. Open year-round Mon–Sat 9am–1pm & 5:30–8pm; Sun 9am–1pm.* ☎ *(9) 816-5593.* Above the entrance hangs the Vatican's coat of arms, along with the Pope's tiara and St. Peter's keys. It is believed that this bastion once served as a holding cell for those condemned by the Spanish Inquisition. Today it is used to exhibit handicrafts from the state of Campeche. It also houses a tourist information and orientation center. Across from this building stands the Iglesia de San Juan de Dios.

★**Puerta de Tierra** – *Calle 18, opposite Calle 59. Open year-round daily 8am–8pm. Sound & Light Show Tue, Fri & Sat at 8:30pm; P$20.* Connected by the longest stretch of wall still standing, this land gate, flanked to the northeast by Baluarte de San Francisco and to the southwest by **Baluarte de San Juan**, is remarkable for its size and for its great arch. A small room underneath the arch exhibits arms and documents from the pirate era. Peek through the arch to spot the sea gate at a short distance, which affords an indication of the city's dimension during colonial times. The sound and light show illustrates the history of Campeche.

Baluarte de Santa Rosa – Calle 67, between Calle 12 and Calle 14. Open year-round daily

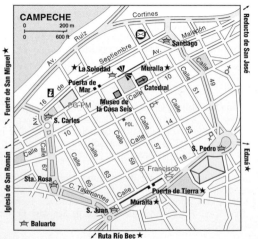

8am–2pm & 5–8pm. ☎ (9) 816–7364. Among the first to be built, this bastion originally protected one of the city's oldest districts, San Román, and was dedicated to Santa Rosa de Lima. In the 19C it served as a poorhouse.

Baluarte de San Carlos – *Calle 8, at the corner of Calle 65. Open year-round Tue–Sat 8am–8pm, Sun 9am–1pm.* ☎ *(9) 816-5593.* Completed in 1686, this bastion-the city's most ancient fortress-now the town museum, houses models, photographs, maps and information about Campeche's historical development. Its damp and lugubrious cellars, once used to store gunpowder, are now open to visitors.

ADDITIONAL SIGHTS

Iglesia de San Román – *Corner of Calle Bravo and Calle 10. San Román district. Open year-round daily 7am–noon & 3–9pm.* On the main altar of the church stands the ebony image of the venerated *Cristo Negro* (Black Christ), whose miracles and protection are highly esteemed by the people of Campeche. Local Catholics pay homage to this image every September during the feast of the Holy Cross, the most popular religious celebration in the state.

★**Fuerte de San Miguel** – *Head south on Av. Ruiz Cortines and Justo Sierra. After 2.5km/1.5mi, turn left and continue 300m/325yd on the Camino Escénico (Scenic Road). Open year-round Tue–Sun 8am–1pm & 2–7pm. P$10.* ☎ *(9) 816-5593.* Situated on a hilltop, this imposing fortress-one of the last fortifications to be built for defense of the city-was completed in 1801. General Santa Anna used it in 1842 as his headquarters to smother a separatist uprising in the peninsula. The fort's moat, drawbridge, ramp, terrace and lookout posts have been preserved. Inside, magnificent pre-Hispanic artifacts found at state archaeological sites are on display; of particular interest are the **jade masks and jewels**★ discovered at the archaeological site of Calakmul. From atop the fortress, one can appreciate a panoramic **view**★ of the sea and the city.

Reducto de San José (El Alto) – *Head northeast on Av. Ruiz Cortines and Pedro Sáinz de Baranda; turn right at Plaza 4 de Octubre and continue to Av. Morazán; then turn right and go 100m/110yd past the Benito Juárez monument. Open year-round Tue–Sun 8am–8pm. P$4.* ☎ *(9) 816–5593.* From this quadrangular military facility, enjoy a wonderful **view** of the sea and the city, especially at sunset. Go inside to the lower level to view a model of the city, scale models of ships that once docked in this port, antique weapons and various artifacts from colonial times.

EXCURSIONS

★**Edzná** – *55km/34mi. Head east on Av. Central and take Carr. Fed. 180 via Chiná, crossing the town to the intersection; turn left and continue another 10km/6mi along Carr. Fed. 188. Open year-round daily 8am–5pm. P$20.* In the middle of a green valley emerges Edzná, "House of the Itzaes," an important Maya ceremonial center that reached its peak between AD 600 and 900, a period during which it was inhabited by priests, merchants and craftsmen. At that time the temples and edifices were finished in a red painted stucco. Decorative traces can still be seen on some buildings.

Besides its architecture designed according to heavenly phenomena and significant Maya dates, the archaeological site of Edzná boasts an ingenious multileveled water system designed to catch, store and release rainwater. It consisted of 29 canals, 27 cisterns, over 70 water troughs and numerous underground deposits. Discovered by farmers in 1906, with exploration beginning in 1927, Edzná was first excavated by archaeologists in 1958. About 20 buildings and adjacent spaces covering some 8ha/20 acres can be visited.

After passing the ticket booth, follow the directional arrows for 300m/328yd, through a path lined with trees, to reach the Plaza Principal. To the left lies the Plataforma de los Cuchillos.

Plataforma de los Cuchillos – The Platform of the Knives was built in the Puuc style and so named because of the copious offering of flint knives discovered here. Vaulted chambers located at both ends of the structure may have housed important officials.

Nohoch-Na (Casa Grande) – *On the west side of Plaza Principal.* This imposing palace measures 135m/443ft in length, 31m/102ft in width and 9m/30ft in height. On the way up 15 enormous steps that span the front of the building, visitors can see four large galleries, which probably played an administrative role. Each year, during the first three days of May, occurs an interesting astronomical phenomenon: the sunlight illuminates the doors of the Templo de los Cinco Pisos; this event can be observed perfectly well from Nohoch-Na.

Templo del Sur – *On the southern end of the Plaza Principal.* This temple of five sections reflects the architectural style characteristic of the Petén region. It is believed that the temple on the summit was built in the Late Classic period, between AD 600 and 900. Beside this temple, to the east, lies the **ball court**.

Pequeña Acrópolis – *Behind the ball court, towards the southeast.* Most of the 32 stelae registered in Edzná were discovered in this complex, the most ancient one in the site (built around 200 BC). Particularly noteworthy is the **Templo de los Mascarones** (Temple of the Masks), which boasts two large masks of modeled stucco painted in red. They represent **Kinich Ahau**, the sun god, at dawn (left) and dusk (right).

Several anthropomorphic reliefs, crouching jaguars and geometric motifs decorate the staircase of the building located to the east.

Gran Acrópolis – *Return to the Plaza Central and climb the east steps.* Nucleus of the ancient city, the Great Acropolis is composed of large bases on which temples and palaces were constructed in a symmetrical fashion. Note the small plaza with its ceremonial platform.

★★★**Templo de los Cinco Pisos** – *To the east side of the Gran Acrópolis.* A majestic 31.5m/105ft-high construction with 27 bays, the Five-Story Temple possibly housed residential quarters for important Maya rulers. The monolithic columns found in most of the temple's doors are characteristic of the Chen style. Its first four steps are noteworthy because of hieroglyphics representing AD 652, year in which an important event must have occurred. The structure at the top is incomplete due to the fact that it has been struck by lightning on more than one occasion. The north side of the temple displays several different Maya architectural features: from the Petén, Chenes, Puuc and Chontal (or Late) styles.

★**La Ruta Río Bec** (Xpuhil, Becán, Chicanná and Kohunlich) – *292km/181mi from Campeche. Leave Campeche south on Carr. 261 toward Escárcega (139km/86mi); then take Carr. 186 east; Xpuhil is at 153km/95mi. Description p 324.*

Templo de los Cinco Pisos

CANCUN★★

Quintana Roo
Population 300,000
Map of Principal Sights
🅱 Av. Tulum, 26 ☎ (9) 884-8073 or www.gocancun.com

This Mexican Caribbean island, 17km/10.5mi long by 2km/1.2mi wide, is linked to the mainland peninsula by two bridges, one at Punta Nizuc, the other at Punta Cancun, which connects the island to the airport and to the downtown area. Building of this great tourism complex began in 1970, thus facilitating access for numerous visitors to enjoy its transparent waters and white-sand beaches.

Between the island and the mainland lies Laguna de **Nichupté★**, which is surrounded by large luxury hotels, restaurants, dance clubs, countless clothes boutiques and hand-icraft shops, as well as water-sport stores.

SIGHTS

★★★**Beaches** – *Along Blvd. Kukulcán.* The soft sand of the beaches is a constant invitation to relax while watching the roll of the emerald green and turquoise-blue waters. Cancun offers numerous beaches from which to choose-between km 3 and km 19-the most popular include **Linda, Langosta, Caracol, Tortugas, Chac-mool, Ballenas** and **Delfines**.

Museo Arqueológico de Cancún – *Blvd. Kukulcán km 9.5, Convention Center Annex. Open year-round daily 9am–8pm. P$16, free Sun.* ☎ *(9) 883–0305.* Housed in a one-story building, the archaeological museum displays representative Mayan artifacts such as pottery, stelae and the *Cabeza del Rey* (King's Head) sculpture that gave its name to that archaeological site. Sketches and photographs illustrating the history of Maya civilization, the Spanish Conquest and local cultural traditions are also exhibited.

El Rey – *9km/5.6mi south of the Centro de Convenciones. Enter at km 18.5 along Blvd. Kukulcán, hotel zone. Open year-round daily 8am–5pm. P$17.* ☎ *(9) 883-3671.* Thus named for a richly attired, anthropomorphic statue that was found here, this archaeological site-the largest in the island of Cancun-dates back to the post-Classic period (AD 1200–1550). Its coastal location facilitated trading of products from the sea. The objects found here, made of obsidian, basalt, flint, jade and quartz, are indicative of the highly developed stage that El Rey's inhabitants reached in their maritime endeavors.

Measuring 520m/569yd by 70m/76.5yd, the site is divided into two plazas enclosed by buildings. In the southern plaza lies an L-shaped platform with a stairway and two rows of columns. To one side of this building stands a temple with a colonnade, beside which rises yet another temple. Archaeologists believe that religious rituals were held in this plaza. By contrast, the northern plaza served as a commercial center and contained housing for the ruling class. Huge columns supported roofs made of perishable materials on structures that most likely served as markets. The tallest building was constructed in stages, with three superposed pyramids, crowned by a throne.

Several platforms, probably foundations of buildings that housed the elite, flank the Calzada Norte (Northern Road). Beside the walls of some of these, researchers have found human skeletons in seated positions, together with objects meant to accompany them into the netherworld.

EXCURSIONS

★★**Isla Mujeres** – *Accessed by plane from Cancun, by boat from Cancun or Puerto Juárez (8km/5mi north of Cancun), or by ferry from Punto Sam (14km/8.7mi north of Cancun).* Discovered by the Spaniards in 1517, Isla Mujeres (Island of Women) was thus named by Francisco Hernández de Córdoba for the goddess Ixchel and other female deities venerated in its shrine. At present this inviting and friendly island offers a peaceful atmosphere that contrasts with Cancun's hustle and bustle. Due to its marvelous reefs and excellent opportunities for snorkeling and diving, a great number of tourists frequent the island each year. Water-sport excursions are organized at **Playa Cocos** *(from Downtown follow Av. Hidalgo until it ends),* characterized for its clear and tranquil waters.

In **El Garrafón Marine Park★** (Punta Azul, at km 6; open year-round daily 9am–5pm; P$20; ✗ ☎ 9-877-0098), which faces one of the island's large coral reefs, visitors can enjoy snorkeling among a variety of marine species that inhabit this wonderful ecosystem. Another option is to take a boat ride to Los Manchones, a series of coral reefs in open sea, which offers an excellent opportunity for scuba diving. South of the island lies what is popularly known as the Observatorio Maya (The Mayan Observatory), believed to have been a 14C or 15C shrine.

★★Cozumel – *By ferry from Puerto Morelos, by boat from Playa del Carmen, or by plane (international airport).* The largest of the islands in the Mexican Caribbean, 52km/32.5mi by 18km/11.2mi, Cozumel sits 19km/12mi offshore from Playa del Carmen. Surrounded by coral reefs that have made it world famous among professional divers and nature lovers, Cozumel is a large tourist complex struggling to protect its natural riches against the constant building boom. It boasts sparkling white beaches and transparent waters that are generally peaceful, although waves can be rough on the eastern side. Discovered in 1518 by Juan de Grijalva, during the pre-Hispanic period Cozumel was an important and much-visited Maya ceremonial center dedicated to the goddess Ixchel, as well as a trading crossroads.

Of particular beauty is **Chankanaab★** Marine Park *(10km/6mi south on the main highway; open year-round daily 7am–7pm; P$66; ✕ ☎ 9-872-0914)*, which protects the Chankanaab reef and the lagoon, unique in the world for its interior coral floor and ideal for snorkeling and scuba diving. The park also includes a small **maritime museum**, a botanical garden, a natural aquarium, dolphin areas and the "Maya site," which displays models of many of the ancient Maya cities. Both **Playa San Francisco** *(14km/8.7mi south, on the main highway)*, a small cove of tranquil waters, and **Playa Sol** *(km12/mi7.5)*-against its background of palm trees-are ideal for swimming and sunbathing. At **Palancar★** *(21km/13mi south on the main highway and 1.7km/1mi from the beach of the same name)* the 9km/5.6mi-long coral reef has brought worldwide recognition to Cozumel among both professional and amateur divers. Visibility is between 150m/490ft and 200m/650ft, which has sufficient light for photography. Oceanographer **Jacques Yves Cousteau** conducted several scientific experiments here. Take the main highway west and visit Laguna Colombia and Punta Celarain. The east side of Cozumel, alongside the Caribbean coast, features magnificent panoramic views of the sea, the most outstanding being that of a steep rugged rock known as El Mirador.

San Gervasio – *14km/8.7mi east on the crossroad; at 8km/5mi turn left and continue straight on for another 6km/3.7mi. Open year-round daily 7am–6pm. P$30.* ✕ ☎ *(9) 872-0528.* Located in the heart of the island, this archaeological site sits atop a major spring. It was built in two different stages-the Late Classic period (AD 1000–1200) and the Late Post-Classic period (AD 1200–1550). Visitors first see **Group III**, which includes the Plaza Manitas (Plaza of the Hands)-so called because of red drawings of hands in one building. Nearby, a Mayan arch indicates the beginning of a *sacbé* (a Maya causeway that was paved with limestone in ancient times), which leads to the structure **Nohoch-Na**, meaning "big house," possibly a temple where offerings to the goddess Ixchel were deposited. Another *sacbé* allows access to **Group II** or **Murciélagos** (Bats), which consists of a platform with the Murciélagos structure and **Pet-Na** (round house), uncommon in Mayan architecture. Through yet another white stone road, one traverses the exuberant jungle to reach the Central Plaza, also known as **Los Nichos** because of the numerous niches decorating one of the structures, which probably held more offerings. Human remains have been found in some of the buildings that comprise this plaza.

Cancun /© Robert Frerck/Odyssey

Museo de la Isla – *Ciudad de Cozumel, corner of Av. Rafael E. Melgar and Av. 6 norte. Open year-round daily 9am–8pm. P$28.* While the first floor, dedicated to Cozumel's natural history, features a display on reefs, the second floor recounts the history of the island from the ancient Mayan era, including objects and artifacts from San Gervasio. The museum also showcases the Spanish conquest and the history of Cozumel during the 19C and 20C.

From Playa del Carmen to Tulum – *Total distance: 131km/81mi. The points mentioned below are all clearly marked with road signs going south from Cancun on Carr. 307 to Chetumal.*

Playa del Carmen – *68km/42mi south of Cancun on Carr. 307 to Chetumal.* A starting point of what is called the "Tourist Corridor," this town of beautiful beaches is awakened daily by the bustle of tourists from all over the world who have turned it into an important recreation center. The Quinta Avenida (Fifth Avenue), which runs parallel to the beach, consists of four pedestrian blocks offering a wide variety of restaurants, open-air cafes and shops full of Mexican handicrafts.

★★**X'Caret** – *72km/45mi south of Cancun on Carr. 307 to Chetumal. Open Apr–Oct Mon–Sat 8:30am–10pm, Sun 8:30am–6pm; Nov–Mar Mon–Sat 8:30am–9pm. P$390. ✗ ☏ (9) 883-3144.* This beautiful marine park boasts cenotes, or sinkholes, a subterranean river and enchanting beaches. Travelers can pause to catch a glimpse of colorful sea creatures or stroll around the aquarium, the butterfly museum and the birdhouse. Later enjoy the night shows, which include an equitation program *(Mon–Sat 4:15pm)*, a Maya ball game *(Mon–Sat 6:30pm)* and a performance of traditional dances from Jalisco *(Mon–Sat 7:15pm)*.

Akumal – *104km/64.5mi south of Cancun on the Carr. 307 to Chetumal. Enter through the Club Maya Akumal.* A wide cove framed by a wide and luxurious complex of tourist facilities invites visitors to enjoy the beach or go snorkeling in the beautiful **Yal-ku**★ lagoon *(Open year-round 8am–5pm; P$45; ☏ 9-875-9060)*. Also located here, the **Centro Ecológico de Akumal** is dedicated to studying the ecological effects of tourism development in the region.

★★**Xel-Ha** – *122km/75.7mi south of Cancun on Carr. 307 to Chetumal. Open year-round daily 8am–6pm. P$190. ✗ ☏ (9) 884-9422.* This exquisitely beautiful cove, whose name means "water source," is the biggest in the Mexican Caribbean Sea. Currently an ecological park, Xel-Ha offers a variety of diversions, such as snorkeling, tubing down a small river, swimming with dolphins, or delving into the jungle by train or on foot. Following a well-marked 2km/1.2mi trail, visitors can admire cenotes, grottoes, overlooks facing the Caribbean and diverse flora and fauna, including macaws, water birds, colorful fish and enormous iguanas.

About 100m/110yd from the park, across the road, is the **Zona Arqueológica Xel-Ha** *(open year-round daily 8am–5pm; P$17; ☏ 9-883-3671)*. This settlement began in AD 300 and was deserted in 1527. It consists of Las Pilastras (The Pilasters) and a *sacbé* that leads to the Casa del Jaguar (House of the Jaguar), Las Alfardas (The Ramps), and, to the left of this platform, the huge blue-water cenote.

★★**Tulum** – *131km/81mi south of Cancun. Description p 325.*

★★★**Chichén Itzá** – *201km/125mi west of Cancun. Description p 308.*

CHETUMAL

Quintana Roo
Population 200,000
Map of Principal Sights
🅷 Road to Calderitas, 622 ☎ (9) 832-0855

Located close to the Belize border, on the banks of the bay where the Río Hondo reaches the sea, this capital of the young state of Quintana Roo was originally founded in 1898 to control the smuggling of the *palo de tinte* (dye tree) and arms that were reaching the rebel natives during the Caste War. Inhabited only with great difficulty, the city has been destroyed by hurricanes on several occasions-the reason why few of the original typical wooden houses are still standing. Surrounded by a rain forest dotted with archaeological artifacts, Chetumal has been called **Cuna del Mestizaje** (The Cradle of the Mixture of Races) because in 1511 Spaniard **Gonzalo Guerrero** was married in a Maya ceremony and had children with a prominent woman from the local chief's court.

SIGHT

★**Museo de la Cultura Maya** – *Av. Héroes and Mahatma Gandhi. In front of the market, city center. Open year-round Tue–Thu, Sun & holidays 9am–7pm, Fri & Sat 9am–8pm. Closed Jan 1, May 1, Dec 25. P$20.* ☎ *(9) 832-6838.* This modern museum presents on three levels an overview of pre-Hispanic Maya civilization-earthly life, the underworld and the heavenly vault, joined by the image of the sacred silk-cotton tree. Replicas of important discoveries, large models and visitor-friendly interactive screens and **communication systems** help illustrate the physical, daily and architectural features as well as the scientific advances of the ancient Maya.

EXCURSIONS

★**Bacalar** – *38km/23.5mi NW from Chetumal. Take Carr. 186; at km18/mi11.2 take Carr. 306; continue 20km/12.4mi to Bacalar.* The ancient city "Bakjala of the Itzaes," was founded on the banks of the Bacalar Lagoon. From the beginning of the Spanish Conquest to the early 20C, foreigners attempted unsuccessfully to gain total domination of the city. Not even when Bacalar was rebuilt by authorities in the 18C to repel the penetration of English pirates, were the natives driven into submission, as the fort that was intended for this fell into rebel native hands during the Caste War. From here, the natives controlled this remote corner of Mexico from the mid 19C until 1901, when the federal army attacked, entering through Chetumal. Today, not far from the fort, several seafood restaurants line the banks of the peaceful lagoon.

★★**Cenote Azul** – *At the southern entrance to Bacalar, next to Carr. 306. Open year-round daily 8am–6pm* ✗. This very deep sinkhole, known as the "Blue Cenote," is so transparent that the twisted roots of the low surrounding tropical vegetation are visible. Its depth has been explored as far down as 90m/295ft; thus, swimming across the cenote's 250m/820ft-wide surface can be a daunting experience. A restaurant, a small collection of exotic birds and a handicraft shop are located at the water's edge.

★★**Laguna de Bacalar** – *On the eastern edge of Bacalar town.* Mangroves and palm trees line the banks of this clear, fresh-water lagoon, with a length of 68km/42mi. It is also known as the **Laguna de los siete colores** (Lagoon of Seven Colors) because of the gamut of shades created by the variations in depth; the darker colors reveal the presence of the seven cenotes feeding the lagoon. A series of small waterways connects it to Chetumal Bay and to Río Hondo.

★**Fuerte de San Felipe Bacalar** – *To the east of Bacalar's Plaza Principal. Open year-round Tue–Sun 9am–5pm. Closed national holidays. P$5.* ☎ *(9) 832-3600.* In response to attacks by pirates and *palo de tinte* (dye tree) smugglers, construction of this fortress was begun in 1729 to protect the lagoon. With its thick walls, four bastions-each one dedicated to a patron saint-cannons at the corners, high observation tower, and its 4m/13ft moat, the fort is one of the few colonial buildings left in the state; a fact that reflects the weak hold the Spaniards had over this remote area. The **museum** inside presents a historical review of the region, from the pre-Hispanic Maya to the end of the Caste War, when the rebellious native people held sway here.

Dzibanché and Kinichná – *81km/50mi from Chetumal. Head west on Carr. 186; after 58km/36mi take a right, and 17km/10.5mi later continue on the paved path another 6km/3.7mi. These archaeological sites are at 34km/21mi before reaching Kohunlich (see Río Bec Route p 324).* These two sites, opened to the public in 1994, are protected by forested hillocks through which flocks of parrots and other colorful birds still fly.

Laguna de Bacalar

Dzibanché – *Open year-round daily 8am–5pm. P$12.* The hieroglyphics carved on the lintels of **Edificio 6** (Building 6) that consist of four elements with embankments and panels give the site its name, which means "writing on wood." An original lintel with a calendar inscription of AD 733 adorns the opening in the southern wall of the upper temple. South of Edificio 6 lie two plazas. The one to the east is surrounded by long **palaces** and by **Edificio 2**, the tallest building in the site. Both are considered funeral monuments due to their tombs with rich offerings.

Kinichná – *Same times and charges as Dzibanché.* The inhabitants of Dzibanché settled an area of 40,000sq km/15,500sq mi and constructed sites for worshipping their gods and rulers. **Kinichná**, 2km/1.2mi from Dzibanché, may have been one of these. An elevated architectural complex of three-tiered elements where temples of ceremonial and funerary character were built, it possesses on the top tier a tomb of two rulers with some of the most refined jade artifacts ever discovered in the region. Remains of large masks flank the steps.

★**La Ruta Río Bec (Kohunlich, Xpuhil, Becán and Chicanná)** – *124km/77mi west of Chetumal on Carr. 186, beginning at Kohunlich and ending at Chicanná. Description p 324.*

When planning your trip, consult the Practical Information section
for travel tips, useful addresses and phone numbers, and information on sports and
recreation, and annual events.

CHICHÉN ITZÁ★★★

Yucatán
Map of Principal Sights – Map below
🛈 ☎ (9) 851-0124

The majestic ruins of Chichén Itzá, one of the most attractive ancient cities in the world, rest on the Yucatán Peninsula's characteristic permeable limestone floor that nurtures the low-growing vegetation that surrounds and protects the site.

Around the cenotes, natural water holes that appear when the ground's limestone crust gives way, human settlements sprang up, gradually developing into this ceremonial center that was declared a World Heritage Site in 1988.

Chichén Itzá, "city on the edge of the water-sorcerers' well," was the regional capital of the Maya from AD 750 to 1200. Despite being the most explored and visited Maya archaeological site, Chichén Itzá, like every sacred city, still keeps many of its secrets. *(See the Maya, p 32 and 314.)*

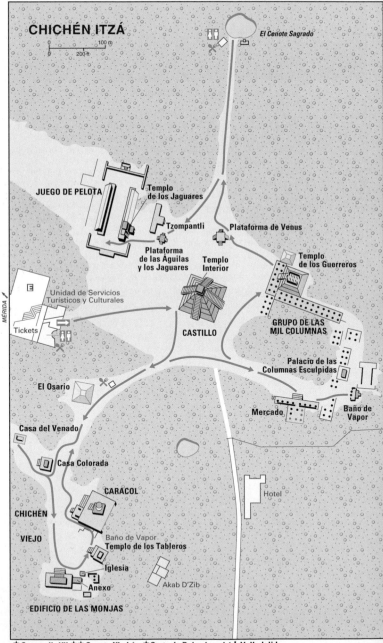

CHICHÉN ITZÁ

0   100 m
0   200 ft

El Cenote Sagrado

JUEGO DE PELOTA

Templo de los Jaguares

Tzompantli

Plataforma de Venus

Plataforma de las Águilas y los Jaguares

Templo Interior

Templo de los Guerreros

MÉRIDA

Unidad de Servicios Turísticos y Culturales

Tickets

CASTILLO

GRUPO DE LAS MIL COLUMNAS

Palacio de las Columnas Esculpidas

El Osario

Mercado

Baño de Vapor

Casa del Venado

Casa Colorada

CARÁCOL

Hotel

CHICHÉN

VIEJO

Baño de Vapor

Templo de los Tableros

Iglesia

Akab D'Zib

Anexo

EDIFICIO DE LAS MONJAS

★ **Cenote Ik-Kil**, ★★ **Cenote Xkekén**, ★ **Gruta de Balamkanché** ↓ **Valladolid**

Historical Notes

Old Chichén and the Itzás – Fanciful and contradictory chronicles about Chichén Itzá created by Spaniards and Maya were disproved in the 19C, when numerous travelers–some with a more adventurous than scientific spirit–began studying the area. In 1924 the great archaeological excavations began.

Occupied by a small agricultural community since 300 BC, and founded as a city in the 5C AD, Chichén (not yet Itzá), meaning "edge of the well," first flourished between the 7C AD and the 9C AD. At that time what is known today as Chichén Viejo (Old Chichén) was built. Despite the 9C decline of the entire Maya region, Chichén was not abandoned, and at the beginning of the 10C different cultural features began to appear. The "Itzás," Chontal Maya for "water-sorcerers," who came to Chichén about AD 918 from Campeche, possessed a hybrid culture with diverse influences that resulted from extensive commerce, particularly that of the Mexican Central Plateau.

Kukulcán and Civil War – Around AD 980 Chichén Itzá received a new wave of settlers of Toltec origin, probably led by **Kukulcán** (Maya translation of the Náhuatl word *Quetzalcóatl*, meaning "Plumed-serpent"), a priest-king expelled from the city of Tula. These groups imposed a military theocracy, worship of the plumed serpent, as well as religiously motivated human sacrifices. Chichén's power grew and the buildings around the Castillo were erected. Around 1185 as a result, it seems, of a civil war between Uxmal, Mayapán and Chichén Itzá, the inhabitants abandoned the city and migrated to the Petén rain forest (present-day Guatemala) where they were finally conquered by the Spaniards under Joaquín de Ursúa in 1697.

ARCHAEOLOGICAL SITE

Open year-round daily 8am–6pm (services 8am-9pm). P$75 (admission to the archaeological site during the day and also to the sound and light show at night); P$30 (admission to the sound and light show only) (p 312). ☎ *(9) 944-0033. We suggest arriving the night before in order to see the sound and light show.*

Though spread over an area of 3km/1.9mi by 1.5km/0.9mi, the buildings are grouped together in distinct complexes in which esplanades for public worship abound. Buildings constructed south of the old city, called **Chichén Viejo**, display Puuc style features. The area around the Castillo, known as **Chichén Nuevo** (New Chichén), displays a more rigid, less embellished architectural style, clearly of Toltec influence.

El Castillo (Pirámide de Kukulcán) – This imposing building stands in the great plaza. Of Toltec influence mixed with elements of Maya classical art, it is composed of three superimposed tiers. With a base 60m/197ft long and nine sloping elements that diminish as they rise, the monument seems taller than it actually is (24m/78ft). Its four sides are fitted with flights of steps; the main flight stands out for its bordering ramps that end at ground level in serpents' heads.

Due to El Castillo's orientation with respect to the cardinal points, during the Spring equinox (March 21) and the Fall equinox (September 22), a play of light and shadow gives the impression that Kukulcán, the plumed serpent, slithers down one of the pyramid's edges to fertilize the earth. This phenomenon further adds to the mystery of this pyramid, which has also been said to have an astronomical function: each flight has 91 steps, multiplied by the number of sides (four) plus one for the upper shrine, equals 365 steps, a number associated with the Maya civil calendar (18 months of 20 days, plus 5 additional days, which were considered of ill omen). Furthermore, each of the pyramid's sides has 52 panels, which correspond to the 52 years in the Toltec calendrical cycle.

Adoratorio – Built atop the pyramid and plainly decorated, the shrine's entrance has three openings flanked by serpentine columns, with the head as the base, and the tail and rattles as the capitals that support the lintels. The jambs and two interior columns bear reliefs of Toltec warriors that are repeated on the wooden beams. The breathtaking **view★★★** from the top takes in the entire archaeological site and embraces the enormous plain stretching like a verdant carpet to the horizon.

Templo Interior – *Open year-round 11am–3pm & 4–5pm.* A tunnel in which even the stones seem to perspire leads to the inner pyramid over which El Castillo was built. At the top, a statue of Chac-mool stands in front of a jaguar-shaped throne painted in bright red with jade incrustations representing his eyes and spots.

The next building leads to the old city known as Chichén Viejo. This section covers all of the following structures, up to and including El Caracol.

El Osario (Tumba del Gran Sacerdote) – The Tomb of the High Priest, a pyramidal structure, boasts four flights of steps and ramps in the form of serpents' bodies which end in serpents' heads at the base. The Ossuary's importance derives from the deep hollow over which it was built and from whence tombs containing skeletons and offerings have been extracted. Carved warrior figures decorate the columns at the top.

Casa Colorada – So called because of the red paint fragments that were found inside, the Red House's facades are smooth, and the friezes are plain. Two Puuc style crestings portray the faces of the god Chac. Its other Maya name, Chichanchoob, meaning "small holes" refers to its perforated cresting. Within this same complex there are vestiges of other structures, such as the **Casa del Venado** (House of the Deer), named for the painting of a deer found on one of its walls.

Edificio de las Monjas – Named because the numerous cells of the structure reminded the Spanish conquerors of a convent, the Nunnery was originally a one-story palace at the level of the plaza. Later, higher bases were added, along with a second story building with murals and stone mosaics of the late Puuc period. On the right side of the main staircase, different stages of construction can be seen–a result of early explorers dynamiting this section to inspect the interior.

Anexo – Actually the first stage of the Nunnery, the Annex consists of a series of rectangular-shaped interconnecting rooms and corridors. The overall decorative style of the facades links it to the Chenes style. Noteworthy is the main entrance, located on the east and adorned with large masks of the god Chac and a godlike figure, ancestor, or ruler, seated on a feathered throne. Below, the entrance resembles the shape of the deity's mouth, typical of the Chenes style.

Iglesia – This one-room church is a true gem of the Puuc style. The smooth walls of the lower section effectively counterbalance the unrestrained ornamentation of the upper areas, whose cornices are decorated with writhing serpents and the friezes boast representations of the rain god Chac, with a seated figure inserted over the nose of the central mask. Flanking the central mask are the four *bacabes*-Maya gods that support the heavens and mark the corners of the earth. The crest, adorned with giant frets in relief, adds to the grandeur of this building.

Templo de los Tableros – The name of the Temple of the Panels is derived from the panels carved on the north and south sides of the structure. The bas-reliefs display warriors, animals and plants. To the east lie the ruins of Akabdzib.

El Caracol – This cylindrical structure, situated on top of two tiered platforms, is also known as the Observatory because of its shape and possible astrological association. The latter is evident in the three bays or windows at the top where a series of astronomical alignments, among them Venus and the equinoctial sunsets, can be observed. The Snail gets its name from a spiral staircase that led to the top. At present, visitors can only access the two circular rooms around a central column. Built around AD 900, and possessing strong Puuc and Toltec features, it belongs to a transitional stage between the Classic and post-Classic periods.

Exit Chichén Viejo by heading back north and crossing the path.

Grupo de las Mil Columnas – The Toltec influence on the northern buildings of Chichén Itzá is evident in the Group of the Thousand Columns, which is surrounded by rows of columns used to support beams that held its roof. This rectangular complex contains the ruins of 50 partially explored buildings. On the extreme west is the **market**, on whose central patio stand 25 slender columns.

Baño de Vapor – *150m/164yd east of the market.* This unique building's waiting area clearly reveals its function. A narrow passageway leads to the steam room and its

El Caracol and El Castillo

Chac-mool, Templo de los Guerreros

oven used to heat the stones over which water was then poured, producing steam. The baths were intended to purify the body for certain rituals, or for healing purposes. Called a *temascal* in native languages, the bathhouse is one of the most ancient cultural elements of the peoples of Mesoamerica.

Palacio de las Columnas Esculpidas – *50m/164ft northwest of the Baño de Vapor, northeastern colonnade.* The Palace of Sculpted Columns, with columns and jambs displaying intricate bas-reliefs, had civic and religious functions. Small architectural pieces that display geometric drawings are assembled here, along with Chac masks that adorned the three facades.

Templo de los Guerreros – Behind a row of 200 pilasters with reliefs of Toltec warriors and on top of an old temple dedicated to Chac-mool, stands the four-tiered pyramid Temple of the Warriors. Its panels display reliefs of eagles and jaguars devouring human hearts, images that bear witness to the bloody practices of the Toltecs. The ample staircase is flanked by ramps of plumed serpents whose heads protrude at the top of the platform, while their bodies support two standard-bearers.

A statue of Chac-mool contemplating El Castillo rests at the summit. Behind it two serpentine columns flank the main entrance to a temple whose roof was supported by pilasters decorated with reliefs of warriors and priests.

Plataforma de Venus – Its location between El Castillo and the *sacbé*, or "white road," leading to the Cenote Sagrado (Sacred Cenote) leads historians to believe that this 4m/13ft–high podium may have been used for important rituals. Decorations on its panel represent the planet Venus, both as a half-flower with a cluster of years and as the figure of Quetzalcóatl-Kukulcán emerging from the mouth of a plumed serpent with jaguar claws.

El Cenote Sagrado – *500m/535yd north of the Plataforma de Venus.* Pilgrims to the Sacred Cenote entered Chichén Itzá by the *sacbé*. They were willing to render impressive homage to the gods that dwelled at the bottom of this 60m/195ft-diameter well with vertical walls that drop 22m/71ft to the water's surface. Following purification in the *temascal* (bathhouse)—the ruins of which are on the cenote's edge—the sacrificial victims, mostly children, dressed and adorned with jewels, were cast into the 20m/65ft—deep well, considered the mouth of the underworld. Most of the treasures recovered from the cenote, consisting of jewels of jade and gold, were smuggled out of Mexico. At the beginning of the 20C, Edward Thompson, the American consul in Mérida, bought the Chichén Itzá hacienda for USD$520 and then proceeded to dredge the cenote, donating his findings to the Harvard Peabody Institute. Mérida's Regional Museum contains a small collection of jade artifacts.

Plataforma de las Águilas y los Jaguares – Similar to that of Venus, the Platform of the Eagles and Jaguars has ramps flanking its four staircases. Each is decorated with carvings of climbing plumed serpents ending in serpents' heads at the top. The recessed panels portray reclining figures that could be representations of Quetzalcóatl-Kukulcán; below these are eagles and jaguars-perhaps representing warriors-preparing to devour human hearts.

311

El Tzompantli (The Stake) – On this platform the scalped heads of enemies and victims of sacrifice were put on display. This macabre Toltec custom was practiced to create lasting memorials of wars and sacrifices, as well as to intimidate the enemies of Chichén Itzá. On its wall are reliefs of three rows of skulls and carvings of eagles devouring hearts, warriors and plumed serpents.

Juego de Pelota – The dimensions of the ball court (16m/52ft by 70m/224ft) make it the largest in Mesoamerica. Symbol of the universe and representation of the struggle between light and darkness, it also reflects the splendor achieved by Chichén Itzá toward the 11C. The esplanade is laid out in the classic double T-shape, enclosed by two high parallel walls for spectators and connected to the outside by wide stairways. At both ends of the court, close to the temples, a curious acoustical phenomenon occurs: a person at one end of the enclosure can clearly hear what is said by a person at the opposite end, even if he speaks in a very low voice.

Six **reliefs** on the lower walls show the decapitation ritual associated with the game. The central motif is a ball with a skull on it, toward which the seven-man teams run. The probable leader of the left-hand group carries a knife in one hand and in the other the head of the leader of the opposing band. The latter is kneeling on one knee, while streams of blood from his neck turn into serpents, symbols of fertility. Another relief portrays entwined serpents on the stone rings in the center of the walls. The height of the stone rings, 8m/26ft above ground level, and the court's large dimensions do not seem to correspond to the rules of games known at the time of the Conquest, in which the players would have to send the ball through the rings using only their hips.

Templo de los Jaguares – Above the ball court, two thick and impressive serpentine columns topped with a plume of feathers mark the entrance to the Temple of the Jaguars.

On the courtyard level, opposite the Tzompantli and between the Kukulcán motif staircases, stands the **Chapel of Kukulcán** (Capilla de Kukulcán). Its interior depicts governors, warriors and Maya priests carved in minute detail. A sculpture of a jaguar appears to stand guard.

★★★**Sound and Light Show** – *Apr–Oct daily 8pm; Nov–Mar daily 7pm. Admission requires either the all-inclusive site visit ticket or a separate P$30 ticket. Headphones (P$15), with simultaneous interpretation into English, French, German and Italian, are provided upon request.* This wonderful, 45min evening show describes the evolution and history of Chichén Itzá and the Maya.

EXCURSIONS

★**Gruta de Balamkanché (Balamkanché Grotto)** – *6km/3.8mi from Chichén Itzá, take Carr. 180 west (passing by Chichén Itzá toward Valladolid); at 5.8km/3.5mi turn left onto a gravel road. Guided tour (30min) year-round daily 9am–4pm (English at 11am, 1pm & 3pm). Arrival before the hour is recommended, because the visits begin punctually and no entry without a guide is allowed P$34* ☎ *(9) 924-9495.* The name Balamkanché means "throne of the jaguar-priest." Because of the scarcity of water in this zone, it is logical that the Maya considered the grottoes sacred. For them these grottoes symbolized the journey to the underworld, the dwelling place of Chac the rain god, whose tears in the shape of stalactites bathe the grottoes. In 1959 a river well and an altar with numerous 11C and 12C vessels and incense burners, adorned with images of Toltec and Maya water deities, were discovered here. Through a path of almost 1km/0.6mi, accompanied by sound effects with pre-Hispanic music, visitors can admire these artifacts in their original setting.

At the entrance to the grotto lies a small botanical garden, with tropical plants and descriptive labels. In addition, a museum room provides information about the place.

★**Cenote Ik-kil** – *3km/1.9mi east of Chichén Itzá on Carr. 180, in front of the Hotel Dolores Alba. Open year-round daily 8am–6pm. P$30.* Surrounded by exuberant vegetation and tropical flowers, this beautiful cenote, whose name means "place of wind," was open to the public in 1997. Approximately 90 steps carved from limestone allow visitors to descend 25m/82ft to the surface of a crystal-clear, natural pool of water, the depth of which reaches an additional 48m/157ft. In this heavenly setting, one can swim alongside a variety of fish and rejuvenate under small waterfalls. A lifejacket is provided upon request. The site also includes a restaurant, dressing rooms and bathrooms.

★★**Cenote Xkekén** – *39km/25mi east of Chichén Itzá on Carr. 180, take the road to Dzitnup; follow it for 2km/1.3mi. Open year-round daily 7am–5pm, P$12.* This marvelous cenote derives its name from the way it was discovered: a wayward piglet (*Xkekén*, in Maya) led its owner to the hidden entrance. One of the few cenotes that still preserves most of its roof, the deep water hole can turn turquoise on a bright day if a shaft of sunlight streams through the opening-beckoning onlookers for a swim under the enormous stalactites.

Cenote Xkekén

Valladolid – *42km/26mi from Chichén Itzá. Go east and continue on Carr. 180.* A colonial city and important trading center for agricultural products and handicrafts, Valladolid is the second most important city in the state of Yucatán. It is also famous for its regional cuisine. The town was founded in 1543 by Francisco de Montejo, nephew of the conqueror of Yucatán of the same name. It has a combative history, as it was the scene of many bloody episodes in the **Caste War**, begun in 1847 when indigenous peoples rose up in an attempt to improve their living conditions. When this civil war finally ended in 1912, the population of the Yucatán had decreased from 500,000 to 200,000.

All visits to this city begin in the main plaza, a pleasant park abounding in trees and flowers. On the south side of the plaza stands the **cathedral**, which dates from the 16C. It is characterized by a solid and restrained style, whose strength reminds one of the indigenous resistance against the region's conquest. On the plaza's east side, the **Palacio Municipal** features important works by painter Manuel Lizama, showing the various stages of the history of Valladolid.

The **Templo y Ex Convento de San Bernardino de Sisal** (Church and Monastery of San Bernardino de Sisal) merits a visit. (*From the main plaza, take Calle 41 west two blocks and turn left along Calle 41-A for four blocks: open year-round daily 8am–noon and 5-7pm).* Founded by the Franciscans in 1552 amidst controversy, the church possesses an austere facade; its lack of bell gables or towers gives it a fortress-like appearance. The monastery and the cloister to the north, as well as the open-air chapel-now chapel of Saint Anthony-to the south, reaffirm its austere design. The **Cenote Zaci** *(Calle 36 between Calles 37 and 39; open year-round daily 8am–6pm; P$4; ☎ 9-856-2107)* is another of those indispensable water sources without which the Maya could not have thrived. A diameter of 45m/140ft and a depth of approximately 80m/260ft make it one of the largest in the peninsula.

Mural by Manuel Lizama, Palacio Municipal, Valladolid

■ The World of the Maya

Maya, p 32. One of the most evolved of all Mesoamerican cultures, the Maya, because of their numerical system, calendars and hieroglyphic writing, have attracted the attention of researchers. Maya territory embraced the present-day states of Tabasco, Chiapas and the Yucatán peninsula, as well as the neighboring countries of Guatemala, Belize, Honduras and El Salvador.

Their origins are undetermined, but the archaeological record places their inception as a culture in the Formative pre-Classic period (2000 BC to AD 100) and their fall during the post-Classic period (AD 800–1500).

In the Classic period (AD 100–800) Maya culture, under a theocratic system, reached the peak of its glory in science and the arts, while its religion became more complex with the proliferation of gods and deities.

In the post-Classic period it appears that a great drought in Mesoamerica led to political and social strife among the Maya peoples. At the same time, the Toltec invaders arrived from Tula (Mexico state), perhaps also driven by a lack of water. They conquered the Maya and intermarried. During this time the science of war flourished while the arts cultivated by the Maya languished.

Recently the governments of Mexico, Guatemala, Belize, Honduras and El Salvador have developed **La Ruta Maya** (The Maya Route) project to protect and promote Maya culture. The route offers the opportunity to visit this most extraordinary region; unique not only for its pre-Hispanic treasures but also because of the diversity of its natural and biological riches.

MÉRIDA★

Yucatán
Population 649,770
Map of Principal Sights – City Map p 316
🚹 Calle 60, between 59 and 57 (next to the theater) ☎ (9) 924-9290

Capital of the state of Yucatán and often decked in flame-colored *flamboyán* blossoms, the tranquil city of Mérida is popularly known as "the White City" *("la Ciudad Blanca")* because of its many whitewashed facades. Mérida was founded in 1542 by Francisco de Montejo y León and his son, on the ruins of the ancient Maya city of **Ichcansihó** or **T'ho**, whose appearance reminded the conquistadors of the Roman ruins of the Spanish city of Mérida.

Following the complicated period of colonization, during the tumultuous 19C, Yucatán made attempts to secede from Mexico, and then was convulsed by the outbreak of the brutal **Caste War**.

The **henequen boom** toward the end of the 19C brought prosperity to a small group of local inhabitants. Thanks to the commercialization of this agave plant, which was stripped to make hemp for worldwide export, the prosperous people of the Yucatán brought back from their travels customs that are alive to this day-as Paris was more accessible than Mexico City.

The mixture of different cultures (with many businesses under the domain of Arab immigrants) has enriched the Yucatán cuisine with a variety of tasty regional dishes such as *pollo pibil (photo p 54)* which can be taken with a cool local beer or a glass of cold *horchata de arroz* (rice drink). In Mérida, the romantic groups of strolling musicians, known as the **trova yucateca**, with their humorous lyrics are never far away; one can also dance the *vaquería* to the rhythms of the traditional **jarana**.

★CITY CENTER

Plaza de la Independencia (Zócalo) – *Calles 60, 61, 62 and 63.* This lovely square provides a tree-shaded refuge from the Mérida heat. It always appears bustling with life and conversation, exemplified by the courting couples seated on the S-shaped benches called **confidentes**. The horse-drawn carriage rides, the vendors of fans, hammocks and hats, the shoeshine men, the daily lowering of the flag at 6pm, and the obligatory ice cream purchase add color and life to the already convivial atmosphere. Adjacent structures, such as the 18C **Palacio Municipal (PM)** built atop the ceremonial center of ancient T'ho surround the square and form the nucleus of the plaza's buildings.

Cathedral – *Corner of Calle 60 and 61. Open year-round daily 6am–noon & 4–7pm.* Built between 1561 and 1598 on the site occupied by the original church of the ancient city of Ichcansihó, the cathedral ranks as the oldest on the American continent. The **facade**★, constructed in a restrained Renaissance style, consists of five sections. Corinthian pilasters with prominent figures of St. Peter and St. Paul flank the main entrance. Above the choir window, a shield in relief bore the royal coat of arms until its replacement by the crowned eagle and serpent, emblems of General Iturbide's empire.

Its **interior** boasts three naves with Tuscan-style columns supporting vaults. The Christ figure on the main altar, called the Christ of Unity, is the biggest wood carving on the continent (7.7m/25ft) and is attached to a mahogany cross (12m/37ft). Located in the northeastern chapel, the popular *Cristo de las Ampollas* (Christ of the Blisters) miraculously survived a fire that destroyed the church of Ichmul with only smoke stains and the blisters that give it its name. The cathedral preserves one of the finest pipe organs in all of Mexico.

Palacio de Gobierno (PG) – *Calle 61, between Calles 60 and 62, north of the Plaza de Independencia. Open year-round daily 8am–8pm. Closed national holidays.* ☏ *(9) 923-1944.* The Governmental Palace is an elegant building with a wide, arched facade built at the end of the 19C on the site of the Royal Houses. The three paintings on the main staircase, representing the creation of humans, the cornhusk and Maya cosmology, are the work of Fernando Castro Pacheco, as well as the 17 monumental oil paintings in the elegant **Salón de la Historia**★ (History Hall) on the second floor. These depict scenes from Yucatán history, such as the harshness of Bishop Landa and the punishment of the rebellious native, Canek. Note the good view of the zócalo from this room.

■ Folklore in Mérida

Music, folkloric dance and poetry play an important role in Mérida's socio-cultural life. Below follows a schedule of weekly events, all of which are free of cost.

Sundays: Mérida on Sundays – *City center, 9am–9pm.* Several streets are closed off to vehicles to create a great pedestrian zone around the Zócalo. With the streets full of peddlers, musicians and townspeople of all ages, one can enjoy and participate in a very festive atmosphere.

Mondays: Regional Vaquería – *The Zócalo, in front of the Palacio Municipal, year-round, 9pm.* Presents the *jarana* and other colorful, traditional dances of the Yucatán.

Folkloric Dancer

Paula Heusinkveld Medina

Thursdays: Serenade – *Plaza de Santa Lucía, calle 60 x 55 (3 blocks north of the Zócalo), year-round, 9pm.* Sentimental Yucatecs of all ages attend this traditional weekly concert of Yucatec music, *trova*, poetry and folklore, which has been celebrated uninterruptedly since 1965.

Fridays: Folkloric Ballet – *Universidad Autónoma de Yucatán, calle 60 x 57 (2 blocks north of the Plaza Principal), year-round, 9pm.* The cultural programs of the university's Ballet Folclórico incorporate various music styles from the Yucatán and other regions.

Saturdays: Mexican Night – *Beginning of the Paseo de Montejo, calle 47 between 56 and 58, year-round, 8pm.* This popular show includes folkloric dances from all over Mexico, marimba music, mariachis, poetry readings and comedy acts.

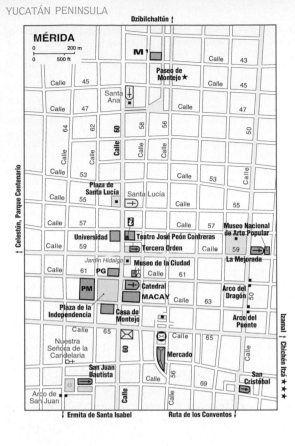

Museo de Arte Contemporáneo Ateneo de Yucatán (MACAY) – *Calle 60, between 61-A and 63, just south of the cathedral. Open year-round Wed–Mon 10am–5:45pm. Closed national holidays. P$20. ✗ ☎ (9) 928-3258.* Once the Palace of the Archbishop, where the controversial Bishop Fray Diego de Landa lived, the 17C building that now houses the Museum of Contemporary Art was connected to the cathedral until the *Pasaje de la Revolución* (Revolution Passageway) was built in 1916. On the upper floor works of the Yucatán painters Fernando Castro Pacheco (b. 1918), Fernando García Ponce (1933–87), and Gabriel Ramírez Aznar (b. 1938) are on display along with beautiful examples of Yucatán embroidery and many other articles.

Casa de Montejo – *Calle 63, 506, south of Independence Square.* This mid-16C residence was the home of Mérida's founding family. The original facade★★ carved by native craftsmen is considered a masterpiece of Mexican Plateresque architecture. It consists of two sections; the upper, less refined but no less ornate, bears the Montejo coat of arms in the center flanked by conquistadors stepping on Maya heads. The busts on the upper frieze presumably represent the conquistador Montejo, his wife and his son.

Museo de la Ciudad – *Calle 61, between 58 and 60, almost one block east of the Zócalo. Open year-round Tue–Fri 10am–2pm & 4–8pm, Sat–Sun 10am–2pm.* A colonial stone door serves as the entryway to this interesting museum, which recounts the history of Mérida in its various periods (pre-Hispanic, colonial, henequen boom and modern).

Calle 60 – Departing from the cathedral, this street leads visitors north, past tranquil plazas, numerous colonial buildings and attractive handicraft shops. Only one and two blocks away from the Zócalo, one finds the Jardín Hidalgo and the Plaza de la Maternidad, respectively, two green areas with a colonial ambiance abounding in open-air cafes. Between these two parks stands the **Templo de la Tercera Orden**, built by the Jesuits in 1618. The main facade, framed with a curved pediment, is noteworthy for its plant motifs and its Corinthian carved columns. Behind the church is the state's **Pinacoteca** (Art Gallery) *(enter from Calle 59, open year-round Tue–Sat 8am–8pm, Sun 8am–2pm; P$17, free Sun; ☎ 9-924-5233).* Most noteworthy among its permanent exhibits is the room dedicated to the work of Enrique Gottdiner Soto, a sculptor whose bronze depictions of rural life in the Yucatán have enjoyed international fame.

Just north of the Plaza de la Maternidad stands the handsome **Teatro José Peón Contreras** *(open year-round daily 9am–9pm)*, a theater constructed in a French Neoclassical style during the early 20C, an era of wealthy henequen estates. The view from its enormous terrace includes the **Universidad Autónoma de Yucatán**. This 18C building, restored in the 20C, is graced by a beautiful inner patio surrounded by Mudéjar style porches. Every Friday at 9pm the University's Folkloric Ballet performs for the public. One more block farther north lies the peaceful **Plaza de Santa Lucía**, where every Thursday the famous Serenade takes place.

Mercado – *Calle 56 x 65, 2 blocks south and 2 blocks east of the Plaza Principal.* Located behind the Post Office (built in 1901), this colorful market is the biggest in the entire peninsula. The upper level is dedicated to a wide variety of handicrafts, such as *guayaberas* (elegant, loosely-fitting men's shirts), *huipiles* (loosely-fitting blouses), silverwork, onyx, ceramics, hammocks, leather goods and much more. Bargaining is fundamental here.

ADDITIONAL SIGHTS

★**Paseo de Montejo** – *Just north of the city center, the promenade begins at Calle 47, between Calles 58 and 56. Horse-drawn carriage rides are available at one side of the cathedral.* As a result of the boom of henequen, then called "green gold," sumptuous residences were erected along this wide tree-lined promenade *(paseo)*. After World War II, when synthetic fiber began to take the place of natural materials in the manufacture of ropes, the mansions were left as reminders of the grand henequen landowners, rich military men and aristocratic families that had emulated a European lifestyle. Today some of these mansions have been converted into tourist agencies, boutiques and restaurants, while others have been replaced by modern buildings, hotels and banks. Along its 1.7km/1mi route stand three monuments: the first to Felipe Carrillo Puerto, a dynamic state governor, executed by firing squad in 1924, and now a leftist symbol; the second to Justo Sierra, a well-known Mexican historian and educator; and the third to patriotism, called **Monumento a la Patria** (Monument to the Fatherland), created by the Colombian poet and sculptor Rómulo Rozo. The latter represents all of Mexico's history; the concave section towards the north portrays the sacred ceiba tree surrounded by numerous bas-relief figures of Mayas and conquistadors. Amid a small pond surrounded by the coat of arms of the 31 Mexican states, rises a sculpture of an eagle devouring a serpent, Mexico's national symbol. The convex section, on the southern end of the monument, is characterized by its bas-reliefs depicting important historical figures, from Mexico's Independence to the modern-day era.

Paseo de Montejo

Museo Regional de Antropología (Palacio Cantón) (M¹) – *Corner of Calle 43 and Paseo de Montejo. Open year-round Tue–Sat & holidays 8am–8pm, Sun 8am–2pm. P$20. ☎ (9) 923-0557.* This beautiful **building★**, housing the Regional Museum of Anthropology, was constructed in the 1910s by order of General Francisco Canton, and designed by the Italian engineer Enrico Deserti, who used both Italian Renaissance and Neoclassical elements. Its interior marble staircase is particularly noteworthy. The museum presents an overview of pre-Hispanic Maya culture–from its customs to its achievements–through halls dedicated to agriculture, social evolution, mathematics, trade, sacrifices and burial customs. Among the most significant archaeological artifacts are the **Estela de Tabi**, a stela showing two hunters with a deer, and the ceramic plate, **Plato Blom**, which depicts a colorful scene from the Popul Vuh, sacred book of the Quiché Maya.

Templo y Ex Convento de la Mejorada – *Calle 50, between Calles 57 and 59. Open year-round daily 7am–noon & 4–8pm.* Founded in 1640 on the old city's limits, this Franciscan monastery features a pair of double bell-gables, which adorn its austere stone facade. Inside, the side chapels and a small Baroque altarpiece stand out among enormous white walls. In 1820, when church property was confiscated, the monastery became the only Franciscan haven in the city; during the Mexican Revolution, it was used as military quarters. Today, its great halls and courtyards harbor the School of Architecture.

Museo Nacional de Arte Popular – *Calle 59, between 48 and 50. Open year-round Tue–Sat 9am–6pm, Sun 9am–2pm. P$10.* Occupying part of the Ex Convento de la Mejorada, this museum exhibits diverse samples of Mexico's beautiful handicrafts. It includes fine work in wood, ceramic, cloth, tin, baskets, leather, palm leaves and seashells. Don't miss the ceremonial masks and the Yucatec embroidery.

Walk down Calle 50, heading south.

Arches – Above Calle 50, on Avenues 61 and 63, rise two huge arches known as El Dragon and El Puente, respectively. Of the eight arches that originally (17–18C) marked the boundaries of the old city, only three remain standing: these two and St. John's arch (see San Juan Bautista).

Parroquia de San Cristóbal – *Calle 50 x 69, five blocks south of La Mejorada. Open year-round daily 5:30am–noon & 3–7:30pm.* This beautiful church stands in the old San Cristóbal (St. Christopher) district, and is very similar to the main cathedral because of its receding semicircular arch and twin towers. A majestic Baroque building, it is one of several churches that underwent restoration in the 18C. A vault composed of a series of very ornate panels graces its handsome interior, while an austere Neoclassical, stone altarpiece adorns the apse. Four enormous paintings, representing the Virgin's apparitions before Juan Diego in 1531, decorate the side walls. For this reason, the church is also known as the Parroquia de Nuestra Señora de Guadalupe.

Templo de San Juan Bautista – *Calle 62, between Calles 67A and 69. Open year-round Tue–Sat 7–10am & 5–7pm, Sun 7am–noon & 4–7pm.* This unusual 17C church features a semicircular arch adorned with plant motifs, which creates an undulating movement on its facade. On the south side, the priest's house portal is notable for its Moorish-style ogee arches resting on quarry-stone columns. The back of the chancel is adorned with a Gothic altarpiece with three vaulted niches. In front of the church is the leafy San Juan Bautista Park. Directly across from the plaza stands one of Mérida's eight original arches, known as the **Arco de San Juan**.

Ermita de Santa Isabel – *Calle 77 x 66. From the Templo de San Juan Bautista take Calle 64 south four blocks and turn right one block on Calle 77. Open year-round daily 8:30am–noon.* Located on the outskirts of the city in the old San Sebastián district, this little 18C chapel crowned by a three-bay bell gable is set on a small rise of land. Inside, worshipers venerate the image of Nuestra Señora del Buen Viaje (Our Lady of Safe Journeys) as it was once a place of restful prayer for travelers. The old cemetery to one side of the hermitage has been transformed into a tranquil **garden** *(open year-round daily 6am–midnight)* adorned with tropical plants native to the Yucatán, as well as archaeological artifacts.

Parque Centenario – *Av. Itzáes, between Calles 59 and 65; from the city center, head west on Calle 57 to reach Itzáes. Open year-round daily 6am–6pm; zoo open 8am–5pm.* Founded in 1910, centennial of Mexican Independence, this spacious park is home to a zoo with animals from all parts of the world, an aquarium, a reptile area and a great aviary. In addition, the park offers a jetty with small boats, a train, a cable railway and children's games.

EXCURSIONS

Progreso – *25km/15.5mi north of Mérida. Exit the city by way of the prolongation of Paseo Montejo and continue on Carr. Progreso.* This is the primary port in the state of Yucatán. Due to the shallowness of its waters, a pier extending 6.4km/4mi towards the sea was built to receive ships from the world over. By keeping vessels far from the shore, the city has been able to conserve the beach's natural beauty. The attractive waterfront is defined by a short undulating wall that separates the beach's white sand from the cobble-stoned sidewalk. Numerous restaurants specializing in seafood flank the zone that faces the waterfront.

Dzibilchaltún – *20km/12.4mi from Mérida. Take Carr. 261 north and at 15km/9.3mi turn right, then go 5km/3.1mi to Dzibilchaltún. Open year-round daily 9am–5pm. P$45 ⅙ ☎ (9) 924-9495.* This archaeological site, a trading and religious center for the Maya, reached its peak between the 8C and the 10C AD and suddenly flourished again in the 13C. It was declared a national park in 1987.

★**Museo del Pueblo Maya** – *Open year-round Tue–Sun 9am–4pm.* ☎ *(9) 924-9495.*
Displaying general information about Maya culture, this museum provides an
overview of the 2,500 years during which they inhabited this area. On display are
its primary gods and world vision, represented by the sacred silk-cotton tree *(ceiba
sagrada)* that supports the Maya worlds. Calendars and writing-of which 800 hieroglyphs have already been deciphered-are also explained in the first hall, which is
adorned by a 7-8C AD round incense burner and the seven dolls found in the
temple that bears the same name as the museum.
The second hall describes the development of Maya culture from the Conquest to
the present day, including subjects such as religious syncretism, folklore and the
Caste War. On the way out, one can view first-hand a typical Maya hut, complete
with hammocks, kitchen utensils and other objects. After this, walk the ecological
path that leads 350m/383yd through the jungle to the archaeological site.

El Templo de las Siete Muñecas – At the eastern end of the area, the Temple
of the Seven Dolls, so named because of the deformed dolls that were found
nearby, has a feature unusual in Maya buildings-windows beside the doors on its
four sides. Through the east and west door the **sunrise** can be seen clearly during
the equinoxes; the same is also true of the rising moon around March 21 and
September 22.

Estructura 44 – *On the southern side of the Plaza Central.* This 130m/426ft-long
palace was built in four different stages, culminating in the Late Classic period (AD
600–1000). Its 16 steps, spanning the length of the structure, may well be the
largest in Mesoamerica. From the top of the building protrude approximately
30 huge columns that delimit a single gallery. It is believed that this palace's function was linked to the rituals and ceremonies of the Plaza Central.

Capilla Abierta – *In the center of the Plaza Central.* This open-air chapel was built
by indigenous hands between 1590 and 1600, by order of the Spaniards, and consists of a short nave covered with a barrel vault and a one-room sacristy.

Cenote Xlacah – At the western end of the main *sacbé* (white stone road) lies one
of the twelve cenotes found in this area. A transparent, natural swimming pool
that has been explored to a depth of 44m/144ft, Xlacah is inhabited by six species
of fish native to the Yucatán Peninsula, three of them found only in this cenote.

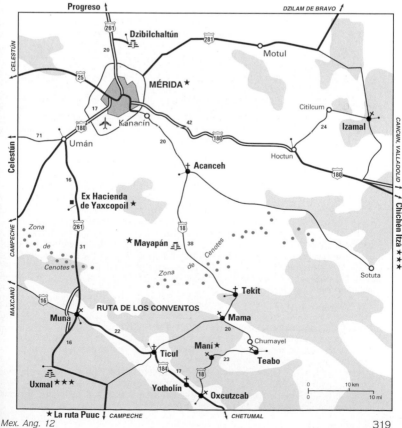

Celestún – *98km/61mi from Mérida. Go west from Mérida on Carr. 180 to Umán (18km/11.2mi); continue 22km/13.7mi to Kinchil; cross the town, and continue 49km/30.5mi on Carr. 281 to Celestún. Arrive early to observe the highest concentration of birds.* This fishing village is located on a strip of land bordered on the north by the Gulf of Mexico and on the south by a tideland estuary that extends for 25km/15.5mi. A wildlife refuge for flora and fauna, it represents a "dry tropical ecosystem." Launches are available *(P$70/pers. for groups of 6; less than 6 people: P$300/launch plus P$20/pers.)* to take visitors closer to the flocks of flamingos, which from March to August feed on the marshes rich in plankton and shrimp larvae. It is a breathtaking **spectacle★** to see the birds take off and paint the sky with pink clouds. A freshwater spring in the midst of the mangroves invites visitors to swim in its clear waters. Don't leave Celestún without sampling the delicious, fresh seafood served in the restaurants along the beach.

★★★Chichén Itzá – *119km/74mi from Mérida. Take Carr. 180 east; after 69km/43mi, in Cantunil, take either the toll road or continue on the freeway. Description p 308.*

Izamal – *66km/41mi from Mérida. Take Carr. 180 east toward Tixcocob (where hammocks are made) for 24km/15mi, crossing the towns of Euan, Cacalchén and Citilcum; then take a narrow road another 11km/6.8mi to Izamal.* A city of three cultures, Izamal testifies to the blend of pre-Hispanic, colonial and present day cultures amidst the ochre color of its constructions. Meaning "Place of Itzamná," creator of life, its name refers to the most important of ancient Maya gods. Believed to have been the greatest ceremonial center after Chichén Itzá, it is still a very important place of pilgrimage for the Maya, due to the cult to the Virgin of Izamal, which dates back to colonial times. Some of the most important ancient structures, oriented to the four cardinal points, flank the great plaza. To the south stood the largest pyramid, called **Ppapp-Hol-Chac**, "House of the heads and lightning bolts," whose enormous base was chosen by the Franciscan friars as the foundation for their monastery. To the north stands **Kinich-Kak-Moo**, "sun-eye of the fire-macaw," the next most important temple. Its base (200m/656ft by 180m/591ft) is the third largest in Mesoamerica. The top affords a beautiful view of the city, with the pyramid to **Itzamatúl** dedicated to the god Zamná to the east, and to the west **Kabul** of which only traces remain.

★Convento de Izamal – *Open year-round daily 5:30am–8:30pm.* Due to its importance as a Maya ceremonial center, the Spaniards, guided by the controversial **Fray Diego de Landa** (1524–79), chose this place to build the largest Franciscan monastery in all of Mexico. The building, constructed between 1549 and 1562 and designed by architect Fray Juan de Mérida, stands on the foundations of a pyramid. Three ramps lead to a majestic **atrium★★** with corner chapels. The large space (120m/394ft x 60m/197ft) embraces the church with its beautiful facade facing west, the large monastery to the north, and an open-air chapel to the south, which was later transformed into a side chapel for the church. It is believed to be the world's second largest enclosed atrium, next to Saint Peter's Plaza in Rome. Inside, a famous altarpiece dedicated to the Virgin of Izamal, patron saint of the Yucatán, makes the church the most important shrine to the virgin in southeastern Mexico.

★Mayapán – *Head southeast on Carr. 18 until reaching Acanceh, 20km/12.4mi; continue south for another 19km/11.8mi, following the "Zona Arqueológica Mayapán" signs. Open year-round, daily, 8am–5pm, P$12.* This visit can be incorporated into the monastery route excursion. The post-Classic (12-15C) city of Mayapán formed part of the "Triple Alliance" with Uxmal and Chichén-Itzá (and for some time served as its capital), until it was destroyed in a civil war in 1447. Mayapán was surrounded by a 9.7km/6mi-long stone wall, which protected its inhabitants from the enemy. The current archaeological site was once the ceremonial center of the ancient city. It exhibits a great deal of influence from the Maya-Toltec style, as can be seen in several structures that appear to emulate those of the New Chichén Itzá, characterized by motifs of eagles, serpents, warriors and sacrifices. It also displays elements of the Puuc style, with numerous masks of Chac, the rain god. During the first investigations initiated by the Carnegie Institute between 1945 and 1950, seven structures were restored. From 1996 to 1998, with the support of the INAH, archaeologists restituted twelve more buildings, including the Gran Pirámide.

Gran Pirámide – This nine-terrace pyramid was dedicated to Kukulcán. It presents the same equinoctial phenomenon as El Castillo in Chichén-Itzá: a play of light and shadow that occurs every year on March 21 and September 22, giving the impression that a serpent is descending down the pyramid. The rear part of this building, towards the left, is adorned with bas-reliefs depicting war scenes and mural paintings portraying eagle-warriors with spears.

To the right of the Gran Pirámide stands a great palace with multiple columns, which probably served as the private residence of priests or the elite.

To the left of the plaza rises a round tower, an observatory that resembles the one in Caracol at Chichén-Itzá. More Chac masks can be seen behind the tower.

■ The Monastery Route

The Franciscan monasteries along this route possess architectural characteristics unique to regional 16C monasteries. Often they stand on pyramidal foundations of ancient Maya temples; are enclosed by an atrium wall; and sometimes the atrium has corner chapels. The church usually faces west and has a monastery and an open-air chapel, behind which lie an orchard, a cemetery and a well. These plain, austere buildings, with buttressed walls and few windows, conjure images of medieval fortresses. Such complexes were not just for evangelization, but were also meant to educate and urbanize.

The single most common external ornamentation in this zone is the **bell gable**, a kind of belfry with a purely decorative function. Smaller ones characterize the Guadalupe chapel in **Acanceh**, where a pyramid stands in the Town Square; others are ornamented like those in **Tekit**, scene of bloody battles during the Caste War. Some bell gables are so large they cover the whole facade, as is the case in **Yotholín**. Still, others are connected by complicated pediments that resemble towers, like those in **Ticul**, or built in threes and ornately decorated, like those of **Muna**.

Ruta de los Conventos (Monastery Route) – *A 148km/92mi circuit from Mérida to Muna. Leave Mérida on Carr. 18 southeast to Acanceh 20km/12.4mi; continue south 38km/23.6mi to Tekit (The archaeological site of Mayapán can be visited in between Acanceh and Tekit.), 7km/4.3mi to Mama, 13km/8mi to Teabo, 12km/7.5mi to Maní, 11km/6.8mi to Oxcutzcab, 5km/3mi to Yohtolín, 12km/7.5mi to Ticul and 22km/13.7mi to Muna.* This trek leads visitors far away from the main tourist routes to immerse them in a rural Maya setting. It is remarkable to see that in spite of the mission to evangelize the natives, as evidenced in the ancient monasteries and churches found here, the towns and peoples remained distinctively Mayan, with their typical huts, their women dressed in white, embroidered *huipiles* (loose-fitting blouses). Their ancestors' traditions are still very much alive here, and in the markets of these villages, Maya is still the preferred language.

Parroquia de la Asunción, Mama – *Open year-round daily 8am–noon & 4–8pm.* Despite its simplicity of design, the portal of this parish church is one of the most richly ornamented. The scaled bell gable was added in the 18C. In the baptistry, to the right of the entrance, stands an enormous **baptismal font** carved from quarry stone. To one side of the monastery lies the well.

★**Parroquia de San Miguel Arcángel, Maní** – *Open year-round Mon–Sat 9:30am–noon & 5–9pm, Sun & holidays 6am–8pm.* This is the most important monastery in the area. Its open–air chapel, the largest in the entire route, rivals the size of the church itself. Inside, the **altarpieces** are, together with those in **Teabo**, the finest in the Yucatán Peninsula. It was in Maní that Fray Diego de Landa conducted the *Auto de Fé* when he called 13 of the principal local chiefs to a town meeting. He proceeded to judge and condemn them, castigating them for their pagan customs and burning them alive along with thousands of Maya religious objects and codices.

© Robert Holmes

Maya Woman in Typical Dress

Parroquia de San Francisco de Asís, Oxcutzcab – *Open year-round Mon-Sat 7am–1pm & 4–8pm, Sun & holidays 7am–8pm.* The tower-like bell gables, the ornamentation of the facade and the Moorish-style double arch leading to the cemetery merit attention.

★**Ex Hacienda de Yaxcopoil** – *3km/1.9mi from Mérida. Go west on Carr. 180 to Umán, from there take Carr. 261 south and continue 15km/9.3mi until you reach the hacienda. Open year-round Mon-Sat 8am–6pm, Sun 9am–1pm. P$30.* ☎ *(9) 927-2606 or* www.mayanroutes.com/yaxcopoil.html. Development of the haciendas in the Yucatán began in colonial times as cattle and corn farms. Starting in 1765, they were transformed into henequen haciendas. The henequen boom (late 19C and early 20C) ended in 1935 due to parceling of the haciendas into common land and the entry of synthetic fibers into the market. Yaxcopoil, "place of the green poplars," is a clear example of the stages of this development, as it was considered one of the largest (over 11,000ha/27,181 acres) and most magnificent estates of its time. Founded in the 17C, this Neoclassical hacienda-museum is composed of the **main house**, a chapel, an orchard, corrals, a well, huge rooms containing the machinery for processing sisal, storehouses, workshops, a pay office, a school and an infirmary-all the facilities needed to run a self-sufficient hacienda.

★★★**Uxmal** – *80km/50mi from Mérida. Head southwest on Carr. 180 to Umán (18km/11mi); then take Carr. 261 south. Uxmal is 16km/10mi past Muna. Description p 328.*

La Ruta PUUC★

Yucatán

Map of Principal Sights – Map p 319

🅱 ☎ (9) 924-9290

On one of the few elevations of the Yucatán Peninsula, almost hidden in the jungle vegetation, lie the ruins of important ceremonial centers built in the Late Classic period (AD 600 and 900), during which the Puuc architectural style flourished. A style exclusive to this area, it has influenced modern decorative designs such as the Palacio de Bellas Artes in Mexico City.

ARCHAEOLOGICAL SITES

Full circuit: 38km/23.6mi leaving from Uxmal.

★★★**Uxmal** – *Description p 328.*

★**Kabah** – *23km/14.3mi from Uxmal. Go east on Carr. 261 for 15km/9.3mi to Santa Elena, then continue another 8km/5mi south. Open year-round daily 8am–5pm. P$17.* ☎ *(9) 944-0033.* This archaeological site is the second largest ceremonial center of the Puuc zone. Meaning "the lord of strong and powerful arm" the Kabah site, famous for its profusely ornamented facades, is composed of a complex of buildings situated on the edge of the highway. Three groups of structures comprise the east side.

Palacio de los Mascarones (Codz Pop) – *First building to the right of the entrance, facing the highway.* On a broad, three-level terrace stands the Palace of the Large Masks with one of the most extraordinary **facades**★★★ of the Mayan area. In Codz Pop, Puuc Baroque style, it is remarkable for the quality and quantity (over 100) of large masks of Chac the rain god, represented with his typical elongated nose associated with the lightning bolt. This repetition of the rain symbol creates a mesmerizing litany. Vestiges of pierced crestings adorn the roof. A repaired **cistern**, still in use, stands in front of the building. Two unusual statues of figures wearing loin clothes, bead necklaces and a carved plume decorate the east side of the building. The jambs of the left entrance contain reliefs depicting battle scenes.

El Palacio – *Northeast of the Palacio de los Mascarones.* Located on an elevated esplanade, which forms a quadrangle with excellent acoustics, the two-story Palace contains remains of crestings and is surrounded by partially restored structures.

Tercera Casa (Templo de las Columnas) – *200m/232yd east of El Palacio.* Situated in the jungle, the Third House, with columns on the upper facade still preserves its cistern with two outlets for the collection and storage of rainwater.

Return and cross the highway.

The largest part of the ceremonial center on this side of the highway has been partially destroyed; nevertheless, at about 200m/232yd appears a majestic **arch**★ 10m/32.8ft tall, which possibly marked the beginning of an 18km/11.2mi *sacbé* that connected Kabah to Uxmal.

Palacio de los Mascarones, detail

© Robert Frerck/Odyssey

Sayil – *9km/5.6mi from Kabah. Go south and at 5km/3mi turn left. Sayil is 4km/2.5mi down this road. Open year-round daily 8am–5pm. P$17.* ☎ *(9) 944-0033.* Situated in the midst of silence, Sayil, whose Mayan name means "house of the ants," was constructed on this reddish clay between the years AD 700–1000. Overrun by vegetation, the elegant **El Palacio★** contains more than 50 double chambers on three stories. The intermediate level is outstanding for its frieze of small columns alternating with Chac masks, along with two representations of Amuxincab (also known as the Diving God), whose head is upside-down and who in the Puuc region is associated with honey. These sculptures are flanked by fantastical reptiles. Farther along the southern walk there are several other buildings in a dilapidated state, of which only the **Mirador** preserves its cresting.

Xlapak – *5km/3mi from Sayil. Open year-round daily 8am–5pm. P$12.* ☎ *(9) 944-0033.* Between AD 600 and 1000 flourished this small site whose name means "touching walls." The best-preserved building, **El Palacio** consists of nine vaulted chambers and boasts a richly decorated frieze. At one time, three rows of superimposed Chac masks adorned each of the entrances. Two masks of the large-nosed god, slightly larger than those on the northern facade, stand guard over the center of the southern facade.

★Labná – *4km/2.5mi from Xlapak. Open year-round daily 8am–5pm. P$17.* ☎ *(9) 944-0033.* The earliest traces of human occupation of Labná (a Mayan word meaning "old house") date back as far as the 1C AD. Nevertheless, the main structures were built between AD 750 and 1000. Labná was probably part of a larger political complex with its capital in Uxmal or Sayil. A broad and well-preserved *sacbé* connects the buildings.

★El Palacio – *First building on the left.* Similar to that of Sayil but larger and two tiered. The Palace consists of 67 chambers, seven courtyards and several stairways that offer interesting perspectives. On the west corner of the building, in front of a Chac mask, is the figure of a serpent's head with a human face between its jaws, which either symbolizes an astronomical element or the underworld. The mask of the large-nosed deity on the northwestern side is one of the largest representations of Chac found to date. A cistern on the roof is still operational.

El Mirador – *At the rear, on the left of the sacbé.* The top of this lookout temple is embellished with fragile cresting. A figure resembling the lower part of a watchman adorns the southwestern corner, confirming the belief that the building was an observatory.

★★★Arco – *To the right of the Mirador.* The decoration distinguishes this structure as the best preserved and most elaborate example of the Mayan arches. It appears to have been the entranceway to the residential complex of a wealthy family. The false bays harbored seated human figures, of which only the feathers of the headdresses remain. A Chac mask is located on the northwestern corner.

EXCURSION

★★Grutas de Loltún – *14km/8.7mi northeast of Labná take the turnoff that leads 5km/3mi to Loltún. Guided visit (1hr). Open year-round daily 9:30am, 11am, 12:30pm, 2pm, 3pm, 4pm. P$37. ☎ (9) 944-0033.* Along a stretch of nearly 2km/1.2mi, twelve caverns, first inhabited by man as early as 3000 BC, contain the grottoes whose name means "stone flower." In this dark cavity the ancient Maya performed rituals related to the underworld. Today the stalactites-considered tears of the god Chac-and stalagmites are colorfully illuminated. While admiring the cave paintings and carvings listen to the guides narrate the legends of **aluxes**-clay idols that came to life in the form of small sprites-bringing drafts of fresh air into the grottoes when they were invoked. During the Caste War, Maya rebels sought refuge in these depths.

La Ruta RÍO BEC★

Campeche and Quintana Roo
Map of Principal Sights
🛈 ☎ (9) 816-6767

In Quintana Roo and southern Campeche, cities of the ancient Maya civilization such as Becán, Chicanná, Xpuhil, el Hormiguero and Calakmul exercised control over extensive cultural subregions still distinguishable by their location and architectural styles. Calakmul fought against Tikal (Guatemala) for political leadership in this region during the Late Classic period and is presently heart of the **Biosfera de Calakmul** (Calakmul Biosphere Reserve). The subregion **Río Bec** lies less than 100km/62mi from the Guatemalan border and includes more than 50 archaeological sites. All of these cultures reached their peak between AD 500 and 800. Considered a link between the Petén (Guatemala) and Chenes (Northern Campeche) styles, Río Bec's distinctive features are tall, steep towers with false stairways flanking the principal buildings, structures built on broad platforms, large constructions with rounded corners, fretwork motifs and large masks of the god **Itzamná**, also called the "Earth Monster," represented by reptiles with open jaws. Despite the heat and lack of water in this area-where hot chili peppers are currently cultivated-the rain forest allows for a proliferation of green foliage, which has hidden rich archaeological treasures for more than 1,200 years.

ARCHAEOLOGICAL SITES

116km/72mi west of Chetumal on Carr. 186 or 290km/180mi from Campeche via Escárcega, 155km/96mi west of Xpuhil.

Xpuhil – *116km/72mi west of Chetumal on Carr. 186. Open year-round daily 8am–5pm. P$17; free Sun & national holidays. ☎ (9) 816-9111.* Of the 17 groups of constructions that have been identified, only four big structures have been restored. The most important is **Estructura I★**, an 18m/59ft-tall building characterized by having three towers-an atypical example of Río Bec architecture-and by the dangerous verticality of these towers. The central tower, comprised of 11 sections, is the best preserved of all the structures and, like its companions, was once crowned by a simulated temple. It was once flanked by a 6m/19.6ft-wide staircase with three large fantastic masks that are still partly visible. Vestiges of stucco ornamentation representing Chac, the rain god, are preserved on the lower portions of the sidewalls. Towards the left side of the southern tower, a narrow and steep staircase leads to an opening at the top of the tower. Xpuhil means "cat's tail," which is what a plant typical of this area resembles.

★Becán – *6km/3.7mi west of Xpuhil turn to Becán, located 500m/547yd from the highway. Open year-round daily 8am–5pm. P$20; free Sun & national holidays. ☎ (9) 816-9111.* This once very large city can be appreciated from the highway. Its main buildings were protected by a moat 5m/16.4ft deep and 16m/52.5ft wide that ran 1.9km/1.2mi around the city. Boasting seven entrances with their respective bridges, it testifies to the constant invasions that took place during the Classic period. Becán, which means "gully" or "water canyon," was the political, economical and religious capital of the province now called Río Bec. This archaeological site was discovered in 1934 by two researchers from the Carnegie Institute. The first excavations took place between 1969 and 1971, and the greatest restoration progress occurred from 1991 to 1994.

In **Plaza A** lies a circular altar associated with Kukulcán, the wind god. To the south stands **Estructura I**, featuring 15m/49ft-high towers, and on whose upper level were found openings that may have allowed for astronomical observations.

To the northeast, the **vaulted passageway★** served as a street in ancient Becán and was covered by a Mayan arch along its length of nearly 60m/65.6yd. This passageway leads to the **Plaza B**, bordered to the west by the monumental **Estructura VIII**, which supports two large towers at its north and south ends; eight dark chambers with a height of 8m/26ft that may have been used for religious ceremonies were found here. To the north is the relatively unexplored Structure IX, which is the site's tallest building (32m/105ft). To the west is **Estructura X**, atop which was built a temple with a facade adorned with a representation of Itzamná. Behind this building is the **Juego de Pelota** (ball court).

Chicanná – *From Becán return to Carr. 186, continue west 2km/1.3mi and turn left onto the dirt road continuing for 500m/547yd. Open year-round daily 8am–5pm. P$17; free Sun & national holidays. ☎ (9) 816-9111.* Chicanná's beginnings date back to the Late pre-Classic period (300 BC–AD 250), but it flourished around AD 850. A hunter discovered the site in 1966. Archaeologists called this House of the Serpent's Mouth (*Chicanná* in Maya) because of the **facade**★★ of Structure II, one of the most complete and best-preserved images of Itzamná. The door bay simulates the open jaws of a serpent, the fangs of which descend menacingly from the lintel. The facade symbolizes the entrance into the bowels of this powerful deity, creator of all things according to Maya mythology. Above can be seen the remains of crestings that held images for worship. Painted hieroglyphics adorn the sides of the portal.

★**Kohunlich** – *From Chicanná, return to Carr. 186; return toward Chetumal, and after 64km/40mi take the right turn for Kohunlich. It can also be reached 69km/43mi from Chetumal; leave the city west on Carr. 186; 60km/37mi farther on take the left-hand turn for Kohunlich, which lies 9km/5.6mi ahead. Open year-round daily 8am–5pm. P$25. ☎ (9) 832-0855.* Amid tall corozo palms rise the ruins of this site, named by archaeologists "the hillock of corozo palms." This ceremonial center had ample ties to the Petén region of Guatemala, which possesses features similar to Río Bec architecture revealed in the remains of the tall towers in the **acropolis**.

At the rear of the site stands the main building that was discovered by a Maya hunter in the 1960s. The five **masks**★★ that adorn the facade are impressively large (1.5m/5ft tall). Their fine stucco decoration still preserves some of its reddish pigment. Representing Kinich Ahau, the "Sun-face," one of the Maya's most important deities, the masks' eyes are inscribed with a hieroglyph representing the symbol *Kin*, which signifies the sun, day and time. A few steps from the Temple of the Masks, towards the right, lies a **ball court** that still remains in excellent condition. Approximately 400m/437yd south stands the **Estructura de los 27 Escalones** (The 27 Step Structure). This was recently consolidated (there are only 22 steps at present) from the remains of an enormous residential complex constructed between AD 600 and 1200. From the top there is a splendid **view** of some 200 buildings discovered in the area completely covered in jungle vegetation.

TULUM★★

Quintana Roo
Map of Principal Sights
🅸 ☎ (9) 884-8073

Tulum, which in Maya means "wall," alludes to the wall that surrounds the area, although its original name **Zamá**, or "sunrise," refers to the site's unique location, perfect for enjoying the sunrise.

The city, located on the coast of the Caribbean Sea, is surrounded by a 380m/416yd north-south wall of three series, which reflects the violent political conditions of its era. A thick outer wall prevented enemy access, and two inner walls separated the commercial and ceremonial areas. Tulum's coastal location made it an important maritime commercial center.

The archaeological site was inhabited during the Late Post-Classic period (AD 1200–1521) and was one of the last cities to be built and inhabited by the Maya of the Yucatán Peninsula. An important seaport trading center, the site's archaeological remains of obsidian, jade and copper testify to its trade with Central America.

ARCHAEOLOGICAL SITE

Open year-round daily 7am–5pm. P$25. ✗ ☎ (9) 883-3671. The path from the parking lot to the archaeological site spans almost 1km/0.6mi, a distance that can be covered on foot or by train (P$10).

A **wall** with a thickness of 6m/20ft and a height of 3-5m/10-16ft bounds the ceremonial center to the north, west and south. The site can be accessed from a narrow entrance on the west side. There are four additional entrances, two to the north and two to the south. From the wall, one can see several large, fortified towers that undoubtedly served as watchtowers. At each place along the complex, there are steps that lead to the wall.

Religious temples, tombs and official buildings, as well as residential platforms, originally occupied the area known as the **recinto interior**. The site boasts over 50 structures, most of which are found along the two "roads" that run from north to south.

Templo de las Pinturas – *More or less in the center of the city, in front of the Plataforma Funeraria.* Probably Tulum's most interesting structure, the Temple of the Paintings features frescoes and a small altar. The lower level facade consists of four stout columns, large corner masks and three niches with sculptures. An image of the *Dios Descendente* (Diving God), apparently associated with the planet Venus, decorates the upper level.

El Castillo – *With its back wall to the sea.* This largest structure was built taking advantage of the rock cliff from where it dominates land and sea. The building reveals several stages of construction. Two vaulted chambers, each with three bays, compose the upper part of the castle, while two columns that resemble serpents flank the entrance. Sculptures adorn its facade, and the remains of masks are visible on the corners.
At ground level, two small temples flanking the stairway possess altars for offerings. From behind the sanctuary, a magnificent **view★★★** of the Caribbean Sea unfolds.

Templo del Dios Descendente – *Located on the north side of the small inner building, whose main monument is El Castillo.* The niche above the door on this small temple houses a clear stucco sculpture of the Diving God, a figure with an upside-down head. It is believed that this god, who appears on many of the buildings in Tulum, was associated with the netherworld.

EXCURSIONS

★**Cobá** – *47km/29mi west of Tulum; this archaeological site can also be reached from Valladolid (59km/36.6mi) via Carr. 180 east, to the junction on the right with signs to Cobá and Tulum. Open year-round daily 8am–6pm. P$25. ☎ (9) 883-3671.* Nestled beside the lake of the same name and surrounded by thick jungle vegetation, this ancient ceremonial complex bears a Maya name that means "water ruffled by the wind." In this 70sq km/27sq mi site, the principal architectural complexes are near the Cobá and Macanxoc lakes. Cobá's structures are connected by means of a **sacbeob** (network of *sacbés* or white stone roads) which also links the city with other groups of buildings and pre-Hispanic settlements such as Yaxuná, near Chichén Itzá, 100km/62mi away.
Its religious center is divided into four groups of structures: Cobá, Pinturas, Nohoch Mul and Macanxoc. These groups are dispersed throughout the thickness of the jungle, but linked to each other by means of trails whose distance ranges from 200m/656ft to 2km/1.2mi. The architectural style of Cobá, which flourished from the Early Classic (AD 300–600) to the Terminal Classic period (AD 900–1000), resembles more the Petén style than that of Chichén Itzá. Therefore, its constructions are less embellished, obvious in the Cobá group as well as the Nohoch Mul.

El Castillo

Grupo Cobá – Of the 43 structures that comprise this group, the most important is the church. Built in the center of a plaza, the church features a stela where offerings of candles and flowers are left by present-day Maya peasants who claim that this stone statue represents the Virgin called "Colebí." The pyramid consists of nine sections with rounded corners 24m/78ft tall. The Cobá Group also boasts a **ball court**, in excellent condition, and a large residential palace.

Grupo Nohoch Mul – *Located 2km/1.2mi from the Cobá Group.* This Maya name means Large Hillock, because it rises 42m/138ft into the sky, making it the tallest structure on the northern part of the peninsula. It consists of seven round-cornered tiers with two staircases. The main staircase leads to a temple decorated with eastern coastal elements-niches and images of the Diving God. Approximately 100m/109yd ahead stands an enormous stela from the 8C AD that depicts a richly dressed Maya ruler, with a scepter, flanked by diminutive warriors who appear kneeling and tied down.

Muyil – *18km/llmi south of Tulum, on Carr. 306. Open year-round daily 8am–5pm. P$12.* Located only 15min away from the frequently visited Tulum, the archaeological site of Muyil offers visitors the jungle tranquillity lacking in the previous site. On the banks of the beautiful Muyil Lagoon, this 450ha/1,112-acre site shows evidence of human occupation from as early as 300 BC, but did not reach its zenith until the Late Classic period (AD 600–900).

El Castillo – This temple of six layered sections, the site's tallest structure, is dedicated to Ixchel, goddess of fertility, maternity, wisdom and the moon. Nearly 300 jade figures, all of them offerings to Ixchel, were found inside the building in 1997. Some of these offerings may have been brought here by sea from places as far away as Belize and Tikal, as Muyil was probably an important ceremonial center associated with this goddess.

Templo del Sacerdote – To the left of El Castillo stands the Temple of the Priest, comprised of two levels. It is believed that the first level housed priests who conducted religious rituals from the small temple superimposed directly above this one. A **sacbé** (white-stone path), of which traces still remain, linked Muyil and Cobá, a distance of more than 50km/31mi.

Guides lead visitors on a 3hr boat excursion around the Muyil Lagoon, located inside the Reserva de la Biosfera Sian-Ka'An (P$100 per person).

★★ Reserva de la Biosfera Sian-Ka'An – 10km/6.3mi south of Tulum on the path to Boca Paila/Punta Allen. *Guided visit (5hr) year-round Mon–Thu & Sat. Reservations needed. P$360 (with car), P$450 (without car).* △ ✗ ▣ ☎ *(9) 884-9583.* This reserve, whose Maya name means "Gift from Heaven," was declared a World Heritage Site in 1987 in order to protect its vastly diverse fauna (350 species of birds, as well as turtles, jaguars, monkeys, deer, anteaters and other endangered species) and ecosystems (including coral reefs, a tropical jungle, sandy grounds and mangrove swamps) found within its 6,000sq km/2,316sq mi.

From Punta Allen, a small fishing village, sport fishing or sightseeing by motor launch is available by reservation. Guided walks lead further into the reserve, which also contains Maya ruins such as Muyil.

★★ Xel-ha – *9km/5.6mi north of Tulum, via Carr. 307 to Cancun. Description p 305.*

Akumal – *27km/16.7mi north of Tulum, via Carr. 307 to Cancun. Description p 305.*

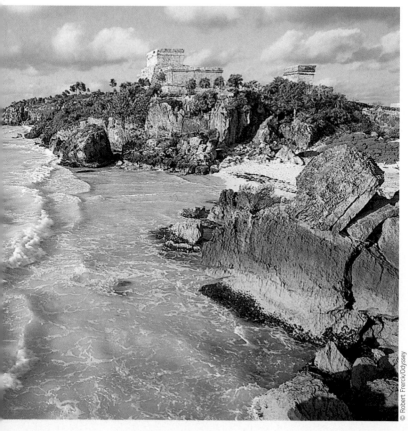

© Robert Frerck/Odyssey

UXMAL★★★

Yucatán
Map of Principal Sights – Map below
☎ (9) 923-9674

The undulating hill country of the Puuc region has one of the highest densities of archaeological sites in the American continent, and the imposing ruins of Uxmal are the most important example of Puuc architecture from the Late Classic period (AD 600–900).

The largest buildings of the "three times built" Uxmal are laid out around quadrangles, a recurrent feature in Puuc architecture *(Description of Maya, p 32 & 314)*. Other characteristics of the style are the Mayan arch, plain walls with ornate stucco friezes, and an abundance of masks of Chac, the rain god with the hooked nose. The intense devotion to Chac reflects the inhabitants'-mostly farmers-concern with a lack of rain and cenotes for which they compensated by building cisterns (*chultún*, in Maya) to store water.

Following its period of power and prosperity, Uxmal was abandoned in AD 1200, probably as a result of civil war.

John Lloyd Stephens and Frederick Catherwood began to explore the ruins in the 1840s. Today Catherwood's drawings adorn many walls in the region and are sold throughout Yucatán. A hundred years later, in 1940, archaeological research was initiated again under the direction of Frans Blom, and in 1996 Uxmal was declared a World Heritage Site.

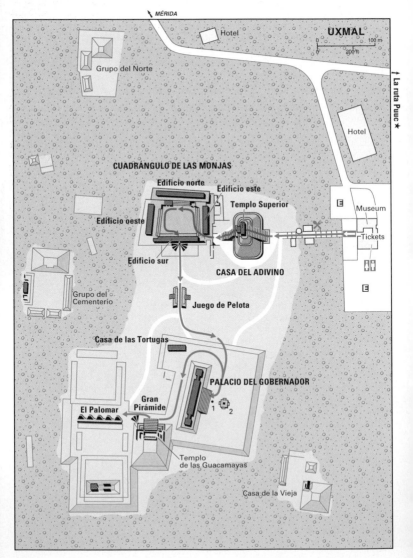

ARCHAEOLOGICAL SITE

Open year-round daily 8am–5pm (winter) & 8am–6pm (summer); service unit open 8am–10pm. P$75 (admission to the site and the sound & light show); P$30 (admission to the sound & light show only); free Sun. ✗ ☎ (9) 944-0033.

Casa del Adivino – One of the most magnificent buildings of the pre-Hispanic world, the oval-shaped Pyramid of the Magician rises to a height of 35m/115ft. According to legend, it was built by a dwarf who, after playing the *tunkul* (drum) and the *soot* (maracas), and solving several riddles, was made king. The steep staircase that faces east leads to a great tunnel opened recently by archaeologists.

Templo Superior – The Upper Temple belongs to the fifth and last phase of construction. As throughout the building, the western facade is exquisitely ornamented. Do not miss the sweeping **view★★★** of the site from here. A temple faced with finely carved stone masks of Chac adorns the first landing descending the western staircase. An impressive zoomorphic mask, whose mouth is the temple entrance, marks the eastern facade, calling forth images of the priest that emerges from Chac's jaws bearing a message from the gods.

The first stage of construction, a type of palace, forms part of a dilapidated quadrangle that contains the **Casa de los Pájaros** (Birdhouse), featuring a frieze adorned with birds associated with the corn harvest.

Casa del Adivino, detail

Cuadrángulo de las Monjas – Named the Nunnery Quadrangle because the Spanish colonizers thought it had been the residence of Maya priestesses, this complex of four buildings built on different levels surrounds a courtyard of exceptional acoustics. The lower walls are usually smooth and plain whereas repeating geometric and zoomorphic motifs full of fantastic representations, create a mesmerizing visual image on the upper areas.

Edificio Este – The frieze adorning the facade of the East Building is composed of a fretwork and resembles snake skin pattern, creating the impression of a snake's undulating movement. A column with three large Chac masks stands above the central doorway and at the corners of the edifice. Across the remainder of the frieze sprawl six groups of eight two-headed serpents arranged according to size and crowned with heads of owls, alluding to this bird's association with death and night in Maya mythology.

Edificio Norte – The high platform of the North Building, which consists of a series of 26 rooms, accentuates the importance of this elegant structure. Its upper facade is adorned with frets and representations of human figures, birds and monkeys, as well as several columns, each adorned with four Chac masks. Interspersed among these are representations of palm huts topped with roofs of two-headed serpents. Two annexes at the courtyard level further enhance the beauty of the complex. The temple of Venus, on the left, is outstanding for its monolithic columns and the representations of the planet that adorn its frieze.

Edificio Oeste – An intricate stone mosaic with human figures in high relief decorates the upper part of the West Building. In particular, the work above the central doorway shows a sculpted throne on which a dignitary with a feathered headdress is seated. Alternating with these sculptures are columns of three masks and palm

329

huts with Chac images on the roofs. The two, feathered rattlesnakes that slither between the frets of the frieze were added at a later date. At one end is the rattle; at the other is a head from whose jaws emerge human faces.

Edificio Sur – The South Building features the same fretwork decoration as the East Building. Groups of columns tied together, reminiscent perhaps of the interlaced poles that form the sides of Maya huts, ornament its upper portion. Its panels preserve images of huts crowned by Chac faces with waves coming out of their eyes-Chac's tears raining down on the homes in the town. From beyond the courtyard's Mayan arch, a panoramic view unfolds of the rest of the ceremonial center, creating the sensation of emerging from underground.

Juego de Pelota – In the ball court, two teams met in a ritual test of a divinatory or prestigious nature. The teams competed in passing the rubber ball through the openings of the stone rings, found along the inner surface of either side of the court and decorated with hieroglyphic inscriptions and reliefs of feathered serpents.

Palacio del Gobernador – On a gigantic platform rises the Governor's Palace, a monumental structure almost 100m/328ft long, 12m/39ft wide and 9m/30ft tall. The exclusive ceremonial and civic rites that took place in its 24 chambers are reflected in its exquisite facade, a magnificent sample containing many elements of the symmetry and precision characteristic of Mayan art. The simplicity of the lower facade, composed of a smooth wall perforated by entrance openings, serves to enhance the frieze, framed by a double cornice, the upper one in the form of an undulating serpent. The stone mosaic simulates snakeskin. To this geometric rigor is added the omnipresent Chac, with his hooked nose, slithering between step-and-fret motifs and dice patterns and adorning the corners. Above the central doorway appears the stunning figure of a ruler with a plume of feathers framed by a trapezoidal composition of two-headed serpents. Two vaulted passageways, later closed off by the Maya, divide the palace into three sections.

Facing this structure, stands the **adoratorio de la picota (1)**, also known as the flagellation post; farther on, the **trono del jaguar (2)** (two-headed jaguar) stands guard. About 100m/110yd southeast of the Governor's platform is the building known as the **Casa de la Vieja** (House of the Old Woman).

Casa de las Tortugas – This temple dedicated to the worship of water rests on the northwest corner of the Governor's platform. The Turtle House consists of three central chambers with four side entrances. Associated with the rain, turtles of different shapes and sizes adorn the upper cornice.

La Gran Pirámide (Templo Mayor) – On the upper level of the Great Pyramid, consisting of nine sections with stairways, rests the partially restored **Templo de las Guacamayas** (Temple of the Macaws), named for the bird associated with sun worship that graces the facade. It affords a wonderful **view**★★ of the site.

El Palomar – The openwork of the elaborate roofcomb adorning the ruins of this architectural complex appears ready to receive all wandering doves; hence its name, the Pigeon House. As elsewhere in Uxmal, the exterior walls were once finished in reliefs of painted stucco.

Mayan Arch, Cuadrángulo de las Monjas

★★★**Sound and Light Show in Spanish** – *Apr–Oct daily 8pm; Nov–Mar daily 7pm. P$30 or general admission. Headphones (P$25) are available for simultaneous interpretation into English.* ☎ *(9) 923-9674.* Every night under the same stars studied by the Maya, the pyramids recover their color under the lights. Accompanied by the sounds of the ancient *tunkul* (tree-drum) and the *soot* (maracas), the drama and tragedy of ancient Uxmal is narrated. "Chac, Chac, Chac...," once more the people implore the gods for rain. The story is told of how Sac Nicté, daughter of the king of Mayapán, was abducted by the ruler of Chichén Itzá just before her wedding to the prince of Uxmal. Apparently, this crime unleashed a civil war that caused the gods and the people to abandon Uxmal.

EXCURSION

★**La Ruta Puuc** – *23km/14mi from Uxmal. Description p 322.*

PRACTICAL INFORMATION ....Area Code 9

Getting There – By Plane: Cancun International Airport is serviced by major international airlines with nonstop flights from major US and European cities; domestic and some US airlines provide service to Mérida International Airport with connecting flights to Cozumel and Chetumal. Taxi service and car rental agencies are available at all airports.

By Bus: Bus terminals in the main cities provide transportation to tourist sights in the region. For information on destinations, rates and schedules: Campeche, ADO ☎ 811-2381; Cancun, ADO ☎ 886-8610; Chetumal, Omnitur del Caribe ☎ 832-7889; Mérida, ADO ☎ 924-9518.

By Car: Main roads throughout the Yucatán Peninsula are paved and in good condition. Driving in the Yucatán Peninsula is safe but travelers are advised to make sure their vehicle is in good working condition, because roads outside major towns and tourist areas may be deserted. An eight-lane highway (toll) connects Mérida with Cancun. Route 307 runs from Cancun to Tulum (4 lanes). Car rental agencies are located in major tourist areas; it is recommended to reserve a car in advance.

By Boat: Passenger and car ferry service from Cancun to **Isla Mujeres** – points of departure: Puerto Juárez, Marítima Magaña ☎ 877-0618 *(daily, every 30min, between 6am & 9pm; 30min one way; P$22/pers)*; Playa Tortugas, Cruceros Marítimos del Caribe ☎ 834-3583 *(4 departures daily, 9:15am–3:45pm; 45min one way; P$130 round trip; 4 return trips 10am–5pm; or one–day trip in Barco Carnaval; departs at 9am, returns at 5pm; P$320/pers)*; Punta Sam, Naviera Contoy ☎ 877-0065 *(cars and passengers, 5 departures daily 8am–8:15pm; 40min one way; P$12.50/pers or P$130/car and driver; 5 return trips 6:30am–7:15pm)*. Cancun to **Cozumel** – points of departure: Playa Tortugas *(meeting place to travel by land to Playa del Carmen or by sea to Cozumel; daily 8:45am–11:30am; 1 3/4hrs one way; P$150 round trip, returns at 6pm)*; Puerto Morelos ☎ 871-0008 *(recommended for those traveling by car; three departures daily 5am–5pm; 2 1/2hrs one way; P$550/car and driver)*. Playa del Carmen, Cruceros Marítimos del Caribe 872-1508 *(14 departures daily 5am–11pm; 45min one way; P$102 for round trip; 14 return trips 4am–10pm)*. International cruise ships (Celebrity, Cunard, Royal Caribbean, Norwegian, Holland America Line) dock at Cozumel and Playa del Carmen.

Tourist Information – For more information on hotels, a list of travel agencies and tour operators, as well as maps and brochures, contact tourist offices listed below or *http://www.wotw.com/Mundo Maya.*

		☎
Campeche: Secretaría de Turismo del Estado	Plaza Moch Couoh, City Center, Camp., C.P. 24000	816-6767
Mérida: Módulo de Información Turística	Calle 60, between 57 & 59, City Center, Yuc., C.P. 97000	924-9290
Cancun: Secretaría de Turismo del Estado	Av. Tulum, 26, City Center, Q. Roo, C.P. 77500	884-8073
Chetumal: Oficina de Turismo	Calz. del Centenario, 622, Col. del Bosque, Q. Roo, C.P. 77010	832-8661

Consulate offices provide assistance to its citizens in these locations:

			☎
US Consulate	Cancun	*Open Mon–Fri 9am–2pm & 3–6pm*	884-2411
Canadian Consulate	Cancun	*open Mon–Fri 11am–1pm*	884-6716
Consulate of the United Kingdom	Mérida	*open Mon–Fri*	928-6152

Accommodations – Most major hotel chains and resorts can be found in the Yucatán region. Hotels with numerous properties near archaeological sites and beaches include Mayaland Resorts ☎ 925-0621 and (800) 235-4079 (US); Misión Park Plaza Internacional ☎ 52-07-07-68 or (01-800) 900-3800 (Mexico City). Resorts favored by families with children: Club Med located on a secluded beach close to Cancun; for rates and reservations ☎ 885-2300; Calinda Cancun/Choice Hotels International ☎ (800) 221-2222 (US and Canada).

Mexico Accommodations ☎ (800) 262-4500 (US) and ☎ (800) 654-5543 (Canada) offers a wide range of condominiums and villas. Luxury suites, villas or individual hotel rooms are offered at four properties at Cancun's beaches through Vacation Club Rentals, San Antonio, TX, ☎ (210) 826-1753 or (800) 531-7211 (US and Canada) or *www.mexonline.com/vcr.htm.* Reservations are suggested, especially during high season *(Dec-March)* when rates are higher. For the budget-minded traveler, hostels associated with Hostelling International *(p 397)* are located in Campeche ☎ 816-1802, Chetumal ☎ 832-3465 and Playa del Carmen ☎ 873-1508. These places also offer cabins *(P$180/double occupancy and P$240/4 people)*. For **weather** and **time zones** *(pp 391 and 399)*.

Recreation – A wide variety of **water sports**, including deep-sea fishing, water-skiing and sailing, can be enjoyed. The coral reef off Isla Mujeres is perfect for scuba diving and snorkeling. Many hotels can arrange excursions that include transportation, equipment and instruction. **Cancun:** Parque Nizuc ☎ 881-3000, Aqua Tours ☎ 883-0400, Aqua World ☎ 885-2288; **Cozumel:** Dzul-Ha Water Sports ☎ 872-1385. To swim with dolphins: Xcaret *(p 305)* and Dolphin Discovery, Isla Mujeres ☎ 883-0777.

Local travel agencies and many hotels arrange excursions to nearby islands, archaeological sites, monasteries and other attractions: Uniterra, Cancun ☎ 884-8606; Gray Line Bus Tours, Cancun ☎ 886-7901 or (800) 235-4079 (US); Turismo Bolontikú, Mérida ☎ 928-1480 also offers excursions to the Puuc Route, the Monastery Route and Kabah. Contact Picaz in Campeche ☎ 816-4426 for trips to **Edzná**. To visit **Chicanná**, **Xpuhil** and **Ruta Río Bec**, as well as **Dzibanché** and **Kinichná**: Agencia Ecoturística Xcalak, Chetumal ☎ 832-1661. For **Ecotourism and Adventure Tourism** *(p 401)*.

Organized all-inclusive tours led by knowledgeable guides to archaeological sites are offered by Far Horizons, P.O. Box 91900, Albuquerque, NM 87199; ☎ (800) 552-4575 or *www.farhorizon.com.*

Handicrafts and markets – **Campeche:** Casa de Artesanías Tukulna ☎ 816-9088 (ceramics, textiles, Panama hats and a selection of handicrafts from around the state). **Cancun:** Mercado de Artesanías. **Mérida:** El Tixcocob ☎ 928-6210 (hammocks and handicrafts); El Aguacate ☎ 923-1838 (hammocks and handicrafts); El Becaleño (Panama hats); for textiles, hammocks and traditional wares: Casa de las Artesanías del Gobierno del Estado de Yucatán ☎ 928-6676; Mercado García Rejón and Bazar Lucas de Galves.

Semana Santa en Zunil

Guatemala

LAND OF COLORFUL MAGIC

Guatemala, a country with a diverse geography and myriad ecosystems, is located in the northwestern part of Central America, southeast of Mexico. With its varied climate, this country not only offers visitors its marvelous natural riches, but also the uniqueness of its syncretic customs, kept alive by indigenous peoples with magical and colorful ancestral traditions.

It is common to observe religious ceremonies in which copal smoke envelops the rituals and their participants, thus creating a mystical ambiance. The attractive colors of the native costumes present a vivid contrast with Guatemala's green forests and jungles, as well as its white mist in the highlands.

The inhabitants of these territories still preserve their ancient customs and languages. Guatemala is the land of the quetzal, the exotic national bird of soft, iridescent green and red plumage. The warmth of Guatemala's inhabitants is present in their friendly smiles, a clear manifestation of their overflowing hospitality.

335

Geographical Notes

Across its 108,899sq km/67,517.5sq mi extends a chain of towering mountains belonging to two systems: the **Sierra Madre** and the **Cordillera de los Cuchumatanes**. Whereas the former runs parallel to the Pacific Coast, the latter intersects the country through the middle and reaches the Caribbean Sea.

Over 30 volcanoes dot the country. The highest and most impressive are **Pacaya** (2,552m/8,371ft), south of Lake Amatitlán; **Agua** (3,765m/12,349ft), 16km/10mi from La Antigua Guatemala; and **Acatenango** (3,975m/13,038ft) and **Fuego** (3,763m/12,343ft), both to the west of La Antigua. **Tolimán** (3,134m/10,280ft), **Atitlán** (3,536m/11,598ft) and **San Pedro** (3,020m/9,906ft) surround Lake Atitlán.

Guatemala has two river drainage systems delineated by the mountains: one with an outlet to the Pacific Ocean, the other to the Caribbean Sea. The most important rivers flowing into the Pacific Ocean are the Suchiate, Naranjo, Samalá, Michatoya, Paz and Esclavos. Those flowing into the Caribbean Sea are Polochic, Rio Dulce, Motagua and Sarstún. The Petén region includes the rivers **Usumacinta** (which forms a natural border with Mexico), Pasión, Salinas and the Rio Azul, marvelous for rafting or fishing.

Diego Molina/Guatemala Tourist Commision

Quetzal

Fauna and Flora – Its wooded canopy covers 44,600sq km/27,652sq mi, representing 41% of the national territory. These forests are divided into coniferous, mixed and wide-leafed areas, the last two being the most abundant. Guatemala also boasts a tropical forest and a region of mangrove swamps. Guatemalan fauna is diverse, and many species that are at risk of becoming extinct are found in protected areas. **Manatees, crocodiles** and **otters** inhabit the mangrove region of the Rio Dulce, in the department of Izabal and the Biotopo Chocón Machacas reserve. Likewise, **pumas** and **jaguars** inhabit the protected Petén region. **Spider monkeys** and **howler monkeys** tranquilly roam the National Park of Tikal, with 300 registered species of birds, ranging from **hummingbirds** to enormous birds of prey. Reptiles, especially serpents, also inhabit this region of Guatemala. There is a natural park dedicated to the conservation of the **quetzal**; this park is located in the municipality of Purulhá, in the department of Baja Verapaz. The Biotopo Mario Dary Rivera, one of Guatemala's misty forests covers 1,253ha/3,096 acres, home to a variety of broad-leafed conifers, as well as orchids, mosses and ferns. Due to the richness of its natural resources, the conservation of its ecosystems and its pleasant climate, Guatemala has been referred to as the "Land of Eternal Spring."

Historical Notes

Pre-Hispanic Era – While vestiges of Maya civilization dating back to 2000 BC have been found in Guatemala, Mayan origins may date back even further to 3113 BC, according to the Maya's own system of recording time. The Maya culture lasted nearly thirty centuries and reached its peak in the Classic period (AD 100–800).

The Conquest of America – When the Spaniards, led by **Captain Pedro de Alvarado**, reached Guatemala in 1524, they only found indigenous groups that were heirs of the Maya culture: the Quichés, Cakchiquels, Tzutuhils, Kekchís, Pokomams, Mams and Chortís.

After having pacified the natives of Soconusco, Pedro de Alvarado, known for his cruelty against the natives, launched a bloody battle against the Quichés in Quetzaltenango. Later on, he selected the capital city of the Cakchiquels' kingdom as the place to establish the first Spanish city. However, the Cakchiquels rebelled against the conquistadors and drove them out of the city, by then known as Santiago de Guatemala (see Guatemala City).

■ The Legend of Tecún Umán

The ancient Maya believed that each human being had a corresponding spiritual animal, called *nahual*. The *nahual* had to be protected because any harm to it would also endanger its human counterpart. However, the law also applied inversely, as was the case of the indigenous hero, Tecún Umán, who during a terrible battle against the conquistadors was wounded in the chest by a lance and, consequently, died. The chest of a quetzal flying nearby also became red, and the bird and warrior died simultaneously.

Colonial Era and Independence – In 1542, the **Audiencia de los Confines** (High Court of the Horizon) was created. This high court ruled over all the provinces, from the Isthmus of Tehuantepec in Mexico to that of Darién in Panama, that is, the entire area known today as Central America. In 1564 the Audiencia was annulled and the provinces were annexed to the Viceroyalty of New Spain (present-day Mexico), until the high court was reactivated in 1568.

Two hundred years later, in the 18C, King Charles III of Spain granted some privileges to the commerce of the **Capitanía General** (Captaincy General), which caused the textile and **cochineal** (a natural red dye) industries to flourish. However, when the king died, his son Charles IV rescinded the reforms. The new provisions caused the decline of the textile industry, resulting in a large number of unemployed and infuriated townspeople. All this, along with news of the independence movements in the Americas at the beginning of the 19C, promoted a spirit of struggle for independence, which reached its culmination on September 15, 1821.

However, Independence encouraged some of the provinces to proclaim their autonomy, which brought about chaos. Thus, Iturbide, the newly self-appointed emperor of Mexico, tried to protect the **ancient Kingdom of Guatemala**, but when he was defeated, the provinces declared their independence from Mexico. Since then, Chiapas (formerly part of Guatemala) was integrated as a state into Mexican territory, while the rest of the territories formed the **Provincias Unidas de Centroamérica** (United Provinces of Central America).

The Nineteenth Century – During the first half of the 19C, the states of the newly created federation became independent in five countries: Guatemala, El Salvador, Honduras, Nicaragua and Costa Rica (Panama was a Colombian territory until the end of the 19C). From 1838 to 1871, the conservatives, who sought a return to colonial ways, governed Guatemala. This period is known as the **Thirty Years' Government**, during which a treaty was signed with England ceding it the territory of Belize in exchange for its help in the construction of a highway.

Guatemala Today

Area	108,899sq km/42,500sq mi, divided into 22 departments
Population	8,331,874 (10,517,448 est. 1997), with 23 Mayan indigenous groups and the Garífunas in the Caribbean.
Time Zone	GMT – 6
Languages	Spanish (official), 23 indigenous dialects (Quiché, Cakchiquel and Mam are the most important). The Garífunas speak Creole.
Capital	Guatemala City
Government	Democratic, representative, federal republic, with three powers: Executive, Legislative and Judicial
Religion	Catholic; indigenous groups practice syncretic rituals; Protestant and Evangelical
Climate	Generally mild, with a temperature of about 20°C/68°F year-round; in the coastal areas, the temperature reaches up to 37°C/99°F; in the mountainous areas, it falls below freezing point. **Precipitation:** varies from 500mm/19.5in to 5,000mm/195in annually, **rainy season:** May–October, especially in the afternoons and at night.
Economy	Agriculture and tourism; **primary exports:** coffee, plantains, corn, beans, cotton and cacao. Textile manufacturing industry remains very important.

When to Go

The **climate** varies according to the altitude and region; the coast and the north are hot year-round, while the highlands have a milder climate. Humid conditions prevail in the tropical regions. The average temperatures are 24°C/75°F (high) and 13°C/55°F (low). The **rainy season** extends from May to October. Peak tourist season is from November to May. Temperatures are fairly cold at night.

Planning Your Trip

Citizens of the US, Canada, Mexico, the European Union, Central America and South America need a valid **passport** and a return ticket. Citizens of other countries, and visitors planning to stay over 30 days, may need a **visa**. Regulations on travel documents change frequently and without prior notice. It is strongly recommended to consult with the Guatemalan Embassy in your country of origin before traveling. **A word of caution:** Due to possible guerrilla activity, it is advisable to check with local authorities before venturing into remote areas. **Vaccines** are not mandatory; however, in some regions malaria is found in areas with elevations below 1,500m/4,920ft. When traveling in the jungle, apply insect **repellent** with DEET. The water in Guatemala City is drinkable, but in other regions only bottled water is recommended.

Getting There

By Plane – **La Aurora International Airport:** 7km/4.3mi south of Guatemala City. Major international airlines fly into this airport. Tourist information booth (near the immigration office) ☎ 331-4256 *(Mon–Fri 6am–9pm; Sat–Sun 8am–8pm)*; foreign currency exchange office *(daily 6am–7pm)*, and car rental agencies. Transportation to downtown: by bus, on the first level *(every 30 minutes, Q$1)* and taxis *(Q$40)*. Some international airlines fly into the **Santa Elena Airport** (Petén region); car rental available. Many landing strips offer service by **domestic airlines:** Aeroquetzal ☎ 337-3469; Inter Grupo Taca ☎ 361-2144; Aerovías ☎ 334-7935; Tapsa ☎ 331-4860; Tikal Jets ☎ 332-5070; Mayan World ☎ 339-1519, as well as numerous charter companies. Service between **Guatemala and Belize:** Aviateca ☎ 334-7722 with a stop in El Salvador, and Aerovías ☎ 334-7935. Early arrival at the airport is advisable for departures. Upon leaving Guatemala, passengers must pay an **airport tax** *(USD$20)*.

By Car – Coming from **Mexico**, point of entry is through San Cristóbal de las Casas and Tapachula; coming from **Belize**, through the Yucatán Peninsula. The Pan-American Highway, from Mexico to El Salvador, goes through Guatemala. Many other highways connect Honduras and El Salvador with Guatemala.

By Boat – International cruises from Barrops in the Caribbean, as well as in Puerto Quetzal on the Pacific Ocean, dock in Guatemala.

Getting Around

By Car and Taxi – Major highways are paved and generally in good condition. INGUAT sells maps showing locations of gasoline stations. There are fewer **gas stations** on less traveled roads; thus, it is advisable to take extra gasoline, as well as water and basic tools. Secondary roads are gravel and difficult to pass, especially during heavy rains. The road from Guatemala City to the Petén region is difficult to navigate, and traveling by bus can take up to 24 hours. Traveling after sunset is not advisable. **Avis**, **Budget**, **Dollar**, **Hertz** and **National** have offices in Guatemala City. Local companies offer car rentals in big cities and in tourist areas. Advance reservations are recommended. A valid driver's license and a credit card are required. Costs start at USD$40 daily, with unlimited mileage, plus a 10% tax. **Taxis** available in Guatemala City are Yellow taxis ☎ 332-1515 and Corporación Blanco Rotativo ☎ 444-0959. They may also be rented by the hour.

By Bus – Buses in Guatemala City are numerous and inexpensive, but crowded. Buses to other regions generally depart very early in the morning. First-class buses connect to some cities with tourist areas. Contact INGUAT for routes and schedules.

By Train – The Pacific route extends from Guatemala City to Tecún Umán, near the border with Mexico. There is another route that extends to Puerto Barrios on the Caribbean coast. Traveling by train is inexpensive, but trains offer few modern conveniences and the trip may take longer than a bus trip.

General Information

Tourist Information – The **Guatemalan Tourist Commission (INGUAT)** Séptima Avenida 1–17, Zona 4, Civic Center, 01004 Guatemala ☏ 331-1333 or 1-801-464-8281 (in Guatemala) and 1-888-464-8281 (from the US) or *www.guatemala.travel.com.gt (Mon–Fri 8am–4pm, Sat 8am–1pm)* provides information and brochures on lodging, transportation, shopping, entertainment, tour guides and travel agencies.

INGUAT maintains offices in the following countries: ☏

Canada	ACA, 72 McGill St., Toronto ON M5B 1H2	16-348-8597
UK	3 Fawcett St., London SW10	171-351-3042
US	299 Alhambra Circ., Ste. 510, Coral Gables FL 33134	305-442-0651

Accommodations – Guatemala offers a wide range of accommodations, from international hotel chains in Guatemala City and tourist areas, to small family establishments in big cities. Ranging from guesthouses to rustic huts with thatched roofs, accommodations in the interior are more modest. In remote areas, running water and electricity may be restricted from 10pm–6am. Hotels charge an additional 20% hotel tax. Credit card payments may be limited to big cities. For a listing of the establishments, contact INGUAT. **Camp grounds** abound throughout the country.

Banking, Foreign Exchange, Credit Cards, Taxes and Tips – The local currency is the **Quetzal**. Banco del Quetzal, Lloyd's Bank and Banco Internacional de Guatemala *(open Mon–Fri 9am–3pm)* accept foreign currency and traveler's checks. Airlines, hotels and restaurants in Guatemala City accept credit cards (American Express, Diner's Club, MasterCard/EuroCard and Visa), as well as traveler's checks. **American Express Agent:** Banco del Café, Avenida de la Reforma 9-00 ☏ 234-7463. When traveling to the interior, visitors should carry Guatemalan currency. A 10% **value-added tax (VAT)** is levied on most goods and services. Hotels charge a 20% room tax. A 10% **tip** is customary in restaurants.

Sightseeing – Organized tours are the easiest way to discover a country. Guatemala Clark Tours, Guatemala City, ☏ 339-2888, offers tours on air-conditioned buses with English-speaking tour guides. Unitours, Guatemala City, ☏ 231-4166, organizes archaeological and ecological trips, nature trips, and fishing trips, with multilingual guides. A boat trip through the subtropical ecosystem at the **Biotopo Monterrico** offers the possibility of **birdwatching** in the mangroves and lagoons. Farther north lies the Iztapa Spa. To arrange a **guided walking tour** of Antigua, contact: Antigua Tours ☏ 832-0140 *(year-round Mon–Sat, English & Spanish; USD$15; reservations required)*. Fly to Flores and take the paved road to Tikal National Park. Transportation via buses or mini-vans can be arranged locally. There are many hotels in Flores, but accommodations in the National Park are limited. Book well in advance, especially during high season (Nov–May). Other **archaeological sites** are within easy reach; check with your hotel or local tour agencies. Far Horizons, PO Box 91900, Albuquerque, NM 87199, ☏ 505-343-9400, 800-552-4575 (US & Canada) or *www.farhorizon.com*, and Holbrook Travel, Inc. 3540 NW 13th St., Gainesville, FL 32609 ☏ 352-377-7111 or 800-451-7111 (US & Canada) offer **escorted tours**.

Recreation – Water-skiing, **swimming** and boating are popular forms of recreation in Guatemala. In the central mountains, **rafting** and spelunking (cave exploration) appeal to visitors and locals alike. Hire the services of an outfitter to enjoy rafting excursions on the Motagua and Cabón rivers (Nov–May). Maya Expeditions, 15 Calle 1–91, Zona 10, Guatemala City, Guatemala ☏ 363-4955, specializes in all-inclusive rafting, **volcano climbing** and nature travel weekend trips, including transportation, lodging, tour guide and equipment. Ecotourism specialists offer all-inclusive white-water rafting and **kayak** expeditions to the jungle, lasting from weekend trips to two-week excursions. For schedules and reservations contact Area Verde Expeditions, 4a. Avenida Sur, 8, Antigua, ☏ 832-38-63 or 507 McClelland Ave., Pueblo, CO 81005; ☏ (719) 564-4944 (US) or *www.areaverde.com*.

Useful Numbers – Police ☏ 120; Fire Department/Ambulance ☏ 123; Assistance Directory (local) ☏ 1524; Long-distance Operator ☏ 1671.

National Holidays

New Year's Day	Jan 1	Revolution Day	Oct 20
Maundy Thu., Good Fri.	Mar–Apr	All Saints' Day	Nov 1
Labor Day	May 1	Christmas Eve	Dec 24
Army Day	June 30	Christmas Day	Dec 25
Independence Day	Sept 15	New Year's Eve	Dec 31

Dictators and the Twentieth Century – The Thirty Years' Government ended due to the revolution of 1871, which gave way to the **Reform** period under the administration of Miguel García Granados who created the national flag and coat of arms. **Justo Rufino Barrios**, García Granados' successor, ended privileges to enroll in the university, expropriated the church's possessions, suppressed monastic orders and proclaimed the Constitution of 1879.

The years that followed were full of turmoil, given that presidents gained office through coups d'état and used force to become reelected. Thus, two major dictators emerged: **Manuel Estrada Cabrera** (in power from 1898 to 1920) and **General Jorge Ubico** (in power from 1931 to 1944). The latter was defeated by the popular movement unleashed in 1944 by university students and professors, under the leadership of Jorge Toriello, Francisco J. Arana and Jacobo Arbenz. These men formed a government junta and proclaimed the new constitution in 1945.

The Arbenz Administration – In 1950, for the first time, power was peacefully surrendered to a new president, **Jacobo Arbenz**. His administration was characterized by an openly hostile attitude toward the United States and US companies operating in Guatemala, especially toward the **United Fruit Company**. Two years later, he issued a new agrarian law, which drastically affected landholders. In 1954, Carlos Castillo Armas, a general who sought asylum in Honduras, gained the support of the Honduran governor and that of the US to invade Guatemala that same year, forcing Arbenz to leave office. Upon assuming the presidential office, Castillo Armas abolished the Constitution of 1945 and Arbenz's agrarian law.

Modern Era – In the 1960s and 70s, Guatemala underwent permanent revolts, while Central America was shaken by the civil war in El Salvador and later that of Nicaragua. Throughout these years, diverse military officers, including Fernando Romero Lucas, Aníbal Guevara and Ríos Montt, succeeded each other into office until 1980, when the second civil government in 40 years, headed by **Vinicio Cerezo**, regained the presidency. In recent years the "Land of Eternal Spring" has witnessed the bloodstaining of its countryside, as a result of the civil war that was unleashed in the provinces, where the primary victims were indigenous groups who represented 80% of the entire population. Repression and continuous persecutions forced millions of these people, as well as some farmers, to seek refuge in Mexico.

In the last decade of the 20C, the aim was to reconcile the differences between the guerrillas and the government, and although the dialogue was often severed, a peace treaty was finally signed on **December 29, 1996**, allowing thousands of refugees to return to their homeland.

Culture

Outstanding Figures – Among the illustrious people of the colony were **Fray Bartolomé de las Casas**, great defender of the indigenous peoples, as well as Brother **Pedro**

de Betancourt, a Franciscan who dedicated his life to helping the poor. Bishop **Francisco Marroquín** founded the first school of Spanish letters and donated his estate upon his death, with the objective of creating a university. Father **Rafael Landívar** was a great poet of the 18C. One of the most famous sculptors of the era was **Quirio Cataño**, creator of the *Cristo de Esquipulas (Christ of Esquipulas)*, located in one of the most important religious centers in Central America. In the 19C, noteworthy figures included painter **Francisco Cabrera** and writer **José Milla**, author of *La hija del Adelantado* (in which he recounts the history of Pedro de Alvarado).

The most outstanding writers of the 20C are **Miguel Ángel Asturias** (1899–1974), awarded the Nobel Literature Prize in 1967, **Luis Cardoza y Aragón**, (1904–92) and **Augusto Monterroso** (b.1921). Most prominent in the fine arts are painter **Carlos Mérida** and **Efraín Recinos** (architect, sculptor and painter). **Rigoberta Menchú Tum** was awarded the Nobel Peace Prize (1992) in recognition for her humanitarian work.

Handicrafts – An important element of the economy, the textiles of Guatemala, as well as its clay ceramics, basketry, straw hats, fabrics and woodcarvings, are renowned worldwide.

Food – Like in Mexico, **tortillas** and **frijoles** (beans) are basic staples of the Guatemalan diet. The typical dishes are **rellenitos**, fried plantains filled with sweet beans or with a mixture prepared with milk and sugar; **chuchitos**, little tamales with meat or herbs, such as chipilín; **dobladas**, small tortillas stuffed with chicken or beef and vegetables; **fiambre**, a sample of cold meats and vegetables, prepared especially for the Day of the Dead (All Saints' Day); and **ponche de frutas**, a fruit beverage prepared during the Christmas season. Also popular are **atol de elote** (a hot beverage prepared with cornmeal gruel) and **beef tamales**. While a variety of international restaurants can be found in Guatemala's major cities, Guatemala City abounds with Chinese restaurants due to the strong Chinese influence in that city's economy.

World Heritage Sites

City of ANTIGUA GUATEMALA (1979)

TIKAL Archaeological Site (1979)

COPÁN Archaeological Site
(1980, located in Honduras)

QUIRIGUÁ Archaeological Site (1985)

Traditional Music and Dance – Guatemala's traditional dances correspond to each of the 22 ethnic groups that comprise most of the Guatemalan population. Generally, they are performed during holidays or during religious rituals. Each ethnic group wears a special costume that distinguishes it from the other groups, and specific costumes on festive days.

The **Ballet** of the Guatemalan Tourist Commission (INGUAT) customarily presents the traditional dances of the entire country at the Miguel Angel Asturias Cultural Center (in Guatemala City).

Guatemala's traditional music includes the indispensable **marimba** (an instrument that resembles a large xylophone with a wooden keyboard). Radio stations also play popular music, characterized by tropical or contemporary rhythms.

Six Days in Guatemala

Day 1

Guatemala City – Flights from Mexico City, Cancun, Belize and other international areas service Guatemala City.

Days 2 and 3

Tikal – Located 548km/340mi north of Guatemala City, in the Petén region, Tikal can be accessed by plane from Guatemala City (30min), Cancun, Belize and other international points.

Days 4 and 5

Antigua Guatemala – Located 45km/28mi west of Guatemala City, in the department of Sacatepéquez. Tour buses departing from Guatemala City service Antigua.

Day 6

Lake Atitlán – Located 80km/50mi west of Antigua Guatemala, in the department of Sololá. Tour buses departing from Antigua service Lake Atitlán.

La ANTIGUA GUATEMALA★★★

Department of Sacatepéquez
Population 34,168
Map p 341 – City Map p 346
Palacio de los Capitanes Generales, Plaza Central ☎ 832-0763

This magnificent city was designated as a World Heritage Site in 1979, for its majestic constructions, today in ruins, which enhance the natural beauty of the valley, along with the three volcanoes surrounding it (Agua, Fuego and Acatenango). Together they form a breathtaking natural **landscape★**.

Historical Notes – Antigua is the third Spanish capital of Central America and was established by the Spaniards after the terrible flood of Almolonga on September 11, 1541. Founded in 1543 and named **Ciudad de Santiago de los Caballeros de Guatemala** in 1566, this city has always been struck by misfortune—which may explain the sturdiness of its buildings and the pride of its inhabitants. Following plagues, earthquakes, eruptions and floods, the earthquake known as the Telluric Movement of 1773 finally destroyed the city. Despite having been banished and abandoned for the creation of a new capital (see Guatemala City), the city was brought back to life gradually. Today its truly colonial flavor makes Antigua one of Guatemala's main tourist attractions.

★PLAZA MAYOR AND SURROUNDINGS

45km/28mi west of Guatemala City. Take Av. Roosevelt west (which later becomes the Carr. Panamericana CA-1); at km 29, take the exit (the bridge to the right) to San Lucas Sacatepéquez and follow that road to La Antigua.

Plaza Mayor – *In the plaza formed by 5a and 4a Av. and 5a and 4a Calle.* This angular, tree-filled esplanade boasts in its center the beautiful **Fuente del Conde de La Gomera** or **Conde de las Sirenas (1)**. Count de La Gomera commissioned the fountain in remembrance of the popular legend about a king whose daughters gave birth and did not want to nurse their babies. As punishment, the king ordered they be tied to a pole in the middle of a freshwater spring, where they died of thirst and hunger. Ironically, the fountain's four mermaids, portrayed holding their breasts in their hands, served as a water source for the city.

Mercado de Artesanía – *6a Av. Sur and 4a Calle Poniente, one street from Plaza Mayor. Open year-round daily 10am–6pm.* Visitors to Antigua flock here to buy a great number of handicrafts-from textiles, sculptures and toys to leather goods, which, piled up in a variety of shapes and colors, provide a feast for the eyes.

Palacio de los Capitanes Generales – *South of Plaza Mayor. Open year-round daily 8am–5pm.* This beautiful building with double archways, formed by sturdy Tuscan columns, gave lodging to the king's representatives in this region during the 17C and 18C. At present, the upper level houses governmental offices, while tourist information offices occupy the lower level.

Palacio del Ayuntamiento – *On the north side of Plaza Mayor.* Constructed in 1743 to house the city council, like the Palace of the Captains General, this building boasts a double archway of carved stone. Due to its sturdy construction the edifice once served as a prison. Guatemala's first printing shop was established here. Today it is home to City Hall and the tourist police offices. The small **Museo Santiago** *(in the lower level of the palace; open year-round Tue–Fri 9am–4pm, Sat–Sun 9am–noon and 2–4pm; donations accepted; ☎ 832-2868)* holds a collection of weapons, paintings, sculptures and furniture of the colonial era. On one side is the **Museo del Libro Antiguo** *(open year-round Tue–Fri 9am–4pm, Sat–Sun noon and 2pm–4pm; Q$10)*, which exhibits first editions of 16C to 18C books and facsimile copies of literary works printed in Guatemala. Its collection includes the first book printed in Guatemala, as well as important texts documenting academic achievements of that period. Also featured is a fragment of the original *Catholicon* printed by Gutenberg in 1460.

Catedral Metropolitana – *On the east side of Plaza Mayor. Open year-round daily 9am–noon and 2–5pm. Q$2.* ☎ 832-0909. Inaugurated in 1680, this cathedral can be seen from the Plaza Mayor. Its elaborate Baroque facade created in white stucco presents a style characteristic of Antiguan churches. It consists of columns with smooth shafts, a main body, and a belfry that had to be reconstructed after the earthquake of 1773.
Behind the cathedral lie the ruins of the previous structure. These include the dome's columns and **pendentives★**, decorated with carved angels. From here, one can also access the catacombs found in the basement of the ruins.

★★Museo de Arte Colonial (M) – *5a Calle Oriente, 5, to the south side of the cathedral. Open year-round Tue–Fri 9am–4pm, Sat–Sun 9am–noon and 2–4pm. Q$25.* ☎ 832-0429. The museum is located in the former headquarters of the University of San Carlos de Borromeo, founded in 1767. Since then it has preserved its beautiful **courtyard★** with an arcade clearly reminiscent of the Mudejar style combined with elements of classic Baroque typical of Antigua, such as its pierced columns. The museum exhibits religious paintings of the 18C, as well as sculptures of the 17C and 18C. Most noteworthy are four beautiful **paintings★** portraying Jesus' appearance before Herod, His arrival before Pilate, His selection for the Crucifixion, and one of the falls from Passion. Room 6 displays an excellent **collection★** of paintings by Cristóbal de Villalpando.

■ Guatemala's Volcanoes

Besides its cultural wealth, Guatemala offers diverse natural attractions, such as its spectacular volcanoes. The Land of Eternal Spring is home to 324 eruptive peaks, of which only 32 rank as volcanoes. Among the best known, **Pacaya** measures 2,552m/8,371ft and has a secondary duct called "Mackenney Peak," which is currently active.

Other awe-inspiring volcanoes include **Acatenango** (3,976m/13,041ft), located between the departments of Chimaltenango and Sacatepéquez; **Fuego** (3,763m/12,343ft), which displays impressive eruptions but cannot be visited because its summit is covered with lava; and **Agua**, or Hunapú, with an elevation of 3,766m/12,352ft.

Some of the lesser known, but no less beautiful, are **San Pedro**, **Ipala**-located in the department of Jutiapa-with a green crater lake, **Suchitán** and **Tecuamburro**, which forms part of a series of three volcanoes-**Tecuamburro**, **Miraflores** and **Soledad**, highly recommended for its vegetation and for the sulphur fumaroles in its foothills.

To climb any of these volcanoes, one must be in good physical condition, and it is advisable to visit as part of an excursion led by an experienced guide from one of the specialized agencies, most of which are found in La Antigua.

★EX CONVENTO DE CAPUCHINAS AND SURROUNDINGS

Ex Convento de Capuchinas – *2a Av. Norte, between 2a and 1a Calle Poniente. Open year-round daily 9am–5pm. Q$10.* The city's last convent for nuns, whose real name was Nuestra Señora del Pilar de Zaragoza (Our Lady of the Pillar of Zaragoza), was completed in 1736 by Diego de Porres, principal architect of La Antigua Guatemala. Its interior features a circular courtyard with archways that marked the nuns' cells. This complex was known as Torre del Retiro (Retreat Tower). A second courtyard led to the main cloister and included a central fountain and archways formed by Tuscan columns. To the west, one street away, lie the ruins of the **Templo de Santa Teresa**.

Templo del Carmen – *3a Av. Norte, between 2a and 3a Calle Poniente. Open year-round daily 9am–5pm.* This church is a prime example of Baroque influence in La Antigua, particularly highlighted in its **facade★**, which stands out for its group of columns in both of the temple's main sections. Those in the second section still preserve their variegated ornamentation depicting plant motifs.

Ex Convento de Santa Catalina – *5a Av. Norte, between 2a and 1a Calle Poniente. Open year-round daily 9am–5pm.* The convent was built in 1613 and the church in 1647. Years later, there was a petition to close off the street and unite the property across the street with that of the nuns. Given the neighborhood's refusal, a passageway was constructed to connect the two buildings. The only original sections that still remain from the convent are some of its walls and this archway with its clock. At night it is illuminated and sheds a pleasing, orange light on the surrounding streets.

Iglesia de la Merced – *6a Av. Norte and 1a Calle Poniente. Open year-round Mon–Sat 6:30am–12:30pm and 3–8pm; Sun 6:30am–7:30pm.* This church was constructed in 1546 and was expanded in 1688 to include three naves. Destroyed in 1717 and repaired in 1765, the edifice was struck again by an earthquake in 1773. Its beautiful Baroque **facade★★** of white stucco covered with ivy is in aesthetically pleasing contrast with its yellow walls. The church's interior consists of a cruciform ground plan, columns with rectangular capitals, an apse with arches, and the base of a minor cupola with stonework in mixtilinear and plant motifs. The church's Baroque altarpieces were dismantled so they could be transported to a church of the same name in Guatemala City.

To the left side of the entrance, a similar facade gives way to part of what once was the convent. Here stands an imposing and beautiful **fountain★★** with a Baroque carved post and angels at the base of the water receptacle.

★Hotel Casa Santo Domingo – *3a Calle Oriente, 28.* ☎ *832-0140.* This magnificent hotel is located in what once functioned as the Convento de Santo Domingo (Monastery of St. Dominic), also destroyed by the 1773 earthquake. The hotel lobby boasts an 18C **anda** (a portable platform used during Holy Week processions to transport religious effigies), the sculpture of an archangel and a Baroque altarpiece. From the gardens, one can access the catacombs, where monks were buried. The underground Capilla del Calvario houses a beautiful **painting** of the Crucifixion with a sculpture of Christ in high relief, while the rest of the personages are painted on the wall. At night the hotel is illuminated by candlelight, giving it a mystical ambiance reminiscent of the colonial era.

Museo Arqueológico – *Open year-round daily 9am–4pm. Q$10 (includes admission to the convent's ruins and to the Museo Colonial).* Across from the ruins of the original monastery is this museum dedicated to exhibiting ceramic artifacts and Maya sculptures from Guatemala's south coast, high tableland and lowlands. Among the most notable are two Teotihuacán-style **censers**★ in the shape of a man with a great headdress. This section also displays polychrome bowls and basins, as well as clay figurines and colorful cups. Next to the museum, the **Casa de la Cera** (House of Wax) offers visitors a chance to observe the wax-making process.

Museo Colonial – *Open year-round daily 9am–6pm.* This museum houses a wonderful collection of Guatemalan works from the colonial period. The display includes wooden sculptures, silver artifacts and neo-Hispanic paintings. Among the most beautiful pieces is a sculpture of **San Miguel Arcángel**★, possibly from the 17C or 18C, made of flesh-colored wood covered in silver.

SAN FRANCISCO AND SURROUNDINGS

Casa Popenoe – *5a Calle Oriente and 1a Av. Sur. Open year-round Mon–Sat 2pm–4pm. Q$5.* This museum preserves furniture, miscellaneous objects, a kitchen and a lovely pigeon house that give it the ambiance of a 17–18C Antiguan home. Dr. Wilson Popenoe purchased the building in 1929 and restored it, thus allowing visitors the opportunity to appreciate an aristocratic mansion of that era. The current owners, relatives of Popenoe, have resumed the restoration work.

Ex Convento de Santa Clara – *6a Calle Oriente and 2a Av. Sur. Open year-round daily 9am–5pm. Q$10.* The convent was founded by nuns from Puebla, Mexico. Although its construction was begun in 1699, the church was not inaugurated until 1734. In spite of the 1773 earthquake, some parts of the convent remain intact, such as the **facade**★ and its cloister, with a lovely **garden**★ and fountain.

Hospital de San Pedro – *6a Calle Oriente and 3a Av. Sur. Open year-round daily 8am–noon and 3–6pm.* Founded in 1663, this hospital, still in use, was named in honor of Brother Pedro de Betancourt, who used it to help the poor.

Iglesia de San Francisco – *Calle de los Pasos and 7a Calle Oriente. Open year-round daily 6am–5:30pm.* The church was constructed in 1579. Surrounded by a wall with merlons, its western **portal** is noteworthy for its beautiful Solomonic bossed columns. Once inside the atrium, visitors can observe the main facade of the temple, which contains twelve niches. The interior, accessed by a side door, houses magnificent Baroque **altarpieces**★★ with mixtilinear figures, all gilded. The chapel preserves the body of the beloved Brother Pedro de Betancourt.

Ex Convento de Santa Clara and Iglesia de San Francisco

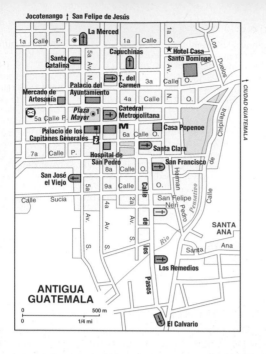

Calle de los Pasos – *From the Church of San Francisco to the Calvary.* This street is lined by the **chapels** where reenactments of the Passion of Christ are held during Holy Week's "Way of the Cross." Seven of the 14 chapels that comprise the procession and that are open to the public exclusively during these festivities are located here. Also gracing the street are the Templo y Convento de San Felipe Neri or Escuela de Cristo (School of Christ) and the 17C **Parroquia de los Remedios** (Parish Church of Remedies). At the end of the street stands the **Iglesia de El Calvario**, where the procession ends.

Iglesia de San José el Viejo – *5a Av. Sur, between the Callejón de San José and 9a Calle Oriente. Open year-round daily 9am–5pm.* Due to its small size this building, completed in 1761, is representative of Antiguan earthquake-resistant architecture. Its facade displays pierced pilasters and columns with fluted shafts. A hollow (recessed) tympanum constitutes the doorframe, while the belfry consists of two small bell towers and a choir window.

EXCURSIONS

Jocotenango – *2km/1.2mi northwest of La Antigua. Head northwest via La Calle Ancha de Los Herreros.* The small town of Jocotenango was founded in 1541 by former natives of Almolonga (Guatemala's second capital) who survived its destruction. Jocotenango's founders earned their livelihood through masonry and hog breeding. Today the town's plaza boasts the **Iglesia de Nuestra Señora de la Asunción** built in the 17C. The church's Baroque **facade** consists of beautiful Solomonic columns, four of which are pierced, as well as an octagonal choir window. Jocotenango was once the official delivery point of the mail pouch sent from New Spain (Mexico) to Guatemala. It also stood on the obligatory path of high-ranking religious figures traveling to the Captaincy General of the ancient Kingdom of Guatemala.

San Felipe de Jesús – *0.7km/0.4mi northwest of Jocotenango.* A pleasant town with a market of handicrafts and typical Guatemalan food, such as the famous **atol de elote**, **rellenitos** and **dobladas**. Visitors and members of the Church of San Felipe congregate at the food stands next to the church.

When planning your trip, consult the Practical Information section for travel tips, useful addresses and phone numbers, and information on sports and recreation, and annual events.

Lago de ATITLÁN★★

Department of Sololá
Map p 340

🏛 Calle Santander, Edificio Rincón Sai, Panajachel ☏ 762-1392

With a surface of 125sq km/77.5sq mi, at an elevation of 1,560m/5,117ft, Lake Atitlán is undoubtedly one of Guatemala's major natural attractions. The crystalline body of water was formed following a volcanic catastrophe over 85,000 years ago, in which an eruption erased every trace of life from southeastern Mexico to Costa Rica. In time, the water that had accumulated in the basin and that had been covered by lava began to flow from the newly formed volcanoes Tolimán, Atitlán and San Pedro. At present, 12 villages surround the lake. Of particular interest are Santa Catarina Palopó, Santiago Atitlán, San Lucas Tolimán, San Pedro La Laguna and Panajachel, with a spectacular **view★★** of the landscape comprised of blue skies and the silhouettes of the volcanoes. Especially beautiful in summer, orange shimmering sunsets enhance the view.

Take in the beautiful colors of the local indigenous costumes, noting the **tocado**, a long piece of woven material worn by many **Cakchiquels** around their heads.

© Edward Thomas

Lake Atitlán

SIGHT

Panajachel – *80km/50mi west of La Antigua. Take the road to Guatemala City. Upon reaching San Lucas (after 9km/5.6mi) take the exit to Chimaltenango, toward Los Encuentros. Once there, head toward Sololá; 9km/5.6mi past Sololá, on that same road, is Panajachel.* Most hotels and restaurants in the region are concentrated around this village. In addition to enjoying the tranquillity this place has to offer, tourists may go shopping at the handicrafts markets or browse through the street vendor stands. At night, explore the local entertainment scene at Panajachel's dance clubs and bars. To tour the villages around the lake, one can hire the services of a boat operator or take a direct boat to one of these villages.

■ Maximón, a saint out of this world

The tradition of worshipping St. Simon, known as Maximón or Maximom in Santiago Atitlán, came about during the 19C and is still practiced to this day. One of Guatemala's most comical saints, Maximón is characterized for his eagle nose and small stature. A wooden statue representative of the saint is clothed with whatever the townspeople gave him during Holy Week; Maximón usually wears up to five hats, one on top of the other, as well as handkerchiefs, sports coats and shirts. Within the syncretic tradition, he seems to be the only saint that receives *aguardiente* (a spirituous liquor), beer and cigars, as offerings in exchange for help in matters of health, love and wealth.

The villagers communicate with Maximón through a *cofradía* (brotherhood), thanks to the intervention of a *Sanjorín* or witch doctor, who with his prayers carries out the favors requested by petitioners. Petitions are made inside the brotherhood's house, in a mystical ambiance full of smoke, candles, flowers and fruit. Also accompanying Maximón are the other representatives of the brotherhood who console the petitioners.

This charming tradition is preserved thanks to the interest of the Tzutuhil community of Santiago Atitlán and to the respect of those tourists who silently observe the ceremony.

EXCURSIONS

From Chichicastenango to San Francisco el Alto

Chichicastenango – *37km/23mi north of Panajachel. Return to Los Encuentros and take the Carr. Nacional 15 to Chichicastenango.* Capital of the department of Quiché, Chichicastenango can be accessed from a modern road offering a breath-taking **view★★★** of the ever-green Guatemalan mountains. Full of enthusiasm and dressed in colorful traditional costumes, the natives of this village gather at the main plaza to sell their merchandise. The **market★★** of Chichicastenango *(open year-round Thu and Sun 8am–4pm)*, Guatemala's biggest and one of the most famous, is visited by indigenous groups from faraway villages, such as Santiago Atitlán. Also of interest is the **Iglesia de Santo Tomás** *(open year-round daily 7am–6pm)*, where vil-lagers practice **rituals★★** characteristic of the syncretism of Maya and Spanish cultures. Spectators should observe these rituals with the utmost respect.

Market, Chichicastenango

Quetzaltenango – *94km/58mi west of Chichicastenango. Return to Los Encuentros and take the Carr. Panamericana (CA-1) to Huehuetenango; drive for 60km/37mi, and upon reaching Cuatro Caminos, take the exit to Quetzaltenango, found 14km/8.7mi ahead (via the Carr. Nacional 1).* Located in the department of the same name, this city, also known by its Maya name, **Xela**, is situated in an exten-sive valley that still preserves the traditions of its Maya-Quiché population. Its main plaza, **Parque Centroamérica**, consists of well-kept gardens, as well as a semicircle of stylized columns. Surrounding the park are treasured buildings, such as the **Catedral**, whose facade is the only portion still standing, the **Casa de la Cultura** *(open year-round daily 8am–noon and 2–6pm; ☎ 761-4931)*, which also houses the tourism office, and the **Pasaje Enríquez**.

San Andrés Xecul – *14km/8.7mi northeast of Quetzaltenango. Go back 14km/8.7mi to return to Cuatro Caminos and at the gas station take a left turn onto the mountain ridge dirt road. Follow that road for 3km/1.9mi to the main plaza, where the church is located.* Falling within the jurisdiction of the depart-ment of Totonicapán, this small town holds perhaps the only sample of indigenous art molded on the impressive **facade★★** of its church (16C). The art features saints, angels, flowers and maize, in an array of colors combining blue, green and red with the temple's blazing yellow. Although its style is unique, the facade resem-bles the work, also indigenous art, of the Tonantzintla Church in Puebla, Mexico.

San Francisco el Alto – *22km/14mi northeast of San Andrés Xecul. Retake the dirt road heading back to San Andrés Xecul, and drive for 3km/1.9mi; then take the Carr. Nacional 1 to Cuatro Caminos (approx. 2km/1.2mi); from there, take the Carr. Panamericana (CA-1) and drive 7km/4.3mi to Huehuetenango; at the Totonicapán-San Francisco el Alto sign, turn right and continue straight on for 1km/0.6mi.* The peaceful town of San Francisco receives a multitude of visitors on Fridays, when various indigenous groups gather at the local **market★** *(open year-round Fri 3am–noon)* to sell their merchandise. The market is divided into sections ranging from the sale of animals and spices to furniture. Do not miss the **view**★ of this part of western Guatemala, as seen from the roof of the town's recently restored 16C **church** *(open year-round daily 6am–noon and 3–7pm; Q$1 to ascend to the roof on market day)*.

Zunil and Abaj Takalik

Zunil – *14km/8.7mi southeast of Quetzaltenango. Follow the Carr. Nacional 9S, also known as "the hot lands highway" ("la de tierra caliente") for 14km/8.7mi southeast, past Almolonga, to reach Zunil. Photo, p 334.* Inhabited mainly by indigenous peoples, Zunil is noted for the white stucco **facade** of its church *(open year-round daily 8am–noon and 2–6pm)* amidst a beautiful **view**★ of the misty mountains. The facade boasts exquisitely carved, bossed Solomonic columns, adorned with plant motifs in both sections, niches with sculptures, and intricate stone carvings with mixtilinear and plant motifs. The austere interior features a Baroque **altarpiece** in the high altar and an enormous **cross**★ in repoussé silver.

★**Abaj Takalik** – *From Zunil follow the road (CITO) south for 50km/31mi to Retalhuleu. Once you reach this village, take the first street to the right and go straight on to reach the Carr. Centroamericana 2 (CA-2); turn right and follow this road for 14km/8.7mi to reach the entrance to the town of El Asintal (4km/2.5mi); from there, take the Carr. 6W (dirt road) for another 4km/2.5mi. Upon reaching the site entrance, turn left and continue straight on for 0.5km/0.3mi. This zone can also be reached from Guatemala City, via the Carr. CA-2 (200km/124mi). Open year-round daily 7am–5:30pm. Q$25. ☎ 331-1333 ext. 206.* Its Quiché name means "standing rock," and it is one of Guatemala's most important archaeological sites, because it holds vestiges of Olmec and Maya cultures. Here visitors can appreciate two architectural styles: one belonging to the mid pre-Classic period (800–300 BC), characterized by earthen constructions (Ball Court), and the other belonging to the late pre-Classic period (300 BC–AD 250), which includes structures made of earth and round smooth stones. The latter was Abaj Takalik's peak period.

The structures that compose the southern area of the Central Group all belong to the late pre-Classic period. **Ceremonial Structure 12** (main pyramid) is surrounded by **Olmec-style** monolithic, zoomorphic and anthropomorphic monuments, shaped like frogs and jaguar heads, as well as **Maya-like** monuments, such as **Altar 8** and **Stela 5** (AD 126), which display two standing figures separated by a column of glyphs. Also exhibited is **Monument 67**, which represents a human figure emerging from a jaguar's mouth.

Next on the tour are the remnants of **Structure 10** a former temple now covered by

a palm roof. At the south-eastern base is **Monument 99**, in the shape of a human head with earmuffs, nick-named "baby face" by anthropologists. The western central base displays **Altar 28**, with the face of a skull and two human foot-prints above. It appears to represent a figure traveling from day to night; the foot-prints symbolize the character's journey.

Farther ahead, the structure named **Nim-Ja** ("Big House"), which may have been the house of an ancient ruler, holds **Monument 93**, an anthropo-zoomor-phic structure (with a human face and the body of a jaguar) facing west.

Lastly, the tour includes archaeological objects found in the area known as *El Escondite* (The Hiding Place), a ceremonial enclosure dedicated to water and located a few meters west of the site.

© Fernando García Aguinaco

Iglesia de San Andrés Xecul

GUATEMALA CITY★

Department of Guatemala
Population 823,301
Map p 341 – City Map p 352
▌ 7a Avenida 1-17, Centro Cívico (Zona 4) ☏ 331-1333 ext. 206

More than two centuries after its founding, Guatemala City is the country's most populated metropolis, as well as its center of political and economic power. Here, one may see indigenous men and women dressed in regional costumes, cohabiting with the mestizos, who make up the majority of the population.
Full of contrasts, the city has also survived the natural disasters that have struck the area, such as the 1976 earthquake that left the entire urban area in need of reconstruction.

Historical Notes

The First Two Capitals – After conquering this region, the Spaniards chose the capital of the Señorío Cakchiquel, then known as **Iximché**, to found the first city of Guatemala in 1524. However, indigenous revolts forced the Spaniards to find a tranquil place where they could establish a new settlement. Thus, in 1527 the Valley of Almolonga was granted the privilege of becoming the capital of the ancient Kingdom of Guatemala. However, in 1541, due to its location to the west of the Agua Volcano, the city fell victim to a terrible flood that drove out its inhabitants.

Antigua and the Present-Day Capital – In 1543 the city of Santiago de Guatemala (today known as La Antigua Guatemala) was founded once again in the Valley of Panchoy, where, with its colonial society, it became the center of political power and of the arts. Two hundred and thirty years later, the third capital of the ancient Kingdom of Guatemala suffered the consequences of its highly seismic location, as the earthquake of 1773 irreparably devastated the city. This destruction and the imminent danger of new catastrophes forced its inhabitants to flee. The people of Antigua were divided into two factions: the *terronistas* who demanded that the capital remain in the same place, and the *traslacionistas*, people without land or whose properties were mortgaged. The second faction won. Thus, the Valley of Ermita gained the fourth and definitive capital of the country on January 2, 1776, as ordered by King Charles III of Spain, who named it **Nueva Guatemala de la Asunción** (New Guatemala of the Assumption).

Guatemala City is divided into 19 zones, which are frequently used as reference points for giving directions.

PLAZA DE LA CONSTITUCIÓN AND SURROUNDINGS

Plaza de la Constitución – *In the center of the city, between 6a and 7a Av.* Throughout the week, the locals frequent this busy rectangular plaza, with few trees. It is host to a colorful, festive ambiance on Sundays, when vendors exhibit their beautiful textiles and women, dressed in traditional fabrics, rendezvous with their friends. To the west lies the **Parque Centenario** (Centennial Park), where the Declaration of Independence was signed in 1821.

Palacio Nacional – *On the north side of Plaza de la Constitución. Open year-round daily 9am–5pm. Q$5.* Completed in 1943 by engineer Rafael Pérez de León, this greenish building is a prime example of eclectic style. It features the Guatemalan coat of arms, with carvings of the quetzal, the national bird, as well as the five round windows representing the five countries of the former federation of the United Provinces of Central America.
Inside, magnificent **stained-glass windows** by Julio Urruela, an accomplished Guatemalan artist, represent the history of Creation, according to Maya tradition. One can also visit the Salón de Protocolo, where a marvelous chandelier made of Czechoslovak crystal, with four gold quetzals at each cardinal point, stands out. The palace is also home to a museum dedicated to plastic art works, both national and international.

Catedral Metropolitana – *On the east side of Plaza de la Constitución. Open year-round Tue–Fri 8am–noon & 3–7pm.* Although construction began in 1781, the Neoclassical cathedral was not completed until 1815; its towers were built later, between 1863 and 1868. In addition to its colonial paintings found in the interior, this cathedral boasts, according to a popular saying, the city's most ancient bell, endearingly referred to as *"la Chepona"* ("the Hunchback").
As part of the Peace Agreements, signed in December 1996, and in honor of Monsignor Gerardi, assassinated in 1998, marble tiles bearing the names of some of the Civil War victims have been placed on the atrium's twelve columns.

Catedral Metropolitana

Mercado Central – *Behind the cathedral, between 8a and 9a Av. Open year-round Tue–Sat 8am–7pm; Sun 8am–1pm.* Built in 1869 on the lot of what once was the city's first cemetery, this market suffered extensive damage during the earthquake of 1976, and thus was demolished and reconstructed underground. Visitors may shop at a variety of stands, including vegetables, fruit, meats and handicrafts.

Iglesia de la Merced – *5a Calle and 11a Av. Open year-round daily 8am–noon and 3–6pm.* While the church's exterior is Neoclassical in design, its interior preserves the Baroque **altarpieces**★ that were transported here from its namesake church in La Antigua Guatemala, after the 1773 earthquake. The Baroque style of these altarpieces, referred to as **Antiguan**—where curved and straight lines intersect to create an intricate pattern of interlaced lines—is remarkable. The pulpit also displays mixtilinear motifs and a gilded wooden crown at the top.

Iglesia de Santo Domingo – *12a Av. and 10a Calle. Open year-round daily 8am–noon and 3–6pm.* This Neoclassical church presents a pink and white facade that was constructed in 1792. Its interior houses 18C sculptures and a collection of **paintings**★ by the Spanish master Zurbarán, which represent passages from the Bible. The church was destroyed by the earthquakes of 1917 and 1918 and later reconstructed.

Iglesia de San Miguel de Capuchinas – *10a Av. and 10a Calle. Open year-round Mon–Fri 9am–noon and 3–6pm; Sat 7:30am–noon and 3:30–7pm; Sun 9am–7:45pm.* The church was inaugurated on August 7, 1789. Due to its whiteness and beautiful Baroque **facade** with rare bossed columns that are unique in all of Guatemala City, the structure stands out among the other buildings around it. Of particular interest in its interior are the Baroque **altarpieces**★★-restored following the Antiguan style, rich in mixtilinear shapes.

Palacio de la Policía – *6a Av. and 14a Calle.* Police Headquarters, a fortress-like structure with four stories and two towers, boasts an arcade reminiscent of Mudejar architecture, with a final touch of Arabesque pointed merlons.

CENTRO CÍVICO

Centro Cívico – *On 7a Av. (Zona 4).* The complex houses the Palacio Municipal (PM), the National Hypothecary Credit building, the Bank of Guatemala and the Guatemalan Social Security Institute (IGSS). The upper level of each of these buildings is decorated with reliefs created by Carlos Mérida, Guillermo Grajeda Mena and Dagoberto Vásquez, all of them prominent Guatemalan artists. The **Guatemalan Tourist Commission (INGUAT)** building is also found on this street.

Centro Cultural Miguel Ángel Asturias – *24a Calle, 3–81 (Zona 1). Open only during performances.* ☎ *232-4042 to 44.* Part of this cultural center was built on the space once occupied by the Fuerte de San José (Fort of St. Joseph). Designed by architect and creator of fine arts, Efraín Recinos, the complex consists of the National Theater, the Chamber Theater and the open-air theater. Its boatlike shape stands out among the adjoining buildings. ·

ZONAS 9 AND 10

La Torre del Reformador – *7a Av. and 2a Calle (Zona 9).* Inspired by the Eiffel Tower, the Reformer's Tower was inaugurated by Jorge Ubico Castañeda on July 19, 1935, during the centennial of the birth of reformer Justo Rufino Barrios. It spans an important intersection. It is 72m/236ft tall and its upper level houses a bell donated to Guatemala City in 1986 by the Belgian government.

★★**Museo Popol Vuh** – *6a Calle Final (Universidad Francisco Marroquí; Zona 10). Open year-round Mon–Fri 9am–5pm, Sat 9am–1pm. Q$15.* ☎ *361-2311.* The museum exhibits an important collection of pre-Hispanic and colonial art. The pre-Classic room features a stela from the Kaminal Juyú archaeological site and a sculpture named the *barrigón* (the big-bellied one). The Classic period area displays a tubular **censer** with three spouts, an **earthen bowl** with a ring-shaped base, a **scale model** of Tikal's North Acropolis showing its construction and the colors of the altars, and a **polychrome bowl** with a chamá-style lid.

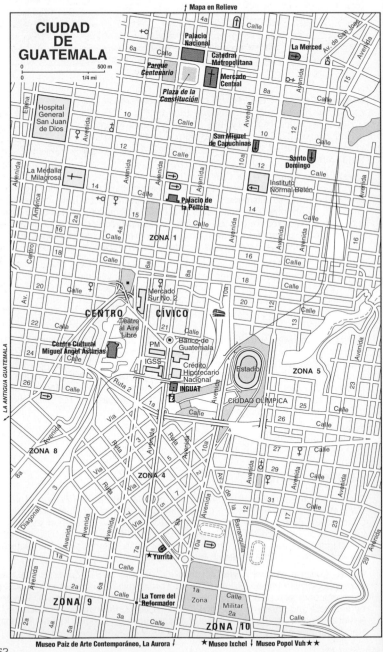

The post-Classic room exhibits **funeral urns**★★★ from Nebaj, San Juan Cotzal and Chajul, in the Quiché region, and from Zaculeu and Huehuetenango. In the center of the showcase, the great urn with a lid in the shape of a jaguar's head constitutes one of the masterpieces of the Late Classic period. The **Colonial Room**★ holds a collection of crowns, emblems with the image of Christ, ornamental silver plaques, large religious sculptures from 18C processional crosses and an 18C **Baroque altarpiece**★★ dedicated to the Virgin of the Assumption.

★**Museo Ixchel** – *6a Calle Final (Univ. Francisco Marroquí, Zona 10). Opposite the Popol Vuh Museum. Open year-round Mon–Fri 8am–5:50pm; Sat 9am–12:50pm. Closed Jan 1, Holy Week, Jun 30, Aug 15, Sept 15, Oct 20, Nov 1, Dec 24 (1/2 day), 25 and 31. Q$15.* ✗ ☎ *331-3739 or* www.ixchelfriends.org. The tour begins with a 15min video on the history of Guatemalan textiles. The museum boasts a valuable collection of regional costumes belonging to Guatemala's indigenous populations. It also exhibits a sample of popular art. The visit ends with an exhibit of watercolor paintings by **Carmen Pettersen**, who dedicated herself to capturing, on canvas, the colors of regional native costumes.

Museo Paiz de Arte Contemporáneo – *7a Av. 8–35 (Zona 9). Open year-round Tue–Sat 9am–5pm; Sun 9am–2pm.* ☎ *334-1040.* The Paiz commercial organization sponsors an annual arts contest and exhibits its winning creations in this building. Among them are the works of Efraín Recinos, Grajeda Mena and Carlos Mérida, as well as works created by young Guatemalan artists.

LA AURORA (ZONA 13)

★**Museo Nacional de Arqueología e Historia** – *Edificio 5, Finca La Aurora (Zona 13). Open year-round Tue–Fri 9am–4pm, Sat–Sun 9am–noon & 1:30–4pm. Q$30.* ☎ *472-0489.* Founded in 1931, the National Museum of Archaeology and History boasts the most important **collection**★★ of pre-Columbian art in Central America, featuring artifacts from the archaeological sites of Kaminal Juyú, Santa Rosa, Malacatán and Uaxactún.

The Classic period room contains beautiful **censers**★ from Guastlán and an Altar of Sacrifices, as well as a human-shaped **basin**★. The adjoining South Coast room houses female figures from this region, a male human **face**★ and the upper part of a female-shaped **censer** from Santa Ana Mixtán. The front room displays a **scale model** of Tikal, as well as different ceramic utensils and a tomb, found at the site.

After viewing the South Coast room, one can admire a wooden **lintel**★ that was found in Temple I at El Zotz, in the Petén region, and was returned by the Denver Art Museum. The lintel dates back to the Classic period (AD 550–650).

Another attraction is the museum's collection of **Maya stelae**★, as well as a **Jade Room**★, which exhibits masks re-created from bits and pieces found, as well as jewelry from different parts of the country. On the left side of this room stands the beautiful **Throne 1**★ brought here from Piedras Negras.

Museo de Arte Moderno – *Edificio 6, Finca La Aurora (Zona 13). Open year-round Tue–Fri 9am–4pm. Q$10.* ☎ *472-0467.* This Neoclassical building features modern works of art created by Guatemala's most renowned artists. The exhibit spans three periods: 1900–1950, 1950–1970, and 1970 to the present. Of particular interest are Carlos Mérida's murals, **Glorificación del Quetzal**, and Efraín Recinos' **El Pintor**. The museum also displays sculptures cast in plaster, stone and wood, such as **Música Grande** and **Caballero Quetzal**, both by Efraín Recinos. Another sculpture of great beauty is the **Cristo Arcaico** by Guillermo Grajeda Mena.

Mercado de Artesanías – *11a Av. (Zona 13). Open year-round Tue–Sat 8am–6pm; Sun 9am–1pm.* ☎ *232-4042 to 44.* A few streets from the museum area is this market, consisting of permanent kiosks surrounding a small plaza where visitors may enjoy a brightly colored display of Guatemalan textiles, ceramics, woodwork and leather work.

ADDITIONAL SIGHTS

★**Iglesia de Yurrita** – *Ruta 6, 8–52 (Zona 4). Open year-round Tue–Sun 8am–noon and 2–4pm.* Dedicated to Our Lady of Sorrows, this church was built in 1928 by the Yurrita family, to give thanks after the eruption of the Santa María Volcano. Due to its eclectic style spanning Art Nouveau, Mudejar influences and Gothic art, this building is unique in the city. The church is well known for its towers with cone-shaped balconies decorated with conches and statues. Of particular interest are the main doors, whose intricate woodcarvings portray historical buildings from La Antigua, as well as Pedro de Alvarado and Brother Pedro de Betancourt. Its **interior**★ is a jewel of the imagination. The side doors present a Mudejar frame, and the second section features balconies made of diamond-shaped stones.

Relief Map – *Av. Simeón Cañas Final. Hipódromo del Norte (Zona 2)*. This large scale model (1,809sq m/5,934sq ft) represents Guatemala's striking topography. Inaugurated in 1905 after 18 months of work, the map was created by engineer Claudio Urrutia-inventor, geographer and scientist who also designed the Avenida Reforma and the National Observatory building.

EXCURSIONS

Las Verapaces – *Northeast of Guatemala City*. Las Verapaces were and have been an Indian territory since the era before Christ. The Kekchí group, which was the strongest in resisting Spanish attacks, predominated here until Fray Bartolomé de Las Casas evangelized and pacified the region, and named it Vera-paz or true peace. Since then, the area is known as Las Verapaces, divided into Alta and Baja (High and Low).

Besides their spirituality and customs, Las Verapaces offer numerous natural attractions, such as the **Biotopo Mario Dary Rivera** (Biotopo del Quetzal) in the Purulhá region, which preserves the habitat of this mystical endangered bird. Besides the national bird, this natural reserve of 1,253ha/3,096 acres is home to more than 80 different species of birds.

Also of interest are the **Grottoes of Lanquín**, 59km/37mi northeast of Cobán, characterized for the whimsical shapes of their boulders and for the **Cahabón River**, one of the most frequented by rafters.

Cobán – *In Alta Verapaz, 214km/133mi north of Guatemala City*. Cobán is an important city, both for its handicrafts and commercial activity and for its bordering coffee plantations, which have belonged to the descendants of Germans who arrived in Verapaz in the 19C.

Despite the European influence of the coffee plantation owners, Cobán and Las Verapaces, in general, preserve their ancestral spirit. Proof of this is the **National Folkloric Festival**, which usually takes place annually, at the end of July. One of the festival's most important events is the indigenous beauty pageant or **Rabín Ahau**, which in Kekchí signifies the King's Daughter. Beauty queens from all regions and ethnic groups in the country, accompanied by an entourage representing each group's ceremonies and dances, participate in this contest.

★**Semuc Champey** – *73km/45mi east of Cobán*. Owing to its beautiful pools of emerald-green waters, which are fed by small waterfalls formed by the Cahabón River, Semuc Champey is often referred to as the paradise of Las Verapaces.

La Democracia – *From Guatemala City head southeast and take Carr. Centroamericana 9 (CA-9) towards Escuintla. Turn right at the exit to Mazatenango, Carr. Centroamericana 2 (CA-2) and follow this road to the junction with Siquinalá and continue straight on; at the sign that says La Democracia, turn left (RD-2). Farther ahead, take another left at the bifurcation of Siquinalá and La Democracia. Upon entering the town, go past three streets and turn left to reach the Archaeological Park.* This town's main attraction is the "Parque Arqueológico Santos Toruño", where rudimentary roofs shelter 12 **statues**★ of indigenous manufacture, apparently of Olmec origin. Some of them were discovered in 1967, in the Monte Alto area, from where they were transported to the park. Several theories link these objects with a previous culture (Early Pre-Classic) or a culture parallel (Mid to Late Pre-Classic) to that of the Olmecs. Some have referred to it as **Cultura Monte Alto**, because the style of its sculptures has been found along Guatemala's Pacific Coast down to Santa Leticia in El Salvador, as well as in Copán, and especially in the central part of Escuintla and Kaminal Juyú, in Guatemala City. These *barrigones* ("big bellied ones") represent individuals seated with their legs crossed and their arms placed over their bellies, apparently naked, although some are wearing necklaces or pectorals. Though there is no certainty as to what they symbolize, they are probably manifestations or allegories of a specific deity. Also notorious are the heads with their eyes shut, some less elaborate than others, but essentially all of them resemble the gigantic Olmec heads found in La Venta, Veracruz. On one side of the park stands the **Museo Arqueológico La Democracia** *(open year-round daily 8am–noon & 2–5pm; Q$10)*, which exhibits ceramic objects, obsidian artifacts, spindles, seals and bowls found in the site's surroundings.

El Baúl – *23km/14.3mi north of La Democracia. From La Democracia return to the exit to Siquinalá and continue along the way to Mazatenango; when you reach Santa Lucía Cotzumala, enter the town and, at the 5th street, turn left and continue straight on. Turn right onto the 3rd Ave. After passing the bridge over the river, take the exit to El Baúl. At the sign "Ingenio El Baúl," continue after leaving a form of identification with the watchman.* Over 70 archaeological objects, currently exhibited here, were found on a plot of land that today constitutes this sugar mill. The findings include two stelae, one called **Stela 1**★, which displays a column of hieroglyphs, engraved with a date of AD 37 in Maya, and a figure with a headdress, over whom rises the representation of a deity in what appear to be clouds of volutes, as well as a beautiful **jaguar**★ in a squatting position.

The remaining objects represent human and zoomorph heads, as well as decorated sidewalks and other carved stones. It is known that Stela 1 contains one of the most ancient inscriptions in Mesoamerica and is classified as the *Izapa style*, a name that characterizes a great deal of the sculptures in the Late Pre-Classic period along the Gulf Coast, Abaj Takalik and Kaminal Juyú. The name is derived from a place in Tapachula, Chiapas, which underwent a great flourishing during the Late Pre-Classic period, manifested in huge structures that were grouped into a series of plazas covering an area of 3.6km/2.2mi.

***Copán** – *Guatemalan tour operators offer excursions to Copán; map, p 340.* This Honduran archaeological site, related to Quiriguá, is located 13km/8mi from the border of Guatemala. Like Tikal, Copán constituted a great ceremonial center, which once had up to 20,000 inhabitants. This high population figure may have brought about the city's collapse due to the exploitation of its forests.

Jaguar, El Baúl

Carlos Quezada García

■ María Ticún and Rey Ticún

Several kilometers from El Baúl, on the way back to Santa Lucía, just past the sugarcane plantations, one reaches a small hill where two enormous trees stand alongside two Maya ceremonial stones, one engraved and the other sculpted. These respectively represent María Ticún and **Rey Ticún★**, also known as Señor del Mundo (Lord of the World). Indigenous peoples and mestizos offer them flowers, incense, chocolate and even spirituous liquor, to request a favor through a shaman or healer. In a manner similar to that celebrated before the **Pascual Abaj** stone in the outskirts of Chichicastenango, this is yet another tradition kept alive by Guatemala's indigenous culture. It should be observed with the utmost respect.

Rey Ticún, El Baúl

Carlos Quezada García

Declared a World Heritage Site in 1980, Copán was considered by archaeologist Sylvanus G. Morley as the Athens of the New World. It encompasses three groups: the Main Group, the Residential Zone of the Forest and the Residential Zone of the Tombs.

At present, visitors may explore only the Main Group, which consists of the Great Plaza and the Acropolis. The **Great Plaza** houses beautiful **stelae★★**, while another part of the complex features an impressive work, the **Escalera de los Jeroglíficos★★** (Staircase of the Hieroglyphs), depicting some of the city's rulers and scenes from selected battles.

On the eastern part of the **Acropolis** is Temple 10L-16, whose base houses **Altar Q** (AD 763) one of Copán's most renowned historical monuments. Inside the altar, 16 seated figures represent the city's rulers and their successors throughout nearly four centuries.

QUIRIGUÁ★

Department of Izabal
Map p 341
🄳 ☏ 331-1333 ext. 206

One must pass through a banana plantation to arrive at Quiriguá. Declared a World Heritage Site in 1985, this archaeological site astounds visitors with its magnificent stelae, the tallest in the Maya world.

Historical Notes

Quiriguá flourished during the Late Classic period and had close ties to the enormous city of Copán, on which it depended for a long time and which it later conquered. The carved stelae found in these cities contain vestiges of the names of the rulers of both cities. An interesting fact is that in Quiriguá's Stela L, Humo Jaguar, Copán's twelfth ruler, was represented as the godfather of Quiriguá's new governor. Six years later, in AD 737, the descendants of the King of Quiriguá seized the city of Copán (in present-day Honduran territory) and beheaded Humo Jaguar's successor, known as "18-Conejo" (18-Rabbit). With this event Quiriguá acquired a much-desired autonomy and underwent an artistic explosion, which resulted in the carving of magnificent stelae that narrated the glory of the king who had liberated them from Copán's oppressive power.

Quiriguá remained hidden until the 19C when three Guatemalans, the Peyés brothers, discovered it shortly before 1840. Subsequently, Frederick Catherwood and John Lloyd Stephens explored the site. Beginning in 1930, it underwent partial restoration by the University of Pennsylvania.

ARCHAEOLOGICAL SITE

210km/130mi northeast of Guatemala City. Take Carr. Centroamericana 9 (CA-9) and drive for 206km/128mi to reach the town of Quiriguá; at the Quiriguá sign, turn right and follow the dirt road for 4km/2.5mi. Open year-round daily 7:30am–5pm. Q$25.

The highlights of this well-preserved park are its **stelae★★★**, dating back to the Late Classic period. Profuse carvings adorn all four sides of the stelae's monoliths. Both the front and back of the stelae portray the faces of ancient rulers or kings, while the sides contain glyphs recording historical events. Of note are the bearded figures carved on the stelae. Stone carvings managed to reach such a sophisticated artistic level that the artisans of Quiriguá perfected the high-relief technique.

The site preserves nine stelae, six altars and seven intricately carved zoomorphs.

★★Stela E – With a height of 10.6m/35ft this stela, created in AD 771, is undoubtedly the tallest carved stone in the Maya world. Its front portrays a human figure with a headdress, and its back depicts a ruler with a scepter.

Stela T – The most ancient and smallest stela at this site dates back to AD 692. It displays rough carvings and portrays a rounder human face.

Altars – Some altars, such as L and M, represent zoomorphic figures, while one of the altars near the entrance to the main plaza depicts a possibly dismembered figure.

Main Plaza – This consists of a quadrangular plaza surrounded by perimetric stone structures whose temples remain without vaults, but there is clear evidence that they were used. The structures are decorated in polychrome stucco.

Ball Court – Its architectural remains are found inside one of the plazas. Stairways along three of its sides characterize this ball court.

EXCURSIONS

Castillo de San Felipe and Livingston

47km/29mi north of Quiriguá, at the northern edge of the Rio Dulce. From Quiriguá retake Carr. Centroamericana CA-9 northeast and drive for 43km/26.7mi to reach La Ruidosa; there, take the exit to Rio Dulce (34km/21mi).

★★**Castillo de San Felipe** – *At the village of Rio Dulce, cross the bridge and turn left onto the first street; follow the dirt road and signs for 4km/2.5mi. Open year-round daily 8am–5pm. Q$10.* This fortress, constructed in 1652, is situated at the edge of the **Rio Dulce**★, whose 30km/18.6mi connect Lake Izabal (Guatemala's largest lake) with the Gulf of Honduras. Its castle-like construction served as a defense against attacks from English pirates, who in 1686 burned down the fortress. Even after its reconstruction, the attacks continued, until the Spanish and English governments put an end to piracy.

This stone fortress includes barracks, canons, a drawbridge, a central courtyard and two large fortified towers, with a splendid **view** of the Rio Dulce.

Livingston – *From the Castle of San Felipe return to the bridge, the departure point for boat rides to Livingston (approx. Q$300, direct dealings with the boatmen). Also accessible from the Castillo de San Felipe (44km/27.3mi to the northeast through the Rio Dulce), or from Puerto Barrios through the Bahía de Amatique (25km/15.5mi to the northwest).* Located very near the Caribbean Sea, Livingston is inhabited mainly by **Garífunas**, a blend of African and Caribbean cultures. Its Afro-Caribbean population speaks Creole, a melodic language resulting from the combination of English, Spanish and Dutch.

Livingston's Caribbean-style architecture consists of brightly painted wooden houses with palm roofs. Cars are a rarity, and the roads are narrow. Although small, the town offers great entertainment at night, as restaurants and bars have Garífuna music shows, featuring **punta rock**.

Monument at Quiriguá (c.1840)
by Frederick Catherwood

From Livingston there are excursions to **Playa Blanca**, to the **Siete Altares** waterfall or to the **Biotopo Chocón Machacas** reserve, located in the zone called "El Golfete," where the Rio Dulce becomes wider. On the return voyage through the river, one may enjoy an unforgettable **view**★ full of mangroves and wild birds.

TIKAL★★★

Department of El Petén
Map p 341 – Site Map p 360
🛈 ☎ 926-0669 and 331-1333 ext. 206

Tikal is located in the region of El Petén, home to the **Maya Biosphere Reserve** with 1,844,900ha/4,558,748 acres of protected territory. Land of the tallest pyramids of Maya civilization, Tikal is one of the most important cities of the ancient Maya world. It was declared a World Heritage Site in 1979.

The Petén region also has other archaeological sites of lesser importance, such as Uaxactún, Yaxha, Nakum, Rio Azul and El Mirador. The first two can be accessed without problems, but the others are more difficult to reach, especially during the rainy season *(Maya, p 32 and 314)*.

Historical Notes

Beginning and Splendor – Around 800 BC, the ancient Maya began to occupy the Petén region, perhaps due to the abundance of flint that allowed them to create arrowheads and knives. From the moment they settled here, the Maya began building ceremonial structures, and in 200 BC they initiated the construction of the North Acropolis. It was not until the Christian era that the Great Plaza took on its current appearance, and by AD 250 Tikal was an important commercial, cultural and religious center, with a population that reached an estimated total of 100,000. Around AD 500 Tikal suffered the invasion of Señor Agua (Lord Water) hailing from the Caracol region, today part of Belize. In AD 700 the city recovered its military strength and regained its splendor under the leadership of **Ah Cacao** (AD 682–734). Some of the stelae found in this archaeological site commemorate this ruler, who facilitated the construction of the Great Plaza. In the 9C AD the decline that affected the rest of Maya culture also brought about the collapse of this magnificent city.

Archaeological Exploration – Tikal was not discovered until 1848, the year in which the first official expedition was conducted by Modesto Méndez, Ambrosio Tut and artist Eusebio Lara, who painted several of the stelae and lintels. In 1877 Dr. Gustav Bernoulli visited Tikal, from where he transported carved wooden lintels corresponding to the doors of Temples I and IV. These lintels were later sent to Basel, Switzerland.

In 1895 and 1904, German Tobert Maler explored Tikal on behalf of the Peabody Museum of Harvard University. Later on, Sylvanus G. Morley visited this site several times to record the monuments' inscriptions. In 1956 the University Museum of Pennsylvania inaugurated an eleven-year program for the study and excavation of Tikal. Since 1965 the Guatemalan government, through the Tikal National Project, has financed research and restoration of Tikal's buildings.

Plaza Mayor

ARCHAEOLOGICAL SITE

Accessed by plane from Guatemala City. We recommend contracting the services of a travel agency. Open year-round daily 6am–5.30pm. Q$50. ☎ 926-0669.

Tikal's core covers 16sq km/9.9sq mi and contains 3,000 different types of structures, from temples and palaces to terraces and wide roads. The period of construction spans the pre-Classic, Classic and post-Classic periods. It was during the Classic period, and particularly during the late Classic period, that Tikal's architectural development reached its peak.

Complex Q – Here stand two twin pyramids, as well as a false arch behind which are **Stela 22**★★ and **Altar 10**★. The stela, which still preserves part of its original color, portrays a sculpted figure that was subsequently mutilated by the inhabitants of the post-Classic period. The altar displays a bound figure, apparently captive.

Temple I – *Located inside the Great Plaza.* Known as the **Temple of the Great Jaguar** for a motif that is engraved on one of its lintels, this temple is 500m/1,640ft wide and 52m/171ft high. Facing west, it was built in AD 700. Most impressive is its cresting, which, both here and on the other temples, provides the finishing touch to the pyramid's peak. In this case it is crowned with stone blocks that form the barely visible figure of a seated character flanked by serpents and spirals. The temple's interior held the tomb of ruler Ah Cacao, in a vaulted space of 4.5m/15ft x 2.4m/8ft and 4m/13ft high. Also found in the interior were 180 jade objects, as well as 90 bone artifacts and other objects of pearls, ceramic and alabaster, some of which are displayed at the Sylvanus G. Morley Museum.

Temple II – *Opposite Temple I.* This structure is also known as the **Templo de las Máscaras** (Temple of the Masks) for its facade decorated with the motifs, two at either side of the staircase, which have physically been erased, and another on the cresting in the shape of a face. Today it is 38m/125ft tall, but it is believed to have originally reached a height of 42m/138ft.

Central Acropolis – With a length of almost 215m/705ft from east to west, this acropolis contains diverse structures called *palaces*, smaller than the temples. Located at different levels, the buildings correspond to various construction stages; that is, the Maya constructed structures one on top of another. The Central Acropolis includes six courtyards or open spaces that are interconnected by stairways and corridors, but not all of them can be visited.

North Acropolis – The structure rises above a platform of approximately 1ha/2.5 acres, 12m/39.4ft above the surface of the Great Plaza. Like the Central Acropolis, it boasts a variety of buildings-among them temples-constructed atop previous stages dating back to 200 BC. It was not until AD 250 that this part of Tikal assumed its current configuration. The left side of the staircase leading to one of the temples of the Acropolis, situated on the platform, displays a stunning large **grotesque mask**★★ with a long-nosed human face. This can be accessed by way of a descending stairway.

© Robert Frerck/Odyssey

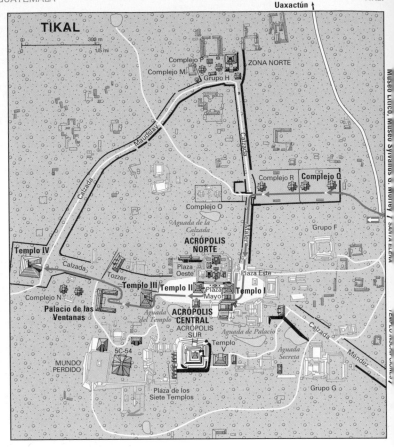

Temple III – *West of the North Acropolis*. It is known as the **Temple of the Jaguar Priest** because of a scene depicted on an inner lintel. Partly covered by the jungle, this temple rises to a height of 55m/180.4ft and was built in the Late Classic period, around AD 810. With a certain amount of agility and effort, visitors may access this temple from its eastern side.

Palacio de las Ventanas – *Inside the palatial compound, to the left of Temple III*. The upper level of the Palace of Windows consists of a gallery with layered vaults, as well as benches in the interconnected rooms.

Temple IV – A path to the west leads to the foot of Tikal's tallest structure, **Templo de la Serpiente de Dos Cabezas** (Temple of the Two-Headed Serpent), named for a motif on its lintel. This Late-Classic-period structure rises to a height of 64.5m/211.6ft from the platform and was built in AD 741, with the same features as Temples I and II. Strategically placed wooden stairways lead to the summit, where climbers are rewarded by a wonderful **view★★** of the jungle with its dense canopy of trees, as well as a view of the cresting of Temple III to the right and Temples I and II in the background.
Temple V and the South Acropolis are located south of the Central Acropolis and are accessible from a path through the jungle. It is advisable to visit them with a guide or be sure to take care not to lose sight of the path.

Museo Lítico – *At the entrance to the archaeological site. Open year-round daily 9am–5pm*. This museum displays stelae found in Tikal, as well as some brought from neighboring archaeological sites. One of the most noteworthy, **Stela 16★★** features intricate carvings portraying ruler Ah Cacao, also known as Señor "A." This monolith was found in Temple I. **Altar 5★★**, opposite the aforementioned stela, depicts two figures standing behind a platform, between them a skull with bones and 31 glyphs. Another noteworthy stela carved in pink stone and found at Ceibal, portrays a standing figure with an elegant headdress and a shaft in his hand.

Sylvanus G. Morley Museum – *To the right of the Lithic Museum. Open year-round Mon–Fri 9am–5pm, Sat–Sun 9am–4pm. Q$10*. Unlike the Lithic Museum, this museum exhibits ceramic artifacts from Tikal. Its highlights include a few polychrome receptacles, such as those in showcase 7, as well as a **censer** of the "God of Sacrifice and War" and a **polychrome bowl** with a lid. Showcase 13 displays a collection of **polychrome glasses** belonging to the tomb of Ah Cacao, with figures dressed in traditional Mayan attire. It also features the only **stela** (AD 445) that portrays the ruler Cielo Tormentoso (Stormy Sky) richly attired. The back of the stela shows a series of glyphs, while its sides present a distinguished individual.

EXCURSIONS

Isla de Flores – *In the peninsula, 65km/40mi from Tikal.* The capital of this department was built across from Lake Petén Itzá, on this small peninsula. Here, visitors from Tikal can find first-class accommodations and restaurants. They may also enjoy boat rides to nearby towns or to the zoo.

Zoológico Petencito – *On the island of El Petencito, 3km/2mi northeast of Flores. Open year-round daily 8:30am–5pm. Q$10.* This zoo not only displays animals native to this region, but also serves as an environmental educational center, where children learn to respect the environment and can enjoy swimming in the lagoon during the summer.

Uaxactún and Ceibal *Map p 341*

Aside from the majestic Tikal, in the surroundings of El Petén lie numerous archaeological sites that have gradually been rescued from the jungle, and some of their structures have been restored, as can be seen in Uaxactún and Ceibal.

Uaxactún – *25km/15.5mi north of Tikal.* This site is located in a town that bears the same name and is divided by a landing strip. The first group of structures, situated to the east, is **Group E**. Its main plaza includes a pyramid, named **E-VII**, whose staircases are flanked by jaguar heads. Excavations were initiated in 1926, after the finding of a well-preserved stucco face. Researchers believe that pyramid E-VII served as the foundation for a temple built of wood and straw, because four deep holes for lodging posts were found at the base. To the left side rises another complex of buildings, one of which displays a dark cresting that contrasts with the whiteness of the edifice.

Only 0.9km/0.6mi from here, on the other side of the landing strip, lies the second part of the archaeological complex, consisting of the West Plaza, which houses stelae and carved stones, and **Group A**, comprised of two pyramids: one crowned with cresting and the other with columns.

Behind the first pyramid, in Group A, another group of buildings stands on a semicircular space and, behind this compound, a pyramid crowned with black cresting.

Ceibal – *81km/50.2mi southwest of Flores, accessed from the riverbanks of the Río de la Pasión.* In 1892 Federico Artes discovered this site, declared an archaeological park in 1985. Its first name was that of a white bird native to this region: Saxtanquiqui. In 1895 Teobert Maler visited the ruins and called them Ceibal due to the great number of trees of this species that abound in the present-day park. In 1914 Sylvanus G. Morley also came here, but it was the Peabody Museum of Archaeology and the Ethnology Department at Harvard University that, between 1964 and 1968, conducted research work and erected stelae here.

Ceibal constituted the largest settlement of the Late Pre Classic period and held sway in the western region of Río de la Pasión, as its geographic location was very favorable in commercial, transportation, political and military activities. The place is composed of a ceremonial center with an area of 1sq km/0.6sq mi over three tall hills, each one separated by depressions.

Group A, the largest in the ceremonial center, consists of three plazas. Over the west side of the South Plaza rises the enormous, pyramid-type building **A-24**. Buildings A-7 and A-8 separate the Central Plaza from the South Plaza on the north side. At the center of the plaza stands building A-3, flanked by four stelae at each of the cardinal points and a fifth one in the center, resting atop the upper platform. The trail that intercepts the path originating from the river leads to the already restored **Structure 79**, known as the observatory, across from which sits an altar with a jaguar's head. Due to the rapid spread of the jungle's lush vegetation, many structures still have to be rescued; however, the grandeur of Ceibal's stelae attests to the organization and importance of this archaeological site.

Ambergris Caye

Belize

© Fernando García Aguinaco

Natural and Social Enclave

South of the Yucatán Peninsula and east of Guatemala, at the heart of the ancient Maya world, lies Belize, a small Central American and Caribbean country possessing striking natural resources that coexist with a wonderful diversity of people, fauna and flora. Belize's vivid jungle houses the country's three tallest structures-all of them pyramids built by the Maya. Just off Belize's coasts, dozens of islands caressed by the alluring blue waters of the Caribbean Sea constitute a tropical paradise from which visitors never want to depart. This country, where different natural and social currents converge, offers endless possibilities to those in search of adventure.

Geography and Nature

Belize is 173.6mi/280km long and 67.6mi/109km wide, a size similar to that of the Mexican state of Tabasco or the US state of Massachusetts. Its primarily flat terrain consists of tropical lowlands. Over 20 rivers, many of them of crystalline waters, run through its imposing jungles, coniferous forests and savannas. Covered in lush vegetation, the **Mountain Pine Ridge** is located to the west, and the **Maya Mountains** run parallel to the southern coast and include **Victoria Peak** (3,673.6ft/1,120m), the country's highest summit.

Approximately 12.4mi/20km from Belize's mangrove shoreline extends the world's second largest **barrier reef**, spanning a length of 184.8mi/298km, surpassed only by that of Australia's Barrier Reef. Nearly 200 cays are scattered along both sides of the reef. While some consist of mangrove forests, others form heavenly islands with white sandy beaches and palm trees.

East of the barrier reef, three of the Western Hemisphere's four **atolls** grace Belize's waters. These immense reefs, formed by the calcareous deposits of corals accumulated over thousands of years, encompass cays of incomparable beauty, lagoons linked to the sea by narrow canals and a diverse marine life, which combined make Belize one of the world's most attractive sites for scuba diving.

© Lynn M. Stone

Jaguar

Jungles – Although up until the 1950s Belize's primary export products were precious woods from its tropical rain forests, at present Belize preserves 75% of its jungles. This rare case in Central America-where according to ecologists' predictions, by the year 2000 only 10% of the jungles in the rest of the region will remain standing-was achieved due to the selective felling of mahogany and cedar trees, leaving the rest of the vegetation intact.

Today, along with coniferous forests and marshes, Belize's jungles cover 70% of the country's territory and-together with the Barrier Reef, cays and atolls-constitute Belize's main tourist attractions.

Nearly 40 protected areas occupy almost half of Belize's territory. Some of these reserves serve as pioneers and admirable models for environmental conservation worldwide.

Flora and Fauna – Excepting the national flag and hymn, Belize's national symbols reside in its jungles: the **black orchid** figures among the 72 varieties found in Belize, and **mahogany** among the 700 trees native to this small country. The **toucan** represents one of the 533 bird species flying across Belize's clear skies; the **tapir** and **jaguar** two of the 155 varieties of mammals that, along with 107 species of reptiles, maraud Belize's vegetation-dotted with up to 4,000 types of flowering plants.

No less striking, Belize's underwater landscape consists of colorful gardens with up to 50 varieties of corals, friendly **dolphins**, majestic **manta rays**, harmless **sharks** that tolerate quiet observation, zigzagging **barracudas** and gentle **sea turtles**, as well as 400 species of fish.

Historical Notes

Formerly known as British Honduras, the country was renamed Belize in 1973, a name whose true origins are still debated to this date. Three versions stand out among all the rest. It was derived from the Maya words **Belikin** "path to the east," or **Beliz** "muddy waters." It is a deformation of the last name of Peter Wallace, a Scottish pirate purported to be the first to take shelter in Belize's reefs. Or it was derived from the Spanish words *bella isla* (beautiful island), in reference to its cays.

The Maya – North of Belize stands the Maya site of Cuello, which dates back to 2500 BC and embodies one of the most ancient sites of the Maya world. Archaeologists believe that three thousand years later, during the Classic period (AD 100–800), the territory today known as Belize represented the center of Maya civilization. Most of the numerous ceremonial centers located in Belize lived their era of splendor during this period when the population exceeded one million Maya, four times higher than the current total population. At the end of the Classic period, a general decadence swept the region. In spite of this, some sites remained occupied even after the arrival of the Spaniards.

Spaniards, Pirates and Slaves – Due to Belize's dense jungles, its scarcity of mines and the fact that its reefs posed a risk to ships, the Spaniards were late in arriving to this region and never succeeded in gaining control of it.

In contrast, English pirates of the 17C and 18C found in these reefs an ideal refuge after looting Spanish galleons on the high seas. Despite resistance from the jealous Maya and Spaniards, these corsairs began to establish settlements during the mid 18C. Subjecting African slaves to manual labor, they exploited a rich market of woods exported to England, where they were converted into furniture or used to produce dyes destined for their important textile industry.

The constant dispute between Englishmen and Spaniards over Belizean territory was prolonged until 1798, when the Spaniards were finally defeated in the **Battle of St. George's Caye**. During this battle, commemorated every year on September 10, the slaves played a decisive role because at that time they constituted almost half of the territory's population. The other half consisted of freed slaves; Caucasians made up only 10% of the population.

In the 19C the Belizean territory was formally declared a British colony and, in 1884, received the name of British Honduras, which it retained until 1973 when it was renamed Belize.

The Making of a Nation – Mexico recognized British sovereignty over the territory as early as the 19C. With the objective of stopping the sale of arms to rebel natives in the Caste War and gaining recognition from the British government, Mexican President Porfirio Díaz signed treaties that defined the boundaries between Mexico and British Honduras. Guatemala, on the other hand, reclaimed the territory even after Belize achieved independence in 1981. In 1961 a ministerial government system was adopted, elections were held, and even road regulations were changed (that is, the British system of driving on the left side of the road was abandoned, and the system that prevails in the rest of the world was adopted). That same year **Hurricane Hattie** struck Belize's former capital, Belize City, causing extensive damage. This resulted in the creation of a new capital, the city of Belmopan, founded a decade later in 1971. On September 21, 1981 Belize gained its independence and became a member of the British Commonwealth. Queen Elizabeth II symbolically remains as the Head of State.

Belize Today

Area	14,238.3sq mi/22,965sq km, including 427sq mi/688sq km of islands and 239mi/386km of mainland
Population	238,500
Time Zone	GMT -6
Languages	English (official), Spanish (gaining popularity), Maya, Garífuna and the Creole dialect
Capital	Belmopan
Districts	Belize, Cayo, Corozal, Orange Walk, Stann Creek and Toledo
Government	Parliamentarian democracy, presided over by the Prime Minister; the National Assembly consists of two chambers: the House of Representatives (29 members) and the Senate (8 members)
Religion	Catholic (62%), Protestant (30%), there is freedom of worship
Climate	Subtropical, humid. Temperatures range from 78°–88°F/24°–29°C. **Precipitation:** 170in/4,250mm annually in the south, 50in/1,250mm annually in the north, **rainy season:** June–October.
Economy	Agriculture and tourism; **primary exports:** citric products, sugar, bananas and wood

PRACTICAL INFORMATION ....Country Code: 501

When to Go

Belize's **climate** is subtropical. Winds predominating from the Caribbean preserve the average annual temperature at 79°F/26°C. Average humidity is 85%. The **rainy season** lasts from June to October, with average temperatures of 72°F/22°C to 85°F/30°C, precipitation can be heavy but brief. Peak tourist season is from November to May. Because the region is located at the hurricane belt, storms usually occur from August to October. While tap water is drinkable in major tourist areas, bottled water is recommended when traveling in the country's interior.

Planning Your Trip

Citizens of the US, Canada, Mexico, the British Commonwealth, the European Union and Australia need a valid **passport** and a return ticket. Citizens of other countries and visitors planning to stay over 30 days may need a **visa**. Regulations on travel documents generally change constantly and without prior notice. Consult with the Belizean Embassy or Consulate in your country of origin before initiating your trip. Although **vaccines** are not mandatory, visitors should be warned that malaria is found in areas below an elevation of 400m/1,312ft. When traveling in the jungle, apply **insect repellent** with DEET.

Getting There

By Plane – **Philip Goldson International Airport:** 9.9mi/16km northwest of Belize City. American Airlines (Miami), Continental Airlines (Houston) and Taca International Airlines (Houston) fly into Belize. Flights from Europe are recommended by way of the US or Mexico. Taxis service the downtown area *(BZ$30, 15min)*. Air transportation between **Belize and Guatemala:** Tropic Air ☎ (2) 456-71 and Maya Island Air ☎ (2) 523-36, 311-40 & 353-71. Upon leaving the country, all visitors must pay a **tax** of BZ$30 at the airport or at the border.

By Bus – Several bus lines offer transportation from Cancun, Mérida and Playa del Carmen to Chetumal. Buses depart from Chetumal *(BZ$10, 3 1/2hrs)* to Belize City: Venus Bus Lines ☎ (2) 733-54 *(every hour from 4am–10:30am)*; Batty Brothers Bus Service ☎ (2) 720-25 *(12 departures daily, the first one at 4am, the last one at 6:30pm; BZ$9, premier BZ$12)*. Passengers must disembark at the border. From Santa Elena (El Petén, Guatemala): Línea Dorada ☎ (502) 926-0070 *(daily at 5am, 5hr trip, USD$20)*. For information on buses to Flores and Tikal (Guatemala), or Chetumal and Playa del Carmen (Mexico), inquire at the maritime taxi stations in Belize City and Caye Caulker.

By Car – From Mexico, the point of entry is through Corozal Town, from Guatemala through Benque Viejo (west). Car insurance is mandatory and can be acquired at any point along the border.

By Boat – Daily boat service between Punta Gorda (Belize) and Puerto Barrios (Guatemala): BZ$25. On Saturdays, Sundays and Mondays, there are also trips to Livingston, Guatemala: BZ$25. For reservations and schedules ☎ (7) 228-70.

Getting Around

By Car and Taxi – The Northern and Western Highways are in good condition. Paved roads that may deteriorate during heavy precipitation interconnect Belize's major cities. Four-wheel drive vehicles are recommended for traveling south of Belize City and driving on roads other than the two main highways. **Avis**, **Budget**, **Hertz** and **National** operate car rental offices in Belize City. Advance reservations are recommended. Only four-wheel drive vehicles are available *(from BZ$126 per day with unlimited mileage, plus 15% in taxes and insurance)*. Road conditions may be difficult, especially on Hummingbird Highway, Southern Highway and Manatee Road. **Gasoline** may be obtained along major highways and in big towns. Driving at night is not recommended. *Emory King's Driver's Guide to Beautiful Belize* is a good backup reference source for touring Belize. Recognizable by their green license plates, **taxis** service cities and tourist areas. Although the government regulates taxi rates, it is advisable to ask the driver what the approximate cost will be, as taxis do not have taximeters *(a trip within Belize City costs BZ$5 per person)*.

By Bus – Venus Bus Lines (heading north) ☎ (2) 733-54, Batty Brothers Bus Service (heading north and west) ☎ (2) 720-25, Novelo's Bus Service (heading west) ☎ (2) 773-72 and (9) 320-54, Z-Line Bus Service (heading south) ☎ (2) 739-37, and James Bus Service (heading south) ☎ (7) 220-49 provide regular bus service between major cities and the borders with Mexico and Guatemala.

General Information

Tourist Information – **Belize Tourist Board** PO Box 325, New Central Bank Bldg., Gabourel Ln., Belize City, Belize ☎ (2) 319-13 or *www.travelbelize.org (Mon–Thu 8am–noon & 1–5pm, Fri 8am–5:30pm)* provides information on accommodations, transportation, shopping, entertainment, tour operators and travel agencies; within the US and Canada ☎ (800) 624-0686. UK: Belize High Commission, 10 Harcourt House, 16A Cavendish Sq. London W1M 9AD ☎ (441) 71-499-9728. US: Belize Tourist Board, 421 7ᵗʰ Ave., New York, NY 10001 ☎ (212) 563-6011.

Accommodations – Small hotels offer clean rooms with private bathrooms. While some hotels have air conditioning, most rely on electric fans. With the exception of those found in Belize City and in some tourist areas, few luxury hotels exist in Belize. The interior and coastal regions offer small guesthouses and country inns, some very exclusive. Hotels charge an additional 7% tax and 5%–10% service fee of the total room cost. Reservations should be made between December and March. Most establishments do not accept credit cards. For hotel listings, contact the Belize Tourist Board or the Belize Hotel Assoc., 4 Fort Street, Belize City ☎ (2) 301-16. **Campsites** abound along the coast and in the cays; camping on the beach is prohibited.

Banking, Foreign Exchange, Credit Cards & Tips – The **Belizean dollar** has a fixed exchange rate of BZ$2 per USD$1. Atlantic Bank Ltd., Scotia Bank, Barclays Bank and Belize Bank *(open Mon–Thu 8am–1pm, Fri 8:30am–4:30pm)* offer currency exchange in Belize. The major branches of Barclays and Scotia Bank, as well as major gas stations, offer ATMs (automatic teller machines) where one can withdraw money in Belizean currency; these are found primarily in Belize City. Although it is preferable to travel with Belizean dollars, most establishments also accept US currency. Most hotels, restaurants, shops and tour operators accept traveler's checks. Only major establishments accept credit cards (American Express, Visa and MasterCard/EuroCard). Occasionally there is a 5% fee for the use of credit cards. American Express agent: Global Travel Service, 41 Albert St., Belize City ☎ (2) 773-63. Most restaurants include gratuities; otherwise, a 10% or 15% tip is customary.

Sightseeing – Organized tours are the best way to get to know the country and many of its attractions, often located in hard-to-find spots. Local travel agents and tour operators offer packages that include transportation, accommodations and recreational activities. Most cays can be reached by water taxis. **Water taxis** to Ambergris Caye and Caye Caulker depart from Belize's Marine Terminal (Belize City) ☎ (2) 319-69: Belize City–Ambergris Caye *(departure 9am, noon & 3pm; 75min trip, BZ$25, return to Belize City at 8am, 11:30am & 2:30pm, Sat & Sun also at 4:30pm).* Belize City–Caye Caulker *(departure every 1 1/2hrs, 9am–5pm, 45min trip; BZ$15; return to Belize City: six departures from 6:45am to 3pm, Sat & Sun also at 5pm).* To visit **other islands** it is possible to rent a boat and hire the services of a captain. Escorted excursions in well-equipped vehicles to Belize's **interior** and Guatemala's **archaeological sites** are organized through: Henry Menzies Travel & Tours, Box 210, Corozal District, Belize City ☎ (4) 237-25 and 234-14; Far Horizons, PO Box 91900, Albuquerque NM 87199, ☎ (505) 343-9400, 800-552-4575 (US & Canada) or *www.farhorizon.com.* Discovery Expeditions Belize Ltd. offers trips from Belize City, Ambergris Caye and San Ignacio ☎ (2) 307-48. Holbrook Travel, Inc. 3540 NW 13th St. Gainesville FL 32609 ☎ (352) 377-7111 or 800-451-7111 (US & Canada) offers guided **natural history tours**. For a complete listing of tour operators, contact the Belize Tourist Board or the Belize Tour Operators Assoc. ☎ (2) 305-15.

Recreation – Boating, snorkeling, scuba diving, windsurfing, kayaking and canoeing are some of the recreational activities possible in Belize. Experienced divers may explore the **dive sites** along Belize's reefs and atolls. Out Island Divers ☎ (2) 739-37 offers daily boat dives, as well as night dives and 4-day dive trips. Ambergris Caye has several diving agencies, including Hustler Tours ☎ (2) 625-38 and Blue Hole Dive Center ☎ (2) 629-82. For fishing, inquire at your hotel or make arrangements with a local fisherman. Deep-sea fishing is plentiful outside the reef. Most beach communities have dive shops that rent equipment and can help with arrangements. Backpacking, hiking, nature walks and biking are popular. Belize also offers many caves, but they should only be explored with an experienced guide.

Useful Numbers – Police ☎ 911; Fire Department/Ambulance ☎ 90; Assistance Directory (local) ☎ 113

National Holidays

New Year's Day	Jan 1	St. George's Caye Day	Sept 10
Baron Bliss Day	Mar 9	Independence Day	Sept 21
Good Friday	Mar–Apr	Pan American Day	Oct 12
Easter Monday	Mar–Apr	Garífuna Settlement Day	Nov 19
Labor Day	May 1	Christmas Day	Dec 25
Commonwealth Day	May 24	Boxing Day	Dec 26

Society and Economy

From the onset Belize has been a country of immigrants. Here three groups of Maya (Kekchí, Mopán and Yucatec) coexist with the Afro-Belizeans, Creoles and Garífunas. Also present are Mestizos, Mennonites, Chinese, English and North Americans. Unlike its neighboring countries, Belize has not suffered violent civil strife, which explains why large numbers of survivors from Central American wars have sought refuge here. As a result, Mestizos have become Belize's largest ethnic group (44%), as shown in the 1991 census, exceeding the numbers of Creoles (30%), Maya (11%) and Garífunas (7%).

While agriculture is the foundation of economic activity, tourism, with 18% partici-pation in the GNP, is increasing in importance. Belize's natural and cultural heritage attracts annually 260,000 visitors, approximately one tourist per inhabitant. Another valuable source of income for the country is the money sent home by Belizeans working in the United States.

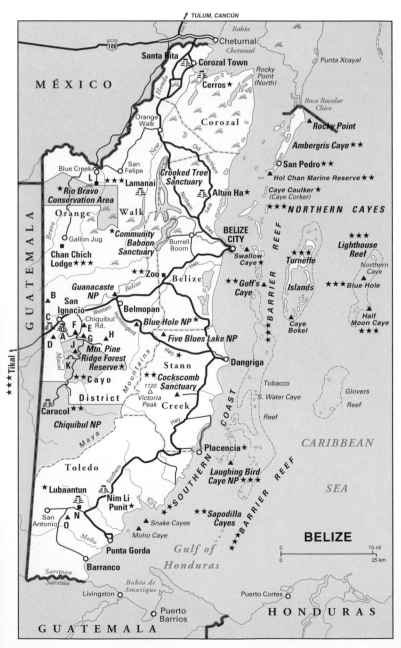

Culture

Handicrafts – Throughout the country visitors can acquire a diverse collection of handicrafts. The most popular include hand-carved slates with reproductions of Maya relics, cericote wood sculptures, baskets woven with jipijapa leaves, wood furniture, cloth dolls and wooden drums made by Garífunas, straw hats, Maya weavings and hand-painted or silk-screened T-shirts.

Food – **Rice and beans** constitute the staples of the Belizean diet. Fried green plantains, stewed chicken and cabbage salad usually accompany these foods. Fresh fish and seafood, especially shellfish and lobster, abound in Belize. On the southern coast, seafood may often be served with coconut milk. Some of the mestizo dishes include **escabeche** (onion soup with chicken), **tamales**, fried **garnachas**, and **empanadas**. The most exotic dishes contain **iguanas** (in season), **turtles** (the most popular being freshwater turtles, such as *Bucatora* and *Hickatee*), **armadillo** and gibnut-a rodent whose "delicious" meat was served to Queen Elizabeth during one of her visits to Belize. The country's bottled hot sauces are world-famous. Also, numerous Chinese restaurants cater to locals and visitors alike.

Traditional Music and Dance – Known even beyond the Atlantic Ocean, **punta rock**, a rhythm based on traditional Garífuna music, is characterized by the sound of Garífuna drums (made from a single piece of wood) and turtle shells. Belize's punta rock king, **Andy Palacio**, enjoys worldwide fame. Also popular in Belize are the **soca** and **calypso** rhythms; **reggae** is heard everywhere and at all hours. Many of northern Belize's locals favor Mexican music. Mestizos and Maya groups usually play **marimba** music in their communities. **Garífuna dances** are spectacular and seductive. In 1993 Belize founded its own National Dance Company, which also performs internationally.

Five Days in Belize

Day 1

Northern Cayes: Ambergris Caye – Accessible from Belize City by 70min boat ride or 15min airplane ride. Join an excursion to **Hol Chan Marine Reserve**, **Shark Ray Alley** and **Caye Caulker**.

Day 2

Lamanai – Excursions available from Belize City and Ambergris Caye.

Day 3

Belize City – Visit the Swing Bridge, the Government House Museum, St. John's Cathedral, the Fort George Area and the **Belize Zoo**.

Day 4

Southern Coast: Placencia Peninsula – Accessible from Belize City by a 1hr airplane ride. Join an excursion to **Laughing Bird Caye National Park**. On the way back, visit **Placencia Village**.

Day 5

Cockscomb Basin Wildlife Sanctuary – 39mi/63km from Placencia.

Dangriga – 26mi/42km from Cockscomb.

BELIZE CITY

Belize District
Population 55,810
Map p 368
🖪 New Central Bank Bldg., Gabourel Lane ☎ (2) 319-13 or www.travelbelize.org

On the shores of the Caribbean Sea, at the mouth of the Belize River lies the largest city of this small Central American country, the only one of British culture and language in the region. Although replaced as capital in 1971 by Belmopan-as a result of the extensive damage caused in 1961 by Hurricane Hattie-Belize City continues as the commercial and cultural center of this newly independent nation. Despite the hurricanes and fires that have devastated the city, most of its houses preserve their typical Caribbean wood appearance, painted in white with red roofs and shady terraces on which their dwellers take shelter from the heat and greet passers-by.

The prettiest homes are found downtown, along **Albert** and **Regent** streets, and in the **Fort George District** located north of **Haulover Creek**, which runs through the city.

SIGHTS

Swing Bridge – *On Haulover Creek.* Dating from 1900, this bridge is the only manually operated swing bridge in the world. Twice a day, at 5:30am and 5:30pm, a group of men turn the crank that swings open the bridge, allowing boats to sail through.

Court House – *Regent St., two streets south of Swing Bridge.* The elegant edifice with wrought-iron columns and a two-ramp staircase currently houses the Palace of Justice. It was reconstructed after 1918, when a fire extensively damaged the original. Its tower is dedicated to the memory of Gov. William Hart Bennetles, who died from the blow he received when the flagstaff collapsed during the fire.

Government House Museum – *South of Regent St., in front of the river's mouth. Open year-round Mon–Fri 8:30am–4:30pm. BZ$5.* Located by the seashore, this 19C **mansion★★** is overlaid in wood, following traditional Caribbean style. From 1815 to 1993 it was home to the various governors who looked after the interests of the British Crown. At present the museum exhibits part of the original furnishings and utensils, as well as photographs that reflect the importance of this house in the country's social, economic and political life.

St. John's Cathedral – *Albert St., in front of the Government House Museum. Open year-round Mon–Fri 9am–noon and 2–4pm, Sat 9am–noon. BZ$5.* ☎ *(2) 721-37.* Slaves built this Protestant cathedral at the beginning of the 19C. It was the site for the coronations of three kings from the indigenous tribe of the Mosquito Coast (located in Honduras and Nicaragua).

Maritime Museum and Terminal – *North Front St., 89. After crossing the Swing Bridge, heading north, turn right. Open year-round daily 9am–5pm. BZ$4.* ☎ *(2) 319-69.* Formerly the firehouse, this white wooden building currently holds a **museum** dedicated to marine life. The terminal is the departure point for boats servicing Caye Caulker, St. George's Caye and San Pedro (Ambergris Caye).

Belize City

Across the street stands the **Paslow Building**, a classical wooden edifice that houses the post office.

Fort George District – *East of the Maritime Museum and Terminal.* Located at the northern end of the city, this area is characterized by its elegant mansions, such as two inns, the **Colton House** and **Fort Street Guest House.** Across the street stands the **National Handicraft Center** *(open year-round Mon–Fri 8am–5pm, Sat 8am–1pm; ☎ 2-336-36).* The area also includes Fort George, a pier located in front of the Radisson Hotel, and the lighthouse-monument **Baron Bliss Lighthouse**, under which lie the remains of English Baron Victor Bliss, Belize's benefactor.

To the north, on Gabourel Lane, near the former prison stands the **US Embassy**, a beautiful wooden building filled with history, which was constructed in New England, United States (1866) and later assembled here.

EXCURSIONS

★**Community Baboon Sanctuary** – *26.2mi/42km from Belize City. Take the Northern Hwy., after 13.5mi/21.5km turn left onto a paved road, cross Burrell Boom and head west on the dirt road for 9mi/14.4km. Open year-round daily 8am–5pm. BZ$10.* ✗ △ ☎ *(2) 772-13.* The treetops of this jungle are home to the black howler monkey, locally known as the "baboon." With the grassroots support of the communities in this region, the sanctuary was founded in 1985 to protect the howler monkey, which the ancient Maya considered to be sacred. Today up to 2,000 of these monkeys inhabit the sanctuary. A brief stroll through the jungle will remove any doubt as to what emits the ear-piercing howl that can be heard from afar.

★**Altun Ha** – *34mi/54.4km from Belize City. Take the Northern Hwy. and after 20mi/32km, turn right and take the Old Northern Hwy.; 12mi/19km later take the exit to the left and continue straight on for 2mi/3km. Open year-round daily 9am–5pm. BZ$10.* ☎ *(2) 772-13.* The ruins of this ceremonial center of the Classic period surround two main plazas. The archaeological site features two temples: the **Temple of the Green Tomb**, where jade objects have been found, and the **Temple of the Sun God**★, the site's tallest structure (59ft/18m). From atop these temples visitors can appreciate a splendid view of the jungle's dense canopy.

In 1968 the famous 15cm/5.9in-tall jade head representing the sun god, Kinich Ahau, was found in one of the seven tombs of the Temple of the Sun God. The original usually resides in the Department of Archaeology or is lent to itinerant exhibits, which makes it difficult to see. However, a reproduction of this smiling sculpture appears on the upper left corner of every Belizean banknote in circulation and the image of the temple adorns the label of a popular local beer, Belikin.

Crooked Tree Wildlife Sanctuary – *34mi/55km from Belize City. Take the Northern Hwy. and after 31.5mi/51km turn left and continue straight on for another 3.5mi/5.6km. Open year-round daily 8am–5pm. BZ$8.* ✗ △ ☎ *(2) 350-04.* Sheltered by towering trees, the sanctuary is located on the outskirts of the peaceful town of Crooked Tree. It was established in 1984 to protect resident and migrant birds, which abound here between November and April.

★★**The Belize Zoo** – *29ml/46km west of Belize City via the Western Hwy. Open year-round daily 8:30am–4:30pm. Closed Good Friday and Sept 21. BZ$15.* ✗ △ ☎ *(8) 130-04 or* www.belizezoo.org. Over 100 animals native to Belize reside in wide spaces with plenty of vegetation. Informative signs explain the animals' habits and characteristics. The zoo features Belize's national animals: the tapir, toucan and jaguar-even a black jaguar.

BELMOPAN
Cayo District
Population 7,105
Map p 368
🛈 ☎ (2) 319-13

Located in Belize's geographical center, between San Ignacio and Belize City, Belmopan was founded as the country's capital in 1971-ten years after Hurricane Hattie struck the former capital, Belize City. Home to Belize's government buildings, Belmopan is inhabited mainly by bureaucrats and some refugees from other Central American countries. Nonetheless, the so-called "modern capital for a newly born nation" has not succeeded in replacing the lively Belize City.

On the outskirts of Belmopan begins **Hummingbird Highway★**, a 55mi/88km road with beautiful scenery, which crosses the Maya Mountains before reaching the south coast.

EXCURSIONS

Guanacaste National Park – *1.4mi/2km north of Belmopan, at the intersection between Hummingbird and Western Highways. 22.5mi/36km east of San Ignacio. Open year-round daily 8am–5pm. BZ$5.* ☎ *(2) 350-04.* Visitors may tour the jungle of this small national park by way of three 2.5mi/4km-long trails. Created in 1990 to protect over 100 bird species that inhabit the area, the park derives its name from the huge, 150-year-old **Guanacaste tree★** growing in the southwestern part of the park.

★**Blue Hole National Park** – *From Guanacaste National Park head south on Hummingbird Hwy. for 12.5mi/20km. Open year-round daily 8am–5pm. BZ$8.* ⚠ ☎ *(2) 350-04.* The extensive jungle area (575 acres/230ha) is home to diverse fauna. This protected area also contains **St. Herman's Cave★**, used by the ancient Maya as a sacred place. The sapphire-blue **natural pool★** for which the park was named is located 1.2mi/2km from the cave.

Five Blues Lake National Park – *Exit Belmopan on Hummingbird Hwy. After 22mi/35.2km, turn left onto a dirt road and continue 4.3mi/7km. Open year-round daily 8am–4pm. BZ$8.* ⚠ ☎ *(2) 319-13. Before arriving, be sure to inquire about road conditions.* Declared a national park in 1991, this place owes its name to the different hues of blue in the lake, accessed via several pedestrian trails through the jungle. *(Take a map at the information booth located 200m/656ft from Hummingbird Hwy.).* In the middle of the lake (10 acres/4ha), which is really a cenote whose roof collapsed, lies a small island colonized by a wide variety of orchids. The limestone hills surrounding the lake house caves, which can also be visited. Managed by a community, the reserve (4,292 acres/1,717ha) is home to 277 species of birds and the five types of wildcats that exist in Belize.

CAYO DISTRICT★★
Cayo District
Population 11,290
Map p 368
🛈 ☎ (9) 242-36

This mountainous region was isolated until the 1940s, when the road that connects Cayo District with Belize City was built. Prior to the road's existence, the journey to this area would take up to 21 days along the Belize River, by way of which precious woods were transported to the port for exportation.

Today, located less than two hours from Belize City, this region offers a wide variety of attractions, such as Maya ruins-many of which are still undergoing excavation-rivers, popular for swimming and rowing, as well as horseback riding trails. Charming **cottage inns** dot the region's wooded hilltops. Also, easily accessible from Cayo District stands the archaeological site of Tikal in Guatemala, whose border lies 9mi/15km southwest of San Ignacio.

SAN IGNACIO AND SURROUNDINGS

San Ignacio – *70mi/107km west of Belize City.* In the heart of the Cayo District, this peaceful village with colorful houses is located just beyond the **Hawksworth Bridge**, a narrow suspension bridge that crosses the Macal River. For generations it served as the main point for logging mahogany and *chicle*, the region's economic foundation. Today it attracts numerous tourists who can find affordable hotels, restaurants and travel agencies that offer organized excursions, on **Burns Avenue**—San Ignacio's main street.

Green Iguana Conservation Project – *In the Hotel San Ignacio, 437yd/400m west of San Ignacio. Guided tour (1hr). Open year-round daily 8am–4pm. BZ$10.* ☎ *(9) 220-34.* Inside the hotel's reserve one can visit the iguana center, created to protect this endangered reptile and to raise people's awareness on the species. Visitors can see the incubators and touch the baby iguanas, most of which are set free nearby.

★**Cahal Pech (A)** – *1mi/1.6km south of San Ignacio on Buena Vista Rd. Open year-round daily 9am–5pm. BZ$5.* ☎ *(9) 242-36.* The reconstructed ruins of this acropolis-like archaeological site, occupied from 1,000 BC to AD 800, perch on a hill offering an excellent panoramic view of the jungle.

Visitor Center – *164yd/150m from the site. Open Tue–Sat 9am–4:30pm, Sun 9am–noon. BZ$5.* Besides providing tourist information, this visitor center features an interesting **collection**★ of ceramic objects that were found mainly in Cahal Pech, but also in various other Belizean sites.

★**El Pilar Archaeological Reserve for Maya Flora and Fauna (B)** – *Exit San Ignacio heading southwest past Bullet Tree Village (3.1mi/5km from San Ignacio); after crossing the bridge, turn left and continue 7.5mi/12km. Open year-round daily 8am–5pm.* ☎ *(8) 221-06.* In this magnificent jungle, decreed a reserve in 1998, several structures made up the ancient administrative center occupied by the Maya during a period spanning 13 centuries, from 250 BC to AD 1000. The visit helps one understand how the Maya lived off the jungle without exploiting it. A great number of birds and wildlife can still be seen or heard in this reserve. Rest on one of the comfortable benches and experience the jungle from the same points where it is believed the ancient rulers observed the rising and setting of the sun. At the foot of the 12 main structures or in the 15 Maya plazas, one can appreciate scenes very similar to those encountered by the archaeologists who discovered the site. Today the challenge lies in having this reserve, supported by community involvement, serve as a model for conserving the environment and preserving the culture of the Maya, both ancient and contemporary.

★★**Xunantunich (C)** – *Board the manually piloted ferryboat located 6.6mi/11km west of San Ignacio. After crossing the Mopán River, drive for 1mi/1.6km. Open year-round Mon–Fri 9am–5pm, weekends 9am–4pm. BZ$10.* ☎ *(8) 221-06.* Located amidst a highland jungle, the high plateau is the site of the ruins of this important, Classic-period ceremonial center whose name means "Maiden of the Rock." The center was probably once under the control of the nearby El Naranjo site, which today belongs to Guatemala. The main structures situated around the three plazas were built between AD 600–1000.

★★**El Castillo** – *South of the three main plazas.* With a height of 135ft/40m including the remains of its cresting, the temple is Belize's second highest building. Its upper level contains the remnants of a remarkable **frieze**★★, which originally covered all four sides of the pyramid with representations of rulers, masks and astral symbols. Today only the east side and a replica of the west side can be seen. From the summit visitors can appreciate a magnificent **view**★ of a seemingly endless jungle.

Chaa Creek Natural History Centre (D) – *Exit San Ignacio and drive to the Benque Viejo Rd. Head west and after 4.8mi/7.7km turn left (follow the road signs) and continue straight on for 3mi/5km. Guided tour (1hr), year-round daily 7am–4pm. BZ$10* ⚒ ⚑ ☎ *(9) 120-10 or* www.chaacreek.com. Set on a hilltop on the premises of Chaa Creek Cottages, the center provides information on the region's natural and archaeological history. It was the first of its kind to be established in Belize. Guided tours are offered to the **Blue Morpho Butterfly Breeding Centre**★, where visitors may follow the different developmental stages of the beautiful blue-winged butterfly, native to the jungles of Belize. Chaa Creek Inland Expeditions offers one-day excursions departing from San Ignacio, which include a walk through the **Chaa Creek Natural Reserve** (330 acres/132ha) home to four Maya sites, howler monkeys and migratory birds. Participants can also choose to explore the reserve on horseback. The expedition ends with a canoe trip back to San Ignacio by way of the Macal River *(BZ$120 per person or BZ$178 for the horseback riding option, includes lunch and transportation from San Ignacio).*

★**Ix Chel Farm Rain Forest Medicine Trail** – *219yd/200m east of the Chaa Creek Natural History Centre. Open year-round daily 8am–noon & 1–5pm. BZ$11.50.* ☎ *(9) 238-70 or* www.ixchelbelize.com. The Ix Chel Farm tour takes place along the Macal River and through the jungle. It covers the usage and properties of over 35 **medicinal plants**, many of which were discovered by the Maya shaman Don Elijio Panti (1891–1996).

The following sights are found along the way to Mountain Pine Ridge Forest Reserve.

★**Barton Creek Cave (E)** – *From San Ignacio head east for 7mi/11km, then take Chiquibul Rd. southbound; 4.8mi/7.8km later, turn left and continue 3.8mi/6.6km on a road accessible only by four-wheel-drive vehicles. Open year-round daily*

8am–5pm. BZ$5 plus the excursion rate (one must be equipped with a canoe and potent flashlights). For further information, inquire in your hotel or at a travel agency in San Ignacio. ☎ (2) 319-13. During a journey of approximately 1mi/1.6km through this enormous cave, one can marvel at the huge stalactites and stalagmites formed over thousands of years. Some of these formations, inhabited by tiny bats, reach the surface of the river. In addition, one can see the remains of a Maya burial ground. Upon turning off the flashlights, one can imagine how the ancient Maya traversed this cave with only the lighting of torches.

Green Hills Butterfly Centre (F) – *Exit San Ignacio to the west; after 7mi/11km, take Chiquibul Rd. and continue 7.8mi/12.5km. Guided tour. Open Christmas–Holy Week daily 8am–5pm; outside this season, visit by appointment only (minimum of 2 people). BZ$5. ☎ (9) 233-10.* Inside a pleasant hut with regional plants, one can observe up to 20 different species of butterflies, which are often difficult to see in the jungle.

★**Mountain Equestrian Trails (G)** – *The entranceway is almost directly across Green Hills. Guided tours in English, Spanish and German. Open year-round daily; reservation required. ✗ ☎ (8) 231-80 or (800) 838-3918 (from the US) or* www.metbelize.com. Located in the Slate Creek Preserve, this place offers horseback rides through 60mi/96km of nature trails; these can last four hours to several days and are suitable for beginners and experts. During the journey one can explore caves and archaeological sites, and admire the fauna and flora in the more remote areas, impossible to reach by car. The reception area, which also functions as a bar, restaurant and common area, affords a great **view** of Mountain Pine Ridge Forest Reserve.

★MOUNTAIN PINE RIDGE FOREST RESERVE

7mi/11km east of San Ignacio take Chiquibul Rd. heading south; continue 10mi/16km to the entrance gate. www.belizex.com/pine/mntpine.htm.

On a red terrain the jungle transforms itself into a coniferous forest. Pine trees and fog rise amid this forest reserve surrounded by an exuberant neotropical jungle. Tumbling waterfalls, white-water rapids and enormous limestone caves are some of the attractions accessible by four-wheel drive vehicle or on horseback. The mountain ridge is home to some of Belize's most charming and frequented **inns**★★. Several of these inns are luxurious—such as the Blancaneaux Lodge, owned by the famous movie director Francis Ford Coppola. Due to the location of a military training camp in this unique reserve once exploited by lumbermen, there is a strong military presence on the premises.

Hidden Valley Falls (H) – *Follow Chiquibul Rd. and go past the gate; 3.6mi/6km later take the exit to the left and after 7mi/11km, turn left and continue straight on for another 3mi/4.5km.* The 18,000-acre/7,200ha Hidden Valley Inn reserve boasts a lookout over a 1,600ft/480m-tall waterfall, also known as the **1,000 Foot Falls**, the highest in the country. On a clear day, Belmopan can be seen from here.

Rio On Pools (J) – *After passing the gate follow Chiquibul Rd.; 11.5mi/18.5km later, take the exit to the right and continue straight on for 1,312ft/400m.* Forming in the bed of the Rio On, the largest in the reserve, these natural pools provide an enjoyable swimming place during the dry season, when the water is crystal clear.

★**Rio Frío Cave (K)** – *From Rio On, take Chiquibul Rd. and continue heading south 3mi/4.4km to the Douglas D'Silva Forest Station. From there turn right and continue straight on for 1mi/1.6km. Open year-round daily.* The breathtaking 2,624ft/800m-long limestone cave arches over the river, whose name literally means "cold river," and is open at both ends. During the dry season visitors may swim in the natural blue pools that form beneath the cave's stalactites.

★★CARACOL

From the Mountain Pine Ridge Forest Reserve gate, head south on Chiquibul Rd. for 14mi/23km to the Douglas D'Silva Forest Station; from here turn left and after 10mi/16km cross the Macal River. Then continue for another 12mi/19km heading southwest. Open year-round daily 8am–5pm. BZ$10. ☎ (8) 221-06 or www.belizereport.com/sites/caracol.html. *Visits to this archaeological site are recommended only during the dry season, and it is advisable to inquire in San Ignacio (which offers excursions to the site) with respect to road conditions.*

In the **Chiquibul Forest Reserve** (National Park) lie the ruins of the immense Maya city that remained hidden under the dense canopy of the jungle for nearly a millennium. Although discovered in 1939 by Rosa Mai, a local logger in search of mahogany and cedar, Caracol's importance was not determined until much later, after decades of extensive research. In 1986 an elaborately carved, 7C altar stone denoting Caracol's victory over Tikal was uncovered in the site's **ball court**. After the battle of AD 562, Caracol retained control over the Petén region for a little over a century, during which period the population of this urban and ceremonial center reached 150,000 inhabitants *(Maya, p 32 and 314)*.

The extensive hieroglyphic records discovered after ten years of intense excavations have provided valuable information about Caracol or Ox Witz Ha (Mayan for "place of the three hills"), which, according to a recent finding, was the site's original name.

The hieroglyphic inscriptions have been found in stelae or slates, which narrate the history of the great accomplishments linked to the ruling class. Based on these, archaeologists have identified a large dynasty that governed the site from AD 331–859 and conquered Tikal and Naranjo (Guatemala), the latter in 1636. The discovery of several bones bearing hieroglyphic inscriptions, in residential areas, suggests that a large proportion of Caracol's population had access to written documents.

This huge city, today covered by a dense canopy of trees in a jungle whose sky is dotted with hundreds of parakeets and other birds, is characterized by its sophisticated **sacbeob** design (road network). Covering 37mi/60km, this network led to various architectural groups and agricultural fields within a radius of 3mi/5km. Caracol spanned approximately 110sq mi/177sq km, of which only 10.5sq mi/17sq km have been mapped. At present, only 5,000 of the site's estimated 36,000 structures have been uncovered.

The visit is limited to the city's center, which extends over a plateau at an elevation of 1,640ft/500m. Start in the **visitor center**, which exhibits some ceramic objects and photographs of some of the site's most important findings.

Group B – *On the north side of Caracol, the first plaza in sight.* The site's largest architectural complex includes Caana, a ball court and Barrio, a residential complex once inhabited by Caracol's elite. On the north edge of the plaza stands the **Caana★** complex whose Maya name signifies "place of the sky," a nickname befitting of its stature—it rises 141ft/43m above the plaza and is the tallest manmade structure in all of Belize. It consists of four residential compounds and three religious compounds. Following several reconstructions, the final version was completed after AD 800. Halfway through the building, one encounters a series of bedrooms. A small plaza, edged by small pyramids, crowns the summit. In the eastern pyramid, four tombs were found, one of which contained the remains of a female body, jade earflaps and ceramic bowls. The climb to these structures is rewarded with an impressive **view★★** of the jungle and the rest of Group B.

Central Acropolis – *Between Group A and Group B.* This residential complex encompasses two temples, two palaces and a funerary building. In the latter, archaeologists found a royal tomb with the remains of four people.

Group A – *On the northwest end of the acropolis.* Judging from the distribution of the buildings, it is believed that this group constituted an astronomical observatory. On the east side lies a platform with four structures, including the **Templo del Dintel de Madera** (Temple of the Wooden Lintel). This place was named for its wooden beams, one of which is inscribed with the date of construction, IC AD, making it one of Caracol's most ancient buildings. The first structure dates back to 300 BC and was used until AD 1100, year in which the city was abandoned. During the excavations, a stone box with a mask from AD 70 was found in the center of the temple. The box contained a rag placed over 684g of liquid mercury. The rag enveloped an earflap made of jadeite and a seashell, inside which another jadeite mask rested in a bed of cinnabar. Across from building A2, located on the west edge of the plaza, in Group A, rises **stela 22**, engraved with Belize's most extensive hieroglyphs.

COROZAL TOWN

Corozal District
Population 8,085
Map p 368
🅱 ☎ (4) 231-76

The tranquil town with colorful wooden houses is located by the seashore, only 9mi/14km from the Mexican border. It was founded in 1849 by the Maya who fled from Yucatán, Mexico, after the massacre of Bacalar, which took place during the Caste War. The growing and thriving sugar industry took advantage of the manual labor provided by the refugees, who proved to be efficient farmers. This activity, along with tapping of the sapodilla tree for *chicle*, predominated in the region until 1955 when **Hurricane Janet** changed Corozal's life and appearance. Along with the hurricane, the fluctuation in the price of sugar created a need to diversify crops.

SIGHTS

Corozal Town is located 87mi/139km north of Belize City.

Corozal Museum – *Coronation Park. Two streets from Santiago Ricalde Central Park, on Costera St. Open year-round Tue–Sun 9am–4:30pm. BZ$3.* ☎ *(4) 231-76.* This quaint wooden **building★** constructed in 1886 housed the market until 1959. At present the museum provides tourist information and displays temporary exhibits. It also features a collection of objects related to the history of Corozal. Of particular interest are the figure of **St. Narcissus** and a collection of **ancient bottles** rescued from the sea. These bottles called *chaparras*—which when empty were thrown to the sea—today serve as typical decorative objects in Belize.

City Hall Mural – *South of Santiago Ricalde Central Park. Open year-round Mon–Thu 8am–5pm, Fri 8am–4:30pm.* ☎ *(4) 220-72.* City hall boasts a **mural** painted by Manuel Villamor Reyes. This work of art, completed in 1953 and retouched in 1986, narrates the history of Corozal. One of the scenes depicts the massacre of Bacalar (1848), which forced many Mexican Maya to cross the border and take refuge in Belize.

Santa Rita – *1mi/1.5km northwest of Corozal, behind the Coca-Cola warehouse. Open year-round daily 9am–5pm. BZ$10.* ☎ *(8) 221-06.* This archaeological site contains the remains of a structure that formed part of the ancient Maya city (occupied between 2000 BC and AD 1550), which probably was the origin of the present-day Mexican city of Chetumal. Most of this ancient commercial center rests buried beneath the town of Corozal.

EXCURSION

★**Cerros** – *15min boat ride from Corozal, located at the tip of the Corozal Bay. Open year-round daily 9am–5pm BZ$5.* ☎ *(8) 221-06.* By the seaside lie the remnants of the three major temples of this important commercial center where jade and obsidian were traded. Los Cerros (The Hills) were, occupied from 300 BC to AD 100.

LAMANAI★★★

Orange Walk District
Map p 368
🅱 ☎ (2) 319-13 or www.travelbelize.org/guide/ma/ma03.html

The boat excursion on the New River to reach the archaeological site of Lamanai provides a picturesque **journey★★**, during which tiny bats and swift yellow birds can be observed walking on the leaves that float on the river's surface. In addition, one may appreciate a variety of wild vegetation and even taste the sweetness of its fruits. With luck, visitors may also see crocodiles, turtles and manatees.

ARCHAEOLOGICAL SITE

North of Belize City. Take the Northern Hwy. and drive 52mi/83.5km to the toll bridge, which is the point of departure for all 2hr boat rides to Lamanai. Excursions also depart from Belize City and Ambergris Caye. The site may also be accessed from a dirt road that goes through Orange Walk Town and San Felipe. Open year-round Mon–Fri 8am–5pm, Sat–Sun 8am–4pm. BZ$10. ☎ *(8) 221-06.*

The ruins of the ancient ceremonial center, whose name means "submerged crocodile," are located on the banks of the **New River**, amid a jungle full of rare aromas and exotic fruits, and beneath the screams of the howler monkeys and the swinging of the spider monkeys. The structures seen today were built between AD 100 and 900. Despite the decline of most of the Maya sites, in AD 900, Lamanai remained occupied for ten more centuries until the 19C, long after the arrival of the Spaniards, who were drawn to the region in the 16C in search of gold *(Maya, p 32 and 314)*.

Museum – This small cabin exhibits figures found in the archaeological site, mostly ceramics, which date back prior to the Christian era.

The Mask Temple – Completed between the 3C and the 6C, the temple was named after a huge 13ft/4m-tall **mask★★** carved in limestone, which is located to the right of the central staircase. Eighty-seven jade beads were found in the temple's tomb.

The High Temple (N 10-43) – Lamanai's tallest temple, it was probably dedicated to the cult of the Sun, given that the front part of the edifice contains remnants of the masks of Kinich Ahau, the sun god. With a height of 111.5ft/34m, the temple constitutes the third tallest structure in all of Belize. From its summit, visitors may admire a breathtaking **view★★** of the lagoon, the jungle and the Guatemalan and Mexican mountains. In front of this structure lie the ruins of the **ball court**, known here as **pok-ta-pok**, from which were extracted traces of mercury, apparently used together with obsidian either to create mirrors or to amplify the reflection of the stars.

★**Stela 9** – *East of the ball court.* This carved, stone slate portrays a ruler whose face emerges from the open mouth of his celestial progenitor, the crocodile. This reptile was the main sacred figure in Lamanai, probably the last city to be abandoned by the ancient Maya.

NORTHERN CAYES★★★
Belize District
Map p 368
🛈 ☎ (2) 319-13

Parallel to Belize's coast, with a length of almost 186mi/300km, extends the largest **coral barrier reef★★★** in the Western Hemisphere, designated a World Heritage Site in 1996. The barrier reef protects the archipelago formed by hundreds of cays (small islands) dotting the blue waters of the Caribbean Sea, just off Belize's coasts. Many of these cays represent the ideal image of a paradisiacal island: they are isolated and have beautiful, white sandy beaches adorned with palm trees.

Beyond the barrier reef, atolls formed by reefs thousands of years old sustain an intriguing variety of marine life, including over 50 types of corals and 400 different species of fish. Some of these cays serve as springboards to world-renowned dive sites, especially those to the northeast of Belize City. The attractions of the underwater world range from schools of exotic fish, corals and geological formations, to sharks and shipwrecks. The sun, music, sea, seafood and Belizean hospitality beckon one to visit and enjoy this paradise.

Far-away islands offer a variety of hotels. Visitors may also opt to spend several days exploring the cays from a full-service yacht.

★★AMBERGRIS CAYE

A channel that marks Belize's border with Mexico separates this 20mi/32km-long island from the Yucatán Peninsula. Lush vegetation, rich in mangroves, lines the cay's peaceful **beaches★★** *(photo p 363)*, from which may be heard the roaring sound of the waves crashing against the barrier reef.

★★**San Pedro** – *35mi/56km northeast of Belize City (70min by boat).* Ambergris' only town is located on the southern end of the island. Founded in the mid 19C by immigrants who fled the coasts of the Yucatán Peninsula escaping the Caste War, this tranquil fishing village has gained worldwide fame as a diving mecca and constitutes Belize's main tourist destination. Outlining San Pedro in profile, several **piers** serve as points of departure for early excursions to the different reefs.

Numerous golf carts—the most widely used means of transportation, along with bicycles—circulate the sand roads of San Pedro. The small town features the cemetery, located by the seashore, and the lovely Caribbean-style **Hotel Barrier Reef**, one of San Pedro's oldest. The town also offers shops, restaurants and travel agencies. Excursions with inland destinations to Belize's principal sights may also be arranged from here. Many of the tours offered last only one day, making it possible to return to San Pedro for dinner or to enjoy its informal **nightlife**.

Several **hotels** can be found on the outskirts of town. To reach the most remote ones, on the north end, visitors must cross a channel aboard a rustic **ferryboat** and walk or bike along the **beach**.

★**Ambergris Museum and Cultural Centre** – *Island Plaza, Barrier Reef Dr. Open year-round Mon–Sat 2pm–8pm. BZ$5.* ☎ *(2) 626-05.* Located on San Pedro's main street, this handsome museum presents a complete panorama of Ambergris

Caye, including its geological formation, as well as a history of the island during ancient Maya times and when it served as a refuge for pirates. It also covers the founding of San Pedro, and how it was transformed from a single-family (Blake) property to an important tourist center. Three small rooms display a variety of objects (ancient Maya ceramics, bottles, tools, etc.), most of which were donated or lent by Ambergris' inhabitants. The museum also provides tourist information.

Rocky Point – *North of Ambergris. For further information on how to join an organized excursion to this place, inquire at your hotel or in the dive shops. BZ$100 (lunch included).* The barrier reef and Ambergris Caye meet at Rocky Point, one of the preferred sites for sport fishing. The excursion to this location includes three stops for snorkeling. Lunch features fish and lobster, or other seafood (varies according to season), grilled on the beach. On the northern edge of Rocky Point lies the protected area known as Bacalar Chico National Park and Marine Reserve, with its delicate ecosystems.

★★ Hol Chan Marine Reserve – *On the southern tip of Ambergris Caye. Only a 10min boat ride from San Pedro. It may also be accessed from Caye Caulker. BZ$5, plus excursion fee.* www.ambergriscaye.com/holchan. In the 5sq mi/8sq km underwater coral park surrounding the barrier reef, visitors can observe beautiful parrotfish and enormous groupers, as well as some of the moray eels that reside in crevices and small caverns. This marine reserve will especially fascinate night divers.

★★★ Shark Ray Alley – *A 20min boat ride from San Pedro or 10min from Hol Chan Marine Reserve. It may also be reached from Caye Caulker. An underwater camera is recommended.* www.ambergriscaye.com/pages/town/parksharkrayalley.html. In this protected zone, visitors may enjoy snorkeling at a depth of only 6.5ft/2m, alongside harmless nurse sharks and rays that span nearly 3ft/1m in diameter.

OTHER CAYS, ATOLLS AND REEFS

★ Caye Caulker – *10mi/16km south of San Pedro (25min boat ride). Boat rides departing constantly from Belize City cover the 20mi/32km distance in 50min.* www.cayecaulker.org *or* www.gocayecaulker.com. South of the 4.3mi/7km-long and 0.5mi/0.8km-wide cay, there is a charming **villa★**, primarily a fishing community whose economy is now enjoying the benefits of tourism. Along with heaps of lobster traps, masks and fins are provided to the growing number of tourists who select this island for being more peaceful and economical than San Pedro. Its surroundings boast over 20 diving and snorkeling sites. Lively bars, restaurants and places that offer slide shows depicting the natural beauty of Belize, flank Caye Caulker's tranquil streets.

★ The Cut – *North of the villa.* This channel of crystalline water divides the island in two. Created by Hurricane Hattie in 1961, today it attracts snorkelers and sunbathers.

Caye Caulker Mini Reserve and Resource Centre – *Next to the landing strip. Open year-round, Mon–Fri 8am–noon & 2–6pm (the reserve is open 24hrs). Donations accepted.* ☎ *(2) 222-51.* Located on the seashore, this small reserve (1.5 acres/0.6ha) shelters more than 20 species of regional flora, as well as iguanas, birds and crabs. A brochure provided at the resource centre explains the characteristics of the different species found here. Besides offering a library with literature on Belize's history, culture and natural life, the center provides online service and computer access *(open 10am–noon, by appointment only after noon).*

Blue Hole

Goff's Caye

Swallow Caye and Goff's Caye (The Manatee Tour) – *South of Caye Caulker. For further information on how to join this excursion, inquire at your hotel or in a travel agency. BZ$55. From San Pedro: BZ$150.* After 22mi/35km (45min from Caye Caulker) through mangrove cays, the boat reaches **Swallow Caye★**, home to a protected area inhabited by endangered manatees. From the boat, visitors can observe this gentle mammal, measuring approximately 10ft/3m in length, which feeds on the mangroves and can stay submerged for up to five minutes.

★★**Goff's Caye** – The second destination is this tiny island situated on the barrier reef. Its transparent waters are ideal for snorkeling. Beneath the shade of a wide thatched hut or a group of palm trees, one can relax on the white sand while enjoying the sun and a view of the sea.

★★★**Turneffe Islands** – *Approximately 25mi/40km southeast of San Pedro (1hr by boat).* www.ambergriscaye.com/pages/town/diveturneffe.html. These islands comprise the largest of Belize's three atolls. Nearly 200 cays surround the three, crystal-clear **lagoons★**, forming a marine labyrinth. Various sizes of cays abound–from small cays that sustain the manatees, to **Caye Bokel**, an island that boasts a lighthouse and three hotels.

The currents that reach this atoll, whose waters can descend to depths of 984ft/300m, along with a proliferation of mangroves rich in nutrients, favor the existence of a diverse marine fauna. Solitary hammerhead sharks, majestic manta rays, as well as sea turtles and dolphins can be seen. Divers may also explore the remains of a 1793 shipwreck.

★★★**Lighthouse Reef** – *Some 50mi/80km southeast of San Pedro (2 1/2hrs by speedboat).* The farthest atoll offers divers the deep enchantments of its reef, home to a wide variety of marine species, as well as an idyllic tropical island with a bird reserve. Six ships have wrecked on the shores of this reef. Although one of the wrecks has been used as a target for military bombing drills, divers may explore the other five. On Northern Caye, one of the atoll's six cays, most divers stay at the Lighthouse Reef Resort *(www.scubabelize.com)*. Several excursions to the Lighthouse Reef offer overnight stays on this idyllic tropical island.

★★★**Blue Hole** – *At the center of the reef.* A marvelous, almost perfect circle, 1,312ft/400m in diameter, marks the entrance to the underwater cave, with a depth of 475ft/145m. Named for its intense blue water, the "hole" has become a world-renowned dive site due to its geological formations. The famous French oceanographer, Jacques Yves Cousteau, explored it in 1972. The stalactites indicate that this cave, whose roof collapsed millions of years ago, became inundated at the end of the Ice Age with the rising of the ocean level.

★★★**Half Moon Caye Natural Monument** – *On the southeastern corner of the reef.* www.nps.gov/centralamerica/belize. The small heavenly island houses a colony of 4,000 red-footed booby birds and 98 other species. For this reason, it was declared a National Park in 1982, the first in all of Belize. Two species of endangered sea turtles lay their eggs on these **beaches★**. The 19C **lighthouse** currently functions with solar energy. The waters surrounding the reserve offer a marvelous dive site with a visibility that exceeds a depth of 164ft/50m, where enormous manta rays can be spotted.

RIO BRAVO CONSERVATION AREA★

Orange Walk District
Map p 368
🛈 ☎ (2) 756-16

This protected area of tropical forests is located to the northwest of Belize. A **trail system**★★ leads visitors through the natural and archaeological riches of the area, managed by a local conservation organization known as the Programme for Belize. Plans are underway to unite the reserve with Guatemala's Maya Biosphere and Mexico's Calakmul reserve, to establish a tri-national park with a surface of 4.9 million acres/2 million hectares, which would constitute the largest in the Western Hemisphere.

SIGHTS

La Milpa Field Station (L) – *94mi/150km from Belize City. In Orange Walk Town take the 24mi/38.4km dirt road west to San Felipe; there turn right and head northwest toward Blue Creek; 6mi/10km beyond this villa, head south and continue straight on for 6.5mi/10.5km. Open year-round 24hrs daily. Reservations or prior notice needed. BZ$40.* ☎ *(2) 756-16.* Most **paths** originate from the field station that offers lodging. Visitors may reach the archaeological site of (3mi/5km) **La Milpa** *(same times and charges as those of La Milpa Field Station;* www.belizereport.com/sites/lamilpa.html*)*, still undergoing excavation and one of the 60 Maya sites found in the area.

★★★**Chan Chich Lodge** – *23mi/37km south of La Milpa Field Station lies the Gallon Jug villa; from here head west on a 5mi/8km road that leads to Chan Chich. Open year-round daily. Reservations or prior notice needed.* ☎ *(2) 756-34, 344-19. From the US and Canada:* ☎ *(800) 343-8009.* www.chanchich.com. Nestled in the lower plaza of an ancient Maya ceremonial center, the rustic but luxurious hotel, unique in the whole world, is located in the southern part of the Rio Bravo area, within a private reserve. A dense jungle, crossed by several rivers and inhabited by more than 300 bird species, surrounds the lodge. Covering over 8mi/13km, an extensive **trail system**★★ maximizes opportunities to explore the jungle's diverse vegetation. Guests of the lodge may partake in guided excursions, especially enjoyable at night when more wildlife can be seen. The howler monkeys' screams and the parrots' chatter serve as a natural alarm clock that goes off before 6am.

Chan Chich Lodge

SOUTHERN COAST★★

Districts: Stann Creek and Toledo
Map p 368
🏠 ✆ (2) 319-13

Some of the wildest but most attractive areas of Belize are nestled in the foothills of the **Maya Mountains**, overlooking the Caribbean Sea and its pristine **cays**. Towns with definite character, such as **Dangriga**, **Placencia Village** and the isolated town of **Punta Gorda**, line Belize's southern coast and provide a perfect base for undertaking fascinating expeditions both to the depths of the sea and to the innermost recesses of the jungle. The towns can be accessed from the Southern Highway-a slow dirt road with a total length of 100mi/160km—or by means of short rides on small airplanes offering magnificent views.

DANGRIGA

75mi/120km from Belize City. Head west and after 31mi/50km, in the town of La Democracia, take the exit to the south and continue straight on for 36.5mi/58.4km until the intersection with Hummingbird Hwy. Follow the highway for 7mi/11km to the coast. www.travelbelize.org/guide/di/di09.html.

Located by the seashore, the village is inhabited mainly by **Garífunas** or Black Caribs, proud descendants of Africans who settled in this area during the 19C. Dangriga resembles a small-scale replica of Belize City. Here, local artists can be seen at work.

Dangriga provides easy access to the barrier reef and nearby cays, such as **South Water Caye**, which offers lodging *(for more information, contact the Pelican Beach Resort* ✆ *5-220-44 or www.pelicanbeachbelize.com).*

★★**Cockscomb Basin Wildlife Sanctuary** – *Exit Dangriga, heading west; after 4.5mi/7km turn left onto Southern Hwy.; 15.5mi/25km later turn right at the Maya Centre onto a 6mi/10km road that leads to the Cockscomb Sanctuary. Open year-round daily 8am–5pm. BZ$10. △ ✆ (2) 350-04 or www.belizeaudubon.org/html/parks/cbws.html. Visits to the jungle are recommended early in the morning or late in the afternoon to maximize the possibilities of observing wildlife.* The exuberant tropical forest reserve is inhabited by 55 species of mammals, among them the elusive **jaguar** (difficult to spot due to its nocturnal habits), as well as 290 species of birds. Sixteen miles (26km) of trails cover the reserve, which is home to deer, howler monkeys, hummingbirds, serpents and lush flora. Established in a basin formerly exploited by loggers, the sanctuary is crossed by rivers where visitors may swim surrounded by towering mountains that include **Victoria Peak** (3,675ft/1,120m), Belize's highest summit.

★★PLACENCIA PENINSULA

From Cockscomb Basin Wildlife Sanctuary take the Southern Hwy. and turn right, heading south; 8mi/13km later turn left and continue straight on for 25mi/40km to Placencia. www.travelbelize.org/guide/di/di10.html.

The 16.2mi/26km-long peninsula lies between the sea and a mangrove lagoon. Used in the 17C as a refuge for buccaneers and inhabited by fishermen since the 19C, today it is considered one of Belize's loveliest tourist sights. Secluded, peaceful hotels can be found on its white sandy **beaches★**, caressed by the Caribbean Sea.

★**Placencia Village** – Located on the southern tip of the peninsula, this pleasant town enjoys the charm of its kind and friendly people. The village's 3.3ft/1m-wide and 0.6mi/1km-long main street is really a sidewalk-designed for pedestrian use only-and appears in the *Guinness Book of World Records* as the world's narrowest street. It is lined by traditional Caribbean-style wooden structures, such as private residences, restaurants, hotels, gift shops and bars, where at night one can enjoy the sounds of live music to the rhythm of **punta**, **soca** and **calypso**.

Placencia offers many recreational activities, from kayaking in the **lagoon**, where manatees can be observed, to sportfishing or diving near the barrier reef.

Even more peaceful than the village are the virtually unspoiled cays in the open sea. Some of them offer overnight stays, be it in cabins or camping grounds.

★★★**Laughing Bird Caye National Park** – *12.4mi/20km from the coast (1hr boat ride from Placencia). Open year-round daily 24hrs. Reservations or prior notice required. BZ$40.* ✆ *(2) 319-13 or www.laughingbird.org.* The long, narrow island boasts gorgeous **beaches★★** whose waters feature coral gardens and a diverse marine life. First declared a protected area in 1981, Laughing Bird Caye is one of the premiere protected areas within the World Heritage Site of Belize's Barrier Reef.

■ The Garífuna

The origin of the Garífuna dates back to the 17C, when two slave ships from Africa landed in the Caribbean. Some of the slaves reached the island of San Vicente, where they found refuge among the Carib Indians. This fusion gave birth to the Garífuna culture, characterized by its free spirit, which drove them to migrate for years until arriving at this coast.

Other traits of this culture include the religious ceremonies with African roots, the food, punta music, as well as its seductive dances. The best day to appreciate them is November 19, a celebration of the Garífuna settlement.

© Fernando García Aguinaco

Garífunas

PUNTA GORDA AND SURROUNDINGS

Punta Gorda – *168mi/269km south of Belize City, 107mi/172km from Dangriga or 86mi/138km from Placencia. On the south side of Southern Hwy.* ☎ *(7) 222-74. www.travelbelize.org/guide/di/di11.html.* This small town, the most important in Toledo District, is located on the coast and inhabited by Garífunas, Maya, Creoles, Mestizos, Chinese, Lebanese and Englishmen, among whom one finds very friendly people. From Punta Gorda, visitors can explore the dense jungle or venture out to the open sea. On market days (Wednesdays and Saturdays), the town's two principal streets—Main and Front—make a colorful scene with jewelry, plastic utensils, fruit and vegetables on sale by the inhabitants of nearby villages. Punta Gorda offers several hotels and good restaurants.

Along the road and street that run parallel to the sea, one can find valuable tourist information in the following places: **Toledo Institute for Development and Environment** (TIDE) *(0.6mi/1km north of the downtown area, open Mon–Fri 8am–5pm,* ☎ *7-222-74 or www.belizetour.com/tide),* **Toledo Visitor's Centre** *(main pier, open Tue–Wed & Fri–Sat 7–11:30am,* ☎ *7-224-70)* and **Nature's Way Guesthouse & Restaurant,** *(65 Front St;* ☎ *7-221-19).*

From "PG," as the town is also known, boats depart daily for Guatemala; BZ$25; ☎ *(7) 228-70.*

Joe Taylor Creek – *On the north side of town. Excursions starting at BZ$30.* ☎ *(7) 222-74.* Here, visitors can see mangroves, bromeliads and orchids, while kayaking down the river. During certain seasons, when the water is agitated at night, it becomes illuminated by tiny living organisms, a phenomenon known as bioluminescence.

★★**Sapodilla Cayes** – *38mi/61km into the open sea. 2hr boat trip. BZ$400–BZ$600.* ☎ *(7) 222-74. Overnight stay recommended.* This secluded group of five of the country's most beautiful cays is located south of Belize. In fact, its proximity to Guatemala and Honduras make it a popular destination with the inhabitants of those nations. The area closest to these islands, which encompasses the barrier reef, is ideal for sportfishing, scuba diving and snorkeling. Hunting Caye, the main and largest island, serves as an army facility, but also provides a place for sea turtles to lay their eggs. Like this cay, the rest of the group offers white sandy beaches and palm trees. In Nicolas Caye and Frank's Caye, tourist development will soon make way for new hotel resorts. Camping is allowed in Lime Caye, a private island. Other cays closer to Punta Gorda include **Moho Caye** and **Snake Cayes**, a group of four small islands.

Barranco Village – *Exit PG towards Southern Hwy., after 8.4mi/13.4km, turn left onto a dirt road and continue 17mi/27.6km. Before departing, inquire about road conditions. Also accessible by boat.* ☎ *(7) 228-41.* This pleasant and tranquil Garífuna village is located on the seashore. During a guided tour, friendly locals welcome visitors, who are then invited to see the making of the traditional *cassava* bread, canoes and fishing nets. Here, the Toledo Ecotourism Association (TEA) offers guesthouse accommodations: www.plenty.org/TEAguesthouses.htm.

Dem Dats Doin Living Resource Centre (N) – *Exit PG toward Southern Hwy., after 13mi/21km, continue straight on via the dirt road to San Antonio; 1mi/1.6km later, turn right; after 1.5mi/2.4km, turn left. Guided tour, by appointment only. BZ$10.* ☎ *(7) 224-70.* Since 1980 a Hawaiian couple resides in this totally self-sustainable house and farm. During the guided tour, visitors can see how they produce electric energy from methane gas—a natural byproduct of organic decomposition—and the system for collecting rainwater, to meet all their basic needs. The couple also tends a botanical garden and breeds hogs.

★**Lubaantun** – *Exit PG toward Southern Hwy.; after 13mi/21km, continue straight on via the dirt road to San Antonio; 1mi/1.6km later, turn right toward San Pedro Columbia; after 3mi/5km, turn left and continue for 0.4mi/0.6km. Follow the signs to Fallen Stones Butterfly Ranch and Jungle Lodge. Open year-round Mon–Fri 8am–5pm, Sat–Sun 8am–4pm. BZ$5.* ☎ *(8) 221-06.* Perched on a hill, in between two rivers, this archaeological site was inhabited from AD 730–890. It is believed to have constituted the center of a political, religious and commercial domain spanning 625sq mi/1,618sq km, ranging from high plateaus in the mountainous region to islands in the open seas. It was discovered in 1875 by indigenous peoples. Its name means "place of the fallen stones", due to the fact that its plazas, terraces and structures were built by means of laying loose stones one over another and, when necessary, cutting them to allow for a tight fit. At the summit of the tallest temple, which rises 39ft/12m above the plaza, stand two imposing trees: one from the "naked tree" species, the other a pepper tree. In the south side lies the ball court where, in 1915, three score boards were found and later transferred to the Peabody Museum in Boston, Massachusetts.

Fallen Stones Butterfly Ranch and Jungle Lodge – *219yd/200m from the Lubaantun parking lot; head north on a 1.1mi/1.7km trail. Visit by guided tour only. Open year-round daily 7am–noon & 1–3pm. BZ$10.* ✗ ☎ *(7) 221-67 or www.fallenstones.co.uk.* Situated atop a hill, this luxurious hotel offers a splendid **view★** of the Maya Mountains and Guatemala. A 10min walk along the luxuriant jungle leads to the **butterfly farm**.

Lubaantun

© Fernando García Aguinaco

■ Ecotourism in Toledo District: An Up-close Experience

Baking tortillas in a *comal* (flat clay dish), visiting a *milpa* (corn plantation), learning to bake bread or make handicrafts, listening to a legend in the evening, dancing to the rhythm of the drums or the harp, and eating and sleeping in a Mayan hut are some of the activities possible in the Toledo District. Diverse villas, inhabited by Garífunas or by the Kekchi and Mopán Maya groups, are found throughout this region—Belize's most remote area, nestled at the foot of the Maya Mountains, one of the world's most ancient geological formations. Despite being the country's poorest district, Toledo enjoys abundant plant and animal life.

The **Toledo Ecotourism Association** (TEA) fully carries out its mission of ensuring that all tourist activities include the participation of and directly benefit the local people. Throughout 13 Maya villages and one Garífuna, TEA has developed the Village Guesthouse Program, which includes meals and lodging and offers guided tours to those interested in cohabiting with the people of these communities, an experience both unique and economical. Each meal is prepared in a different home. Some of the locals serve as guides, while different families take turns attending to the rustic guesthouse. The objective of this task distribution is for tourism to benefit the vast majority of the community and not just a few members. In addition, a certain percentage of the earned income goes toward a common fund, intended to improve the community and conserve the environment. Surrounding every village, rich protected areas, or on their way to becoming protected, are home to a virgin jungle, to caves once inhabited by the ancient Maya and to small archaeological sites, as well as secluded rivers and waterfalls.

In 1997, during the Berlin Tourism Fair, TEA won the "To Do" award in the "Most Socially Responsible" category.

For more information, contact TEA *(65 Front Street, PO Box 75, Punta Gorda, Belize;* ☎ *7-221-19 or www.plenty.org/TEA.html)* or Nature's Way Guesthouse in PG.

★**Blue Creek Cave (O)** – *Exit PG toward Southern Hwy.; after 13mi/21km, continue straight on via the dirt road to San Antonio; 4.2mi/6.7km later, turn left and continue for 5.7mi/9.1km. After parking your vehicle, walk alongside the river for 20min. It is necessary to take a guide equipped with a miner's lantern. To hire the services of Ignacio Coc, leave a message for him at the telephone office in PG* ☎ *(7) 222-74.* The transparent Blue Creek, abounding in fish, originates in this long cave whose total extension is still unknown and inside which visitors can enjoy a swim. On the way to the cave, next to the river, sits **Blue Creek Lodge**. One of its attractions consists of a series of hanging bridges and platforms that tower some 49ft/15m above the river and jungle, at the same height as the canopy of trees.

★**Nim Li Punit** – *Exit PG and head north on Southern Hwy. After 24mi/38.7km, turn left and continue for 0.4mi/0.7km. Open year-round Mon–Fri 8am–5pm, Sat–Sun 8:30am–4pm. BZ$5.* ☎ *(8) 221-06.* Nestled in the foothills of the Maya Mountains, this archaeological site dates back to the Late Classic period (AD 600–900). Its importance lies in the number and size of the **stelae**★ found here. Inside the visitor center, one can admire some of these elaborately carved stone slates, such as **Stela 14**, whose relief portrays an individual with a great headdress, thus giving origin to the site's name signifying "Big Hat." Nim Li Punit consists of three plazas and one ball court. The most interesting group—believed to have been used for astronomical observations—lies on the southern end, where most of the stelae were found.

BELIZEAN FAIRS AND FESTIVALS

Date	Event
February	**Carnival** San Pedro's carnival is the most famous.
March 9	**Baron Bliss Day** Celebration in honor of Belize's benefactor, English Baron Victor Bliss.; Rregatta held in front of the Baron Bliss lighthouse where the baron's remains rest; also bike and horse races.
March/April	**Good Friday** Celebrated mainly in Ambergris Caye and Caye Caulker, with a procession through the towns; the Passion of Christ is usually represented in the towns of San Ignacio and Benque Viejo del Carmen.
May	**Toledo Arts Festival** The weeklong festival takes place in Punta Gorda.
May 24	**Commonwealth Day** Belizeans celebrate the birthday of the Queen of England. In addition to horse races held in Belize City and Orange Walk Town, there is a bicycle race from Belmopan to San Ignacio.
June 27	**St. Peter's Day** During this three-day festival in honor of St. Peter, Belizeans hold special masses, christenings of ships and popular fiestas.
July	**Benque Viejo del Carmen Fair** Local fair in honor of the patron saint of this town, located west of San Ignacio near the Guatemala border; cultural events, marimba bands, food and games.
August (3rd week)	**San Pedro International Sea and Air Festival** Music, dance and traditional dishes from Belize and neighboring countries.
September 10	**St. George's Caye Day** National celebration to commemorate the triumph at the 1798 Battle of St. George, where the English defeated the Spaniards. Carnival, sport activities, and fireworks; musical concerts begin several days in advance.
September 21	**Independence Day** Includes cultural, sport and religious activities, raising of the flag ceremony, parades, music, dance and food.
October 12	**Pan American Day** Celebration of the discovery of America, including beauty pageants that celebrate the mestizo culture. In addition, Belize City hosts a regatta.
November 19	**Garífuna Settlement Day** Festival held primarily in Dangriga and the rest of the Southern Coast to celebrate the Garífunas' arrival in Belize; includes Garífuna music, dance, food and traditions.
December 26	**Boxing Day** Fiestas, horse races and Garífuna dances.

Caribbean Coast South of Tulum

Practical
information

Calendar of events

Traditions, p 47. Mexico has a celebration for every day of the year. Festivals may last one day to two weeks. Fairs take place every year and may last up to two months. The list below includes the most important holidays.

Date	Event	City/State
Jan 6	Epiphany	*Entire country*
Jan 17	Day of St. Anthony the Abbot	*Coyoacán, D.F.*
Jan 18	Day of Santa Prisca & St. Sebastian	*Taxco, Gro.*
Jan 7–23	Festival of St. Sebastian (for children)	*Chiapa de Corzo*
Jan 20	Day of St. Sebastian	
Jan 20–22	Day of the Immaculate Conception	*Pátzcuaro, Mich.*
Jan 22	Coronation of the Virgin	
early Feb	Carnival of Campeche	*Campeche, Camp.*
Feb 2	Candlemas	*Entire country*
Feb 2–9	Encuentro de Jaraneros	*Tlacotalpan, Ver.*
Feb 3	Festival of the Charros Taurinos	*Colima, Col.*
end of Feb	Carnival	*Veracruz, Ver.*
end of Mar	International Horse Fair	*Texcoco, Mex.*
Mar–Apr	Holy Week (rep. of Christ's Passion)	*Taxco, Gro.*
	Ash Wednesday (pilgrimage, dances)	*Amecameca, Mex.*
	Good Friday	*San Luis Potosí, SLP*
	Easter Saturday	*Entire country*
	Palm Sunday	*Entire country*
	Corpus Christi Thursday	*Mexico City*
Mar 21	Flower Festival	*Cuernavaca, Mor.*
Apr 10–May 10	National Fair of San Marcos *(pp 47 & 159)*	*Aguascalientes, Ags.*
May 3	Day of the Holy Cross (fireworks, dances)	*Tepozotlán, Mex.*
Mid June	Festival of June and Ceramics Fair	*Tlaquepaque, Jal.*
June 24	Day of St. John the Baptist	*Tlayacapan, Mor.*
Jul 15–18	Festival of Dance (folklore)	*Cuetzalan, Pue.*
Mid Jul	Festival of Guelaguetza *(p 272)*	*Oaxaca, Oax.*
Aug 17–20	Patronal Festival of St. Bernard	*Vicente Guerrero, Dgo.*
mid Aug	Festival of the Virgin of Charity (handicrafts)	*Huamantla, Tlax.*
Aug 15	Cajeta Fair & Festival of the Assumption of the Virgin	*Celaya, Gto.*
Aug 27–29	Festival of the Moors	*Pradera del Bracho, Zac.*
Sept 3–5	Festival of Candles	*Juchitán, Oax.*
Sept 7	Regional Indigenous Dance at the Ruins	*Tepozteco, Mor.*
Sept 14	Festival of the Virgin of Patronage	*Zacatecas, Zac.*
Sept 29	Day of the Archangel St. Michael	*San Miguel de Allende, Gto.*
Oct 4	October Festival (fair, exhibits)	*Guadalajara, Jal.*
Oct 12	Procession of the Virgin of Zapopán	*Guadalajara, Jal.*
mid Oct	International Cervantes Festival *(p 169)*	*Guanajuato, Gto.*
Nov 1–2	Day of the Dead *(pp 47 & 283)*	*Entire country*
end of Nov	Mariachi Festival	*Zapotitlán, Jal.*
early Dec	Silver Fair (jewelry, objects, utensils)	*Taxco, Gro.*
Dec 1	Festival of St. Andrew (procession)	*Coyutla, Ver.*
Dec 12	Day of Our Lady of Guadalupe	*Entire country*
Dec 16–24	Posadas (door-to-door processions)	*Entire country*
Dec 31	Holy Sacrament Procession	*St. Clara del Cobre, Mich.*

■ Consult the practical information sections written specifically for the following places: Mexico City *(pp 62-65)*, Guadalajara *(p 163)*, Copper Canyon *(p 189)*, Baja California Peninsula *(pp 202-205)*, Oaxaca *(p 267)*, San Cristóbal de las Casas *(p 287)*, Yucatán Peninsula *(pp 331-332)*, Guatemala *(pp 338-339)* and Belize *(pp 366-367)*.

Carnival, Tenosique

Explanation of Mexican Holidays

Epiphany – traditionally the 12 days of Christmas when the Three Kings came bearing gifts for Christ. On this day, gifts are given to children in Mexico.

St. Anthony the Abbott – commemorates the hermit saint of healing of animals; household pets are brought to churchyards and blessed by priests with holy water.

St. Sebastian – nine-day celebration that includes pantomime, dancing and ritual meals.

Carnival – involves folk and ritual dances, fireworks, parades, street dances and costume balls.

Posadas – nine-day Christmas celebration that commemorates Mary and Joseph's journey from Nazareth to Bethlehem; children form a door-to-door procession and break piñatas to obtain candy.

Corpus Christi – A reenactment symbolic of the battle between the Moors and Christians.

Festival of the Charros Taurinos – pre-Lenten festival that includes children's parades, rodeos and bullfights.

Our Lady of Guadalupe – homage to the patron saint of Mexico.

All Soul's Day and Day of the Dead – festive atmosphere commemorating the spirits of the dead of friends and relatives.

Good Friday – somber holiday with religious processions representing the funeral that Jesus Christ never had.

Easter Saturday – effigies of Judas are burned for his betrayal of Jesus; Judas' effigies are stuffed with candy for children or hung in the streets with fireworks attached to them, and are ignited after holy mass.

Guelaguetza – costumed dancers from various Oaxaca tribes perform traditional dances during this week-long celebration.

National Fair of San Marcos – ten-day festival that showcases more than 200 forms of ritual and folk dance, art exhibits, parades, cockfights, bullfights, sports competitions and the battle of flowers.

Holy Cross – observed by miners, masons and construction workers who build crosses to place on buildings where they are working; a day of fiesta with fireworks.

Day of St. John the Baptist – honors the patron saint of waters by decorating fountains and wells; bathing takes place in local streams and rivers; street vendors sell small mules made of cornhusks, decorated with flowers and filled with candy.

Candlemas – 40-day period of purification following the birth of Christ; blessing of candles in celebration of Christ's birth.

Planning your trip

Tourist Information – **Tourism Board (Sectur)**, Av. Presidente Masaryk, 172, P.B., Col. Polanco, C.P. 11587, Mexico, D.F. ☎ (52) 52-50-01-23 or 52-50-01-51 *(24hrs)* and ☎ (01-800) 903-9200 (anywhere within Mexico) or *www.mexico-travel.com* provides information on rates, accommodations, guided tours and brochures. From the US ☎ (800) 482-9832 provides assistance in English and Spanish, as well as brochures in English, Spanish and French. Tourist information in English can be obtained by calling **FaxMeMexico**, ☎ (541) 385-9282 (US), and choosing documents from a recorded menu.

Mexico Tourist Board Offices (by region)

Region 1: Mexico City

Mexico City	Amberes, 54, P.B., Col. Juárez, C.P. 06600, Mexico, D.F. ☎ 55-25-93-80

Region 2: Central Mexico

Hidalgo	Av. Revolución, 1300, Col. Periodista, Pachuca, Hgo., C.P. 042060 ☎ (7) 718-4489 or 718-3937
Mexico (state)	Av. Urawa, 100, Pta. 110, Col. Izcalli Ipiem, Toluca, Mex., C.P. 50150, ☎ (7) 219-5190 or 219-6158
Morelos	Av. Morelos Sur, 187, Col. Las Palmas, Cuernavaca, Mor., C.P. 62050, ☎ (7) 314-3920 or 314-3872
Puebla	5 Oriente, 3, Col. Centro, Puebla, Pue., C.P. 72000, ☎ (2) 246-2044
Querétaro	Luis Pasteur Nte., 4, Centro Histórico, Col. Centro, Querétaro, Qro., C.P. 76000, ☎ (4) 212-1412
Tlaxcala	Av. Juárez, corner of Lardizaval, behind the Ex Palacio Legislativo, Tlaxcala, Tlax., C.P. 90000, ☎ (2) 462-0027 or 462-2787

Region 3: Central West

Aguascalientes	Plaza de la Patria, Palacio de Gobierno, ground floor, Aguascalientes, Ags., C.P. 20000 ☎ (4) 915-1155 or 916-0347
Colima	Calle Hidalgo, 96, Col. Centro, Colima, Col., C.P. 28000, ☎ (3) 313-7540
Guanajuato	Plaza de la Paz, 14, Guanajuato, Gto., C.P. 36000, ☎ (4) 732-8275 or 732-4565
Jalisco	Morelos, 102, Plaza Tapatía, Guadalajara, Jal., C.P. 44100, ☎ (3) 613-0306 / 668-2222 / (01-800) 363-2200
Nayarit	Av. México y Ejército Nacional, Ex Convento de la Cruz, Tepic, Nay., C.P. 63168 ☎ (3) 214-8071 to 73

Region 4: Northwest

Chihuahua	Libertad, 1300, 1er piso, Palacio de Gobierno, Centro, Chihuahua, Chih., C.P. 31000 ☎ (1) 410-1077 or (01-800) 49-52-48
Durango	Florida, 100, 2° piso, Col. Barrio del Calvario, Zona Centro, Durango, Dgo., C.P. 34000 ☎ (1) 811-2139 or 811-1107
Sinaloa	Av. Camarón Sábalo, esq. Tiburón, 4, Edif. Banrural, 4° piso, Fracc. Sábalo Country Club, Mazatlán, Sin., C.P. 82110, ☎ (6) 916-5160 to 65
Sonora	Centro de Gobierno, Comonfort y Paseo Canal, North, 3rd level, Hermosillo, Son., C.P. 83280, ☎ (6) 217-0044

Region 5: Baja California Peninsula

BC (North)	Paseo de los Héroes, 10289, Zona Río, Edif. Nacional Financiera, 4° piso, Tijuana, B.C., C.P. 22320, ☎ (6) 634-3085 or 634-6330
BC Sur	Carretera Norte, Km 5.5, Edif. Fidepaz, Apdo. Postal 419, La Paz, B.C.S., C.P. 23090, ☎ (1) 124-0100 / 124-0103

Region 6: Northeast

Coahuila	Periférico Luis Echeverría Álvarez, 1560, Edif. Torre Saltillo, piso 11, Saltillo, Coah., C.P. 25286 ☎ (8) 415-1714, 415-4053 or (01-800) 718-4220
Nuevo León	Hidalgo, 441, Ote., Col. Centro, Monterrey, N.L., C.P. 64000, ☎ (8) 345-0870 or 345-0902
San Luis Potosí	Álvaro Obregón, 520, Col. Centro, San Luis Potosí, S.L.P., C.P. 78000 ☎ (4) 812-9906, 812-2357 or 812-9939

Tamaulipas	16 Rosales, 272, Ote., Col. Centro, Cd. Victoria, Tamps., C.P. 87000 ☎ (1) 312-7002 or 312-1057
Zacatecas	Av. Hidalgo, 403, 2° piso, Zacatecas, Zac., C.P. 98000 ☎ (4) 924-4047 or 922-3426

Region 7: Gulf of Mexico

Tabasco	Av. los Ríos, esq Calle 13, Tabasco 2000, Villahermosa, Tab., C.P. 86035 ☎ (9) 316-2889 / 316-3633
Veracruz	Blvd. Cristóbal Colón, 5, Frac. Jardines de las Ánimas, Jalapa, Ver., C.P. 91190 ☎ (2) 812-8500 ext. 127 or (01-800) 712-6666

Region 8: Pacific Coast

Chiapas	Blvd. Belisario Domínguez, 950, Edif. Plaza de las Instituciones, P.B., Tuxtla Gutiérrez, Chis., C.P. 29060, ☎ (9) 613-4499 or (01-800) 280-35
Guerrero	Costera Miguel Alemán, 4455, Centro de Convenciones, Acapulco, Gro., C.P. 39850 ☎ (7) 484-4416 or 484-4583
Michoacán	Nigromante, 79, Col. Centro, Palacio Clavijero, Morelia, Mich., C.P. 58000 ☎ (4) 317-2371
Oaxaca	Av. Independencia, 607, corner of García Vigil, Col. Centro, Oaxaca, Oax., C.P. 68000 ☎ (9) 516-0123 or 516-4828

Region 9: Yucatán Peninsula

Campeche	Av. Ruiz Cortínez, s/n, Plaza Moch-Couhuo, Col. Centro, Campeche, Camp., C.P. 24000 ☎ (9) 816-5593 or 816-7364
Quintana Roo	Calz. del Centenario, 622, Col. del Bosque, Chetumal, Q. Roo, C.P. 77100 ☎ (9) 832-8661 or 832-8682
Yucatán	Calle 59, 514, (between 62 & 64), Col Centro, Mérida, Yuc., C.P. 97000 ☎ (9) 924-9290 or 946-1300

When to Visit – Mexico's geographical location between the 14° and 32° parallels of the northern latitude places it between two important climatic zones in the Northern Hemisphere. The northern desert and southern tropics, modified by the uneven relief as well as the influence of sea air from the Pacific and the Gulf of Mexico, generate countless climatic and vegetation changes. This makes it an agreeable place to vacation during all seasons. The coast and interior have a warm **climate**. The average annual temperature is 25–28°C/77–82°F, with a maximum of 38°C/100°F, and in certain coastal areas, such as the Yucatán, 41°C/106°F. The temperate zone is located in higher elevations (930 – 1 8 6 0 m / 3069–6138ft) with temperatures at 17–21°C/62–70°F. With an elevation close to 2,134m/7,142ft in the cold zone, the average temperature is 15–16°C/59–60°F. The **rainy season** falls during the months of May through October. **Winter** (October through January) is the best season of the year on the Pacific Coast, with temperatures that fluctuate from 24–31°C/75–88°F with a precipitation of 0.08mm/0.3in. In the Yucatán Peninsula, the temperature averages 21–32°C/70–90°F with precipitation at 0.77–2.05mm/3–8in. **Tourist season** occurs during Holy Week, June–August and December.

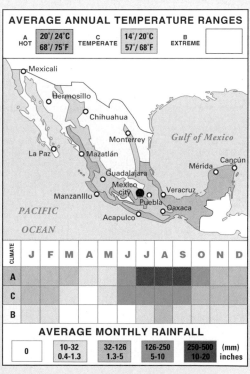

International visitors

PLANNING YOUR TRIP

Foreign visitors can obtain information on Mexico from the Tourism Board **(Sectur)** *(p 390)*, a travel agent, or the Mexican embassy or consulate in their country of residence.

Mexican Government Tourist Offices: ☏

Canada	2 Bloor St. West, Suite 1801, Toronto Ontario M⁴W 3ᵉ2	416-925-2753
France	4, rue Notre Dame des Victoires, 75002 Paris	142-86-56-20
Germany	726 Wiesenhüttenplatz, Frankfurt/a.Main	69-25-3413
UK	60/61 Trafalgar Sq., London WC2N 5DS	171-839-3177
US	5075 Westheimer, Suite 975, Houston, TX 77056	713-780-3740

Entry Requirements – Foreign visitors entering Mexico need proof of citizenship such as a valid **passport** and, in some cases, a visa. US citizens may enter with a notarized copy of a birth certificate, a permanent resident card, or a valid voter registration card (non-photo ID documents must be accompanied by a valid driver's license). For Canadian citizens the "Canadian Identification Card" is accepted. Travelers who drive through Mexico en route to Central America must carry a passport and visa for the country they will visit. **Inoculations** are generally not required. Before departing, consult the Mexican embassy or consulate nearest you for entry regulations. All visitors who plan to remain more than 72 hours require a **tourist card**. These are available from Mexican government tourist offices, travel agents, airline companies and Mexican border offices at points of entry. **Business travelers** must ask for a Business Entry Form *(Formulario Migratorio de Negocios)*. Children under 18 years of age who are traveling alone or with a guardian need an authorized statement from their parents, unless the minor is in possession of a valid passport. Tourist cards must be returned to Mexican immigration officials at the time of departure.

Customs – You are allowed to bring in to Mexico: 3 liters of alcoholic beverages, 400 cigarettes or 20 cigars (if the person carrying them is over 18 years of age); gifts that do not exceed USD$300. **Prohibited items:** illegal drugs, plants and perishable goods, firearms or weapons of any kind. It is recommended to check with the Mexican embassy or consulate before entering Mexico regarding strict regulations on bringing in firearms for hunting activities. The export of **archaeological objects** and certain antiquities is forbidden.

Health Insurance – Prior to departure, check to see whether your insurance company covers emergency consultations, medical expenses, medication and hospitalization while abroad. All **prescribed drugs** should be properly identified on the label and accompanied by a copy of the prescription. Insurance companies offer policies as do some credit card companies, such as American Express' Global Assistance.

Vehicle Entry requirements – *see Getting to Mexico section, opposite page.*

GENERAL INFORMATION

Currency Exchange, Credit Cards and Traveler's Checks – *(p 398)* Mexican currency is the *peso*, available in coins and paper bills. The major banks in Mexico are **Banamex** and **Bancomer**. Many banks provide Automatic Teller Machines (ATMs) throughout the country connected to Cirrus and Plus systems. **Money exchange offices** *(open 9am–4:30pm)* accept all types of currency and offer quick service and extended hours. Major credit cards (American Express, Diners Club, Mastercard/Eurocard and Visa) are accepted at many hotels, restaurants and shops. Most establishments accept traveler's checks, which some hotels will exchange for cash. Inquire beforehand in all establishments.

Electricity – Voltage in Mexico is 120 volts AC, 60Hz. Some foreign-made appliances require an adapter and flat plugs.

Embassies and Consulates – Embassies and consulates are located in Mexico City. Many foreign countries also maintain consulates in some of Mexico's larger cities. Consult the *Yellow Pages* in the telephone book for telephone numbers and addresses.

Postal Service – *p 398*

Telephones and Telegrams – *p 399*

Time Zones – *p 399*

Weights and Measures – Mexicans use the metric decimal system. Speed limits are represented in kilometers and temperatures are measured in centigrade degrees; the conversion from °C to °F (1.8 x °C) + 32. Below are equivalencies:

1 meter (m)	3.28 feet
1 centimeter (cm)	0.39 inches
1 millimeter (mm)	04 inches
1 kilometer (km)	0.62 miles
1 liter (lt)	33.8 ounces
1 kilogram (kg)	2.2 pounds
0 °C	32 °F
100 °C	212 °F

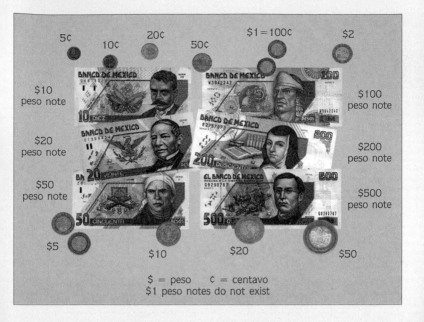

$ = peso   ¢ = centavo
$1 peso notes do not exist

Getting to Mexico

By Air – Major international airports in Mexico serviced by international airlines are Mexico City's International Airport, as well as airports in Guadalajara, Acapulco, Monterrey, and Cancun. Aeromexico and Mexicana offer daily, direct flights to Mexico from many foreign cities. Approximate flight time London–Mexico City: 10hrs, Los Angeles–Mexico City: 5 1/2hrs, New York–Mexico City: 5hrs. An airport departure tax, which varies constantly, is charged on international flights. *(For air travel within Mexico see p 394.)*

As of July 1999, international visitors arriving in Mexico by air or land have to pay a P$150 fee for entering the country.

By Ship – Along the Caribbean and the Pacific coasts, many **cruise ships** dock at major ports in Mexico. **Cozumel:** Clipper, Cunard, Norwegian, Royal Caribbean, Celebrity, Princess, Carnival, Holland, Royal Olympics; **Acapulco:** Princess, Holland, Seabourn, Royal, Carnival, Celebrity; **Cancún:** Norwegian; **Mazatlán, Puerto Vallarta and Cabo San Lucas:** Carnival. For more information, contact the cruise-line companies directly.

By Bus – **Greyhound** bus line provides service to all border cities in Mexico. For more information, contact Greyhound in the US ☎ (800) 531-5332 or in Mexico City ☎ 56-69-12-87. Travel within Mexico is by Mexican bus lines only *(p 394)*. Mexican buses, such as ADO, cross the border to Brownsville and McAllen, TX. **Information and reservations:** ADO, North Terminal (Mexico City) ☎ 51-33-24-24.

At the **southern border**, Galgos buses cross the Guatemala border when heading to Tapachula, Chiapas. Bally Brothers Bus Service (501) 272-025 cross the Belize border when heading to Chetumal, Q. Roo. Mexican bus lines, such as ADO and Cristóbal Colón, have bus terminals on the border with Tapachula, Chis. and Chetumal, Q. Roo to connect to the interior of Mexico.

By Train – Train connections with Mexican railways can be made at Nuevo Laredo, a city on the northern border with the US, and at Tapachula, on the southern border with Guatemala. If you wish to continue your trip by train in Mexico, you must purchase your ticket in Mexican train stations. Consult the *Yellow Pages*, contact tourist offices or ask for information at Buenavista Station in Mexico City ☎ 55-47-10-97 / 55-47-10-84.

By Car – *(p 395)* For information, contact the local tourism office (they provide road maps, brochures on traffic regulations, and phone numbers for emergency road service). **Ángeles Verdes** ☎ 52-50-82-21 (highway patrol assistance) provides bilingual, English-Spanish, service in the interior of Mexico. The **Mexican Automobile Association** (AMA) ☎ 52-08-83-29 offers publications, travel tips, maps and **emergency road service:** ☎ 55-88-70-55 or (01-800) 010-7100.

The **Automobile Association** ☎ 55-27-51-60 and 55-27-38-08 carries out transactions in governmental offices, granting permits and licenses to members of the **American Automobile Association** (AAA), the **Canadian Automobile Association** (CAA), and affiliates of the **Federación Internacional ́de Automóviles Asociados** (FIA) in Venezuela and Puerto Rico. Branches of the AMA can be found in most large cities.

Vehicle Importation Requirements – If you wish to enter Mexico by car 24km/15mi beyond the border, a temporary importation permit for your vehicle (forms are available at AAA, CAA or FIA offices) is required by presenting proof of citizenship, a valid driver's license and the vehicle's title and registration. A fee of USD$15 is charged to be paid with a major credit card only (Visa, MasterCard, American Express or Diner's Club). Originals and copies of all documents for each driver must be presented. Upon leaving the country, you will need to submit all documents to customs officials. In Baja California, permits to enter with your own vehicle are not required unless your vehicle is being transported by ferry to the Mexican mainland.

Automobile Insurance – Car insurance is mandatory. An insurance policy can be purchased from Mexican insurance companies at points of entry. Central American and South American and US insurance policies are not valid in Mexico. AAA offices can help you obtain an insurance policy prior to departing the US, or contact Sanborns, P.O. Box 310, McAllen, TX 78505, ☎ (956) 686-3601, which provides insurance only for car rentals and has agencies in California, Arizona, Texas and Mexico. The insurance becomes valid upon crossing the US border. Canadian drivers should inquire at their local CAA office prior to traveling.

Travelling in Mexico

By Air – Mexico has several national airlines that offer service to most major cities. For information on packages offered by some airlines, consult your travel agent. Reserve well in advance during the major tourist season (Holy Week, June–August and December).

Airline	☎ Reservations
Aeroméxico	800-237-6639 (from the US) or 55-71-36-00
Mexicana	800-531-7921 (from the US) or 54-48-09-90/ (01-800) 502-2000
Aero California	800-237-6225 (from the US) or 52-07-13-92
Aerolíneas Internacionales	55-43-12-23 or (01-800) 004-1700
Aviacsa	54-48-89-00/ (01-800) 006-2200
Taesa	800-328-2372 (from the US) or 52-27-07-00/ (01-800) 904-6300
Aeromar	56-27-02-07 or (01-800) 904-2900

By Train – Mexico has an extensive railway system linking main towns. For reservations and schedules, contact the **Estación Central de Buenavista**, Insurgentes Norte, Col. Buenavista, Mexico City, C.P. 06358, ☎ 55-47-10-84. Among the main train stations figure: Chihuahua-Pacific, Los Mochis, Guadalajara, Veracruz and Mérida. Prices vary according to the destination and type of service desired. First-class travel is recommended. A complete overhaul of Mexico's trains was initiated in August 1999.

By Bus – Mexico has a well-developed bus system reaching virtually every town. Rates are affordable, schedules are frequent, including express service, and most of the time buses run on time. There are several types of buses, but travel by **deluxe class** with air-conditioning, snack service, restrooms, TV/video, assistants and reclining seats, or **first class** with air-conditioning, restrooms, TV/video and reclining seats, is recommended. It is a good idea to reserve seats in advance. In most towns the bus station is located near the downtown area. Information and tickets can be obtained from local bus stations.

Bus Line	Destinations (from Mexico City)	☎ Reservations
ADO	**Southeastern Mexico:** states of Chiapas, Oaxaca, Tabasco, Campeche, Yucatán and Quintana Roo	51-33-24-24 or (01-800) 702-8000
AU	**Southeastern Mexico** (see above)	51-33-11-00
ETN	**Bajío Area:** states of Aguascalientes, Guanajuato, Jalisco, Michoacán, San Luis Potosí, Querétaro and Zacatecas	55-67-94-66
Estrella de Oro	Acapulco, Cuernavaca, Taxco, Zihuatanejo (states of Morelos and Guerrero)	55-49-85-20 to 29
UNO	**Parts of the Gulf of Mexico:** states of Veracruz, Tamaulipas and Tabasco, as well as connections to the southeast	51-33-24-24 or (01-800) 702-8000
Estrella Blanca	**Northern, eastern & western Mexico:** states of Querétaro, San Luis Potosí, Jalisco, Aguascalientes, Zacatecas, Nuevo León, Coahuila, Chihuahua, Michoacán, Nayarit, Sinaloa, Durango, Tamaulipas and Veracruz	57-29-07-07

By Taxi – Every city has a fleet of taxis, and stands are located at airports, bus terminals, train stations and hotels. It is recommended to use radio service taxi transportation or those located at official taxi stands only.

By Car – Mexico has a modern and safe highway system throughout the country that connects all major cities. Before departing by highway, check your car to make sure it is in good condition; carry necessary tools and use the seat belt. On expressways *(autopistas)* a toll is charged. These stretches of highway are regularly patrolled and offer clean rest rooms; however, tolls are high. Many secondary roads are unpaved. Travel at night is not recommended.

There is bilingual (English–Spanish) highway patrol assistance available: **Ángeles Verdes**, Presidente Masaryk, 172, Col. Chapultepec, Mexico D.F., C.P. 11570, ☏ 52-50-82-21 (radio call boxes). You can find information on where this service is available throughout the country by contacting **Sectur** ☏ (01-800) 903-9200 *(24hrs)*. They offer mechanical assistance, first aid and tourist information, and assist travelers in emergency situations. Service is free. The driver pays only for gas and car repairs. **Emergency telephones** can be found alongside some highways and can be identified by a sign of a yellow telephone with the SOS symbol.

Gasoline can be purchased (cash only) in any PEMEX station, in both cities and along highways. **Magna Sin** gas is unleaded and found at green gas pumps. Premium is found at red gas pumps. Most gas stations operate from 6am-10pm. There is no self-service; it is customary to tip the attendant (P$2-$3).

Car Rental – Major rental agencies have offices at airports and downtown locations. Packages may include unlimited mileage and weekly rates. It is recommended to reserve a car in advance. If the vehicle is returned at a different location from where it was rented, drop-off charges may be incurred. Minimum age for rental is 18. A valid driver's license, an international driver's license and a credit card (cash is not accepted) are required for car rental. Insurance is mandatory and is provided by the rental company. Be sure to check limitations and add additional coverage if needed. Rental documents and the agency's emergency phone number should be kept in the car. Numerous Mexican companies offer car rental; their rates may be lower, but vehicles are less reliable. Consult the *Yellow Pages* for other agencies.

☏

Avis	800-331-1212 (US) or 57-62-32-62 (Mexico)
Budget	800-527-0700 (US) or 55-66-68-00 (Mexico)
Hertz	800-654-3131 (US) or 57-84-76-28 (Mexico)
Europcar	800-227-7368 (US) or 57-85-93-30 (Mexico)
Fresno	55-88-38-19 or 55-78-90-16 (Mexico)

Road and Safety Regulations – On all public roads, traffic circulates on the right-hand side. Cars may overtake each other on the left. The **speed limit** is indicated in **kilometers/hour**. In **cities**, the speed limit is 50km/hr (30mph). On **highways:** 100km/hr (60mph) during the day and 90km/hr (55mph) at night. Be careful at railroad crossings and reduce speed. The use of **seat belts** is mandatory. Double parking is forbidden. Avoid parking on the street and use parking lots.

SITIO EXCLUSIVO TAXIS

© Edward Thomas

In Case of Accident – Under Mexican law an automobile accident is a criminal offense; the police detains all parties involved until responsibility has been assessed. In some cases vehicles are impounded until damages are paid. A driver involved in a **serious accident** is detained until the appropriate authority arrives; in this case it is recommended to contact your embassy.

THE GREEN GUIDE is updated periodically... do you have the latest edition?

Accommodations

Mexico offers accommodations to suit every taste and pocketbook ranging from international hotels in large cities, luxury resorts along the coastlines and islands, to modest hotels along highways, as well as youth hostels. A 17% hotel occupancy tax is added to all hotel bills. Hotels are required to display officially approved rate schedules. The Ministry of Tourism rates all establishments. There are six classifications: Gran Turismo and a five-star rating system. Room rates vary greatly according to season and location. A 10–15% tax is added to all international telephone calls made from your hotel room. It is recommended to make reservations well in advance especially when traveling during Holy Week and peak travel season. All reservations should be confirmed with a credit card and, if possible, by a written confirmation. It is advisable to inquire in advance about cancellation policies. Outside major tourist areas, some hotels may not accept credit cards. Special rates are offered through packages available from international hotel chains, airlines or travel agencies.

Reservation Service – Within Mexico, contact **Sectur** *(p 390)* ☎ 52-55-10-06, a travel agency or a hotel chain.

Hotels – **Luxury** (five stars/diamonds): *double rooms P$1,200–$3,000 per night.* Amenities offered include central air-conditioning, multilingual staff, restaurants, nightclubs, meeting facilities, satellite TV, handicap access, exercise facilities, pool, 24hr room service, ATMs, shops, travel agency. **First class:** *double rooms P$800–$1,200 per night.* Amenities include multilingual staff, restaurant, bars, exercise facilities, pool, 24hr room service, safety deposit box, satellite TV, shops. **Commercial & Economy:** *double rooms P$100–500 per night.* Amenities include restaurant or coffee shop, ceiling fans and other basic services.
Generally, hotels with a five-star/diamond rating are located in or near the main tourist areas; four-star hotels are found in more secluded areas; and commercial and economy hotels are located in the outskirts of cities.

Major Hotel Chains	☎ Reservations / Information
Camino Real	800-722-6466 (US) or 52-03-21-21 / (01-800) 901-23
Hotel Marquis Reforma	52-11-36-00 / (01-800) 901-7600
Calinda (Quality) Hotels	800-221-2222 (US) or 01-800-900-0000
Club Med	800-258-2633 (US) or 52-03-30-86 / (01-800) 901-7000
Fiesta Inn or Americana	800-263-3508 (US) or 53-26-69-00 / (01-800) 504-5000
Holiday Inn	800-465-4329 (US) or 56-27-02-99 / (01-800) 009-9900
Hyatt	800-228-9000 (US) or 56-26-78-70 / (01-800) 005-0000
Krystal	800-231-9860 (US) or 56-05-96-95 / (01-800) 903-33
Marriot	800-228-9290 (US) or 52-07-10-16 / (01-800) 900-88
Sheraton	800-325-3535 (US) or 52-07-39-33 / (01-800) 900-88
Westin	800-228-3000 (US) or 52-30-17-77 / 52-27-05-55/ (01-800) 902-23

Motels – Motels are found in every state in Mexico, generally alongside the highways or on the outskirts of cities. Some first-class motels will not accept credit cards. Rates for modest rooms, some with air-conditioning, range from P$200–$400.

© Robert Frerck/Odyssey

Colonial-Style Hotels and Haciendas – Some historical buildings-such as haciendas, monasteries and colonial homes-have been converted into hotels. Most of them date from the 19C and are decorated with locally made furniture. Some have original paintings on the walls and ceilings, and guests can enjoy beautiful lush gardens.

Some of these inns once served as the private residences of famous people. The estate of Barbara Hutton has been transformed to the Camino Real Sumiya in Cuernavaca, and the B&B Quinta Quetzalcóatl near Guadalajara was once home to D.H. Lawrence. Usually restaurants in these establishments are well known for their cuisine of regional specialties prepared by renowned chefs; many offer packages that include breakfast and dinner. Reservations should be made well in advance, because most of these hotels have a limited number of rooms. These establishments offer outstanding quality service and amenities; thus, rates tend to be high *(P$600–$1,200)*.

State	Hotel	☏ Reservations
Mexico City	Hotel de Cortés *(p 85)*	55-18-21-81 to 85
Cuernavaca	Las Mañanitas	(7) 314-1466
	Camino Real Sumiya	(7) 320-9199
Guadalajara	El Francés	(3) 613-1190
	Quinta Quetzalcoatl (Chapala, Jalisco)	(3) 765-3653 or
		(415) 898-0644 (US)
Guanajuato	Museo Posada Santa Fe	(4) 732-0084
Monterrey	Radisson Plaza Gran Hotel Ancira	(8) 150-7000
Morelia	Virrey de Mendoza	(4) 312-0636
	Hotel Villa Montana	(4) 314-0231
Querétaro	Mesón de Santa Rosa	(4) 224-2623
Oaxaca	Ex Convento de Santa Catalina de Siena *(p 270)*	(9) 516-0611
San Miguel de Allende	Casa de Sierra Nevada	(4) 152-0415
Taxco	Monte Taxco *(p 293)*	(7) 622-1300
	Hacienda del Solar	(7) 622-0323
	Hotel Posada La Misión	(7) 622-0533
Valladolid, Yuc.	Hotel Hacienda Chichén	(9) 851-0045
	Hacienda Mayaland, Chichén Itza	(9) 851-0077 or
		(800) 235 4079 (US)
	Hacienda Uxmal, Uxmal	(9) 946-2333 or
		(800) 235-4079 (US)
Zacatecas	Quinta Real Zacatecas *(p 232)*	(4) 922-9104
	Mesón de Jobito *(p 230)*	(4) 924-1722

Spas – Exclusive spas offer a variety of programs from fitness, beauty and wellness, to weight management and stress relief. These hotels include Misión del Sol, Cuernavaca ☏ (7) 321-0999; Ixtapan de la Sal, Mexico City ☏ 52-64-26-13; and Avándaro, Valle de Bravo ☏ (7) 266-0366. However, a great number of deluxe hotels in major cities or at beach resorts include facilities offering everything from beauty treatments, massages, Jacuzzis, saunas, steam rooms, pool and spa facilities to exercise programs. For more information, contact Sectur *(p 390)* or your travel agent.

Condominiums and Villas – For families with children, furnished apartments or villas are more cost-effective than hotels. Amenities include living rooms, fully equipped kitchens with dining areas, several bedrooms and bathrooms, TV (some with cable or satellite stations), air-conditioning or ceiling fans. Maid service can be arranged. Some properties offer transport to local attractions. Average price runs between USD$60–70 per person per day during high season. An oceanfront villa will run USD$300 additional. Reservations should be made well in advance. Check carefully regarding cancellation policies. For more information contact **Sectur** *(p 390)* or your travel agent. In the US: Condo & Villa Authority, 305 N. Pontiac Trail, Walled Lake MI 48390 ☏ (248) 669-7500; Villas of Mexico, P.O. Box 3730, Chico, CA 95927 ☏ (916) 893-3133 or (800) 456-3133. Mexico Accommodations, 5801 Soledad Mountain Rd., La Jolla CA 92037, ☏ (619) 275-4500 or (800) 262-4500 (US) and (800) 654-5543 (Canada) or *www.mexico-accommodations.com*.

Youth Hostels – The association **Instituto Mexicano de la Juventud**, Serapio Rendón, 76, Col. San Rafael, Mexico, D.F. 06470, ☏ 57-05-60-72 and (01-800) 716-0092 or *www.causajoven.gob.mx*, allows both Mexican residents and foreigners, between the ages of 12-29, a Youth Hostel card *(P$25)*. Double rooms are P$100 per person for members; however, nonmembers are welcome. **Causa Joven** is a member of the International Youth Hostel Federation (IYHF). Reservations should be made by contacting the hostel directly or checking with Hosteling International, Washington DC, ☏ (202) 783-6161 and in Ottawa, Canada ☏ (613) 237-7884, or *www.hiayh.org*.

Camps and RV Parks – Campgrounds can be found in the following states: Quintana Roo, Ixtapa-Zihuatanejo, Jalisco, Loreto, Durango, Guerrero and Morelos. Some camps offer cabins and rooms. Tent sites only are less common. Camping in isolated areas is not recommended. Trailer parks can be found almost everywhere. Amenities vary but can include full hook-up service, drinkable water, flush toilets, cable TV, showers, pool and laundry service. Additional services (groceries, recreational facilities, sight-seeing) are available at extra cost. Some campgrounds accept international credit cards. Reservations are recommended, particularly during high season and during the months of December and January. Rates for RV trailer parks range from P$30–$50. Travel to Mexico in your own RV or rent one with a knowledgeable tour operator (Nov–Apr). Explore Copper Canyon "piggyback" on a train or go as far south as Panama with Point South RV Tours, Inc., 11313 Edmonson Ave., Moreno Valley, CA 92555; ☎ (909) 247-1222, (800) 421-1394 or *www.RVTOURS.com*. For more information, contact **Sectur** *(p 390)*, **Instituto Mexicano de la Juventud** or the **American Automobile Association** (AAA) offices in the US and CAA offices in Canada.

General information

Business Hours – Banks are usually open Mon–Fri 9am–1:30pm and in larger cities on Saturday (9am–noon). Businesses and retail stores operate Mon–Sat 9am–8:30pm. Government offices are open Mon–Fri 8:30am–7pm. Business hours may vary according to each state or region. In some towns, stores close from noon–2pm.

Credit Cards – *(p 392)* Shops, hotels, restaurants, insurance agencies and car rental companies all accept international credit cards (MasterCard, EuroCard, Visa or American Express). Automatic Teller Machines (ATMs) can be found at airports, in hotel lobbies and at Bancomer and Banamex branches throughout Mexico. Don't forget your personal identification number (PIN). To report a lost or stolen credit card or traveler's checks: Diner's Club ☎ (01-800) 500-30; American Express ☎ (01-800) 055-55; MasterCard ☎ (800) 307-7309.

Language – Spanish is the official language of Mexico. English is widely understood particularly in tourist areas. If you don't speak Spanish, it would be wise to bring a dictionary with basic words and useful phrases, especially when traveling in remote areas.

Liquor Laws – The legal drinking age is 18. All types of alcoholic beverages are sold in self-service stores and wine shops. Dry laws are enforced during national holidays (i.e. Election Day, Labor Day, Sept 16). Driving under the influence is prohibited.

National Holidays – During official holidays, banks, government offices, schools and some stores and businesses are closed.

New Year's Day	January 1
1917 Constitution Day	February 5
Benito Juarez's Birthday	March 21
Holy Week (Thu & Fri)	March–April
Labor Day	May 1
Day of the Battle of Puebla	May 5
Independence Day	September 16
Change of executive power (every 6 years)	December 1
Christmas	December 25

Brigitta L. House

Postal Service – Post offices are open Mon–Fri *(8am–7pm)*, and some on Saturday morning. Airmail to Europe takes about 6 days, surface mail within Mexico as well as to other countries is very slow. Postage for international letters (20g) P$3. You may also receive mail at the post office by registering *poste restante*. For more information, contact the post office in each state or the Central Post Office in Mexico City ☎ 57-09-96-00 or 57-22-95-00.

Independent companies, such as UPS, Federal Express, DHL and Mail Boxes, offer overnight mail and package service in Mexico and abroad. For addresses, telephone numbers and information on courier services, consult the *Yellow Pages*.

Shopping – *For arts & crafts organized by the state or region see pp 49-54.*

Taxes and Tipping – In Mexico, the Value Added Tax (VAT) is 15% and is applied to goods and services. In Cancun, Isla Mujeres and Cozumel, the VAT is 10%. Throughout Mexico the hotel occupancy tax is 17%. Tips for hotel maids and porters are 15–20%. It is customary to tip 15% of the total bill in restaurants. In Mexico, gas station attendants should be tipped.

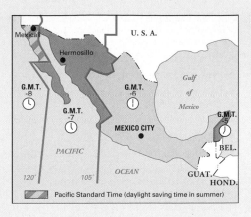

Pacific Standard Time (daylight saving time in summer)

Telephones and Telegrams – Emergencies: ☎ 060. Local calls cost P$0.50/minute. Domestic long-distance operator: ☎ 020; international long-distance operator: ☎ 090. Direct, domestic long-distance calls: 01 + city/state area code + number. Long distance to the US and Canada: 001 + country code + area code + number. For listing of area codes, check the local phone book in the *Yellow Pages* section. Public phones operate with a **Ladatel telephone card** available at airports, in pharmacies, supermarkets, stores and subway stations. Telegrams can be sent from Telecom offices *(Mon–Fri 8am–4:45pm, Sat–Sun 9am–9pm)* or by phone: national telegrams; P$1.15/word; ☎ 57-09-85-00 *(Mon–Fri 8am–9pm)*; international telegrams; P$1.20/word; ☎ 57-09-86-25 *(Mon–Fri 9am–1pm)*.

Time Zones – There are four different time zones in Mexico: Baja California Norte (120° meridian, 2 hours behind Mexico City); Baja California Sur, Chihuahua, Nayarit, Sinaloa and Sonora (105° meridian, 1 hour behind Mexico City); Quintana Roo (75° meridian, 1 hour ahead of Mexico City) and Mexico City and the rest of the country (90° meridian). Time is moved forward 1 hour in all time zones during summer hours (from the first Sunday in April through the last Sunday in October).

Nature and personal safety

For **emergencies** contact the National Center for Communication and Civil Protection (CENACOM), ☎ (01-800) 004-13. Persons needing legal assistance should contact Protección Legal al Turista (SECTUR) at ☎ 250-6603 (English). For medical emergencies check at the hotel's front desk for a listing of English speaking doctors and hospitals with English speaking staff. Local police, especially in Mexico City, is oftentimes slow in handling emergencies (robbery, car jacking, etc.), foreigners may be better served contacting the hotel management, the nearest tourist office or the embassy or consulate:

Australia	Jaime Balmes 11, Mexico DF	53-95-99-88
Canada	Schiller 529, Mexico DF	52-54-32-88
UK	Rio Lerma 71, Mexico DF	52-07-20-98
US	Paseo de la Reforma 305, Mexico DF	52-11-00-42

Visitors to Mexico should be aware that most tap water is unpurified. Only bottled water should be used for drinking and even brushing teeth and rinsing contact lenses. Do not forget that this does include ice cubes. It is recommended to rely on bottled water, which is readily available in hotel shops, restaurants, grocery stores and pharmacies. As a precaution, it is best to avoid all foods that have to be washed (salads, fruit, etc.) and stick to dishes that have been cooked or broiled. In some outlying tropical regions refrigeration may not always be available when preparing foods. An effective medicine is Lomotil, available at local pharmacies.

Travelers not used to high altitude should keep to a light diet and limit alcoholic beverages for the first few days. The same precautions should be taken in hot and humid tropical regions of the country. The risk of malaria is present in Campeche, Chiapas, Guerrero, Michoacán, Nayarit, Oaxaca, Quintana Roo, Sinaloa and Tabasco. For additional information, US residents can contact the Centers for Disease Control and Prevention (CDC), Atlanta, GA; ☎ (404) 332-4559 or *www.cdc.gov*.

Hurricanes – From June through September, hurricanes are very common on the Atlantic Coast, the Gulf of Mexico and the Yucatán Peninsula. On the Pacific Coast there are heavy tropical storms during May. When warnings are issued, boating and swimming are prohibited. Take the following precautions:

▲ Make sure you have a battery-operated radio, flashlight and extra batteries.

▲ Pay attention to radio information provided by the authorities.

▲ Stay in the house, hotel or, preferably, in shelters.

▲ Have life preservers, a first-aid kit, canned food and large amounts of drinking water.

▲ Do not try to cross flooded rivers or lakes.

Volcanic Eruptions – Certain volcanoes are still active in Mexico; one of these is Popocatépetl. Others are located in the states of Puebla, Mexico and Morelos. Take special precautions when ashes are overflowing.

▲ Close all doors and windows.

▲ Place wet towels at thresholds.

▲ Have a wet mask or cloth, a first-aid kit, canned food and large amounts of drinking water (a minimum of 1 liter per person per day).

▲ Keep candles, flashlights and an extra supply of batteries on hand.

▲ Have blankets and toiletries.

▲ Have a battery-operated radio with an extra supply of batteries.

Earthquakes – Mexico City, along with the states of Oaxaca and Guerrero, are regions predisposed to earthquakes on a regular basis. The moment the earth begins to tremble, emergency alarms go off on all radio stations. If you find yourself inside a building, take the following precautions:

▲ Stay calm.

▲ Put out all fires.

▲ Move away from windows and breakable objects.

▲ Do not use elevators; take the stairs instead.

▲ Go to safe areas.

▲ Locate the emergency exit.

▲ Have a first-aid kit, canned food and large amounts of drinking water.

▲ Have a battery-operated radio with an extra supply of batteries.

Beach Security – Sunburn is a common occurrence for visitors who remain in the sun too long and don't use **sunblock**. Wear sunglasses and a hat and bring a sufficient supply of bottled water. Avoid the sun at midday when the ultraviolet rays are strongest.

Respect signs that limit swimming or boating as well as buoys that divide the area designated for swimming from the open sea. Occasionally there are red flags that indicate an extremely dangerous, forbidden area. Supervise children at all times. In the event of an accident, immediately advise a lifeguard or hotel authorities. Never sail alone. Always wear a lifejacket and have plenty of drinking water, a first-aid kit and flare lights. During tropical storms, warning signs advise of swimming and boating restrictions. Some beaches have jellyfish that sting; be aware of sea urchins, morays and sharks. When diving, make sure you are accompanied by someone who knows the area well.

© Robert Holmes

Adventure tourism and ecotourism

Today Mexico boasts more than 8 million hectares/19 million acres of ecological reserves. These include: 70 protected areas divided into 24 **biosphere reserves**, 44 **national parks**, as well as **protected areas** for flora, fauna and **marine parks**.

Mexico offers countless activities that can lead to an unparalleled experience of being in contact with nature and Mexican culture. Rates for packages depend largely on the nature of the activity, equipment, level of comfort, season and location. Some outfitters require a minimum number of participants.

For more information about associated agencies, contact the **Asociación Mexicana de Turismo de Aventura y Ecoturismo (AMTAVE)** at Av. Insurgentes Sur, 1971-251, Col. Guadalupe Inn, Mexico City, C.P. 01020, ☎ 56-63-53-81.

ADVENTURE TOURISM

General Excursions, Hiking and Biking

Amigos de Sian Ka'an	Apartado Postal 770, Cancún, C.P. 77500, Q. Roo. ☎ (9) 884-9583
	Excursions across various ecosystems on the Sian-Ka'an Biosphere Reserve.
A.T.C. Touroperadores	Av. 16 de Septiembre, 16, C.P. 29200, San Cristóbal de las Casas, Chis. ☎ (9) 678-2550
	Excursions to the Yumka (Tab.) ecological park and to the Yaxchilan and Bonampak archaeological sites (Chis.) in the Lacandon Jungle.
Bike Mex	Guerrero, 361, Centro, C.P. 48300, Puerto Vallarta, Jal. ☎ (3) 223-1680 or www.bikemex.com.
	Mountain biking at the Bay of Banderas.
Biodiversidad Mexicana	Antonio Narro, 70, Col. Centro, Quinta Trinidad, C.P. 25000, Saltillo, Coah. ☎ (8) 412-8490
	Hiking and mountain biking in Cuatro Ciénegas.
Coscati (Villa Calmecac)	Zacatecas, 114, esq. Tanque, Col. Buenavista, C.P. 62130, Cuernavaca, Mor., ☎ (7) 313-2146 or www.giga.com/~meliton.mx
	Mountain biking and hiking in the Morelos region.
Ecocolors	Uxmal, 36, A-1, Super Manzana 2A, Cancún, C.P. 77500, Q. Roo, ☎ (9) 884-9580 or www.Cancún.com.mx/ecocolors
	Excursions to the Sian-Ka'an Biosphere Reserve, Yum Balam, Botanical Garden, cenotes, archaeological sites, grottoes, rivers and colonial enclaves throughout the peninsula.

Eco-Discover Tours Huatulco	Paseo Benito Juárez, Plaza las Conchas L-6, Col. Bahía de Tangolunda, C.P. 70989, Bahías de Huatulco, Oax. ☎ (9) 587-0678 *Mountain biking in the Bay of Huatulco.*
Ecogrupos	Centro Comercial Plaza Inn, Insurgentes Sur, 1971-251, Col. Guadalupe Inn, C.P. 01020, Mexico, D.F. ☎ 56-61-91-21 and Ignacio L. Vallarta, 243, Col. Emiliano Zapata, C.P. 48380, Pto. Vallarta, Jal. ☎ (3) 222-6606 *Excursions to the Copper Canyon (Chih.), the Mazunte Ecological Reserve (Oax.), Palenque, Yaxchilán, Bonampak, Agua Azul, Cañón del Sumidero, Montebello lagoons and Lacandon forest (Chis.), and to Catemaco and Nanciyaga in Tuxtlas (Ver.).*
Ecoturismo Yucatán	Calle 3, 235, between 32A and 34, Col. Pensiones, C.P. 97219, Mérida, Yuc., ☎ (9) 925-2187 or 920-2772 or *www.imagenet.com.mx* *Excursions to Dzitnup cenote, Balamkanché grotto, Celestún, archaeological sites, the entire Yucatán Peninsula and Belize.*
Far Horizons	P.O. Box 91900, Albuquerque, NM 87199; ☎ (505) 343-9400, (800) 552-4575 or *www.farhorizon.com* *All-inclusive tours led by English-speaking archaeologists; limited to 15 participants to destinations throughout cities of Maya civilization in Mexico, Guatemala and Belize.*
Iguana Expediciones	Tiburón, 1516, Costa de Oro, C.P. 94299, Boca del Río, Ver. ☎ (2) 921-1550 *Mountain biking in Veracruz. Eco-archaeological hikes to Cotlamani (Ver.) and El Zapotal, herbal steam baths (Temazcal) in Dos Bocas, Ver.*
Intercontinental Adventures	Homero, 526-801, Col. Polanco, C.P. 11570, Mexico, D.F. ☎ 52-55-44-00 *Excursions to various places in Mexico; in particular, to the Sierra Gorda missions, Route of Cortés (Ver.) and colonial cities.*
Kamino Tours	Calzada las Águilas, 1075, Col. San Clemente las Águilas, C.P. 01740, Mexico, D.F. ☎ 56-35-58-45 *Adventure excursions, hikes and mountain biking in the Oaxacan mountains and beaches.*
Lindblad Special Expeditions	720 Fifth Ave., New York, NY 10019, ☎ (212) 765-7740 or *www.expeditions.com* *All-inclusive tour (leave from Phoenix, AZ, to La Paz, return by plane from Chihuahua to Phoenix): explore the Sea of Cortés by private ship, watch whales, snorkel or visit uninhabited islands in the company of a naturalist— and then ride through the spectacular mountains and canyons of the Copper Canyon. Limited railroad.*

Copper Canyon

Mexican-American Railway Co.	16800 Greenspoint Park Dr., Houston TX 77060-2308 ☎ (281) 872-0190 or (800) 659-7602 *Round-trip travel between Houston, TX, and Copper Canyon is offered on the luxurious South Orient Express several times a month from January–May and October–December.*
Quinto Sol	Presa Las Pilas, 37 PH, Col. Irrigación, C.P. 11500, Mexico, D.F., ☎ 53-95-52-52 or *www.quinto-sol.com.mx* *Journeys to the Mazatec mountain range, the city of Oaxaca and the coast, passing through the Bays of Huatulco, Mazunte and Zipolite to the Chacahua lagoons.*
Trek & Trail	P. O. Box 906, Bayfield WI 54814, ☎ (715) 779-3320 or (800) 354-8735 or *www.trek-trail.com.* *Multiactivity fully guided tours include kayaking, snorkeling, scuba diving, birdwatching and camping along the Yucatán coast or a stay at the Sian Ka'an Biosphere Reserve; exploration of archaeological sites on the Yucatán Peninsula while staying in colonial hotels.*
Reserva Ecológica El Edén	Teocaltiche, 207, Super Manzana 45, Manzana 4, Lote 3, Cancún, Q. Roo. ☎ (9) 880-5032 *Ecological tours to El Edén Ecological Reserve (Q. Roo) the Yum Balam Reserve (Q. Roo) and Ría Lagartos (Yuc.).*

Hiking, Rappel and Rock Climbing

Río y Montaña Expediciones	Prado Norte, 450-T, Col. Lomas de Chapultepec, C.P. 11000, Mexico, D.F. ☎ 55-20-20-41 *High mountains in the Iztaccíhuatl, Pico de Orizaba and La Malinche volcanoes. Rappel in Santa María (SLP).*

Scuba Diving and Snorkeling

Asociación Nacional de Operatours de Actividades Acuáticas y Turísticas (ANOAAT)	15 Avenida Norte, 299-B, C.P. 77600, Cozumel (Q. Roo). ☎ (9) 872-5955 or *www.cozumel.nct/diving/anoaat* *Diving in Cozumel.*
Ecocolors	(p 401) *Diving at the islands of Akumal, Isla Mujeres, Contoy, Holbox, Chinchorro and Cozumel. Natural cenotes along the Cancún-Tulum tourist corridor.*
Open Air Expeditions	Guerrero, 339, Centro, C.P. 48300, Pto. Vallarta, Jal., ☎ (3) 222-3310 or *www.vivamexico.com* *Diving and snorkeling in Bahía de Banderas.*

Canoeing, kayaking and rafting

Baja Expeditions	2625 Garnet Ave., San Diego, CA 92109; ☎ (619) 843-6967, (800) 843-6967 or *www.bajaex.com* *Sea kayaking, exploration of caves and natural reserves, scuba diving.*
Coscati (Villa Calmecac)	(p 401) *Kayaking and rafting on the Dos Bocas (Mor.) and Amacuzac (Gro.) rivers.*
Ecogrupos	(p 402) *Rafting on the Antigua, Pescados and Filobobos rivers in Veracruz.*
Open Air Expeditions	(above) *Kayaking in Bahía Banderas, Pto. Vallarta.*
Expediciones México Verde	José María Vigil, 2406, Col. Italia Providencia, C.P. 44640, Guadalajara, Jal. ☎ (3) 641-5598 *Rafting on the Filobobos, Pescados and Antigua rivers in Veracruz.*
Expediciones Tropicales	Magdalena, 311-10, Col. del Valle, C.P. 03100, Mexico, D.F. ☎ 55-43-79-84 *Canoeing on the Santa María River and rafting on the Tampaon-Santa María (San Luis Potosí), Antigua, Pescados and Actopan rivers in Veracruz.*
Iguana Expediciones	(opposite) *Rafting on the Actopan, Filobobos and Pescados rivers; sea kayaking at the Isla de los Sacrificios, all in Veracruz.*
Kayak	Carrillo Puerto, 76-A, Col. Coyoacán, C.P. 04000, Mexico, D.F. ☎ 55-54-84-87 *Specialized kayak expeditions on the ocean and rivers in Chiapas, Veracruz, Puebla and San Luis Potosí.*

Miramar Adventures	P.O. Box 12094, Seattle, WA 98102 ☎ (206) 322-6559, (800) 297-3111 or *www.miramar-adventures.com* *All-inclusive sea-kayaking expeditions from base camp in Bahía de los Angeles.*
Outdoor Odysseys	12003 23rd Ave., Seattle, WA 98125 ☎ (206) 361-0717, (800) 647-34621 or *www.pacificim.net/~bydesign/odyssey.html* *Snorkeling, scuba diving (Apr–Nov) and kayaking (Nov–Apr).*
Pápero Aventuras	41 Poniente, 2120, Col. Ex Hacienda la Noria, C.P. 72410, Puebla, Pue. ☎ (2) 240-6455 *Rafting on the Filobobos, Antigua, Pescados and Actopan rivers in Veracruz, the Amacuzac River in Guerrero, and the Pahuatlán River in Puebla.*
Río y Montaña Expediciones, D.F. *(p 403)*	*Rafting and canoeing on the Pescados, Tonto, Antigua, and Actopan rivers in Veracruz and the Santa María y Gallinas River in San Luis Potosí.*
Veraventuras	Santos Degollado, 81, int 8, Xalapa, Col. Centro, C.P. 91000, Xalapa, Ver. ☎ (2) 818-9579 and Av. Ejército Nacional, 1136, 1er piso, Col. Chapultepec Morales, C.P. 11570, Mexico, D.F. ☎ 55-57-12-77 or *www.dpc.com.mx/veraventuras* *Rafting on the Filobobos, Antigua, Pescados and Actopan rivers in Veracruz.*
Hot Air Ballooning	
Globo Aventuras	Canteras de Oxtopulco, 20-22, Col. Oxtopulco Universidad, C.P. 04310, Mexico, D.F. ☎ 56-61-26-91 *Hot-air balloon rides in Tenancingo, Mexico state (14km/8.5mi from Malinalco).*

ECOTOURISM

For this type of journey, visitors should follow the rules requiring them to protect the flora and fauna of the area they are visiting. They should avoid using sunblock or suntan lotion when swimming in natural waters; wear comfortable clothing, sunblock and a hat when embarking on excursions in forests or jungles. Do not litter and only use designated paths.

© Fernando García Aguinaco

San José del Cabo Estuary, Baja California Sur

Baja Expeditions	San Diego, CA ☎ (619) 843-6967 or *www.bajaex.com* *Whale watching (Dec–March).*
Ecogrupos	*(p 402)* *View the humpback whale in the Bay of Banderas (Nay.) and the gray whale in San Ignacio, BCS.*
Open Air Expeditions	*(p 403)* *View the humpback whale in the Bay of Banderas (Nay.).*
Kuyima	Morelos, Col. Centro, C.P. 23930, San Ignacio, BCS. ☎ (1) 154-0070 *View the gray whale in San Ignacio.*
Malarrimo Ecotours	Blvd. Emiliano Zapata, Col. Fundo Legal, Guerrero Negro, C.P. 23940, BCS ☎ (1) 157-0100 or *www.malarrimo.com* *View the gray whale in Guerrero Negro.* *Excursion to see the cave paintings and salt mines; 3-day, all-inclusive camping.*
Museo de Ciencias (Science Museum)	Calle Obregón, 1463, Centro, C.P. 22800, Ensenada, BC ☎ (6) 178-7192 *View the gray whale in Bahía Todos Santos, Ensenada, BC.*

Amigos de Sian-Ka'an	*(p 401)* *At the Sian Ka'an Biosphere Reserve in Q. Roo.*
Ecogrupos	*(p 402)* *In the Islas Marietas (Bahía de Banderas, Nayarit) and the Sanctuary of the Monarch Butterflies in Michoacán.*
Ecoturismo Yucatán	*(p 402)* *Calakmul Biosphere Reserve in Campeche and Celestún in Yucatán.*
Open Air Expeditions	*(p 403)* *In Punta Mita and Islas Marietas, Bahía de Banderas (Nayarit).*
Holbrook Travel	3540 NW 13th St., Gainesville, FL 32609, ☎ (352) 377-7111 or (800) 451-7111 (US and Canada) or *www.holbrooktravel.com* *Knowledgeable naturalists lead nature tours (that combine birdwatching with local cultural diversity and stays in first-class hotels) to areas like Yucatán, Belize and Guatemala.*
Caribbean Habitat	Super Manzana 32, Manzana 6, lote 2, Depto. A, Av. Kabah, C.P. 77500, Cancún, Q. Roo ☎ (9) 884-9063 *At the Sian Ka'an Biosphere Reserve in Quintana Roo.*
Victor Emanuel Nature Tours	P.O. Box 33008, Austin, TX 78764; ☎ (512) 328-5221 or (800) 328-8368 (US and Canada) or *www.ventbird.com* *Knowledgeable naturalists lead nature tours (that combine bird watching with local cultural diversity and stays in first-class hotels) to areas like the Copper Canyon, Colima, Jalisco, El Triunfo, Oaxaca, Yucatán, Cozumel, Belize and Guatemala.*

Biodiversidad Mexicana	*(p 401)* *Appreciation of the geological, paleontological, archaeological and natural wealth of northeastern Mexico.*
Ecocolors	*(p 401)* *Sian Ka'an Biosphere Reserve, Botanical Gardens, Reserva del Edén, and Punta Laguna in Quintana Roo.*
Ecogrupos	*(p 402)* *Sian Ka'an Biosphere Reserve in Quintana Roo and Cuajilote, Veracruz.*
Open Air Expeditions	*(p 403)* *In the Islas Marietas, Bahía de Banderas, Nayarit.*
Parque Ecológico de Xochimilco	Periférico oriente, 1, between Canal de Chalco and Canal de Cuemanco, Mexico, D.F. ☎ 56-73-80-61. *Observation of flora and birds in Xochimilco, D.F.*

Monarch Butterflies

GLOSSARY

A selection of foreign terms found in this guide.

avenida (av.)	avenue	jardín	garden
bahía	bay	lago	lake
barranca	canyon, ravine	laguna	lagoon
barrio	district, quarter	mercado	market
cabo	cape, headland	mesa	Plateau
calle	street	mestizo	person of Spanish & indigenous blood
calzada	avenue	mina	mine
capilla	chapel	mirador	lookout
capilla abierta	open-air chapel	museo	museum
capilla posa	corner chapel	nevado	snow-covered peak
carretera (carr.)	road, highway	palacio gubernamental	government palace
carretera federal	federal highway	palacio municipal	city hall
carr. de cuota	toll road	palapa	palm sunshade
casa	house	parque nacional	national park
cascada	waterfall, cascade	parroquia	parish church
cerro	hill	paseo	promenade
ciudad	city	patio	courtyard, patio
claustro	cloisters	piso	floor (story)
colegio	school, seminary	plaza (principal)	plaza (main)
conjunto	archit. complex	planta (baja, alta)	floor (ground, upper)
convento	monastery, convent	portada	portal, entrance
edificio	building	portales	arcade
estructura	structure	sierra	mountain range
fachada	facade	sor	sister (nun)
fray	friar	templo	church, temple
fuente	fountain	tezontle	a pink or red building stone
fuerte	fort	tianguis	market or trading district
gruta	grotto	valle	valley
hacienda	large ranch or farm	zócalo	main plaza
iglesia	church	zona arqueológica	archaeological site
isla	island	zoológico	zoo

USEFUL WORDS AND PHRASES

Spanish	**English**
sí, no	yes, no
ayer	yesterday
hoy	today
mañana	tomorrow
por la mañana	in the morning
por la tarde	in the afternoon
por favor	please
muchas gracias	thank you very much
perdón	pardon, excuse me
suficiente	enough
buenos días	good morning
buenas tardes	good afternoon
buenas noches	good night
adiós	goodbye
mucho, poco	a lot, little
más, menos	more, less
caro/barato	expensive/inexpensive
¿Cuánto?	How much?
grande, pequeño	big, small
¿La carretera hacia...?	The road to...?
¿Dónde?, ¿Cuándo?	Where? When?
¿Dónde está?	Where is?
¿Se puede visitar?	May we visit?
¿Qué hora es?	What time is it?
No comprendo.	I don't understand.
No hablo español.	I don't speak Spanish
Hable más despacio, por favor.	Speak more slowly, please.

At the bank

¿Dónde está el banco más cercano?	Where is the nearest bank?
Quisiera cambiar unos dólares.	I would like to exchange some dollars.
¿Dónde está el cajero automático?	Where is the automatic teller machine (ATM)?
¿A cuánto está el tipo de cambio?	What is the exchange rate?

At the hotel

Tengo una reservación.	I have a reservation.
habitación sencilla/doble	single/double room
cama matrimonial	king-size bed
con/sin ducha	with/without a shower
con/sin baño	with/without a bathroom
agua caliente/fría	hot/cold water
Quisiera un cuarto con baño y ducha.	I would like a room with a bath/shower.

At the restaurant

¿Tiene usted una mesa para dos?	Do you have a table for two?
¿Qué va a pedir?	What will you have?
Quisiera... (una cerveza bien fría).	I would like... (a cold beer).
No puedo comer nada hecho con...	I cannot eat anything made with...
No puedo comer nada frito (salado).	I cannot eat anything fried (salted).
¿Es muy picante?	Is this very spicy?
¿Tienen platos sin carne?	Do you have any dishes without meat?
¿Dónde está el baño?	Where is the bathroom?
La cuenta, por favor.	The check/bill, please.
Cuentas separadas.	Separate checks.
¿Está incluido el servicio?	Are gratuities included?
No he pedido esto.	I haven't ordered this.
No creo que la cuenta esté bien.	I don't think the bill is right.
Tenemos prisa.	We are in a hurry.
¿Acepta usted tarjetas de crédito o cheques de viajero?	Do you accept credit cards or traveler's checks?
Esto es para usted.	This is for you.

Index

D – E

F – G

H – I

J – K – L

M

N – O

P

Q – R

S

T

U – V

X – Y – Z

Belize

Guatemala